Germany
day BY day

1st Edition

by George McDonald & Donald Olson

WILEY

John Wiley and Sons, Inc.

> To hear traditional German music, visit a historic beer hall or plan your trip around one of the country's many festivals.

Contents

PAGE 91

PAGE 150

PAGE 231

PAGE 282

PAGE 339

PAGE 359

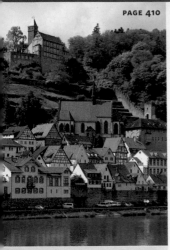

PAGE 526

PAGE 564

PAGE 599

PAGE 626

PAGE 627

PAGE 643

PUBLISHED BY
Wiley Publishing, Inc.
111 River St., Hoboken, NJ 07030-5774

ISBN 978-0-470-58252-7

Frommer's®

Editorial by Frommer's

EDITOR	PHOTO EDITOR
Christine Ryan	Cherie Cincilla
CARTOGRAPHER	CAPTIONS
Elizabeth Puhl	Mike Hammer
COVER PHOTO EDITOR	COVER DESIGN
Richard Fox	Paul Dinovo

Produced by Sideshow Media

PUBLISHER	MANAGING EDITOR
Dan Tucker	Megan McFarland
PROJECT EDITOR	PHOTO EDITOR
Pamela Nelson	John Martin
PHOTO RESEARCHER	DESIGN
Jennifer Senator	Kevin Smith, And Smith LLC

SPOTLIGHT FEATURE DESIGN
Em Dash Design LLC

For information on our other products and services or to obtain technical support, please contact our Customer Care Department within the U.S. at 800/762-2974, outside the U.S. at 317/572-3993 or fax 317/572-4002.

Wiley also publishes its books in a variety of electronic formats. Some content that appears in print may not be available in electronic formats.

MANUFACTURED IN CHINA

5 4 3 2 1

How to Use This Guide

The Day by Day guides present a series of itineraries that take you from place to place. The itineraries are organized by time (The Best of Berlin in 1 Day), by region (The Black Forest & the Bodensee), by town (Dresden), and by special interest (The Rhineland & Mosel Valley for Wine Lovers). You can follow these itineraries to the letter, or customize your own based on the information we provide. Within the tours, we suggest cafes, bars, or restaurants where you can take a break. Each of these stops is marked with a coffee-cup icon ☕. In each chapter, we provide detailed hotel and restaurant reviews so you can select the places that are right for you.

The hotels, restaurants, and attractions listed in this guide have been ranked for quality, value, service, amenities, and special features using a **star-rating system.** Hotels, restaurants, attractions, shopping, and nightlife are rated on a scale of zero stars (recommended) to three stars (exceptional). In addition to the star-rating system, we also use a kids icon **kids** to point out the best bets for families.

The following **abbreviations** are used for credit cards:

AE American Express   **MC** MasterCard
DC Diners Club   **V** Visa
DISC Discover

A Note on Prices

Frommer's lists exact prices in local currency. Currency conversions fluctuate, so before departing consult a currency exchange website such as **www.oanda.com/convert/classic** to check up-to-the-minute conversion rates.

How to Contact Us

In researching this book, we discovered many wonderful places—hotels, restaurants, shops, and more. We're sure you'll find others. Please tell us about them, so we can share the information with your fellow travelers in upcoming editions. If you were disappointed with a recommendation, we'd love to know that, too. Please e-mail us at frommersfeedback@wiley.com or write to:

Frommer's Germany Day by Day, 1st Edition
Wiley Publishing, Inc.
111 River Street
Hoboken, NJ 07030-5774

Travel Resources at Frommers.com

Frommer's travel resources don't end with this guide. **Frommers.com** has travel information on more than 4,000 destinations. We update features regularly, giving you access to the most current trip-planning information and the best airfare, lodging, and car-rental bargains. You can also listen to podcasts, connect with other Frommers.com members through our active reader forums, share your travel photos, read blogs from guidebook editors and fellow travelers, and much more.

An Additional Note

Please be advised that travel information is subject to change at any time—and this is especially true of prices. We suggest that you write or call ahead for confirmation when making your travel plans. The authors, editors, and publisher cannot be held responsible for the experiences of readers while traveling. Your safety is important to us, so we encourage you to stay alert and be aware of your surroundings.

About the Authors

George McDonald (chapters 1, 2, 3, 4, 10–12, and 14) is a freelance journalist and travel writer, formerly based in Amsterdam and Brussels, who has written extensively for Frommer's guides. He is author of *Frommer's Belgium, Holland & Luxembourg* and *Frommer's Amsterdam* and coauthor of *Frommer's Europe* and *Frommer's Europe by Rail*. He lives with his German wife and his daughter in northern Germany, which he covered for this first edition of Frommer's *Germany Day by Day*.

Donald Olson (chapters 1, 2, 5–9, 13, and 15) is a novelist, playwright, and travel writer. His travel stories have appeared in the *New York Times, Travel + Leisure, Sunset, National Geographic,* and other publications. His guides include *Frommer's Vancouver & Victoria, Best Day Trips from London* (as coauthor), *England for Dummies* (winner of the Lowell Thomas Travel Journalism Award for best guidebook), *Germany for Dummies, London for Dummies,* and *Great Britain Day by Day* (as coauthor). His novels include *The Confessions of Aubrey Beardsley* and, under the pen name Swan Adamson, *Memoirs Are Made of This, My Three Husbands,* and *Confessions of a Pregnant Princess.* His play *Beardsley* was produced in London. His essay "Confessions of a Faux Pa" is featured in *What I Would Tell Her: 28 Devoted Dads on Bringing Up, Holding On To and Letting Go of Their Daughters* (2010).

Acknowledgments

George McDonald I'd like to thank coauthor Donald Olson for taking time from his schedule to make valuable proposals for handling the "interface" between his area in the South and mine in the North. To my wife, Tanja, goes thanks for her enthusiasm for the many beauties of her native land and her joy when others come to appreciate them. I'd like to dedicate "my" half of the book to my 10-year-old daughter Lara, with a promise to try harder to obey her injunction: *"Daddy, sprich Deutsch."*

About the Photographers

Anne Ackermann (www.anneackermann.com) lives in Hamburg and does assignment work for such national and international medias as GEO, chrismon plus, and Caritas. In 2010 she was nominated for the World Press Photo Joop Swart Masterclass. Argentina-born **Alejandro Arditi** is a documentary photographer based in Berlin. He has shown his work on the Israeli-Palestinian conflict in Italy and Israel and has contributed to such publications as Israeli Y-net websites, *bthere!,* and the annually published Jewish diary *Durch das jüdische Jahr.* **Benjamin Hiller** (www.benjamin-hiller.com) is a photojournalist currently working with NGOs in crisis zones and on long-term projects involving international politicians as well as different religious communities. **Katja Heinemann** is a German photographer based in Brooklyn, NY. She regularly produces photo essays, news media stories, and portraiture for editorial, commercial, and institutional clients in the U.S. and abroad. She is represented by Aurora Select photo agency in New York City. German photojournalist **Max Kesberger** works primarily as a travel photographer and on in-depth, long-term reportages about human beings and environmental issues. Award-winning photographer **Clay McLachlan** (www.claymclachlan.com) is based in Paris and Piedmont, Italy. His work can be seen in such magazines as *Condé Nast Traveler, National Geographic Traveler, Wine Spectator, Decanter,* and *Food & Wine.* **Dean Nixon** shot for newspapers and magazines in New Zealand before hitting the road to work on personal documentary projects interpreting the expression of individual identity within various political, economic, and ideological cultures. He's now based in Germany. **Joao Paglione** (www.joaopaglione.com) works as a photojournalist in Berlin and has been published by *Reuters,* the *Guardian,* Getty Images, and various other international publications. He is currently working on a project involving abandoned places in former East Germany. Photographer **Hans Peter Schöne** (www.hps-pro.de) has worked for travel organizations around the world, but since 1996 has been based in southern Bavaria, primarily working for tourism associations and holiday magazines. **Damian Stanulla** (www.damian-stanulla.de) was born in Poland and studied journalism in Germany. He is currently working as a freelance photojournalist worldwide. His last project involved 360-degree panorama photography for a major German online magazine. Berlin-based photojournalist **Gregor Zielke** regularly contributes to national and international magazines, newspapers, and corporate clients.

1
The Best of Germany

Our Favorite Germany Moments

> **PREVIOUS PAGE** *View of Tübingen from Castle Hill.* **THIS PAGE** *One of Munich's festive beer gardens.*

Enjoying a bird's-eye-view of Berlin. After riding the turbo elevator up to the observation deck and rotating Telecafé restaurant of the Fernsehturm (Television Tower), more than 200m (656 ft.) above Alexanderplatz, you'll find many of the best-known landmarks in Germany's capital laid out at your feet. See p. 91, **13**.

Taking in a performance at the Semperoper. Dresden's baroque opera house and ballet theater, designed by architect Gottfried Semper and re-created after its destruction in World War II, is among Europe's most magnificent cultural venues. See p. 174.

Escaping from Schloss Colditz. In truth, all you need to do is stroll nonchalantly through the front gate—but there's a certain *frisson* in getting into, and then out of, this handsome yet notorious 16th-century castle, where some of the most escape-prone Allied prisoners were held during World War II. See p. 152, **11**.

Discovering the work of Tilman Riemenschneider in Creglingen. The Romantic Road is full of surprises—lovely landscapes, medieval towns, and a small church in the tiny hamlet of Creglingen that houses an amazing altarpiece carved by the 15th-century genius Tilman Riemenschneider. You'll see Riemenschneider's expressive sculptures in museums and churches throughout Bavaria, but the elaborate altarpiece in the Herrgottskirche qualifies as a tourist attraction in its own right. See p. 208, **3**.

Sipping beer in a Munich beer garden. Sit down in the shade of a chestnut tree, order a glass of beer, and enjoy life. That's what Munich is all about. Your musings may be accompanied by a zither, an accordion, or an oom-pah-pah band, all part of the sudsy sentimentality and good-natured *Gemütlichkeit* (coziness) found in beer gardens. See p. 280.

Wandering through Munich's Viktualien-markt. Wouldn't you agree that public markets show off the soul of a city? The Viktualienmarkt in the heart of Munich has been around for 200 years now, with shops and stalls open daily to lure your nose, tempt your taste buds, and beguile your senses on all fronts. Nab a nosh and take it to the market's beer garden for an alfresco meal. See p. 286, ⑤.

Reveling in the rococo in the Wieskirche. If you're a fan of rococo, step into this church in southern Bavaria and be prepared to have your aesthetic socks knocked off. Light floods in through the cupola, illuminating an interior sparkling with swags and swirls and garlands of gold-frosted stuccowork and lots of little angels. See p. 328, ❸.

Ascending the Zugspitze. From the train station at Garmisch-Partenkirchen in the Bavarian Alps, a cog railway and a cable car take you up to the top of the 2,960m-high (9,711-ft.) Zugspitze, Germany's highest peak. The whole experience makes you want to yodel. See p. 324, ❸.

Strolling through Lindau's Altstadt (Old Town). What a pleasure to wander around this lovely, laid-back little island-town. The Germans think of it as their "little Mediterranean" because the weather is so balmy, the light so mellow, the flowers so vivid. The giant expanse of the Bodensee (Lake Constance), Germany's largest lake, makes you feel like you're at the seaside. See p. 390.

Getting the full bath treatment in Baden-Baden. If cleanliness is next to godliness, you may feel deified by the time you leave the Friedrichsbad bath complex. Following the ancient Roman-Irish bathing procedures, you progress through a series of tepid, warm, and hot steam rooms, stopping along the way to be vigorously scrubbed down by a bath attendant, until you reach the cool-down pools and, finally, are wrapped up and left to doze in blissful, fully sanitized comfort. See p. 382, ❼.

Finally seeing Schloss Neuschwanstein. How many photographs have you seen of "Mad King Ludwig's" castle? It's the most photographed site in all of Germany. And one of the most visited. But even so, trekking up to the front entrance and touring the interior—matching the images to the reality—has to provide some of the most memorable moments of any trip to Germany. See p. 338, ❷.

Dressing up for Karneval in Cologne. The Rhine River city celebrates the annual pre-Lenten Carnival with a riot of color and a display of fervid revelry that handily overturns the serious character generally attributed to the Germans. See p. 442.

Wine-tasting in the Mosel Valley. The autumn grape harvest is the best time to visit the Mosel River vineyards, yet local wineries welcome visitors to sample their vintages year-round. Among the best are Schloss Landenberg near Cochem and the Prüm Winery at Wehlen. See p. 456.

Letting the kids play with rats. The rodents in question are Hameln's and—you'll be pleased to hear—are not real. In this famously rat-infested town, you can watch an open-air theater piece that retells the Pied Piper of Hamelin tale, buy all kinds of rat souvenirs, and dine in the Rattenfängerhaus (Rat-Catcher's House). See p. 515, ❽.

Walking on water. Or walking where water was a few minutes earlier, and will be again before many hours have passed. Low tide in the Wadden Sea exposes the seabed, and on special *Wattwandern* (mudflat-hiking) tours you hike across this remarkable landscape—or seascape—to the Frisian Islands. See p. 535.

Crossing to Helgoland. Most ferries can't dock at this North Sea island, so passengers must board small open boats to get to the island from ships anchored in the bay, and then return the same way. It gets . . . *interesting* when there's any kind of a sea running. See p. 565.

Our Favorite Small Cities & Towns

> *The Gothic Heiliggeistkirche towers over Munich's Marktplatz, the city's bustling main square.*

Meissen. The Elbe River town near Dresden has, since 1710, been a beneficiary of its connection to the exquisite porcelain produced in Meissen. Gothic monuments from earlier centuries and the towering Albrechtsburg castle add their considerable weight to Meissen's charms. See p. 151, ⑩.

Quedlinburg. This historic town close to the Harz Mountains is quite extraordinarily beautiful and yet is not well known outside Germany. Its origins go back to a Saxon settlement in the early 10th century. The town survived World War II intact and has more than 1,600 half-timber buildings—more than any other town in the country. The entire Old Town is a UNESCO World Heritage site. See p. 186.

Nuremberg. It's a city with a past, for sure. During the Renaissance it was the home of Albrecht Dürer, the greatest artist of the period, and thrived as a center of the arts. During the Nazi era, it served as a rallying ground for massive *Heil Hitler!* rallies. During World War II it was almost leveled. But as it reemerged from the rubble, Nuremberg managed to rebuild itself into one of the most attractive and appealing urban centers in Germany, with extensive pedestrian areas, great museums, and an overall ambience that looks back to the past but sits firmly in the present. See p. 226.

Rothenburg ob der Tauber. The Romantic Road takes you to several medieval towns, but Rothenburg out-medievals all of them. It's hard not to love this picturesque piece of Old Germany, where walking down the cobbled lanes wafts you back hundreds of years, to a time before cars, coffee, computers, cellphones, and GPS. Can you imagine? See p. 236.

Lindau. There's not all that much to do in this lovely little town on the Bodensee (Lake Constance)—except enjoy the place. Yes, there's a casino if you're into gambling, and a small museum or two, but basically Lindau is about taking it easy: poking around the charming Altstadt (Old Town), connected to the mainland by a causeway; sipping a coffee or glass of wine at a lakeside cafe; and dining beside the harbor with its twinkling lights. See p. 390.

Heidelberg. The view from Heidelberg Castle, looking down on the tiled roofs of the Altstadt (Old Town) nestled alongside the Neckar River, is a classic. And Heidelberg itself is pretty classic, too; for many, in fact, it's the quintessential "romantic" German town. Home of Germany's oldest university, Heidelberg has an urban core that was almost entirely untouched by World War II. What that means is that you can see an architectural footprint that starts in the Middle Ages and strides all the way to today. See p. 424.

Monschau. During World War II, German commanders refused to order artillery to fire on this U.S.-occupied post, so great would be the loss to Germany's heritage. And so the small town's original timber-frame buildings with slate roofs survived to delight visitors down to the present day. See p. 443, ⑤.

Bad Karlshafen. A scenic setting on the Weser River, among the Weserbergland's hills and forests, and a historic connection to the French Huguenots mean that this 18th-century spa town has even more to recommend it than its whitewashed baroque buildings and cobblestoned streets. See p. 514, ④.

Lüneburg. Salt might seem an unlikely source of enchantment, but back in the day it was salt that laid the foundations for Lüneburg's ascent to wealth and status in the Hanseatic League. Much of the Old Town maintains a medieval air, even if it does come across as a little too pristine. See p. 550.

Goslar. Even medieval German kings and emperors liked to see and be seen in this center of the silver-mining industry in the Harz Mountains, so there's every reason for you to be out and about in today's bustling resort.

> *Once a center of the silver mining industry, Goslar is now a charming reminder of medieval life in the Harz Mountains.*

The entire Old Town is a UNESCO World Heritage site. See p. 544.

Friedrichstadt. You might think you're in Holland in little Friedrichstadt, founded in 1621 in a forlorn effort to rival Amsterdam and populated by Dutch settlers who made themselves at home by way of canals and gabled buildings. See p. 568, ①.

Stade. Overshadowed by nearby Hamburg as a maritime trading town, Stade settled into backwater status along its tributary of the Elbe. The spirit of centuries past envelops it like a North Sea mist, and even the contemporary touristic bustle doesn't quite overcome the museum-piece ambience. See p. 612.

Germany's Top 10 Must-See Landmarks

> *The Prussian-designed arch known as Brandenburger Tor is one of Berlin's most recognizable landmarks.*

Reichstag. The seat of Germany's imperial-era parliament carries a large burden of 20th-century history. It now houses the nation's Federal Parliament, and its contemporary glass dome symbolizes the openness and transparency of Germany's 21st-century democracy. You can attend a session of parliament (reserve ahead of time), go up onto the roof for fine views over Berlin, and dine in a rooftop restaurant. See p. 69, ➏.

Brandenburger Tor (Brandenburg Gate). Adjacent to the Reichstag, this Prussian triumphal arch shares some of that building's historical associations. It has since become a popular symbol of Berlin and has a distinctly laid-back air, with people strolling back and forth between Tiergarten and Unter den Linden through its colonnaded passages. The quadriga, or four-horse chariot, on top bears a figure who, at different times, has been identified as the goddess of peace and the goddess of victory. See p. 69, ➐.

Schloss Sanssouci. Prussia's 18th-century king Frederick the Great constructed this neat little—well, relatively little—single-floor rococo palace in Potsdam to be his "carefree"

private escape from the strains of government. He entertained guests here, sometimes treating them to performances of his own classical music compositions. The palace—which neighbors grander Prussian state palaces—looks out onto a large ornamental garden. See p. 130, ➊.

Zwinger. First among Dresden's many spectacular monuments, the graceful 18th/19th-century Zwinger, built in a mixture of baroque and neoclassical styles, is a large and multifaceted complex of pavilions, galleries, gardens, and water ornaments, designed originally to house state collections of fine art, scientific instruments, and more. It still does so, and ideally you should set aside at least a half-day for your visit. See p. 166, ➊.

BMW Welt (BMW World). This isn't a plug for BMW but rather for the stunning building that serves as the auto company's Munich showroom and anchors a BMW complex that includes a museum and factory. Designed by the Coop Himmelb(l)au architecture firm and opened in 2007, BMW Welt is notable for its hourglass-shaped tower and solar-fueled "customer experience and exhibition facility," where the latest-model BMWs sit enshrined like four-wheeled gods. It makes your local Toyota dealership look like a Wal-Mart. See p. 269, .

Schloss Nymphenburg. Unlike the Wittelsbachs' city palace in Munich, which looks like a forbidding fortress, their summer digs just outside the city center is unusually elegant and almost airy. That's because in 1702 Elector Max Emanuel decided to enlarge the original Italianate villa by adding four large pavilions connected by arcaded passageways. Set within magnificent gardens with vast pools and jetting fountains, Schloss Nymphenburg (Nymphenburg Palace) is a monument to power and prestige from an era that was beginning to lighten up its aesthetic sensibilities. See p. 274, **②**.

Wieskirche. From the outside it's not exactly what you'd think of as a "must-see" landmark. True, it sits by itself in a gorgeous Alpine meadow (*Wieskirche* means "church in the meadow") and has many of the structural trademarks of a Bavarian baroque-era church. But step inside and you'll understand why the Wieskirche has become a world-famous example of rococo at its most joyfully flamboyant. Once seen, it's never forgotten. See p. 328, **③**.

Schloss Neuschwanstein. If there's a German landmark more iconic than Neuschwanstein Castle, we'd like to know what it is. For decades now, images of this "fairy-tale castle" built atop a crag in southern Bavaria have been seen on travel posters and the covers of guidebooks. Seeing it in person is like visiting that fairy-tale castle of your childhood dreams. See p. 338, **②**.

Schloss Heidelberg. It's mostly in ruins, having been shelled and hit by lightning over the years, but Heidelberg Castle still dominates the town and attracts visitors from around the world. Frankly, it's more the setting than the castle itself—or what remains

> *The ornate Kölner Dom took more than 600 years to complete and is a symbol of Cologne's historical religious devotion.*

of it—that makes visiting such a memorable experience. Standing on the ramparts, with Heidelberg and the Neckar River far below, it's easy to see why the German Romantic poets and painters were so enamored of Heidelberg and found such inspiration here. See p. 427, **⑧**.

Kölner Dom (Cologne Cathedral). More than 300 years of work spread out over 6 centuries (including postwar repair work) went into creating Germany's grandest Gothic cathedral and, indeed, one of Europe's greatest. Visible from a long way beyond the Rhine River city, the dizzyingly high twin spires are a symbol both of the medieval ecclesiastical city that saw itself as a "northern Jerusalem" and of the modern, vibrant city of Cologne. See p. 482, **①**.

The Best of Germany Outdoors

> *The rolling hills and lakes of the Thüringer Wald draws both summer and winter outdoor enthusiasts.*

Grunewald. Berlin has plenty of parks, but as is the nature of city parks most of them are manicured affairs that don't bear much relation to the natural world. Not so the extensive Grunewald (Green Forest), formerly a Prussian royal hunting reserve, on the city's doorstep. It's the perfect place for a long walk or run. See p. 65, **10**.

Nationalpark Sächsische Schweiz (Saxon Switzerland National Park). *Switzerland* is European for "mountainous," and even though Saxony's peaks fall short of Alpine heights, they reach respectable altitudes. Germany's piece of the Elbe Sandstone Mountains makes up in rugged charm for what it lacks in height. See p. 163, **3**.

Naturpark Thüringer Wald (Thuringian Forest Nature Park). This hilly forest sprawls through a considerable chunk of the state of Thuringia; it makes a great arena for summer hikes as well as winter sports that include

downhill skiing (though most local skiing is cross-country). See p. 164, **5**.

Hiking around the Alpspitz in the Bavarian Alps. Be sure you have good hiking boots. A walking stick would be useful, too. Then take the Kreuzeckbahn cable car from Garmisch-Partenkirchen up to one of two areas on the Alpspitz where you can get out and hike along well-tended trails. You'll revel in the gorgeous Alpine scenery, the fresh air, and the physical exercise. The Bavarian Alps offer an endless variety of hiking trails of varying degrees of difficulty. See p. 350, **5**.

Skiing in Garmisch-Partenkirchen. Garmisch-Partenkirchen has been Germany's number one ski resort since the Winter Olympics were held here in 1936. The main runs are easily accessible by bus, train, or even by foot from the town, and the separate Zugspitze glacier ski area can be accessed by cog railway and cable car. Heading to the top of the

> *Garmisch-Partenkirchen, the site of the 1936 Winter Olympics, still draws accomplished, thrill-seeking skiers to the Bavarian Alps.*

Zugspitze, Germany's highest peak, is a popular activity for non-skiers as well. See p. 348.

Biking along the Bodensee. The terrain along the lakeshore is fairly flat, the weather is mild and often sunny when the rest of Germany isn't, and the lovely scenery includes fruit orchards, charming little towns, and the clear waters of the Bodensee (Lake Constance). No wonder about 380,000 people ride bicycles around the Bodensee every year. You'll find a 4-day self-guided Bodensee bike tour, plus lots of valuable information about biking in Germany, at www.bicyclegermany.com. See "Travel Tip," p. 376.

Eifel. Lying roughly between Cologne and Trier (and "rough" is a word that suits the Eifel well), this sparsely populated, hilly, and forested region even runs to dormant volcanoes in its southern reaches, the Vulkaneifel. Winding country roads make for great motorcycling. See p. 464, **5**.

Nationalpark Harz. Northern Germany's highest mountain, the Brocken, lies within the old, weathered Harz Mountain range. Lakes,

forests, bustling mountain towns, fine dining, and winter sports attract visitors from near and far to Harz National Park. See p. 527, **3**.

Naturpark Lüneburger Heide. It's ironic that Lüneburg Heath Nature Park—a large patch of open heath, moor, and bog—is characterized as "natural," since the forests that once covered it have been cleared. Still, the wide, flat landscape is fine country for hiking, bicycling, and horseback-riding. See p. 528, **6**.

Sylt. Germany's northernmost island is an odd mixture of chic vacationers and a wild nature due to it lying full in the path of North Sea storms. Drag yourself away from the hedonistic offerings to experience challenging windsurfing and some great, if often breeze-buffeted, beaches. See p. 571, **5**.

Nationalpark Jasmund. Blink, and you might just miss Jasmund National Park—the smallest of Germany's national parks, on Rügen island. Not to mention that you'd run the risk of toppling over its dazzlingly white-chalk sea cliffs and plunging into the sparkling blue of the Baltic Sea. See p. 566.

The Best Festivals

> *Cologne's elaborate and colorful pre-Lenten Karneval attracts costumed revelers from around the world.*

Berlin International Film Festival. Big international names join German stars for this annual shindig. Berlin's mascot is a brown bear, and the top movies screened at Germany's premier film festival compete for the Golden Bear and Silver Bear awards. See p. 125.

Dresdner Musikfestspiele (Dresden Music Festival). Continuing the festival tradition of the old Electors of Saxony, the city's annual music festival makes use of its baroque venues to put on a feast of symphonic and chamber music, along with opera, ballet, and jazz. See p. 170.

Historisches Festspiel, Rothenburg ob der Tauber. Set in the medieval town of Rothenburg, the Historisches Festspiel (History Festival) centers around an annually performed play called *Der Meistertrunk* ("The Master Draught"), which tells the story of how a mayor saved the town from destruction in 1631 by accepting the challenge of a general who said he would spare Rothenburg if a citizen could drink an enormous goblet of wine in one draught. The festival takes place over a 4-day period every Whitsuntide (Pentecost, the seventh Sunday after Easter). See p. 238.

Mozartfest Würzburg. Founded in 1921, the annual Mozartfest Würzburg is one of the leading music festivals in Europe. Some 50 concerts featuring the world's greatest musicians are given from late May to early July in the ornate Residenz palace in Würzburg. Würzburg marks the beginning of the Romantic Road; how civilized to attend a concert or two before heading south along one of Germany's most beautiful scenic drives. See p. 242.

Oktoberfest, Munich. Even if you're not a beer drinker, you've probably heard of Munich's Oktoberfest (www.oktoberfest.de). Ironically, despite its name, the world's biggest and beeriest beer-fest mostly takes place in September. For Oktoberfest, which can draw up to five million people annually, local breweries erect huge tents, each holding up to 6,000 people, and sell their beer and food (including roast oxen) in a sometimes raucous atmosphere that includes bands, singing, rides for the kiddies, and lots of Bavarian dirndls and lederhosen. You don't have to drink beer, of course, although the brew serves as a communal lubricant. See p. 278.

Fasching (Carnival), Munich. Fasching, or Carnival, is often referred to as Germany's "Fifth Season" or "Season of Fools." Basically, it's a late-winter party that began as a way for Germans in the Catholic south to let their hair down and have a good time before the fasting of Lent began. Events include parties, balls, and a street festival with food and music. See p. 249.

Weinkost (Wine and Food Fair), Freiburg im Breisgau. Munich and Stuttgart celebrate their beers, but Freiburg in the southern Black Forest celebrates its local wines. Weinkost, a public wine-tasting featuring wines produced in the Freiburg area, starts in July or August and lasts for 9 days. Local vintners set up tents and offer wines and local food specialties. Visit www.freiburg.de for more information. See p. 384 for more on Freiburg.

Beer Festival, Stuttgart. Germany's second-largest brew-haha after Munich's Oktoberfest, the Stuttgart Beer Festival originated in 1818 as a harvest festival following a famine. It takes place at the end of September and provides 2 weeks of fun with oom-pah-pah bands in traditional costume inside the drinking tents and fairground rides outside. Attracting more than five million visitors every year, this Swabian event is a fave for Germans and a great option if you've already bellied up to the beer in Bavaria. Visit www.stuttgart.de for more information. See p. 430 for more on Stuttgart.

Richard-Wagner-Bayreuther-Festspiele, Bayreuth. Since tickets are as scarce as hen's teeth, it's probably a bit of a tease to even mention this world-famous summer music festival. In cultural terms, however, the festival is one of Germany's most important annual events. The Festspiele (www.bayreuther-festspiele.de) is a program of operas written by Richard Wagner and performed in the

> *Oom-pah-pah bands and horse-drawn beer wagons kick off Stuttgart's 2-week Beer Festival with style.*

Festspielhaus, which he designed and opened in 1877. See p. 222 for more on Bayreuth.

Cologne Karneval (Carnival). See "Dressing up for Karneval in Cologne" under "Our Favorite Germany Moments (p. 3). See p. 442.

Bremer Freimarkt. For 17 days (and a considerable part of their nights) in October, the Bürgerweide behind Bremen's central train station and the Marktplatz in the Old Town reverberate with the noise and excitement of the annual Bremen Free Market, northern Germany's largest fair. See p. 541.

Walpurgisnacht (Walpurgis Night). On Walpurgisnacht (Apr 30–May 1) in the Harz Mountains, revelers dress as witches, dance with the devil, and gather on the Brocken mountain for a last fling before spring dispels them. Many Harz villages join in the fun. See p. 526.

The Best Boat, Cable Car & Train Experiences

> *A cog railway takes travelers up the Zugspitze, Germany's highest mountain.*

Heading up the Zugspitze in the Bavarian Alps. Getting to the top of the Zugspitze, Germany's highest mountain, begins with a cog railway in Garmisch-Partenkirchen and continues in a cable car. You can make this unforgettable Alpine excursion any season of the year. See p. 324, ❸.

Taking the Belchen Seilbahn (Cable Car) in the Black Forest. The Belchen is a famous peak in the Black Forest near Freiburg where, tradition has it, witches and demons once gathered to dance on the witches' Sabbath. But nowadays you don't need a broom to reach the top of the Belchen because you can ride in an enclosed cable car. A panoramic view of mountains, hillside pastures, small villages, and the vast Rhine plain is your reward. See p. 358, ❺.

Ferrying to Mainau in the Bodensee. The scenic Bodensee (Lake Constance), Germany's largest lake, exudes a kind of warm, watery magic that reminds sun-starved Germans of the Mediterranean. Daily passenger ferries ply the clear waters of the Bodensee, stopping at the fabled garden-isle of Mainau, a perfect day trip from Lindau. See p. 361, ❺.

Cruising on the Mosel River. Day-trip cruising on the river from historic Trier down to Koblenz, passing famed winery towns along the way, is the perfect way to experience the scenic Mosel Valley—especially during the late-summer grape-harvesting season. See p. 461.

Riding the Harz Mountains steam railway. Walking might be the healthy, eco-friendly way to reach the top of the Brocken, northern Germany's highest mountain, but the Harzer Schmalspurbahn's narrow-gauge steam trains from Wernigerode and Drei Annen Hohne do add romance to the ascent. See p. 527, ❸.

Taking a Hamburg harbor cruise. Tour boats crewed by salty Hamburg rivermen depart from the St. Pauli Landungsbrücken dock on the Elbe River on jaunts both upstream and down, through the port city's great ocean harbor and into narrow warehouse-lined canals. See p. 598.

Canoeing on the Mecklenburg lakes. There are around a thousand lakes in the Mecklenburg Lake District, many of them connected by river or canal, so lack of choice isn't a problem. Rental canoes are widely available, as are campsites, hotels, and restaurants. See p. 588.

The Best Scenic Drives

> *Charming pastoral scenery abounds along the Black Forest Crest Road.*

The Romantic Road. The well-traveled Romantische Strasse (Romantic Road), which stretches between the Main River and the beginning of the Bavarian Alps, is dotted with lovely medieval towns. See p. 206.

The German Fairy-Tale Road. The colorful characters of the Brothers Grimm live again along the Deutsche Märchenstrasse (German Fairy-Tale Road), a 600km (373-mile) stretch that begins in the little town of Hanau and stretches all the way north to Bremen (our itinerary takes in about a quarter of the route). This is one of the great motor trips of Germany for those who thrilled to those nursery-room favorites. See p. 512.

The German Alpine Road. Scenic majesty and architectural charm combine for an unforgettable experience on the Deutsche Alpenstrasse (German Alpine Road), a 488km (303-mile) route through the foothills of the Bavarian Alps. See p. 332.

The Black Forest Crest Road. The Schwarzwaldhochstrasse (Black Forest Crest Road) is one of the most popular car trips in Germany. The twisting secondary roads that run from Baden-Baden to Freiburg im Breisgau pass through lots of charming scenery and architecture. See p. 362.

The Rhine & Mosel valleys. Driving along the Rhine and Mosel rivers will take you past historic castles, wine villages, and some of the country's most famous vineyards. See "Along the Rhine from Mainz to Bonn," p. 450, and "The Rhineland & Mosel Valley for Wine Lovers," p. 456.

The Best Luxury Hotels

> *Munich's magnificent Mandarin Oriental hotel, located near the heart of the city, is known for the warmth and friendliness of an attentive staff.*

Adlon Kempinski, Berlin. Any hotel at the western end of Unter den Linden, adjoining Pariser Platz and overlooking the Brandenburg Gate, has at least three things going for it: location! location! location! Today's Adlon Kempinski is a worthy re-creation of the old Adlon hotel, the most famous and glamorous hotel in prewar Britain. See p. 115.

Taschenbergpalais Kempinski, Dresden. In the early 18th century, the Elector of Saxony built a baroque palace for his favorite mistress, Countess Cosel. Though ruined in the last war, the five-story building has been lavishly restored and is now Dresden's finest and most luxurious hotel. See p. 175.

Kempinski Hotel Vier Jahreszeiten München. For over 150 years, this famous hotel has been considered the preeminent star of the Munich hotel scene, attracting the rich and famous and everyone else who can afford it. The rooms and bathrooms are large and luxurious, and the spa,

pool, and fitness center are the best in Munich. Great on-site dining, as you would expect. See p. 309.

Mandarin Oriental, Munich. Munich is hardly lacking in high-end hotels, but the Mandarin Oriental stands out because of its contemporary elegance and the superior quality of its in-room amenities. The staff at this boutique luxury hotel are warm, personable, and genuinely eager to please. The restaurant has earned a Michelin star. And the central location is absolutely perfect. See p. 309.

Der Kleine Prinz, Baden-Baden. Der Kleine Prinz (the name derives from the children's classic *The Little Prince*) is a full-service boutique hotel with impeccably high standards of comfort and personal service. The rooms are individually decorated, unusually comfortable, and close to all the main attractions in Baden-Baden. Der Kleine Prinz also has a first-class restaurant. See p. 383.

Der Europäische Hof–Hotel Europa, Heidelberg. Family owned and operated, this palatial establishment just minutes from Heidelberg's famed Altstadt (Old Town) is the only 5-star hotel in the entire Rhine-Neckar region. The rooms are large and traditionally furnished, the service is impeccable, and the rooftop pool and sauna area is perfect for relaxing after your climb to Heidelberg Castle. See p. 428.

Park Hotel Bremen. This palatial hotel occupies an enviable site, in a park with meandering lakes and exotic trees, on the edge of the Old Town. Its terra-cotta dome and evenly proportioned side wings were rebuilt in 1955 to emulate a turn-of-the-20th-century pleasure pavilion. See p. 542.

Fairmont Hotel Vier Jahreszeiten, Hamburg. Founded in 1897, this connoisseurs' hotel on the Binnenalster could be the finest in Germany. It has a baronial-style interior replete with Oriental rugs and dignified period furnishings, yet also has modern luxuries and a touch of Hamburg's saltwater zestiness. See p. 604.

Our Favorite Guesthouses & Inns

> *The comfortable innlike ambience of Regensburg's Grand Hotel Orphée exudes old-fashioned charm and features a fine French restaurant.*

Grand Hotel Orphée, Regensburg. Three different buildings in different parts of Regensburg house three Orphée hotels, but the Grand Hotel Orphée in the Altstadt (Old Town) feels the most like an old-fashioned inn and has the added advantage of being connected to the French-inspired Restaurant Orphée. See p. 235.

Zum Roten Bären, Freiburg im Breisgau. "At the Red Bear" claims to be Germany's oldest inn, but it also has a newer wing and, like much of Freiburg, had to be considerably rebuilt after the war. It's not fancy, but it's comfortable, friendly, and has a noteworthy restaurant that serves regional specialties and local wines. See p. 389.

Luisenhof, Berlin. A severely dignified house, built in 1822, contains one of the most desirable small hotels in eastern Berlin. Its five floors of high-ceilinged rooms have been outfitted in a conservative and traditional style. See p. 119.

Galerie Hotel Leipziger Hof, Leipzig. This 19th-century town house resides in a district of similar buildings just east of Leipzig's Hauptbahnhof (main train station). Contemporary paintings and sculptures by local artists turn each room into a mini art gallery. See p. 185.

Alte Thorschenke, Cochem. Both a hotel and a restaurant (with its own winery), the centrally located Alte Thorschenke is one of the oldest and best-known establishments along either side of the Mosel. The romantically conceived building, with its timbers and towers, was originally built in 1332. See p. 461.

Christinenhof, Hameln. The gabled windows of this 300-year-old timber-frame building overlook a cobblestoned street in the middle of the bustling Old Town. The antique facade belies the hotel's updated, streamlined interior and modern amenities. See p. 517.

The Best Dining Experiences

> The Fischereihafen in Hamburg serves up the best seafood in the city, along with a delicious view of the Elbe River.

Alt Luxemburg, Berlin. The service is both unpretentious and gracious in master-chef Karl Wannemacher's elegant piece of Old Berlin. A finely balanced wine list complements seductively sensual dishes prepared with quality market-fresh ingredients. See p. 107.

Lutherstuben, Eisenach. In a historic town that's a gateway to the Thuringian Forest—a region where old-fashioned virtues hold sway—this restaurant entertains with its medieval style and satisfies with robust dishes served from an open kitchen. See p. 179.

Hofbräuhaus am Platzl, Munich. It's not the food—hearty and filling rather than refined—that makes dining at the world-famous Hofbräuhaus such an experience. When you're seated at a communal table in the vast *Schwemme* (taproom) with a band playing Bavarian tunes and waiters racing past carrying trays laden with enormous glasses of beer and heaping plates of sausages and ham hocks, the din of conversation and laughter becomes as important as the meal itself. See p. 302.

Zum Roten Bären, Freiburg im Breisgau. The restaurant in Freiburg's oldest inn isn't overly fancy, but it has one of the best kitchens in the region. This is a great spot to sample seasonal specialties made with local ingredients, such as fresh *Spargel* (white asparagus, available in May and June) and roasted goose (November and December). Enjoy a glass of fresh young wine from the nearby Kaiserstuhl vineyards with your meal. See p. 389.

Der Kleine Prinz, Baden-Baden. The menu at The Little Prince showcases the bounty of food and wine produced in the Black Forest—everything served here is homemade from the best and freshest local ingredients. (The cooking traditions of nearby France also influence the cuisine.) Menu offerings change daily, but you won't go wrong with one of the tasting menus. See p. 383.

Fischereihafen, Hamburg. This Altona eatery serves true local fare and the best seafood in town. Government bigwigs and international stars have been spotted dining here—but ordinary folks won't be turned away. Picture windows open onto a view of the Elbe River. See p. 605.

Ratskeller zu Lübeck. You'll eat like a lord in the Town Hall's cellar restaurant, or at any rate like a city alderman or merchant. Enjoy a hearty meal amid mementoes of Lübeck's glory days as a powerhouse of the medieval Hanseatic League. See p. 609.

The Best Markets

> *Berlin's well known street market, Markt am Winterfeldtplatz, offers a landscape of local wares, from fine food to clothing and more.*

Markt am Winterfeldtplatz, Berlin. Both popular and tolerably sophisticated, this street market on a prominent Schöneberg square has stalls retailing a variety of artisanal food and drink products, along with clothes, household items, and much more. See p. 105.

Dresdner Striezelmarkt (Dresden). This is among Germany's most highly regarded Christmas markets. During the 4 weeks leading up to Christmas, 250 stalls set up in the heart of town sell traditional ornaments from the Ore Mountains and many other handcrafted items. See p. 173.

Christkindlesmarkt, Nuremberg. Every December, some two million visitors make their way to Nuremberg to enjoy the ancient and ever-delightful Christkindlesmarkt, Germany's most famous Christmas market. About 180 wooden stalls, festooned with red-and-white cloth, are set up right in the center of town and sell traditional food and craft products such as Nuremberg spicy gingerbread, fruit loaves, Christmas-tree angels, cribs, tree ornaments, candles, roast sausages, and mugs of mulled wine. See p. 230.

Viktualienmarkt, Munich. For 200 years, the Viktualienmarkt has served as Munich's primary outdoor market. Wandering through this daily, year-round food and drink festival is a treat for the senses. Hundreds of stalls sell every kind of victual you can think of, beautifully displayed and enticing to the eyes, nose, and palate. See p. 286, ⑤.

Old Town Flea Market, Hannover. Should you be passing through Hannover on a Saturday, perhaps on the way to visit the Herrenhausen Gardens in the north of the city, be sure to stop by this busy and colorful flea market along the Leine River on the edge of the Old Town. See p. 548.

Fischmarkt, Hamburg. Starting at the unearthly hour of 5 o'clock on a Sunday morning (in summer), the riverside Fish Market on Grosse Elbstrasse, in Hamburg's Altona district, attracts night owls and is in reality a general street market with long lines of stalls. See p. 603.

2
The Best
All-Germany
Itineraries

Germany Highlights

Germany is a large country. How much of it can you see in a week? Quite a bit, if you follow our suggestions. For this tour we've chosen five unique, exciting, and very different cities that epitomize specific regions of the country. There won't be time for exploring the countryside on this weeklong whirlwind, but the itinerary will help you gain an overview of the country as a whole and a few of the cities that make it so special.

> **PREVIOUS PAGE** Schwerin's impressive Schweriner Schloss. **THIS PAGE** Berlin's Alexanderplatz.

START Fly into Frankfurt. TRIP LENGTH 1 week.

❶ Frankfurt. The city's attractions, though respectable enough, can't match those of Berlin and Munich, so a visit here is a case of getting the best out of flying into (or out of) Frankfurt Airport. Head first to **Römerberg** (p. 474, **❷**), the city's medieval main square (reconstructed after World War II), in the heart of the **Altstadt** (Old Town; p. 474, **❶**). On the square stands the **Römer,** which houses Frankfurt's city hall. If you're up for a museum, make it either the **Städel** (p. 480,

❼), the most important art gallery in town, or the **Liebieghaus** (p. 480, **❽**), for its wonderful collection of sculpture. For a moving alternative to high culture, visit either or both of the houses where **Anne Frank** lived during her childhood (see "Anne Frank in Frankfurt," p. 475). ⏱ 1 day.

Board an ICE (high-speed) train at Frankfurt's Hauptbahnhof (main station) bound for Cologne's Hauptbahnhof (travel time 1 hr. 20 min.).

DENMARK

Bornholm
(DENMARK)

*North
Sea*

Sylt
North Frisian Islands

Flensburg
Schleswig
Kiel

Kiel Bay

*Baltic
Sea*

Hiddensee
Rügen
Stralsund
Greifswald
*Pomeranian
Bay*

**SCHLESWIG-
HOLSTEIN**

Lübeck

*Mecklenburg
Bay*

Rostock
Wismar

**MECKLENBURG-
VORPOMMERN**

*Stettin
Bay*

East Frisian Islands
Cuxhaven
Wilhelmshaven
Bremerhaven

Hamburg

Schwerin
Neubrandenburg

Müritzsee

Emden
Oldenburg
Bremen
Lüneburg

**NETHER-
LANDS**

NIEDERSACHSEN

Celle

BRANDENBURG

POLAND

Brandenburg
★ **Berlin** ❸
Potsdam
Frankfurt
an der Oder

Hannover

Osnabrück
Minden
Hildesheim
Hameln
Braunschweig
Magdeburg

Münster
Bielefeld
Detmold
Goslar

Rhein

NORDRHEIN-WESTFALEN

HARZ

**SACHSEN-
ANHALT**

Cottbus

Duisburg
Essen
Dortmund
Mönchengladbach
Düsseldorf
Kassel
Göttingen
Halle
Leipzig

SACHSEN

Görlitz

Cologne
(Köln)
❷
Aachen
Bonn

Siegen
Marburg

HESSEN

Eisenach
Erfurt
Weimar
Jena
Gera
Zwickau
Chemnitz

Dresden
❹

ERZGEBIRGE

Rhein
Mose
Koblenz
Bad
Homburg
Fulda

THÜRINGER WALD

THÜRINGEN

Hof
Cheb

CZECH

Wiesbaden
Frankfurt am Main ❶
Aschaffenburg
Bad
Kissingen
Coburg
Bayreuth
Prague ★

**RHEINLAND-
PFALZ**
Mainz
Worms
Darmstadt
Bamberg
Plzeň
REPUBLIC

Trier
Ludwigshafen
Mannheim
Würzburg

SAARLAND
Saarbrücken
Homburg
Speyer
Heidelberg
Rothenburg
ob der Tauber
Nuremberg
(Nürnberg)

FRÄNKISCHE ALB

České
Budějovice

Karlsruhe
Schwäbisch
Hall

BAYERN

Regensburg

BAYERISCHER WALD

Linz

FRANCE
Pforzheim
Stuttgart
Ingolstadt
Donau
Passau

Strasbourg
Baden-
Baden
Tübingen
**BADEN-
WÜRTTEMBERG**
Heidenheim
Landshut

Freiburg
im Breisgau

*SCHWARZWALD
(BLACK FOREST)*

Ulm
SCHWÄBISCHE ALB
Donau
Augsburg

Munich (München) ❺

Rosenheim
Salzburg

Lörrach
Konstanz
Lindau
Füssen
Garmisch-
Partenkirchen
Berchtesgaden

Basel
Zürich
Bodensee
▲ *Zugspitze*
Innsbruck

AUSTRIA

LIECHTENSTEIN

SWITZERLAND

ITALY

SLOVENIA

0   50 mi
0   50 km

❶ Frankfurt
❷ Cologne
❸ Berlin
❹ Dresden
❺ Munich

> *Cafes and people fill the Römerberg, Frankfurt's historic and bustling medieval market square.*

2 Cologne (Köln). Be sure to see the **Kölner Dom** (Cologne Cathedral; p. 482, **1**), Germany's greatest Gothic cathedral and an awesome piece of the Middle Ages in the heart of the city. Cologne's Roman-era history as the legionary base and city of Colonia Claudia Ara Agrippinensium is laid out for you in the **Römisch-Germanisches Museum** (Roman-Germanic Museum; p. 484, **2**), which is built around one of the most important period mosaics in the country. Good alternatives for a museum visit are the **Museum Ludwig** (p. 485, **3**), for its large collection of Picassos and other modern art, and the **Wallraf-Richartz-Museum** (p. 485, **4**), for Old Masters. Among the best ways to view Cologne's cityscape is from the Rhine; several companies offer **boat tours** on the river (see "Tours of Cologne," p. 485). Be sure to leave time and energy for the city's nightlife and entertainment options (p. 485). ☉1 day.

Board an ICE train at Cologne's Hauptbahnhof bound for Berlin's Hauptbahnhof (travel time 4 hr. 20 min.).

3 Berlin. The long-ish train ride from Cologne means you won't get to start on Berlin until around midday. Hit the ground running with a stroll from the **Reichstag** (p. 69, **6**) through the **Brandenburger Tor** (Brandenburg Gate; p. 69, **7**) and along **Unter den Linden** (p. 54, **9**), a long boulevard that has plenty to take in as you go along "under the linden trees."

There's **Bebelplatz** (p. 72, **8**), for instance, a square that contains some imposing historical architecture and that was made infamous by the Nazis, who in 1933 used it as a setting for burning "un-German" books. At the end of Unter den Linden, cross over the Spree River to **Museumsinsel** (Museum Island; p. 80, **17**) and visit one of a constellation of stellar museums there. In the evening, hang out in the nightlife and entertainment zone around the **Hackesche Höfe** (p. 90, **4**).

On Day 2, get to the **Fernsehturm** (Television Tower; p. 91, **13**) on Alexanderplatz before it opens to secure an early place in the line to ride the elevator on its ear-popping ascent to the tower's viewing deck. From Alexanderplatz, take a bus to Pariser Platz and walk downhill to tour the **Holocaust Memorial** (p. 54, **7**). Return to Pariser Platz at the Brandenburg Gate, and walk westward through **Tiergarten** (p. 96), Berlin's central park, to the **Siegessäule** (Victory Column; p. 69, **4**). Board a bus here to take you to the start of **Kurfürstendamm** (p. 95, **15**), the long shopping street Berliners know as the "Ku'damm." Have lunch in this area,

Taking the Train

We've set up this entire 1-week itinerary to be car-free. Train service between all of our recommended cities is frequent and convenient.

and then go by bus to **Schloss Charlottenburg** (Charlottenburg Palace; p. 68, **1**). Either make this palace your big museum visit of the day or settle for an outside view before returning to the city center, from where you can reach the **Gemäldegalerie** (Picture Gallery; p. 78, **7**) by bus, to view some of the world's greatest art masterpieces. An evening **boat tour** (p. 139) on the Spree would be a good way to wind up your day. ⊕ **2 days.**

Board an ICE train at Berlin's Hauptbahnhof bound for Dresden's Hauptbahnhof (travel time 2¼ hr.).

4 **Dresden.** This queenly baroque city on the Elbe River offers so much to see and do that compressing the highlights into a single day is going to involve some unkind cuts. Just strolling through the reconstructed and restored **Altstadt** (Old Town) is something of a marvel, considering that Dresden was so badly damaged during World War II that postwar planners considered abandoning it altogether. Even choosing just one museum to visit won't help you much with time constraints, because the best museums are BIG. Top of the list has to be the amazing **Zwinger** (p. 166, **1**), with the **Residenzschloss** (Royal Palace; p. 169, **3**) coming in a close second. One of many heartening aspects of Dresden's rebirth was how people from around the world—including former enemies—chipped in to help reconstruct the **Frauenkirche** (Church of Our Lady; p. 170, **6**), a baroque masterpiece. A **boat tour** (p. 172) on the Elbe is called for, doubly so since the antique paddle-steamers that ply the river are attractions all by themselves. Try to fit in a visit to **Schloss Pillnitz** (Pillnitz Palace; p. 150, **9**), even if only for a walk in the gardens of this riverside palace complex. ⊕ **1 day.**

Munich is about 460km (286 miles) south of Dresden. There are frequent trains from Dresden; the trip takes about 5¾ hours and requires a change at Nuremberg. Along the way, you'll be able to enjoy the scenery of northern and southern Bavaria.

5 ★★★ **Munich.** Finish up the week with 2 days in Munich. Try to arrive in the early afternoon so that you can still do some sightseeing. After checking into your hotel, you might want to orient yourself by taking one of the 1- or 2½-hour

> *Fans of baroque architecture should be sure to visit the Frauenkirche in Dresden.*

sightseeing tours that depart from in front of the Hauptbahnhof (main train station) where you arrived. Otherwise, you can get an instant hit of the city just by strolling around **Marienplatz** (St. Mary's Square; p. 252, **1**), the heart of bustling Munich, and the adjacent **Viktualienmarkt** (p. 286, **5**), where food stalls, snack shops, and a beer garden beckon. If it's early enough, head over to visit one of Munich's great art museums in the Museum Quarter (keep in mind most museums are closed on Monday). The **Alte Pinakothek** (Old Masters Gallery; p. 262, **1**), with its magnificent collection of German Old Masters, is a must-see. For a more detailed 1-day itinerary of Munich, see p. 252.

On Day 2, you may want to make a visit to the **Residenz** (p. 274, **1**), the city palace of the Wittelsbach family, which ruled Bavaria, or **Schloss Nymphenburg** (p. 274, **2**), their summer palace. You need about 2 hours to browse through the Residenz, about 4 to visit Nymphenburg, a 20-minute tram ride from central Munich.

If you're not interested in palaces, you can roam through the Altstadt (Old Town) and surrounding area visiting world-class art or science museums (the **Deutsches Museum** of science and technology is the most popular museum in Germany; p. 266, **1**), Gothic and baroque churches, and, of course, Munich's famed beer halls and beer gardens. ⊕ **2 days.**

The Best of Germany in 2 Weeks

With 14 days at your disposal you can make a fascinating circuit of Germany, hitting all of the high spots. For this itinerary we've chosen a route that will take you to the most exciting cities, the most famous castles and palaces, the most charming towns, and the most scenically rewarding landscapes. It's a "greatest hits" tour that introduces you to Germany's past and present, showing off the best of its urban treasures and natural pleasures.

> *A striking modern glass dome now crowns Berlin's historic Reichstag, home to the government's lower house of Parliament, the Bundestag.*

START **Fly into Frankfurt, and take the ICE (high-speed) train from Frankfurt Airport station to Cologne's Hauptbahnhof (main station; travel time 1 hr.). If you arrive in Frankfurt too late to make it to Cologne, see our Frankfurt hotel suggestions on p. 481.**

❶ Cologne (Köln). ⏱ 1 day. See p. 22, ❷.

Board an ICE train at Cologne's Hauptbahnhof bound for Berlin's Hauptbahnhof (travel time 4 hr. 20 min.).

❷ Berlin. ⏱ 2 days. See p. 22, ❸.

❸ Potsdam. On your third day based in Berlin, take the *S-Bahn* (urban rail) train for the short ride to neighboring **Potsdam** (p. 130), a city beautified by a succession of Prussian kings and German emperors. Return to Berlin in the afternoon, leaving yourself time for one of the city's less-trafficked neighborhoods—we suggest either **Prenzlauer Berg** (see p. 59, ❸) or **Kreuzberg** (see p. 56, ❷). ⏱ 1 day.

On Day 5, board an ICE train at Berlin's Hauptbahnhof bound for Dresden's Hauptbahnhof (travel time 2¼ hr.).

1 Cologne
2 Berlin
3 Potsdam
4 Dresden
5 Munich
6 Garmisch-Partenkirchen
7 Wieskirche
8 Schloss Neuschwanstein
9 Schloss Hohenschwangau
10 Füssen
11 Lindau
12 Freiburg im Breisgau
13 Baden-Baden
14 Heidelberg
15 Frankfurt

> *Freiburg im Breisgau hosts the annual Weinkost (Wine and Food Fair) each July or August.*

4 Dresden. ⊕1 day. See p. 23, **4**.

Munich, your stop for Days 6 and 7, is about 460km (286 miles) south of Dresden. There are frequent trains from Dresden; the trip takes about 5¾ hours and requires a change at Nuremberg. You won't need a car while in Munich, but arrange to pick one up on the morning of Day 8.

5 ★★★ Munich. Spend 2 days in the capital of Bavaria and you'll understand why so many Germans say this is the city they'd live in if they could. Munich can be enjoyed on many different levels. It can be coolly sophisticated or boisterous and rowdy, but the *Gemütlichkeit*—that indefinable sense of "friendly coziness"—is constant. ⊕2 days. See p. 23, **5**.

Taking the Train

The first part of this itinerary does not require a car. You can easily reach Cologne, Berlin, Dresden, and Munich by train, saving yourself the expense and hassle of driving. From Munich, the itinerary ventures off into the countryside and includes a scenic driving tour, so having a car is necessary. You can easily rent one in Munich and return it in Stuttgart or Frankfurt.

Drive south on Day 8 from Munich to Garmisch-Partenkirchen via A95, B2, and B23 (90km/56 miles). The trip should take a little over an hour.

6 ★★ Garmisch-Partenkirchen. Your overnight stay for Day 8 is a famed sports and ski resort lying beneath the Wetterstein mountain range of the Bavarian Alps. Ski, hike, climb, or simply stroll around the resort and enjoy the Alpine views. But don't miss a trip on a cog railway to the top of the **Zugspitze** (p. 324, **3**), Germany's highest peak. ⊕1 day. See p. 348.

On Day 9 you'll be driving from Garmisch-Partenkirchen to Füssen, making three important stops along the way. The first, the Wieskirche near Steingaden, is 45km (28 miles) northwest of Garmisch-Partenkirchen via B23 and St2059.

7 ★★★ Wieskirche (Church in the Meadow). Looking at the rather sedate exterior of this church, you'd never guess the interior is world-famous for its exuberant rococo decoration. ⊕30 min. See p. 328, **3**.

From the Wieskirche, drive southwest on B17 to Schloss Neuschwanstein (24km/15 miles), about a 30-minute drive.

8 ★★★ Schloss Neuschwanstein.
Neuschwanstein Castle, the most famous castle in Germany, crowns its rocky crag like a collective fantasy worked out between the "Dream King" Ludwig, the illustrator Maxfield Parrish, and Walt Disney. However you view it, visiting this architectural icon is a memorable experience. ⏱ 35 min. once inside. See p. 338, **2**.

Take the shuttle bus or a horse-drawn carriage, or walk to Schloss Hohenschwangau.

9 ★★ Schloss Hohenschwangau. The "parent castle" of Neuschwanstein was built by Ludwig's father, Maximilian II of Bavaria, and was used as a summer retreat by the family, including little Ludwig, who later built his own castle above this one. ⏱ 35 min. once inside. See p. 340, **4**.

Füssen is 4.5km (2¾ miles) west of Neuschwanstein via St2008, a drive of about 10 minutes.

10 ★ Füssen. Your overnight stay for Day 9 is this lovely old town in the foothills of the Bavarian Alps. You can see the sights in a couple of hours; the **Lechfall**, a nearby waterfall, makes for a pleasant walk. ⏱ 2 hr. See p. 204, **6**.

From Füssen, take B12 west to Lindau (106km/66 miles), a drive that should take you about 1¾ hours.

11 ★★ Lindau. It's hard not to enjoy this balmy little town on the Bodensee (Lake Constance). Make it your overnight for Day 10 and forget about strenuous sightseeing. Instead, take a leisurely stroll through the charming Altstadt (Old Town), go biking or swimming, and enjoy a meal beside the picturesque harbor with its thousands of twinkling lights. ⏱ 1 day. See p. 390.

From Lindau, take B31 west to Freiburg im Breisgau (176km/110 miles), a drive of about 2½ hours. Part of this drive runs along the scenic northern shore of the Bodensee (Lake Constance).

12 ★★ Freiburg im Breisgau. Freiburg is your overnight destination for Day 11. If you arrive early enough, you might want to visit a couple of wineries on the nearby Kaiserstuhl (see the "Black Forest Vineyards" tour, p. 370).

Otherwise, stroll around and enjoy the charms of this attractive university town with its rose-colored Gothic cathedral and numerous wine-restaurants. ⏱ 1 day. See p. 384.

To reach Baden-Baden, 111km (69 miles) north of Freiburg, you have several options. By car, we recommend the 232km (144-mile) Schwarzwaldhochstrasse (Black Forest Crest Road), one of Germany's prettiest and most popular scenic drives, if you have the time—it takes about 6 hours with stops. (See the "Black Forest Crest Road" tour on p. 362; it's set up from Baden-Baden to Freiburg, so you would be doing the tour in reverse). A second option is a more direct route, which will get you to Baden-Baden in about 1¼ hours: From Freiburg, take B3 north and continue on B500 and L84a/Lichtentaler Strasse. A third option is to drop off your car in Freiburg and take the train; direct trains will get you to Baden-Baden in under an hour, regional trains in about 1½ hours.

13 ★★ Baden-Baden. Germany's most famous spa resort is your overnight stop for Day 12. You'll enjoy your stay even more if you visit the giant **Friedrichsbad** bath complex (p. 382, **7**) and go through the full Roman-Irish bath ritual. ⏱ 1 day. See p. 380.

Heidelberg, your destination for Day 13, is 93km (58 miles) north of Baden-Baden via B500, A5, and L600a; the drive should take about 1 hour. By train, you can get there in about 1 hour 20 minutes, with a change in Karlsruhe.

14 ★★ Heidelberg. For many, Heidelberg epitomizes "romantic Germany." With its famous **castle** (p. 427, **8**), its ancient university centered around the charming **Universitätsplatz** (University Square; p. 426, **3**), and its architecturally distinctive streets, this is one of the loveliest small cities in Germany. ⏱ 1 day. See p. 424.

Frankfurt, where this 2-week itinerary ends, is 89km (55 miles) north of Heidelberg, about an hour's drive on A5. Direct trains will get you there in under an hour.

15 Frankfurt. ⏱ 1 day. See p. 20, **1**.

Undiscovered Germany in 8 Days

Germany is a heavily populated country in heavily populated western Europe. In consequence, there is little of this country that is truly undiscovered. Still, it is big enough that in remote areas there are invariably many ways to avoid crowds, especially with a backpack and some decent hiking boots at your disposal. This itinerary seeks out some little-trafficked spaces, including a 1-day loop through the Swabian Alb—a fascinating area in southwestern Germany that visitors seldom explore (see chapter 9 for more on this region).

> *Northern Germany's Harz Mountains feature lakes, forests, mountain villages, and a popular national park that draws masses of adventuring tourists.*

START **Fly into Hamburg, then rent a car and drive east along the Baltic Sea coast, past Lübeck, Wismar, and Rostock, to Ahrenshoop (226km/140 miles).**

❶ **Ahrenshoop.** This small seacoast resort and artists' colony is a convenient gateway to the **Nationalpark Vorpommersche Boddenland-schaft** (West-Pomeranian Lagoon Landscape National Park; see "Northern Germany's National Parks," p. 566). A considerable part of the national park is set on the Fischland-Darss-Zingst peninsula. Ahrenshoop stands astride the narrow peninsula, stretching from the sandy

Baltic shore to a painterly harbor on the lagoon. The majority of visitors stick to the coast, meaning that the peninsula's interior is relatively undiscovered for those willing and able to tramp through it. The landscapes range from sand dunes along the seacoast that "wander" under the influence of waves and wind, to wetlands that just about qualify as rainforest, to areas that are only accessible via signposted hiking trails and wooden boardwalks that snake through the park. Shallow coastal waters around the peninsula are good spots for observing cranes and many other species of seabirds and wading

1. Ahrenshoop
2. Stralsund
3. Neustrelitz
4. Quedlinburg
5. Harz Mountains
6. Goslar
7. Tübingen
8. Urwelt-Museum Hauff
9. Burgruine Reussenstein
10. Uracher Wasserfall
11. Bärenhöhle
12. Burg Hohenzollern

> *A historic royal castle and church sit imperiously atop the pinnacle of Quedlinburg's Burgberg.*

birds, both indigenous and transient. From the seacoast resort of **Zingst** (p. 584, ⑤), you gain access to the peninsula's eastern end, the Sundische Wiese heathland. The *Bodden* of the national park's name refers to shallow lagoons that afford calm recreational waters for beginners or anyone who's not up to venturing out on the open sea. Canoes, kayaks, rowboats, and windsurf boards are available for rent from harbors along the seacoast and around the lagoons.

A colorful alternative, and easier on the muscles, is a short cruise onboard the replica Mississippi stern-wheel paddle steamer *River Star,* out of Prerow, operated by **Reederei Poschke** (☎ 038234/329; www.reederei-poschke.de). ⊕ At least 1 day.

From Ahrenshoop, head south and then east on B105, to Stralsund (66km/41 miles), from which you'll cross over to Rügen.

② **Stralsund.** Spend some time in this busy fishing port (p. 580, ⑥) and use it as a base to cross over to **Rügen** (p. 585, ⑦). Allot one of your 2 days to making a circuit of Rügen by car; take in the island's extremities at **Putgarten, Sassnitz,** and **Thiessow,** for a round-trip of around 200km (124 miles). ⊕ 2 days.

On Day 4, head south on B96, A20, and B104 to Neubrandenburg, and continue on B96 to Neustrelitz (138km/86 miles).

③ **Neustrelitz.** This town on the Zierker See is a good starting point for touring the **Mecklenburgische Seenplatte** (Mecklenburg Lake District; p. 588). With more than a thousand lakes to choose from, you'll have plenty of

options for getting away from the crowds that gather at the most popular choke points. Follow a route that trends northwest through the lake district, via **Waren** (p. 590), **Krakow am See, Dobbertin,** and **Sternberg,** to **Schwerin** (p. 610), on the western shore of Schweriner See. This journey runs to around 160km (99 miles). With an early enough start to the day, you could easily add another 50km (31 miles) for diversions to small lakes that take your fancy. ⊕ 1½ days.

From Schwerin, hit the Autobahn south and southwest (A24, A10, and A2) for a fast transfer to Quedlinburg, a total distance of 365km (227 miles).

④ **Quedlinburg.** Stay overnight in one of Germany's loveliest towns. ⊕ 4 hr. See p. 186.

From Quedlinburg on Day 6, take L239 south and then L92 west to Thale (10km/6 miles).

⑤ **Harz Mountains.** Northern Germany's most important, and highest, mountain range affords multiple avenues of escape from crowds and stress. At **Thale,** a town that's an eastern gateway to the mountains, you can spend a rewarding few hours hiking into the rugged **Bodetal** (Bode River valley). Pick up the trailhead by driving or walking 5km (3 miles) south on Friedrichsbrunner Strasse (L240) to the **Hexentanzplatz** (Witches' Dancing Ground). Or ride the cable car operated by **Seilbahnen Thale** (☎ 03947/2500; www.seilbahnen-thale.de) from the cable-car station on Goetheweg up to the Hexentanzplatz. Along the Bodetal trail, place names such as **Goethe-Felsen** (Goethe Rock), **Königsruhe** (King's Rest), and **Teufelsbrücke** (Devil's Bridge) provide a flavor of this romantic and scenic gorge. Back at Thale, after a round-trip hike of about 8km (5 miles), return to your car and head deeper into the Harz. A good route to follow from Thale is through Blankenburg, Elbingerode, Wernigerode (p. 153), Drei Annen Hohne, Schierke, Braunlage, Torfhaus, Altenau, Schulenberg, and Clausthal-Zellerfeld, ending at Goslar; the winding mountain roads will make the 125km (78-mile) distance seem longer. ⊕ 1 day. Thale tourist information: Bahnhofstrasse 3. ☎ 03947/2597. www.thale.de.

⑥ **Goslar.** A bustling mountain town—and former imperial residence—Goslar is a good place to overnight, with the intention of getting an early start the next day on the long ride to southern Germany. See p. 544.

On Day 7, from Goslar—just 24km (15 miles) from the A7 north-south Autobahn—take A7 and A81 south all the way to Tübingen (520km/323 miles).

7 ★★ **Tübingen.** This picturesque town on the banks of the Neckar and Ammer rivers is famous for its university, founded in 1477, and for its medieval Altstadt (Old Town). Wander around the town's narrow lanes and admire its half-timber houses before you turn in for the night. See p. 402, **4**; for hotel and restaurant recommendations, see p. 403.

Spend your last day touring the Swabian Alb. Holzmaden is 69km (43 miles) northeast of Tübingen, about a 50-minute drive. Head east on B28, and continue north on B27 and then east on A8; in Holzmaden, follow signs to Urwelt-Museum Hauff.

8 ★ **Urwelt-Museum Hauff.** You gain an overview of the prehistoric origins of the Swabian Alb in this small museum. ⏱ 15 min. See p. 416, **2**.

Burgruine Reussenstein is 9km (5½ miles) south of Holzmaden on L1200.

9 ★ **Burgruine Reussenstein (Castle Ruins).** This impressive ruin atop a 760m-high (2,500-ft.) escarpment is all that remains of a 13th-century castle. A lookout point in the castle ruins provides a dramatic view of the entire valley below. ⏱ 30 min. See p. 416, **3**.

From Burgruine Reussenstein, take L1200 east to the village of Wiesensteig and follow the marked roads of the Schwäbische Albstrasse (Swabian Alb Road) south and west via Westerheim and Donnstetten to Bad Urach (23km/14 miles).

10 ★ **Uracher Wasserfall (Urach Falls).** A path leads from the delightfully picturesque town of Bad Urach with its half-timber houses to this impressive cascade hidden in the surrounding forest. ⏱ 20 min. to and from the waterfall. See p. 418, **4**.

Follow the signposted Schwäbische Albstrasse (K6708) via Ohnastetten and Holzelfingen, and then head southwest on B313

> *Colorful half-timber houses line the Neckar River in Tübingen.*

to Erpfingen, a 34km (21-mile) drive that will take about 40 minutes.

11 kids **Bärenhöhle (Bear Cave).** This cave with its stalactites and stalagmites offers a glimpse of what lies beneath the Alb. ⏱ 30 min. See p. 418, **6**.

Burg Hohenzollern is 43km (27 miles) southwest of Bärenhöhle via K6767, L382, K7103, L360, and K7111, about a 1-hour drive.

12 ★★ **Burg Hohenzollern.** Hohenzollern Castle—the ancient seat of the Hohenzollern dynasty—crowns a pinnacle and provides a stunning panorama. ⏱ 90 min. See p. 419, **8**.

After visiting Burg Hohenzollern you can easily head back to Tübingen, which is only 28km (17 miles) north via B27, about a 30-minute drive.

Travel Tip

If you have time to extend your stay in the region, I'd recommend spending some time in either charming, romantic Heidelberg (p. 424) or vibrant, modern Stuttgart (p. 430). Neither city is "undiscovered," but they are both well worth your time.

Northern Germany in 1 Week

The bright lights of Cologne, Hamburg, Berlin, and Dresden are in here, as indeed they must be, even though getting to and around them uses up a big chunk of your time-budget. Hameln is a convenient and notable stop along the way, and both Lübeck and Schwerin are so close to Hamburg that it would be a pity to pass them up. In addition, there are a few suggestions for detours that no self-respecting North German itinerary could bring itself to leave out.

> *Six warehouses that once stored salt from Lüneburg are among the beautiful buildings that line the Trave waterfront in Lübeck.*

START **Fly into Frankfurt, then rent a car and drive northward through Limburg, the Rhine Valley, and Bonn to Cologne. It's 215km (133 miles) from Frankfurt to Cologne.**

❶ **Cologne (Köln).** Stroll around the historic heart of town, or take a boat tour on the Rhine, unwind, visit a bar or two, and set yourself up for a good evening meal. ⏱ 1 day. See p. 482.

For **Day 2**, you'll want to get out of the industrial Ruhr region quickly. Go north on A1 and east on A44, skirting the scenic Sauerland region's western and northern rim. At War-

Taking the Train

This grand tour around some of the highlights in the northern half of Germany is designed to be done by car, and a few extras and options have been included that can only be done by car in the time available. The itinerary's main elements are, however, eminently doable by train, and what you lose by missing out on some places along the way, you gain by being able to sit back and watch northern Germany flow past your window.

> A parade and play recreate the famed children's fable of the Pied Piper of Hamelin each Sunday at noon.

burg, switch to **B252, B241, B64, and B83,** which lead north to the **Weser River** at **Holzminden** (p. 502), and then head north along the river, through **Bodenwerder** (p. 515,), to **Hameln,** a total distance of 310km (193 miles).

② **Hameln.** For children, visiting Hameln is a chance to imagine the legend of the Pied Piper of Hamelin. ⏱ 1 day. See p. 515, ⑧.

On the morning of **Day 3,** take **A2** and **A7** north from Hameln toward Hamburg (208km/129 miles).

③ **Hamburg.** A good plan is to visit a single museum, either the **Hamburger Kunsthalle** (p. 595, ②) or **BallinStadt—Das Auswanderermuseum Hamburg** (p. 601, ⑫), and then stick to the city's waterfront. Since this includes the Elbe River, the Binnenalster and the Aussenalster lakes, and the old harbor, that still leaves you plenty to see and do. Don't forget that Hamburg is known for its great dining and nightlife. ⏱ 1 day. See p. 594.

From Hamburg, the route on **Day 4** leads to Berlin by way of **Lübeck, Wismar,** and **Schwerin** (380km/236 miles). If you're short on time you could skip the three intermediate stops and head straight to Berlin (290km/180 miles). From Hamburg to Lübeck is 66km (41 miles) northeast on A1.

④ **Lübeck.** This historic city was the seat of the Baltic Sea–based Hanseatic League medieval trade federation (see p. 578 for more on the League). It retains many points of interest from those days and is also a vibrant and sophisticated small city that is still the mistress of Germany's Baltic coast. ⏱ 4 hr. See p. 606.

From Lübeck, take **B105** east to Wismar (58km/36 miles).

⑤ **Wismar.** Make a brief stop at this attractive old Hanseatic port. Strolling around the restored —and now bustling—Altstadt (Old Town) gives you a taste of how former East German towns are shaping up 2 decades after Germany's reunification. ⏱ 2 hr. See p. 579.

From Wismar, take **B106** south to Schwerin (32km/20 miles).

⑥ **Schwerin.** Even more so than Wismar, Schwerin is a poster-boy for grim and crumbling East German towns that since reunification have made their way confidently into a new era. Mecklenburg-Vorpommern's elegant state capital had a lot going for it to begin with—a history as seat of the powerful

Side Trips on the Way to Hamburg

On the way from Hameln to Hamburg, there are three diversions you should consider. Leave the highway at Wunstorf, west of Hannover, for a short stop at **Steinhuder Meer** (p. 527, ④), the largest lake in Niedersachsen (Lower Saxony), at the resort town of Steinhude, before returning to the highway and continuing north. If you're traveling with children, consider leaving the highway at Hodenhagen, to visit **Serengeti-Park** (p. 522, ④). Farther north, another easy diversion is through Egestorf to **Undeloh,** a village in the heart of the **Naturpark Lüneburger Heide** (Lüneburg Heath Nature Park; p. 528, ⑥).

> *The tree-lined Unter den Linden is Berlin's central boulevard, stretching from the Brandenburg Gate to Museumsinsel in the Spree River.*

grand dukes of Mecklenburg-Schwerin, and a scenic setting on the shores of **Schweriner See** (Schwerin Lake; p. 610, ❹). ⏱ 4 hr. See p. 610.

From Schwerin, settle down for the long ride on A14, A24, and A10 to Berlin (210km/130 miles). Aim to arrive in the evening with enough time for dinner in one of the national capital's plethora of fine restaurants.

❼ **Berlin.** Ah, Berlin . . . where to begin? You should aim to stay 2 nights in the capital, since that's the only way to get a full day out of it. For suggestions on making the most out of your day, see "The Best of Berlin in 1 Day" on p. 50. ⏱ 1 day.

Side Trips Around Dresden

On the way from Berlin to Dresden, consider a 16km (10-mile) detour to **Lübbenau** (p. 136, ❷), which affords you a taste of the fascinating **Spreewald** (p. 136). Should you have even a smidgen of spare time on the way from Dresden to Frankfurt, spend it on **Eisenach** (p. 178) and its stunning castle, the **Wartburg** (p. 178, ❹), at a cost of just an additional 12km (7½ miles).

From Berlin, it's a fast charge down Autobahn A13 to Dresden (194km/120 miles) for Day 6.

❽ **Dresden.** Once ensconced in Dresden, you'll want to see something of how the city has bounced back from virtually complete devastation in World War II to regain its crown as the queen of German baroque cities. Then break into one of the big palace complexes—the **Zwinger** (p. 166, ❶), the **Residenzschloss** (Royal Palace; p. 169, ❸), or **Schloss Pillnitz** (Pillnitz Palace; p. 150, ❾). Relax on a short **boat tour** (p. 172) of the magical Elbe River valley, onboard an antique steamer. ⏱ 1 day.

On Day 7, go southwest from Dresden on A4 and A5 to Frankfurt. This is a long drive (465km/288 miles), even if it is Autobahn all the way.

❾ **Frankfurt.** Spend whatever time you have left on your last day exploring Frankfurt. Some good options include strolling through the **Römerberg** (p. 474, ❷), Frankfurt's historic core, or admiring the works of such European masters as Renoir, Monet, and van Eyck at the **Städel Museum** (p. 480, ❼). See p. 474.

Southern Germany in 1 Week

Northern Germany has the lion's share of big, exciting, culturally rich cities, but southern Germany has great scenic splendors like the Black Forest, the Bodensee (Lake Constance), and the Bavarian Alps. And it has Munich, of course. In short, southern Germany has all the ingredients necessary for a week of stimulating exploration.

> *Munich bursts into beer-inspired song and celebrations each September and October during Oktoberfest.*

START Fly into Munich.

❶ ★★★ Munich. It may be Germany's third-largest city (after Berlin and Hamburg), but it's number one in the hearts of almost all who visit (and is, in fact, the city where most Germans would live if they could). Give yourself 2 days to explore this big, fun-loving, artistically rich metropolis. To see the city in full party mode, visit during **Oktoberfest** (p. 278), the giant beer and food festival that takes place in September and October. But you can enjoy beer year-round in Munich because the city is famous for its giant beer halls, especially the **Hofbräuhaus am Platzl** (p. 283, ❹). The city is not all beer steins and oom-pah-pah, however. Far from it. Munich is one of the most artistically and culturally rich cities in Europe, with world-class art museums (the **Alte Pinakothek,** for instance, houses a stunning collection of Old Masters; p. 262, ❶), opera and ballet companies, and an urban core full of architectural treasures, including the **Residenz** (p. 274, ❶), the palace the ruling Wittelsbachs called home for hundreds of years. Stroll or bike around the giant **Englischer Garten** (p. 288, ❷), the oldest public park in the world; sniff around the food stalls in the **Viktualienmarkt** (a giant public market; p. 286, ❺); and, for a hit of the new, head out to **BMW Welt** (p. 269, ❺), an auto showroom/museum that's one of the most striking pieces of contemporary architecture in Europe. ☺ 2 days.

1 Munich

2 Schloss Neuschwanstein & Schloss Hohenschwangau

3 Wieskirche

4 Garmisch-Partenkirchen

5 Lindau

6 Mainau

7 Freiburg im Breisgau

8 Baden-Baden

> *Lindau's picturesque harbor on the Bodensee (also known as Lake Constance).*

Neuschwanstein and Hohenschwangau castles are located 116km (72 miles) southwest of Munich via A8 and B17. With a car, you can make the castles and the nearby Wieskirche a day trip from Munich. There is no train service to these places, but several tour operators in Munich offer guided bus tours.

② ★★★ **Schloss Neuschwanstein & Schloss Hohenschwangau.** Neuschwanstein, the "fairy-tale castle" built by Ludwig II, is the most popular and most photographed tourist attraction in Germany. Some advance planning is required if you want to see it and neighboring Hohenschwangau Castle, built by Ludwig's father, Maximilian II, without waiting in line for hours. ⏱ 35 min. to tour each castle once you're inside. See p. 338, **②**, & p. 340, **④**.

The Wieskirche, is 25km (15 miles) northeast of Neuschwanstein, about a 25-minute drive. Head north on St2016, and continue on St2059 and St2559; the church is near the village of Steingaden.

③ ★★★ **Wieskirche.** The name translates as "Church in the Meadow," but the Wieskirche is no ordinary church. From the outside it's fairly sedate-looking, but step inside. If you've never seen rococo in full bloom, you're in for a dazzling surprise. ⏱ 30 min. See p. 328, **③**.

If you're returning to Munich from the Wieskirche for your overnight on Day 3, head north on St2559 and St2059, then follow B17 and St2054 to the A96, which will bring you to Munich; the 114km (71-mile) drive takes about 1½ hours. Or you can spend Nights 3 and 4 in Garmisch-Partenkirchen, 45km (28 miles) south of the Wieskirche. Head south on St2559, turn right at St2059 and right again at B23; the drive should take about 45 minutes. You can also reach Garmisch-Partenkirchen by train from Munich in about 1½ hours.

④ ★★ **Garmisch-Partenkirchen.** These combined towns in the Bavarian Alps became Germany's most famous ski resort in 1936, when the Winter Olympics were held here. The towns themselves aren't particularly exciting, but their setting, below several major peaks, is spectacular. What I'd suggest you do here is check into your hotel and then head over to the train station to get the cog railway that will carry you on the first leg of a trip up the **Zugspitze** (p. 324, **③**), Germany's highest mountain. ⏱ 1 day. See p. 348.

Taking the Train

You might want to consider going carless for most of this itinerary. Except for visiting Ludwig II's Neuschwanstein Castle and the Wieskirche, you can reach all the recommended places by train. To see Neuschwanstein and the Wieskirche you could rent a car in Munich for 1 day and make those destinations a day trip.

On Day 5, take A7 and A96 east to Lindau (194km/121 miles), a drive of a little over 2 hours. Spend the next 2 nights in Lindau.

⑤ ★★ Lindau. Shimmering in the foothills of the Alps, the Bodensee (Lake Constance) is Germany's largest and Europe's third-largest lake, stretching some 74km (46 miles). The island-city of Lindau is the most charming and picturesque town on the Bodensee's shores. This is a small, mostly car-free town where simple pleasures, not frenzied sightseeing, are the order of the day. Stroll through the historic Altstadt (Old Town), sip an aperitif or coffee at a harborside cafe, go swimming or biking, and maybe visit the casino. Don't rush, whatever you do. ⏱ 1 day. See p. 390.

On Day 6, the island of Mainau makes a lovely, relaxing, car-less day trip from Lindau. Take one of the daily passenger ferries that leave from Lindau's picturesque harbor.

⑥ ★★ Mainau. It's a small jewel of an island, blessed with a semitropical climate and famous for the colorful and luxurious gardens planted by the Bernadotte family. Sniff the roses, smell the orange blossoms, wander through the baroque palace, and enjoy the views of the lake all around you. ⏱ 1 day. See p. 361, **⑤**.

On Day 7, take B31 northwest to Freiburg im Breisgau (177km/110 miles), about a 2½-hour drive.

⑦ ★★ Freiburg im Breisgau. Little brooks called *Bächle* run alongside the streets in Freiburg, adding to the charm of this old university town. You can see everything in a couple of hours, and then perhaps make an excursion to the nearby vineyards. ⏱ 2 hr. See p. 384.

Baden-Baden is 111km (69 miles) north of Freiburg. You can easily get there by direct train in under an hour. But if you have a car and the time, consider taking the wonderfully scenic 232km (144-mile) Black Forest Crest Road (Schwarzwaldhochstrasse), which runs almost the entire length of the Black Forest at heights of about 1,000m (3,280 ft.). See the "Black Forest Crest Road" tour on p. 362.

⑧ ★★ Baden-Baden. The thermal springs beneath Germany's most famous spa resort have been used to treat arthritis and various ailments for over 2,000 years, and continue to be used in various Baden-Baden clinics today. The town became fashionable in the 19th century, which is when the amazing **Friedrichs-bad** bath complex (p. 382, **⑦**) was built. And we'd recommend a visit to Baden-Baden is worth it just to experience the 3-hour Roman-Irish bath ritual you get there. You couldn't end your tour of southern Germany on a more relaxing note. ⏱ At least a half-day. See p. 380.

From Baden-Baden you can return to Munich by train in about 3½ hours, or get to Frankfurt Airport (Germany's main international hub) in about 1½ hours.

> *A perfect day trip from Lindau, the fabled garden island of Mainau in the Bodensee is a breathtaking vision when in bloom.*

Germany with Your Family

Be realistic: No kid wants to go on a vacation and spend hours, day after day, in museums. Make a museum or two part of your plans, of course, but your trip to Germany will have more impact on your kids if you expose them to Germany's vibrant urban life, its fairy-tale castles, and its majestic natural wonders. Thrill them by traveling at least part of this suggested itinerary on one of Germany's sleek high-speed trains.

> Husum makes a great jumping-off point for outdoor adventures along Germany's northern coast.

START Fly into Hamburg. TRIP LENGTH 10 days.

❶ Hamburg. The great city of the north has many family-friendly attractions. The city's **Tierpark Hagenbeck** (p. 602, ❶) is one of Germany's leading zoos. **Miniatur Wunderland** (p. 600, ❿) is the largest scale-model railway in the world, taking up a sizeable chunk of the old harbor warehouse it occupies. Also in the old port area is **BallinStadt—Das Auswanderermuseum Hamburg** (Emigrants Museum; p. 601, ❶), an amazing museum covering the city's history as an outlet point

for generations of emigrants to the New World. Boat tours on the **Elbe River** and on the **Binnenalster** and **Aussenalster** lakes (see "Hamburg by Boat," p. 598) are other good options. In summer, you can sail on a day trip from Hamburg to the North Sea island of Helgoland (p. 565). ⏱1 day for Hamburg, plus an optional 1 day for Helgoland. See p. 594.

Go east on A24 to the Kreuz Hamburg-Ost interchange, and then northeast on A1 to Lübeck, a distance of 66km (41 miles). It's a 36-minute ride on the high-speed ICE train.

1 Hamburg
2 Lübeck
3 Husum
4 Bremerhaven
5 Munich
6 Zugspitze
7 Schloss Neuschwanstein
8 Lindau
9 Mainau
10 Schwarzwald

> *The Figurentheater-Lübeck offers puppet shows right next door to the impressive Puppet Theater Museum in seaside Lübeck.*

2 Lübeck. A good day trip from Hamburg in summer is to nearby Lübeck. In the town, the kids might like to visit the **TheaterFigurenMuseum** (Puppet Theater Museum; p. 607, **3**), which boasts that it holds the world's largest marionette collection. Check out what's playing next door (unless the language barrier is too much of a problem) at the marvelous **Figurentheater-Lübeck** puppet theater. Just beyond Lübeck is **Timmendorfer Strand** (see "Linging in Lubeck"p. 564), one of the best beach resorts hereabouts. ⏱1 day. See p. 606.

From Hamburg, go north on A23 and its continuation, B5, for a distance of 143km (89 miles), which you can do in around 1¾ hours. By train from Hamburg, you're looking at a ride of around 2 hours.

3 Husum. For a second day trip from Hamburg, head up Schleswig-Holstein's west coast to Husum. A unique activity on the shallow Wattenmeer (Wadden Sea) is *Wattwandern* (see "Mudflat Hiking," p. 570), literally walking on the seabed. Be sure to book with a registered guide; this is not something you should attempt on your own. Consider a cruise to the **Nord-Friesische Inseln** (North Frisian Islands) or the small islets known as the **Halligen** (see "North Frisian Ferries," p. 563); even better would be a boat tour that allows you to stroll on an exposed sandbank that will soon be underwater again (these tours, operated by Halligreederei MS Hauke Haien, leave from Schlüttsiel, p. 570, **3**). ⏱1 day. See p. 570, **2**.

Go west from Hamburg on B73 and B71 to Bremerhaven, a pleasant drive of 124km (77 miles). The train to Bremerhaven (transfer at Bremen) takes around 1¾ hours.

4 Bremerhaven. A third day trip from Hamburg takes you west to this port town on the Weser River. Among possible activities here are visits to the **Deutsches Schiffahrtsmuseum** (German Maritime Museum) and to **Zoo am Meer** (Sea Zoo; p. 523, **8**). ⏱1 day. See p. 542, **9**.

Ride the rails from Hamburg to Munich. The fastest ICE (high-speed) trains do the 775km (482-mile) journey in 5½ hours.

5 ★★★ **Munich.** It's big, it's boisterous, but it's also safe and friendly, and a great place to explore with your family. Give yourself at least 2 days in Munich. If you have kids in tow, you'll definitely want to explore **Marienplatz** (p. 252, **1**) and watch the Glockenspiel (Carillon) display on the **Neues Rathaus** (New Town Hall; p. 254, **2**). Also make a point to wander through the nearby **Viktualienmarkt** (p. 286, **5**), Munich's marvelous outdoor food market. Visit either the **Deutsches Museum** (p. 266, **1**), a gigantic treasure trove devoted to science and technology through the ages, or to the **Deutsches Museum Verkehrszentrum** (p. 268, **4**), a transportation museum filled with historic and modern vehicles of all kinds. To boost the cultural-historical ante, visit either the **Residenz** (Royal Palace; p. 274, **1**) or nearby **Schloss Nymphenburg** (Nymphenburg Palace; p. 274, **2**). ⏱ 2 days. See p. 247.

Garmisch-Partenkirchen is about 97km (60 miles) southwest of Munich. You can easily make this a day trip; trains are frequent and take about 1½ hours from Munich. Just behind the train station at Garmisch-Partenkirchen is the station for the cog railway up the Zugspitze.

6 ★★★ **Zugspitze.** An adventure on a grand scale awaits you at Garmisch-Partenkirchen, where you board a cog railway to begin your ascent of the Zugspitze, Germany's highest mountain. ⏱ 1 day. See p. 324, **3**.

Neuschwanstein is located 116km (72 miles) southwest of Munich via A8 and B17 (to Schwangau). With a car, you can make this a day trip from Munich and spend whatever time you have left on Day 7 there. If you want to stay near the castle, spend some time in Füssen (p. 204) after your castle tour and spend the night there.

7 ★★★ **Schloss Neuschwanstein.** Your kids' reference point (and maybe your own) to this "fairy-tale castle" will probably be Disney-based, since it served as a prototype for the Sleeping Beauty Castle in Disneyland. Its location, perched atop a high crag, makes getting up to the castle an adventure in itself. ⏱ 35 min. to tour the castle. See p. 338, **2**.

Lindau is 179km (111 miles) southwest of Munich on the Bodensee (Lake Constance), the largest lake in Germany. If you're staying in Munich and don't want to drive, you can get to Lindau by direct train in about 2¼ hours. By car from Munich, take the A96 Autobahn and then B31. If you're driving from Füssen (147km/91 miles), follow B310 and B308 west, turning south on B12.

8 ★★ **Lindau.** This little, laid-back resort-town on an island in the Bodensee is a surprise to many, and a delight for families. Stroll, ride bikes, swim in the lake or in one of the municipal pools—Lindau is about kicking back and relaxing. ⏱ 1 day. See p. 390.

The island of Mainau, about 53km (33 miles) west of Lindau, makes a great day trip and doesn't require a car.

9 ★★ **Mainau.** Reached by ferry from Lindau, this semitropical garden-island in the Bodensee enchants visitors with its lush plantings, lake views, and baroque palace. ⏱ 1 day. See p. 361, **5**.

From Lindau, you can reach Freiburg im Breisgau by direct train, but once there, rent a car so you can explore the Black Forest countryside. To drive from Lindau, take B31 northwest (177km/110 miles).

10 ★★★ **Schwarzwald (Black Forest).** There are many ways to enjoy the Black Forest with your family. If you base yourself in **Freiburg im Breisgau** (p. 384), for instance, you can make an easy 145km (90-mile) side trip that loops around to a lake, a waterfall, and two cable cars (see "High Points of the Black Forest," p. 359). Or you can take one of the most scenic and popular car trips in Germany by driving from Freiburg im Breisgau to **Baden-Baden** (p. 380) along the **Schwarzwaldhochstrasse** (Black Forest Crest Road), which runs almost the entire length of the forest (p. 362). ⏱ 1 day.

From Baden-Baden you can return to Munich by train in about 3½ hours or via the A8 southeast by car (331km/206 miles). You can get to Frankfurt (Germany's main international airport) by train in about 1½ hours; by car take the A5 north (177km/110 miles).

3
Berlin

Our Favorite Berlin Moments

Berlin has it all. This world city has raised itself from the ashes of destruction and decades of division and now offers visitors world-class museums and attractions, wild-and-wonderful nightlife, shopping fit for both kings and commoners, and food rustled up from all ends of the earth. Above all, Berlin has spirit and is happy to show it. Complement your dips into cultural treasures and history by getting out to less-advertised areas and experience Berlin in all its parts.

> PREVIOUS PAGE *The modern glass dome that sits atop the Reichstag.* THIS PAGE *Take in the Berlin sights from the Spree River, which flows through the heart of this beautiful city.*

❶ Sailing on the Spree River. You'll absorb a fascinating variety of cityscapes and an array of noteworthy sights as you float along. Start out at Schloss Charlottenburg in the west of the city and cruise gently eastward through the old heart of Berlin. See p. 139.

❷ Hanging out like ancient Greeks and Romans, on the Pergamon Altar's stairway of the gods. Rest your museum-weary feet with a stop on the massive stairway in the Pergamonmuseum, a striking vantage point from which to indulge in some people-watching. See p. 80, ❶⓱.

❸ Strolling like Nebuchadnezzar through ancient Babylon's Ishtar Gate. It's fascinating to consider that during the 6th century B.C., the great Babylonian ruler—along with nobles, soldiers, and commoners—passed through the monumental gateway that's been partially reconstructed inside the Pergamonmuseum. See p. 80, ⓱.

❹ Soaking up some rays on Tiergarten's grassy acres. You'll find it hard to believe you're in the heart of a great city. Later, stroll through the greenery and peruse sculptured monuments to various Teutonic big names. See p. 96.

❺ Downing a beer at Café am Neuen See. What could possibly go together more harmoniously than a *Biergarten* in Tiergarten? The Bavarian-style beer garden on the south shore of Neuer See (New Lake) serves up liquid refreshments that should hit the spot on a hot day. See p. 69, ⑤.

❻ Passing a morning or afternoon at Zoo Berlin. Check out the various feeding times posted at the gates of what was once called the Zoologischer Garten, and save some time for the fantastic aquarium. See p. 64, ⑨.

❼ Reading a book on Bebelplatz. Agreed, this is not the most exciting thing you can possibly do in Berlin. Still, savor your freedom to do so on the square where the Nazis kicked off their reign of terror in 1933 by publicly burning 20,000 "un-German" books. See p. 72, ⑧.

❽ Giving ear to a musical evening at the Philharmonie. The Berlin Philharmonic Orchestra's masterly musicians perform at this cool, modern concert hall. See p. 128.

❾ Taking in the spectacular views from the Fernsehturm's rotating Telecafé, 207.5m (681 ft.) above the ground. The Telecafé's eats, drinks, and fabulous views (virtually the entire city is laid out below your feet) are well worth an ear-popping ascent aboard the turbo-elevator of the Fernsehturm (Television Tower). See p. 83, ⑧.

❿ Celebrating diversity in Kreuzberg. Everyday life in Berlin's most multiethnic and multicultural (and in some parts poorest) district is not always smooth sailing. Yet much of the place has a vibrancy that's missing from areas where "mono-" is the prevailing social prefix. Our "The Best of Berlin in 2 Days" tour starts off in Kreuzberg; see p. 56.

⓫ Shopping for a steal at Kaufhaus des Westens. Hah! Small chance of that. Experiencing the awesome variety of upmarket consumer goods and goodies inside Germany's best-known department store will need to be its own shopping reward when you visit "KaDeWe." See p. 104.

> *Drink in some beer and beautiful sights by taking a seat at Café am Neuen See in Tiergarten's scenic greenery right in the heart of Berlin.*

⓬ Picking out bargains at Markt am Winterfeldtplatz. This large and much-loved street market has plenty of buzz, color, aromas, and general goodies; it's definitely worth going out of your way for. See p. 105.

⓭ Feeling the chill at Checkpoint Charlie. "Leaving the American Sector" is now easy to do at this former Cold War checkpoint since the Berlin Wall has all but vanished and U.S. and Soviet tanks no longer face off across a short, fateful space. See p. 55, ⓭.

⓮ Hitting the beach at Wannsee. A lake on the Havel River in southwest Berlin, the Wannsee is a popular get-away-from-it-all spot for city-stressed Berliners. Some like to peel off their outer skin on the FKK (naturist/nudist) stretch of Wannsee Beach. See "Wonderful Wannsee," p. 80.

⓯ Acting like a König or Königin in Potsdam. Germany's version of Versailles is at the end of an easy Metro-train ride from the heart of Berlin. It's easy to imagine you're a king or queen among the spectacular palaces, villas, and ornamental gardens from the 18th and 19th centuries that abound in this right royal showcase. See p. 130.

⓰ Eating a Berliner. No, not cannibalism! Just like U.S. president John F. Kennedy, this humble jam donut can proclaim (if only it could talk), "Ich bin ein Berliner!" Pick up one, or many, from almost any *Bäckerei* (bakery) or *Konditorei* (cafe or pastry shop).

Our Favorite Berlin Moments

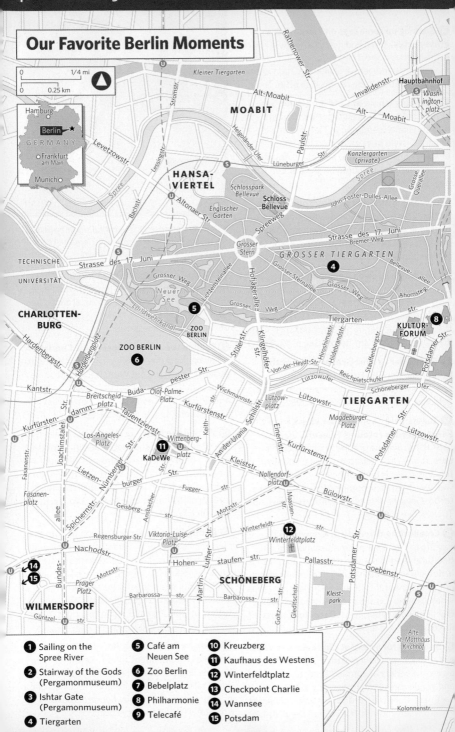

1. Sailing on the Spree River
2. Stairway of the Gods (Pergamonmuseum)
3. Ishtar Gate (Pergamonmuseum)
4. Tiergarten
5. Café am Neuen See
6. Zoo Berlin
7. Bebelplatz
8. Philharmonie
9. Telecafé
10. Kreuzberg
11. Kaufhaus des Westens
12. Winterfeldtplatz
13. Checkpoint Charlie
14. Wannsee
15. Potsdam

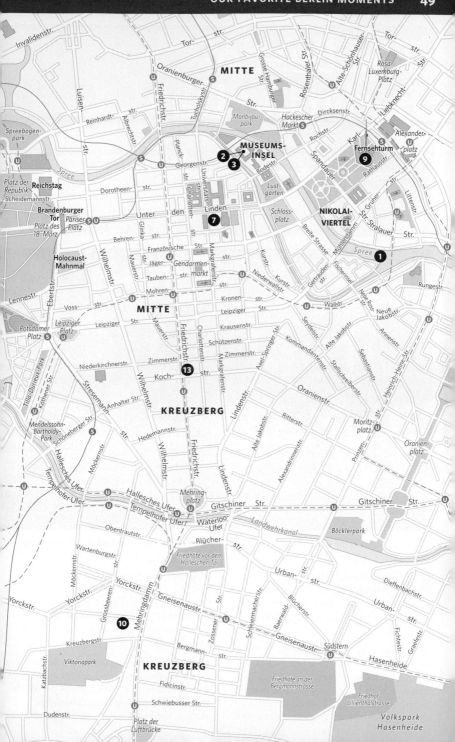

The Best of Berlin in 1 Day

You have a full itinerary ahead of you if you intend to absorb the best of Berlin (pop. 3.5 million) in a single day, so be sure to start out early. Working in your favor: Berlin's public transportation system, which makes it easy to get around the city center. In addition, some of the sights are very close together, and for others, like the iconic Brandenburg Gate, a few minutes are all you'll need to invest before checking it off your list.

> The broken links of this sculpture, titled Berlin, symbolize the former separation of East and West Berlin.

START Take the *U-Bahn* to Sophie-Charlotte-Platz or Richard-Wagner-Platz; or the *S-Bahn* to Westend; or bus no. M45, 109, or 309, all of which stop outside Schloss Charlottenburg.

1 ★★★ **Schloss Charlottenburg.** Named by a grieving Friedrich I, the first king of Prussia, for his wife Sophie Charlotte, who died in 1705 at age 36, Schloss Charlottenburg (Charlottenburg Palace) seems to reflect the young queen's sophistication allied with

a certain youthful verve. Its mix of graceful baroque and rococo architecture is complemented by gilded statues, delicate pastel tones, and the natural grace imparted by extensive gardens and a wooded park. ⏱ 90 min. See p. 68, **1**.

It's one heck of a long walk from Schloss Charlottenburg to the next sight. Instead, hop aboard bus no. M45 outside the palace and ride it to Zoologischer Garten bus station, then take bus no. 100 to the church.

> The Café am Neuen See, within Berlin's Tiergarten, offers a great place to grab some local refreshment amid pastoral beauty.

2 ★★ **Kaiser-Wilhelm-Gedächtniskirche.** Dating from 1895, the Kaiser Wilhelm Memorial Church, or what's left of it, has in effect become Berlin's memorial to itself—to the version of the city that was bombed to rubble in World War II. Take a few minutes to reflect amid the subdued bluish light inside the modern octagonal chapel. ⏲ 15 min. See p. 69, **3**.

3 ★★★ **Kaufhaus des Westens.** This is an optional stop for die-hard shoppers—feel free to give it a miss if you're pressed for time. Better known to Berliners as "KaDeWe," the giant Department Store of the West is a plush one-stop shopping emporium, and its bustling food department a great (if pricey) place to assuage the munchies. ⏲ 30 min. See p. 104.

Walk up to Budapester Strasse, and take bus no. 100 or 200 to the Grosser Stern stop, at the Siegessäule (Victory Column) in Tiergarten.

4 ★★★ **Tiergarten.** The city's central park provides a breath of fresh air and a chance to come face to face with sculptured images of the great and good from Germany's past—Bismarck, anyone? There are lakes, ponds, and waterways, grass and trees, a beer garden, and the spectacular **Siegessäule** (Victory Column; p. 69, **4**) at its heart. ⏲ 1 hr. See p. 96.

5 ★★★ **Reichstag.** Few edifices are burdened with as much historical freight as Germany's old imperial parliament building, with its bronze inscription to *Dem Deutschen Volke* (The German People) on the pediment. Gutted by a mysterious fire at the start of the Nazi era, and a target of Red Army troops who raised the Soviet Union's hammer-and-sickle banner over its ruins in 1945, the restored building houses the Bundestag, the lower house of Germany's Federal Parliament. ⏲ 30 min. See p. 69, **6**.

Getting Around Berlin

There are multiple options for getting around easily in Berlin, among them going by taxi. Many first-time visitors choose to take one of the hop-on-hop-off bus tours that run on a fixed circular route and take in many of the main sights. A cheaper alternative is to ride bus no. 100 or 200. Both cover a lot of the same ground, and with a public-transportation day-ticket for zones A and B, you'll come out ahead with a significant reduction over the tour-bus price. For information on Berlin's *U-Bahn* and *S-Bahn* system, see "Fast Facts" at the end of this chapter.

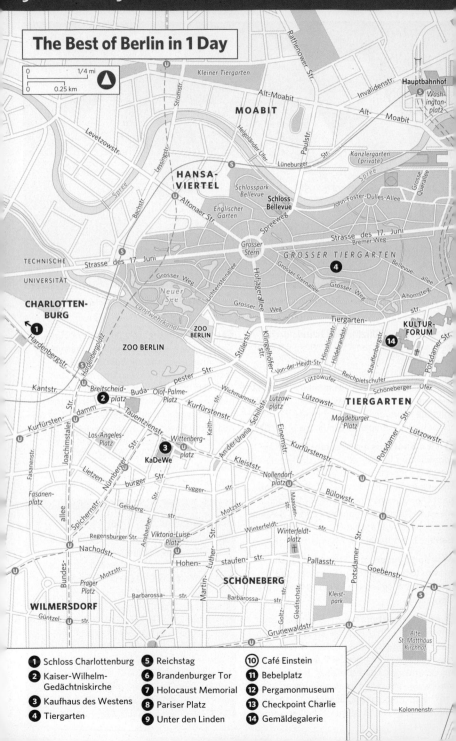

The Best of Berlin in 1 Day

0   1/4 mi
0   0.25 km

MOABIT

Kleiner Tiergarten

Alt-Moabit

Hauptbahnhof

Washington-platz

HANSA-VIERTEL

Schlosspark Bellevue

Schloss Bellevue

Kanzlergarten (private)

GROSSER TIERGARTEN

Grosser Stern

Strasse des 17. Juni

John-Foster-Dulles-Allee

TECHNISCHE UNIVERSITÄT

Strasse des 17. Juni

CHARLOTTEN-BURG

Hardenbergstr.

ZOO BERLIN

KULTUR-FORUM

Tiergarten-

TIERGARTEN

Kantstr.

Breitscheidplatz

Buda-

Olof-Palme-Platz

Kurfürstenstr.

Lützow-platz

Lützowstr.

Magdeburger Platz

Kurfürstendamm

Los-Angeles-Platz

Wittenberg-platz

KaDeWe

Kleiststr.

Nollendorf-platz

Bülowstr.

Fuggerstr.

Geisbergstr.

Winterfeldt-platz

Regensburger Str.

Viktoria-Luise-Platz

Winterfeldtstr.

Pallasstr.

Goebenstr.

Nachodstr.

Hohen-   staufen-   str.

SCHÖNEBERG

Kleist-park

WILMERSDORF

Prager Platz

Barbarossa-   str.

Barbarossa-

Grunewaldstr.

Alte St. Matthäus Kirchhof

Günzel-   str.

Kolonnenstr.

1 Schloss Charlottenburg
2 Kaiser-Wilhelm-Gedächtniskirche
3 Kaufhaus des Westens
4 Tiergarten
5 Reichstag
6 Brandenburger Tor
7 Holocaust Memorial
8 Pariser Platz
9 Unter den Linden
10 Café Einstein
11 Bebelplatz
12 Pergamonmuseum
13 Checkpoint Charlie
14 Gemäldegalerie

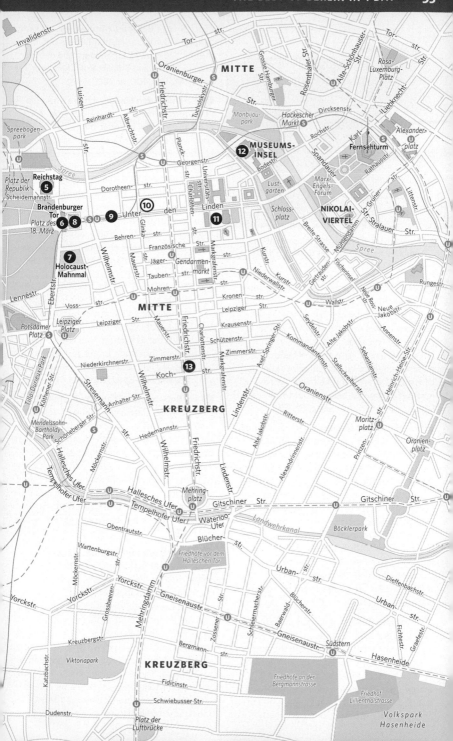

> *The enormous and sobering Holocaust Memorial features a maze of passages through a field of massive granite slabs.*

6 ★★★ **Brandenburger Tor (Brandenburg Gate).** Invading foreign armies have paraded through Brandenburger Tor (1791), as have German armies just back from invading, or setting out to invade, some nearby country. It's kind of a neat little piece of historical payback, then, to flit back and forth under the triumphal arch yourself without having invaded anyone, or being about to invade anyone, or being invaded. See p. 69, **7**.

7 ★★ **Holocaust Memorial.** Formally known as the Denkmal für die Ermordeten Juden Europas (Memorial for the Murdered Jews of Europe), this monument to the six million Jews murdered by the Nazis is a vast and somber sight. Its 2,711 gray concrete stelae cover a substantial swath of prime central Berlin real estate. Visitors stroll pensively through its narrow, mazelike passages. And in a sad yet hopeful echo of the many child victims whose laughter was silenced, children clamber over the slabs. ⏲ 45 min. Stresemannstrasse 90. ☎ 030/2639-4336. Free admission. *S-Bahn:* Unter den Linden.

8 ★ **Pariser Platz.** Though it's still graceful enough, it's likely fair to infer that "Paris Square" isn't what it was back in the day, when it was dubbed the "salon of Berlin," before World War II bombs and shells razed it to the ground. A museum on the rebuilt square is dedicated to the Kennedy family, one of whom—U.S. president John F. Kennedy—won

the hearts of Berliners during the Cold War by famously declaring that he was one of them. ⏲ 20 min. At the western end of Unter den Linden. *U- and S-Bahn:* Brandenburger Tor. Bus: M41, TXL, 100, or 200.

9 ★★ **Unter den Linden.** If there's a single Berlin street that's worth walking from end to end and perusing in detail, the central boulevard lined with a double row of linden (lime) trees, has to be it. At one end is Pariser Platz and the Brandenburg Gate, and at the other a bridge that leads to Museumsinsel, an island in the Spree River that's packed with some of Germany's most noteworthy museums. In between is an array of elegant buildings, among them Madame Tussauds, the Guggenheim Gallery, Humboldt University, the city's opera house, and the German Historical Museum. ⏲ 1 hr.

10 🍴 ★★ **Café Einstein.** This Berlin institution is a no-brainer for a break involving something light like coffee and *Apfelstrudel,* or even a full-scale lunch. It's tempting to linger in the cafe's own art gallery, but don't forget you have a lot of the city left to see. Unter den Linden 42. ☎ 030/204-3632. 8€-16€.

11 ★★ **Bebelplatz.** Opening off Unter den Linden, Bebelplatz is the scene of a chilling historical event. A small memorial recalls the 1933 book-burning on the square by Nazi brownshirts, a premonitory episode of far worse to come. But it's also worth visiting in its own right to view the imposing 18th- and 19th-century buildings that line the square in an array of architectural styles—from neoclassical to baroque to rococo. ⏲ 15 min. See p. 72, **8**.

12 ★★★ **Pergamonmuseum.** It seems astonishing that just by going to Berlin you get to see such awesome reconstructed ancient monuments as Babylon's Ishtar Gate, with its cobalt-blue glazed tiles, Nebuchadnezzar's Throne Room, the Altar of Zeus and the Telephos Frieze from Pergamon, and the gate to the Agora of Miletus, along with more recent works such as the cupola from the Alhambra in Granada. There are a bunch of other museums on Museumsinsel (Museum Island), all within a few minutes walking distance at most, so if none of the above gets your juices

> *Marvel at rebuilt ancient monuments at the magnificent Pergamonmuseum; shown here, the Pergamon Altar, a massive reconstructed stairway, colonnade, and frieze from the Temple of Zeus.*

flowing, fear not, multiple alternatives are right at hand. ⏱ 90 min. See p. 80, **17**.

Walk along Georgenstrasse to *U-Bahn* Friedrichstrasse and take the train to *U-Bahn* Kochstrasse; the station is on Friedrichstrasse, just south of Checkpoint Charlie.

⓭ ★★ **Checkpoint Charlie.** A tough little mind game at this spot on Friedrichstrasse is to try to think yourself back in time to the Cold War and the Berlin Wall, and to take seriously the once-ominous sign: YOU ARE LEAVING THE AMERICAN SECTOR. The original guardhouse at Checkpoint C—"Charlie" in NATO parlance—is at the Allied Museum in the city's Dahlem district. A replica now holds the fort, and there's a museum, the **Haus am Checkpoint Charlie,** Friedrichstrasse 43–45 (☎ 030/253-7250; www.mauermuseum.de), just across the street. ⏱ 30 min. *U-Bahn:* Kochstrasse.

Take bus no. M29 from Kochstrasse to Potsdamer Strasse.

⓮ ★★★ **Gemäldegalerie (Picture Gallery).** Seeing two world-class museums in a single day can be a tall order for anyone, but this is well worth trying to fit in if you can—you've got until 6pm (or 10pm on Thursday). The bumper crop of European masters

represented here includes Rembrandt, Vermeer, Van Eyck, Bruegel, Titian, Caravaggio, and more. If you'd like to focus on German artists, head to rooms I through III and cabinets (side rooms) 1 through 4, where you'll see works by the likes of Lucas Cranach, Albrecht Dürer, and Hans Holbein. If you're more interested in modern art, head instead to the Neue Nationalgalerie (p. 75, **6**), just across the way. ⏱ 90 min. See p. 78, **7**.

Museumsinsel Reconstruction

Museumsinsel (Museum Island) as a whole, and most of the individual museums that give the island its name, are caught up in a decades-long, big-bucks (or euros) reconstruction, consolidation, and renovation project. Right now, and for some time to come, the Pergamonmuseum is taking its turn. However, the museum's management is keeping almost all of it open, doing the work one section at a time. At worst, some of the large-scale exhibits will be covered with clear plastic sheeting for protection. If that should change on short notice, you can always switch to one of the other stellar museums on the island, all of them within easy reach.

The Best of Berlin in 2 Days

On your second day, start out by gaining an insight into everyday life in bustling, multiethnic Kreuzberg, before heading, by way of the Jewish Museum, to the stellar museums on Museumsinsel and to a booming shopping and entertainment district in and around the old Jewish Quarter, in what used to be blighted East Berlin. From here, it's an easy tram ride out to trendy and blossoming Prenzlauer Berg, which in Communist times was a dreary residential zone.

> Berlin's Jüdisches Museum honors the memory of the millions of Jewish people who perished in the horrors of World War II.

START From the city center, take bus no. M19 to Katzbachstrasse.

1 ★ **Viktoriapark.** A fresh-air infusion from an early stroll through this park should help to shake off any lingering fatigue from the day before. At the park's southern edge, on a 66m-high (216-foot) hill, a memorial in the shape of an Iron Cross (1821) honors Prussia's war dead from the wars against Napoleon and gives Kreuzberg (Mountain of the Cross) its name. You can enjoy fine views from this point. ⊕ 30 min. The park is bordered by Katzbachstrasse, Kreuzbergstrasse, and Methfesselstrasse. *U-Bahn:* Platz der Luftbrücke. Bus: 140.

2 ★ **Bergmannstrasse.** Walking eastward along the first half of this modest shopping street acts as a kind of easy Kreuzberg primer. You can either call a halt at the low-budget indoor-market stalls on Marheineplatz, or continue along the second, residential half of Bergmannstrasse as far as the big neo-Gothic church (1897) on Südstern. ⊕ 20–40 min. *U-Bahn:* Mehringdamm. Bus: M19 or 140.

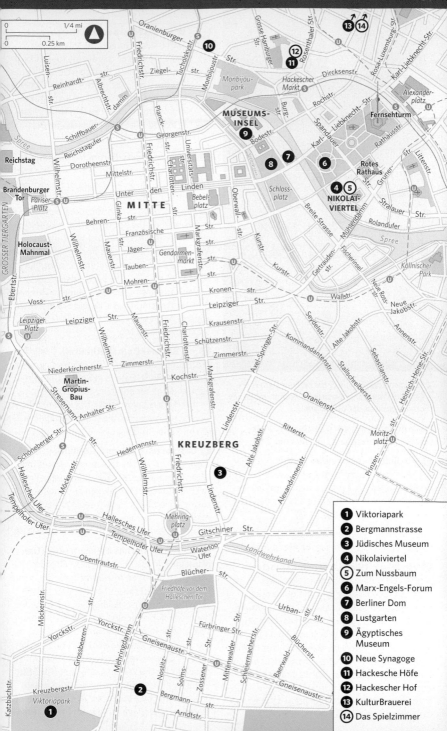

1. Viktoriapark
2. Bergmannstrasse
3. Jüdisches Museum
4. Nikolaiviertel
5. Zum Nussbaum
6. Marx-Engels-Forum
7. Berliner Dom
8. Lustgarten
9. Ägyptisches Museum
10. Neue Synagoge
11. Hackesche Höfe
12. Hackescher Hof
13. KulturBrauerei
14. Das Spielzimmer

> The spectacular dome of the Berliner Dom is the German Protestant response to the architecturally ornate basilicas of Catholicism.

From either point, go to the bus stop on Gneisenaustrasse and take bus no. 248.

❸ ★★ Jüdisches Museum. Inevitably, a Jewish Museum in Berlin shines a powerful light on the Holocaust, yet the exhibits go beyond this, to the wider story of Germany's Jewish community. ⏱ 1 hr. See p. 79, **15**.

Bus no. 248 is your trusty steed again, on the way to Spandauer Strasse, at Alexanderplatz.

❹ ★★ Nikolaiviertel (Nicholas Quarter). Named after its Church of St. Nicholas (1230), the Nikolaiviertel can't quite cut it as a restored medieval district. It does make a brave attempt—handicapped as it was by destruction in World War II and East German restorers who were likely more at home with Socialist Realism. Still, it's worth strolling through the atmospheric little quarter and admiring a handful of prim baroque and rococo mansions scattered along its streets. ⏱ 45 min. See p. 91, **16**.

❺ ☕ ★ Zum Nussbaum. Fitting in nicely with the faux-medieval Nikolaiviertel, this little *Kneipe* (local bar) looks like it dates from 1571, though it actually goes "all the way back" to the district's 1980s restoration. It is based on an original in a nearby part of town that was lost in World War II. Am Nussbaum 3. ☎ 030/242-3095. 5€–10€.

❻ kids Marx-Engels-Forum. As the founding duo of Communism, Karl Marx and Friedrich Engels might have had a word or two to say about their 19th-century vision's 20th-century decline and fall. Their bronze statues (1986) in this park on the Spree riverbank keep their own counsel. Small kids like to climb into Marx's lap and tweak his beard—since he was seemingly a jovial character in life, he likely doesn't mind a bit. The park is bordered by the Spree, Rathausstrasse, Spandauer Strasse, and Karl-Liebknecht-Strasse. *U-* and *S-Bahn:* Alexanderplatz. Bus: M48, TXL, 100, 200, or 248. Tram: M4, M5, or M6.

❼ ★★ Berliner Dom (Cathedral). Berlin's Protestant cathedral (1905) was designed to rival Catholic St. Peter's in Rome. Climb the central dome for stunning views of the city, visit the graves of royals in the Hohenzollern Crypt, and marvel at the massive Sauer organ. ⏱ 1 hr. See p. 73, **14**.

❽ Lustgarten (Pleasure Garden). In this garden, bordered by the cathedral and the Altes Museum (p. 80, **17**), pleasure is limited to sunbathing on the lawn in summer and perusing a clutch of modern sculptures. On the main street is a memorial to Jewish Resistance fighters killed in 1942. Bus: TXL, 100, or 200.

❾ ★★★ Ägyptisches Museum (Egyptian Museum). In 2009, the Neues Museum (New Museum, 1850) on Museumsinsel (Museum Island) reached the end of a 6-year reconstruction. The Ägyptisches Museum, which had been hopscotching around Berlin since World War II, promptly moved in. At last, the famous sculptured bust (c. 1340 B.C.) of Egypt's Queen Nefertiti had a permanent residence fit for the wife of a pharaoh (the 18th Dynasty's Akhenaten). Her colorful image is supported by a huge cast of other ancient Egyptian objects, ranging from the pharaonic

> *The lush lawn of the Lustgarten is a haven for Berliners, with magnificent vistas of the Dom (cathedral) and Altes Museum.*

to the everyday. Look out for the papyrus collection and the African contribution from Nubia (modern Sudan). ⏱ **2 hr.** See p. 80, ⓱.

⑩ ★★ **Neue Synagoge-Centrum Judaicum.** Oriental domes topped by gilded Stars of David mark Berlin's New Synagogue, which dates from 1866 and miraculously survived the first 10 years of Nazi rule before being felled by Allied bombs in 1943. The rebuilt synagogue is a focal point for the city's small Jewish community, which, before the Holocaust, spread into the neighboring Scheunenviertel (Barn Quarter). ⏱ **30 min.** See p. 88, ❶.

⑪ ★★ **kids Hackesche Höfe.** This restored courtyard complex (1907) stands at the heart of a tolerably alternative shopping district around the Hackescher Markt. Since some elements of this tour have touched on Jewish heritage, you might want to drop by the Anne Frank Zentrum, a foundation dedicated to the young diarist and Holocaust victim, next door at Rosenthaler Strasse 39. ⏱ **30 min.** See p. 90, ❹.

⑫ 🍽 ★ **Hackescher Hof.** Seats are often hard to get at this casual-chic cafe-restaurant inside the Hackesche Höfe, but the *Kaffee und Kuchen* (coffee and

cake) is worth a wait. Rosenthaler Strasse 40–41. ☎ 030/283-5293. 8€–16€. See also p. 101.

Take tram (streetcar) M1 from outside the Hackesche Höfe for the run north to Prenzlauer Berg, and get out on Kastanienallee at Eberswalder Strasse.

⑬ ★★ **KulturBrauerei.** A highlight of the cultural and entertainment scene in trendy Prenzlauer Berg—dubbed "Prenz'l" in Berlin—is this complex of venues, among them a clutch of cafes and restaurants, located in a rambling former brewery. There's something happening at most times of the day and night. In addition, it's worthwhile strolling around the nearby residential streets, speckled with cafes and restaurants with sidewalk tables. ⏱ **30 min.– 1 hr.** See p. 129.

⑭ 🍽 **kids Das Spielzimmer.** A boon for frazzled moms and dads touring with kids. While the little darlings use up their spare energy in the delightful playroom of the cafe's name, drained parents can recharge their batteries over a coffee. Schliemannstrasse 37. ☎ 030/4403-7635. 4€–6€.

The Best of Berlin in 3 Days

You start out your third morning in the beating heart of the city and stay in that mode for a good half of the day, absorbing artistic treasures and places of architectural interest, along with some sites associated with the Nazi dictatorship and World War II. Berlin's green credentials are on full display during most of the afternoon, however, with a visit to the downtown zoo and an excursion to the suburbs for a tour of grand Grunewald.

> The domed French and German cathedrals frame the awe-inspiring architecture of the Gendarmenmarkt, a large square in the heart of Berlin.

START Take the *U-Bahn* to Französische Strasse; or bus no. 147 to Gendarmenmarkt.

① ★★★ **Gendarmenmarkt.** A large rectangular space in the heart of the city, Gendarmenmarkt—named after the *Gens d'Armes,* a Prussian guards cavalry regiment—is among Berlin's most handsome squares. That's not to say it has intimate charm. The neoclassical and baroque buildings lining three of its four sides are too massively monumental for

that, though trees, bushes, and lawns soften the overall scene. On the square's north side, the **Französischer Dom** (French Cathedral, 1705), built for Berlin's French Protestant Huguenot refugees, now houses the small Hugenotten-Museum (admission 2€ adults, 1€ kids; Tues–Sat noon–5pm, Sun 11am–5pm). At the far end is the **Deutscher Dom** (German Cathedral, 1708). The domes from which both churches take their names—and their

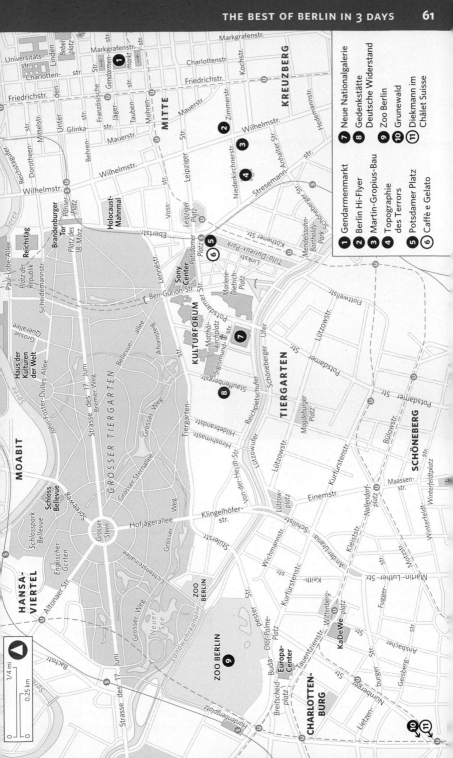

1 Gendarmenmarkt
2 Berlin Hi-Flyer
3 Martin-Gropius-Bau
4 Topographie des Terrors
5 Potsdamer Platz
6 Caffè e Gelato
7 Neue Nationalgalerie
8 Gedenkstätte Deutsche Widerstand
9 Zoo Berlin
10 Grunewald
11 Diekmann im Châlet Suisse

> *Colorful remnants of the Berlin Wall are not only decorative features of bustling Potsdamer Platz but reminders of the Cold War.*

matter; takeoffs are canceled when the wind blows too strong. ⊙ 30 min. (plus waiting time). Air Service Berlin, corner of Zimmerstrasse and Wilhelmstrasse. ☎ 030/5 -5321. www.air-service-berlin.de. Flights: 19€ adults, 13€ kids 7–18, 3€ kids 3–6, 49€ families. From 10am in summer, 11am in winter. *U-Bahn:* Kochstrasse.

❸ ★ **Martin-Gropius-Bau.** The Renaissance-style Martin Gropius Building (1881) takes its name from one of the two architects who designed it to be the city's Museum of Decorative Arts (now housed at the Kulturforum; p. 78, ❾). Visit for a tour of the building's graceful interior or for a temporary exhibit or cultural event. ⊙ 30 min. Niederkirchnerstrasse 7. ☎ 030/254-860. Ticket prices vary, depending on what's on. Wed–Mon 10am–8pm. *U-* and *S-Bahn:* Potsdamer Platz; *U-Bahn:* Kochstrasse; *S-Bahn:* Anhalter Bahnhof.

❹ ★ **Topographie des Terrors.** Few spots in all of history can have such images of fear and horror (and, undoubtedly, defiant courage) attached to them as this piece of Berlin, where once stood the headquarters of the Gestapo, SS, and Reich Security Service (Sicherheitsdienst, or SD), the Nazi triad of terror and genocide. In May 2010, the Topography of Terror exhibit and documentation center opened in a new, permanent building, replacing a previous open-air photographic exhibit on the site, which had been left vacant by a combination of wartime destruction and postwar demolition. The new building provides a purpose-built space for exhibits and a research and documentation center focused on the site's role in the Nazi machinery of repression. ⊙ 1 hr. Niederkirchnerstrasse 8. ☎ 030/254-5090. www.topographie.de. Free admission. Apr–Oct Tues–Sun 10am–6pm; Nov–Mar Tues–Sun 10am–5pm. *U-* and *S-Bahn:* Potsdamer Platz; *U-Bahn:* Kochstrasse; *S-Bahn:* Anhalter Bahnhof.

❺ ★★★ **Potsdamer Platz.** From 1945 to the 1990s, this formerly racy square and its environs were a war-devastated wasteland slashed in two by the Berlin Wall. It's hard to believe now, as you stroll through this riot of modern commercial architecture and signature image of the new Berlin. The **Sony Center**—no longer owned by the Japanese giant but still home to the Sony Style Store—is the heart of the

towering scale—were added in the 1780s. In between stands the **Konzerthaus** (Concert Hall, 1821; p. 128). During the Cold War, this was the home base of the old East Germany's elite Berliner Sinfonie-Orchester (Berlin Symphony Orchestra), now reinvented as the Konzert-hausorchester Berlin. Out front is a fountain built around a sculpture (1871) of dramatist and philosopher Friedrich Schiller, who died in 1805. ⊙ 30 min. *U-Bahn:* Französische Strasse. Bus: 147.

❷ ★★ **Berlin Hi-Flyer.** To get a bird's-eye view of Berlin, all you need to do is climb aboard this tethered balloon, which launches from a point a block west of Checkpoint Charlie, and let helium lift you up where you belong. At an altitude of 150m (492 ft.), memorable views are guaranteed. Actual flights are another

> *The Neue Nationalgalerie houses the work of masters of modern art, from Ernst Kirchner to Salvador Dalí.*

redeveloped zone. Its steel-and-glass dome seems to float like a parachute above boutiques, restaurants, and movie theaters, and lights up in a rainbow of color once the sun goes down. Office towers rise up all around, among them the BahnTower and Kollhoff-Tower. Fans of modern architecture should be sure to check out celeb architect Renzo Piano's clay-colored Debis-Haus (1997), along Schellingstrasse. ⏱ 1 hr. See p. 86, **11**.

---

⑥ 🍽 **kids** **Caffè e Gelato.** The name says it all: Stop here for great Italian coffee and ice cream, inside the Arkaden mall. Alte Potsdamer Strasse 7. ☎ 030/2529-7832. 4€–8€.

⑦ ★★★ **Neue Nationalgalerie.** Most of the Kulturforum complex of cultural institutions (see "Museum Tip," p. 75) forms an ensemble based on 1960s organic architecture (some elements were not completed until the 1990s). An exception is the New National Gallery, designed by Bauhaus pioneer Ludwig

Mies van der Rohe, which set up shop in 1968. Inside is a feast of 20th-century art, led by German artists from Ernst Ludwig Kirchner to Georg Baselitz, supported by an international cast that includes Edvard Munch, Karel Appel, Salvador Dalí, and Barnett Newman. (For more on 20th century German artists, see p. 628.) The gallery puts on a strong program of temporary shows, previewed on the Berlin State Museums website: www.smb.spk-berlin.de. If 20th-century art doesn't float your boat and you haven't yet made it to the Gemäldegalerie (p. 78, **7**), consider a visit there instead. ⏱ 2 hr. See p. 75, **6**.

⑧ ★ **Gedenkstätte Deutsche Widerstand.** In July 1944 Count Claus von Stauffenberg and three other German army officers who conspired to assassinate Hitler were summarily shot in the courtyard here. The Gedenkstätte Deutsche Widerstand (German Resistance Memorial) honors their sacrifice. Codenamed Valkyrie, the coup attempt came close to success when von Stauffenberg placed a

> *You'll find wild boar and deer, as well as beautiful natural vistas, in Grunewald, a former Prussian royal hunting reserve.*

> *German artist Ernst Kirchner's* Potsdamer Platz *is on view at the Neue Nationalgalerie in the Kulturforum.*

briefcase bomb right next to the Führer during a conference at his headquarters in East Prussia. Miraculously, as Hitler saw it, he survived the blast. Key scenes from the 2008 Tom Cruise movie *Valkyrie* were filmed here, after considerable local controversy. ⏱ 20 min. Stauffenbergstrasse 13–14. *U-Bahn:* Kurfürstenstrasse or Potsdamer Platz. Bus: M29 or M48.

Head south along Stauffenbergstrasse to Reichpietschufer, then take bus no. M29 to Breitscheidplatz.

❾ ★★ kids **Zoo Berlin.** A large area adjoining Tiergarten, on the south side of the Landwehrkanal (one small section is on the canal's north side), is taken up by this fine zoo. As with any big-city zoo, there's a multitude of animals to get around. A highlight is the polar bear enclosure, where the once cuddly and now too big to cuddle Knut was born in 2006. There are pandas, wild horses, an African savannah, and seemingly any number of pools where wading birds and marine and river creatures disport. The attached aquarium is worth a visit. Feeding times are posted at the gates and at points around the zoo. A full-scale restaurant and multiple cafe and snack options cater to your own feeding time. ⏱ 4 hr. Budapester Strasse 34 and Hardenbergplatz 8. ☎ 030/254-010. www.zoo-berlin.de. Admission: Zoo alone 12€

> Knut the Polar Bear is just one of the many exotic animals that make Zoo Berlin their home.

adults, 9€ teens 16–18, 6€ kids 5–15, 20€–32€ families; Zoo and Aquarium 18€ adults, 14€ teens 16–18, 9€ kids 5–15, 30€–45€ families. Daily 9:30am to 5, 6:30, or 7pm (varies with season). *U-* and *S-Bahn:* Zoologischer Garten. Bus: M19, M29, M45, M46, X9, X10, X34, 100, 109, 110, 200, 204, 205, or 249.

Those who prefer to skip the zoo should go directly to *S-Bahn* Zoologischer Garten and take the train to Grunewald.

⑩ ★★ **Grunewald (Green Forest).** When you walk in the Grunewald, you are strolling through what was once a Prussian royal hunting reserve. You won't get to hunt these days (though there are wild boar and deer in the forest), but you can chase down some peace and quiet and fresh air. Follow the signs to the 18th-century Jagdschloss (Hunting Lodge), on the shore of Grunewaldsee (Grunewald Lake). To the west, on the far side of Autobahn A115, is Teufelsberg (Devil's Hill, 115m/377 ft.), raised using rubble from Berlin's wartime destruction and now covered with grass and trees. ⏱ 2 hr. Multiple entrances along Clayallee. Free admission. Open 24/7. *U-Bahn:* Dahlem-Dorf; *S-Bahn:* Grunewald.

⑪ 🍴 ★★ **Diekmann im Châlet Suisse.** Finish off your day at this Swiss farmhouse–style restaurant. See p. 110.

Queen Luise

The nation mourned in 1810, when, at age 35, Luise Auguste Wilhelmine Amalie, Princess of Mecklenburg-Strelitz and Queen of Prussia, died at Schloss Hohenzieritz north of Berlin. She had borne ten children in 17 years of marriage to King Friedrich Wilhelm III, endured the shock of Napoleon's conquest of Prussia in 1806, and served as an almost mythical figure of loving mother, loyal wife, and patriot woman. Her early death added eternal youth and beauty to a legend future generations would revere.

It was a heavy weight to have placed on the shoulders of a gay young princess, who valued feeling over learning and who shunned aristocratic manners. A glimpse of the teenage girl behind the princess—girls behind the princesses, in fact—can be seen in Johann Gottfried Schadow's superb marble sculpture (1797) in the Alte Nationalgalerie (p. 80, ⑰), depicting Luise and her younger sister, Friederieke, arm in arm.

Luise rests inside a sculptured sarcophagus in a mausoleum on the grounds of Schloss Charlottenburg (p. 68, ①). Friedrich Wilhelm, who died in 1840, was interred at her side. Given the passage of time and the many tribulations of German history since then, Luise's star has faded. Yet visitors still place flowers on her sculpture-bust in Schloss Charlottenburg's park.

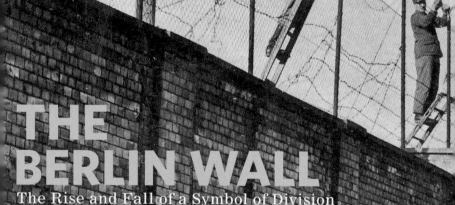

THE
BERLIN WALL
The Rise and Fall of a Symbol of Division

BY GEORGE MCDONALD

THEY CAME IN THE NIGHT, with barbed wire entanglements, fencing, and mechanical construction equipment. By the morning of August 13, 1961, work crews from East Germany's National People's Army and paramilitary workers' militia had split Berlin in two. The city was divided by what the Communist regime began calling an "Anti-Fascist Protection Wall," ostensibly aimed at fending off imperialist aggression from the West, and which would be known to history as the Berlin Wall.

At the end of World War II in 1945, a defeated Germany and its capital were occupied by the victorious Allied powers. The United States, Great Britain, France, and the Soviet Union divided the country into four zones of occupation. Berlin, in the heart of the Soviet zone, was divided into four sectors. In 1949 the Soviets established the German Democratic Republic in their zone. In response, the Federal Republic of Germany was established in the American, British, and French zones. In 1961 the GDR sealed off its borders and erected the Berlin Wall, which instantly became a stark symbol of the Cold War. It was evident that the newly constructed barrier was designed not to keep external enemies out but to keep East Germany's own citizens in by ending the emigration from East to West Germany that was crippling the East German state.

ANTI-VEHICLE▶
TRENCH

PATROL PATH

ALARM

◀GUARD DOG
LEAD WIRE

Killing Ground

Over the almost 3 decades of its existence, the Berlin Wall was steadily "improved." The initial rudimentary barrier was replaced by a concrete wall, and later by an in-depth network of deadly obstacles and traps culminating in a barrier of reinforced concrete. This was supported by armed guards with orders to shoot would-be defectors on sight, attack dogs on long lines, watchtowers, and bunkers. Around 5,000 people are thought to have successfully defected to the West by getting through, under, or over the Wall. Estimates of the number killed in the attempt vary from an official 136 to over 200 in unofficial figures. Among the best-known cases are that of East German soldier Conrad Schumann, who successfully leapt over the barbed wire in 1961; 18-year-old Peter Fechter, who bled to death after being shot by East German border guards in 1962; and 20-year-old Chris Gueffroy, the last person to be fatally shot while attempting to cross the Berlin Wall, in 1989.

And the Wall Came Tumbling Down

Standing at the Wall in front of the highly symbolic Brandenburg Gate in 1987, U.S. President Ronald Reagan called on the reformist Soviet leader, Mikhail Gorbachev, to "tear down this wall." Two years later, Gorbachev's program of liberalization in the Soviet Union had spread to Eastern Europe and encouraged East Germans to demand the same of their own hard-line Communist leadership. Huge popular demonstrations across the country forced the old leaders to stand down and prompted the new ones to open the border to West Berlin at selected points. On November 9, 1989, East Berliners took matters into their own hands and peacefully besieged the crossing points. Unwilling to confront the massed populace with force, the border guards opened the gates. The Wall was history, though it took a year of both enthusiastic chipping and organized demolition before it had all but disappeared.

Berlin's Best Royal & Imperial Monuments

There was far more to Prussia than "blood and iron," and some of the vanished land's positive entries in history's ledger meet the eye on this tour. Architecture and sculpture are the most obvious legacy of Hohenzollern rule in the capital, though much was pulverized in World War II and later painfully reconstructed—a process that continues to this day. Behind the elegant facades of royal buildings, you catch glimpses of the art and philosophy that informed a monarchy that, although despotic, was often enlightened.

> Visitors can tour the opulent halls and gardens of Berlin's 17th-century Schloss Charlottenburg, the palatial home to Prussian and German rulers.

START Take the *U-Bahn* to Sophie-Charlotte-Platz; or bus no. M45, 109, or 309 to Schloss Charlottenburg.

❶ ★★★ **Schloss Charlottenburg (Charlottenburg Palace).** Prussian and German rulers spent lavishly from the late 17th century onward to expand and beautify Schloss Charlottenburg. In the vast, elegantly domed main building, visit the original royal apartments (guided tours only) and the later Neuer Flügel (New Wing, 1747). Though there's enough to see in the long echoing corridors of the main building, any kind of decent weather is an incentive to stroll in the extensive ornamental garden and wooded park along the Spree River. Then, catch up with Prussia's King Friedrich Wilhelm III and his wife Queen Luise (see "Queen Luise," p. 65) in their his-and-hers 19th-century sarcophagi in the mausoleum at the rear of the gardens. In the Belvedere, a museum collection covers antique porcelain. A snack or a full meal at the palace's own Café

Schliemann in the Kleine Orangerie (Small Orangery) helps to break up a long visit. ⏱ 2 hr. Spandauer Damm 10–22. ☎ 030/320-910. www.spsg.de. Admission: Old Palace 10€ adults, 7€ kids 7–14; New Wing 6€ adults, 5€ kids 7–14. Tues–Sun 10am to 5 or 6pm (some elements of the palace complex are open on fewer days and/ or for shorter hours). *U-Bahn:* Sophie-Charlotte-Platz or Richard-Wagner-Platz; *S-Bahn:* Westend. Bus: M45, 109, or 309.

② 🍺 ★ **Brauhaus Lemke am Schloss.** Right across the street from Schloss Charlottenburg, this rustic bar-restaurant is a fine place in which to quaff a beer and tuck into a pub-type snack. Luisenplatz 1. ☎ 030/341-9388. 6€–12€.

Take bus no. M45 from outside Schloss Charlottenburg to the Zoologischer Garten bus station, and transfer there to bus no. 100 to Breitscheidplatz.

❸ ★★ **Kaiser-Wilhelm-Gedächtniskirche (Kaiser Wilhelm Memorial Church).** A 1943 Allied air raid destroyed the neo-Gothic Protestant church (1895) built by Kaiser Wilhelm II in memory of his grandfather. The church tower's ruined stump, joined in 1961 by a modern chapel and belfry, serves as a war memorial. ⏱ 20 min. Breitscheidplatz. Free admission. Daily 9am–7pm. *U-Bahn:* Kurfürstendamm. Bus: M19, M29, M46, 100, or 200.

Take bus no. 100 from Breitscheidplatz to the Grosser Stern.

❹ ★★ 🔲kids **Siegessäule (Victory Column).** The Siegessäule, 67m (220 ft.) high, celebrates various thrashings the 19th-century Prussian military dished out to less martial neighbors. Climb the interior stairway for great views over Tiergarten. ⏱ 30 min. Grosser Stern. Admission 2.50€ adults, 1.50€ kids. Daily 9:30 or 10am–from 3 to 7pm (varies with time of year). *U-Bahn:* Hansaplatz. Bus: 100, 106, or 107.

⑤ 🍺 ★★ **Café am Neuen See.** There's no better place in Berlin for a liquid break and a snack when the weather's good than this Bavarian-style beer garden on the shore of Tiergarten's New Lake. Lichtensteinallee 2. ☎ 030/254-4930. 5€–10€.

> The battered spire on the neo-Gothic Protestant church Kaiser-Wilhelm-Gedächtniskirche is a dramatic reminder of the Allied air raids of World War II.

❻ ★★★ **Reichstag.** Grandiose imperial architecture (1894), Nazi-era and Cold War memories, and British architect Sir Norman Foster's light-flooded glass dome (1999)—the home of Germany's Bundestag (the Federal Parliament's lower house) doesn't lack for symbolism. The grassy square at the front is a pleasant place to hang out, and the Käfer Dachgarten roof restaurant affords fine food and a grand outlook. ⏱ 30 min. Platz der Republik 1. ☎ 030/2273-2152. www.bundestag.de. Free admission. Daily 8am–midnight. *U-Bahn:* Bundestag. Bus: M41, TXL, or 100.

❼ ★★★ **Brandenburger Tor.** Brandenburg Gate (1791), with its bronze quadriga (a chariot pulled by four horses) guided by Nike (Greek goddess of victory), has become a Berlin symbol. There's not much you can do with a triumphal arch these days, except look at it and walk through it—which is what people do. Pariser Platz. *U-* and *S-Bahn:* Brandenburger Tor. Bus: M41, TXL, 100, or 200.

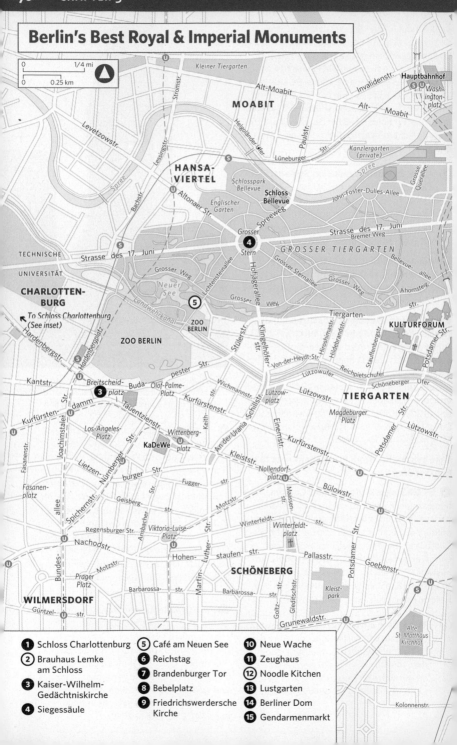

Berlin's Best Royal & Imperial Monuments

1. Schloss Charlottenburg
2. Brauhaus Lemke am Schloss
3. Kaiser-Wilhelm-Gedächtniskirche
4. Siegessäule
5. Café am Neuen See
6. Reichstag
7. Brandenburger Tor
8. Bebelplatz
9. Friedrichswerdersche Kirche
10. Neue Wache
11. Zeughaus
12. Noodle Kitchen
13. Lustgarten
14. Berliner Dom
15. Gendarmenmarkt

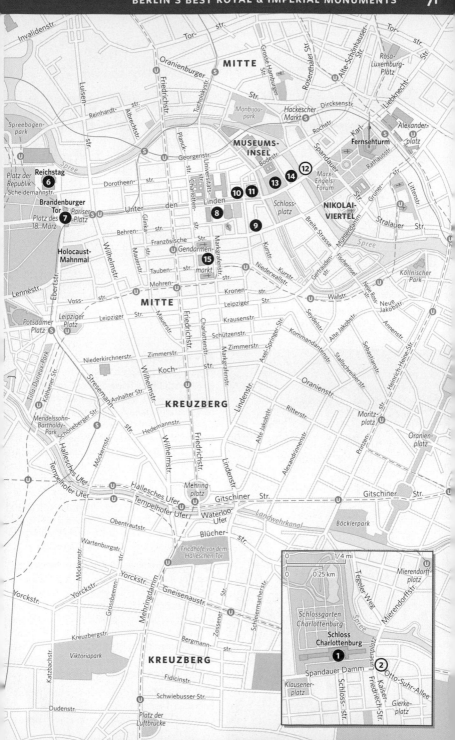

> *ABOVE The impressive steps of the historic Reichstag. BELOW The elaborate interior of Berlin's first neo-Gothic church, Friedrichswerdersche Kirche.*

8 ★★★ **Bebelplatz.** This monumental square owes a lot to Prussia's 18th-century enlightened despot King Friedrich der Grosse (Frederick the Great), who planned a Roman-style Forum Fridericianum. The three elements that were completed are the Staatsoper Unter den Linden (Opera House, 1742), the Alte Bibliothek (Old Library, 1780), and Berlin's Catholic cathedral, the large-domed St.-Hedwigs-Kathedrale (1773). A glassed-in memorial recalls the Nazis' 1933 book-burning episode. If you're in Berlin around Christmas and New Year, look out for the open-air ice-skating rink set up on the square. ⏱ 30 min. *U-Bahn:* Französische Strasse. Bus: TXL, 100, 147, or 200.

9 ★★ **Friedrichswerdersche Kirche.** Berlin's first neo-Gothic church (1830), festooned with tracery and tinted glass, was designed by Karl Friedrich Schinkel. It's now a museum of the architect and sculptor's life and work, and of 19th-century portrait sculpture. ⏱ 30 min. Werderscher Markt. ☎ 030/2090-5577. www.smb.spk-berlin.de. Free admission. Daily 10am-6pm. *U-Bahn:* Hausvogteiplatz. Bus: 147.

10 ★ **Neue Wache.** New Guardhouse may not be a user-friendly kind of name, but for a neo-classical Prussian royal guardhouse that was new when built (1818), it fits. A larger copy of Käthe Kollwitz's 1938 anti-war sculpture, *Mother with Her Dead Son,* occupies the hall behind the colonnade. ⊙ 15 min. Unter den Linden 4. Free admission. Daily dawn–dusk. Bus: TXL, 100, or 200.

⓫ ★ Zeughaus (Arsenal). This graceful, domed baroque edifice (1706) once housed Prussia's Royal Arsenal, though it looks more suited to being some fluttering aristocrat's town *palazzo.* It's now home to the Deutsches Historisches Museum (German Historical Museum, p. 79, **⓰**). ⊙ 15 min. (without museum visit). Unter den Linden 2. *U-* and *S-Bahn:* Friedrichstrasse. Bus: TXL, 100, or 200. Tram: M1 or 12.

⓬ 🍴 **★ Noodle Kitchen.** You'll dine speedily but tolerably fine here, on multiethnic Asian cuisine that's a cut above fast food. Radisson Blu Hotel, Karl-Liebknecht-Strasse 3. ☎ 030/238-283-464. 8€–16€.

⓭ Lustgarten. The name may mean Pleasure Garden, but this miniature park between the Berliner Dom and the Altes Museum is not quite in Babylon league. Berlin society once paraded its finery and breeding here. Times have changed. In summer, teens in jeans and T-shirts now hang out on the lawn. ⊙ 10 min. Bus: TXL, 100, or 200.

⓮ ★★ Berliner Dom (Cathedral). Berlin's sumptuous Protestant cathedral (1905), rebuilt after World War II and renovated during the 1990s, was the family church first of Prussia's and then of Germany's ruling dynasty. Electors and Great Electors of Brandenburg, kings of Prussia, and members of their families are buried here, most of them in the Hohenzollern Crypt. This somber scene of massed royal tombs includes little caskets for child princes and princesses. A 270-step ascent allows you to see the great central dome from the inside. Step outside onto an open-air platform that rings the cupola and affords fine all-round city views. The church's restored Sauer organ, a massive instrument with no fewer than 113 registers, occupies the entire space under one arch. An earlier Gothic church on the same site, dating back to the Middle Ages, was demolished so that this fanciful

> *The Schiller Monument is an imposing landmark in Berlin's Gendarmenmarkt square, which also features two fabulous churches and the Konzerthaus.*

confection of Renaissance-style and baroque domes, pediments, and pillars could be raised in its place. ⊙ 1 hr. Am Lustgarten. 030/2026-9119. www.berliner-dom.de. Admission 5€ adults, 3€ teens 14–18; free for kids 13 and under. Mon–Sat 9am–8pm, Sun noon–8pm (until 7pm daily Oct–Mar). Bus: TXL, 100, or 200.

To go by bus from the Berliner Dom/ Schlossplatz area to Gendarmenmarkt, take no. M48 from Spandauer Strasse to Leipziger Strasse.

⓯ ★★★ Gendarmenmarkt. The imposing buildings lining this attractive square include two grand churches and the Konzerthaus (Concert Hall). ⊙ 30 min. See p. 60, **❶**.

Berlin's Best Museums

Arguably, Berlin does not have quite as many world-class museums and galleries as you might expect to find in a major European capital, but it does have a sufficient stock, along with a supporting bench of institutions that add their own distinctive notes to the city's cultural symphony. Many museums hunt in packs, concentrated in several clusters speckled around town, and this makes both getting to them and around them quite easy. Even so, it would be impossible to visit all of these great museums in 1 day, so look at this as a list of Berlin's top museums rather than a place-to-place tour.

> *Visitors to the Pergamonmuseum stroll through the ornate reconstruction of ancient Babylon's Ishtar Gate, which dates from the 6th century B.C.*

START **Take the *U-Bahn* to Sophie-Charlotte-Platz; or bus no. M45, 109, or 309 to Schloss Charlottenburg.**

➊ ★ **Museum Berggruen.** A former Prussian Guards officer barracks houses the wide-ranging European art collection the late Heinz Berggruen, a Jewish American and onetime

refugee from the Nazis, bequeathed to Berlin. ⏱ 1 hr. Schlossstrasse 1. ☎ 030/3269-5815. www.smb.spk-berlin.de. Admission 8€ adults. Tues–Sun 10am–6pm. *U-Bahn:* Sophie-Charlotte-Platz. Bus: M45, 109, or 309.

➋ ★ **Sammlung Scharf-Gerstenberg.** Complementing the nearby Museum Berggruen,

> *You'll see one of Europe's greatest collections of art masterpieces at the Gemäldegalerie.*

the Scharf-Gerstenberg Collection covers some of the same artistic ground, and in particular has a large haul of works by Paul Klee. ⏱ 1 hr. Schlossstrasse 70. ☎ 030/3435-7315. www.smb.spk-berlin.de. Admission 8€ adults. Tues–Sun 10am–6pm. *U-Bahn:* Richard-Wagner-Platz. Bus: M45, 109, or 309.

③ 🍽 ★ **Brauhaus Lemke am Schloss.** See p. 69, ②.

④ ★ **Käthe-Kollwitz-Museum.** A small collection of works by the artist Käthe Kollwitz, whose traumatic loss of a son in World War I and a grandson in World War II informed her pacifist and socialist creations. ⏱ 1 hr. Fasanenstrasse 24. ☎ 030/882-5210. www.kaethe-kollwitz.de. Admission 6€ adults, 3€ kids 5–18. *U-Bahn:* Uhlandstrasse. Bus: M19, M29, X10, 109, or 110.

⑤ 🍽 ★★ **Wintergarten im Literaturhaus.** Next door to the Käthe-Kollwitz-Museum, this cafe-restaurant in the Literature House cultural foundation has a garden terrace and serves *Kaffee und Kuchen* (coffee and cake) as well as full meals. Fasanenstrasse 23. ☎ 030/882-5414. 6€–12€.

⑥ ★★★ **Neue Nationalgalerie.** One of the two main Kulturforum (Culture Forum) museums (along with Gemäldegalerie), the New

Museum Tip

Combination day tickets are available for Berlin State Museums, a group of 17 museums located in five clusters (such as Museumsinsel) that are funded by the German federal government. Combination tickets are based on the "cluster" in which the museum is located. For instance, the Museumsinsel ticket is 12€ for adults and 6€ for teens 16 to 18 (free for kids 15 and under). It's valid for four of the five museums on the island (not for the Neues Museum) and represents a considerable saving over the admission for each museum. Area tickets also are available for the Kulturforum (which includes Neue Nationalgalerie, ⑥, and Gemäldegalerie, ⑦), Charlottenburg, and other areas. Note that exceptions may be in force from time to time—due, for instance, to a special exhibit. For a full list of Berlin State Museums (Staatliche Museen zu Berlin), go to www.smb.museum.

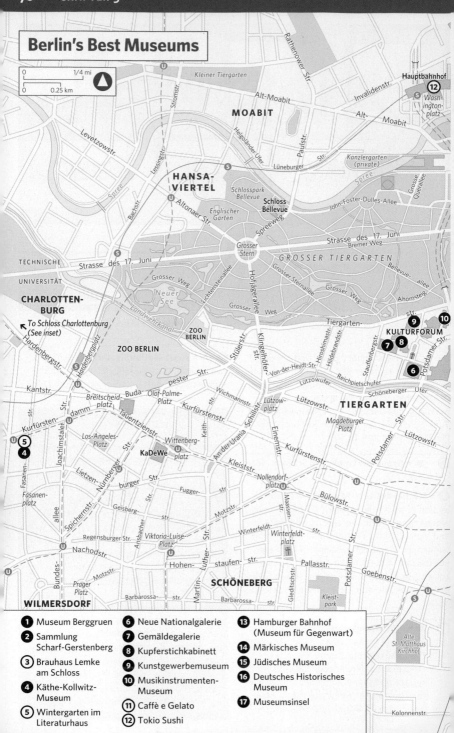

Berlin's Best Museums

MOABIT

Kleiner Tiergarten

Kleiner Tiergarten

Alt-Moabit

Schlosspark
Bellevue

HANSA-
VIERTEL

Englischer
Garten

Schloss
Bellevue

Kanzlergarten
(private)

Hauptbahnhof

Wash-
ington-
platz

Grosser
Stern

GROSSER TIERGARTEN

Strasse des 17. Juni

Bremer Weg

Bellevue-
allee

John-Foster-Dulles-Allee

TECHNISCHE

UNIVERSITÄT

Strasse des 17. Juni

Grosser Weg

Grosser Weg

Grosser Sternallee

Ahornsteig

CHARLOTTEN-
BURG

Neuer
See

Grosser   Weg

Tiergarten-

KULTURFORUM

To Schloss Charlottenburg
(See inset)

Landwehrkanal

ZOO
BERLIN

ZOO BERLIN

Stülerstr.

Klingelhöfer-

Von-der-Heydt-Str.

Reichpietschufer

Schöneberger Ufer

TIERGARTEN

Breitscheid-
platz

Olof-Palme-
Platz

Lützow-
platz

Lützowufer

Lützowstr.

Magdeburger
Platz

Kantstr.

Buda-
pester   Str.

Wichmannstr.

Kurfürstenstr.

Lützowstr.

Hardenbergstr.

Kurfürsten-
damm

Tauentzienstr.

KaDeWe

Wittenberg-
platz

An der Urania

Einemstr.

Kurfürstenstr.

Potsdamer Str.

Los-Angeles-
Platz

Kleiststr.

Nollendorf-
platz

Bülowstr.

Fasanen-
platz

Lietzen-
burger   Str.

Fugger-
str.

Bülowstr.

Geisberg-
str.

Motzstr.

Maassen-
str.

Spichernstr.

Regensburger Str.

Viktoria-Luise-
Platz

Winterfeldt-
str.

Winterfeldt-
platz

Potsdamer   Str.

Goebenstr.

Nachodstr.

Hohen-   staufen-   str.

Pallasstr.

Prager
Platz

Motzstr.

Martin-   Luther-   Str.

Gleditschstr.

Kleist-
park

SCHÖNEBERG

Barbarossa-
str.

Barbarossa-   str.

Alte
St. Matthäus
Kirchhof

WILMERSDORF

Kolonnenstr.

1 Museum Berggruen

2 Sammlung
Scharf-Gerstenberg

3 Brauhaus Lemke
am Schloss

4 Käthe-Kollwitz-
Museum

5 Wintergarten im
Literaturhaus

6 Neue Nationalgalerie

7 Gemäldegalerie

8 Kupferstichkabinett

9 Kunstgewerbemuseum

10 Musikinstrumenten-
Museum

11 Caffè e Gelato

12 Tokio Sushi

13 Hamburger Bahnhof
(Museum für Gegenwart)

14 Märkisches Museum

15 Jüdisches Museum

16 Deutsches Historisches
Museum

17 Museumsinsel

0   1/4 mi

0   0.25 km

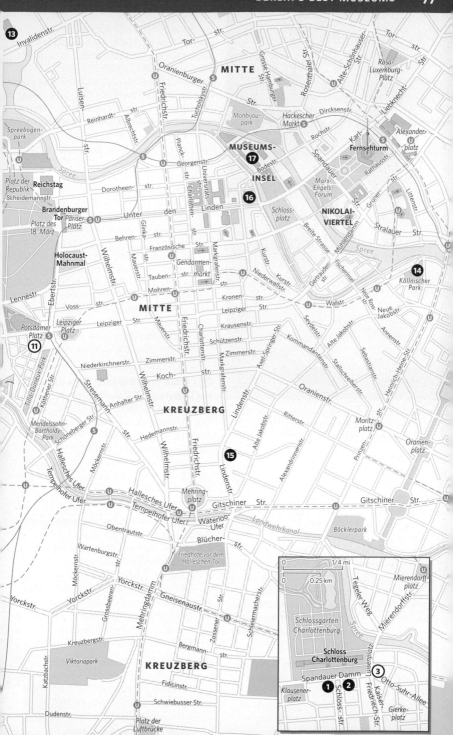

> *The Roman-era Xanten Boy sculpture is one of the renowned classical attractions of Berlin's Pergamonmuseum.*

the grand periods and schools of painting, and many big-name artists, are represented in a stunning array. German masters kick off the show, with works by Albrecht Dürer, Lucas Cranach (both Elder and Younger), and others. Look for Hans Holbein the Younger's powerful *The Merchant Georg Gisze* (1532), in Room 4.

Flemish and Dutch painters take up the challenge from their neighbors to the east, with highlights being Vermeer's typically delicate *The Glass of Wine* (c. 1660) and Rembrandt's tender portrait of his mistress, Hendrickje Stoffels (1657). French, Spanish, Italian, and English artists ranging from the 14th to the 19th centuries fill out a museum that will leave you wanting far more than the bare-bones minimum 2 hours suggested here.

The museum's own cafeteria spreads tables outdoors in good weather and is a decent, time-saving place for a snack or meal. ⏱ 2 hr. Matthäikirchplatz 4–6. ☎ 030/266-424-242. www.smb.spk-berlin.de. Admission 8€ adults, 4€ teens 16–18, free for kids 15 and under. Tues–Wed and Fri–Sun 10am–6pm, Thurs 10am–10pm. *U-* and *S-Bahn:* Potsdamer Platz. Bus: M29, M48, M85, 200, or 347.

⑧ ★ Kupferstichkabinett (Museum of Prints and Drawings). Through a series of changing exhibits, the Kupferstichkabinett displays its hoard of European engravings and sketches, among them works by Albrecht Dürer. ⏱ 1 hr. Matthäikirchplatz. ☎ 030/266-424-242. www.smb.spk-berlin.de. Admission 8€ adults, 4€ teens 16–18, free for kids 15 and under. Tues–Sun 10am–6pm (until 10pm Thurs). *U-* and *S-Bahn:* Potsdamer Platz. Bus: 200 or 347.

⑨ ★★ Kunstgewerbemuseum (Museum of Decorative Arts). This museum holds an astonishingly large and rich array of applied arts, including lavish collections like the medieval ecclesiastical Welfenschatz (Guelph Treasury). ⏱ 1 hr. Matthäikirchplatz. ☎ 030/266-424-242. www.smb.spk-berlin.de. Admission 8€ adults, 4€ teens 16–18, free for kids 15 and under. Tues–Fri 10am–6pm, Sat–Sun 11am–6pm. *U-* and *S-Bahn:* Potsdamer Platz. Bus: 200 or 347.

⑩ ★ Musikinstrumenten-Museum. Many of the 3,500 antique and rare musical instruments in this museum next to the Philharmonie concert hall are still playable, and are played on occasion. ⏱ 1 hr. Tiergartenstrasse 1

National Gallery (1968) takes over the baton of Berlin's historical art scene from the Alte Nationalgalerie (⑰) and the Gemäldegalerie (❼) and runs with it through the 20th century. Die Brücke artist Ernst Ludwig Kirchner's *Potsdamer Platz* (1914) shows (kind of) how the nearby city square once looked. American Color Field painting is represented by works by Barnett Newman and others. ⏱ 2 hr. Potsdamer Strasse 50. ☎ 030/266-424-242. www.smb.spk-berlin.de. Admission 8€ adults, 4€ teens 16–18, free for kids 15 and under. Sun and Tues–Wed 10am–6pm, Thurs 10am–10pm, Fri–Sat 10am–8pm. *U-* and *S-Bahn:* Potsdamer Platz. Bus: M29, M48, or M85.

❼ ★★★ Gemäldegalerie (Picture Gallery). Top dog among the museums of the Kulturforum (Culture Forum) complex, just west of Potsdamer Platz, the Gemäldegalerie is one of the greatest European art collections. All (enter on Ben-Gurion-Strasse). ☎ 030/2548-1178. www.mim-berlin.de. Admission 4€ adults, 2€ teens 16–18, free for kids 15 and under. *U-* and *S-Bahn:* Potsdamer Platz. Bus: 200 or 347.

⑪ 🍴 kids **Caffè e Gelato.** See p. 63, ⑥.

⑫ 🍴 **Tokio Sushi.** A fast-food sushi place inside Berlin's main railway station. Berlin Hauptbahnhof, Europaplatz. ☎ 030/3377-6000. 6€–16€.

⑬ ★★ **Hamburger Bahnhof (Museum für Gegenwart).** Operating out of the neoclassical former terminal (1847) of the Berlin–Hamburg railway, the Museum für Gegenwart (Museum of Contemporary Art) gives the city a second outstanding modern-art gallery, to go with the Neue Nationalgalerie (⑥). The large exhibition space allows for a host of movements and styles—Naim June Paik, Roy Lichtenstein, and Andy Warhol are a few of the featured artists—and for extensive temporary exhibits. ⏱1 hr. Invalidenstrasse 50–51. ☎ 030/3978-3411. www.hamburgerbahnhof.de. Admission 8€ adults, 4€ teens 16–18, free for kids 15 and under. Tues–Fri 10am–6pm, Sat 11am–8pm, Sun 11am–6pm. *U-* and *S-Bahn:* Hauptbahnhof. Bus: 120, 147, or 245.

⑭ ★ **Märkisches Museum.** Take a stroll down Berlin's memory lane at the Museum of the Mark (region) of Brandenburg, from the city's foundation in 1244 right up to the present day. ⏱1 hr. Am Köllnischen Park 5. ☎ 030/3086-6215. www.stadtmuseum.de. Admission 6€ adults, 3€ kids 6–15. Tues and Thurs–Sun 10am–6pm, Wed noon–8pm. *U-Bahn:* Märkisches Museum. Bus: 147.

⑮ ★★ **Jüdisches Museum.** Berlin's Jewish Museum is a surprising sight—and not for its mere existence alone. Polish-American architect Daniel Libeskind designed the new wing (1999), which looks something like a jagged lightning bolt. Inside, there's a raw character to much of the design, exemplified by the 10,000 ragged steel "faces" of the installation *Shalechet* (*Fallen Leaves,* 2001), and an eerily empty tower that's a memorial to the Holocaust. Other exhibits take a wider view of Germany's Jewish community over the centuries, and there's kosher food in the cafe-restaurant. ⏱1 hr. Lindenstrasse 9–14. ☎ 030/2599-3300. Admission 5€ adults, 2.50€ kids 7–18. Mon

> *Ernst Kirchner's stirring 1929 oil rendering of the Brandenburg Gate is just one of the impressive pieces on display at Berlin's Neue Nationalgalerie.*

10am–10pm, Tues–Sun 10am–8pm. *U-Bahn:* Hallesches Tor. Bus: M29, M41, or 248.

⑯ ★★ **Deutsches Historisches Museum.** For visitors who imagine that Germany's history is not a subject for polite conversation, touring the Deutsches Historisches Museum (German

Restoring Museums and Collections

When World War II in Europe ended in 1945, Berlin was a gigantic *Trümmerfeld* (field of rubble). Among the debris of the once proud capital were the ruins of its museums and galleries. Their collections were scattered, hidden away for safekeeping or removed as reparations. It took decades to reconstruct and restore the buildings that had housed the institutions before the war. When the Berlin Wall came down in 1989, that process was still underway. Since then, more buildings have been restored and collections reshuffled between museums from the former West Berlin and East Berlin, a painstaking process that still has years to run.

Wonderful Wannsee

During the hot months, after spending a day or two inside museums, take the *S-Bahn* to Nikolassee and follow the hordes of bathers to **Wannsee** (pictured), one of Europe's largest lake beaches. The beach is lined with *Strandkörbe*, snazzy basketlike reclining beach chairs that afford shade from the sun and protection from wind. Some like to bare all on the FKK (naturist/nudist) stretch of the beach.

A darker sight is chillingly elegant ★★ **Wannsee Villa,** Am Grossen Wannsee 56–58, on the western shore, across the water from Nikolassee. This was the site of the notorious conference in January 1942 where Nazi bureaucrats and SS officials, among them Reinhard Heydrich and Adolf Eichmann, met to plan the "Final Solution"—the annihilation of European Jewry. The villa is now a memorial to the Holocaust, the **Haus der Wannsee-Konferenz** (☎ 030/805-0010; www.ghwk. de; bus: 114). It includes photographs of men, women, and children who were sent to concentration camps. Nearly all the pictures are official Nazi photographs, including some of

atrocious medical experiments. Nearby on the lakefront, you can visit an art and historical exhibit in the **Liebermann-Villa,** Colomierstrasse 3 (☎ 030/8058-5900; www.maxliebermann.de; bus: 114), the pink summer villa that belonged to Jewish-German Impressionist artist Max Liebermann (1847–1935).

A bay in the lake's southwest corner holds ★ **Pfaueninsel** (Peacock Island), a UNESCO World Heritage site. Designed by King Friedrich Wilhelm II in the 1790s, it showcases Prussian royal pomp and romantic folly. The small island contains the Schloss, a miniature castle sporting mock ruins, in which Friedrich kept assignations with his mistress, Wilhelmine Encke. Among the island's oak trees are also an enclosed garden occupied by the island's namesake peacocks; a neo-Gothic mansion, the Kavaliershaus (1825); the Meierei (dairy), built to resemble a ruined monastery; and a memorial portico dedicated to Prussia's Queen Luise. You reach the island, which is just 100m (330 ft.) from the mainland, aboard a tiny ferry.

Historical Museum) is a useful antidote. It is housed in a handsome former Prussian arsenal, the Zeughaus (1706), enlarged in 2004 with a striking cylindrical wing by Chinese-American architect I. M. Pei. The story starts with national hero Hermann (Arminius) zapping invading Roman legions and runs up to the Nazi period, Cold War division, and reunification. ◷ 2 hr. Unter den Linden 2. ☎ 030/203-040. www.dhm. de. Admission 5€ adults. Daily 10am–6pm. *U-* and *S-Bahn:* Friedrichstrasse. Bus: TXL, 100, or 200. Tram: M1 or 12.

SITE GUIDE
PAGE 81

⑰ ★★★ **Museumsinsel (Museum Island).** Museumsinsel's five majestic museums occupy the northern third of a long island in the Spree River in the oldest part of Berlin. Each building holds more than one museum or collection, and together they comprise one of Europe's most dazzling cultural constellations.

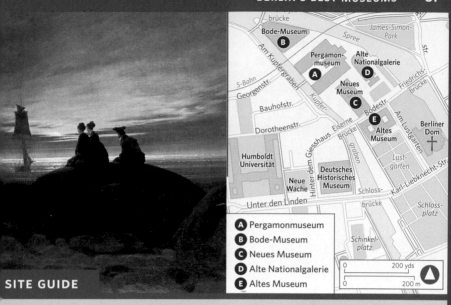

A Pergamonmuseum
B Bode-Museum
C Neues Museum
D Alte Nationalgalerie
E Altes Museum

⑰ Museumsinsel

The lower floor of the **A** ★★★ **Pergamonmuseum** houses works from classical antiquity and the ancient Near East, most notably the **Pergamon Altar,** a reconstructed stairway, colonnade, and frieze from ancient Pergamon's Temple of Zeus (c. 160 B.C.). Babylon's Ishtar Gate and Nebuchadnezzar's Throne Room are offerings from an earlier period. There are also smaller works, such as the Roman-era Xanten Boy sculpture, plus Islamic art and architecture upstairs.

Named after its 1904 founder, Wilhelm von Bode, the **B** ★ **Bode-Museum** covers Byzantine art, European sculpture, and ancient and medieval coins. Religious mosaic art from Justinian-era Constantinople and sculptures from Renaissance Italy are highlights.

Opened in 1850, the **C** ★★★ **Neues Museum** lives up to its New Museum moniker, having been heavily bombed in World War II and restored in 2009. Here, in the **Ägyptisches Museum** (Egyptian Museum), look for the 14th-century B.C. bust of Queen Nefertiti. The **Museum für Pre- und Vorgeschichte** (Prehistory and Early History) also has its collections here.

The **D** ★★★ **Alte Nationalgalerie** (Old National Gallery, 1876) should appeal to lovers of 19th-century European art, with paintings by Karl Friedrich Schinkel, Caspar David Friedrich (his *Moonrise Over the Sea* is pictured above), Adolph Menzel, Hans Thoma, Max Liebermann, and others. Paintings by French artists includes works by Monet, Gauguin, and Renoir. A standout among the sculptures is Johann Gottfried Schadow's sensuous marble work (1795) depicting the Prussian princesses Luise and Friedericke arm in arm.

The main emphasis in the **Antikensammlungen** (Antiquities Collection), housed in both the neoclassical **E** ★★ **Altes Museum** building (1828) and the Pergamonmuseum, is on classical Greek and Roman sculpture. ⏱ Per museum on average 2 hr. Spread visits out over 2 or 3 days if possible. ☎ 030/2090-5577. www.museumsinsel-berlin.de and www.smb.spk-berlin.de. Admission: combination day ticket for Alte Nationalgalerie, Altes Museum, Bode-Museum, and Pergamonmuseum 12€ adults, 8€ teens 16–18 (exceptions for special exhibits); single museums 8€ adults, 4€ teens 16–18; Neues Museum 10€ adults, 5€ teens 16–18; all museums free for kids 15 and under. Daily 10am–6pm (until 10pm Thurs). *U-Bahn:* Friedrichstrasse; *S-Bahn:* Friedrichstrasse or Hackescher Markt. Bus: TXL, 100, or 200. Tram: M1 or 12.

Berlin's Best Modern Architecture

Berlin had the worst of reasons for dabbling in modern architecture. The city was entirely devastated in World War II, first by years of increasingly heavy Allied bomber raids and finally by having one of the war's most cataclysmic ground battles fought through its streets. Reunification provided an additional incentive for creative experimentation and more space in which to indulge it. As a result, speckled through the capital are highlights of modern architecture, large and small. If you want to fit this tour into a single day, you'll probably have to skip a few stops or spend less time at each than we've recommended.

> *The Westend district's classic example of postwar design is the 17-story Corbusierhaus, which was built in 1958.*

START **Take the** *S-Bahn* **to Olympiastadion; or bus no. M29 or 218 to Flatowallee.**

❶ ★ **Corbusierhaus.** Swiss architect Le Corbusier's "machine for living in" (1958), near the Olympic Stadium in the Westend district, won't be everyone's idea of Home Sweet Home. The single block of 557 apartments on 17 floors is, however, a landmark in postwar residential architecture. ⏱ 20 min. Flatowallee 16. *S-Bahn:* Olympiastadion. Bus: M29, X34, X49, or 218.

Take the *S-Bahn* **from Westend to Tiergarten.**

> *Known locally as the "pregnant oyster," the Haus der Kulturen der Welt is a stunning postmodern performance venue.*

2 ★ **Hansaviertel (Hansa Quarter).** Named after the medieval Hanseatic League (see the box on p. 578), the small Hansaviertel lies between the Tiergarten and a bend in the Spree River. Its apartment blocks (1957–61), designed by such architects as Bauhaus pioneer Walter Gropius and Brazilian Oscar Niemeyer, make for an interesting comparison with the Corbusierhaus. ☺1 hr. *U-Bahn:* Hansaplatz; *S-Bahn:* Tiergarten or Bellevue. Bus: 106.

3 ★★ **Haus der Kulturen der Welt.** Housed in a futuristic building dubbed the "pregnant oyster" by Berliners, the Haus der Kulturen der Welt (House of World Cultures) is a multicultural performance venue. Look for Henry Moore's bronze sculpture *Large Divided Oval: Butterfly,* 1986) in the Spiegelteich (Mirror Pond) out front. ☺20 min. John-Foster-Dulles-Allee 10. Bus: 100. See p. 129.

4 ★ **Bundeskanzleramt.** The postmodern office (2001) of Germany's head of government, the Bundeskanzleramt (Federal Chancellery), is eight times larger than the White House in Washington, D.C. Part of it bridges the Spree, making a kind of "paper clip" holding the former East and West Berlin together. ☺20 min. Willy-Brandt-Strasse 1. *U-* and *S-Bahn:* Hauptbahnhof. Bus: M85 or 100.

5 ★★ **Reichstag.** It's not the famous Reichstag building as a whole that's a modern-architecture marvel, but the glass dome (1999) designed by British architect Sir Norman Foster. The transparent structure is meant to symbolize the openness of democratic government. ☺30 min. See p. 69, **6**.

Take bus no. 100 or walk to the far end of Unter den Linden.

⑥ 🍴 ★★ **Café Einstein.** See p. 54, ⑩.

7 ★★ **Zeughaus (Arsenal).** When its former arsenal building proved too small for the collections of the German Historical Museum (p. 79, **16**), the Chinese-American architect I. M. Pei was commissioned to create this striking, cylindrical extension (2004). ☺20 min. (without museum visit). Unter den Linden 2. www.dhm.de. *U-* and *S-Bahn:* Friedrichstrasse. Bus: TXL, 100, or 200. Tram: M1 or 12.

⑧ 🍴 ★★ **kids Telecafé.** Besides getting you inside the Fernsehturm (Television Tower, 1969; see p. 91, **13**), a spectacular piece of modern architecture, the rotating cafe-restaurant over 200m (655 ft.) up affords fabulous city views. Alexanderplatz. ☎ 030/242-3333. 6€–12€.

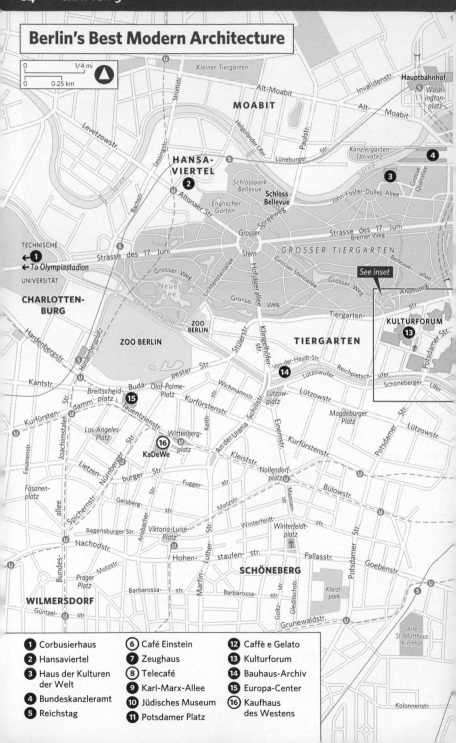

Berlin's Best Modern Architecture

| 0 | 1/4 mi |
| 0 | 0.25 km |

Kleiner Tiergarten

Alt-Moabit

MOABIT

Invalidenstr.

Hauptbahnhof

Wash-
ington-
platz

Levetzowstr.

Helgoländer Ufer

Lüneburger

Alt-

Moabit

Kanzlergarten
(private)

4

Stromstr.

Lessingstr.

HANSA-
VIERTEL

2

Schlosspark
Bellevue

Schloss
Bellevue

Spree

John-Foster-Dulles-Allee

3

Grosse
Querallee

Bachstr.

Altonaer Str.

Englischer
Garten

Spreeweg

TECHNISCHE

←**1**
← To Olympiastadion

UNIVERSITÄT

Strasse des 17. Juni

Grosser

Stern

GROSSER   TIERGARTEN

Strasse des 17. Juni
Bremer Weg

Grosser Sternallee

Bellevue-
allee

CHARLOTTEN-
BURG

Grosser Weg

Neuer
See

Lichtensteinallee

Hofjägeralle

Grosse

Weg

Grosser   Weg

See inset

Ahornste
str.

Tiergarten-

KULTURFORUM

13

Hardenbergstr.

Landwehrkanal

ZOO
BERLIN

ZOO BERLIN

Stülerstr.

Klingelhöfer Str.

Tiergarten-

Potsdamer Str.

Hardenbergplatz

TIERGARTEN

Kantstr.

pester   Str.

Buda-
Olof-Palme-
Platz

Wichmannstr.

Von-der-Heydt-Str.

14

Lützowufer

Reichpietsch-
ufer

Schöneberger   Ufer

Breitscheid-
platz

15

Tauentzienstr.

Kurfürstenstr.

Schillstr.

Lützow-
platz

Lützowstr.

Lützowstr.

Magdeburger
Platz

Kurfürstendamm

damm

Los-Angeles-
Platz

Wittenberg-
platz

An der Urania

Einemstr.

Kurfürstenstr.

Potsdamer Str.

Fasanenstr.

Joachimstaler Str.

16

KaDeWe

Kleiststr.

Nollendorf-
platz

Lietzen-
burger   Str.

Keithstr.

Bülowstr.

Fasanen-
platz

Spichernstr.

Fugger-

Maassenstr.

allee

Geisberg-
str.

Motzstr.

Nürnberger Str.

Ansbacher   Str.

Regensburger Str.

Viktoria-Luise-
Platz

Winterfeldtstr.

Winterfeldt-
platz

Luther-
Str.

Potsdamer   Str.

Goebenstr.

Nachodstr.

Motzstr.

Hohen-
staufen-   str.

Pallasstr.

Prager
Platz

Martin-

Kleist-
park

WILMERSDORF

Barbarossa-   str.

Barbarossa-
str.

SCHÖNEBERG

Goltzstr.

Gleditschstr.

Alte
St. Matthäus
Kirchhof

Güntzel-   str.

Grunewaldstr.

Kolonnenstr.

---

1 Corbusierhaus	**6** Café Einstein	**12** Caffè e Gelato
2 Hansaviertel	**7** Zeughaus	**13** Kulturforum
3 Haus der Kulturen der Welt	**8** Telecafé	**14** Bauhaus-Archiv
4 Bundeskanzleramt	**9** Karl-Marx-Allee	**15** Europa-Center
5 Reichstag	**10** Jüdisches Museum	**16** Kaufhaus des Westens
	11 Potsdamer Platz	

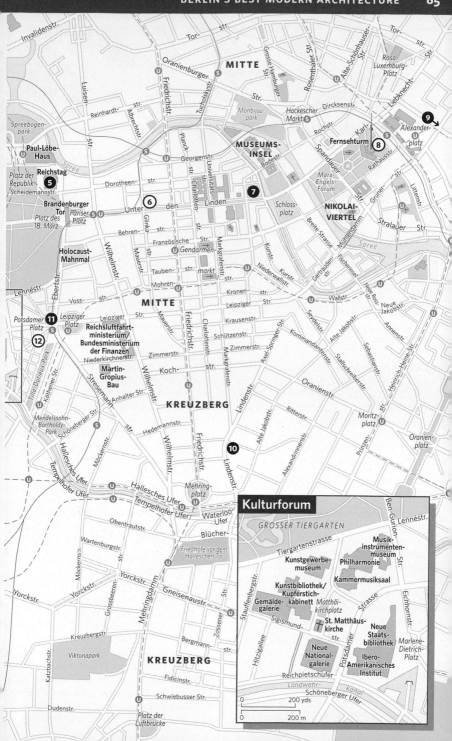

Invalidenstr.

Spreebogen-
park

Paul-Löbe-
Haus

Reichstag **5**

Platz der
Republik
Scheidemannstr.

Brandenburger
Tor

Platz des
18. März

Holocaust-
Mahnmal

Pariser
Platz

6

Lennéstr.

Potsdamer
Platz **11**

12

Tilla-Durieux-Park

Reichsluftfahrt-
ministerium/
Bundesministerium
der Finanzen
Niederkirchnerstr.

Martin-
Gropius-
Bau

Mendelssohn-
Bartholdy-
Park

Leipziger
Platz

Oranienburger

Friedrichstr.

Tucholskystr.

Luisenstr.

Reinhardt-

Albrechtstr.

Dorotheen-   str.

Unter   den   Linden

Behren-

Französische   Str.

Gendarmen-
markt

Tauben-   str.

Mohren-

Kronen-

Leipziger

MITTE

Grosse Hamburger   Str.

Monbijou-
park

**MUSEUMS-
INSEL**

Universitäts-

Charlotten-

7

Bodestr.

Schloss-
platz

Glinka

Mauerstr.

Markgrafenstr.

Niederwallstr.

Krausenstr.

Hackescher
Markt

Rochstr.

Marx-
Engels-
Forum

Breite Strasse

Mühlendamm

Gertrauden-   str.

Fischerinsel

Neue Ross-

Wallstr.

MITTE

Voss-   str.

Leipziger   Str.

Mauerstr.

Charlottenstr.

Friedrichstr.

Schützenstr.

Zimmerstr.

Koch-

Zimmerstr.

Anhalter Str.

KREUZBERG

Hedemannstr.

Wilhelmstr.

Friedrichstr.

10

Mehring-
platz

Waterloo-
Ufer

Blücher-

Friedhöfe vor dem
Hallerschen Tor

Obentrautstr.

Wartenburgstr.

Möckernstr.

Yorckstr.

Yorckstr.

Grossbeeren-

Kreuzbergstr.

Katzbachstr.

Viktoriapark

KREUZBERG

Fidicinstr.

Dudenstr.

Schwiebusser Str.

Platz der
Luftbrücke

Bergmann-

Gneisenaustr.

Zossener

Oranienstr.

Lindenstr.

Alte Jakobstr.

Ritterstr.

Prinzenstr.

Moritz-
platz

Oranien-
platz

Lindenstr.

Alexandrinenstr.

Heinrich-Heine-Str.

Sebastianstr.

Stallschreiberstr.

Kommandantenstr.

Alte Jakobstr.

Axel-Springer-Str.

Seydelstr.

Kurstr.

Kurstr.

**NIKOLAI-
VIERTEL**

Spree

Rathausstr.

Spandauer

Fernsehturm **8**

Karl-

Liebknecht-

Alte Schönhauser

Rosenthaler   Str.

Dircksenstr.

Karl-

MITTE

Tor-

Oranienburger   Str.

Planck-

Georgenstr.

Str.

Rosa-
Luxemburg-
Platz

Tor-   str.

Alexander-
platz   **9**

Gruner-

Littenstr.

Rathausstr.

Stralauer   Str.

Neue
Jakobstr.

Annenstr.

Spree

Kulturforum

GROSSER TIERGARTEN

Tiergartenstrasse

Kunstgewerbe-
museum

Musik-
instrumenten-
museum

Philharmonie

Kammermusiksaal

Kunstbibliothek/
Kupferstich-
kabinett

Gemälde-
galerie

*Matthäi-
kirchplatz*

Neue Staats-
bibliothek

St. Matthäus-
kirche

Neue
National-
galerie

Ibero-
Amerikanisches
Institut

Reichpietschufer

Landwehr-

Schöneberger Ufer

kanal

Ben-Gurion-

Lennéstr.

Potsdamer-

Strasse

Eichhornstr.

Marlene-
Dietrich-
Platz

Staufenbergstr.

Hitzigallee

Sigismund-

| 0 | | 200 yds |
| 0 | | 200 m |

> *The Jüdisches Museum, also known as the Blitz (lightning bolt), is as memorable for its jagged exterior design as its contents.*

9 ★ **Karl-Marx-Allee.** This long boulevard leading east from Alexanderplatz was dreary Communist East Berlin's 1950s showcase of socialist neoclassicist architecture (its original name was Stalinallee). The apartment blocks have been restored since reunification. ⏱ 30 min.–1 hr. *U-* and *S-Bahn:* Alexanderplatz. Bus: M48, TXL, 100, or 200. Tram: M4, M5, or M6.

Take bus no. 248 from Alexanderplatz to the Jewish Museum.

10 ★★ **Jüdisches Museum.** The jagged outline of Polish-American architect Daniel Libeskind's new wing (1999) for the Jewish Museum led to it being dubbed the *Blitz* (lightning bolt). In 2007, he added a glass courtyard to the original baroque building. ⏱ (without museum visit) 30 min. Lindenstrasse 9–14. For museum information, see p. 79, **15**. *U-Bahn:* Hallesches Tor. Bus: M29, M41, or 248.

Take bus no. M29 from the Charlottenstrasse stop to Potsdamer Strasse.

11 ★★★ **Potsdamer Platz.** Berlin's largest and most impressive concentration of large-scale postmodern commercial architecture arose on and around a once-vibrant city square

destroyed in World War II and left desolate during the Cold War. Among the first pieces completed was Renzo Piano's Debis-Haus (1997), an office tower 106m (348 ft.) high. Then followed in regular succession the Potsdamer Platz Arkaden mall (1998); the Kollhoff-Tower (1999), 103m (338 ft.) high; Helmut Jahn's Sony Center entertainment complex, the BahnTower, and the Park Kolonnaden offices (all 2000); and the Beisheim-Center (2004). ⏱ 1–2 hr. *U-* and *S-Bahn:* Potsdamer Platz. Bus: M29, M41, M48, M85, 200, or 347.

12 🍽 **kids** **Caffè e Gelato.** See p. 63, **6**.

13 ★★★ **Kulturforum.** The Culture Forum's individual buildings seem built to a human scale, even if structures like the Gemäldegalerie (1998; p. 78, **7**), Neue Nationalgalerie (New National Gallery, 1968; p. 75, **6**), and Philharmonie concert hall (1963; p. 128) are not exactly Lilliputian. German architect Hans Scharoun, who drew up the plans, aimed to fulfill his vision of organic architecture. Only his masterpiece, the Philharmonie, was completed during his lifetime. Most of the other buildings—except for Ludwig Mies van der Rohe's Neue Nationalgalerie—followed Scharoun's general lines,

> *The seamless symmetry of the renowned Kulturforum is a testament to architect Hans Scharoun's focus on organic architecture.*

while differing in many details. Across the street from the Philharmonie is the equally harmonious Kammermusiksaal (Chamber Music Hall, 1987). ☺ (exteriors only) 1–2 hr. Either side of Potsdamer Strasse, down to the bridge over the Landwehrkanal. *U-* and *S-Bahn:* Potsdamer Platz. Bus: M29, M48, M85, 200, or 347.

Take bus no. M29 to Von-der-Heydt-Strasse.

⓮ ★★ **Bauhaus-Archiv.** Despite its distinctively curved gables, the Bauhaus Archive (1979) follows only in outline the plans Bauhaus pioneer Walter Gropius proposed in 1964 for a museum of the influential German school of art, design, and architecture that flourished in the 1920s and was suppressed by the Nazis (see p. 466 for more on the Bauhaus movement). ☺ (exterior only) 20 min. Klingelhöferstrasse 14. *U-Bahn:* Nollendorfplatz. Bus: M29, 100, 106, or 107.

Take bus no. M29 to the Europa-Center.

⓯ **Europa-Center.** This multifloor mall (1965), in the shadow of the bombed-out Kaiser-Wilhelm-Gedächtniskirche (p. 69, ❸), was a symbol of West Germany's postwar economic miracle and of West Berlin's success as a capitalist island surrounded by a Communist sea. ☺ 20 min. Tauentzienstrasse 9–12. *U-Bahn:* Kurfürstendamm. Bus: M19, M29, M46, 100, or 200.

⓰ ★★ **Kaufhaus des Westens.** The bustling Gourmet Floor (sixth floor) in the giant KaDeWe department store (p. 104) serves everything from coffee to caviar. Tauentzienstrasse 21–24. ☎ 030/21210. 8€–24€.

Nazi Architecture

Two emblematic works of Nazi architecture are about all that survive of Hitler's plans for a new Berlin, to be renamed Germania and constructed on a megalomaniac scale. They are the Olympiastadion (Olympic Stadium, 1936), where African-American athlete Jesse Owens famously won four gold medals at the 1936 Berlin Olympics, and the Reichsluftfahrtministerium (Reich Air Ministry, 1938), which now houses the Bundesministerium der Finanzen (Federal Finance Ministry). Both buildings have been extensively remodeled, but their Nazi-era heritage remains.

Mitte

Inevitably, a tour through Berlin's Mitte (Central) district takes in some of the city's most heavily touristed streets and areas. The itinerary followed here, however, aims as far as possible to duck into side streets and offbeat neighborhoods, some of them the haunts of trendy shoppers and nightlife hounds. It should thereby afford strollers an insight into how the old East Berlin has taken its place in the reunited city.

START Take the *U-Bahn*, bus no. 142, or tram no. M1 or M6 to Oranienburger Tor.

① ★★ **Neue Synagoge-Centrum Judaicum.** A remarkable survivor of the Nazi period (though it was vandalized during the 1938 *Kristallnacht* pogrom), and subsequently partly reconstructed after being hit by World War II Allied bombs, the Moorish-style New Synagogue (1866) was the heart of Berlin's Jewish Quarter. Although no longer a functioning synagogue, it holds an exhibit on Jewish history in Berlin and its own history, in addition to special exhibits, and is worth visiting just to view its ornate gilded dome. ⊕ 30 min. Oranienburger Strasse 28–30. ☎ 030/8802-8300. www.cjudaicum.de. Admission 3€ adults, 2€ kids 6–18. Mar–Oct Sun–Mon 10am–8pm, Tues–Thurs 10am–6pm, Fri 10am–5pm (until 2pm Mar and Oct); Nov–Feb Sun–Thurs 10am–6pm, Fri 10am–2pm.

② ★ kids **Monbijoupark.** Where neat little Monbijou Park now spreads its few leafy acres beside the Spree once stood a Prussian royal palace, rococo Schloss Monbijou (1706), which suffered bomb damage in World War II and was later demolished. A playground and (in summer) an "urban beach" along the Spree make this a worthwhile spot for children. ⊕ 20 min. Monbijoustrasse and Oranienburger Strasse.

③ ★ **Sophienkirche.** Named after its royal patron, Prussian queen Sophie Luise, the church (1712) is rarely open outside of services but is worth passing by for a look. Its tower (1735) is Berlin's only surviving original baroque church tower. Along the street is a small park that was Berlin's Alter Jüdischer Friedhof (Old Jewish Cemetery). Grosse Hamburger Strasse 29–31.

> *The dome of Berlin's Neue Synagogue.*

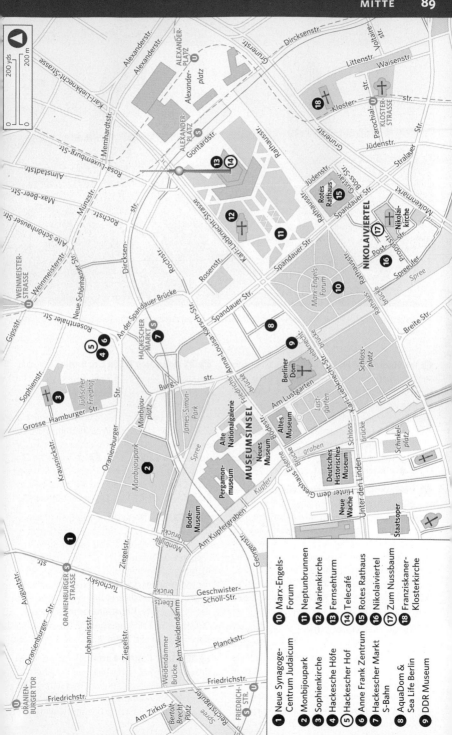

200 yds
200 m

> *Ride 200 meters (655 feet) up the Fernsehturm, Berlin's tallest structure, to the Telecafé for a breathtaking view of the city.*

4 ★★ **Hackesche Höfe.** Eight lovingly restored Art Nouveau courtyards (1907) cluster to form this chic symbol of the new East Berlin. Behind an elegant facade are trendy stores, cafes, restaurants, bars, and clubs, and it stands at the heart of a lively shopping and entertainment district. ⏱ 30 min. Rosenthaler Strasse 40–41.

5 ☕ ★ **Hackescher Hof.** See p. 59, **12**.

6 ★ **kids Anne Frank Zentrum (Center).** The German-born teenage Jewish diarist and Holocaust victim Anne Frank is honored at this small exhibit and documentation center. A short film about her life is accompanied by material about the diary she kept while in hiding from the Nazis in Amsterdam. ⏱ 40 min. Rosenthaler Strasse 39. ☎ 030/288-865-610. Admission 5€ adults, 2.50€ kids over 10, free for kids 10 and under. Tues–Sun 10am–6pm.

7 **Hackescher Markt S-Bahn.** Few of Berlin's rapid-transit stations are special enough to be worth pointing out. This one (1882) is an exception, due to its red-brick arches and iron-and-glass main hall, and the trendy boutiques, bars, and restaurants under the arches that mark it out as part of the area's commercial success story. Hackescher Markt.

8 **kids AquaDom & Sea Life Berlin.** The kids might want to visit the Sea Life aquarium chain's Berlin branch, with its elevator ascent through AquaDom's wraparound, see-through cylindrical tank, 25m (82 ft.) high, filled with more than 2,500 tropical fish. All in all, though, the marine environment is better presented at the aquarium at **Zoo Berlin** (p. 64, **9**). A tolerable (and free) substitute here is to eyeball the fish tank from below, in the Radisson Blu Hotel atrium (p. 120). ⏱ 10 min. Karl-Liebknecht-Strasse 3.

9 ★ **kids DDR Museum.** A glimpse of everyday life in the old, Communist-era German Democratic Republic. You get to "drive" a *Trabbie*—a Trabant car that was the bizarre little standard-bearer of East German automotive engineering—and stroll through an apartment furnished in typical Communist-era style. ⏱ 1 hr. Karl-Liebknecht-Strasse 1. 030/847123731. Admission 5.50€ adults, 3.50€ kids 6–18. Sun–Fri 10am–8pm, Sat 10am–10pm.

10 **kids Marx-Engels-Forum.** A sculpture-group (1986) of Karl Marx and Friedrich Engels, the founders of Communism, is the main (or only) point of interest in this park. There's not much to do besides leaving a red rose if you've a mind to, or, if you're a kid, climbing up and tweaking Marx's beard. Along the Spree, btw. Karl-Liebknecht-Strasse and Rathausstrasse.

11 ★ kids Neptunbrunnen. Neptune, the Roman god of the sea, stands at the heart of this monumental bronze fountain (1891), accompanied by water nymphs representing Germany's Elbe, Oder, Rhine, and Weichsel (Vistula) rivers. Kids can get away with splashing in the fountain when the weather is good; adults should probably not risk it. **Spandauer Strasse.**

12 ★ Marienkirche. Berlin's second oldest church (after the Nikolaikirche; see below), the red-brick Marienkirche (Church of St. Mary) contains a variety of Gothic and baroque styles, representing centuries of building and rebuilding from its foundation around 1250. Look for the fine alabaster pulpit (1703) and the grand Joachim Wagner organ (1721). A bronze statue of Protestant reformer Martin Luther stands outside. ⏲ 30 min. Karl-Liebknecht-Strasse 8.

13 ★★★ kids Fernsehturm (Television Tower). At 368m (1,207 ft.) high, the Fernsehturm (1969) is Berlin's tallest structure. Riding the turbo elevator up about 200m (655 ft.) to the observation deck or the rotating Telecafé restaurant can seem exciting enough, and the superb views from both places should be compensation for any ear-popping along the way. When the sun shines on the stainless steel dome, it reflects in the shape of a cross—a symbolic irritant for East Germany's atheist rulers and a phenomenon its citizens dubbed "the Pope's Revenge." ⏲ 45 min. Alexanderplatz. ☎ 030/242-3333. www.tv-turm.de. Admission 10€ adults, 5.50€ kids 4–16. Mar–Oct daily 9am–midnight; Nov–Feb daily 10am–midnight.

14 ☕ ★★ kids Telecafé. See p. 83, ⑧.

15 ★ Rotes Rathaus. Just across the way from the Television Tower is Berlin's town hall (1869). Calling it "Rotes Rathaus" (Red Town Hall) was doubly appropriate when the building was Communist East Berlin's seat of government, though the nickname actually refers to the facade's fiery-red bricks. A frieze along the facade tells tales from the city's history. Rathausstrasse 15.

> The Nikolaiviertel is Berlin's faithfully recreated medieval district, featuring a Gothic church and three 17th-century mansions.

16 ★★ Nikolaiviertel (Nicholas Quarter). Escape now for a time from bustling streets and heavy traffic into Berlin's only surviving medieval district. Well, "faux-medieval" might be a more accurate description for this restored and reconstructed quarter in the heart of Old Town Berlin, but the 1980s effect is more or less believable, and the specialty stores and bars go a long way toward canceling any misgivings. The Nikolaiviertel is centered on the twin Gothic spires of the Nikolaikirche (c. 1230), a church dedicated to St. Nicholas, which contains fine baroque funerary monuments. Speckled around the district is a trio of elegant 17th-century mansions. ⏲ 45 min. Btw. Spandauer Strasse and the Spree.

17 ☕ ★ Zum Nussbaum. See p. 58, ⑤.

18 ★ Franziskaner-Klosterkirche. A remnant of medieval Berlin, this tree-shaded ruin is the church of the Franciscan "Gray Cloister," a monastery founded around 1250 close to the original city wall. The church—which no longer had a religious function—did not survive World War II. It does, however, add to the atmosphere of Berlin's oldest area. ⏲ 20 min. Klosterstrasse 73.

Charlottenburg

The Charlottenburg district has lots of interesting residential, shopping, and nightlife zones, along with some stellar attractions (like Schloss Charlottenburg; p. 68, ❶). It is, however, too spread out to get around easily on foot. This tour includes the part closest to the city center, which can be seen as a kind of microcosm, containing many of Charlottenburg's attributes concentrated into a relatively tight space.

> *The Kaiser-Wilhelm-Gedächtniskirche's spire suffered severe damage in the bombings of World War II, but its lavish interior remains breathtaking.*

START Take the *U-Bahn* to Kurfürstendamm; or the *U-Bahn* or *S-Bahn* to Zoologischer Garten; or bus no. M19, M29, M46, 100, or 200 to Breitscheidplatz; or bus no. M45, M46, X9, X10, X34, 109, 110, 204, 245, or 249 to Zoologischer Garten.

❶ ★★ **Kaiser-Wilhelm-Gedächtniskirche.** Berliners have dubbed the bombed-out tower of the ruined Kaiser-Wilhelm-Gedächtni- skirche (Kaiser Wilhelm Memorial Church, 1895)—an unmissable and unmistakable sight at the start of the tour—the *Hohler Zahn* (Hollow Tooth). The church, together with a modern chapel of remembrance and belfry, is a memorial to the city's destruction in World War II. ⏱ 20 min. See p. 69, ❸.

❷ kids **Weltkugelbrunnen.** Its formal name translates as Globe Fountain in English, but with typical sardonic humor Berliners have relabeled this stepped red granite fountain (1983) in the form of a misshapen sphere the *Wasserklops* (Water Meatball). Small bronze figurines of humans and animals are speckled around. Breitscheidplatz.

❸ ★★ kids **Zoo Berlin.** There's not much point in spending less than 4 hours in this marvel- ous zoo, so unless you have plenty of time on this tour, it's best to just note it for possible future use and move on. ⏱ 4 hr. See p. 64, ❾.

❹ ★★ **Museum für Fotografie/Helmut Newton Stiftung.** Berlin native son, and later Australian citizen, the photographer Helmut

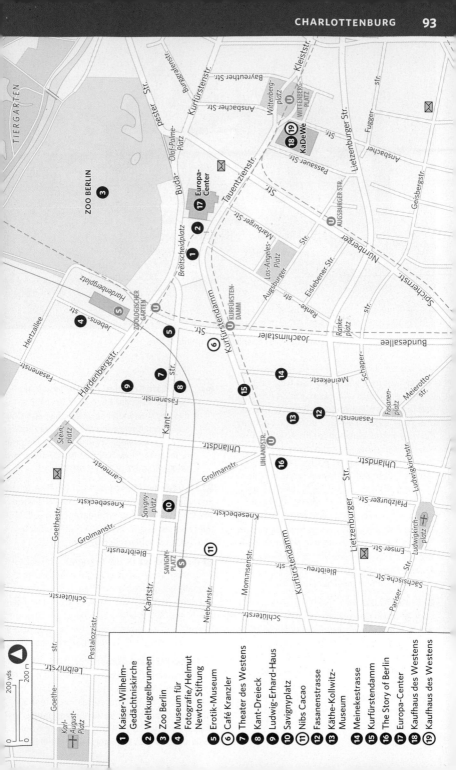

1 Kaiser-Wilhelm-Gedächtniskirche
2 Weltkugelbrunnen
3 Zoo Berlin
4 Museum für Fotografie/Helmut Newton Stiftung
5 Erotik-Museum
6 Café Kranzler
7 Theater des Westens
8 Kant-Dreieck
9 Ludwig-Erhard-Haus
10 Savignyplatz
11 Nibs Cacao
12 Fasanenstrasse
13 Käthe-Kollwitz-Museum
14 Meinekestrasse
15 Kurfürstendamm
16 The Story of Berlin
17 Europa-Center
18 Kaufhaus des Westens
19 Kaufhaus des Westens

> *Galleries, bookstores, and boutiques line charming Savignyplatz square.*

Newton (born Neustädter) was forgiving enough to donate pictures to the city he had had to flee as a Jewish teen during the Nazi era. The Helmut Newton Foundation displays his work in the Museum for Photography. Newton's photographs and those of his wife, June Brown (aka Alice Springs), include erotically charged black-and-white pictures of women, the so-called Big Nudes. Along with other photography exhibits, these are displayed in a restored neoclassical building (1908) that originally served the German army as an officers' club. ⏱ 40 min. Jebensstrasse 2. ☎ 030/266-2188. www.smb.spk-berlin.de. Admission 8€ adults, free for kids 15 and under. Tues–Sun 10am–6pm (Thurs until 10pm).

⑤ Erotik-Museum. This almost sinfully popular attraction reveals images of undraped ladies, often with accompanying gentlemen, along with accessories both historical and modern pertaining to the mysteries of the flesh. ⏱ 20 min. (to all day, I guess). Joachim-staler Strasse 4. Admission: before noon 10€; after noon 14€ per person, 25€ per couple; minimum age 18. Mon–Sat 9am–midnight, Sun 11am–midnight.

⑥ ☕ ★ Café Kranzler. The heir to a grand-cafe tradition dating to 1825 (to 1932 at this spot), Kranzler serves highly regarded *Kaffee und Kuchen* (coffee and cake) and other snacky delights in its rotunda interior or on an outdoor balcony. Kurfürstendamm 18. ☎ 030/887-183-925. 6€–12€.

⑦ Theater des Westens. Marlene Dietrich is just one of the name actors who have graced the stage at this elegant theater (1896). ⏱ 5 min. Kantstrasse 12. ☎ 030/259-244-555. *U-* and *S-Bahn: Zoologischer Garten.*

⑧ Kant-Dreieck (Kant Triangle). One of Berlin's many pieces of modern architecture that scarcely get noticed other than by specialists, the Kant-Dreieck is a prize-winning 11-story office tower (1995) with a sail-like appendage on the roof and windows connected in a distinctive crisscross pattern. ⏱ 10 min. Kantstrasse 155.

⑨ Ludwig-Erhard-Haus. With its 15 giant arches causing it to look something like a large and not entirely tame armadillo set down on a city street, English modernist architect Sir Nicholas Grimshaw's Berlin Chamber of Commerce and Industry (1998) is nothing if not striking. ⏱ 15 min. Fasanenstrasse 83–84.

10 ★★ Savignyplatz. This handsome square with a small park in the middle is at the center of a bustling residential zone. You need to be careful in this area—not due to any physical threat but because the streets radiating in all directions from Savignyplatz are speckled with appealing boutiques and designer stores, bookstores, small galleries, and offbeat stores of all kinds; to-die-for bars, cafes, and restaurants; and small-scale nightlife venues. The catch is that the distances involved are longer than they seem on a map, and the points of interest are scattered, so you can easily end up walking your socks off. ⏱ 30 min.

11 🍽 ★ kids Nibs Cacao. Chocolate, in many and varied shapes and guises, including hot liquid, is the sweet-tooth allure at this tiny gathering place for cocoa junkies. Drink up, eat up, and stock up on artisanal chocolate goodies to take home with you. Bleibtreustrasse 46. ☎ 030/2637-6740. 4€–10€.

12 ★★ Fasanenstrasse. Among the Jugendstil (Art Nouveau) villas and townhouses on this well-to-do street are two that house the Käthe-Kollwitz-Museum and the Literaturhaus cultural foundation, with its Wintergarten cafe-restaurant (see p. 75, **4** and **5**). At nos. 79–80, the Jüdisches Gemeindehaus (Jewish Community Center, 1959) stands on the site of a liberal synagogue built in 1912 and destroyed by the Nazis in 1938. ⏱ 30 min.

13 ★ Käthe-Kollwitz-Museum. ⏱ 1 hr. See p. 75, **4**.

14 Meinekestrasse. This street boasts handsome villas and townhouses dating from the late 19th and early 20th centuries. Some of them now house cafes, restaurants, or hotels. At no. 10 (Mark Hotel Meineke), a plaque recalls the building's time as the Zionist Palästinaamt (Palestine Office), which helped 50,000 German Jews emigrate to Palestine before the Nazis closed it in 1941. ⏱ 5 min.

15 ★★★ Kurfürstendamm. The warning about long distances provided under Savignyplatz (above) goes double or triple for the long boulevard Berliners call simply "Ku'damm." If you live to shop, or at least window-shop, you'll surely love it (that's why it rates 3 stars),

> *Wintergarten im Literaturhaus, on Fasanenstrasse.*

because every and any kind of shop is to be found along its length of 3.5km (2.2 miles). Kids, though, are sure to hate being dragged up and down it, especially since this busy street is intersected by many traffic-heavy side streets—you may have a youthful rebellion on your hands by the time you reach the end. ⏱ 30 min.–1 hr.

16 ★ kids The Story of Berlin. Finally, a waypoint on this tour that's of interest to kids and (unlike the zoo) doesn't need hours to get around. It's a hands-on tour with multimedia support through 2 dozen themed rooms that present Berlin's history from its founding in the 13th century and through such highs and lows as the rise of Prussia, the blossoming German capital, the Third Reich, wartime destruction, and the divided-then-reunited postwar city. You even get a guided tour of a Cold War nuclear shelter. ⏱ 1 hr. Kurfürstendamm 207–208. ☎ 030/8872-0100. www.story-of-berlin.de. Admission 9.80€ adults, 3.50€ kids 6–13, 21€ families. Daily 10am–8pm (last admission 6pm).

17 Europa-Center. ⏱ 20 min. See p. 87, **15**.

18 ★★★ Kaufhaus des Westens. Even if you preferred to pass on Kurfürstendamm's extended shopping miles (**15**), the "KaDeWe" department store has a lot of the same stuff under one roof. ⏱ 30 min. (or more, if you like to shop). See p. 104.

19 🍽 ★★ Kaufhaus des Westens. KaDeWe's "Gourmet Floor" is a great place to end the day, whether you're in need of a snack or a full meal. See p. 87, **16**.

Tiergarten

Berlin's central park, the "Animal Garden" was once a Prussian royal hunting reserve and was landscaped into a park—at that time known as Grosser Tiergarten—in the 1830s. Nowadays, it is the city's principal lung, a place to get away for a time from the noise and stress of urban life and to breathe fresh air. It's not perfect, since busy streets pass right through and around it. Quiet paths abound, however, and its leafy acres are a valuable resource.

> *The Tiergarten's lush lawns provide an idyllic destination for Berliners and tourists seeking sun or escape from city stress.*

START Take the *U-Bahn* or *S-Bahn* to Zoologischer Garten; or bus no. M45, M46, X9, X10, X34, 109, 110, 204, 245, or 249 to Zoologischer Garten. **Then walk up along Stadtbahnbogen, a path that runs alongside the elevated *S-Bahn* line.**

❶ ★ kids Landwehrkanal. The canal, which curves through central Berlin south of the Spree, was dug between 1845 and 1850. Walk along the south bank on the leafy Gartenufer canal-side path. Kids might be tickled to discover that they can peek through the fence and see the animals in Zoo Berlin (p. 64, **❾**). ◷ 30 min.

② 🍴 **★ Schleusenkrug.** In summer you can sit out under sun-umbrellas in the beer garden; at other times, or when the weather doesn't cooperate, the cafe-bar-restaurant should do fine for a snack or even just a coffee. Müller-Breslau-Strasse (at Gartenufer). ☎ 030/313-9909. 4€–12€.

❸ ★ Strasse des 17 Juni. Cross over the canal island (Schleuseninsel) to the Landwehrkanal's north bank to join this east-west boulevard that slices Tiergarten in two. On weekends, you'll be able to visit the flea market (p. 105) here, which is popular with Berlin students. ◷ 30 min.

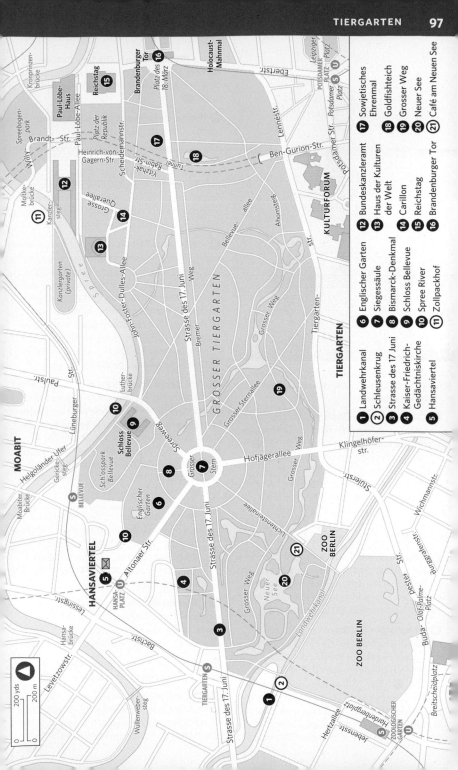

> *The towering 67-meter (220-foot) Siegessäule celebrates the long history of German and Prussian victories in battle.*

4 Kaiser-Friedrich-Gedächtniskirche. Not to be confused (obviously) with the more famous Kaiser-Wilhelm-Gedächtniskirche (p. 69, **3**), the Kaiser-Friedrich-Gedächtniskirche (Kaiser Friedrich Memorial Church, 1957) replaced a neo-Gothic church dating from 1895 that was built in memory of Kaiser Friedrich III. That church was destroyed in World War II. The modern skeletal bell tower reaches a height of 68m (223 ft.). ⏱ 20 min. Händelallee 20.

5 ★ Hansaviertel. Going around this modern residential quarter may be too much to do on this walk, but if you have the time, there are some Bauhaus buildings here that make an interesting diversion. ⏱ 1 hr. See p. 83, **2**.

6 ★ Englischer Garten. A handsome, English-style garden inside Tiergarten, Berlin's diminutive English Garden in no way compares with the vast scale or interest of Munich's (p. 288, **2**). Still, its fountains, sundial, tea house, flowers, clipped bushes, and lawns are pretty enough in their way. Jazz performances and other concerts (www.konzertsommer. info) take place here in summer. ⏱ 30 min.

7 ★★ kids Siegessäule (Victory Column). Climbing the Siegessäule affords grand views over Tiergarten and beyond. ⏱ 30 min. See p. 69, **4**.

8 Bismarck-Denkmal (Bismarck Monument). Cross to the north side of the Grosser Stern traffic circle, inside which the Siegessäule stands, and you will find, half hidden among the trees, this lavish monument (1901) to Otto von Bismarck (1815–98), dubbed the "Iron Chancellor" and the man who more than anyone else unified Germany under strong, militaristic Prussian leadership.

9 ★★ Schloss Bellevue. Flanked by the Spree and its own extensive gardens, Bellevue Palace (1786) was built originally for Prussia's Prince Ferdinand. Today, it is the official residence of Germany's head of state, the federal president, a largely ceremonial office that commands considerable respect in the country. Nearby is the oval Bundespräsidialamt (1998), the offices of the presidency staff. ⏱ 20 min. Spreeweg 1 (in the Tiergarten).

10 ★★★ Spree River. Cross over the meandering river on the graceful Lutherbrücke (1892), a bridge named after the leader of the Protestant Reformation, Martin Luther, and go east along the north-bank park walkway. Cross back over the Spree on the equally graceful Moltkebrücke (1891), named after Helmuth von Moltke, a 19th-century chief of the Prussian general staff. ⏱ 40 min.

11 🍴 ★★ Zollpackhof. The elegant beer garden and restaurant here is a fine place to relax, and an exemplar of creative traditional German cuisine. Elisabeth-Abegg-Strasse 1. ☎ 030/3309-9720. Entrees 17€–20€.

12 ★ Bundeskanzleramt. The white, postmodern office (2001) of Germany's head of government, the federal chancellor, is remarkable for its size and clean lines. See p. 83, **4**.

13 ★★ Haus der Kulturen der Welt (House of World Cultures). ⏱ 20 min. See p. 83, **3**.

14 kids Carillon. This bell tower will only really be of interest to children if the Glockenspiel's 68 bells actually ring out some tune or other, which they do from time to time in summer.

> *The beer garden at Tiergarten's Café am Neuen See.*

Across the path is a sculpture garden containing a bunch of modern-art masterpieces. Well, they might in future be considered masterpieces—anything's possible! ⏲ 10 min.

⓯ ★★★ Reichstag. ⏲ 30 min. See p. 69, **❻**.

⓰ ★★★ Brandenburger Tor (Brandenburg Gate). See p. 69, **❼**.

Berlin's Best Parks

Berlin is green (it is, to a considerable degree, Green as well, but that's another story). Parks, gardens, and other green spaces, both large and small, are scattered through the urban area. The city's rim is a mass of green in which rivers and lakes are embedded. Among the best known and easiest to reach are the central **Tiergarten**; the gardens and riverside park at **Schloss Charlottenburg** (p. 68, **❶**) in the west; small **Viktoriapark** in Kreuzberg (p. 56); tiny **Monbijoupark** in Mitte (p. 88, **❷**); and the large **Grunewald** (p. 65, **❿**) along the Havel River in the southwest.

In addition, fans should consider visiting other parks inside the city: Volkspark Jungfernheide in Charlottenburg-Nord; Volkspark Humboldthain in Gesundbrunnen (Mitte); Heinrich-von-Kleistpark in Schöneberg; and Volkspark Hasenheide in Neukölln. Farther out, **Wannsee** in the southwest (p. 80), **Tegeler See** in the northwest, and **Müggelsee** in the southeast are scenic lakes bordered by forest.

⓱ Sowjetisches Ehrenmal (Soviet Memorial). A pair each of Russian tanks and howitzers and a sculptured Red Army soldier "guard" this memorial (1945), which honors 80,000 Russian troops killed during the Battle of Berlin that same year. Some Berliners have dubbed it the "Monument to the Unknown Rapist," due to the many rapes that accompanied the fall of Hitler's capital. ⏲ 10 min.

⓲ 𝗸𝗶𝗱𝘀 Goldfishteich (Goldfish Pond). Cross over Strasse des 17 Juni to the south side of Tiergarten. The pond here is not, as you might expect, filled with goldfish, though that might change. At the time of writing, it was being cleaned up and restored to its original 1840 condition. Whether that includes goldfish remains to be seen. ⏲ 15 min.

⓳ ★ Grosser Weg. Turn west (to your right) along this path through the park's southern reaches and follow it to its end. Along the way, you'll cross over to a tiny island on which stands a statue of Prussia's fairy-tale princess (and later queen) Luise (see "Queen Luise, p. 65) and pass a monument to composer Richard Wagner. ⏲ 30 min.

⓴ ★★ 𝗸𝗶𝗱𝘀 Neuer See (New Lake). Neuer See is the largest body of water in Tiergarten—though that's not saying too much. Boats are available to rent from Café am Neuen See, and there are a couple of islets to row around. ⏲ 15–20 min.

㉑ 🍴 ★★ **Café am Neuen See.** See p. 69, ⑤.

Berlin Shopping Best Bets

Best for Urban Fashion
Thatchers, Kastanienallee 21 (p. 104)

Best for Teen Threads
EastBerlin, Alte Schönhauser Strasse 33–34 (p. 104)

Best for Toys
Die Puppenstube, Propststrasse 4 (p. 105)

Best for Vinyl Records
Café Horenstein, Fechner Strasse 3 (p. 105)

Best Street Market
Markt am Winterfeldtplatz, Winterfeldtplatz (p. 105)

Best for English Books
Books in Berlin, Goethestrasse 69 (p. 101)

Best for Traditional Gifts
Erzgebirgshaus, Friedrichstrasse 194–199 (p. 104)

Best Department Store
Kaufhaus des Westens, Tauentzienstrasse 21–24 (p. 104)

Best for Gourmet Foods
Galeries Lafayette, Friedrichstrasse 76–78 (p. 101)

Best for Local High Fashion
Anette Petermann, Bleibtreustrasse 49 (p. 104)

Best for Packing a Picnic
Kaufhaus des Westens, Tauentzienstrasse 21–24 (p. 104)

Best for Designer Homewares
House of Villeroy & Boch, Kurfürstendamm 33 (p. 101)

Best for Traditional Marzipan
Wald Königsberger Marzipan, Pestalozis-trasse 54A (p. 104)

Best for Heavenly Scents
Harry Lehmann, Kantstrasse 106 (p. 104)

> *The high-end Kaufhaus des Westens (KaDeWe) is the largest department store in continental Europe, and one of its finest.*

Berlin Shopping A to Z

Art

★ **Lumas** CHARLOTTENBURG

Among the wares at this art-photography gallery run by a New York–based group are signed limited-edition prints from top photographers. Fasanenstrasse 73. ☎ 030/8862-7601. www. eu.lumas.com. AE, MC, V. *U-Bahn:* Uhlandstrasse. Bus: M19, M29, X10, 109, or 110. See map, p. 103.

Books

kids **Books in Berlin** CHARLOTTENBURG

This store focuses on books in English, including new and secondhand (they buy books, too) books and fiction and nonfiction titles for adults and kids. Goethestrasse 69. ☎ 030/313-3233. www.booksinberlin.de. V. *S-Bahn:* Savignyplatz. Bus: 101. See map, p. 103.

Ceramics & Homewares

★ **Art + Industry** CHARLOTTENBURG

Go back to the 20th century (mainly 1930s to 1980s) for refurbished furnishings, fittings, ornaments, and accessories. Bleibtreustrasse 40. ☎ 030/883-4946. www.aiberlin.de. AE, MC, V. *S-Bahn:* Savignyplatz. Bus: M19, M29, X10, 109, or 110. See map, p. 103.

★ **House of Villeroy & Boch** CHARLOTTENBURG

The Saarland-based company's own-label store sells its trademark sleek glassware, crockery, cutlery, and home accessories. Kurfürstendamm 33. ☎ 030/8868-2970. www. villeroy-boch.com. AE, DC, MC, V. *U-Bahn:* Uhlandstrasse. Bus: M19, M29, X10, 109, or 110. See map, p. 103.

Department Stores & Malls

★★ **Galeries Lafayette** MITTE

The French chain's glittering Berlin branch brings *une abondance* of high-end Parisian style in fashion, fragrances, cuisine, and more. Friedrichstrasse 76–78. ☎ 030/209-480. www. lafayette-berlin.de. AE, DC, MC, V. *U-Bahn:* Französische Strasse. Bus: 147. See map, p. 102.

★★ **Hackesche Höfe** MITTE

Stores in this Art Nouveau monument range from purveyors of designer duds to cheap jewelry. Rosenthaler Strasse 40–41 and Sophienstrasse 6. ☎ 030/2809-8010. www.hackesche-hoefe.de. AE, DC, MC, V. *S-Bahn:* Hackescher Markt. Tram: M1 or M6. See map, p. 102.

> *You'll find a taste of Paris in Berlin when you visit the upscale French department store Galeries Lafayette.*

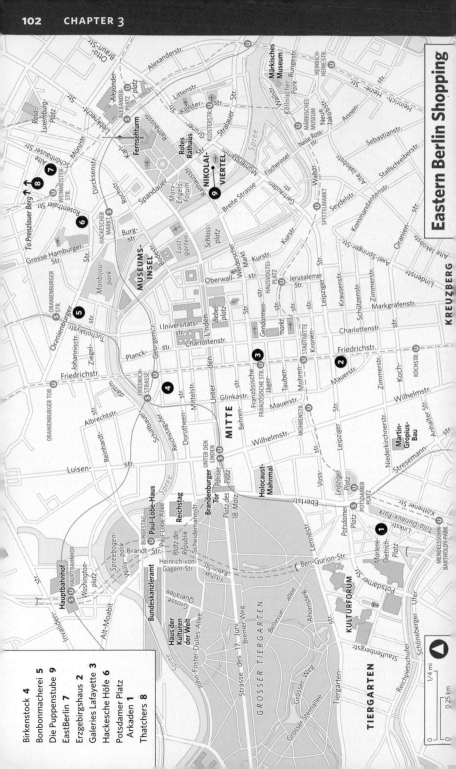

Eastern Berlin Shopping

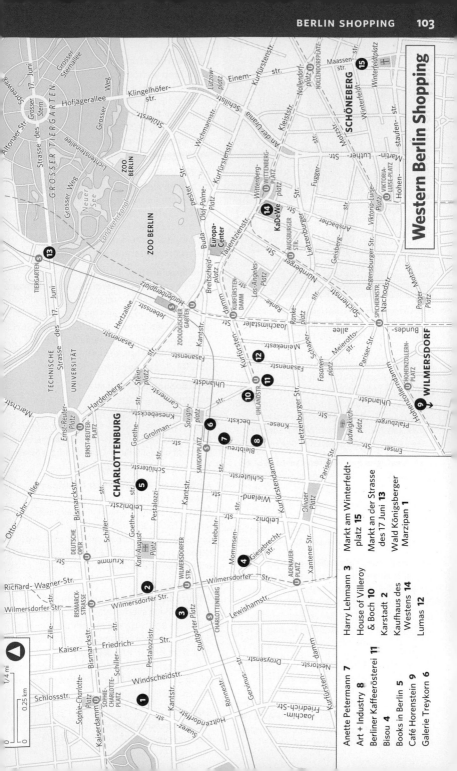

Western Berlin Shopping

Anette Petermann **7**
Art + Industry **8**
Berliner Kaffeerösterei **11**
Bisou **4**
Books in Berlin **5**
Café Horenstein **9**
Galerie Treykorn **6**

Harry Lehmann **3**
House of Villeroy & Boch **10**
Karstadt **2**
Kaufhaus des Westens **14**
Lumas **12**

Markt am Winterfeldt-platz **15**
Markt an der Strasse des 17 Juni **13**
Wald Königsberger Marzipan **1**

> *The beautiful Hackesche Höfe mall is an early 20th-century architectural marvel and houses numerous popular specialty stores.*

Karstadt CHARLOTTENBURG
The Berlin flagship of this midbrow department-store chain sports clothes, fashion accessories, electronics, and more. Wilmersdorfer Strasse 118. ☎ 030-311-050. www.karstadt.de. AE, DC, MC, V. *U-Bahn:* Wilmersdorfer Strasse. Bus: M49, X34, or 309. See map, p. 103.

★★★ Kaufhaus des Westens SCHÖNEBERG
Europe's largest department store, "KaDeWe" stocks virtually every upmarket shopping item known to man, woman, child, and pet. Tauentzienstrasse 21–24. ☎ 030/21210. www.kadewe.de. AE, DC, MC, V. *U-Bahn:* Wittenbergplatz. Bus: M19, M29, or M46. See map, p. 103.

★★ Potsdamer Platz Arkaden MITTE
Architect Helmut Jahn's mall is where the serious shopping gets done, in 150 stores of all kinds. Potsdamer Platz. ☎ 030/255-9270. AE, DC, MC, V. *U-* and *S-Bahn:* Potsdamer Platz. Bus: M41, M48, M85, 200, or 347. See map, p. 102.

Fashion
★★ Anette Petermann CHARLOTTENBURG
The sharp edges of this homegrown haute couture are softened by the tactical use of roses and other indelibly feminine motifs. Bleibtreustrasse 49. ☎ 030/323-2556. www.anette-petermann.de. AE, MC, V. *S-Bahn:* Savignyplatz. Bus: M49 or X34. See map, p. 103.

★ EastBerlin MITTE
A cool step up from rough-and-ready street fashion, for men and women. Bags, accessories, and silver jewelry round out the selection at this inventive boutique. Alte Schönhauser Strasse 33–34. ☎ 030/2472-3988. www.eastberlinshop.com. AE, MC, V. *U-Bahn:* Weinmeisterstrasse. Tram: M1. See map, p. 102.

★★ Thatchers PRENZLAUER BERG
Local innovators Ralf Hensellek and Thomas Mrozek create sexy yet understated clothes for young urbanites heading to the office or on the club trail. Kastanienallee 21. ☎ 030/2462-7751. www.thatchers.de. AE, MC, V. *U-Bahn:* Eberswalder Strasse. Tram: 10. See map, p. 102.

Food Specialists
★ Berliner Kaffeerösterei CHARLOTTENBURG
Old-fashioned charm reigns here, where fresh-roasted coffee is king and tea and pralines are nobility. Uhlandstrasse 173–174. ☎ 030/8867-7920. www.berliner-kaffeeroesterei.de. MC, V. *U-Bahn:* Uhlandstrasse. Bus: M19, M29, X10, 109 110, 204, or 249. See map, p. 103.

★ kids Bonbonmacherei MITTE
Handmade *Maiblätter* (flavored with woodruff are among the delights at this candy store in the Heckmann Höfe. Oranienburger Strasse 32. ☎ 030/4405-5243. www.bonbonmacherei.de. No credit cards. *S-Bahn:* Oranienburger Strasse. Tram: M1 or M6. See map, p. 102.

★★ kids Wald Königsberger Marzipan
CHARLOTTENBURG A heavenly aroma wafts from this family-run store. Pestalozzistrasse 54A. ☎ 030/323-8254. www.wald-koenigsberger-marzipan.de. No credit cards. *U-Bahn:* Sophie-Charlotte-Platz. Bus: M49, X34, or 309. See map, p. 103.

Fragrances
★ Harry Lehmann CHARLOTTENBURG
Even if buying scents by weight seems counterintuitive, mixing and matching your own perfumes comes out smelling like a sweet deal. Kantstrasse 106. ☎ 030/324-3582. www.parfum-individual.de. MC, V. *U-Bahn:* Wilmersdorfer Strasse. Bus: M49, X34, 109, or 309. See map, p. 103.

Gifts
★ kids Erzgebirgshaus MITTE
Hand-carved wooden ornaments and

decorations from the Erzgebirge (Ore Mountains) in Saxony are sold at this delightful store. Friedrichstrasse 194–199. ☎ 030/2045-0977. www.erzgebirgshaus.de. AE, MC, V. *U-Bahn:* Stadtmitte. Bus: M48 or 347. See map, p. 102.

Jewelry & Accessories

Bisou CHARLOTTENBURG
Affordable jewelry made primarily from pearls, but including pieces that employ coral and lava, make this store worth checking out. Giesebrechtstrasse 18. ☎ 030/3101-4908. www.bisou-berlin.de. No credit cards. *U-Bahn:* Adenauerplatz. Bus: M19, M29, X10, 101, 109, or 110. See map, p. 103.

★★★ Galerie Treykorn CHARLOTTENBURG
A respectful air permeates an elegant store where jewelry is considered wearable applied art for connoisseurs. Passage, Savignyplatz 13. ☎ 030/3180-2354. www.treykorn.de. AE, DC, MC, V. *S-Bahn:* Savignyplatz. Bus: M49 or X34. See map, p. 103.

Music

★ Café Horenstein WILMERSDORF
The coffee is good, but the classic vinyl records are the real reason to seek out this store. Fechner Strasse 3. ☎ 030/8639-6897. www. horenstein.de. No credit cards. *U-Bahn:* Blissestrasse. Bus: 101, 104, or 249. See map, p. 103.

Shoes

Birkenstock MITTE
German-made Birkenstocks are the Mercedes of footwear. The shoes and sandals for adults and children keep a firm grip on the ground. Georgenstrasse 24. ☎ 030/2007-7245. www. birkenstock.de. AE, MC, V. *U- and S-Bahn:* Friedrichstrasse. Bus: 147. Tram M1 or 12. See map, p. 102.

Street Markets

★★ Markt am Winterfeldtplatz SCHÖNEBERG
Wednesday and Saturday, the square is alive with the sounds, aromas, and bustle of one of the city's best street markets. Appease your appetite with a selection from the arrays of artisanal, organic, and ethnic food. Winterfeldtplatz. No phone. www.winterfeldt-platz.de. No credit cards at most traders. *U-Bahn:* Nollendorfplatz. Bus: M19 or 204. See map, p. 103.

> *The popular and high-quality Markt am Winterfeldtplatz overflows with options, from artisanal food to fashion and more.*

★ Markt an der Strasse des 17 Juni TIERGARTEN
On weekends, the western end of Tiergarten's long boulevard hosts this popular flea market. Berliners come here to find an appropriate piece of nostalgia, a battered semi-antique, or used clothing. Strasse des 17 Juni. ☎ 030/2655-0096. www.berliner-troedelmarkt.de. No credit cards at most traders. *U-Bahn:* Ernst-Reuter-Platz. Bus: M45, X9, or 245. See map, p. 103.

Toys

★ kids Die Puppenstube MITTE
This old-fasioned toy store fits the surrounding restored medieval Nikolaiviertel quarter perfectly. Come for porcelain dolls, teddies, and hand puppets. Propststrasse 4. ☎ 030/242-3967. www.puppen-eins.de. AE, MC, V. *U-Bahn:* Klosterstrasse. Bus: M48 or 248. See map, p. 102.

Berlin Restaurant Best Bets

Best Michelin-Star Splurge
Gourmet Restaurant Lorenz Adlon, Hotel
Adlon Kempinski, Unter den Linden 77 (p. 111)

Best Tandoori
Masaledar, Feurigstrasse 38–39 (p. 1113)

Best for Sushi
Izumi, Kronenstrasse 66 (p. 112)

Best Turkish
Hasir, Adalbertstrasse 10 (p. 111)

Best Vegan
Hans Wurst, Dunckerstrasse 2A (p. 111)

Best for Budget German Food
Henne, Leuschnerdamm 25 (p. 111)

Best Pizza in Town
Il Casolare, Grimmstrasse 30 (p. 111)

Best Contemporary Italian
Ana e Bruno, Sophie-Charlotten-Strasse 101
(p. 107)

Best French Bistro
Paris Bar, Kantstrasse 152 (p. 113)

Best for Spanish Tapas
Mar y Sol, Savignyplatz 5 (p. 112)

Best for the Humble Spud
Kartoffelkiste, Europa Center,
Tauentzienstrasse 9–12 (p. 112)

Best for Kids
Funkturm Restaurant, Messedamm 22
(p. 110)

Best Posh German
Alt Luxemburg, Windscheidstrasse 31 (p. 107)

Best Leafy Setting
Diekmann im Châlet Suisse, Im Jagen 5,
Grunewald (p. 110)

Best for High-End Seafood
Fischers Fritz, Regent Hotel, Charlottenstrasse
49 (p. 110)

> *You'll find the best Turkish dishes in Berlin at Hasir.*

Berlin Restaurants A to Z

★★★ **Alt Luxemburg** CHARLOTTENBURG *FRENCH-GERMAN* An elegant piece of Old Berlin is the tranquil setting for master-chef Karl Wannemacher's refined cuisine. Windscheidstrasse 31. ☎ 030/323-8730. www.alt-luxemburg.de. Entrees 27€–32€. AE, DC, MC, V. Dinner Mon–Sat. *U-Bahn:* Sophie-Charlotten-Platz. Bus: M49, X34, or 309. See map, p. 109.

★ **Amrit** KREUZBERG *INDIAN* Despite strong competition from neighboring Indian restaurants, Amrit keeps its nose ahead by matching exotic looks with carefully considered cuisine. Oranienstrasse 202–203. ☎ 030/612-5550. www.amrit.de. Entrees 9€–19€. AE, DC, MC, V. Lunch & dinner daily. *U-Bahn:* Görlitzer Bahnhof. Bus: M29 or 140. See map, p. 108.

★★★ **Ana e Bruno** CHARLOTTENBURG *ITALIAN* Owner/chef Bruno Pellegrini and his wife, Ana, mix and match ingredients to chart

unorthodox courses at this sophisticated restaurant. Sophie-Charlotten-Strasse 101. ☎ 030/325-7110. www.ana-e-bruno.de. Entrees 21€–45€. MC, V. Lunch & dinner daily. *S-Bahn:* Westend. Bus: M45 or 309. See map, p. 109.

★★ **Aroma** CHARLOTTENBURG *CANTONESE* Authentic Chinese cuisine is the draw here, with the classic dim sum dinner served into the wee hours. Kantstrasse 35. ☎ 030/3759-1628. Entrees 8€–17€. AE, MC, V. Lunch & dinner daily. *S-Bahn:* Savignyplatz. Bus: M49 or X34. See map, p. 109.

★★ kids **Blockhaus Nikolskoe** WANNSEE *GERMAN* A Russian timber *dacha* (1819) overlooking Wannsee lake is the unlikely setting for this traditional restaurant. Nikolskoer Weg 15. ☎ 030/805-2914. www.blockhaus-nikolskoe.de. Entrees 10€–15€. No credit cards. Lunch & dinner daily (closes 6pm in winter). *S-Bahn:* Wannsee. Bus: 218 or 316. See map, p. 109.

> *Enjoy delicious, traditional Prussian cuisine in a Russian log cabin overlooking the beautiful Wannsee lake at Blockhaus Nikolskoe.*

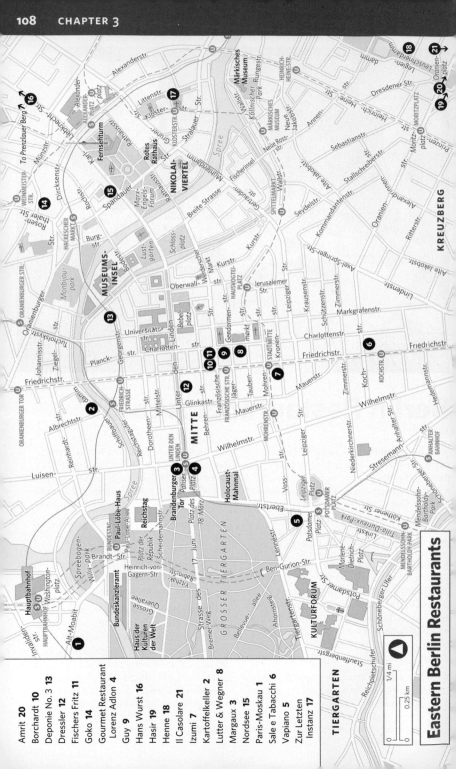

Eastern Berlin Restaurants

Amrit **20**
Borchardt **10**
Deponie No. 3 **13**
Dressler **12**
Fischers Fritz **11**
Goko **14**
Gourmet Restaurant
  Lorenz Adlon **4**
Guy **9**
Hans Wurst **16**
Hasir **19**
Henne **18**
Il Casolare **21**
Izumi **7**
Kartoffelkeller **2**
Lutter & Wegner **8**
Margaux **3**
Nordsee **15**
Paris-Moskau **1**
Sale e Tabacchi **6**
Vapiano **5**
Zur Letzten
  Instanz **17**

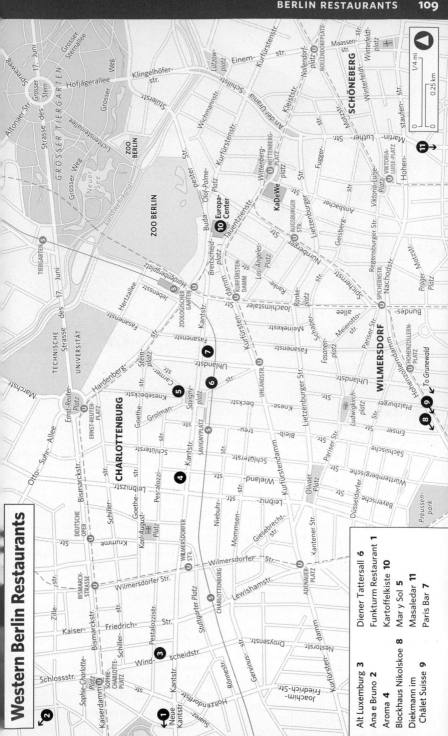

Western Berlin Restaurants

> *Luxurious 19th century–style dining and fine wine is the order at the elegant Alt Luxemburg.*

★★ **Borchardt** MITTE *CONTINENTAL*
An Art Nouveau–style institution among city "names" in politics, media, and the arts, Borchardt can be stuffy but compensates with fine cuisine. Französische Strasse 47. ☎ 030/8188-6262. Entrees 20€–30€. AE, MC, V. Lunch & dinner daily. *U-Bahn:* Französische Strasse. Bus: 147. See map, p. 108.

★ **Deponie No. 3** MITTE *GERMAN*
Artfully designed to look older than its 1990s origins, "Storeroom No. 3" is a repository of traditional taste. Georgenstrasse 5. ☎ 030/2016-5740. www.deponie3.de. Entrees 6€–14€. No credit cards. Breakfast, lunch & dinner daily. *U-* and *S-Bahn:* Friedrichstrasse. Tram: M1 or 12. See map, p. 108.

★★ kids **Diekmann im Châlet Suisse** DAHLEM
CONTINENTAL This Swiss farmhouse–style restaurant suits the forested Grunewald to its roots. Im Jagen 5. ☎ 030/832-6362. www.diekmann-restaurants.de. Entrees 10€–22€. AE, DC, MC, V. Lunch & dinner daily. *U-Bahn:* Dahlem-Dorf. Bus: X10, X83, or 115. See map, p. 109.

★ **Diener Tattersall** CHARLOTTENBURG
GERMAN Simple bar fare and a fine sidewalk terrace attract a sophisticated crowd. Grolmanstrasse 47. ☎ 030/881-5329. Entrees 5€–10€. No credit cards. Dinner daily. *S-Bahn:* Savignyplatz. Bus: M49 or X34. See map, p. 109.

★★ **Dressler** MITTE *CONTINENTAL*
German dishes lead but don't rule the menu, in an Art Deco–style setting. Unter den Linden 39. ☎ 030/204-4422. www.restaurant-dressler.de. Entrees 12€–26€. AE, DC, MC, V. Breakfast, lunch & dinner daily. *U-Bahn:* Französische Strasse. Bus: TXL, 100, 147, or 200. See map, p. 108.

★★★ **Fischers Fritz** MITTE *SEAFOOD*
A brace of Michelin stars glistens amid the exquisite fish dishes in master chef Christian Lohse's palatial dining room. Regent Hotel, Charlottenstrasse 49. ☎ 030/2033-6363. www.fischersfritzberlin.com. Entrees 49€–80€. AE, DC, MC, V. Lunch & dinner daily. *U-Bahn:* Französische Strasse. Bus: 147. See map, p. 108.

★★ kids **Funkturm Restaurant** CHARLOTTENBURG
INTERNATIONAL This restaurant, 52m (171 ft.)

> *Celebrity chef Thomas Neeser's Gourmet Restaurant Lorenz Adlon is acknowledged as Berlin's finest eatery and offers a breathtaking view of the Brandenburg Gate.*

high on the Radio Tower, serves up exceptional views. Messedamm 22. ☎ 030/3038-2900. Entrees 8€–18€. AE, DC, MC, V. Lunch & dinner Tues–Sun. *S-Bahn:* Messe Nord/ICC. Bus: M49, 104, 218, or 349. See map, p. 109.

★★ **Goko** MITTE *JAPANESE*
A cool, almost Scandinavian look sets the scene for masterful sushi and other Japanese dishes, some of them vegetarian. Neue Schönhauser Strasse 12. ☎ 030/2758-2549. www.go-ko.com. Entrees 4€–14€. MC, V. Lunch & dinner daily. *U-Bahn:* Weinmeister Strasse. Tram: M1. See map, p. 108.

★★★ **Gourmet Restaurant Lorenz Adlon**
MITTE *FRENCH* Celeb chef Thomas Neeser presides at Berlin's top restaurant. It has windows overlooking the Brandenburg Gate, walnut paneling, black-and-white marble, and draperies that seem like works of art themselves. Hotel Adlon Kempinski, Unter den Linden 77. ☎ 030/2261-1960. Menus 140€–190€. AE, DC, MC, V. Dinner Tues–Sat. *U-* and *S-Bahn:* Brandenburger Tor. Bus: TXL, 100, or 200. See map, p. 108.

★★ **Guy** MITTE *CONTINENTAL*
Just off Gendarmenmarkt, this inventive restaurant offers fine cuisine outdoors in a romantic courtyard or in an elegant dining room. Jägerstrasse 59–60. ☎ 030/2094-2600.

www.guy-restaurant.de. Entrees 27€–29€. MC, V. Lunch & dinner Mon–Fri, dinner Sat. *U-Bahn:* Französische Strasse. Bus: 147. See map, p. 108.

★ **Hans Wurst** PRENZLAUER BERG *VEGAN*
They're maybe a little too self-aware about "doing good" at this laid-back place, but the 100% organic food has exemplary taste. Dunckerstrasse 2A. ☎ 030/4171-7822. http://hanswurstcafe.com. Entrees 5€–8€. No credit cards. Lunch & dinner Tues–Sun. *U-Bahn:* Eberswalder Strasse. Tram: M10. See map, p. 108.

★★ kids **Hasir** KREUZBERG *TURKISH*
The home of *döner kebab* has been going strong since 1971, serving up this and other Anatolian specialties inside or on the terrace. Multiple locations. Adalbertstrasse 10. ☎ 030/614-2373. www.hasir.de. Entrees 11€–21€. No credit cards. Lunch & dinner daily. *U-Bahn:* Kottbusser Tor. Bus: M29. See map, p. 108.

★★ **Henne** KREUZBERG *GERMAN*
You can't go far wrong here, provided you like roast organic chicken, because that's what this Kreuzberg pub serves up. Leuschnerdamm 25. ☎ 030/614-7730. www.henne-berlin.de. Entrees 6€–8€. MC, V. Dinner Tues–Sun. *U-Bahn:* Moritzplatz. Bus: M29 or 347. See map, p. 108.

★ kids **Il Casolare** KREUZBERG *ITALIAN*
Wood-fired pizza heads the bill at this rustic

Dining Tips

Berlin is a world city with a population that includes many ethnic minorities. In addition, it's a center of government and diplomacy, a home to both wealthy and poor, a place that attracts visitors from around the world, and an arena for both the socially traditional and wildly liberal. What all this adds up to on the plate is that there are dining options to suit all possible tastes. Here are a few general pointers to help you get the most out of dining in Berlin—keep in mind that they are generalizations, but with at least a grain of truth.

- Charlottenburg was the most desirable district of the old West Berlin, and it still has the most settled dining scene. There are plenty of great restaurants here, not all of them expensive, though you are likely to pay somehat more here for location.

- Mitte is perhaps the hardest district to define, covering as it does a relatively new dining scene that ranges from platinum-card establishments around Unter den Linden, Gendarmenmarkt, and Friedrichstrasse, to the trendy eateries around Hackescher Markt. Anything is possible here.

- Kreuzberg is home to many of Berlin's ethnic-minority inhabitants. Most, but by no means all, are Turkish. This means there are plenty of low-cost and often excellent Turkish restaurants and restaurants of other ethnic minorities here.

- Prenzlauer Berg in the old East Berlin is the new trendy "in" district, increasingly a haunt of young professionals, often with kids (something of a rarity in this demographically challenged land). Establishments have been springing up that specialize in New Age, holistic, vegetarian and vegan dining, and ethnic cuisine that goes beyond cheap-and-basic.

- Street markets are a good place to score low-priced grub. There's generally a bunch of food stalls selling low-cost ethnic and German eats, and usually some that have fancy cheeses, cold meats, decent wines, and other artisanal stuff.

canal-side trattoria with a sidewalk terrace. but there's other Italian fare, too. **Grimmstrasse** 30. ☎ 030/6950-6610. Entrees 7€–12€. No credit cards. Lunch & dinner daily. *U-Bahn:* Schönleinstrasse. Bus: M41. See map, p. 108.

★★ **Izumi** MITTE *JAPANESE*
Fittingly restrained decor is the setting for a contender for the accolade of "best sushi in Berlin." **Kronenstrasse** 66. ☎ 030/2064-9938. www.sushi-izumi.de. Entrees 7€–18€. AE, DC, MC, V. Lunch & dinner daily. *U-Bahn:* Stadtmitte. Bus: M48 or 347. See map, p. 108.

kids **Kartoffelkeller** MITTE *GERMAN*
Berliners do love their spuds, and in a cavernous space where the potato is king, the business gets done in more than a hundred ways, ranging from braised with *Schnitzel* to U.S.-style with fillings. **Albrechtstrasse** 14B. ☎ 030/282-8548. www.kartoffelkeller.com. Entrees 8€–15€. MC, V. Lunch & dinner daily. *U-* and *S-Bahn:* Friedrichstrasse. Bus: TXL or 147. See map, p. 108.

★ kids **Kartoffelkiste** CHARLOTTENBURG *GERMAN*
The humble potato is rustled up in a multitude of creative ways, from pizza toppings to fritters. **Europa Center, Tauentzienstrasse** 9–12. ☎ 030/261-4254. www.kartoffelkiste-berlin. de. Entrees 7€–13€. MC, V. Lunch & dinner daily. *U-* and *S-Bahn:* Zoologischer Garten. Bus: M19, M29, M46, 100, or 200. See map, p. 109.

★★ **Lutter & Wegner** MITTE *AUSTRIAN/GERMAN*
Modern art counterpoints restrained dark wood panels and a nice, if pricey, line in *Wiener Schnitzel.* **Charlottenstrasse** 56. ☎ 030/202-9540. www.l-w-berlin.de. Entrees 18€–27€. AE, MC, V. Lunch & dinner daily. *U-Bahn:* Französische Strasse. Bus: 147. See map, p. 108.

★★★ **Margaux** MITTE *FRENCH*
Amid classic surroundings, star chef Michael Hoffmann brings a contemporary touch to his Michelin-star cuisine. **Unter den Linden** 78 (enter on Wilhelmstrasse). ☎ 030/2265-2611. www.margaux-berlin.de. Entrees 35€–60€. AE, DC, MC, V. Dinner Mon–Sat. *U-* and *S-Bahn:* Brandenburger Tor. Bus: TXL or 100. See map, p. 108.

★★ **Mar y Sol** CHARLOTTENBURG *SPANISH*
Browse tapas and specialties like *iberico de bellotta* ham amid tiles and timber beams in an indelibly Andalusian cellar eatery. *Savignyplatz*

. ☎ 030/313-2593. www.marysol-berlin.de. Tapas 2€–10€; entrees 14€–20€. AE, MC, V. Lunch & dinner daily. *S-Bahn:* Savignyplatz. Bus: M49 or X34. See map, p. 109.

★★ **Masaledar** SCHÖNEBERG *INDIAN*
Good things emerge from the tandoor oven in a plain-dealing restaurant that values taste over style. Feurigstrasse 38–39. ☎ 030/781-2546. www.masaledar.de. Entrees 5€–13€. No credit cards. Dinner Mon–Fri, lunch & dinner Sat–Sun. *S-Bahn:* Schöneberg. Bus: M46, M48, M85, 104, 186, or 248. See map, p. 109.

kids **Nordsee** MITTE *SEAFOOD*
The menu at this centrally located branch of the breezy fast-seafood chain runs from kid-friendly fish-and-chips to fresh sushi. Spandauer Strasse 4. ☎ 030/242-6881. www.nordsee.com. Entrees 4€–12€. No credit cards. Breakfast, lunch & dinner daily. *S-Bahn:* Hackescher Markt. Tram: M4 or M5. See map, p. 108.

★★ **Paris Bar** CHARLOTTENBURG *FRENCH*
Tout Berlin has dined, is dining, or plans to dine at this convivial bistro—which makes it hard to get a reservation. Kantstrasse 152. ☎ 030/313-8052. Entrees 10€–25€. AE, DC, MC, V. Lunch & dinner daily. *U-* and *S-Bahn:* Zoologischer Garten. Bus: M49 or X34. See map, p. 109.

★★ **Paris-Moskau** TIERGARTEN *CONTINENTAL*
Politicos from the nearby Bundestag (Federal Parliament) rub shoulders with upscale citizenry in a timber-framed villa with garden terrace. Alt-Moabit 141. ☎ 030/394-2081. www.paris-moskau.de. Entrees 25€–26€. AE, MC, V. Dinner daily. *U-* and *S-Bahn:* Hauptbahnhof. Bus: TXL or 245. See map, p. 108.

★★ **Sale e Tabacchi** KREUZBERG *ITALIAN*
Customers from the media and gallery scenes join Checkpoint Charlie visitors for authentic Italian food that hits the spot. Rudi-Dutschke-strasse 23. ☎ 030/252-1155. www.sale-e-tabacchi.de. Entrees 9€–27€. AE, DC, MC, V. Breakfast, lunch & dinner Mon–Fri. *U-Bahn:* Kochstrasse. Bus: M29. See map, p. 108.

★ kids **Vapiano** TIERGARTEN *ITALIAN*
This chain restaurant does fast food with a sense of *bella figura*, and the pasta is freshly made. Potsdamer Platz 5. ☎ 030/2300-5005. www.vapiano.com. Entrees 7€–15€. AE, MC, V. Breakfast, lunch & dinner daily. *U-* and *S-Bahn:*

> The old-fashioned Henne pub offers up roast organic chicken in a friendly East Berlin style.

Potsdamer Platz. Bus: M48, M45, 200, or 347. See map, p. 108.

★★ **Zur Letzten Instanz** MITTE *GERMAN*
Dine on traditional fare in Berlin's oldest inn. Waisenstrasse 14–16. ☎ 030/242-5528. www.zurletzteninstanz.de. Entrees 10€–18€. DC, MC, V. Lunch & dinner Mon–Sat. *U-Bahn:* Klosterstrasse. Bus: M48 or 248. See map, p. 108.

A Stiff Drink

I really hate to raise this (if you'll pardon the expression), but if your preferred method of ingesting caffeine is drinking a *latte* it may spare some blushes. Be sure to specify the full name—*caffè latte* or *latte macchiato*—when ordering. You see, *latte* is vulgar German for a . . . well, not to beat around the bush (whoops!) . . . male erection. So, either order in full or stick to *espresso*.

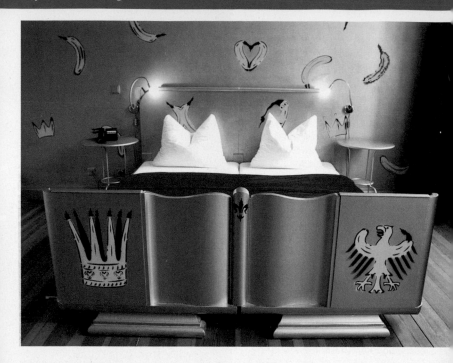

Berlin Hotel Best Bets

Best for Bedroom Art
Arte Luise Kunsthotel, Luisenstrasse 19
(p. 115)

Best for Backpackers
EastSeven Berlin Hostel, Schwedter Strasse 7
(p. 118)

Best for Gay Travelers
Axel, Lietzenburger Strasse 13–15 (p. 115)

Best for Women
Frauenhotel Artemisia, Brandenburgische
Strasse 18 (p. 118)

Best for Quality on a Budget
Circus, Rosenthaler Strasse 1 (p. 115)

Best for Business Travelers
Westin Grand, Friedrichstrasse 158-164
(p. 121)

Best for Old World Opulence
Adlon Kempinski, Unter den Linden 77 (p. 115)

Best for Contemporary Chic
Hotel de Rome, Behrenstrasse 37 (p. 118)

Best 19th-Century Flashback
Luisenhof, Köpenicker Strasse 92 (p. 119)

Best for Garden Tranquillity
Villa Kastania, Kastanienallee 20 (p. 121)

Best for Holistic Philosophy
The Mandala, Potsdamer Strasse 3 (p. 119)

Best for Communist-Era Nostalgia
Ostel, Wriezener Karree 5 (p. 119)

Best Courtyard
Riehmers Hofgarten, Yorckstrasse 83 (p. 120)

Best for Families
Radisson Blu, Karl-Liebknecht-Strasse 3
(p. 120)

> *The bohemian Arte Luise Kunsthotel is a boutique hotel offering rooms individually designed by several top German artists.*

Berlin Hotels A to Z

★★★ Adlon Kempinski MITTE

No other hotel sits as close to the Brandenburg Gate, on an avenue that's reasserting its claim on the city's sense of chic. Step inside for Belle Epoque airs, exquisite dining, and rooms fit for at least minor royalty. **Unter den Linden 7. ☎ 800/426-3135 in North America, or 030/22611111. www.hotel-adlon.de. 382 units. Doubles 380€–580€. AE, DC, MC, V.** *U-* and *S-Bahn:* Brandenburger Tor. Bus: TXL, 100, or 200. See map, p. 116.

★★ Arte Luise Kunsthotel MITTE

The art in each one-of-a-kind "installation" of a room could inspire either creativity or nightmares. No, it's not a communal crash pad for the bohemian fringe but a select boutique hotel where a different German artist designed each of the guest rooms. **Luisenstrasse 19. ☎ 030/84-480. www.luise-berlin.com. 50 units. Doubles 79€–210€. AE, MC, V.** *U-* and *S-Bahn:* Friedrichstrasse. Bus: TXL or 147. See map, p. 116.

★ Axel SCHÖNEBERG

Upscale gays are the main target group for this new boutique hotel, but heteros, both male and female, are welcome, too. A friendly staff and intriguing interior design make up for the impersonal, business-style exterior. **Lietzenburger Strasse 13-15. ☎ 030/2100-2893. www.axelhotels.com. 86 units. Doubles 75€–225€. AE, MC, V.** *U-Bahn:* Wittenbergplatz. Bus: M19, M29, M46, 106, or 187. See map, p. 117.

Berliner City Pension FRIEDRICHSHAIN

The modest rooms in this hotel on a tree-lined street are bright and clean and have new furnishings. **Proskauer Strasse 13. ☎ 030/4208-1615. www.berliner-city-pension.de. 24 units. Doubles 40€–55€. V.** *U-Bahn:* Samariterstrasse or Frankfurter Tor. Tram: 21. See map, p. 116.

★★ Circus MITTE

The youthful owners of this cool new hotel have given budget travelers color, design, and

The garden of the Honigmond, with its beautiful "tropical" landscapes, makes for a romantic getaway.

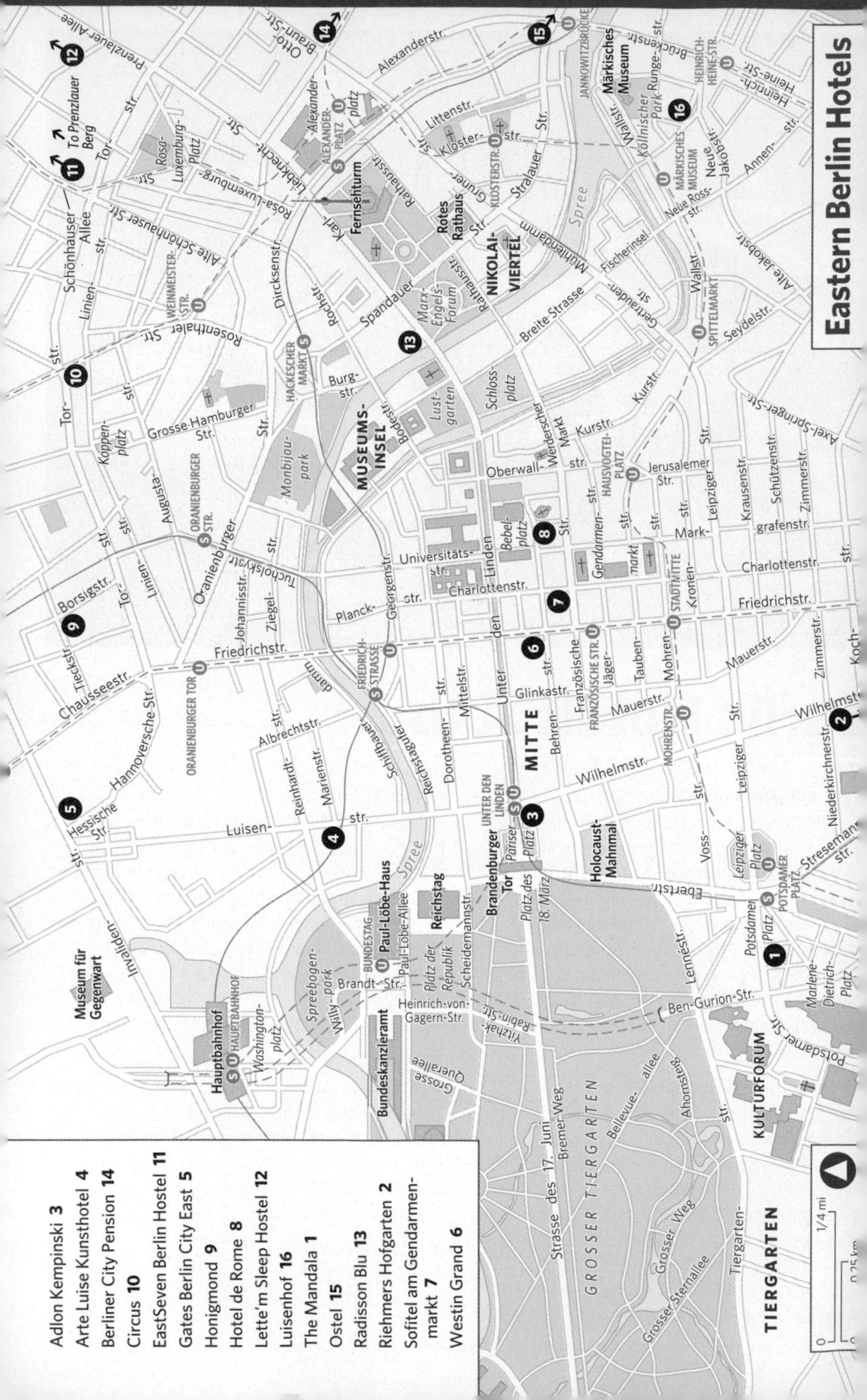

Eastern Berlin Hotels

1/4 mi

0.25 km

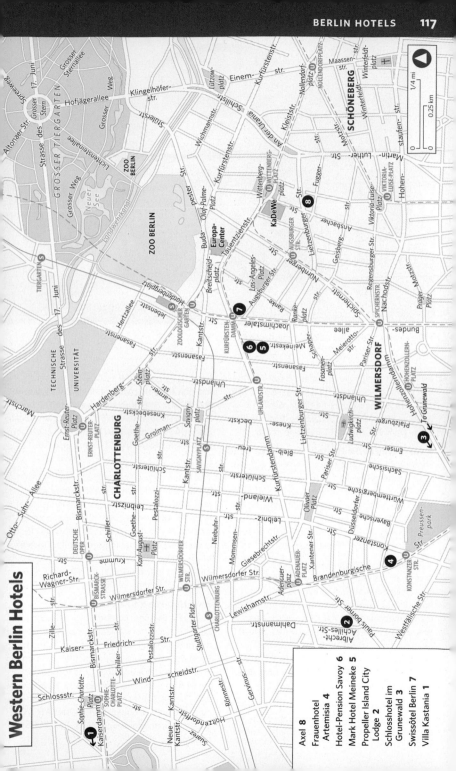

Western Berlin Hotels

Axel **8**
Frauenhotel
Artemisia **4**
Hotel-Pension Savoy **6**
Mark Hotel Meineke **5**
Propeller Island City
Lodge **2**
Schlosshotel im
Grunewald **3**
Swissôtel Berlin **7**
Villa Kastania **1**

> *The elegant lobby of the Adlon Kempinski, on Pariser Platz.*

style, aiming to prove that class is not merely a function of price. **Rosenthaler Strasse 1.** ☎ 030/2000-3939. www.circus-berlin.de. 60 units. Doubles 80€–90€. MC, V. *U-Bahn:* Rosenthaler Platz. Tram: M1, M8, or 12. See map, p. 116.

★ **EastSeven Berlin Hostel** PRENZLAUER BERG
Friendly and contemporary, this "Prenz'l" star has awards as Germany's top hostel under its belt. The immaculate rooms sport wood floors and zingy paintjobs. **Schwedter Strasse 7.** ☎ 030/9362-2240. www.eastseven.de. 25 units. Doubles 42€–50€. MC, V. *U-Bahn:* Senefelderplatz. Tram: M1 or 12. See map, p. 116.

★ **Frauenhotel Artemisia** WILMERSDORF
A woman without a man is . . . only natural, in what was Germany's first ever female-only hotel. It's still women only, and the hotel has maintained a ladylike approach in spotless rooms that have clean, modern lines. **Brandenburgische Strasse 18.** ☎ 030/873-8905. www.frauenhotel-berlin.de. 12 units. Doubles 78€–108€. AE, DC, MC, V. *U-Bahn:* Konstanzer Strasse. Bus: 101 or 104. See map, p. 117.

Gates Berlin City East MITTE
This steady hotel in a contemporary building serves a mixed business and tourist clientele by offering quirk-free standards and service in a comfortable package. **Invalidenstrasse 98.** ☎ 030/203-956-100. www.hotel-gates.com. 39 units. Doubles 75€–175€. AE, MC, V. *U-Bahn:* Zinnowitzer Strasse. Bus: 120, 123, 147, 240, or 245. Tram: M6, M8, or 12. See map, p. 116.

★ **Honigmond** MITTE
The name means "honeymoon" in English, but anyone will appreciate this hotel's leafy grounds, antiques, and stucco ceilings. Real honeymooners can opt for the four-poster treatment. **Tieckstrasse 12.** ☎ 030/284-4550. www.honigmond-berlin.de. 44 units. Doubles 145€–235€ w/breakfast. MC, V. *U-Bahn:* Zinnowitzer StrasseTor. Bus: 240. Tram: M6, M8, or 12. See map, p. 116.

★★★ **Hotel de Rome** MITTE
Rocco Forte's chic contemporary design fits nicely inside a bank building from 1899 just off monumental Bebelplatz. The renovation has been nothing short of spectacular—the underground vault, for example, was turned into a swimming pool. **Behrenstrasse 37.** ☎ 888/667-9477 or 030/460-6090. www.hotelderome.com. 146 units. Doubles 215€–490€. AE, DC, MC, V. *U-Bahn:* Hausvogteiplatz. Bus: 147. See map, p. 116.

★ Hotel-Pension Savoy CHARLOTTENBURG
The rooms in this hotel in a converted 19th-century townhouse on a sober upmarket street are neatly and traditionally furnished. Meinekestrasse 4. ☎ 030/8847-1610. www.hotel-pension-savoy.de. 21 units. Doubles 109€–149€ w/breakfast. AE, DC, MC, V. *U-Bahn:* Uhlandstrasse or Kurfürstendamm. Bus: M19, M29, X10, 109, 110, 204, or 249. See map, p. 117.

Lette'm Sleep Hostel PRENZLAUER BERG
Expect a multinational clientele, multicultural flair, and multilingual staff at this bustling place. Lettestrasse 7. ☎ 030/4473-3623. www.backpackers.de. 46 dorm beds and 10 rooms. Doubles 49€–69€. No credit cards. *U-Bahn:* Eberswalder Strasse. Tram: M2, M10, or 12. See map, p. 116.

★★ Luisenhof MITTE
Period touches in an enchanting 1822 building are melded with contemporary boutique airs and graces. Its five floors of high-ceilinged rooms are outfitted in a conservative and traditional style, a welcome escape from modern Berlin. Köpenicker Strasse 92. ☎ 030/246-2810. www.luisenhof.de. 27 units. Doubles 99€–250€. AE, DC, MC, V. *U-Bahn:* Märkisches Museum. Bus: 147, 248, or 347. See map, p. 116.

★★★ The Mandala TIERGARTEN
Enjoy creature comforts amidst avant-garde design, an all-round wellness philosophy, and stellar French cuisine. Each guest room is upholstered in discreetly plush fabrics, decorated with top-of-the-line stone, tile, or marble, and ringed with big windows that flood the postmodern interiors with sunlight. Potsdamer Strasse 3. ☎ 030/590-050-000. www.themandala.de. 165 units. Doubles 195€–580€. AE, DC, MC, V. *U-Bahn:* Potsdamer Platz. Bus: M48, M85, 200, or 347. See map, p. 116.

★ Mark Hotel Meineke CHARLOTTENBURG
Dark wood and antiques grace a handsome townhouse (and former Jewish emigration office) from 1899. The hotel is a few steps from the shopping, dining, and general bustle of Kurfürstendamm. Meinekestrasse 10. ☎ 030/319-803-190. www.markhotels.de. 59 units. Doubles 89€–195€. AE, MC, V. *U-Bahn:* Uhlandstrasse. Bus: M19, M29, X9, X10, 109, 110, 204, or 209. See map, p. 117.

★ Ostel FRIEDRICHSHAIN
Selling *Ostalgie* (nostalgia for the East), through the very best of Communist-era East German design, makes for a novel, kind of

> *The modern Mandala offers plush comfort and large windows with sensational views of Tiergarten.*

> *The colorful and artistic appointment of every room is distinct and dazzling at the Propeller Island City Lodge.*

retro lodging experience. Wriezener Karree 5. ☎ 030/2576-8660. www.ostel.de. 16 units. Doubles 54€–98€. No credit cards. *S-Bahn:* Ostbahnhof. Bus: 140, 240, or 347. See map, p. 116.

★★ **Propeller Island City Lodge** CHARLOTTENBURG An artist owner's fantasy helps to make this offbeat hotel, occupying three high-ceilinged floors of an 1880s apartment house, a unique lodging proposition. Each guest room is radically different in its decor and theme, and each may delight or appall you with its quirks. Albrecht-Achilles-Strasse 58. ☎ 030/891-9016. www.propeller-island.de. 45 units. Doubles 94€–205€. AE, MC, V. *U-Bahn:* Adenauerplatz. Bus: M19, M29, X10, 104, 109, or 110. See map, p. 117.

★★ kids **Radisson Blu** MITTE Minimalist yet luxurious, this hotel on the banks of the Spree River and facing the Berliner Dom (cathedral) has international class—and a cylindrical fish tank 25m (82 ft.) high. Karl-Liebknecht-Strasse 3. ☎ 800/333-3333 in North America, or 030/238280. www.radissonblu.com.

427 units. Doubles 150€–350€. AE, DC, MC, V. *S-Bahn:* Hackescher Markt. Bus: TXL, 100, or 200. Tram: M4, M5, or M6. See map, p. 116.

★★ **Riehmers Hofgarten** KREUZBERG You trade location somewhat here for 1890s Art Nouveau class, boutique charm, and a tranquil courtyard. The rooms have high ceilings, stucco ornamentation, and creaking floors. Yorckstrasse 83. ☎ 030/7809-8800. www.riehmers-hofgarten.de. 22 units. Doubles 138€–155€. AE, MC, V. *U-Bahn:* Mehringdamm. Bus: M19 or 140. See map, p. 116.

★★ **Schlosshotel im Grunewald** GRUNEWALD Escape from urban cares to a leafy suburban setting at this aristocratic country villa dating from 1912. For anyone who can afford it and prefers a stay in the city's verdant suburbs, the experience can be elegant, historic, and charming. Brahmsstrasse 10. ☎ 030/895-840. www.schlosshotelberlin.com. 53 units. Doubles 215€–325€. AE, DC, MC, V. *S-Bahn:* Grunewald. Bus: M29, X10, 115, 186, or 249. See map, p. 117.

> *Gorgeous greenery provides a unique suburban lodging experience at the converted 1912 mansion that is now the popular Schlosshotel in Grunewald.*

★★ Sofitel am Gendarmenmarkt MITTE

This centrally located hotel of the French chain is a good choice for travelers who like dependable standards and luxuries ready to hand. Charlottenstrasse 50–52. ☎ 030/203-750. www.sofitel.com. 92 units. Doubles 175€–300€. AE, DC, MC, V. *U-Bahn:* Französische Strasse. Bus: 100 or 147. See map, p. 116.

★ Swissôtel Berlin CHARLOTTENBURG

Centrally located and as smooth-running as a Swiss watch, the hotel has a modern minimalist style. Augsburger Strasse 44. ☎ 800/637-4771 in North America, or 030/220100. www.swissotel.com. 316 units. Doubles 180€–290€. AE, DC, MC, V. *U-Bahn:* Kurfürstendamm. Bus: M19, M29, X10, 109, 110, 204, or 249. See map, p. 117.

★★ Villa Kastania CHARLOTTENBURG

For all its up-to-date touches, spa, and pool, the hotel retains the class of the rebuilt villa it occupies. The rooms have large balconies and a posh part of the city to look out on. Kastanienallee 20. ☎ 030/300-0020. www.villakastania.de. 45 units. Doubles 79€–179€. AE, MC, V. *U-Bahn:* Theodor-Heuss-Platz. Bus: M49, X34, X49, 104, 218, or 349. See map, p. 117.

★★ Westin Grand MITTE

Sink back into the arms of dependable luxury at a central hotel where nothing is taken for granted. Belle Epoque features blend with contemporary styling. Guest rooms come in a wide range of styles, from beautifully appointed standard doubles all the way up to the lush-looking Schinkel Suite. Friedrichstrasse 158–164. ☎ 030/20270. www.starwoodhotels.com. 400 units. Doubles 189€–520€. AE, DC, MC, V. *U-Bahn:* Französische Strasse. Bus: TXL, 100, 147, or 200. See map, p. 116.

LIFE IS A CABARET

Come to the *Kabarett*, Old Chum

BY GEORGE MCDONALD

CABARET EXISTED IN GERMANY LONG BEFORE WORLD WAR I, and even in its early days it strained against the boundaries of censorship and the prevailing moral climate. But the form really came into its own during the years that followed defeat in the war. During the 1920s and 30s, the chaos of the Weimar Republic, hyperinflation and economic meltdown, street battles between militias of right and left, and the steady rise of the anti-Semitic Nazi Party formed the backdrop to a collapse of traditional values. Live it up while you can and spend money while you have it was the new morality. Cabaret provided entertainment with a satirical and political bent that suited the mood and circumstances of the times, influenced by cutting-edge artistic and social movements such as Dadaism, social expressionism, and *Neue Sachlichkeit* (new objectivity).

Famous Period Cabarets

DIE KATAKOMBE Comedian Werner Finck (1902–78) founded "The Catacombs" on Bellevuestrasse, just off Potsdamer Platz, in Berlin in 1929. His subtle jibes at Brownshirts, the Gestapo, and other "pillars" of the Nazi establishment made him popular—and brought secret policemen into the audience to "take notes." Nazi propaganda minister Joseph Goebbels ordered the cabaret closed in 1935, and Finck spent 6 weeks in a concentration camp before enlisting in the German army.

KABARETT DER KOMIKER Better known as Kadeko, the Cabaret of Comics took a less risky approach than Die Katakombe in its choice of material by presenting shows for every taste. A well-known Kadeko *Conferencier* (Master of Ceremonies), Fritz Grunbaum, frequently employed his acid wit on his own audiences, ribbing them for, among other things, their disgusting eating habits.

WIEN-MÜNCHEN From 1915 to 1916, the "Vienna-Munich" cabaret in Munich had as its director the comic actor Karl Valentin, a fellow spirit of playwright Bertolt Brecht and author Erich Kästner, and who has been dubbed "the German Chaplin." In the 1930s, Valentin made two failed attempts to get his Panoptikum für Gruseliges und Nonsens (Panopticon for Horror and Nonsense) exhibit in Munich off the ground.

Living the Revival

Popular among visitors to Berlin, Munich, Frankfurt, Dresden, and other German towns is the kind of nightspot depicted in the 1966 Broadway musical *Cabaret* (still from the 1972 movie, starring Liza Minnelli and Joel Grey, shown above), with floor-show patter and acts that satirize the political and social scene. These emporiums of schmaltz have been reborn, though the satire is less biting than it was during the time of the Weimar Republic and the rise of Hitler. Some of today's cabaret shows may remind you of Broadway blockbusters, without much of the intimacy of the smoky, trenchant cellar revues of the 1920s and early 1930s.

Nurtured in Munich

Berlin between the wars generally gets the historical kudos when it comes to cabaret, but in fact the capital was a long way behind prewar Munich in taking to the genre. German *Kabarett* emerged as different from the original French form in that it was nearly always a vehicle for political satire. In clubs like Die Elf Scharfrichter (The Eleven Executioners), founded in 1901 in the Schwabing district, Munich's bohemians, socialists, progressives, and avant-gardistes of all stripes got together to gripe and poke fun at the smug, stultifyingly bourgeois society in which they lived.

Berlin Nightlife & Entertainment Best Bets

Best Cocktail
Bar am Lützowplatz, Lützowplatz 7 (p. 125)

Best Martini (Shaken, not Stirred)
Harry's New York Bar, Lützowufer 15 (p. 125)

Best for Jazz Licks
A-Trane, Bleibtreustrasse 1 (p. 129)

Best Life Is a Cabaret
Die Stacheschweine, Tauentzienstrasse 9–12 (p. 128)

Best for Fetishist Action
KitKatClub, Köpenicker Strasse 76 (p. 128)

Best Opera House
Staatsoper Unter den Linden, Unter den Linden 7 (p. 128)

Best Avant-Garde Opera
Komische Oper Berlin, Behrenstrasse 55–57 (p. 128)

Best Orchestral Maneuvers
Philharmonie, Herbert-von-Karajan-Strasse 1 (p. 128)

Best Classic Drama
Deutsches Theater, Schumannstrasse 13A (p. 129)

Best Vaudeville Glitz
Friedrichstadtpalast, Friedrichstrasse 107 (p. 128)

Best Soccer Action
Olympiastadion, Olympischer Platz 3 (p. 129)

Best Slam-Dunk
O2 World Arena, Mühlenstrasse 12–30 (p. 129)

Best for Grunge and Alternative
SO36, Oranienstrasse 190 (p. 129)

Best for World Cultures
Haus der Kulturen der Welt, John-Foster-Dulles-Allee 10 (p. 129)

> *The Berliner Philharmoniker holds a popular annual concert at the Waldbühne, near the Olympiastadion.*

Berlin Nightlife & Entertainment A to Z

Bars, Cocktail Bars & Lounges

★★ Bar am Lützowplatz TIERGARTEN
A roster of 140-plus champagnes and any number of cocktails make this place along the Landwehrkanal a fixture on the city's sophisto circuit. Lützowplatz 7. ☎ 030/262-6807. www.baramluetzowplatz.co. *U-Bahn:* Nollendorfplatz. Bus: M29, 100, 106, or 187. See map, p. 127.

★ Felsenkeller SCHÖNEBERG
With its handsome 1920s interior, this small but much-loved local *Kneipe* (traditional bar) pours beer with due solemnity. Akazienstrasse 2. ☎ 030/781-3447. *U-Bahn:* Kleistpark or Eisenacher Strasse. Bus: M48, M85, 104, 187, 204, or N7. See map, p. 127.

★★ Harry's New York Bar TIERGARTEN
Taking both New York City and U.S. presidents as its theme, and with a nod to its namesake bar in Paris, Harry's has around 200 different drinks and live piano music. Hotel Esplanade, Lützowufer 15. ☎ 030/254-780. www.esplanade.de. *U-Bahn:* Nollendorfplatz. Bus: M29. See map, p. 127.

★★ Times Bar CHARLOTTENBURG
Named for clocks displaying different time zones, this tony hotel bar has a timeless wood-paneled look. Savoy Hotel, Fasanenstrasse 9–10. ☎ 030/311-030. *U-* and *S-Bahn:* Zoologischer Garten. Bus: M45, M49, X9, X34, or N2. See map, p. 127.

★ Windhorst MITTE
This stylish bar in the heart of town has a big-hearted owner and a large choice of cocktails, many of which you'll find nowhere else. Dorotheenstrasse 65. ☎ 030/2045-0070. *U-* and *S-Bahn:* Friedrichstrasse. Bus: TXL, 100, 147, 200, N2, or N6. Tram: M1 or 12. See map, p. 126.

Berlin's Big-Screen Moment

Stars, would-be stars, directors, and almost anyone with a movie to peddle show up at the annual **Berlin International Film Festival,** or Berlinale (☎ 030/259-200; www.berlinale.de). The festival, which runs for 10 days in February, with screenings at theaters around the city, is a showcase for the work of international directors and the latest German films. Tickets can be purchased at any box office.

> *The A-Trane is one of the best places in the city to listen to jazz.*

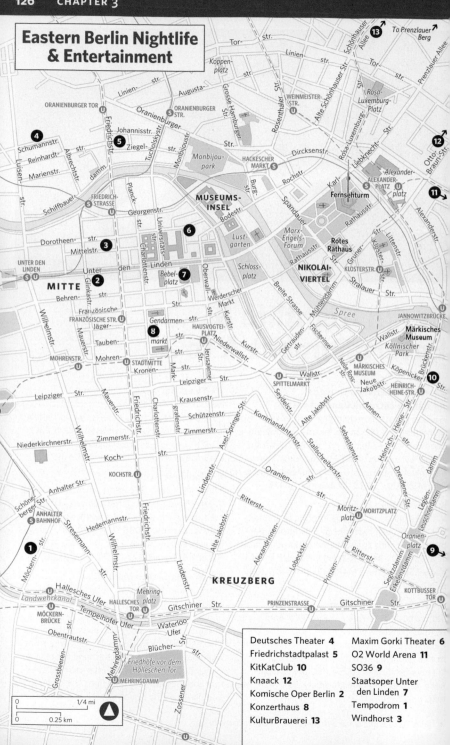

Eastern Berlin Nightlife & Entertainment

Deutsches Theater **4**
Friedrichstadtpalast **5**
KitKatClub **10**
Knaack **12**
Komische Oper Berlin **2**
Konzerthaus **8**
KulturBrauerei **13**
Maxim Gorki Theater **6**
O2 World Arena **11**
SO36 **9**
Staatsoper Unter den Linden **7**
Tempodrom **1**
Windhorst **3**

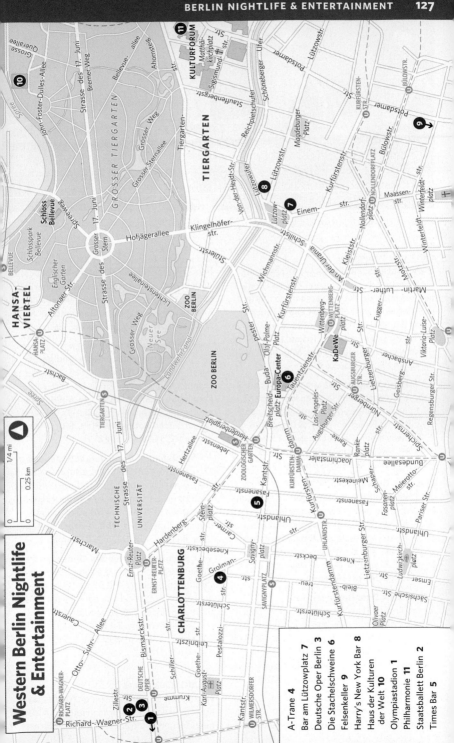

Western Berlin Nightlife & Entertainment

A-Trane 4
Bar am Lützowplatz 7
Deutsche Oper Berlin 3
Die Stachelschweine 6
Felsenkeller 9
Harry's New York Bar 8
Haus der Kulturen der Welt 10
Olympiastadion 1
Philharmonie 11
Staatsballett Berlin 2
Times Bar 5

> *A revue at Friedrichstadtpalast might include comedy, music, acrobats, and plenty of dancing girls.*

Cabaret & Vaudeville

★ Die Stachelschweine CHARLOTTENBURG
This theater—its name means The Porcupines—delivers prickly satire (in German) on matters political and cultural. Europa Center, Tauentzienstrasse 9-12. ☎ 030/261-4795. www.stachelschweine-berlin.de. Tickets 12.50€–30€. *U-Bahn:* Kurfürstendamm. Bus: M19, M29, M46, N1, N2, or N3. See map, p. 127.

★★ Friedrichstadtpalast MITTE
Europe's largest revue theater, with almost 1,900 seats, brings on the long-legged dancing girls. Friedrichstrasse 107. ☎ 030/2326-2326. www.friedrichstadtpalast.de. Tickets 18€–75€. *U-Bahn:* Oranienburger Tor. Bus: 147 or N6. Tram: M1 or 12. See map, p. 126.

Classical, Opera & Ballet

★★ Deutsche Oper Berlin CHARLOTTENBURG
This concrete-and-glass building from 1961 is not exactly a classic opera venue, but the productions are world-class. Bismarckstrasse 35. ☎ 030/3438-4343. www.deutscheoperberlin.de. Tickets 12€–120€. *U-Bahn:* Deutsche Oper. Bus: 101, 109, N2, or N7. See map, p. 127.

★ Komische Oper Berlin MITTE
A magnificent Belle Epoque interior is the setting for opera, operetta, and musical theater in German, plus the occasional ballet. Behrenstrasse 55-57. ☎ 030/4799-7400. www.komische-oper-berlin.de. Tickets 8€–98€. *U-Bahn:* Französische Strasse. Bus: TXL, 100, 147, 200, N2, or N6. See map, p. 126.

★★ Konzerthaus MITTE
The magnificent, Greek temple–style concert hall is home to the highly regarded Konzerthausorchester, under the baton of chief conductor Lothar Zagrosek. Gendarmenmarkt 2. ☎ 030/203-092-101. www.konzerthaus.de. Tickets 12€–105€. *U-Bahn:* Stadtmitte. Bus: M48, 147, 347, or N6. See map, p. 126.

★★★ Philharmonie TIERGARTEN
Sir Simon Rattle leads the elite Berliner Philharmoniker amid this concert hall's distinctive organic architecture (1963). Herbert-von-Karajan-Strasse 1. ☎ 030/2548-8999. www.berliner-philharmoniker.de. Tickets 8€–140€. *U-* and *S-Bahn:* Potsdamer Platz. Bus: M41, 200, 347, or N2. See map, p. 127.

★★ Staatsballett Berlin CHARLOTTENBURG
The city's top-ranked ballet troupe shares the stage—albeit not at the same time—with the Deutsche Oper (see above). Bismarckstrasse 35. ☎ 030/2035-4555. www.staatsballett-berlin.de. Tickets 10€–95€. *U-Bahn:* Deutsche Oper. Bus: 101, 109, N2, or N7. See map, p. 127.

★★★ Staatsoper Unter den Linden MITTE
Daniel Barenboim sets the tone behind the Corinthian columns of Berlin's oldest opera house, a neoclassical pile dating from 1742. Unter den Linden 7. ☎ 030/2035-4455. www.staatsoper-berlin.de. Tickets 10€–120€. *U-Bahn:* Französische Strasse. Bus: TXL, 100, 200, or N5. See map, p. 126.

Clubs

★ KitKatClub MITTE
Fetishism and eroticism are on full display here, as likeminded spirits in latex and leather meet techno and trance. Köpenicker Strasse 76

(enter on Brückenstrasse). ☎ 030/7871-8963. www.kitkatclub.de. From 10€ cover. *U-Bahn:* Heinrich-Heine-Strasse. Bus: 147 or N8. See map, p. 126.

★★ SO36 KREUZBERG
The famous old political-punk venue has moved with the times, and now covers a number of dance styles, among them techno, and puts on club evenings for gays and lesbians. Oranienstrasse 190. ☎ 030/6140-1306. www. so36.de. 3€–25€ cover. *U-Bahn:* Kottbusser Tor. Bus: M29, 140, N1, or N8. See map, p. 126.

Live Music
★★★ A-Trane CHARLOTTENBURG
You might catch an international name in jazz (all kinds) at this great club, owned by a Turkish-German aficionado—and if not, local names serve up some decent licks. Bleibtreustrasse 1. ☎ 030/313-2550. www.a-trane. de. 8€–20€ cover (or no cover). *S-Bahn:* Savignyplatz. Bus: M49 or X34. See map, p. 127.

★★ Knaack PRENZLAUER BERG
There are live concerts several nights a week at this dance club. The bands are German, the audience young, and the music loud and hot. Greifswalder Strasse 224. ☎ 030/442-7060. www.knaack-berlin.de. 2€–8€ cover (often free for women). *U-Bahn:* Senefelderplatz. Bus: TXL, 200, or 240. Tram: M4. See map, p. 126.

Multipurpose Center
★★ KulturBrauerei PRENZLAUER BERG
An old brewery hosts entertainment and nightlife venues: dance club, cinema, theater, beer garden, and more. Schönhauser Allee 36. ☎ 030/4431-5100. www.kulturbrauerei-berlin. de. *U-Bahn:* Eberswalder Strasse. Bus: N2. Tram: M1, M10, or 12. See map, p. 126.

Performance Venues
★ Haus der Kulturen der Welt TIERGARTEN
The House of World Cultures in Tiergarten's futuristic Kongresshalle (1957) lives up to its name with performances of world music, theater, and dance. John-Foster-Dulles-Allee 10. ☎ 01805/570-071. www.hkw.de. Tickets free to 50€. *U-* and *S-Bahn:* Brandenburger Tor. Bus: 100. See map, p. 127.

★ kids Tempodrom KREUZBERG
This tentlike building hosts popular entertainment, such as musicals, live music, theater, and circuses. Möckernstrasse 10. ☎ 01805/554-111. www.tempodrom.de. Tickets 5€–75€. *U-Bahn:* Möckernbrücke. *S-Bahn:* Anhalter Bahnhof. Bus: M29, M41, or N1. See map, p. 126.

Spectator Sports
★ kids O2 World Arena FRIEDRICHSHAIN
Alba Berlin, Germany's top-rated basketball club, plays home games at this giant venue. Mühlenstrasse 12–30. ☎ 030/3009-0555. www. albaberlin.de. Tickets 10€–35€. *U-* and *S-Bahn:* Warschauer Strasse. Bus: 347. Tram: M1 or M10. See map, p. 126.

★★ kids Olympiastadion CHARLOTTENBURG
Hertha BSC, Berlin's main soccer club, brings the top clubs in Germany to matches here. Olympischer Platz 3. ☎ 01805/189-200. www. herthabsc.de. Tickets 8€–64€. *U-Bahn:* Olympia-Stadion. *S-Bahn:* Olympiastadion. Bus: M49, X34, X49, or 218. See map, p. 127.

Theater
★ Deutsches Theater MITTE
Mainstream, highbrow stage productions (in German) of German and international plays are performed in a neoclassical building (1850). Schumannstrasse 13A. ☎ 030/2844-1225. www.deutschestheater.de. Tickets 8€–45€. *U-* and *S-Bahn:* Friedrichstrasse. Bus: 147 or N6. Tram: M1 or 12. See map, p. 126.

★ Maxim Gorki Theater MITTE
This neoclassical theater (1827) features plays (in German) ranging from classical productions to works by young and experimental playwrights. Am Festungsgraben 2. ☎ 030/2022-1115. www.gorki.de. Tickets 10€–30€. *U-* and *S-Bahn:* Friedrichstrasse. Bus: TXL, 100, 147, 200, or N6. Tram: M1 or 12. See map, p. 126.

Nightlife Tip
Because nightlife generally happens, well, at night, your chosen activity might finish only after daytime public transportation has called it a day. Never fear, Berlin has a bus service for night owls. We've provided *Nachtbus* (night bus) line numbers, identified by the letter "N," for venues at or close to a night bus stop.

Potsdam

Brandenburg's state capital, Potsdam (pop. 153,000), is a UNESCO World Heritage site due to its Prussian royal palaces, villas, pavilions, gardens, and parks. It's often been called Germany's Versailles. World attention focused on Potsdam July 17 to August 2, 1945, when the Potsdam Conference helped shape postwar Europe. The palaces and gardens of Sans Souci Park, which lies to the west of Potsdam's historic core, are the major attractions here. It's just 24km (15 miles) southwest of Berlin. On a day trip, you'll need to select from all the possibilities the city has to offer, and not try to squeeze in everything.

> *Schloss Sanssouci was the summer palace of Frederick the Great and is now Potsdam's biggest tourist attraction.*

START Take the *S-Bahn* to Potsdam, a 40-minute ride from central Berlin; then take bus no. 695 from the Hauptbahnhof (main station) to Maulbeerallee at Park Sanssouci.

1 ★★★ **Schloss Sanssouci.** Prussia's 18th-century multifaceted King Friedrich II, better known as Friedrich der Grosse (Frederick the Great), had this light-hearted summer palace (1747) built as a place of retreat from Berlin and the cares of ruling a then militarily belea-guered Prussia. *Sans Souci,* the pastel-toned rococo palace's motto, is French for "carefree." An impression of life at his laid-back country court can be gained from Adolph Menzel's painting *A Flute Concert of Frederick the Great at Sanssouci* (1852), in Berlin's Alte Nationalgal-erie (p. 80, **17**).

Graceful rather than grandiose, Sanssouci is Potsdam's most popular visitor attraction, and among Germany's finest palaces. Its single floor overlooks terraced ornamental gardens, a grand fountain, and the rest of Park Sanssouci. Among many ancient Greek and Roman motifs are the facade's slender Corinthian columns and reliefs depicting Bacchus, the Roman wine god. Your visit takes you through ornate state rooms like the Marmorsaal, encrusted with Tuscan marble and gold embellishments, and Friedrich's pri-vate apartments. Be sure to take time for a stroll outside in the palace courtyard, among the gazebos and gardens and down to the fountain. ⏱ 75 min. Admission: Apr–Oct 12€ adults, 8€ kids 8–18; Nov–Mar 8€ adults, 5€ kids; addi-tional charges may apply. Apr–Oct Tues–Sun 10am–6pm; Nov–Mar Tues–Sun 10am–5pm.

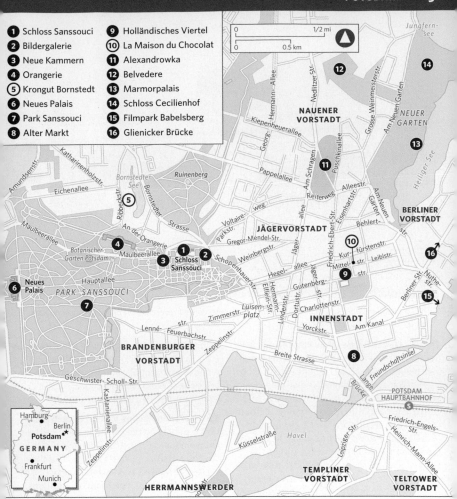

1. Schloss Sanssouci
2. Bildergalerie
3. Neue Kammern
4. Orangerie
5. Krongut Bornstedt
6. Neues Palais
7. Park Sanssouci
8. Alter Markt
9. Holländisches Viertel
10. La Maison du Chocolat
11. Alexandrowka
12. Belvedere
13. Marmorpalais
14. Schloss Cecilienhof
15. Filmpark Babelsberg
16. Glienicker Brücke

② ★★ Bildergalerie (Picture Gallery). Frederick the Great constructed the Bildergalerie next to Sanssouci to house his art collection in style and within easy walking distance. The building's marble-and-gold interior has paintings by Caravaggio, van Dyck, Rubens, and many more artists. ⏱ 45 min. Admission 3€ adults, 2.50€ kids 8–18. May–Oct Tues–Sun 10am–6pm.

③ ★★ Neue Kammern (New Chambers). An idea of the luxurious nature of Frederick the Great's court can be gotten from the Neue Kammern (1775), built next to Sanssouci to house the king's guests. Its opulent style is similar to that of the palace. ⏱ 30 min. Admission 4€ adults, 3€ kids 8–18. May–Oct Tues–Sun 10am–6pm.

④ ★★ Orangerie. The Orangerie Palace (1864) dwarfs nearby Schloss Sanssouci. Constructed a century later in neoclassical style for the Romantically inclined King Friedrich Wilhelm IV, it seems far more pompous. Still, the greenhouse, gardens, and ornate state rooms (such as the Raffaelsaal) make it worth visiting. ⏱ 30 min. Admission 3€ adults, 2.50€ kids 8–18. May–Oct Tues–Sun 10am–6pm.

⑤ 🍴 ★★ Krongut Bornstedt. On the shore of a small lake, this large establishment offers everything from a drink in the beer garden to a full restaurant meal. Ribbeckstrasse 6–7. ☎ 0331/550-650. 4€–16€.

> *The spectacular, 200-room Neues Palais offers a massive baroque presence in Park Sanssouci and hosts theater, music, and opera performances.*

6 ★★★ **Neues Palais (New Palace).** At Park Sanssouci's western end, Frederick the Great's vast Neues Palais (1769) is quite a contrast to Schloss Sanssouci. Where his own *pied-à-terre* seems flighty, the baroque state palace, solidly constructed and with 200 rooms and a monumental central cupola, is a clear declaration of Prussian pride and power designed to impress foreign ambassadors and visitors. Even the scale of the Communs (Commons), a services building at the rear, appears to back up that message. The palace's rococo Schlosstheater is still used for theater, music, and opera performances. ⏱ 1 hr. Admission 6€ adults, 5€ kids 8–18. Apr–Oct Tues–Sun 10am–6pm; Nov–Mar Tues–Sun 10am–5pm.

7 ★★★ **Park Sanssouci.** In addition to the principal palaces and sights described in stops **1** through **6** of this tour, the park is speckled with sights and places of interest that don't justify separate coverage, but still can be admired on a walk around the grounds.

SITE GUIDE PAGE 133

8 ★ **Alter Markt (Old Market).** The Alter Markt, across the Havel River from Potsdam station, was the heart of Old Potsdam. On the square stands the neoclassical **Altes Rathaus** (Old Town Hall, 1755), with Atlas bearing the globe atop its cupola, and the Italianate **Nikolaikirche** (Church of St. Nicholas, 1837). ⏱ 30 min. Tram: X98, 91, 92, 93, 96, or 99.

9 ★★ **Holländisches Viertel (Dutch Quarter).** Not only do the Holländisches Viertel's gabled houses—constructed in the 1730s for Dutch craftsmen invited to Prussia for their skills—seem like a transplanted piece of Amsterdam, they host a plethora of boutiques, craft stores, antiques dealers, cafes, bars, and restaurants. ⏱ 45 min. Around Benkertstrasse. Tram: 92 or 96.

10 🍴 ★ **La Maison du Chocolat.** The Dutch Quarter's ambience is on display in a delightful cafe-restaurant that serves coffees, snacks, and French cuisine—far more, in fact, than its namesake chocolate. Benkertstrasse 20. ☎ 0331/237-0730. 4€–20€.

11 ★ **Alexandrowka.** An interesting contrast to the Holländisches Viertel, Potsdam's Russian quarter was sponsored by Tsar Alexander I during and after the Napoleonic Wars to house Russian guardsmen and a military choir in Prussian service. Among its typical features

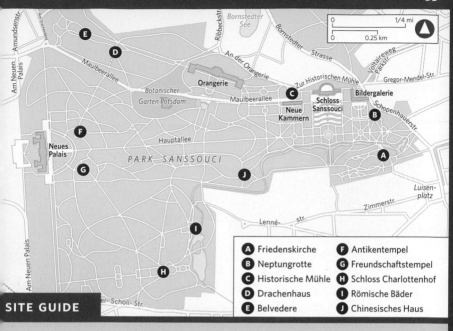

SITE GUIDE

A	Friedenskirche	**F**	Antikentempel
B	Neptungrotte	**G**	Freundschaftstempel
C	Historische Mühle	**H**	Schloss Charlottenhof
D	Drachenhaus	**I**	Römische Bäder
E	Belvedere	**J**	Chinesisches Haus

⑦ Park Sanssouci

Entering the park from the heart of Potsdam, you pass the **A Friedenskirche** (Church of Peace, 1848). In the attached mausoleum are interred scions of the Hohenzollern dynasty. Going around the park counterclockwise, you pass the **B Neptungrotte,** a grotto focused on a sculpture of the Roman sea god Neptune. View also the Bildergalerie (**②**), Schloss Sanssouci (**①**), and the Neue Kammern (**③**).

The **C Historische Mühle** (1791), a historical windmill re-erected here, houses the park's visitor center. Beyond the Orangerie (**④**) and Krongut Bornstedt (**⑤**), a path climbs Drachenberg hill to the **D ★ Drachenhaus** (Dragon

House, 1772), a Chinese-style pagoda with 16 dragon sculptures on its roof. Farther up, the **E ★ Belvedere** (1772) commands fine views of the park. The **F Antikentempel** (1769), modeled on an ancient round temple, functions as a Hohenzollern mausoleum. Beyond is the **G Freundschaftstempel** (Temple of Friendship, 1770), in front of the Neues Palais (**⑥**).

Next up is **H ★ Schloss Charlottenhof** (1829), with columns and pediment inspired by ancient Roman villas. The **I Römische Bäder** (1840), a "Roman Bath" that never actually functioned as a bathhouse, incorporates Roman-style pavilions. The ornately gilded **J ★ Chinesisches Haus** (1764) was built in the style of a Chinese teahouse. ⏲ At least 2 hr. Park Sanssouci: free admission; open 24/7. Friedenskirche: free admission; mid-Apr to Oct daily dawn–dusk. Historische Mühle: 2.50€ adults, 1.50€ kids 6-14; Apr-Oct daily 10am-6pm; Nov and Jan-Mar Sat-Sun 10am-4pm. Belvedere: 2€; May-Oct Sat-Sun and holidays 10am-6pm. Schloss Charlottenhof: (guided tours only) 4€ adults, 3€ kids 8-18; Römische Bäder: 3€ adults, 2.50€ kids 8-18; Chinesisches Haus: 2€; all open May-Oct Tues-Sun 10am-6pm.

> *The heads of the Allied powers, including Truman, Stalin, and Churchill, met at Schloss Cecilienhof in 1945 to hammer out the Potsdam Agreement.*

are timber houses and a Russian Orthodox church, the Alexander-Newski-Gedächtni-skirche (1829). ⏱ 45 min. Off Puschkinallee. Tram: 92 or 96.

⑫ ★ kids **Belvedere.** Like its sidekick in Park Sanssouci (p. 132, ➐), this outlook tower (1863) on Pfingstberg hill commands fine views, in this case over central Potsdam. ⏱ 30 min. Pfingstberg. ☎ 0331/2005-7930. Admission 3.50€ adults, 1.50€ kids 6-16. June–Aug daily 10am–8pm; Apr, May, and Sept daily 10am–6pm; Oct daily 10am–4pm; Mar and Nov Sat–Sun 10am–4pm. Bus: 638, 639, or 697.

Park Sanssouci Tips

Combination tickets are available for some of Park Sanssouci's sights. There are cafes or restaurants at the Historische Mühle (**C**), Drachenhaus (**D**), Neues Palais (**6**), and Krongut Bornstedt (**5**). Several sights have rest rooms. General information is available from ☎ 0331/969-4200 or by visiting www.spsg.de or www.potsdamtourismus.de.

⑬ ★★ **Marmorpalais (Marble Palace).** As if Potsdam hadn't enough royal palaces, Frederick the Great's nephew and successor, King Friedrich Wilhelm II, moving out to Heiliger See's reed-fringed western shore, constructed this lakeside dream pad. The early neoclassical Marmorpalais (1792) is a mountain of red brick and marble set in the English landscape-style Neuer Garten (New Garden). A rooftop belvedere affords grand views over the lake. You can tour the palace's lavish interior and see private royal apartments restored to their 18th-century magnificence. ⏱ 1 hr. Neuer Garten. ☎ 0331/969-4202. www.spsg.de. Admission 5€ adults, 4€ kids 8-18. May–Oct Tues–Sun 10am–6pm; Nov–Apr Sat–Sun and holidays 10am–4pm. Bus: 692.

⑭ ★ **Schloss Cecilienhof.** North of the Marmorpalais is the Tudor manor–style Cecilienhof Palace (1917), famous for having hosted the 1945 Potsdam Conference that divvied up postwar Europe. Though it's now a hotel (with restaurant), you are allowed to visit the royal apartments and the rooms where the conference was held—you can even see the

> *The grim Glienicker Brücke, which linked Potsdam in East Germany and the Wannsee district in West Germany, was the site of many Cold War spy exchanges.*

large round table, made in Moscow, where the actual agreement was signed. ⏱ 45 min. Neuer Garten. ☎ 0331/969-4200. www.spsg.de. Admission 6€ adults, 5€ kids 8–18. Apr–Oct Tues–Sun 10am–6pm; Nov–Mar Tues–Sun 10am–5pm. Bus: 692.

15 ★★ kids **Filmpark Babelsberg.** Experience a hands-on tour of Babelsberg film studio, where some of the best-known German films have been shot. Stars such as Marlene Dietrich and Tom Cruise have worked here. ⏱ 2 hr. Grossbeerenstrasse. ☎ 0331/721-2750. Admission 19€ adults, 13€ kids 4–14, 60€ families. Mid-Mar to Oct daily 10am–6pm (closed Mon and Sat in Sept). Bus: 601, 608, 609, or 690.

16 kids **Glienicker Brücke.** During the Cold War, spies who came in from the cold often did so at this bridge over the Havel River, between Potsdam (East Germany) and Berlin's Wannsee district (West Germany). Downed American U-2 spy plane pilot Gary Powers was one of those exchanged at the bridge, in 1960. ⏱ 20 min. Tram: 93.

Frederick the Cool

Prussia's King Friedrich der Grosse (Frederick the Great) liked to kick back from his duties while at Schloss Sanssouci and to indulge his love of music (he was an accomplished musician and modest composer), art, philosophy, reading from his large library of leather-bound antiquarian books, and learned disputation with some of the sharpest intellects of the day, among them Voltaire.

The enlightened despot's lighter side didn't make him a pushover. Friedrich expanded and improved the formidable army he inherited from his father. He used his command of strategy and tactics to win a series of stunning victories against stronger enemies, notably at Rossbach and Leuthen. Yet he preferred a quieter life. War, he opined, was not a game to play often.

Spreewald

Not much more than an hour's jaunt by car southeast from Berlin, this forest landscape crisscrossed by waterways and speckled with lakes and open fields has been declared a UNESCO Biosphärenreservat (Biosphere Reserve). It's an agricultural region, populated by the Sorbs, descendants of ethnic Slavs who have their own language: Niedersorbisch. Tourism is important in the Spreewald, considering that four million visitors pour in annually, but the pickled gherkin is king (see "Get Your Gherkins Pickled," p. 137).

> Kayakers and rowboats splash through the waterways of the forested Spreewald, which draws four million visitors a year.

START By car, take A113 and A13 south, then go east on B115 to Lübben. There is frequent train service from Berlin to both Lübben and Lübbenau.

① ★ **kids** **Lübben (Lubin).** When you arrive in Lübben (pop. 14,000), the Spreewald's northern tourism center, park your car and leave it.

The favored methods of getting around here are on foot, by pedal-bike rented from one of several local outlets, and aboard a traditional flatbottom *Kahn* (punt) on a tour of the reserve's narrow waterways. In the town itself, visit **Schloss Lübben** (☎ 03546/187-478; www.schloss-luebben.de), a much restored, originally medieval castle on a small island, and take in the castle museum and perhaps a meal in the traditional restaurant. A decent choice in town for Spreewald specialties is at waterfront **Hotel-Restaurant Spreeblick,** Grubener Strasse 53 (☎ 03546/2320; main courses 8€–17€; Mon–Fri 2–11pm, Sat 8am–11pm, Sun 8am–2pm). A lakes area north of Lübben is centered on scenic ★ **Neuendorfer See.** ⏱ 4 hr. Tourist information: Spreewaldinfo Lübben. Ernst-von-Hauwald-Damm 15. ☎ 03546/3090. www.luebben.de.

From Lübben, take local road L49 south and east, through the villages of Ragow and Stennewitz, to Lübbenau (13km/8 miles).

② ★★ **kids** **Lübbenau (Lubnjow).** This small town (pop. 18,000) is equally a center for touring the Spreewald by bicycle, boat, and car. It has its own castle, ★ **Schloss Lübbenau** (1839; ☎ 03542/8730; www.schloss-luebbenau.de), an elegant neoclassical mansion that belongs to the family of one of the executed conspirators in the July 1944 plot to assassinate Hitler and that now hosts a stellar hotel and restaurant. In addition, there's the historical **Spreewaldmuseum** (☎ 03542/2472) in the redbrick Torhaus (Gatehouse, 1899). *Kahn* (punt) tours depart from a dock close to the castle, and rowboats and

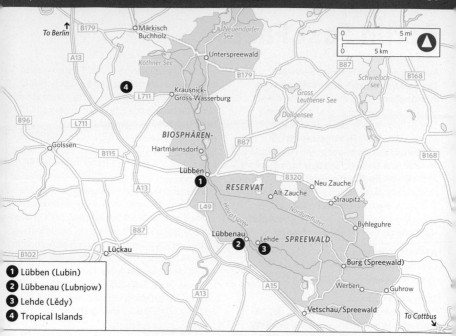

1. Lübben (Lubin)
2. Lübbenau (Lubnjow)
3. Lehde (Lědy)
4. Tropical Islands

pedal-boats are available to rent. When the weather is fine, head into the forest, or pause on a *Kahn* tour to dine on Spreewald specialties on the waterfront terrace at rustic ★ **Gasthaus Wotschofska,** Wotschofskaweg 1 (☎ 03546/7601; main courses 8€–18€; Apr–Oct daily from 9am). ⏲ 4 hr. Tourist information: Ehm-Welk-Strasse 15. ☎ 03542/3668. www.spreewald-online.de.

From Lübbenau, drive (or even walk) eastward on Lehdscher Weg to the hamlet of Lehde (2km/1¼ miles).

Get Your Gherkins Pickled

Throughout Germany, the pickled gherkin is a prized fruit. Trademarked Spreewälder Gurken, produced by scores of small-scale growers and processors in the Spreewald, are the acknowledged state of the art (or craft). This sour and spicy delicacy is protected by a European Union regulation that guarantees geographical authenticity. There's even a scenic pedal-bike Gherkin Trail through the Spreewald, the Gurken-Radweg, a bum-numbing circular route 250km (155 miles) long.

3 ★ kids **Lehde (Lědy).** You step further back into ethnic Sorb history at this village of timber houses just east of Lübbenau. An annex of the Spreewaldmuseum, the open-air ★ **Freilandmuseum Lehde** (☎ 03542/2472; www.freilandmuseum-lehde.de; admission 5€ adults, 1€ kids 6–16, 10€ families; Apr–Sept daily 10am–6pm; Oct daily 10am–5pm) is the main point of interest. In addition to re-creations of folk arts and crafts, you can see reenactors wearing traditional costumes. ⏲ 1 hr.

Return to the north–south expressway, A13, by way of L49 and L526 through Lübbenau and Zerkwitz. Go north on A13 to exit 6 (Staakow), then switch to L711 northeast, bypassing Brand, and following signs to Tropical Islands, for a total distance of 38km (24 miles).

4 ★★ kids **Tropical Islands.** Swimming in warm water from a sand beach at this vast indoor "tropical paradise" makes a great escape, especially in winter, from the capital's often poor weather. ⏲ 2 hr.–all day. Krausnick. ☎ 0354/7760-5050. www.tropical-islands.de. Admission 25€ adults, 19.50€ kids 4–14 (multiple variations available: check website). Open 24/7. Train: To Brand station, and then by shuttle.

Berlin Fast Facts

Accommodations Booking Services
The desks of **Tourist-Information Berlin-Brandenburg** (☎ 0331/200-4747; www.brandenburg-tourism.com) at Tegel and Schönefeld airports can help with accommodations. The **BERLIN Infostore** (☎ 030/250-025; www.visitberlin.de) at the Hauptbahnhof has a similar service. Find apartment rentals from **All-Berlin-Apartments** (www.all-berlin-apartments.com), which also covers hotels and B&Bs; **Apartment Berlin City** (www.ferienwohnung-24-berlin.com); and **ApartmentsApart** (www.apartmentsapart.com).

ATMs/Cashpoints
Central Berlin has plenty of banks with ATMs (*Geldautomaten)* for withdrawing cash 24/7.

Currency Exchange
Exchange AG (www.exchange-ag.de) has eight offices in the city. A central one is at Bayreuther Strasse 37–38 (☎ 030/2147-6292; *U-Bahn:* Wittenbergplatz). Most banks can also handle currency exchange and tend to provide the best rates.

Dentists & Doctors
Call ☎ 01804/2255-2362 to be referred to an English-speaking doctor or dentist. You will be expected to provide proof of health/dental insurance (such as an EHIC card in the case of most residents of Europe), or you will have to pay for treatment. In the event of minor injuries that require speedy treatment, go to the *Notaufnahme* (emergency) department of the nearest *Krankenhaus* (hospital). If injuries are serious, call the emergency doctor/ambulance number (see "Emergencies," below).

Emergencies
To call the police (*Polizei),* dial ☎ **110.** To report a fire or to summon an emergency doctor (*Notarzt)* or an ambulance (*Krankenwagen),* dial ☎ **112.**

Getting There
BY PLANE You'll arrive at either **Berlin-Tegel** (TXL), 8km (5 miles) northwest of the city center, or at **Berlin-Schönefeld** (SXF), 18km (11 miles) southeast of the city center. Express bus service is available from Tegel to the city

center; AirportExpress trains, *S-Bahn* (metro) trains, and express buses go from Schönefeld to the city center; and taxis are available at both airports (taxis to the city center cost around 15€ from Tegel or 24€ from Schönefeld). Tegel is scheduled to close in 2012, and Schönefeld to be expanded and renamed Berlin-Brandenburg International Airport (BER). **BY TRAIN** You'll most likely arrive at either Berlin Hauptbahnhof (main station) or Berlin Ostbahnhof (East Station). Eurolines buses from around Europe arrive at the Zentraler Omnibusbahnhof, or ZOB (Central Bus Station), in the western Charlottenburg district. **BY CAR** Germany's excellent Autobahn network makes getting to Berlin by car fast and easy. Converging on the city are A2/E30 from the west, A24/E26/E55 and A11/E28 from the north, A12/E30 from the east, and A13/E36/E55 and A9/E51 from the south.

Getting Around
Berlin's public transportation *U-Bahn* (metro) trains, buses, trams (streetcars), and ferries are operated by **BVG** (☎ 030/19449; www.bvg.de); **S-Bahn Berlin** (☎ 2974-3333; www.s-bahn-berlin.de) operates the rapid-transit rail net. *U-Bahn* trains run mostly underground, *S-Bahn* trains are mostly elevated. Trams run only in the former East Berlin. In addition to the ordinary bus service, there are Metro (M) buses for main routes, Express (X) buses that make relatively few stops, and a special express bus (TXL) that shuttles to and from Tegel Airport. Buses nos. 100 and 200, stop at key sights around the city and are useful for visitors. Short-distance one-way tickets are 1.30€, regular one-way tickets 2.10€. Day tickets cost 6.10€–6.50€. All tickets must be validated in the time-stamping machines when you board. See also "Taxis," below.

Internet Access
There are many Internet cafes around the city. A reasonably central one that's open 24/7 is **24hr Internetcafé am Adenauerplatz,** Kurfürstendamm 161 (☎ 030/8940-9690; *U-Bahn:* Adenauerplatz). A growing number of hotels, cafes, and bars offer Wi-Fi.

Pharmacies
In German, a pharmacy is an *Apotheke.* For

cosmetics and toiletries, go to a *Drogerie*. Most pharmacies operate during normal business hours but post details of the nearest 24-hour pharmacy. There is a pharmacy at the city's main rail station, Berlin Hauptbahnhof, that's open 24/7 (☎ 030/2061-4190).

Police

The national *Polizei* (police) emergency number is ☎ **110.** In nonemergency situations, go to a local precinct/station, or call the Berlin police at ☎ 030/4664-4664.

Post Office

You'll recognize branches of **Deutsche Post** (☎ 01802/3333; www.deutschepost.de) by their yellow sign with a black horn. Centrally located post offices include one at the city's main railway station, Berlin Hauptbahnhof (Europaplatz); Karl-Liebknecht-Strasse 13 (Alexanderplatz); Friedrichstrasse 69 (Gendarmenmarkt); Potsdamer Platz 2; and Joachimstaler Strasse 7 (Kurfürstendamm). Post offices are open Monday to Friday 8am–6pm, Saturday 8am–noon.

Safety

Speaking generally, Berlin is a safe city, particularly in the city center. That doesn't mean there are no dodgy areas or that violent crime is unknown. The rules of common sense apply. Parts of Kreuzberg and Neukölln can seem threatening after dark, and in parts of the old East Berlin, such as Lichtenberg and Marzahn-Hellersdorf, there may be a threat of neo-Nazi extremism against nonwhites. Pickpockets work the public transportation network.

Taxis

Taxis wait outside major rail and metro (*U-Bahn* and *S-Bahn*) stations and hotels, and at taxicab stands around the city. Most drivers speak some English. There is a minimum fare of 2.50€ plus 1.50€ per kilometer (2.42€ per mile). Reputable cab companies include **City-Funk Berlin** (☎ 030/210-202), **TaxiFunk Berlin** (☎ 030/443-322), and **Funk Taxi Berlin** (☎ 030/261-026)—*Funk* is German for radio. Because taxi fares in Germany already include a charge for service, it is not necessary or automatically expected to tip taxi drivers. Still, many taxi users at least round up the fare to the nearest convenient amount.

Telephones

Call ☎ 11837 for information and ☎ 11834 for international information. Berlin's area code is 030. Dial the area code when calling a Berlin number from outside the city; you don't need to dial it when calling from inside the city. There is no standard number of digits for telephone numbers in Germany. Some public phones accept coins; some take phone cards, available at post offices and newsstands.

Toilets

The city has a number of clean public toilets (*Toilette* in German; pronounced twah-*leh*-teh), many of them automatic and wheelchair-accessible; you need a .50€ coin to unlock the door. More convenient and widespread are toilets in cafes, bars, restaurants, hotels, malls, gas stations, and some stores, which you can generally use by paying .50€ or by buying something. It is customary to leave the attendant .50€.

Tours

Berlin is awash with tour companies offering many kinds of tours. A step-on/step-off circular city bus tour (*Stadtrundfahrt*) is the most popular type; those operated by **Severin+Kühn** (☎ 030/880-4190; www.berlinerstadtrundfahrten.de) are typical (but see the note about buses nos. 100 and 200 under "Getting Around," above). Boat tours through the city on the Spree and Havel rivers and the Landwehrkanal, and longer excursions out to Potsdam, are well worth doing. **Stern und Kreisschiffahrt** (☎ 030/536-3600; www.sternundkreis.de) line has a good selection of such cruises. Tickets for most of these tours are available at Infostore tourist offices (see "Visitor Information," below).

Visitor Information

Berlin's tourist information service, **Berlin Tourismus Marketing** (www.visitberlin.de), operates **BERLIN Infostore** tourist offices at: ALEXA SHOPPING CENTER Grunerstrasse 20; Apr–Oct Mon–Sat 10am–10pm, Nov–Mar Mon–Sat 10am–8pm; *U-* and *S-Bahn:* Alexanderplatz. BERLIN HAUPTBAHNHOF Europaplatz 1, ground floor, north entrance; daily 8am–10pm; *U-* and *S-Bahn:* Hauptbahnhof. BRANDENBURGER TOR (SOUTH WING) Pariser Platz; Apr–Oct daily 10am–8pm, Nov–Mar daily 10am–6pm; *U-* and *S-Bahn:* Brandenburger Tor. NEUES KRANZLER ECK PASSAGE Kurfürstendamm 21; Mon–Sat 10am–8pm, Sun 10am–6pm; *U-Bahn:* Kurfürstendamm.

4

Dresden, Leipzig & Eastern Germany

The Best of Dresden, Leipzig & Eastern Germany in 3 Days

Three days work quite well for this itinerary. Dresden, Leipzig, Weimar, and Eisenach are relatively close together, and traveling between them is both speedy and painless. The one real difficulty is getting enough out of Dresden in a single day, but with a little focus even that can be done. On the first day, you visit Dresden, a city that is gaining rapidly in popularity as a tourist destination. The second day takes you to Leipzig, for its great musical legacy and urban bustle. Spend Day 3 acquiring a taste for elegant Weimar before winding up in the small historical hotspot of Eisenach.

> *PREVIOUS PAGE Luscious Lake Wörlitzer, in the garden-filled town of Wörlitz. THIS PAGE Get a different view of beautiful Dresden on an Elbe River boat tour.*

START Dresden lies on the Elbe River, 194km (120 miles) south of Berlin on A113 and A13; 367km (228 miles) southeast of Hannover on A2 and A14; 464km (288 miles) northeast of Frankfurt on A5 and A4; and 313km (194 miles) northeast of Nuremberg on A9, A72, and A4. By ICE (high-speed) train the trip from Berlin takes just over 3 hours; from Frankfurt, around 5 hours; and from Munich, around 6 hours. **TRIP LENGTH** 322km (200 miles).

1 ★★★ **Dresden.** The city that's the pride of Saxony has so much to see and do, both on the inside (museums, churches, and other sights) and on the outside (baroque architecture, boat tours on the Elbe River, sidewalk cafes, and more), that you'll be hard put to do more than draw a graphic impression and make a resolution to allow more time on your next visit. Amazingly, one can't even say that the vast and astonishing **Zwinger** dominates central Dresden, because there's plenty of competition for that accolade. Unless you are a dedicated museum hound, it's unlikely you will be able to go straight from there to the almost equally captivating **Residenzschloss** (Royal Palace) on the same day. In the event that you can manage this, the way is at least short—just across Sophienstrasse. ⏱ 1 day. For information on Dresden, including hotel and restaurant recommendations, see p. 166.

From Dresden, the fast track to Leipzig is northwest on A4 and A14, a distance of 112km (70 miles) that can be done in not much more than 1 hour. A more scenic, though slower, route is northwest on B6, through Meissen (p. 151, **10**) and Wurzen, a distance of 111km (69 miles).

> *Towering Thomaskirche is known as much for its sounds as its sights—Johann Sebastian Bach was once the church's musical director.*

② ★★ **Leipzig.** Cosmopolitan Leipzig might not have as many top-drawer attractions as Dresden, but it's definitely a worthwhile place to spend the day and soak up some atmosphere. Highlights include **Thomaskirche** (Church of St. Thomas), where Johann Sebastian Bach was musical director for a number of years, and the **Bach-Museum,** in a baroque home once owned by one of Bach's friends. Nightlife options abound thanks to the large student population—round out your day with some live music (options range from a symphony performance to jazz, soul, blues, reggae, and pop), or just do some bar-hopping. ⏲ 1 day. For information on Leipzig, including hotel and restaurant recommendations, see p. 180.

From Leipzig, the fastest, but not shortest, route to Weimar is southwest and west on A38, A9, and A4 (130km/81 miles). Or, take a more interesting way on B87 southwest, through Weissenfels, Naumburg (p. 149, **⑥**), and Apolda (100km/62 miles).

③ ★★ **Weimar.** Don't be fooled by its small size—Weimar is a cultural powerhouse, with multiple UNESCO World Heritage sites within its borders. Unlike many cities in the former East Germany, Weimar retains much of its old flavor: Many of its important historical monuments were spared bombing in World War II. Highlights include the 16th-century **Lucas-Cranach-Haus,** where Lucas Cranach the Elder and Younger lived; **Goethes Wohnhaus,** Johann Wolfgang von Goethe's baroque mansion; **Liszt-Haus,** where composer and pianist Franz Liszt lived, and the **Bauhaus Museum.** A short trip outside the town takes you to **Gedenkstätte Buchenwald,** a memorial to those who suffered and perished in the notorious concentration camp once located there. ⏲ Half-day. For more on Weimar, see p. 188.

Taking the Train

For those riding the rails, this itinerary should be straightforward. There are frequent ICE (high-speed) trains going between Dresden and Leipzig (1 hr. 13 min.), Leipzig and Weimar (50 min.), and Weimar and Eisenach (44 min.). The short distances mean you won't be spending all of your limited time looking out a train window. Basing yourself in Leipzig, the most central point, and visiting the three other places on day trips may make more sense than having to pack up and move each day.

From Weimar, either zip directly to Eisenach on A4 (80km/50 miles), or add in a little extra time (15–20 min.) at the end: Leave A4 at exit 41B (Gotha-Boxberg), and take L126 south to Friedrichroda, B88 west and north through Seebach to Wutha-Farnroda, and B7

west into Eisenach (total distance 90km/56 miles); this enables you to experience at least a piece of the scenic Thüringer Wald.

4 ★ **Eisenach.** The historic town lies between the northern slopes of the Thüringer Wald (Thuringian Forest, p. 164, **5**) and the forested Nationalpark Hainich (p. 165, **6**). It's Johann Sebastian Bach's birthplace (fans should stop in at the **Bachhaus** museum), and just outside of town is **Wartburg,** a UNESCO World Heritage site and one of Germany's finest castles. ⏱ Half-day. For information on Eisenach, including hotel and restaurant recommendations, see p. 178.

At Eisenach, you are on A4, a main east–west Autobahn (highway) that opens up easy connections around the country.

> *Wartburg Castle was once called "the most German of German castles" by the most infamous of German leaders.*

The Best of Dresden, Leipzig & Eastern Germany in 1 Week

Shaped like a letter V lying on its side, this itinerary starts at Eisenach and heads eastward to Weimar, via Gotha and Erfurt, and then on to the V's apex at Dresden and Meissen, passing through Jena, Naumburg, Altenburg, and Freiberg. From Dresden, the direction is generally northwest, through Colditz, Leipzig, Wittenberg, and Dessau, before reaching the western terminus at Wernigerode, by way of Bernburg and Quedlinburg. It's not necessary to stop at all of the suggested waypoints—how many will depend on your interests, how fast you drive, and how much you like to take in along the way.

> Magnificent Albrechtsburg Castle towers majestically above the banks of the Elbe River in Meissen.

START Eisenach is 355km (221 miles) southwest of Berlin on A9 and A4; 214km (133 miles) south of Hannover on A7 and A4; 196km (122 miles) northeast of Frankfurt on A5 and A4; and 263km (163 miles) north of Nuremberg on A73, A71, and A4. An ICE train from Berlin to Eisenach takes about 3 hours, from Frankfurt about 2 hours, and from Hannover about 2½ hours. TRIP LENGTH 705km (438 miles).

❶ ★ **Eisenach.** In addition to being a place of historical interest for its connections to Martin Luther and Johann Sebastian Bach, Eisenach has a formidable castle on its outskirts. ⌚ 4 hr. For information on Eisenach, see p. 178.

From Eisenach, take B7 along the northeastern rim of the Thüringer Wald (p. 164, ⑤) to Gotha (29km/18 miles).

② **Gotha.** It's worth stopping briefly in this town (pop. 46,000) for a stroll through the Altstadt (Old Town) around central Hauptmarkt, on which stands the ornamented Renaissance **Rathaus** (Town Hall, 1577). The town's main attraction is ★ **Schloss Friedenstein** (☎ 03621/823-411; www.stiftungfriedenstein.de; admission 7€ adults, 3€ kids 6–16; May–Oct Tues–Sun 10am–5pm, Nov–Apr Tues–Sun 10am–4pm), a massive

baroque palace (1655). ⊙ 2 hr. Tourist information: Hauptmarkt 33. ☎ 03621/5078-5712. www.kultourstadt.de.

Continue east on B7 to Erfurt (26km/16 miles).

Taking the Train

Once again, you can accomplish most of this itinerary by train. The only exception is Colditz (**⑪**); skip that stop and go from Meissen to Leipzig.

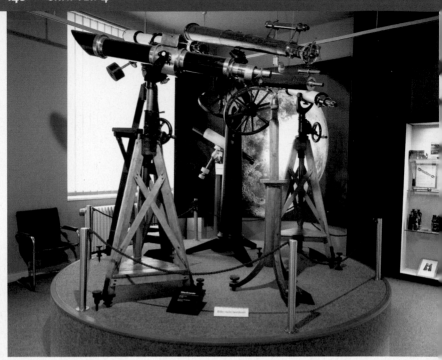

> *There are many things you won't be able to take your eyes off at the renowned Optisches Museum in Jena.*

❸ Erfurt. Like Gotha, Erfurt (pop. 205,000) is worth a short detour, though since Thüringen's state capital is a respectably sized city, you'll want to make sure you don't use up too much time getting in and out. Head for the city center to take in Erfurt's medieval heritage. The **Alte Synagoge** (Old Synagogue, 1094), An der Stadtmünze 4 (☎ 0361/655-1608; www.alte-synagoge.erfurt.de), is Germany's oldest surviving synagogue. Close by, the unique ★★ **Krämerbrücke** (1486), a bridge over the Gera River, is lined with timber-framed houses and shops. On Domplatz are two great churches, the **Erfurter Dom** (Erfurt Cathedral), where Martin Luther was ordained in 1507, and the 15th-century **St. Severikirche** (Church of St. Severus). ⏱ **2 hr.** Tourist information: Benediktsplatz 1. ☎ 0361/66400. www.erfurt-tourismus.de.

Continue east on B7 to Weimar (24km/15 miles). Aim to arrive in the afternoon or evening with enough time in hand for a stroll around town.

❹ ★★ Weimar. Stop here for the night. For information on Weimar, including hotel and restaurant recommendations, see p. 188.

On Day 2, take B7 east from Weimar to Jena (23km/14 miles). If you prefer to pass on Jena, switch at Umpferstedt from B7 east to B87 north, to Naumburg (48km/30 miles).

❺ kids Jena. The only solid reason for visiting Jena (pop. 105,000), the home of the Carl Zeiss Jena optics works, is something that should appeal to kids. The ★ **Zeiss Planetarium,** Am Planetarium 5 (☎ 03641/885-488; www.sternevent.com; admission 8€–11€ adults, 6.50€–9€ kids 6–16; Tues–Fri 10am–4:30pm, Sat 11am–5pm), dates from 1926 and is the world's oldest working planetarium. Across town is the **Optisches Museum** (Optical Museum), Carl-Zeiss-Platz 12 (☎ 03641/443-165; www.optischesmuseum.de; admission 5€ adults, 4€ kids 6–18; Tues–Fri 10am–4:30pm, Sat 11am–4:30pm), which likewise takes its cue from the town's history

> *Altenburg, the 1,000-year-old former imperial palace, provides a magnificent landmark for Erfurt's Altstadt.*

of making optical systems and products. ⏱ 90 min. Tourist information: Markt 16. ☎ 03641/498-050. www.jena.de.

From Jena, follow B88 north to Naumburg (33km/21 miles).

⑥ ★ Naumburg. This town (pop. 29,000) on the Saale River stands in the heart of Europe's most northerly wine district, Saale-Unstrut. Yet vineyards in the hills around the town are not the only attraction. Naumburg has a particularly handsome ★ **Altstadt** (Old Town), containing public buildings, churches, and houses that date from the Middle Ages to the Renaissance and reward a stroll through town. Its most important gem is the Romanesque and Gothic ★ **Naumburger Dom** (Naumburger Cathedral), Domplatz (☎ 03445/23010), dedicated to St. Peter and St. Paul. ⏱ 90 min. Tourist information: Markt 12. ☎ 03445/273-25. www.naumburg-tourismus.de.

From Naumburg, take B180 southeast to Altenburg (54km/34 miles).

⑦ ★ Altenburg. Like Naumburg, Altenburg (pop. 36,000) is one of this region's small and unassuming gems—or as unassuming as a thousand-year-old, former imperial *Residenzstadt* (seat) is likely to be. To a beautifully preserved **Altstadt** (Old Town), Altenburg adds a magnificent baroque palace, ★ **Schloss Altenburg** (☎ 03447/512-712; admission 3.50€ adults, 2.50€ kids 6–18; Tues–Sun 10am–5pm), crowning a rocky hill overlooking the town. Playing cards are produced in Altenburg, and the palace houses, among other things, a museum of playing cards. ⏱ 90 min. Tourist information: Moritzstrasse 21. ☎ 03447/512-800. www.altenburg-tourismus.de.

From Altenburg, take B95 and A72 southeast to A4, A4 northeast to the Frankenberg exit, and S203 east through Frankenstein—you might want to stop for a moment to snap a picture of the village's name board—to Freiberg (86km/53 miles).

8 ★ **Freiberg.** Like many of Saxony's towns that were left untouched by World War II, Freiberg (pop. 42,000) is an exceptionally beautiful mix of historical buildings spanning centuries' worth of architectural styles. Freiberg's wealth during a thousand years was created by the town's silver mines, which Saxony's rulers scooped up to fund their Dresden palaces and self-indulgent way of life. You can go underground on a guided tour of an imperial mine, the **Reiche Zeche** (☎ 03731/394-5781; www.besucherbergwerk-freiberg.de; guided tours 7.50€–12.50€ adults, 5€–10€ kids 6–18, daily 11am–3pm). ⏱ 90 min. Tourist information: Burgstrasse 1. ☎ 03731/419-5190. www.freiberg-service.de.

From Freiberg, take B173 northeast into Dresden (38km/24 miles). Stay overnight in the city—the first of 3 nights you will spend here.

> A visit to Schloss Pillnitz (pictured) and the three other royal residences on-site makes a great day trip from Dresden.

9 ★★★ **Dresden and environs.** One good thing about assigning 2 days to Saxony's splendid capital is that, in the event you see and do all you want in Dresden on the first day, you have a whole day left for trips outside the city center and side trips. For more on Dresden, including hotel and restaurant recommendations, see p. 166. Some suggestions for excursions from Dresden follow.

The **Elbe Valley** in and around Dresden is noted for its pleasure palaces and lavish villas. The villa colony at the suburb of **Loschwitz,** set among vineyards on the Elbe River's east bank, is a good example of the latter, and it's worth spending a little time strolling here. A funicular, the **Standseilbahn,** links Loschwitz to a hillside residential area, Weisser Hirsch, and the Schwebebahn suspension monorail carries passengers from Loschwitz to Oberloschwitz, to the Loschwitzhöhe viewing point. From here you get fine views of the Elbe Valley, which until 2009 was a UNESCO World Heritage site, a status it lost due to a dispute over the construction of a highway bridge. Operating hours and other details for the funicular and the monorail are available from the city's public transportation authority, DVB (☎ 0351/857-1011; www.dvb.de). Loschwitz is a ride of 8km (5 miles) by car from the city center, crossing the Elbe on the Loschwitzer Brücke (1893)—a cantilever bridge dubbed the *Blaues Wunder* (Blue Wonder).

Not satisfied with a single stately residence at their summer palace, 18th-century ★★ **Schloss Pillnitz** (Pillnitz Palace), August-Böckstiegel-Strasse 2 (☎ 0351/4914-2000; www.skd-dresden.de; admission 4€ adults, 2€ kids 6–18; Apr–Oct Tues–Sun 10am–5pm), Saxony's rulers constructed three separate palaces—**Bergpalais** (Hill Palace), **Wasserpalais** (Water Palace), and **Neues Palais** (New Palace)—on the same site, all set around an ornamental garden (free admission open daily from 5am to sunset). The riverside site upstream from Dresden, on the east bank of the Elbe, can be reached by car from the city center (14km/9 miles). Or take tram no. 2 from Postplatz to the Kleinzschachwitz Freystrasse stop, then cross the Elbe on the vehicular ferry between Kleinzschachwitz and Schloss Pillnitz, a walk of 2km (1¼ miles). From May to October, Pillnitz hosts an outpos

> *The Staatliche Porzellan-Manufaktur Meissen produces and sells the region's renowned porcelain.*

of Dresden's ★ **Kunstgewerbemuseum** (Museum of Decorative Arts).

A similar distance by car (15km/9 miles) from central Dresden, but this time northward and inland from the river, stands 18th-century ★★ **Schloss Moritzburg** (Moritzburg Palace; ☎ 035207/8730; www.schloss-moritzburg. de; admission 6.50€ adults, 3.50€ kids 6–18; Apr–Oct daily 10am–5:30pm, Nov 1–10 and Jan Tues–Sun 10am–4pm, Feb–Mar Sat–Sun 10am–4pm). Like Schloss Pillnitz, it is a graphic illustration of the kind of wealth Saxon rulers like August II der Starke (Augustus the Strong) were able to employ when it came to maintaining themselves in style. Set in a large pond, the Schlossteich, on the edge of the Friedewald forest, the huge baroque pleasure palace and hunting lodge is a remodeled enhancement of an earlier version that evidently was not lavish enough.

Garden lovers with enough time on their hands won't want to miss the magnificent 18th-century ★ **Barockgarten Grosssedlitz** ☎ 03529/56390; www.barockgarten-grosssedlitz.de; admission 4€ adults, 2€ kids 6–18; Apr–Aug daily 8am–8pm, Sept–Mar daily 8am–sunset). The baroque garden is 19km (12 miles) southeast of central Dresden on B172, on the road to **Pirna** (p. 157, ❷). 2 days; 1 for the city itself and 1 for side trips.

On Day 5, take riverside B6 northwest from Dresden to Meissen, a distance of 24km (15 miles).

❿ ★★ **Meissen.** A byword around the world for its exquisite porcelain, Meissen (pop. 28,000) would be worth visiting for this aspect alone. But the town, which straddles the Elbe, with the Altstadt (Old Town) on the left bank, has much more to offer. As is usual in German towns, the best place to start out is the central **Markt,** around which are the late-Gothic **Rathaus** (Town Hall, 1486) and the **Frauenkirche** (Church of Our Lady), in the same style and from the same period; the church has a carillon of porcelain bells—Meissen porcelain, of course. Just to the north of the Markt, Burgberg hill rises up over the Elbe, crowned by the 15th- to 16th-century ★★ **Albrechtsburg** (☎ 03521/47070; www. albrechtsburg-meissen.de; admission 3€ adults, 1.50€ kids 6–18; Mar–Oct daily 10am–6pm), a residential castle of spires and gables rather than of fortified towers and turrets, and the neighboring ★ **Dom** (cathedral), from the 13th to 15th centuries, which holds rare Meissen porcelain. On the southern edge of the town is the reason so many people visit Meissen—the combined factory, museum, and shop of ★ **Staatliche Porzellan-Manufaktur Meissen,** Talstrasse 9 (☎ 03521/4680;

> *Dessau's Bauhaus College is famed for launching a revolutionary approach to design.*

www.meissen.com; admission 8.50€ adults, 4.50€ kids 6–18; May–Oct daily 9am–6pm, Nov–Apr daily 9am–5pm). On a tour, you get to see how the centuries-old process of making Meissen porcelain is carried on, visit the museum with its 3,000 Meissen pieces, and arrive ineluctably at the shop, where prices are not noticeably better than elsewhere in Germany. ⏱ 3 hr. Tourist information: Markt 3. ☎ 03521/41940. www.stadt-meissen.de.

From Meissen, drive south on B101 to A14, and then northwest on A14 to Leipzig (100km/62 miles). If you are interested and think you can fit it in, make a short diversion off of A14 to Colditz (68km/42 miles from Meissen; 19km/12 miles from A14).

⓫ **Colditz.** The small town (pop. 5,000) has a picturesque location along the Mulde River, and the kind of handsome old town hall, market square, and church that are town fixtures in this part of Germany. In addition, there is 16th-century ★ **Schloss Colditz** (Colditz Castle), Schlossgasse 1 (☎ 034381/55151; www.schloesser-und-burgen-im-muldental.de; admission 6€ adults, 4€ kids 6–18; Apr–Oct daily 10am–5pm, Nov–Mar daily 10am–4pm), an imposing pile of whitewashed stone and red-tiled roofs atop a rocky pinnacle. During World War II, this was Nazi Germany's infamous Oflag IV C, a prisoner-of-war camp for Allied officers, whose primary pastime was escaping. ⏱ 90 min. Tourist information: Tourismusverein Colditz Mulderland, Markt 1. ☎ 034381/43519. www.fremdenverkehrsamt-colditz.de.

If you did the detour to Colditz, go west and north from there on B176, B95, and B2 to Leipzig (48km/30 miles). Either way, spend the night in Leipzig.

⓬ ★★ **Leipzig.** ⏱ Half-day. For information on Leipzig, including hotel and restaurant recommendations, see p. 180.

On Day 6, depart Leipzig on B2 north to Wittenberg (71km/44 miles), on the way passing through a forested nature park, Naturpark Dübener Heide.

⓭ ★★ **Wittenberg.** This is the town where in 1517 Martin Luther set the ball rolling for the Protestant Reformation. ⏱ 4 hr. See p. 158, ❺.

From Wittenberg, go west on country roads L131 and K2042 to Wörlitz (p. 159, ❻), and then west on L133, through Vockerode, to Dessau (40km/25 miles).

> *An old-fashioned steam train will make your journey into the Harz Mountains as pleasant as your charming destination, the village of Wernigerode.*

⓮ ★ **Dessau.** Standing at the point where the Mulde River flows into the Elbe, Dessau is a multiple UNESCO World Heritage site holder, for a bunch of centuries-old palaces set in landscaped gardens, a Biosphere Reserve on the Middle Elbe, and a constellation of 20th-century Bauhaus school architectural masterpieces. ⏱ 4 hr. See p. 159, ➐.

Go west on B185 to Bernburg (42km/26 miles).

⓯ **Bernburg.** Like Eisenach (p. 178) and Quedlinburg (p. 186), Bernburg (pop. 30,000) is crowned by a magnificent, rambling castle that seems far too big for it. ★★ **Schloss Bernburg,** Schlossstrasse 24 (☎ 03471/625-007; www.museumschlossbernburg.de; admission 4€ adults, 3€ kids 6–14; Apr–Oct Tues–Sun 10am–5pm; Nov–Mar Sat–Sun and Tues–Thurs 10am–4pm, Fri 10am–1pm), overlooking the Saale River, has a bewildering array of parts, dating from the 12th to the 16th centuries. ⏱ 2 hr. Tourist information: Schlossgartenstrasse 6. ☎ 03471/6590. www.bernburg.de.

From Bernburg, go west on B185 and B6 to Quedlinburg (46km/29 miles), where you'll spend the night.

⓰ **Quedlinburg.** ⏱ 4 hr. For information on Quedlinburg, including hotel and restaurant recommendations, see p. 186.

Continue west on B6 to Wernigerode (31km/19 miles).

⓱ **Wernigerode.** A charming mountain town (pop. 35,000) filled with timber-frame houses, Wernigerode is the eastern gateway to the Harz Mountains (p. 527). Its central Gothic ★ **Rathaus** (Town Hall, 1498) is surely one of Germany's quaintest, with its witch's-hat corner towers—an appropriate image for the Harz, where witches seemingly roam (see "Witching Hours," p. 526). Kids might enjoy a ride aboard the narrow-gauge trains of **Harzer Schmalspurbahn** (☎ 03943/5580; www.hsb-wr.de), departing from Wernigerode to the summit of the Brocken (p. 527, ➌), northern Germany's highest mountain. ⏱ 2 hr. Tourist information: Marktplatz 10. ☎ 03943/553-7835. www.wernigerode.de.

At Wernigerode, you are just off A6, allowing rapid access to Germany's Autobahn (highway) network. Should you need one more night in a hotel, Wernigerode is a good place for it (see p. 527).

MEISSEN
PORCELAIN
State-of-the-art China

BY GEORGE MCDONALD

IN 2010 MEISSEN CELEBRATED ITS 300TH ANNIVERSARY as a center for the manufacture of quality porcelain. Since 1710, the Elbe River town has been the home of Meissen porcelain, and you can visit the factory where it's produced. The early makers of this "white gold" were virtually held prisoner here because the princes who ruled both Dresden and Meissen carefully guarded the secret to its production.

Meissen porcelain got its start when Saxon ruler Augustus the Strong commissioned alchemist Johann Friedrich Böttger to transmute gold from base metals. That project went nowhere, naturally, but with the aid of scientist Ehrenfried Walther von Tschirnhaus, Böttger successfully produced Chinese-style porcelain instead. That was enough to keep Augustus happy, since expensive Chinese porcelain had long bedazzled Europe, and until Böttger and von Tschirnhaus got to work, had resisted the best efforts of European craftsmen to re-create it.

FORM AND CONTENT

Among the products that have emerged from the Meissen workshop are dinner services and other tableware, human and animal figurines, clocks, candlesticks, snuffboxes, and classic Chinese and Japanese scenes and motifs. Art Nouveau and Art Deco works were produced between the late 19th and early 20th centuries. Some of the most exquisite antique pieces depict classical Greek and Roman myths and legends.

ART AND TECHNIQUE

Despite its fragile nature, Meissen porcelain is technically a "hard" or "hard-paste" porcelain, made from the feldspar (ore-free) clay kaolin, also known as china clay, that's mined at a quarry in Mehren,

5km (3 miles) west of Meissen. The ingredients are mixed in a proprietary recipe and fired in a kiln at around 1,200°C (2,192°F) to produce the famous translucent white china.

RED PORCELAIN

Production of Meissen porcelain was one of Communist East Germany's few profitable industries, so the Staatliche Porzellan-Manufaktur Meissen was of great importance to the country's economy. At that time, the factory was owned by "the

People," though few East German people outside of the Party elite could afford such a luxury. Purchasers from the capitalist West snapped up the china, causing demand to outstrip supply. Ownership of the factory reverted to the state of Saxony after Germany's re-unification in 1990.

REAL OR FAKE?

To be tolerably sure that you're looking at a real piece of Meissen porcelain (though it's not an absolute guarantee), look on the bottom for the

distinctive cobalt-blue crossed-swords logo, derived from Augustus the Strong's coat of arms, and an official hallmark granted in 1724.

A PORCELAIN FEAST

In addition to viewing Meissen porcelain in the workshop's own museum—and in the factory store, of course—you can take in the world's largest single collection in nearby Dresden's Zwinger Palace (p. 166, ❶). It counts 8,000 pieces. There's even a full-size glockenspiel of Meissen porcelain bells in the palace's gate tower.

BULL MARKET

Delicate antique Meissen porcelain is considered a solid investment, a fact that gives a whole new meaning to the old saw about a bull in a china shop.

Centuries of Tradition

The new homegrown china was made inside Meissen's medieval Albrechtsburg Castle until 1865, when production shifted to the current site overlooking the town. Most of the iconic tableware patterns sold today, such as the Swan and the cobalt-enhanced Blue Onion patterns, have been in production since the 1700s at the Staatliche Porzellan-Manufaktur Meissen (Meissen State Porcelain Manufactory). Meissen

porcelain is for sale in specialized stores and by mail order, but it is far more interesting to go to the workshop in the town to see how it is made. Little has changed over the centuries, and all the ornate painting, decoration, and other effects are still done by hand. This makes Meissen porcelain pricey, but each piece is a unique product, made by craftsmen. The delicacy of the brushstroke, the richness of color, and the sheen of the glazes make the items produced by the firm highly prized.

The Elbe River from Dresden to Magdeburg

Starting out in glorious Dresden, you sidestep briefly southeastward to Pirna, before doubling back and rolling languidly northwest, following the trace of the Elbe River downstream, to Meissen, the home of fine porcelain; Torgau, where U.S. and Russian troops linked up in 1945; then on to Martin Luther's Reformation city, Wittenberg; the garden town Wörlitz and the nearby Bauhaus town Dessau; and finally to Magdeburg, a city that has taken some hard knocks in its time, picked itself up, and got going again.

> Dresden's skyline is best seen from the banks of the Elbe River.

START Dresden is 195km (121 miles) south of Berlin on A113 and A13; and 465km (289 miles) east of Frankfurt on A5 and A4. A direct ICE train from Berlin takes a little over 2 hours; from Munich it's about 6 hours. TRIP LENGTH 311km (193 miles) and 4 days.

❶ ★★★ **Dresden.** ◷ 1 day. For information on Dresden, including hotel and restaurant recommendations, see p. 166.

On Day 2, drive east and south from Dresden along the Elbe's right (north) bank, on Bautzner Strasse (B6). Beyond the suburb of Radeberger

1 Dresden
2 Pirna
3 Meissen
4 Torgau
5 Wittenberg
6 Wörlitz
7 Dessau
8 Magdeburg

Where to Stay & Dine

Grüne Tanne **11**
Hotel Residenz Joop **14**
Kornhaus **13**
Landhaus Wörlitzer Hof **12**
Ratskeller **10**
Vincenz Richter **9**

Vorstadt, shift to S167 south, through the tony villa colony of Loschwitz, before crossing over the Elbe bridge on Hauptstrasse (S164) into Pirna (25km/16 miles).

2 ★ Pirna. Although it's dubbed the "gateway to Sächsische Schweiz" (Saxon Switzerland, p. 163, **3**), Pirna (pop. 40,000), on the Elbe River, is a worthwhile destination in its own right. It was largely spared the deluge of World War II bombs that devastated Dresden and still has many original buildings from the 16th century and earlier. The finest of these

are clustered around the Markt, notably the **Rathaus** (Town Hall, 1556) and the late Gothic **St. Marienkirche** (St. Mary's Church, 1546). No less an admirer of civic beauty than the Italian artist Canaletto painted 11 canvases of the town between 1753 and 1755. A darker part of Pirna's history is recalled in a memorial

Taking the Train

With the exception of Wörlitz, you can reach all the towns on this itinerary by train.

> *Meissen's Altstadt district draws tourists with its classic German architecture.*

in **Schloss Sonnenstein** (1460), a castle on a hill above the town, in which the Nazis gassed 15,000 disabled people. ⏱ **2 hr.** Tourist information: Am Markt 7 (Canaletto House). ☎ 03501/556-447. www.pirna.de.

From Pirna, bypass Dresden on A17 and A4 before switching to riverside B6 for the run northwest into Meissen (54km/34 miles).

❸ ★★★ **Meissen.** ⏱ 4 hr. See p. 151, ❿.

From Meissen, hold to the minor riverside road north through Hirschstein and Leutewitz to Riesa, where you pick up B182 north to Torgau (66km/41 miles).

❹ ★ **Torgau.** This well-preserved old town (pop. 20,000) passed into the history books in April 1945, when the spearheads of the advancing U.S. and Soviet armies connected in the town (see "U.S.-Russian Wartime Link-up"). It was known in earlier centuries as the seat of the Landgraf (count) of Thüringen. The count's Renaissance palace, grandiose ★★ **Schloss Hartenfels,** Schlossstrasse 27

(☎ 03421/70140; Schloss Museum: admission 2€ adults, 1€ kids 6–18; Apr–Oct daily 10am–6pm, Nov–Mar Sat–Sun 11am–4pm; Tower: admission 1€; Apr–Oct daily 10am–6pm, Nov–Mar daily 10am–4pm), dominates the town's Elbe waterfront. Protestant Reformer Martin Luther consecrated the Schlosskapelle (chapel) here in 1544. Luther's widow, Katharina von Bora, died in Torgau in 1552. View her tomb in the **Marienkirche** (St. Mary's Church) and visit a small museum of her life and times in the room where she died, the **Katharina-Luther-Stube,** Katharinenstrasse 11 (☎ 03421/908-043; admission 1€; daily 10am–4pm). ⏱ 2 hr. Tourist information: Markt 1. ☎ 03421/70140. www.tic-torgau.de.

Continue north on B182, which is replaced by B2 as the road rolls across the Elbe into Wittenberg (50km/31 miles). Spend your second night in Wittenberg.

❺ ★★ **Wittenberg.** Just as the cities of the old Hanseatic League (see the box on p. 578) delight in their honorary prefix *Hansestadt*, so does Wittenberg (pop. 48,000) take pride in its handle *Lutherstadt*. This is where the great Protestant Reformer and former Augustinian monk Martin Luther (1483–1546) shook the foundations of the papacy, the Catholic Church, and the Hapsburg Empire. On October 31, 1517, he nailed his Ninety-five Theses disputing certain practices of the Church to the door of Wittenberg's **Schlosskirche** (Castle Church). A statue of Luther stands on the Markt in front of the Gothic **Rathaus** (Town Hall, 1440), and his tomb is in the Schlosskirche, which was reconstructed in 1760 after a fire. ⏱ 3 hr. Tourist information: Schlossplatz 2. ☎ 03491/498-610. www.wittenberg.de.

Recross the Elbe on B2 to Kienberge, and switch to country road L131 west to Riesigk, and then to K2042 for the short remaining stretch into Wörlitz (24km/15 miles).

⑥ ★ Wörlitz. If you like gardens, you're sure to love little Wörlitz (pop. 1,600). UNESCO did, enough to award its gardens World Heritage status. The grandest is ★★★ **Wörlitzer Park,** a naturalistic (up to a point) English-landscape extravaganza begun in 1764 by Prince Leopold III and expanded up until 1813 by his successors. It's built around a series of lakes and islets and has a neoclassical palace, **Schloss Wörlitz** (1773), as its focal point. In addition, there are Greek-, Roman-, and Gothic-inspired pavilions, temples, and grottoes, and even a synagogue (modeled on the Roman Temple of Vesta) and an artificial volcano. You'll need 2 hours to do the park any kind of justice. It's open 24/7 and admission is free, but there's a charge for admission to some pavilions and for boat rental. ⏱ 2 hr. Tourist information: Förstergasse 26. ☎ 034905/20216. www.woerlitz-information.de.

Spend the night in Wörlitz, then on Day 4 go west on L133, through Vockerode, to Dessau (16km/10 miles).

⑦ ★★ Dessau. In a region where ornate Renaissance palaces and baroque gardens are, if not exactly a dime a dozen, not rare, Dessau (pop. 80,000) has something completely different—a Bauhaus connection. The highlight of this unornamented form-follows-function style in architecture and design is the ★ **Bauhausgebäude** (Bauhaus Building,

> *Old World elegance still thrives in Pirna's Markt, which was miraculously spared the devastation of World War II.*

1926), Gropiusallee 38 (☎ 0340/650-8251; www.bauhaus-dessau.de; daily 10am–6pm), a design college created after plans by Walter Gropius. Among the other notable Bauhaus buildings in town are the detached residences

U.S.-Russian Wartime Linkup

On April 25, 1945, patrols from the U.S. 69th Infantry Division probed warily eastward to the Elbe River. At the same time, patrols from the Red Army's 58th Guards Division probed warily westward to the river. Adolf Hitler's armies were disintegrating, but on the roads were many freed prisoners of war and slave laborers, civilian refugees, and other displaced persons, and there were occasional outbreaks of fighting with die-hard Nazis. A series of joyous meetings took place in and around war-battered Torgau that day, as American and Russian troops shook hands, overcame language barriers, danced and sang, and celebrated the linkup of their two armies—and the defeat, soon to be made official, of Nazi Germany.

> *The magnificent Magdeburger Dom houses the tomb of the Holy Roman Emperor Otto the Great.*

Meisterhaus Kandinsky-Klee, Ebertallee 69–71 (☎ 0340/661-0934; www.meisterhaeuser.de), and **Meisterhaus Feininger/Kurt-Weill-Zentrum,** Ebertallee 63 (☎ 0340/619-595; www.kurt-weill.de); both houses are open Tuesday to Sunday from 10am to 5pm (until 6 in summer). A ticket to all three Bauhaus sites costs 15€. ⊕ 4 hr. Tourist information: Zerbster Strasse 2C. ☎ 0340/204-1442. www.dessau.de.

From Dessau, take L63 west, through Aken and Brumby, to the junction with A14 northbound, and stay on this highway into large and busy Magdeburg (76km/47 miles).

❽ ★ **Magdeburg.** The Middle Elbe's big city, Magdeburg (pop. 230,000) has had ups and downs in a 1,200-year history (see "The Sack of Magdeburg"). It was an important medieval town, was heavily bombed in World War II, and was later "developed" as an industrial center in postwar Communist East Germany. Most of its surviving or reconstructed monuments are medieval churches, "supported" by a cast of Stalin-era Socialist neoclassical architecture. And yet Magdeburg, which since Germany's reunification has been Sachsen-Anhalt's state capital, is on the up and up, looking more attractive every year and possessing significant urban energy. In the great Gothic ★ **Magdeburger Dom** (cathedral), Am Dom 1 (☎ 0391/541-0436; www.magdeburgerdom.de), constructed during 3 centuries beginning in 1209, over an earlier church dating from 937, is the tomb of Holy Roman Emperor Otto I "the Great" (912–973), along with a deal of medieval religious art. Nothing could be more different than the nearby ★ **Grüne Zitadelle** (Green Citadel), Breiter Weg 180 (☎ 0391/620-8653; www.gruene-zitadelle.de). This mix of shopping, offices, and apartments was built in 2005 in the marvelously flowing, higgledy-piggledy, bright and colorful lines favored by unorthodox Austrian architect Friedensreich Hundertwasser.

The Sack of Magdeburg

In 1631, during the Thirty Years War, a Catholic imperial army stormed the Protestant fortress town, amid an orgy of killing, raping, looting, and burning that cost 25,000 out of a population of 30,000 their lives and left Magdeburg devastated. It never recovered its former prominence.

Take the kids down to the river, to the east-bank **Elbauenpark,** Tessenowstrasse 5A (☎ 0391/ 593-4263; admission 3€ adults, 2€ kids 6–18; Mar–Apr daily 10am–6pm, May–Sept daily 9am–8pm, Oct daily 9am–6pm, Nov–Feb daily 10am–4pm), a theme-park with gardens, stages, playgrounds, and the ★ **Jahrtausendturm** (Millennium Tower), which holds an exhibit on 6,000 years of human history.

If you have some extra time to kill in Magdeburg, consider taking a short cruise on the Elbe. Boat tours operated by **Magdeburger Weisse**

Flotte (☎ 0391/532-8891; www.weisseflotte-magdeburg.de) depart from a dock on Petriförder, on the left (west) riverbank, just north of the city center. There are multiple cruise options available, ranging from 1 to 4½ hr. (and even a full-day tour). Ticket prices start at 7.50€ for adults, 3.75€ for kids 4–14. ⊕ At least 4 hr. Tourist information: Ernst-Reuter-Allee 12. ☎ 0391/19433. www.magdeburg-tourist.de.

Magdeburg is on Germany's main east–west highway, A2, a road that opens up connections in all directions around the country.

Where to Stay & Dine

★★ **Grüne Tanne** WITTENBERG
Set on a leafy estate, this country-manor hotel 7km (4⅓ miles) north of Wittenberg has tastefully furnished rooms and a traditional German restaurant with a garden terrace in summer. Am Teich 1. ☎ 03491/6290. www. gruenetanne.de. 40 units. Doubles 56€–79€ w/breakfast. AE, DC, MC, V.

★★ **Hotel Residenz Joop** MAGDEBURG
A 1903 villa in a quiet residential district south of the Altstadt (Old Town) has been turned into a refined, family-run hotel that might be a tad chintzy for some tastes. Jean-Burger-Strasse 16. ☎ 0391/62620. www.residenzjoop.de. 25 units. Doubles 98€–142€ w/breakfast. AE, MC, V.

★★ **Kornhaus** DESSAU *SAXON/CONTINENTAL*
Fit right in with Dessau's modernist architectural flavor in this Bauhaus building from 1930 with big windows and a terrace next to the Elbe, while tucking into hearty local dishes. Kornhausstrasse 146. ☎ 0340/640-4141. Entrees 10€–16€. AE, MC, V. Lunch & dinner daily.

★ **Landhaus Wörlitzer Hof** WÖRLITZ
A perfect location on the edge of Wörlitzer Park is complemented by rooms styled to be bright and contemporary (though not luxurious), and a restaurant that serves Saxon cuisine. Markt 96. ☎ 034905/4110. www.vincenz-richter.de. 46 units. Doubles 97€–144€ w/breakfast. AE, MC, V.

★ **Ratskeller** TORGAU *GERMAN/SAXON*
Napoleon dined in this 16th-century cellar restaurant in 1810, and evidently sustained no injury. Look for heaped servings of

> Meissen's intimate Vincenz Richter restaurant dates all the way back to 1523 and features a dazzling array of local wines.

old-fashioned Saxon and German fare, lots of meat (and some fish), and game in season. Markt 1. ☎ 03421/903-477. Entrees 9€–17€. No credit cards. Lunch & dinner daily.

★★ **Vincenz Richter** MEISSEN *GERMAN/SAXON*
Just off the Markt, this restaurant in a vine-sheathed building from 1523 has a cozy setting, a hearty menu of local specialties, and fine wines from the attached winery. An der Frauenkirche 12. ☎ 03521/453-285. Entrees 14€–22€. AE, DC, MC, V. Lunch & dinner Tues–Sun.

The Best of the Outdoors in Saxony & Thuringia

Some of the most scenically beautiful and ecologically diverse parts of this itinerary lie generally south of Dresden, among the mountain ranges that extend across Germany's border with the Czech Republic. From the end of this segment, a bit of determined Autobahn (highway) driving gets you to some significant forested regions, prior to finishing up on the east side of the Harz Mountains (p. 527). We've given directions to each of these parks from the nearest major town. You can use those towns (or one of the hotels we recommend at the end of this section) for overnights if you're stringing this into a park-to-park tour (which would take about a week), or you can pick and choose from these parks and make them side trips as you explore the region.

> The awe-inspiring peaks of Nationalpark Sächsische Schweiz near Dresden are a big draw for hardy hikers and climbers.

START Dresden is 195km (121 miles) south of Berlin on A113 and A13; and 465km (289 miles) east of Frankfurt on A5 and A4.

❶ ★★★ Dresden. ⏱ 1 day. For information on Dresden, including hotel and restaurant recommendations, see p. 166.

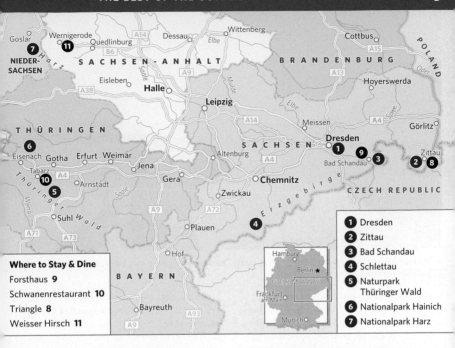

Where to Stay & Dine

Forsthaus **9**

Schwanenrestaurant **10**

Triangle **8**

Weisser Hirsch **11**

① Dresden
② Zittau
③ Bad Schandau
④ Schlettau
⑤ Naturpark Thüringer Wald
⑥ Nationalpark Hainich
⑦ Nationalpark Harz

② ★ kids **Zittau.** Handsome Zittau (pop. 30,000) stands right up against the border in the tri-country Bohemia region where Germany, Poland, and the Czech Republic meet. If you are at all culturally minded, you'll love strolling its graceful streets and viewing a pleasing mix of baroque, neo-Renaissance, and neoclassical buildings. Beyond the town, the wooded ★ **Naturpark Zittauer Gebirge** (Zittau Mountains Nature Park; www. naturpark-zittauer-gebirge.de) forms the German part of the transborder Lausitzer Gebirge (Lausitz Mountains), with peaks up to 793m (2,602 ft.) high. Go by car, or ride the narrow-gauge steam trains of the ★ **Zittauer Schmalspurbahn** (☎ 03583/540-540; www.zoje.de) from the town into the hills around Oybin and Jonsdorf, where there is good hiking country. ⏰ 1 day. Tourist information: Markt 1, Zittau. ☎ 03583/752-174. www.naturpark-zittauer-gebirge.de. From Dresden, drive east on B6, through Bischofswerda, Bautzen, and Löbau, and then take B178 southbound to Zittau (100km/62 miles).

③ ★ kids **Bad Schandau.** This town is a spa resort and the main tourist town in the area. It makes a good jumping-off point for

★★★ **Nationalpark Sächsische Schweiz** (Saxon Switzerland National Park), the German sector of the Elbsandsteingebirge (Elbe Sandstone Mountains), a low range that straddles the German-Czech border and is split by the Elbe River. On the German side, the highest "peak" is the table mountain **Grosser Zschirnstein** (562m/1,844 ft.). You can climb and hike all around this area. Just downriver, the ★★ **Bastei,** a spectacular cliff formation, rears up 190m (623 ft.) above the Elbe. Cross the river at Bad Schandau to reach a dramatically sited 16th-century fortress, ★★ **Königstein** (☎ 035021/64609; www.festung-koenigstein.de; admission 6€ adults, 4€ children and students; daily Apr–Sept 9am–8pm, Oct 9am–6pm, Nov–Mar 9am–5pm). ⏰ 1 day. Visitor center: NationalparkZentrum, Dresdner Strasse 2B. ☎ 035022/50240.

Taking the Train

It's not impossible to do this itinerary by train and bus, using public transportation to get to the nature zones and then doing some hiking from there, but it'll be a far easier proposition by car.

> *The rolling forests and stirring beauty of Naturpark Thüringer Wald are a natural draw for hikers and winter sports enthusiasts.*

www.nationalpark-saechsische-schweiz.de. Admission 4€ adults, 3€ kids 6–16, 7.50€ families. Apr–Oct daily 9am–6pm; Nov–Mar Tues–Sun 9am–5pm. Train: Bad Schandau, then by bus into the mountains. From Dresden, take B170 and A17 south, then B172 east to Bad Schandau (46km/29 miles).

4 **kids** **Schlettau.** The Erzgebirge (Ore Mountains) of ★★ **Naturpark Erzgebirge/Vogtland** (www.naturpark-erzgebirge-vogtland.de; admission 4.50€ adults, 1.50€ kids 6–16; Tues–Fri 10am–5pm, Sat 2–5pm, Sun 1–5pm) are generally higher than the Elbsandsteingebirge—at 1,215m (3,986 ft.), the highest peak on the German side, the **Fichtelberg,** is quite respectable. From Schlettau to the Fichtelberg is 30km (19 miles) by car. Cute handmade wooden Christmas ornaments from the

Erzgebirge are much loved in Germany. To see why, visit the ★ **Erzgebirgisches Spielzeugmuseum** (Ore Mountains Toy Museum; ☎ 037362/8239; www.spielzeugmuseum-seiffen.de; admission 3.50€ adults, 1.50€ kids 4–16; daily 10am–5pm) in Seiffen. Schlettau has a 14th-century palace (rebuilt in the 19th), ★★ **Schloss Schlettau** (☎ 03733/66019; www.schloss-schlettau.de; admission 3.50€ adults, 1.50€ kids 6–18; Tues–Fri 10am–5pm, Sat 2–5pm, Sun 1–5pm). ⏱ At least a half-day. Visitor center: Schloss Schlettau, Schlossplatz 8, Schlettau. ☎ 03733/622-106. www.naturpark-erzgebirge-vogtland.de and www.schloss-schlettau.de. From Dresden, take A4, A72, and S258 south to Schlettau (123km/76 miles).

5 ★ **Naturpark Thüringer Wald.** Ilmenau is the eastern gateway to the Naturpark Thüringer Wald (Thuringian Forest Nature Park). From here, you can pick up hiking trails leading into the forest and spend a happy day living out of a backpack and experiencing a limited segment of these trails. If you prefer to drive, much of this beautiful area opens up to you. A clockwise circular route of 100km (62 miles) that makes a decent and realistic 1-day tour from Ilmenau and takes in a variety of landscapes, villages, and small towns, is through Gabelbach, Frauenwald, Schleusingen, Suhl, Zella-Mehlis, Oberhof, Crawinkel, Gräfenroda, and Eigersburg. ⏱ 1 day. Visitor center:

A Detour Through the Mountains

If you're visiting both Bad Schandau and Schlettau and you'd enjoy a scenic mountain drive, spend the night in Bad Shandau instead of going back to Dresden, then follow mountain roads along the Czech border, through Breitenau, Altenberg, Rechenberg-Bienenmühle, and Seiffen, to Schlettau, a total distance of 170km (106 miles); you'll want to allocate at least 4 hours, plus 4 hours for breaks and sightseeing.

> To get the most out of your visit to Nationalpark Hainich, be sure to spend some time on the nature trails.

Naturparkzentrum Thüringer Wald, Dorfstrasse 16, Friedrichshöhe. ☎ 036704/70990. www.naturpark-thueringer-wald.de. Mon–Fri 8am–5pm. From Weimar (p. 188), take A4 west and A71 south to Ilmenau (60km/37 miles).

6 ★★ kids Nationalpark Hainich. Hainich National Park might be small—a mere 76 sq. km (29 sq. miles) of protected beech forest—but it'll seem bigger on the ground. To get much out of your time here, you need to be willing to hike the nature trails. Or, from the Thiemsburg visitor center (see below), take an easier option that the kids should like. The cool ★★ **Baumkronenpfad** (Treetop Path) is an educational trail literally among the treetops, 44m (144 ft.) above the forest floor. Fantastic views across the canopy of leaves are guaranteed, and there are intriguing little nature puzzles to be solved along the way. ⏱ Half-day. Visitor center: Nationalparkzentrum Thiemsburg (near Bad Langensalza). ☎ 03603/892-464. www.nationalpark-hainich.de. Admission 2€ adults, 1.50€ kids 6–18, 5.50€ families. Apr–Oct daily 9am–6pm; Nov–Mar daily 10am–4pm. From Weimar (p. 188), take A4 west, then L1029 and K15 north to Thiemsburg (85km/53 miles).

7 ★★★ kids Nationalpark Harz. Wernigerode makes a good starting point for touring the eastern Harz Mountains. ⏱ 1 day. See p. 527, **3**. From Quedlinburg (p. 186), take B6 west to Wernigerode (31km/19 miles).

Where to Stay & Dine

★★ Forsthaus BAD SCHANDAU
At the entrance to the bucolic Kirnitzsch Valley, this complex of separate buildings around a main, timber-framed hotel offers Scandinavian-style rooms and great dining. Kirnitzschtalstrasse 5. ☎ 035022/5840. www.veka-hotels.de. 77 units. Doubles 68€–108€ w/ breakfast. AE, MC, V.

★★★ Schwanenrestaurant TABARZ THURINGIAN/CONTINENTAL Watch the chefs at work in the open kitchen of this fine Thüringer Wald restaurant, in an ambiance that's not totally country-manor, but close. Hotel Frauenberger, Max-Alvary-Strasse 11. ☎ 036259/5220. Entrees 13€–19€. AE, MC, V. Dinner Mon–Fri, lunch & dinner Sat–Sun.

★ Triangle ZITTAU CONTINENTAL
Literally on the edge of Bohemia, this moody brasserie eschews the hearty menus typical of the region in favor of a French-influenced style that runs to cocktails on an outside terrace. Bautzner Strasse 9. ☎ 03583/5550. Entrees 9€–17€. AE, DC, MC, V. Lunch & dinner daily.

★★ Weisser Hirsch WERNIGERODE
Across the main square from the medieval Rathaus (Town Hall), this family-run hotel has a conservative style and a feel for quality in both the rooms and the restaurant. Marktplatz 5. ☎ 03493/602-020. www.hotel-weisser-hirsch.de. 55 units. Doubles 115€–220€ w/ breakfast. AE, MC, V.

Dresden

For centuries, Dresden was admired as "Florence on the Elbe," a graceful masterpiece of baroque architecture and a storehouse of art treasures. All that came to a sudden end with a series of devastating Allied firebombing raids in February 1945. Or so it seemed at the time. In the more than 60 years since its near total destruction, Dresden has slowly risen like a phoenix from its own ashes. Today, the fruits of an astonishing restoration can be seen and enjoyed, and the city (pop. 515,000) is once again a major sightseeing destination. You really need 2 days to see all the sights on this tour; if you don't have that much time, you'll need to pick the stops that most appeal to you.

> Dresden's beautiful Frauenkirche escaped the ravages of Allied bombs with its spectacular dome intact.

START The large square called Postplatz, reached by tram nos. 1, 2, 4, 8, 9, 11, and 12, is a good jumping-off point for touring central Dresden's sights and attractions. It's just south of the first stop on this tour; walk toward the river on Sophienstrasse.

❶ ★★★ Zwinger. Even among Dresden's many magnificent baroque confections, this vast complex of pavilions, galleries, and gardens is a scene of jaw-dropping majesty. The Zwinger (1710–1855) was constructed between two belts of the city walls—the name refers to a castle's outer ward, or bailey—as

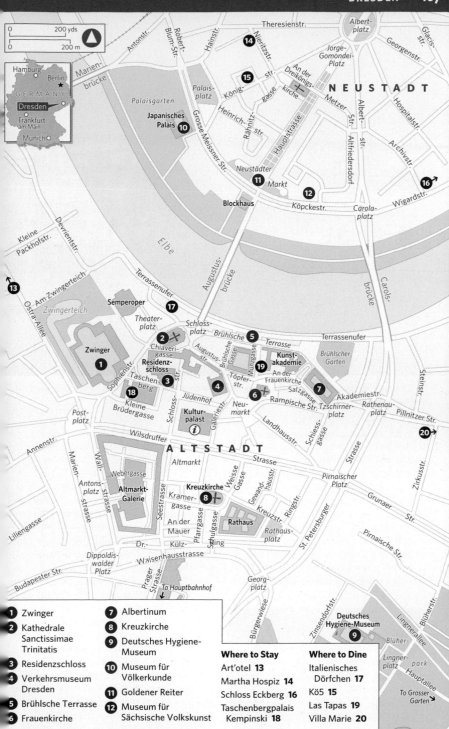

1 Zwinger

2 Kathedrale Sanctissimae Trinitatis

3 Residenzschloss

4 Verkehrsmuseum Dresden

5 Brühlsche Terrasse

6 Frauenkirche

7 Albertinum

8 Kreuzkirche

9 Deutsches Hygiene-Museum

10 Museum für Völkerkunde

11 Goldener Reiter

12 Museum für Sächsische Volkskunst

Where to Stay

Art'otel 13

Martha Hospiz 14

Schloss Eckberg 16

Taschenbergpalais Kempinski 18

Where to Dine

Italienisches Dörfchen 17

Kö5 15

Las Tapas 19

Villa Marie 20

> *The Zwinger's fountains, galleries, and open squares draw people from all over Dresden and the world for moments of connection and reflection.*

a space for festivals, masques, and parades organized by Elector August II (Augustus the Strong) and subsequent members of Saxony's ruling house, and as galleries to house their art collections. Enter from Ostra-Allee, across a moatlike pond, the Zwingerteich, and then go through the crown-shaped Kronentor (Crown Gate) to the courtyard's ornamental garden. The south pavilion, the Glockenspielpavillon, contains a cool carillon of bells made from Meissen porcelain. Inside the main complex, visit the ★★★ **Gemäldegalerie Alte Meister**

Dresden for Less

The Dresden-City-Card costs 21€ and is good for 48 hours. It affords unlimited access to all city trams, buses, and Elbe ferries and free access to many of Dresden's finest museums, along with reductions on sightseeing tours and cultural events.

(Old Masters Picture Gallery), a treasury of great European paintings that includes masterpieces like Raphael's *Sistine Madonna* (1513) and Vermeer's *Girl Reading a Letter at an Open Window* (c. 1659). Dresden china is an international byword, and the ★★ **Porzellansammlung** (Porcelain Collection) has centuries worth of the finest pieces. Historical timepieces and scientific instruments are exhibited in the ★ **Mathematisch-Physikalischer Salon** (Mathematics and Physics Salon), and in the **Rüstkammer** (Armory) are suits of armor, weaponry, uniforms, and other martial stuff from the 15th century onward. Be sure to take in the ★ **Nymphenbad,** an ornate ensemble of fountains and sculptures. ⏱ 4 hr. Theaterplatz 1. ☎ 0351/4914-2000. www.skd-dresden.de. Combined admission: 10€ adults; Porzellansammlung: 6€ adults; Rüstkammer: 3€ adults; Mathematisch-Physikalischer Salon: 3€ adults; free in all cases for kids 16 and under. Wed–Sun 10am–6pm. Tram: 1, 2, 4, 8, 9, 11, or 12

> *The Residenzschloss offers design elements that are as recent as postwar reconstruction and as old as 700 years.*

② ★ **Kathedrale Sanctissimae Trinitatis.**
Designed by Italian architect Gaetano Chiaveri, the Kathedrale Sanctissimae Trinitatis (Cathedral of the Holy Trinity, 1739–55) was originally the Catholic court church and holds the tombs of dozens of Saxony's royals. It is infused with Italianate baroque style, something Chiaveri encouraged by importing craftsmen from Italy. The great organ (1753) is the last work by Dresden master-builder

Gottfried Silbermann. ⏱ 15 min. Theaterplatz. ☎ 0351/484-4712. www.bistum-dresden-meissen.de. Free admission. Mon–Tues 9am–6pm, Wed–Thurs 9am–5pm, Fri 1–5pm, Sat 10am–5pm, Sun noon–4pm. Tram: 4, 8, or 9.

③ ★★ **Residenzschloss (Royal Palace).** The rambling former Residenzschloss comprises some elements that date back 700 years, some from the present day (reconstruction from the World War II bombing continues), and some from just about every period in between. Should you want to get a picture of the diamond-encrusted lifestyle of Saxony's former rulers, Poland's former Saxon monarchs, and assorted aristos, visit the rooms of the ★★ **Historisches Grünes Gewölbe** (Historical Green Vault) and the ★ **Neues Grünes Gewölbe** (New Green Vault), which are pretty much dripping with gold and silver, precious stones, amber cabinets, ivory statuettes, and more such stuff. A particularly lavish piece is the statue *Moor with Emerald Plate* (1724), by Balthasar Permoser, with added bling by Johann Melchior Dinglinger. You can view

Getting Around Dresden

If you plan to see more than the city's historic core, use the excellent tram, bus, and *S-Bahn* (city rail) lines operated by the public transportation authority, DVB (☎ 0351/857-1011; www.dvb.de). A ticket for use inside the central fare zone costs 1.90€ and is valid for transfers for up to 1 hour. Or, purchase a 24-hour pass, prices for which begin at 5€. Maps and tickets are available from automated dispensers outside Dresden Hauptbahnhof (main train station). Service is cut back after midnight.

> *Located in Dresden's former royal stables, the Verkehrsmuseum offers an amazing array of vintage cars, trains, trams, and more.*

different types of historical treasure in the **Kupferstich-Kabinett** (Print Room) and the **Münzkabinett** (Coin Room). Haul yourself up 221 steps inside the **Hausmannsturm** to enjoy fine city views from the tower's 37m-high (121-ft.) observation deck. ⏱ 2 hr. Sophienstrasse. ☎ 0351/4914-2000. www.skd-dresden. de. Admission 10€ adults; Historisches Grünes Gewölbe 10€ adults; Hausmannsturm 3€ adults; free in all cases for kids 16 and under. Wed–Mon

Dresden Music Festival

The annual **Dresdner Musikfestspiele** (☎ 0351/478-560; www.musikfestspiele. com) runs for 18 days in May and June. It dates back to 1978, when it began as a Communist-approved, toned-down revival of the lavish arts and music festivals the 18th-century Electors of Saxony had held in the city's baroque palaces and pavilions. It took off, and it has since developed into one of Germany's best-loved feasts of classical symphonic and chamber music, supported by a cast of opera, ballet, and jazz performances.

10am–6pm (Historisches Grünes Gewölbe until 7pm; Hausmannsturm Apr–Oct only). Tram: 1, 2, 4, 8, 9, 11, or 12.

④ kids **Verkehrsmuseum Dresden.** The Verkehrsmuseum (Transportation Museum) makes a great stop for kids who are going crazy on a steady diet of Dresden's baroque buildings. Housed in the Johanneum (1591), a former royal stables, the museum features vintage trams, steam engines, automobiles, model ships, and lots of other non-baroque stuff. ⏱ 1 hr. Augustusstrasse 1. ☎ 0351/86440. www.verkehrsmuseum-dresden.de. Admission 4.50€ adults, 2.50€ kids 6–16, 11€ families. Tues–Sun 10am–5pm. Tram: 1, 2, or 4.

⑤ ★ **Brühlsche Terrasse.** Take a short stroll eastward from Schlossplatz to Brühlscher Garten (Brühl Garden), along this pleasant raised riverside terrace (1747), dubbed the "Balcony of Europe." ⏱ 10 min. Tram: 4, 8, or 9.

⑥ ★★★ **Frauenkirche (Church of Our Lady).** Of all the many beautiful and historic buildings Dresden lost in the February 1945 firebomb deluge, the one it missed most was the Lutheran Frauenkirche. This baroque

> *The vast collection of sculptures at Dresden's Albertinum museum are a compelling testament to the area's rich artistic history.*

masterpiece (1743) has, like Dresden itself, been restored to life. Reconstructed with the aid of money donated from around the world, the church reopened in 2005, just in time for Dresden's 800th anniversary celebrations the following year. The Frauenkirche's restored dome, 93m (305 ft.) high and crowned by a golden cross, is once again a city symbol. ⏱ 1 hr. Neumarkt. ☎ 0351/6560-6100. www. frauenkirche-dresden.org. Free admission (donation requested). Mon–Sat 10am–6pm, Sun 1–6pm. Tram: 4, 8, or 9.

Dresden Ferries

Six small ferries (five passengers-only and one vehicular) operated by the city's public transportation authority, DVB (☎ 0351/857-1011; www.dvb.de), ply back and forth across the Elbe River at Dresden.

⑦ ★★★ Albertinum. Another large chunk of Dresden's artistic and cultural heritage is up for viewing here, in an 1880s neo-Renaissance building named after Saxony's 19th-century King Albert. In the ★★★ **Galerie Neue Meister** (Modern Masters Gallery) are paintings by many 19th- and 20th-century European artists. This is a good place to get into the Romantic, melancholy landscapes of Caspar David Friedrich (1774–1840), who lived and worked in Dresden for most of his career and is buried in the city's Trinitatisfriedhof (Trinity Cemetery). The ★ **Skulpturensammlung** (Sculpture Collection) covers a lot of ground; look for pieces by Balthasar Permoser (1651–1732), who created a lot of what makes Dresden special today. ⏱ 2 hr. Georg-Treu-Platz 2. ☎ 0351/4914-2000. www.skd-dresden. de. Admission 8€ adults; Skulpturensammlung 2.50€ adults; free in both cases for kids 16 and under. Wed–Sun 10am–6pm. Tram: 3 or 7.

⑧ Kreuzkirche (Church of the Cross). For more than 700 years, the Kreuzkirche, on the old market square, has been the home of the famous Kreuzchor (Cross Choir), Dresden's 150-strong boys' choir. It performs in a space that's a mix of medieval Gothic, 18th-century baroque, and Jugendstil (Art Nouveau) from around 1900. Choral concerts take place every Saturday at 5pm when the choir is in

> *Visitors to Dresden are greeted by the impressive sight of the gilded statue of the city's benefactor, Augustus the Strong.*

residence. ⏲ 20 min. Altmarkt. ☎ 0351/439-3920. www.kreuzkirche-dresden.de. Free admission to church; choral concerts: 5€–39€. Apr–Oct Mon–Sat 10am–6pm, Sun 1–5pm; Nov–Mar Mon–Fri 10am–4pm, Sat 10am–5pm. Tram: 1, 2, or 4.

⑨ ★ kids Deutsches Hygiene-Museum. To any parent, it may sound totally counterintuitive, but the German Hygiene Museum really should appeal to children. The exhibits, many of them hands-on, have more to do with anatomy, health, the senses, playing, working, and creating than with hygiene, but the museum was founded in 1912 by a health-care products entrepreneur, and the name has stuck. ⏲ 1 hr. Lingnerplatz 1. ☎ 0351/484-6400. www.dhmd.de. Admission 7€ adults, free for kids 16 and under. Tues–Sun 10am–6pm. Tram: 10 or 13.

⑩ Museum für Völkerkunde (Ethnology Museum). When Dresden's ruler Augustus the Strong needed somewhere to store his Japanese porcelain collection, he expanded a palace on the right (north) bank of the Elbe to house it. The Japanisches Palais (Japanese Palace, 1731) never did get the porcelain in the end, and the late-baroque palace now hosts the city's Museum für Völkerkunde, with its collection of 90,000 items collected over centuries from cultures around the world. ⏲ 1 hr. Palaisplatz 11. ☎ 0351/814-4840. www.voelkerkunde-dresden.de. Admission 4€ adults, free admission first Tues in month; free for kids 16 and under. Tues–Sun 10am–6pm. Tram: 4 or 9.

⑪ Goldener Reiter. Across the ★ **Augustusbrücke** (Augustus Bridge) from central Dresden, you'll find this gold leaf–embellished

Elbe Cruises

A compelling alternative to sightseeing within the city is a short cruise on the Elbe. Most tour boats that sail on the river under the flag of ★★ **Sächsische Dampfschiffahrt** (☎ 0351/866-090; www.saechsische-dampfschiffahrt.de) are antique paddle-steamers, their vintages ranging from 1879 to 1929. Departing from the company's dock on Terrassenufer, the side-wheelers ply upstream and down, on scheduled routes and fixed cruises that last from 1½ hours to all day. Tickets for the basic city tour are 12€ for adults and 6€ for kids 3–14.

Dresden Shopping

Antiques, modern and historical art, porcelain, handcrafted goods, and gift items
are the kind of things Dresden does best. If
you arrive in the city by train, you can hit the
Wiener Platz mall right outside Hauptbahnhof (main train station) before moving on
to the department stores and chain stores
on nearby Prager Strasse, then to the new
(2009) Centrum Galerie mall at the end of
this street, and then to Altmarkt-Galerie on
Altmarkt. A little farther along are upmarket
stores around Neumarkt. Cross over the
Elbe to the interesting and glamorous shops
on and around Königstrasse in the Innere
Neustadt district. Farther north, the Äussere
Neustadt district is the realm of offbeat and
alternative stores.

A store that's an attraction in its own right
is ★ **Pfunds Molkerei** (pictured), Bautzner
Strasse 79 (☎ 0351/808-080; www.pfunds.
de). The dairy, founded in 1879, has been
installed at this address since 1891, in a
building decorated with thousands of hand-
painted ceramic tiles. It sells cheese and
other dairy products, and has an upstairs
cafe-restaurant.

Dresden's celebrated Weihnachtsmarkt
(Christmas Market), at the colorful ★★ **Dresdner Striezelmarkt** (☎ 0351/160-9158; www.
striezel-markt.de), dates back to at least 1434,
making it one of Germany's oldest Christmas
markets. Some 250 stands are set up on and
around Altmarkt, and the market runs through
the 4 weeks leading up to Christmas.

Dresden Nightlife

A highlight for many visitors is a performance at the ★★★ **Semperoper** (Semper Opera House, 1841), Theaterplatz (☎ 0351/491-1705; www.semperoper.de), designed by architect Gottfried Semper. This magnificent opera house (pictured above) is home to the Sächsische Staatsoper (Saxon State Opera) and the Dresden Semperoper Ballett, accompanied by the Sächsische Staatskapelle (Saxon State Orchestra). The Dresdner Philharmonie (Dresden Philharmonic Orchestra; www.dresdnerphilharmonie.de) performs at the **Kulturpalast** (Culture Palace), Altmarkt (☎ 0351/486-6666; www.kulturpalast-dresden.de). Lighter classical fare is on offer at the **Staatsoperette Dresden,** Pirnaer Landstrasse 131 (☎ 0351/207-9929; www.staatsoperette-dresden.de), 5km (3 miles) southeast of the city center.

Mainstream plays (in German) are put on at the **Staatsschauspiel Dresden,** Theaterstrasse 2 (☎ 0351/491-3555; www.staatsschauspiel-dresden.de).

In the tourist zone south of the river, a decent mainstream dance club is **M.5,** Münzgasse 5 (☎ 0351/496-5491; www.m5-nightlife.de). The Äusser Neustadt district north of the river, around Görlitzer Strasse, Alaunstrasse, and Louisenstrasse, is a good bet for bars and nightlife venues. A student-oriented bar is **Cafe 100,** Alaunstrasse 100 (☎ 0351/273-5010; www.cafe100.de). For dance clubs in this area, head to **Groove-Station,** Katharinenstrasse 11–13 (☎ 0351/802-9594; www.groovestation.de), and neighboring **Downtown Dresden,** Katharinenstrasse 11 (☎ 0351/810-3923; www.downtown-dresden.de).

equestrian statue (1734) of Augustus II (Augustus the Strong), Duke of Saxony and king of Poland, and a key figure in Dresden's history. Though designed to evoke Roman role models, like that of 2nd-century A.D. emperor Marcus Aurelius, it lacks the latter's classical *dignitas.* It is, however, a widely recognized symbol of the city. Neustädter Markt. Tram: 4, 8, or 9.

⑫ kids **Museum für Sächsische Volkskunst.** Housed in a former hunting lodge, the Jägerhof (1569), the Museum für Sächsische Volkskunst (Museum of Saxon Folk Art) has all kinds of locally made antique craft items: woodwork, glass, fabrics, and more. The collection includes handmade Christmas ornaments from the Erzgebirge region (p. 164, ❹). Kids are sure to enjoy both these and the museum's thousands-strong ★ **Puppentheatersammlung** (Theater Puppet Collection). ⏱ 2 hr. Köpckestrasse 1. ☎ 0351/4914-2000. www.skd-dresden.de. Admission 3€ adults, free for kids 16 and under. Wed–Sun 10am–6pm. Tram: 3, 7, or 9.

Where to Stay & Dine

> *The elaborate and popular Taschenbergpalais Kempinski hotel sits inside a fully restored baroque palace that dates back to the 1700s.*

★★ **Art'otel** INNERE ALTSTADT
Original modern art is included in the room rate at this boutique hotel just off the main tourist drag, and there's chic international dining in the unlikely-sounding Factory restaurant. Ostra-Allee 33. ☎ 0351/49220. www.artotels.com. 174 units. Doubles 134€–200€ w/ breakfast. AE, DC, MC, V. Tram: 6 or 11.

★ **Italienisches Dörfchen** INNERE ALTSTADT
SAXON/CONTINENTAL Four restaurants occupy this rambling waterfront neoclassical pavilion (1911), constructed on the site of lodgings for Italian craftsmen. Theaterplatz 3. ☎ 0351/498-160. www.italienisches-doerfchen.de. Entrees 10€–21€. AE, DC, MC, V. Lunch & dinner daily. Tram: 4, 8, or 9.

★ **Kö5** INNERE NEUSTADT *SAXON/INTERNATIONAL*
A restored baroque townhouse from 1737 houses this family-run restaurant, with several differently styled dining rooms, sidewalk tables, and a winebar in the brick-arched cellar. Königstrasse 5A. ☎ 0351/802-4088. www.koe5.de. Entrees 10€–13€. No credit cards. Lunch & dinner daily. Tram: 4 or 9.

★★ **Las Tapas** INNERE ALTSTADT *SPANISH*
Tapas from a menu of 40-some variations flow about as profusely as the *vino* in this stone-floored Iberian-style wine tavern close to the Frauenkirche. An extended menu adds typical dishes like paella. Münzgasse 4. ☎ 0351/496-0108. www.las-tapas.de. Entrees 4€–17€. MC, V. Lunch & dinner daily. Tram: 4, 8, or 9.

★ **Martha Hospiz** ÄUSSERE NEUSTADT
In a 19th-century mansion, this Christian-run hotel has Biedermeier good looks. At street level there's the (separate) rustic restaurant Zum Kartoffelkeller (☎ 0351/817-6358). Nieritzstrasse 11. ☎ 0351/81760. www.martha-hospiz.de. 50 units. Doubles 103€–121€. AE, MC, V. Tram: 4, 6, 9, or 11.

★★ **Schloss Eckberg** RADEBERGER VORSTADT
Atmosphere is guaranteed—along with contemporary furnishings—in a magnificent 19th-century castle overlooking the Elbe River from a wooded north-bank estate. Bautzner Strasse 134. ☎ 0351/80990. www.schloss-eckberg.de. 84 units. Doubles 143€–295€ w/breakfast. AE, DC, MC, V. Tram: 11.

★★★ **Taschenbergpalais Kempinski** INNERE ALTSTADT The reconstructed facade of an 18th-century baroque palace hides Dresden's most opulent hotel, with rooms boasting classy contemporary design. Taschenberg 3. ☎ 0351/49120. www.kempinski.com. 214 units. Doubles 295€–450€. AE, DC, MC, V. Tram: 1, 2, 4, 8, 9, 11, or 12.

★★ **Villa Marie** BLASEWITZ *ITALIAN*
Creative cuisine emerges from the kitchen of this Tuscan-style villa, with a garden terrace overlooking the Blaues Wunder (Blue Wonder) bridge from 1893, upriver from the city center. Fährgässchen 1. ☎ 0351/315-440. Entrees 12€–25€. AE, MC, V. Lunch & dinner daily. Tram: 6 or 12.

REBUILDING DRESDEN

A City Rises from the Ashes of Its Own Destruction

BY GEORGE MCDONALD

THE FIRE-BOMBING OF DRESDEN BY ALLIED PLANES during the final weeks of World War II in Europe remains a painful and controversial subject to this day. When the city's air-raid sirens began to sound just before 10 o'clock on the evening of February 13, 1945, their fear-inducing wail foretold the imminent end to an estimated 25,000 lives, almost all of them civilians, and the loss of a rich cultural heritage in Germany's "Florence on the Elbe." Some 1,300 bombers struck the city over the next 2 days. Historians have variously described the bombing as everything from a fully justified attack on a military target in time of war to an action of little military value and questionable morality to a war crime.

Postwar Reconstruction

So complete was the devastation that postwar planners considered abandoning the site altogether and building a new Dresden at a different location. The first reconstruction efforts were undertaken by East Germany's Communist administration, which rebuilt key cultural institutions such as the Semperoper (Opera House). Much remained still to do when Germany was reunited in 1989, and despite considerable efforts and expenditure since then, decades more of work are needed. Even so, the old Dresden will never be fully re-created.

Slaughterhouse-5

At the time of the bombing, Dresden was crowded with German military personnel, civilians, refugees, concentration camp inmates, and Allied prisoners of war. Among the POWs was author Kurt Vonnegut, Jr. (1922–2007). Taken prisoner during the Battle of the Bulge in December 1944, Vonnegut was held at a meat-packing plant in Dresden. He survived the bombing of the city and was required to help with recovering charred corpses from the rubble. His controversial science-fiction novel *Slaughterhouse-Five* (1969) references (among other things) the events of February 1945.

The Frauenkirche

During the Cold War, the domed baroque Church of Our Lady (1743), one of the city's best-loved monuments, remained in ruins. The East German government left the hulk as it was as a reminder of the horrors of war, and of the threat from U.S.-British "aggression." Reconstruction began in 1993, and the church was reconsecrated for Dresden's 800th anniversary in 2005. Original pieces from the pile of rubble were used along with other materials. Financial and material assistance came from around the world, and included a new dome cross donated by Britain. The church has become a symbol of reconciliation.

Modern Architecture

Not all of the reconstruction efforts in Dresden have gone to restoration. Among the most striking works of modern and postmodern architecture in the city are the new Synagogue (2001), which stands on the site of the old one destroyed by the Nazis, and the transparent Volkswagen plant (pictured; 2002). Another piece of modern construction, the Waldschlösschen Bridge over the Elbe River, due to be completed in 2011, cost the Elbe Valley at Dresden its status as a UNESCO World Heritage site.

Eisenach

The birthplace of Johann Sebastian Bach and refuge of

Martin Luther, Eisenach (pop. 44,000) holds much of historical interest, without ever being reduced to the status of a "living museum." Just outside the town is the Wartburg, one of Germany's finest castles.

> *Detail of a stained-glass window in Wartburg Castle, where Martin Luther hid from the Holy Inquisition.*

START The Markt is a good place to start out. You can pick up information from the tourist office and take some time to peruse the handsome square. From the train station, head west on Bahnhofstrasse, turn left at Karlsplatz, then right on Goldschmiedenstrasse.

❶ ★ **Markt.** On Eisenach's central square stands the **Georgenkirche** (Church of St. George), where Johann Sebastian Bach was baptized and Martin Luther preached. The **Thüringer Museum** (☎ 03691/670-450; admission 2€; Mon–Fri 10am–6pm, Sat–Sun 10am–5pm), housed in the 18th-century Stadtschloss (Town Palace), has a collection of

Thuringian art, antiques, and applied arts such as porcelain, pottery, and glass. ⏱ 30 min.

❷ **Lutherhaus.** Martin Luther lived in this 15th-century timber-frame house while attending school in Eisenach between 1498 and 1501. ⏱ 30 min. Lutherplatz 8. ☎ 03691/29830. www.lutherhaus-eisenach.de. Admission 3.50€ adults, 2€ kids 7–18. Daily 10am–5pm.

❸ **Bachhaus.** The house where Johann Sebastian Bach (1685–1750) was born no longer exists. This 15th-century, timber-framed stand-in contains Bach family mementos and a collection of musical instruments, and there's a statue of the musical maestro outside. ⏱ 30 min. Frauenplan 21. ☎ 03691/79340. www.bachhaus.de. Admission 6.50€ adults, 3.50€ kids 6–18, 13€ families. Daily 10am–6pm.

❹ ★★ **kids** **Wartburg.** A UNESCO World Heritage site, Wartburg Castle is featured in Richard Wagner's opera *Tannhäuser.* Adolf Hitler described it as "the most German of German castles." The Wartburg is no Cinderella castle but rather a businesslike fortification that sits solidly on top of a long wooded hill, 180m (591

Eisenach for Auto Buffs

Eisenach was once a modest player in the world of automotive engineering. Automobiles were produced in Eisenach as long ago as 1898. Automobilewerk Eisenach's last product was East Germany's Wartburg auto, with its three-cylinder, two-stroke engine. Production ended in 1991. Wartburgs and other autos, both vintage and relatively modern, can be seen at **Automobile Welt Eisenach,** Friedrich-Naumann-Strasse 10 (☎ 03691/77212), a museum at the erstwhile plant.

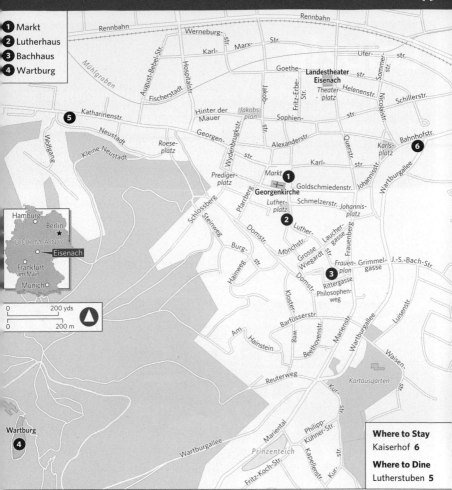

1 Markt
2 Lutherhaus
3 Bachhaus
4 Wartburg

Where to Stay
Kaiserhof **6**

Where to Dine
Lutherstuben **5**

ft.) high, 1.5km (1 mile) southwest of Eisenach. The Romanesque oldest part is called the Palas (Palace). Don't look for much design consistency—the castle was a work in progress for

Spending the Night in Eisenach

The stately **Kaiserhof** (Wartburgallee 2, 03691/88890, www.kaiserhof-eisenach.de) offers spacious, tastefully renovated rooms with comfortable furnishings for 112€–131€, including breakfast. For dinner try the Saxon fare at **Lutherstuben** (Katharinenstrasse 11–13, ☎ 03691/29390), a medieval-style restaurant with an open kitchen and tables with holes for beer pitchers.

centuries after its founding in 1067 by Count Ludwig of Thüringen, then was reconstructed in the 19th century and restored in the 1950s and 1960s to something like its 16th-century state. That was around the time (1521–22) when Protestant Reformer Martin Luther, in hiding here from the Holy Inquisition, which planned to burn him, first translated the Bible into German. Luther's modestly furnished study and living quarters, the Lutherstube, where he "fought the Devil with ink," has been restored and can be visited. ⏱ 2 hr. Auf der Wartburg. ☎ 03691/2500. www.wartburg-eisenach.de. Admission to palace and museum 8€ adults, 5€ kids 6–18, 21€ families; museum only 4€ adults, 2.50€ kids 6–18; 1€ photography permit; 5€ video permit. Bus: 3, 10, or 13.

Leipzig

The city of Bach might not have as much instant appeal as Dresden, but if you dig a little below the surface, you will find that Leipzig (pop. 516,000) has bags of character and plenty going for it. Invigorating nightlife (much of it aimed at a large student population), a cosmopolitan flavor, and established cafe and restaurant scenes go a long way toward making up for a dearth of A-list sights and attractions.

> Leipzig's Altes Rathaus is an impressive amalgam of oddly assembled architecture.

START Even if you arrive in Leipzig by car rather than by train, the huge Hauptbahnhof (main station) is a good place to start out. From here, tram lines 1, 3, 4, 7, 8, 9, 10, 11, 12, 13, 14, 15, 16, and 17, and a bunch of bus lines, fan out around town. To get to the first stop on this tour, walk south on Goethestrasse then west on Brühl, which intersects with Katharinenstrasse.

❶ ★★ **Museum der Bildenden Künste (Museum of Fine Arts).** The museum is housed in a striking, cube-shaped dollop of contemporary architecture (2005). Its painting collection is a tad thin on the modern period—look, though, for Otto Mueller's sultry *Lovers* (1919)—but has a good selection of European Old Masters, as well as Caspar David Friedrich's allegorical seascape *The Stages of Life* (1835). ⏱ 1 hr. Katharinenstrasse

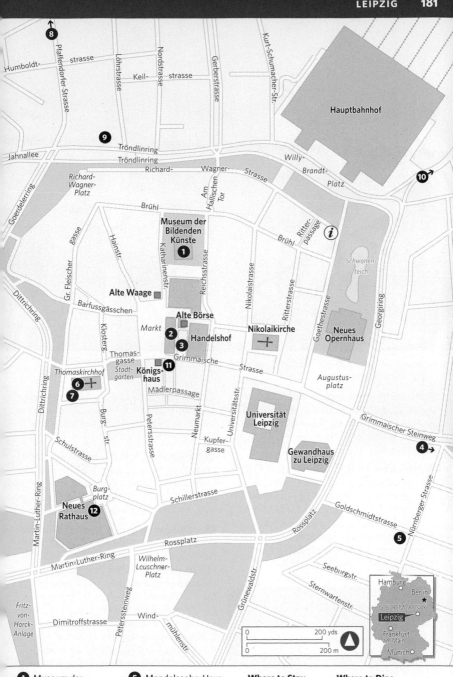

1. Museum der Bildenden Künste
2. Altes Rathaus
3. Naschmarkt
4. Museen im Grassi
5. Mendelssohn-Haus
6. Thomaskirche
7. Bach-Museum
8. Schillerhaus

Where to Stay

Fürstenhof **9**
Galerie Hotel
  Leipziger Hof **10**

Where to Dine

Auerbachs Keller **11**
Ratskeller **12**

> *The Belantis theme park is filled with fun rides and attractions, making it a dream destination for vacationing families.*

10. ☎ 0341/216-990. www.mdbk.de. Admission 5€ adults, 3.50€ kids 14–18; free admission on second Wed in month. Tues and Thurs–Sun 10am–6pm, Wed noon–8pm. Tram: 1, 3, 4, 7, 9, 12, 13, 14, or 15.

❷ Altes Rathaus (Old Town Hall). The Altes Rathaus (1556) is an attractive composition of arcades, gables, and an off-center tower. It was bombed during the war but has been carefully restored. Inside you'll find the **Stadtgeschichtliches Museum** (Museum of City History), chronicling Leipzig's cultural and political history. ◷ 30 min. Markt 1.

☎ 0341/956-1320. www.stadtgeschichtliches-museum-leipzig.de. Admission 4€ adults; free for kids 16 and under. Tues–Sun 10am–6pm. Tram: 9.

❸ Naschmarkt. The elegant old square behind the Rathaus contains the 17th-century baroque Alte Börse (Old Stock Exchange) and a statue of Johann Wolfgang von Goethe, who was a student in Leipzig in the 1760s. Tram: 9.

❹ ★ Museen im Grassi. Named after Italian-German merchant and philanthropist Franz Dominic Grassi (1801–80), the foundation houses three museums: the Museum für Angewandte Kunst (Museum of Applied Arts), the Museum für Völkerkunde (Museum of Ethnography), and the Museum für Musikinstrumente (Museum of Musical Instruments). ◷ 90 min. Johannisplatz 5–11. ☎ 0341/222-9100. www.grassimuseum.de. Admission: combined 12€ adults, single museum 5€ adults; free for kids 16 and under. Tues–Sun 10am–6pm. Tram: 4, 7, 12, or 15.

❺ Mendelssohn-Haus. The composer Felix Mendelssohn Bartholdy (1809–47), who

> *The spectacularly maintained Nikolaikirche offers amazing displays of its original 12th-century design.*

conducted Leipzig's Gewandhaus Orchestra, lived the last few years of his life in this house, which is now a museum of his life and music. ⏱ 30 min. Goldschmidtstrasse 12. ☎ 0341/127-0294. www.mendelssohn-haus.de. Admission 3.50€ adults, free for kids 16 and under. Tues–Sun 10am–6pm. Tram: 4, 7, 12, or 15.

Leipzig with Kids

Kids will likely be interested in the city's **Zoo Leipzig,** Pfaffendorfer Strasse 29 (☎ 0341/593-3385; www.zoo-leipzig.de), just north of the city center, internationally known for its breeding of carnivores. Equally aimed at kids are the rides at the theme park ★ **Belantis,** Zum Weissen Mark 1 (☎ 01378/403-030; www.belantis.de), close to Cospudener See, Leipzig's largest lake. Boat tours on the lake—which locals call the *Cossi*—onboard the small motor cruiser *Neuseenland* (☎ 0341/356-510; www.leipzigseen.de), depart from a dock at Markkleeberg on the eastern shore.

⑥ ★★ **Thomaskirche.** Johann Sebastian Bach was musical director at the Thomaskirche (Church of St. Thomas, 1496) between 1723 and 1750. The great baroque composer and musician is interred in the church, in front of the altar. Martin Luther preached here, and Mozart is among other famous composers

The Battle of Leipzig

On Leipzig's southeast edge, the ★ **Völkerschlachtdenkmal** (Battle of the Nations Monument), Prager Strasse (☎ 0341/241-6870; www.stadtgeschichtliches-museum-leipzig.de), recalls the decisive defeat a coalition of European and Russian armies inflicted on Napoleon at the Battle of Leipzig in 1813. With 520,000 soldiers engaged and 115,000 casualties sustained, the battle was Europe's largest and costliest until World War I. The monument is 91m (299 ft.) high, and if you are willing and able to climb its 500 interior steps, you arrive at a viewing platform with fine views over Leipzig.

to have performed in the church. ⏱ 30 min. Thomaskirchhof. ☎ 0341/2222-4200. www. thomaskirche.org. Free admission. Daily 9am–6pm. Tram: 9.

❼ ★★ Bach-Museum. The baroque Bosehaus (1711), in the shadow of the Thomaskirche, belonged to Johann Sebastian Bach's friend Georg Heinrich Bose, and the composer was a frequent visitor. It now contains this newly expanded, interactive, multimedia museum dedicated to Bach and his family. ⏱ 45 min. Thomaskirchhof 15–16. ☎ 0341/913-7202 www. bach-leipzig.de. Admission 6€ adults, free for kids 16 and under. Tues–Sun 10am–6pm. Tram: 9.

❽ Schillerhaus. Friedrich Schiller (1759–1805) wrote his poem *Ode to Joy* in 1785, while living in this farmhouse in the then village of Gohlis, now a north Leipzig suburb. Beethoven later incorporated the poem into his *Ninth Symphony.* ⏱ 30 min. Menckestrasse 42, Gohlis. ☎ 0341/566-2170. www.stadtgeschichtliches-museum-leipzig.de. Admission 3€ adults, free for kids 16 and under. Apr–Oct Tues–Sun 10am–6pm; Nov–Mar Wed–Sun 10am–4pm. Tram: 4.

> The interactive, multimedia Bach-Museum resides in the former home of the composer's great friend George Heinrich Bose.

Leipzig Shopping & Nightlife

There's a thriving trade in art, antiques, and antiquarian books in Leipzig. The **Galerie für Zeitgenössische Kunst,** Karl-Tauchnitz-Strasse 9–11 (☎ 0341/140-810; www.gfzk. de), is a privately owned gallery that displays international art. Dozens of antiques dealers are to be found around the city's core, and several antiquarian bookstores are in the elegant ★ **Mädler-Passage** (1914), Grimmaische Strasse 2–4 (☎ 0341/216-340; www.maedler-passage-leipzig.de). Leipzig's Hauptbahnhof (main train station) has its own superb mall, the underground ★ **Promenaden** (☎ 0800/226-6444; www.promenaden-hauptbahnhof-leipzig.de). During the 4-week *Weihnachtsmarkt* (Christmas Market), which dates from 1767, 250 stands are set up in front of the Altes Rathaus on the Markt.

The ★★ **Gewandhaus** (1981), Augustusplatz 8 (☎ 0341/127-0280; www.

gewandhaus.de), is home to the city's orchestra, the Gewandhausorchester, founded in 1781. Acclaimed opera company Oper Leipzig has its home in the nearby ★★ **Opernhaus Leipzig,** Augustusplatz 12 (☎ 0341/126-1261; www.oper-leipzig.de). Around the Markt are bars, cafes, and other entertainment options. **Nachtcafe,** Petersstrasse 39-41 (☎ 0341/221-0000; http://nachtcafe.tnc-group.de), plays soul, house, funk, and blues. **Spizz,** Marktplatz 9 (☎ 0341/960-8043; www.spizz. info), does jazz, boogie-woogie, reggae, pop, and disco. Student-friendly **Moritzbastei,** Universitätsstrasse 9 (☎ 0341/702-590; www.moritzbastei.de), is an all-in-one complex—concerts, cabaret, a pub, live bands, DJs, and more. Another multifunction spot is ★ **Werk II Kulturfabriek,** Kochstrasse 132 (☎ 0341/308-0140; www.werk-2.de), in south Leipzig.

Where to Stay & Dine

> *Featuring an elaborate ballroom and banquet hall, the opulent and luxurious Fürstenhof hotel has been one of Germany's finest destinations since 1913.*

★★ **Auerbachs Keller** ZENTRUM SAXON/ INTERNATIONAL Regional cuisine and beer flow in the stately Historic Rooms and the sprawling Big Room of this cellar from 1530, which has 16th-century murals representing the Faust legend. Grimmaische Strasse 2–4. ☎ 0341/216-100. www.auerbachs-keller-leipzig. de. Entrees 15€–35€. AE, MC, V. Lunch & dinner daily. Tram: 9.

★★★ **Fürstenhof** ZENTRUM-NORD A 1913 conversion of an 18th-century mansion is among Germany's best-regarded hotels, and all but dripping with luxury, most notably in the Serpentinsaal ballroom and banqueting room. Rooms are outfitted in a modern interpretation of neoclassical style. Tröndlinring 8. ☎ 0341/1400. www.starwoodhotels.com.

92 units. Doubles 160€–350€. AE, DC, MC, V. Tram: 15.

★ **Galerie Hotel Leipziger Hof** NEUSTADT-NEUSCHÖNEFELD Paintings and sculptures by local artists in the minimalist small-to-midsize rooms add bohemian appeal to an offbeat hotel behind a baroque facade. There is also an on-site art gallery. Hedwigstrasse 1–3. ☎ 0341/69740. www.leipziger-hof.de. 73 units. Doubles 87€–195€ w/breakfast. AE, DC, MC, V. Tram: 1, 3, 8, or 13.

★ **Ratskeller** ZENTRUM SAXON/CONTINENTAL Different rooms in this rambling, arched cellar restaurant have different styles and levels of service but the same emphasis on hearty helpings of local meat and fish dishes. Lotterstrasse 1. ☎ 0341/123-4567. www.ratskeller-leipzig.de. Entrees 12€–25€. AE, DC, MC, V. Lunch & dinner daily. Tram: 2, 8, or 9.

Communist Leipzig

Leipzig has been dubbed *Heldenstadt* (City of Heroes) for its role in toppling East Germany's Communist regime in 1989. The mostly 16th-century Gothic **Nikolaikirche** (Church of St. Nicholas), Nikolaikirchhof (☎ 0341/960-5270; www.nikolaikirche-leipzig.de), which still has elements of the original 12th-century Romanesque church, was one of the focal points of that peaceful overthrow. Entering the round-cornered building that now houses the ★ **Gedenkstätte Museum in der Runden Ecke,** Dittrichring 24 (☎ 0341/961-2443), is not something many East Germans cared to do during the Communist years. This was Leipzig headquarters and the underground bunker of the feared *Stasi* (Staatssicherheit/State Security) police and functionaries. Housed in a former insurance building (1913), the office where they kept their bulging files on "persons of interest" is now a memorial and museum and displays a peculiar mix of the grimness and mind-numbing banality of a police state.

Quedlinburg

In any competition for the title of Germany's most beautiful town, Quedlinburg (pop. 22,000), off the northern rim of the Harz Mountains, would be a definite contender. The entire Altstadt (Old Town), "an extraordinary example of a medieval European city," is a UNESCO World Heritage site, with a magnificent array of timber-framed houses with red-tiled roofs. Almost 800 buildings in the town are classified as historical monuments. Like icing on a colorful cake, the rocky Burgberg (Castle Hill) pinnacle bears the weight of a historic royal castle and church.

> Burgberg started off as a Saxon stronghold in the 10th century; the castle was expanded from the late 16th to the mid-17th centuries.

START The Markt (at Hohe Strasse and Marktstrasse) is a good place to start out. It's a walk of just 1km (⅔ mile) northwest from the train station to the Markt, by way of Bahnhofstrasse and Heiligegeiststrasse. There's no bus that goes all the way from the train station to the Markt, but bus line B goes about two-thirds of the way, to the stop on Neuer Weg, a ride of around 4 minutes.

❶ ★★ Markt. On one side of Quedlinburg's central square stands the Rathaus (Town Hall), a 16th-century Renaissance building. Outside is a statue (c. 1420) representing Charlemagne's heroic 8th-century Frankish knight, Roland. While you're here you can also pick up information from the tourist office, peruse the square, and, in summer, board a little road train for tourists. ⏱ 1 hr.

❷ ★ Finkenherd. Quedlinburg is filled with charming nooks and crannies, none more so than this district of higgledy-piggledy timber-framed houses just below the Burgberg. ⏱ 1 hr.

❸ ★★ Stiftskirche St. Servatius. Take the ramp up to the Burgberg to visit the restored, twin-towered, Romanesque Stiftskirche St. Servatius (Abbey Church of St. Servatius, 10th century). During the Third Reich, the Nazis took over the church and used it as an SS cult site, due to Heinrich Himmler's association of his own name (and possibly his person) with that of Heinrich I (876–936), the first king of Germany, who is interred alongside his wife Mathilde in the crypt. The Domschatz (Treasury) contains ecclesiastical objects made of gold, silver, and precious stones—some of the treasures, "liberated" by a U.S. Army officer in 1945, were recovered in 1990. ⏱ 1 hr. Schlossberg. ☎ 03946/709-900. Admission 4€ adults, 3€ kids 6–18, 21€ families. Apr Tues–Sat 10am–4:30pm, Sun noon–4:30pm; May–Oct Tues–Sat 10am–5:30pm, Sun noon–5:30pm; Nov–Mar Tues–Sat 10am–3:30pm, Sun noon–3:30pm.

❹ ★ Schlossmuseum. Facing St. Servatius is the Renaissance (16th–17th century) palace

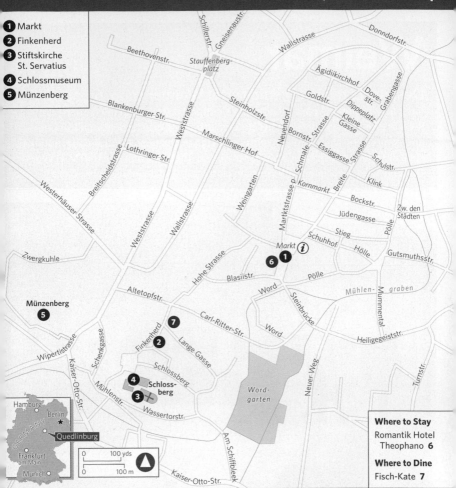

1 Markt
2 Finkenherd
3 Stiftskirche St. Servatius
4 Schlossmuseum
5 Münzenberg

Where to Stay
Romantik Hotel Theophano **6**

Where to Dine
Fisch-Kate **7**

of the Lutheran abbesses. Its rooms afford a good idea of the lavish style in which a religious leader with political connections could live. Be sure to stroll around the gardens on the hill and enjoy the grand views over Quedlinburg's roofs. ⏱ 1 hr. Schlossberg. ☎ 03946/905-681. Admission 4€ adults, 2.50€ kids 6–18, 9€ families. Apr–Oct Tues–Sun 10am–6pm; Nov–Mar Tues–Sun 10am–4pm.

5 ★ **Münzenberg.** Across a narrow valley from the Burgberg, this separate rocky outcrop is crowned by a perfect ensemble of pretty little 16th-century houses. ⏱ 1 hr. Off Wipertistrasse.

Spending the Night in Quedlinburg

The centrally-located **Romantik Hotel Theophano,** Markt 13-14 (☎ 03946/96300), offers homey, small rooms, some with exposed timber beams, and a (separate) cellar restaurant, all of which fits in perfectly with Quedlinburg's ambience. Doubles go for 89€–140€, including breakfast. For lunch or dinner, the seafood at **Fisch-Kate,** Lange Gasse 1A (☎ 03946/989-153), makes a nice change from Quedlinburg's ubiquitous traditional Saxon and German restaurants.

Weimar

Despite its relatively small size, Weimar (pop. 65,000) has played a notable part in Germany's cultural history. The town on the Ilm River was once a kind of German Camelot, attracting artists, poets, philosophers, and composers. During the enlightened reign of Duchess Anna Amalia, notables such as Goethe and Schiller were in residence. There are multiple UNESCO World Heritage sites associated with German classicism and Bauhaus architecture.

> *Goethes Wohnhaus, the former home of writer and philosopher Johann Wolfgang von Goethe, houses a museum dedicated to his work.*

START The Markt is a good place to start out. You can pick up information from the tourist office here. It's a walk of 1.6km (1 mile) south from the train station to the Markt, by way of Carl-August-Allee, Weimarplatz, Karl-Liebknecht-Strasse, Goetheplatz, and Geleitstrasse. There's no bus that goes all the way from the train station to the Markt, but bus nos. 1, 2, 3, 6, 7, and 8 go about two-thirds of the way, to Goetheplatz.

❶ ★★ Markt. Weimar's neo-Gothic Rathaus (Town Hall, 1841) dominates the town's main square. On the Markt's east side, the **Lucas-Cranach-Haus** is the left one of a pair of gabled 16th-century Renaissance town houses that father-and-son artists Lucas Cranach the Elder (1472–1553) and Lucas Cranach the Younger (1515–86) called home; it's now a theater.

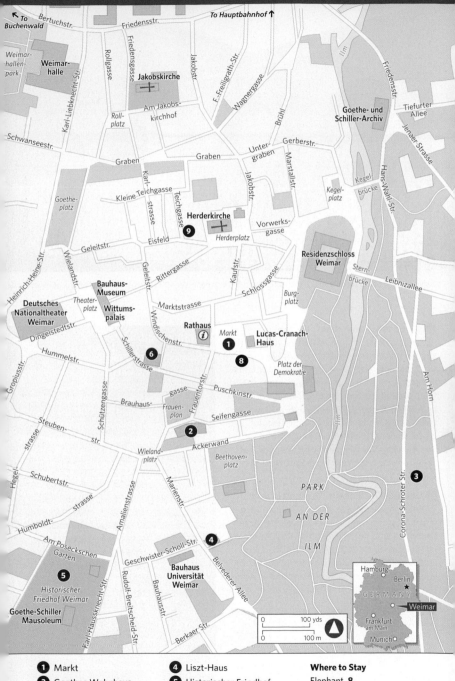

To Buchenwald
To Hauptbahnhof

Bertuchstr.
Friedensstr.
Weimarhallen-park
Weimar-halle
Rollgasse
Friedensgasse
Jakobskirche
Jakobstr.
F. Freiligrath-Str.
Wagnergasse
Ilm
Friedensstr.
Karl-Liebknecht-Str.
Am Jakobs-kirchhof
Roll-platz
Brühl
Goethe- und Schiller-Archiv
Tiefurter Allee
Schwanseestr.
Graben
Graben
Unter-graben
Gerberstr.
Jenaer Strasse
Goethe-platz
Kleine Teichgasse
Karlstrasse
Teichgasse
Herderkirche
Jakobstr.
Marstallstr.
Kegel-platz
Kegel-brücke
Hans-Wahl-Str.
Geleitstr.
Eisfeld
9 Herderplatz
Vorwerks-gasse
Residenzschloss Weimar
Stern-brücke
Leibnizallee
Heinrich-Heine-Str.
Wielandstr.
Bauhaus-Museum
Theater-platz
Geleitstr.
Rittergasse
Kaufstr.
Schlossgasse
Burg-platz
Deutsches Nationaltheater Weimar
Wittums-palais
Marktstrasse
Rathaus
Markt
Lucas-Cranach-Haus
Am Horn
Dingelstedtstr.
Schillerstrasse
Windschenstr.
6
1
8
Platz der Demokratie
Hummelstr.
Gropiusstr.
Frauen-plan-gasse
Frauentorstr.
Puschkinstr.
Schützengasse
Brauhaus-str.
Seifengasse
2
Steuben-strasse
Wieland-platz
Ackerwand
Beethoven-platz
Ilm
3
Hegel-str.
Schubertstr.
Marienstr.
Amalienstrasse
PARK
Corona-Schröter Str.
Humboldt-strasse
Am Poseckschen Garten
Geschwister-Scholl-Str.
4
AN DER
5
Historischer Friedhof Weimar
Bauhaus Universität Weimar
Belvederer Allee
ILM
Goethe-Schiller Mausoleum
Karl-Hausknecht-Str.
Rudolf-Breitscheid-Str.
Bauhausstr.
Berkaer Str.
0 — 100 yds
0 — 100 m

Hamburg
Berlin
GERMANY
Weimar
Frankfurt am Main
Munich

1 Markt

2 Goethes Wohnhaus

3 Goethes Gartenhaus

4 Liszt-Haus

5 Historischer Friedhof

6 Schillers Wohnhaus

Where to Stay
Elephant **8**

Where to Dine
Zum Zwiebel **9**

> *Weimar's Bauhaus Museum is a shrine to revolutionary post–World War I design and its biggest innovators.*

② ★★ Goethes Wohnhaus. German writer and philosopher Johann Wolfgang von Goethe lived in this baroque mansion from 1782 to 1832. It's now a shrine to, and museum of, his life and work, its rooms and library restored to their state at the time Goethe lived here. ⏱ 1 hr. Am Frauenplan 1. ☎ 03643/545-400. www. klassik-stiftung.de. Admission 8.50€ adults, 2.50€ students 16–20, free for kids 15 and under. Apr–Sept Tues–Fri and Sun 9am–6pm, Sat 9am–7pm; Oct Tues–Sun 9am–6pm; Nov–Mar Tues–Sun 9am–4pm.

③ Goethes Gartenhaus. Goethe's first Weimar residence was this cottage in a tree-shaded garden, set in a riverside park that he described as "infinitely beautiful." ⏱ 20 min. Im Park an der Ilm. ☎ 03643/545-400. www. klassik-stiftung.de. Admission 4.50€ adults, 2€ students 16–20, free for kids 15 and under. Apr–Oct daily 10am–6pm; Nov–Mar daily 10am–4pm.

④ Liszt-Haus. Composer and pianist Franz Liszt lived in this garden house from 1869 to 1886, and his recreated apartments can be visited. ⏱ 20 min. Marienstrasse 17. ☎ 03643/545-400. www.klassik-stiftung.de. Admission 4€ adults, 1€ students 16–20, free for kids 15 and under. Apr–Oct daily 10am–6pm; Nov–Mar daily 10am–4pm.

Buchenwald

Gedenkstätte Buchenwald is a memorial to those who suffered and perished in Buchenwald Konzentrationslager, one of Nazi Germany's notorious concentration camps. An estimated 250,000 Jews, Slavs, Roma (Gypsies), homosexuals, political opponents, prisoners of war, Jehovah's Witnesses, social misfits, criminals, and others were confined here from 1937 until 1945. The gate bears the slogan JEDEM DAS SEINE ("to each his own"). Buchenwald—the name means Beech Forest—was a "work camp," so far fewer inmates were killed here than at other camps. Nonetheless, 56,000 people died, and sadistic medical experiments were conducted on prisoners. Only fragments of the camp have been preserved. A memorial with several facets (sculpture, bell tower, and so on) has been raised over the graves of more than 3,000 victims. ⏱ 1 hr. ☎ 03643/4300. www.buchenwald.de. Free admission. Apr–Oct Tues–Sun 10am–6pm; Nov–Mar Tues–Sun 10am–4pm. Buchenwald is just outside the town to the northwest, a car ride of 10km (6 miles) on country roads, or take bus no. 6 from Weimar station.

⑤ Historischer Friedhof (Historical Cemetery). Johann Wolfgang von Goethe and Friedrich Schiller are interred side by side in oak caskets in the cemetery's Fürstengruft (Ducal Vault, 1826). ⏲ 15 min. Am Posekschen Garten. Free admission. Mar–Oct Wed–Mon 9am–1pm and 2–5pm; Nov–Feb Wed–Mon 10am–1pm and 2–4pm.

⑥ ★ Schillers Wohnhaus. German poet, philosopher, and playwright Friedrich Schiller wrote his play *Wilhelm Tell* and other works, while living in this baroque villa (1777) between 1802 and 1805. Some rooms have been restored as a monument and museum. ⏲ 30 min. Schillerstrasse 12. ☎ 03643/545-400. www.klassik-stiftung.de. Admission 5€ adults, 2€ students 16–20, free for kids 15 and under. Apr–Sept Tues–Fri and Sun 9am–6pm, Sat 9am–7pm; Oct Tues–Sun 9am–6pm; Nov–Mar Tues–Sun 9am–4pm.

Bauhaus in Weimar

Although well known for its heritage of 18th-century German classicism, as personified by Goethe and Schiller and reflected in the town's architecture, Weimar was, together with Dessau (p. 159, ⑦), a center of the post–World War I Bauhaus school of architecture and design. Among several hundred exhibits in the ★ **Bauhaus Museum,** Theaterplatz (☎ 03643/545-621; www.klassik-stiftung.de), are works by movement luminary Walter Gropius. In addition, Weimar hosts the **Bauhaus-Universität** (☎ 03643/580; www.uni-weimar.de), an offspring of the Bauhaus school. Several of this university's buildings were based on early 20th-century designs by Belgian architect Henry van de Velde. For more on the Bauhaus movement, see p. 466.

> *The Art Deco Elephant hotel is famous for its colorful rooms, fine dining, and list of luminous guests (including Johann Sebastian Bach).*

Where to Stay & Dine

★★★ Elephant ZENTRUM
The hotel with the memorable name holds memories of 3 centuries of distinguished guests (Bach among them), colorful rooms with an Art Deco look, and several dining options that are among the best in town. Markt 19. ☎ 03643/8020. www.starwoodhotels.com. 99 units. Doubles 125€–245€. AE, DC, MC, V.

★ Zum Zwiebel ZENTRUM *THURINGIAN*
Take a break from Weimar's cool classicism and academic airs in an inviting, brick-walled, bistro-style eatery, where beer and wine gush forth as accompaniments to local meat and fish dishes. Teichgasse 6. ☎ 03643/502-375. www.zum-zwiebel.de. Entrees 7€–13€. No credit cards. Lunch & dinner daily.

Dresden, Leipzig & Eastern Germany Fast Facts

Accommodations Booking Services
Call **Hotel Reservation Service** (☎ 0870/243-0003; www.hrs.de) from anywhere in Germany. Tourist offices around the region can arrange accommodations in local hotels, apartments, and B&Bs, as can tourist info points in train stations and airports.

ATMs/Cashpoints
The main towns in the region have multiple ATMs (*Geldautomaten*) from a range of banks. Even small towns are likely to have at least one bank with an ATM.

Dentists & Doctors
If you have a routine medical issue or dental problem while traveling in Germany, your hotel can likely either refer you to a local English-speaking doctor (*Arzt*) or dentist (*Zahnarzt),* or at least to one who speaks some English. You will be expected to provide proof of health/dental insurance (such as an EHIC card in the case of most residents of Europe), or you will be required to pay for treatment. In the event of minor injuries that require speedy treatment, go to the *Notaufnahme* (emergency) department of the nearest *Krankenhaus* (hospital). If injuries are serious or life-threatening, call the emergency doctor/ambulance number (see "Emergencies," below).

Emergencies
To call the police (*Polizei),* dial ☎ **110.** To report a fire or to summon an emergency doctor (*Notarzt*) or an ambulance (*Krankenwagen),* dial ☎ **112.**

Getting There
This region is served by the three large hub airports on its periphery—**Berlin-Tegel** (TXL) and **Berlin-Schönefeld** (SXF) to the north and **Frankfurt am Main** (FRA) to the southwest—and by three regional airports: **Leipzig/Halle** (LEJ), **Leipzig-Altenburg** (AOC), and **Dresden** (DRS). To a lesser degree, **Hannover** (HAJ) affords access to the region's western zone. All cities and most towns are well served by train. International highways enter the

region from Poland to the east and the Czech Republic to the southeast, and important German highways enter through Berlin, Hannover, and from the Ruhr. **Eurolines** (www.eurolines.com) international buses stop at Dresden.

Getting Around
In much of the region you can travel fast on the Autobahns (A roads) and *Bundesstrassen* (Broads); many of these roads also have a European (E) designation. Most rail service—and all InterCity trains, including the high-speed ICE trains—are operated by **Deutsche Bahn** (German Railways; ☎ 11861; www.deutschebahn.com). Some local and regional services are operated by private train companies. Regional bus service is not great, even in areas not well served by train—Thüringer Wald, the Erzgebirge, and the Elbsandsteingebirge, for instance—and is likely to be slow. Dresden, Leipzig, and Magdeburg have integrated public transportation networks of *S-Bahn* (metro) trains, trams, buses, and trains.

Internet Access
Many hotels have one or more terminals for the use of their guests. Wi-Fi or broadband is often available, though often for a fee. Most towns of any size are likely to have an Internet cafe, and cities like Dresden, Leipzig, and Magdeburg have many.

Pharmacies
In German, a pharmacy is an *Apotheke.* For cosmetics or toiletries, go to a *Drogerie.* Most pharmacies operate during normal shopping hours, and post details of the nearest 24-hour pharmacy. There are pharmacies in even the smallest towns.

Police
To report a lost or stolen article, such as a wallet or passport, visit the local police (*Polizei*) in your location. To call the police from anywhere in Germany, dial ☎ **110.**

Post Office
You'll recognize branches of **Deutsche Post**

(☎ 01802/3333; www.deutschepost.de) by their yellow sign with a black horn. Addresses of some centrally located post offices are as follows: Dresden: Webergasse 1 (Innere Altstadt); Leipzig: Grimmaische Strasse 30 (Zentrum); Magdeburg: Breiter Weg 203–206 (Altstadt); Weimar: Goetheplatz 7–8 (Altstadt). Post offices are open Monday to Friday 8am–6pm, Saturday 8am–noon.

Safety

The risk of being a crime victim in this region is very low, although slightly higher in the larger cities. In one respect, though, the region shares a characteristic of other parts of the old Communist East Germany: There is a small but definite risk of violence by neo-Nazi thugs against members of ethnic minorities and people of color. While this is by no means a common occurrence, and those involved in it are a tiny minority, their willingness to employ massive violence—up to and including homicide—makes it a risk that can't be ignored.

Taxis

In Dresden, call **Funktaxi Dresden** (☎ 0351/211-211); in Leipzig, **Funk-Taxi** 4884 (☎ 0341/4884); in Magdeburg, **Taxi-Ruf G** (☎ 0391/737-373); and in Weimar, **Taxi-Weimar** (☎ 03643/59555).

Telephones

Call ☎ 11837 for information and ☎ 11834 for international information. Dresden's area code is 0351; Leipzig's is 0341; Magdeburg's is 0391; Weimar's is 03643; and Eisenach's is 03691. Dial the area code when calling a town number from outside the town; you don't need to dial it when calling from inside town. There are public phones in many places—some accept coins and some take phone cards, available at post offices and newsstands.

Toilets

In some places you will find clean public toilets (Toilette in German; pronounced twah-*leh*-teh), many of them automatic and wheelchair-accessible; you need a .50€ coin to unlock the door. More convenient and widespread are toilets in cafes, bars, restaurants, hotels, malls, and some stores and at highway services and rest areas. Even if you are not obliged to pay, it is customary to leave the attendant .50€.

Tours

Many different boat-tours depart from Dresden, Magdeburg, and other towns along the Elbe River. On dry land, all kinds of tours are available in national parks and nature parks. Fans of modern architecture can head out on tours of the region's Bauhaus heritage (Dessau, Weimar). Musical fans have Johann Sebastian Bach (Leipzig, Weimar, Eisenach), Felix Mendelssohn Bartholdy (Leipzig), and Franz Lizst (Weimar). Religious folks—of the Protestant variety at any rate—can follow in Martin Luther's footsteps (Eisenach, Wittenberg). Lovers of literature can look up Johann Wolfgang von Goethe and Friedrich Schiller (Weimar). Art aficionados have Lucas Cranach the Elder (Weimar), Caspar David Friedrich (Dresden), and Canaletto (Meissen). Book specialty tours like these at local tourist information offices.

Visitor Information

Tourist offices are ubiquitous. They range from big visitor-centers in Dresden, Leipzig, and Magdeburg to tiny offices in some villages. In addition to those provided with the individual town listings in this chapter, some key tourist offices are as follows:

DRESDEN Tourist Information Kulturpalast, Schloss-strasse; ☎ 0351/5016-0160; www.dresden.de; Apr–Dec Mon–Fri 10am–7pm, Sat 10am–6pm, Sun 10am–3pm; Jan–Mar Mon–Fri 10am–6pm, Sat 10am–4pm, Sun 10am–2pm. **LEIPZIG** Tourist Information, Richard-Wagner-Strasse 1; ☎ 0341/710-4260; www.leipzig.de; Mon–Fri 9:30am–6pm (from 10am Nov–Mar), Sat 9:30am–4pm, Sun 9:30am–3pm. **EISENACH** Tourist Information, Stadtschloss, Markt 24; ☎ 03691/79230; www.eisenach.de; Mon–Fri 10am–6pm, Sat–Sun 10am–5pm. **QUEDLINBURG** Tourismus, Markt 1; ☎ 03946/905-624; www.quedlinburg.de; mid-Apr to mid-Oct Mon–Fri 9:30am–6:30pm, Sat 9:30am–4pm, Sun 9:30am–3pm; mid-Oct to mid-Apr Mon–Fri 9:30am–5pm, Sat 9:30am–2pm. **WEIMAR** Tourist Information, Markt 10; ☎ 03643/7450; www.weimar.de; Apr–Oct Mon–Sat 9:30am–7pm, Sun 9:30am–3pm; Nov–Mar Mon–Fri 9:30am–6pm, Sat–Sun 9:30am–2pm. Welcome Center, Friedensstrasse 1; Mon–Sat 10am–6pm.

5
Northern Bavaria & the Romantic Road

The Best of Northern Bavaria in 3 Days

This itinerary highlights Würzburg, Rothenburg ob der Tauber, and Nuremberg, three intriguing destinations in northern Bavaria and along the Romantic Road, so named for the quintessentially German scenery and quaint medieval towns you'll find along the way. Give yourself an unhurried day and night in each place. With this tour, you'll gain insight into the region's history and artistic wealth and be able to sample the distinctive foods and wines of Franconia, the name of the ancient duchy to which Würzburg belonged before it became part of Bavaria in 1803.

> PREVIOUS PAGE *Alte Mainbrücke in Würzburg, which marks the beginning of the Romantic Road.* THIS PAGE *Visiting the beautiful Marktplatz of Rothenburg ob der Tauber is like stepping into the Middle Ages.*

START **Würzburg is 117km (73 miles) southeast of Frankfurt on A3.** TRIP LENGTH **160km (99 miles).**

❶ ★★ **Würzburg.** The small, lively city of Würzburg, stretching out along the Main River, provides a graceful introduction to the charms of northern Bavaria and marks the beginning of the scenic **Romantic Road** (p. 206). Known for its historic buildings, its ancient university, and its dry, fruity white *Frankenwein* (Franconian wine), Würzburg offers visitors an intriguing medley of sights

1 Würzburg

2 Rothenburg ob der Tauber

3 Nuremberg (Nürnberg)

> *Würzburg is a great place to sample Franconian cuisine and local wines.*

that can easily be enjoyed in a day and a tasty sampling of the regional food and drink of Franconia.

The Altstadt (Old Town), on the east bank of the Main, is where you'll find the **Residenz,** one of the biggest and most impressive baroque palaces in Germany. Built as a residence for Würzburg's powerful prince-bishops, it has an interior embellished with rococo decorations and a staircase graced with a huge and justifiably famous ceiling fresco by Giovanni Battista Tiepolo. On an easy walk through the Altstadt you can also visit **Dom St. Kilian,** the city's Romanesque cathedral, the **Marienkapelle** (Chapel of Mary), a lovely Gothic hall-church, and the **Rathaus** (Town Hall), a 13th-century building with a 16th-century painted facade. Then cross over the nearly 500-year-old **Alte Mainbrücke** (Old Main Bridge) and climb the vineyard-covered slopes to **Festung Marienberg** (Marienberg Fortress), the hilltop

stronghold where the prince-bishops lived from the 13th century to until they moved across the river to the Residenz. The fortress is home to the Mainfränkisches Museum (Franconian Museum of the Main), worth visiting primarily to see the collection of remarkably expressive wood sculptures by Tilman Riemenschneider, a 16th-century master woodcarver whose genius is also on display in Rothenburg ob der Tauber's St.-Jakobs-Kirche (p. 238, ❹) and the Herrgottskirche near Creglingen (p. 208, ❸). ☺ 1 day. For information on Würzburg, including hotel and restaurant recommendations, see p. 240.

From Würzburg, take A3 east then A7 south to Rothenburg ob der Tauber (74km/46 miles).

❷ ★★★ **Rothenburg ob der Tauber.** For sheer historical panache, no other city in Germany can match Rothenburg ob der Tauber. A completely intact walled medieval city located on a high promontory above the Tauber River, Rothenburg offers visitors a fascinating glimpse into the Germany of the Middle Ages. This atmospheric time capsule is the major highlight along the Romantic Road (p. 206). From May through September you'll encounter hordes of visitors, but don't let that deter you from visiting this re-markable reminder of Germany's medieval past.

Taking the Train

You can easily reach all the towns on this tour by train. You will have to change trains on your way to Rothenburg ob der Tauber and Nuremberg.

For an excellent introduction, take a walk on a portion of the town ramparts from the massive 16th-century **Spitalbastei** (a medieval tower-gate) to the **Klingenbastei** (another tower-gate). Down at street level there are plenty of picturesque nooks and crannies to explore. You may or may not want to stop in at the **Mittel-älterliche Kriminalmuseum** (Medieval Crime Museum) to view its gruesome collection of torture instruments. More uplifting is the Gothic **St.-Jakobs-Kirche** (Church of St. James), with a masterful altarpiece created by the Würzburg sculptor Tilman Riemenschneider. The nearby **Reichsstadtmuseum** (City Museum) is housed in a 700-year-old nunnery. One particularly pretty spot with lovely views over the Tauber Valley is the **Burggarten** (Castle Gardens), a park on the site of the imperial castle. Also look for the photogenic corner known as the **Plönlein,** where two streets—an upper and a lower—converge. As you're walking, look for a Rothenburg specialty called *Schneeballen* (snowballs)—crisp, round pastries covered with powdered sugar. You can buy them in bakeries all across town. ⏲ 1 day. For information on Rothenburg ob der Tauber, including hotel and restaurant recommendations, see p. 236.

From Rothenburg ob der Tauber, take A7 south, A6 east, and A73 and B8 north to Nuremberg (109km/68 miles), about a 70-minute drive.

❸★★★ **Nuremberg (Nürnberg).** This fascinating city of half a million residents, large enough to offer several worthwhile attractions but small enough so that you can see everything in a day, has a nice urban buzz. As you wander through the streets of this ancient capital of the Holy Roman Empire, you'll find reminders of Nuremberg's brightest period—the Renaissance, when it bloomed as an artistic powerhouse—and its darkest, when it was the site of massive Nazi rallies.

Looming over the city is the **Kaiserburg** (Imperial Castle), the official residence of German kings and emperors from 1050 to 1571. The city's one must-see museum is the **Germanisches Nationalmuseum** (German National Museum), with collections that include works by Renaissance greats Albrecht Dürer and Veit Stoss. Dürer fans can also visit the **Albrecht-Dürer-Haus,** where he lived

> *The priceless carving* The Angelic Salutation *greets visitors to St.-Lorenz-Kirche in Nuremberg.*

from 1509 to 1528. Nuremberg's other acclaimed museum is the **Spielzeugmuseum** (Toy Museum), with three floors of historic and modern toys.

The colorful, cobblestoned **Hauptmarkt** (Market Square) is filled with stalls selling fruit, flowers, vegetables, and *Lebkuchen,* the delicious honey-and-spice cakes first created in Nuremberg over 500 years ago. On the square's eastern side is the **Frauenkirche** (Church of Our Lady), whose 16th-century mechanical clock chimes the noontime hour as figures appear and pay homage to Emperor Karl IV (Charles IV). Just off the Hauptmarkt is the **Altes Rathaus** (Old Town Hall). The nearby twin-towered **St.-Lorenz-Kirche** (Church of St. Lawrence) is the largest and most beautiful Gothic church in Nuremberg, while the 13th-century **St.-Sebal-dus-Kirche** (Church of St. Sebald), dedicated to Nuremberg's patron saint, represents the stylistic transition from late Romanesque to the early Gothic style. Nuremberg's wartime history comes chillingly alive in the **Dokumentation-szentrum Reichsparteitagsgelände** (Nazi Party Rally Grounds Documentation Center), housed in the former Nazi Congress Hall and providing a chronological overview of the rise of Nazism. ⏲ 1 day. For more on Nuremberg, including hotel and restaurant recommendations, see p. 226.

The Best of Northern Bavaria in 1 Week

The northern Bavaria section of this weeklong tour includes Regensburg and Nuremberg, while the Romantic Road section highlights Würzburg, Rothenburg ob der Tauber, Augsburg, and Füssen. Give yourself a day and night in each of these historic and architecturally rich places (allow 2 days in Nuremberg). The distances are not great between tour stops, usually around an hour by train or car.

> The 12th-century Steinerne Brücke crosses the majestic Danube and offers views of Regensburg, the largest medieval city in Germany.

START Regensburg is 125km (78 miles) north of Munich on B32R, A9, and A93. **TRIP LENGTH** 558km (347 miles).

❶ ★★ Regensburg. With some 1,400 medieval buildings, Regensburg is the largest medieval city in Germany and the only one to survive World War II completely intact. Situated at the northernmost point of the Danube River, it's a lovely little city slightly removed from the restless hustle of modern life and a

Where to Stay & Dine

Altstadt-Hotel
zum Hechten **9**

Feriengasthof
Helmer **8**

Fischerhütte **7**

Zum Schwanen **9**

> A view of Nuremberg's Altstadt from the turrets of the Kaiserburg, the one-time residence of German kings.

good place to begin your weeklong tour. In a day you can easily see, on foot, all of Regensburg's historic highlights. Instead of spending the night, you may prefer to move on to the larger and more cosmopolitan city of Nuremberg (p. 226) and spend 3 nights there.

Start your explorations with a panoramic view of the Altstadt (Old Town) from the 12th-century **Steinerne Brücke** (Stone Bridge) spanning the Danube. Nearby, a fragment of the 2nd-century **Porta Praetoria** marks the northern gate of the Roman camp established here in A.D. 79. A short walk away is the 13th-century **Dom St. Peter** (St. Peter's Cathedral), built in a French Gothic style and illuminated by beautiful stained-glass windows; visit at 10am on Sunday and you'll hear the cathedral's famous boys' choir. If you're interested in religious art, visit the **Diözesanmuseum St. Ulrich** (Diocesan Museum), beside the cathedral. You'll be wafted back to the Middle Ages

as you stroll down **Hinter der Grieb,** an ancient alleyway lined with 15th-century houses with high towers modeled on northern Italian architecture. Step into the **Alte Kapelle** (Old Chapel) to view the riot of rococo decoration. Regensburg's **Altes Rathaus** (Old Town Hall) is notable for its splendid Gothic hall. The **Historisches Museum** (History Museum) exhibits some fine paintings by masters of the Danube School. Finally, for a glimpse into aristocratic life, take a tour of **Schloss Thurn und Taxis** (Thurn und Taxis Palace). ⏱1 day. For information on Regensburg, including hotel and restaurant recommendations, see p. 232.

From Regensburg, take A3 northwest to Nuremberg (103km/62 miles).

❷ ★★★ **Nuremberg (Nürnberg).** One of Bavaria's larger cities, Nuremberg is a delight to explore, with museums, churches, and historic sites that chronicle its history, from capital of the Holy Roman Empire to headquarters for bombastic Nazi rallies. In order to take it all in, plan to spend 2 full days and 2 or 3 nights of your weeklong tour here. ⏱2 days. For information on Nuremberg, including hotel and restaurant recommendations, see p. 226.

Taking the Train

You can also follow this itinerary by train. You'll have to change trains at least once on your way to Rothenburg ob der Tauber, Augsburg, and Füssen.

> *Take in Renaissance-era fountains and statues during a stroll along Maximilianstrasse in Augsburg.*

From Nuremberg, continue northwest on A3 to exit 72, and then pick up B8 to Würzburg (112km/70 miles).

❸ ★★ **Würzburg.** Spend your fourth day and night in this lovely, lively wine town on the Main River, visiting the **Residenz,** its enormous baroque palace, and **Festung Marienberg,** its fortress-museum, and sampling the locally produced Franconian wines. ⏲ 1 day. For information on Würzburg, including hotel and restaurant recommendations, see p. 240.

From Würzburg, take A3 east then A7 south to Rothenburg ob der Tauber (74km/46 miles).

❹ ★★★ **Rothenburg ob der Tauber.** Though it can be packed in the summer, most visitors find this medieval walled city on the Romantic Road an enchanting place. Spend a full day strolling and soaking up the atmosphere, and overnight in one of Rothenburg's old inns. ⏲ 1 day. For information on Rothenburg ob der Tauber, including hotel and restaurant recommendations, see p. 236.

From Rothenburg, follow A7 south and then A8 east to Augsburg 184km (114 miles).

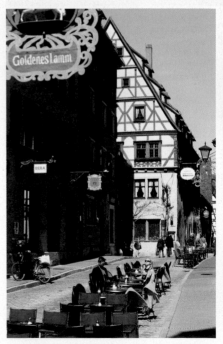

> *Rothenburg ob der Tauber's Altstadt has changed little in the past 400 years.*

> The Lechfall is an easy walk from beautiful Füssen, a city known for its quaint squares and medieval buildings.

5 ★★ **Augsburg.** Augsburg is a city of pleasant surprises. The largest town along the Romantic Road, with a population of about 260,000, it was founded some 2,000 years ago by the Roman emperor Augustus and reached its cultural zenith during the Renaissance, under the patronage of the enormously wealthy Fugger family (see "Meet the Fuggers," p. 220). A stroll through the city reveals an attractive urban landscape loaded with historic buildings, charming corners, and the lively ambience of a university town.

Rathausplatz, the city's main square, is dominated by the 17th-century **Rathaus** (Town Hall) and adjacent **Perlachturm** (Perlach Tower), capped by a distinctive dome called an "Augsburg onion." **St. Anna,** a former Carmelite monastery church dating from 1321, contains paintings by the great Renaissance artist Lucas Cranach the Elder. As you stroll along **Maximilianstrasse,** Augsburg's most elegant boulevard, admire its three large Renaissance-era fountains and duck into the **Schaezlerpalais** (Schaezler Palace) for a look at its baroque and Old Masters painting collections. In the tiny **Fuggerei Museum** you'll get a glimpse of life in the Fuggerei, the world's first almshouse complex, built in 1523 and still in use today. Augsburg's cathedral, **Dom St. Maria,** displays paintings by Hans Holbein the Elder and contains some of the oldest stained glass in Germany. ⊕ 1 day. For information on Augsburg, including hotel and restaurant recommendations, see p. 218.

From Augsburg, follow B17, B12, and B16 south to Füssen (108km/67miles).

6 ★ **Füssen.** The Romantic Road ends in this lovely hamlet situated in the foothills of the Bavarian Alps, 119km (74 miles) southwest of Munich. Divided by the rushing Lech River, Füssen has lovely squares and narrow cobblestoned streets flanked by medieval stone houses. It's a good place to headquarter while exploring the nearby fairy-tale castle of Neuschwanstein (p. 338, **2**).

The town's main attraction is ★ **Hohes Schloss** (High Castle), one of the finest late-Gothic castles in Bavaria and home of the Staatsgalerie, with its collection of Swabian artwork from the 1400s to the 1700s (Magnusplatz; ☎ 08362/903-146; admission 3€; Tues–Sun 11am–4pm, Nov–Mar 2–4pm). **Kloster St.-Mang** (Monastery of St. Magnus) was founded by Benedictine monks in the 8th century on the site where an Irish missionary named St. Magnus died in 750; its Romanesque crypt contains frescoes painted around A.D. 1000. In the early 18th century, Johann-Jakob Herkomer, a local architect, turned the church and monastery into a baroque gem with a strong Venetian influence. Access is through the **Museum der Stadt Füssen** (City Museum), which occupies the former state apartments of the abbey and displays artifacts relating to the history and culture of the region, including a collection of locally produced violins and lutes (Lechhalde 3; ☎ 08362/903-145; admission 3€; Tues–Sun 10am–5pm, Nov–Mar 1–4pm). The **Lechfall,** less than a kilometer (½ mile) south of town, is a popular walk from Füssen. A pedestrian footbridge spans the falls, located where the Lech River squeezes through a rocky gorge and rushes over a high ledge. ⊕ 1 day. Tourist information: Kaiser-Maximilian-Platz 1 and Rathaus, Lechhalde 3. ☎ 08362/93850 for both. www.fuessen.de.

Where to Stay & Dine

> Spectacular mountain vistas are as mouthwatering as the succulent seafood at the Fischerhütte restaurant, in Hopfen am See, near Füssen.

★ **Altstadt-Hotel zum Hechten** FÜSSEN Owned and operated by the same family for generations, this spotless guesthouse with blooming flower boxes exudes an air of old-fashioned Bavarian hospitality and features small to medium-size rooms, most with shower-only bathrooms. Ritterstrasse 6. ☎ 08362/91600. www.hotel-hechten.com. 35 units. Doubles 86€–98€ w/breakfast. AE, MC, V.

★★ kids **Feriengasthof Helmer** SCHWANGAU With its countryside setting near the spa gardens in Schwangau, this traditional, family-run guesthouse offers bright, modern rooms and is convenient to Neuschwanstein Castle. Mitteldorf 10 (4km/2½ miles east of Füssen). ☎ 08362/9800. www.hotel-helmer.de. 10 units. Doubles 64€–104€. MC.

★★ **Fischerhütte** HOPFEN AM SEE SEAFOOD/ BAVARIAN On a small lake with dramatic mountain views, this restaurant with an outdoor summer beer garden specializes in seafood from around the world: Alaskan salmon, North Atlantic lobster, French-style bouillabaisse, fresh local trout, and grilled halibut. Uferstrasse 16 (5km/3 miles northwest of Füssen). ☎ 08362/91970. www.fischerhuette-hopfen.de. Entrees 11€–25€. AE, MC, V. Lunch & dinner daily.

Zum Schwanen FÜSSEN SWABIAN/BAVARIAN Small and old-fashioned, Zum Schwanen (At the Swan) serves a flavorful blend of Swabian and Bavarian cuisine. Specialties include homemade sausage, roast pork, lamb, and venison. Service is helpful and attentive, and portions are generous. Brotmarkt 4. ☎ 08362/6174. Entrees 7€–18€. MC, V. Lunch & dinner Tues–Sat.

The Romantic Road

Germany's best known and most popular tourist route wends its way from the Main River south to the Alps, taking in a host of remarkable medieval towns and scenic landscapes. This is definitely a tour to do by car, so you can go at your own pace, linger wherever strikes your fancy, and enjoy the scenery. You can drive the length of the Romantic Road (Romantische Strasse) in as little as 3 days, but you might want to budget a couple of extra days to enjoy its unfolding charms.

> Cobblestone streets and the medieval buildings that populate them are the signature of charming Bad Mergentheim on the scenic Romantic Road.

START **Würzburg** is 117km (73 miles) southeast of Frankfurt. You can take the train, a 1½-hour trip, or go by car southeast on A3. TRIP LENGTH 375km (233 miles) and at least 3 days.

❶ ★★ **Würzburg.** With its fortress-crowned hilltop, famous baroque palace, and vineyard-covered slopes, this small, amiable city on the Main River is a good place to sample Franconian food and wine and spend your first night on the Romantic Road. ⏲ 1 day. For information on Würzburg, including hotel and restaurant recommendations, see p. 240.

From Würzburg, the Romantic Road leaves the Main River and follows B27 in a southwesterly direction to the town of **Tauberbischofsheim**, where you pick up B290 to **Bad Mergentheim** (47km/29 miles).

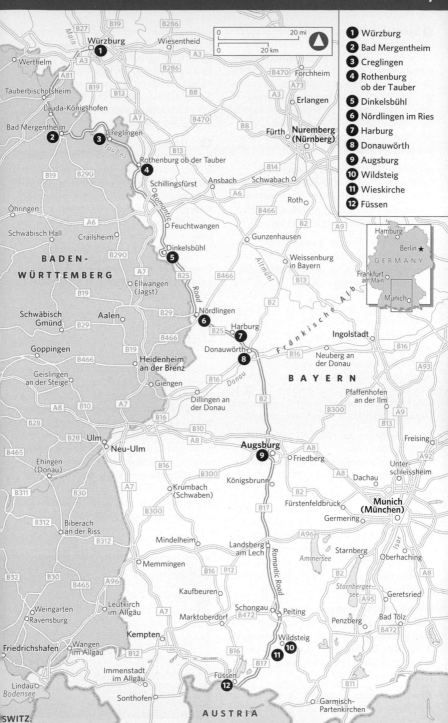

1. Würzburg
2. Bad Mergentheim
3. Creglingen
4. Rothenburg ob der Tauber
5. Dinkelsbühl
6. Nördlingen im Ries
7. Harburg
8. Donauwörth
9. Augsburg
10. Wildsteig
11. Wieskirche
12. Füssen

2 Bad Mergentheim. This spa town is worth a stop to stroll along its pretty cobbled streets and to have a quick look at the **Deutschordenschloss,** a palace used by royal princes and the medieval order of Teutonic Knights (Schloss 16; ☎ 07931/52212; www.deutschordensmuseum. de; Apr–Oct Tues–Sun 10:30am–5pm; Nov–Mar Tues–Sat 2–5pm, Sun 10:30am–5pm). ⏲ 20 min. Tourist information: ☎ 07931/57131; www. bad-mergentheim.de.

Another 28km (17 miles) brings you to Creglingen. To get there, head east from Bad Mergentheim on B19 and continue east on the smaller roads L2251, L1001, and L1003, following signs for Herrgottskirche.

3 Creglingen. The one must-see sight here is the famous carved wooden altar by Tilman Riemenschneider in the ★ **Herrgottskirche,** located on a signposted road about 2km (1¼ miles) south of Creglingen in the tiny hamlet of Herrgottstal (admission 2€, buy your ticket at the machine outside the church; Tues–Sun noon–4pm, closed Jan). Between 1505 and 1510, the master woodcarver from Würzburg created the extraordinarily beautiful altar with figures representing the Assumption of the Blessed Virgin and scenes from her life. ⏲ 15 min. Tourist information: An der Romantischen Strasse 14. ☎ 07933/631. www.creglingen.de.

From Creglingen, take St2268 to Rothenburg ob der Tauber (18km/11 miles). North and south of Rothenburg, the drive parallels the lovely, leafy Tauber Valley.

4 ★★★ Rothenburg ob der Tauber. For many, this amazing medieval walled city on the Tauber River is the undisputed star destination along the Romantic Road. Eminently strollable and delightfully atmospheric, it's also a good place to spend the night. ⏲ 1 day. For information on Rothenburg ob der Tauber, including hotel and restaurant recommendations, see p. 236.

If you have time, stop and spend an hour exploring Dinkelsbühl or Nördlingen im Ries, both located on B25 south of Rothenburg ob der Tauber. Driving time between the two towns, only 32km (20 miles) apart, is about 40 minutes.

5 ★ Dinkelsbühl. Situated in the idyllic Wörnitz Valley, Dinkelsbühl is an enchanting place surrounded by medieval stone walls and with a night watchman who still makes his rounds every evening. It won't take you more than an hour to stroll through this historic gem with its half-timber houses and beautiful late-Gothic **Münster St. Georg** (St. George Minster). ⏲ 1 hr. Tourist information: Marktplatz. ☎ 09851/90240. www.dinkelsbuehl.de.

6 ★ Nördlingen im Ries. Nördlingen im Ries has preserved its medieval Altstadt (Old Town) and is the only town in Germany with walls and battlements that can be walked all the way around. Climb the bell tower of **St. Georg,** a 15th-century hall church, for a bird's-eye view of this remarkable time capsule. ⏲ 1 hr. Tourist information: Marktplatz 2. ☎ 09081/84116. www.noerdlingen.de.

From Nördlingen im Ries, follow B466 south to Harburg (18km/11 miles), about a 20-minute drive.

7 ★ Harburg. The small town of Harburg in the Wörnitz Valley is another fine example of the historic towns laid out like gems along the Romantic Road. Medieval half-timber houses and baroque gabled residences crowd together in the Altstadt (Old Town) between the Wörnitz River and the castle. Towering above the town is the mighty **Schloss Harburg,** one of Germany best-preserved castles (☎ 09080/7823; Mar–Oct Tues–Sun 9am–5pm; guided tour in English by appointment only). You may want to stop here to dine at **Fürstliche Burgschenke** (☎ 09080/1504; www.burgschenke-harburg.de), the castle's restaurant. ⏲ 30 min. Tourist information: Schlossstrasse 1. ☎ 09080/96990.

Shortcuts

If you have limited time for your journey down the Romantic Road, you may want to drive directly from Rothenburg ob der Tauber (**4**) south on B25 to Augsburg (**9**), the next major destination on the Romantic Road, a distance of 184km (114 miles). You can further shorten your trip by driving from Augsburg south on B17 directly to Füssen (**12**), a distance of 108km (67 miles) and about 90 minutes.

> *The Romantic Road takes you through charming towns and scenic Bavarian countryside.*

Donauwörth is 12km (7 miles) south of Harburg on B25, about a 15-minute drive.

8 Donauwörth. Donauwörth, at the confluence of the Wörnitz and Danube rivers, grew from a fishing village to become a Free Imperial City. It's worth a quick stop to stroll down Reichsstrasse with its imposing patrician houses and to poke around in the Altstadt (Old Town). ⏱ 1 hr. Tourist information: Rathausgasse 1. ☎ 0906/789-151. www.donauwoerth.de.

From Donauwörth, take B2 south to Augsburg (44km/27 miles), about a 45-minute drive.

9 ★★ Augsburg. The largest town along the Romantic Road was founded some 2,000 years ago by the Roman emperor Augustus and reached its cultural zenith during the Renaissance. The Renaissance still defines the city's elegant urban core, especially along Maximilianstrasse. ⏱ 1 day. For information on Augsburg, including hotel and restaurant recommendations, see p. 218.

From Augsburg, follow B17 south to Wildsteig (87km/54 miles), a drive of about 1 hour 20 minutes.

10 Wildsteig. Located in the midst of a federally protected conservation area with rare plants and animals, this cluster of small mountain villages is home to a community of farmers who share their idyllic landscape with hikers and outdoor enthusiasts. Stop here for a glimpse of age-old mountain life and a deep breath of fresh Alpine air. ⏱ 30 min. Tourist information: Kirchbergstrasse 208. ☎ 08867/409. www.wildsteig.de.

The Wieskirche is located in Steingaden, 2.5km (1½ miles) beyond Wildsteig on a narrow, signposted road.

11 ★★★ Wieskirche. Rococo runs riot behind the tranquil facade of the most remarkable church on the Romantic Road. ⏱ 30 min. See p. 328, **3**.

Continue south on B17 to Füssen (21km/13 miles) a drive of about 25 minutes.

12 ★ Füssen. This attractive town marks the official end of the Romantic Road and makes a great headquarters for those visiting the fairy-tale castle of **Neuschwanstein** (p. 338, **2**). ⏱ 1 day. For information on Füssen, see p. 204, **6**; for hotel and restaurant recommendations in and around Füssen, see p. 205.

MEN (AND WOMEN) OF NOTE

Germany's Rich Musical History

BY DONALD OLSON

SOME OF THE GREATEST WORKS of Western music have been written by German composers. The roster includes Bach, Handel, Beethoven, Brahms, Mendelssohn, Schumann, and Wagner, as well as 20th-century greats Alban Berg and Kurt Weill. Over the centuries, Germany's musical traditions were fostered in convents, monasteries, and churches where composers were hired to write sacred songs, cantatas, and oratorios. Eventually, as opera houses and concert halls became a fixture in German cities, a wider public clamored for musical performances. Classical music remains an important part of German culture today and can be enjoyed in concert halls and opera houses throughout the country.

THE THREE B'S:
Beethoven, Bach & Brahms

JOHANN SEBASTIAN BACH (1685–1750). After stints as a violinist, an organist, and Kapellmeister, Bach arrived in Leipzig in 1723 and stayed for the rest of his life, writing more than 200 cantatas, the *Passion According to St. Matthew,* and the Mass in B Minor. He was prolific in other ways as well, fathering 17 children. Every June Leipzig celebrates Bach's musical legacy with the famous **Bachfest** (www.bach-leipzig.de), during which Bach's works are performed in the Thomaskirche, where he is buried.

LUDWIG VAN BEETHOVEN (1770–1827). Beethoven brought emotional depth and new tone colors to music in the transitional period between the classical (Bach) and romantic (Brahms) eras. He began his career by composing and performing piano concertos, and he continued to compose (9 symphonies, the opera *Fidelio*) even after his hearing began to deteriorate in the late 1790s. By the time his monumental Ninth Symphony was premiered in 1824, Beethoven was so deaf that he had to be turned around to see the tumultuous applause of the audience. Music lovers can visit his birthplace, **Beethoven-Haus,** in Bonn (p. 455, ❾).

JOHANNES BRAHMS (1833–1897). Like Beethoven, Brahms was a composer and virtuoso pianist who performed many of his own works. He composed for piano, chamber ensembles, and symphony orchestra and for voice and chorus. The structure of Brahms's music is rooted in the traditions of baroque and classical composition, but he developed musical themes in a way pioneered by Beethoven, creating bold new harmonies and melodies. Brahms's glory years as a composer were between 1868, when he premiered *A German Requiem,* his largest choral work, and 1885, by which time he had composed his four symphonies and the Piano Concerto No. 2. In 1889 Brahms made an experimental recording of his first Hungarian dance on the piano, the earliest recording made by a major composer.

Hildegard, Weill & Wagner

Hildegard of Bingen (1098–1179). Known as Saint Hildegard, this Benedictine abbess

is credited with more than 70 surviving compositions, one of the largest repertoires among medieval composers. Hildegard's music is monophonic, consisting of only one melodic line, but her soaring melodies go well beyond the range of medieval chant.

Kurt Weill (1900–1950). Although he was classically trained, it was Weill's musical-theater songs that became popular in Germany in the late 1920s and early 1930s. His best-known work, *The Threepenny Opera,* was written in 1928 in collaboration with the playwright Bertolt Brecht and contained his most famous song, "Mack the Knife." As a prominent Jewish composer, Weill became a target of the Nazis and was forced to flee Germany in 1933.

Richard Wagner (1813–1883). Known for his operas, Wagner pioneered advances in musical language that greatly influenced the development of European classical music. While in exile from Germany, fleeing creditors, Wagner completed his four-act *Ring* cycle and the opera *Tristan and Isolde,* and developed his revolutionary vision of operas as *Gesamtkunstwerk,* or "total artwork," a fusion of music, song, dance, poetry, visual arts, and stagecraft. His fortunes brightened when Ludwig II, king of Bavaria, became Wagner's patron. Wagner built the **Festspielhaus** in Bayreuth (p. 222, ❶), a theater where his operas—and only his—would be performed. He is buried in the garden at **Haus Wahnfried** (p. 224, ❹) in Bayreuth.

The Medieval Towns & Baroque Gems of Northern Bavaria

There are many lovely medieval and baroque towns and cities to visit in northern Bavaria, and this tour takes you to five of them. In addition to visiting Bayreuth, Bamberg, Nuremberg, Regensburg, and Passau, you can take a scenic drive into the forested heights of the beautiful Bavarian Woods. This itinerary is best done in a car.

> The New Palace at Schloss Eremitage, in Bayreuth, houses a cafe in summer and hosts painting exhibitions.

START Bayreuth is 92km (57 miles) northeast of Nuremberg on B14 and A9. TRIP LENGTH 524km (326 miles), including the Bavarian Woods drive, and at least 3 days.

❶ ★ **Bayreuth.** Built between the Richtelgebirge hills and the undulating plateau of Swiss Franconia, this small Bavarian city is indelibly linked with the composer Richard Wagner (1813–83). Music lovers have been flocking here for over a century to attend the annual festival of Wagner operas in the **Festspielhaus** (Festival Theater) and to visit the **Richard-Wagner-Museum** in Haus Wahnfried, where the composer lived and is buried.

More musical memorabilia is displayed in the **Franz-Liszt-Museum,** the house where the Hungarian composer and pianist (and Wagner's father-in-law) died in 1886.

But there was another outsize personality who shaped the city's cultural and architectural landscape long before Wagner's time. When the Margravine Wilhelmine (1709–58), sister of Prussian king Friedrich der Grosse (Frederick the Great), arrived in town, she sparked the most brilliant period in Bayreuth's history. A gifted artist, writer, composer, and decorator, Wilhelmine commissioned the building of the **Markgräfliches Opernhaus** (Margrave's Opera House), one of the finest

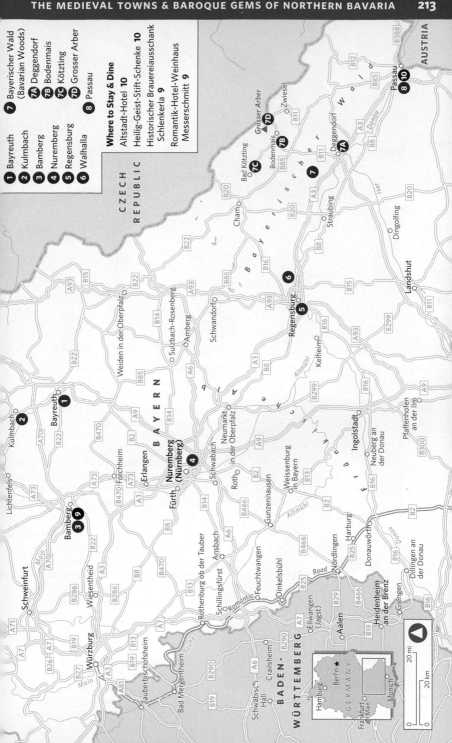

1 Bayreuth
2 Kulmbach
3 Bamberg
4 Nuremberg
5 Regensburg
6 Walhalla

7 Bayerischer Wald (Bavarian Woods)
7A Deggendorf
7B Bodenmais
7C Kötzting
7D Grosser Arber
8 Passau

Where to Stay & Dine
Altstadt-Hotel 10
Heilig-Geist-Stift-Schenke 10
Historischer Brauereiausschank Schlenkerla 9
Romantik-Hotel-Weinhaus Messerschmitt 9

> *The 13th-century* Bamberger Reiter *sculpture is just one of the many artistic wonders adorning the Kaiserdom in Bamberg.*

> *Franz Lenbach's portrait of renowned composer Richard Wagner is displayed in the museum that bears the artist's name.*

and best preserved baroque theaters in Europe, and the **Neues Schloss** (New Castle), in which nearly all the rooms have retained their original baroque and rococo decor. She also transformed **Schloss Eremitage** (Hermitage Castle) into a glamorous country seat with a grand English-style garden. ⊙ 1 day. For more on Bayreuth, including hotel and restaurant recommendations, see p. 222.

If your time is limited, head directly from Bayreuth to Bamberg (❸), 75km (47 miles) west on A70, about a 50-minute drive. Alternatively, round out your day in Bayreuth by visiting nearby Kulmbach, 23km (14 miles) north on B85, about a 25-minute drive.

❷ **Kulmbach.** Famous for its many breweries, the town of Kulmbach hosts a big beer festival each year in July and August. From the town's attractive **Rathaus** (Town Hall), with its rococo facade dating from 1752, you can walk to **Schloss Plassenburg** (Plassenburg Castle), a vast structure built between 1560 and 1570 (☎ 09221/82200; admission 4€; daily

> *Kulmbach prides itself on being a beer town; its summer Bierfest attracts about 100,000 people each year.*

Apr–Sept 9am–6pm, Oct–Mar 10am–4pm). Skip the castle's museum unless you're into tin figurines. ⏱ 30 min.

From Kulmbach, follow B85, B4, and St2190 southwest to Bamberg (63km/39 miles), about an hour's drive.

The Bamberg Christmas Crèche Circuit

One of Bamberg's most popular tourist events—the Bamberger Krippenweg (Bamberg Christmas Crèche Circuit)—takes place in the weeks before Christmas (the traditional season of Advent) and into the first week in January. The citywide event, held in 30 different churches, museums, and squares, features an unusual and highly original array of Christmas crib scenes, everything from life-size figures wearing traditional costumes to a tiny Holy Manger peep show.

❸ ★★ **Bamberg.** With more than 2,300 protected buildings ranging from the Romanesque to the baroque period, Bamberg has by far the largest and best-preserved **Altstadt** (Old Town) in Germany and has been recognized by UNESCO as a World Heritage site. In ages past, this small and remarkably pretty city built on seven hills around the Regnitz River was such an important ecclesiastical center that it was called the "Frankish Rome." On its narrow cobblestoned streets, lined with churches, palaces, and patrician mansions, you can survey an architectural legacy that spans some 1,000 years.

The interior of Bamberg's beautiful ★ **Kaiserdom** (Imperial Cathedral) shows a clear progression from the Romanesque to the Gothic styles, with an overall effect that is both sober and stately and enlivened by masterpieces of early Gothic sculpture, particularly the famous 13th-century equestrian statue known as the *Bamberger Reiter* (Knight of Bamberg; Domplatz; ☎ 0951/502-330; Mon–Fri 9:30am–5pm, Sat 9:30–11:30am & 12:45–5pm, Sun 12:30–1:45pm & 2:45–5pm). Have a look at the exterior of the

> The twin towers of St. Stephan's lavishly decorated baroque cathedral loom over the beautiful city of Passau in the early morning light.

Alte Hofhaltung (Old Residence), the former episcopal and imperial palace located beside the cathedral, and then spend a few minutes visiting the **Neue Residenz** (New Residence), a Renaissance and baroque palace with an impressive Emperors' Hall, Imperial Apartments, and a German Masters painting gallery (Domplatz 8; ☎ 0951/519-390; admission 4€; daily 9am–4pm, Apr–Sept until 6pm). Built between two stone bridges on a small island in the river, Bamberg's ★ **Altes Rathaus** (Old Town Hall), with its frescoed facade and adjacent half-timber house, is picture perfect. Be sure to sample Bamberg's traditional culinary delights, which include carp and *Rauchbier,* a smoked beer first brewed some 400 years ago. ⏱ 3–4 hr. Tourist information: Geyerswöthstrasse 3. ☎ 0951/297-6200. www.bamberg.info.

Nuremberg is 65km (40 miles) south of Bamberg on A73, about an hour's drive.

❹ ★★★ Nuremberg. ⏱ At least 1 day. For information on Nuremberg, including hotel and restaurant recommendations, see p. 226.

From Nuremberg, take A3 southeast to Regensburg (103km/62 miles).

❺ ★★ Regensburg. ⏱ 1 day. For information on Regensburg, including hotel and restaurant recommendations, see p. 232.

It's a short drive (12km/7miles) east on St2125 from Regensburg to Walhalla.

❻ Walhalla. More of a curiosity than a significant tourist attraction, Walhalla is a Doric temple built by King Ludwig I of Bavaria between 1830 and 1842 to honor all the great men in German history. Busts of once-famous soldiers, artists, scientists, and statesmen and plaques dedicated to lesser worthies line the interior of this marble memorial that sits high above the Danube, looking oddly incongruous in the Bavarian landscape. ⏱ 15 min. Free admission. Daily 10am–4pm (closed noon–2pm in winter).

The village of Deggendorf in the Bavarian Woods is 73km (45 miles) southeast of Walhalla on A3, a drive of about 1 hour.

❼ ★★ Bayerischer Wald (Bavarian Woods). One of the oldest mountain ranges in the world, the Bayerischer Wald is Europe's largest protected forest area and contains a national park within its boundaries. Mixed forests of pine, beech, and fir cover the summits and slopes of these low, rounded mountains. The southwestern edge of the forest begins in the Danube plain between Regensburg and Passau, and it's possible to visit the most scenic parts on a tour that takes about 4 hours. From Regensburg drive southeast on A3 for 73km (45 miles) to ❹ **Deggendorf,** turn north on B11 and follow it for 35km (22 miles) to the spa town of ❺ **Bodenmais,** where you turn west on St2132 for another 24km (15 miles) to ❻ **Kötzting.** Here you turn south and north on St2132 for 32km (20 miles) to the ❼ **Grosser Arber** (the highest peak of the Bavarian-Bohemian-mountain ridge), where a chairlift takes you up for a panoramic view of the entire region. ⏱ 4 hr.

Travel Tip

If your time is limited, drive directly from Regensburg (❺) southeast on A3 to Passau (❽), a distance of 119km (74 miles). The drive takes about 1¼ hours.

Continue southeast on A3 to Passau (94km/58 miles).

8 ★★ **Passau.** Situated on a peninsula between the Danube, Inn, and Ilz rivers, Passau is a small, quietly enchanting city with a long history and several venerable buildings and museums. In the 5th century St. Severinus established a monastery here, and in 739 an Irish monk named Boniface founded a bishopric. For many years Passau was the largest diocese of the Holy Roman Empire. Nearly all the major attractions are contained within the Altstadt (Old Town), a narrow tongue of land between the Danube and the Inn rivers, and you can easily walk to all of them.

Dominating the town are the twin towers of ★★ **Dom St. Stephan** (St. Stephan's Cathedral), a masterpiece of Italian baroque with a lavishly decorated interior. Its most unusual feature is the octagonal dome over the intersection of the nave and transept. The organ, rebuilt in 1928 with 17,388 pipes and 231 stops, is the largest in the world (Mon–Sat 8–11am and 12:30–6pm; 30-min. organ concerts May–Oct Mon–Sat noon, 3.50€; Thurs 7:30pm, 5€–8€). On Schrottgasse, have a look at the **Altes Rathaus** (Old Town Hall), with its 14th-century frescoed facade. Try to time your visit to coincide with the Glockenspiel, which plays daily at 10:30am,

2pm, and 7:25pm as well as at 3pm on Saturday. Inside, the huge knights' hall contains two large 19th-century frescoes illustrating incidents from the legend of the Nibelungen. The ★★ **Passauer Glasmuseum** (Glass Museum), housed in the historic Wilder Mann Hotel, displays an outstanding collection of Bavarian, Bohemian, and Austrian glassware from the 18th to the 20th centuries (Am Rathausplatz; ☎ 0851/35071; admission 5€; daily 1–5pm). Stroll down to the quayside along the Inn River and enjoy the ★ **Dreiflusseckspaziergang** (Three Rivers Walk). At the confluence of the three rivers, the green current of the Inn runs alongside the brown waters of the Danube before they finally mingle. From the Danube bank, on the far side of the promontory, a viewpoint looks across to the wooded, rocky height of **Veste Oberhaus,** an imposing hilltop fortress once used by Passau's powerful prince-bishops and now home to a local history museum (Veste Oberhaus 125; ☎ 0851/396-495; www.oberhausmuseum. de; admission 5€; daily 9am–5pm). On Mariahilfweg, high above the banks of the Inn and reached by a steep flight of stairs, stands **Wallfahrtskirche Mariahilf** (Pilgrimage Church of Mary), an early baroque abbey complex. ⏲ Half-day. Tourist information: Rathausplatz 3. ☎ 0851/955-980. www.passau.de.

Where to Stay & Dine

★★ **Altstadt-Hotel** PASSAU
Some of the rooms in this charming, comfortable hotel have a scenic view of the Danube, Ilz, and Inn rivers; an old-fashioned, traditional ambience prevails throughout. Bräugasse 23–29. ☎ 0851/931-5150. www.altstadt-hotel. de. 35 units. Doubles 89€–125€ w/breakfast. AE, DC, MC, V.

★ **Heilig-Geist-Stift-Schenke** PASSAU
BAVARIAN At this rustic inn (established 1358) you can order wine from the restaurant's own vineyard to accompany your hearty meal of fish, boiled rump steak, or roast suckling pig. Heiliggeistgasse 4. ☎ 0851/2607. www. stiftskeller-passau.de. Entrees 10€–18€. MC, V. Lunch & dinner Thurs–Tues.

Historischer Brauereiausschank Schlenkerla
BAMBERG *FRANCONIAN* Hearty Franconian specialties and *Rauchbier,* a local beer with a smoky aroma and taste, are served at long communal tables in this ancient, atmospheric dining room. Dominikanerstrasse 6. ☎ 0951/56060. www.schlenkerla.de. Entrees 7€–12€. No credit cards. Lunch & dinner Wed–Mon.

★★ **Romantik-Hotel-Weinhaus Messerschmitt**
BAMBERG For romantic atmosphere in the heart of the city, book a room in the old building (not the new wing) of this traditional inn; it has a fine restaurant and bistro where you can sample local wines with your meal. Lange Strasse 41. ☎ 0951/297-800. www.hotel-messerschmitt.de. 68 units. Doubles 137€–158€ w/breakfast. AE, DC, MC, V.

Augsburg

Many of the towns and cities along the Romantic Road
are medieval microcosms, but if Augsburg lays claim to any one era, it is the
Renaissance. In Roman times, Augsburg served as an important trading center
on the road to Italy, but it was under the influence of two local banking families,
the Welsers and the Fuggers, that it became a financial powerhouse and a major
player in the political fortunes of the Holy Roman Empire. The city suffered
serious damage in World War II, and much of it had to be rebuilt, but evocative
reminders of its Renaissance past remain. Augsburg is the Romantic Road's
largest city, with 260,000 inhabitants.

> Take some time to stroll down Maximilian-
strasse, Augsburg's most elegant street.

START From the train station, walk east on
Bahnhofstrasse to Rathausplatz (about a
10-min. walk).

❶ **Rathaus & Perlachturm.** Augsburg's main
square, Rathausplatz, is dominated by two
imposing Renaissance-era buildings. The
Rathaus (Town Hall), designed by Elias Holl and
completed in 1620, is one of the most significant secular buildings of the German Renaissance, famous for its sumptuous Goldener Saal
(Golden Hall), completely restored (like the rest
of the building) following its almost complete
destruction during World War II. The Augustus
Fountain in front of the Rathaus was dedicated
on the occasion of the town's 1,600th birthday
in 1594. The Perlachturm (Perlach Tower), next
to the Rathaus, is a soaring spire capped by a
distinctive dome called an "Augsburg onion."
If you climb to the top you'll be rewarded with
a marvelous view of the old town center. ⏱15
min. for Goldener Saal; 15 min. for view from Perlachturm. Am Rathausplatz 2. ☎0821/324-9180.
Rathaus and Goldener Saal open daily 10am–6pm;
tower open May–Oct 10am–6pm.

❷ **St. Anna.** This former Carmelite monastery
church dates from 1321. In 1518, Martin Luther
stayed in the adjoining monastery when he
was called to Augsburg to recant his Ninety-
five Theses before a papal emissary. The
church contains paintings by Lucas Cranach
the Elder and the chapel of the Fugger family.
Augsburg's city market is right next to the
church. ⏱15 min. Im Annahof 2. ☎0821/502-
070. Tues–Fri 10am–6pm.

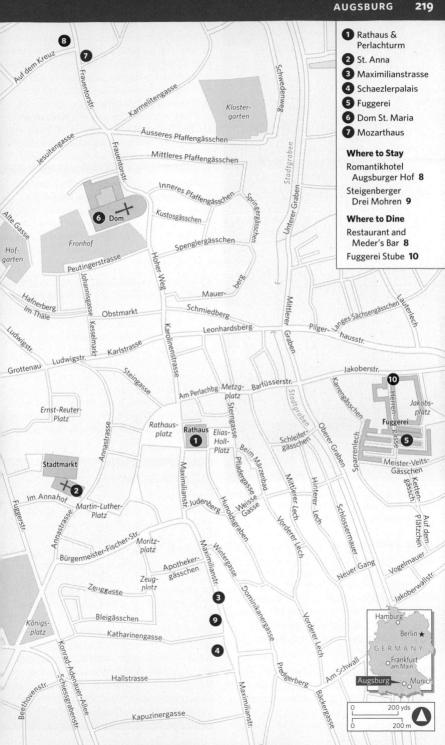

1 Rathaus & Perlachturm
2 St. Anna
3 Maximilianstrasse
4 Schaezlerpalais
5 Fuggerei
6 Dom St. Maria
7 Mozarthaus

Where to Stay

Romantikhotel Augsburger Hof 8
Steigenberger Drei Mohren 9

Where to Dine

Restaurant and Meder's Bar 8
Fuggerei Stube 10

> *The Fuggerei is a mazelike almshouse complex that includes 147 apartments, a park, and a fountain, all surrounded by gated walls.*

paintings by artists active in Augsburg and its vicinity. You probably won't recognize any of the names, but there are some evocative and interesting works on display. Be certain to visit the Festsaal, an enormous banqueting hall lavishly decorated with rococo frescoes, stuccowork, and wall paneling. The adjoining **Katharinenkirche** (St. Catherine's Church) has been transformed into the Stadtgalerie Katharinenkirche, a coolly serene gallery that displays a highly worthwhile collection of 15th- and 16th-century paintings by Augsburg and Swabian masters, including works by Holbein the Elder and a famous portrait of Jakob Fugger the Rich (the Fugger who founded the Fuggerei almshouses) by Albrecht Dürer. ⏱ 45 min. Maximilianstrasse 46. ☎ 0821/324-4125. Admission 7€. Tues–Sun 10am–4pm.

❺ ★★ **Fuggerei Museum.** The first almshouse complex in the world, and still in use today, the Fuggerei was built in 1523 by Jacob Fugger the Rich. Surrounded by walls and gates, the compound looks like a miniature town, with 67 identical cottages containing 147 small apartments, a church, a fountain, and a park. Residents pay an annual rent of 1€ (equivalent to one old Rhenish guilder) and are expected to pray three times a day for the soul of their Fugger benefactor. In the tiny but fascinating Fuggerei Museum you can poke your head

❸ **Maximilianstrasse.** This boulevard, ornamented by three large Renaissance-era fountains and lined with shops and fine patrician houses, stretches south from Rathausplatz. As you stroll along Augsburg's most elegant street, duck into the courtyard of the Damenhof, or Ladies' Court, of what was once the **Fugger-Stadtpalais** (Fugger City Palace, 1512– 15; Maximilianstrasse 36).

❹ ★★ **Schaezlerpalais.** This late-18th-century mansion, the most important rococo building in Augsburg, contains the **Deutsche Barockgalerie** (German Baroque Gallery), with its impressive collection of 17th- and 18th-century

Meet the Fuggers

By the late 1400s Augsburg had become a center of banking and finance thanks to the efforts of the Fuggers, an incredibly wealthy local family. The aptly named Jakob Fugger the Rich (1459–1529) served as the Holy Roman Empire's banker and was the financier behind the Hapsburgs, who were in debt to him to the tune of some 4 million ducats.

Jakob was so rich and so powerful that during an exchange with Charles I of Spain (Holy Roman emperor Karl V) he had the temerity to say, "It is well known that without my help, Your Majesty would no longer wear the crown of the Holy Roman Empire." It was this same Jakob who founded the Fuggerei, the world's first almshouse complex, in exchange for the daily prayers of its impoverished residents.

into the interior of one of the cottages and see how it looked in centuries past. ⏱15 min. Mittlere Gasse 13. ☎ 0821/319-8810. Admission 2€. Mar–Dec daily 10am–6pm.

❻ ★ Dom St. Maria (St. Mary's Cathedral). The south transept of Augsburg's cathedral contains some of the oldest stained-glass windows in Germany, dating from the 12th century. Much altered over the centuries, the cathedral features Gothic frescoes, paintings by Hans Holbein the Elder, and a 14th-century bronze door. ⏱15 min. Hoher Weg. ☎ 0821/316-6353.

❼ Mozarthaus. If you're a fan of Wolfgang Amadeus Mozart, you may want to take a look at this humble house where Wolfgang's father, Leopold, was born in 1719. Wolfie's great-grandfather Franz Mozart, a master mason reduced to penury, lived in the Fuggerei almshouse at Mittlere Gasse 14. Skip the small museum inside unless you're a musicologist. ⏱15 min. if you visit the museum. Frauentorstrasse 30. ☎ 0821/324-3984. Admission 2€. Tues–Sat 10am–5pm.

Where to Stay & Dine

> The beautiful boutique Romantikhotel Augsburger Hof offers visitors old-fashioned German sensibility and cutting-edge comfort at affordable prices.

Fuggerei Stube ALTSTADT SWABIAN
Locals come to this unpretentious local eatery to enjoy generous portions of regional specialties such as potato cream soup with mushrooms and calves' liver with apples, onions, and roast potatoes. Jakoberstrasse 26. ☎ 0821/30870. www.fuggerei-stube.de. Entrees 9€–18€; fixed-price menu 20€. AE, MC, V. Lunch & dinner Tues–Sat, lunch Sun.

★★★ Romantikhotel Augsburger Hof ALTSTADT Some rooms in this boutique-style hotel feature exposed beams; all have small but well-designed bathrooms with showers. Larger (and quieter) rooms face an inner courtyard. Auf dem Kreuz 2. ☎ 0821/343-050. www.augsburger-hof.de. 36 units. Doubles 90€–140€ w/breakfast. AE, DC, MC, V.

★★★ Romantikhotel Augsburger Hof's Restaurant and Meder's Bar and Grill ALTSTADT SWABIAN/INTERNATIONAL Fine food and impeccable service in a lovely lindenwood-paneled dining room make this hotel restaurant the perfect choice for a romantic dinner. Meder's Bar and Grill serves smaller-portion German dishes throughout the day. Auf dem Kreuz 2. ☎ 0821/343-050. Entrees 12€–25€. AE, MC, V. Lunch & dinner daily.

★★ Steigenberger Drei Mohren ALTSTADT Augsburg's only full-service luxury-oriented hotel has rooms that vary in size and level of finesse. The best are large and comfortable, with marble-clad bathrooms with big bathtubs. Maximilianstrasse 40. ☎ 0821/50360. www.augsburg.steigenberger.de. 102 units. Doubles 110€–196€. AE, DC, MC, V.

Bayreuth

Bayreuth was established in 1231 but really came into prominence during the 17th and 18th centuries, when it was the residence of the Margraves of Brandenburg-Bayreuth, and particularly during the reign (1735–58) of Margrave Frederick and Margravine Wilhelmine, sister of the Prussian king Friedrich der Grosse (Frederick the Great). Because of her, this small Bavarian city became one of Europe's capitals of baroque and rococo architecture. Bayreuth is also famous as the place where composer Richard Wagner lived, worked, and is buried. Nearly everything you'll want to see is related in some way to either Wilhelmine or Wagner.

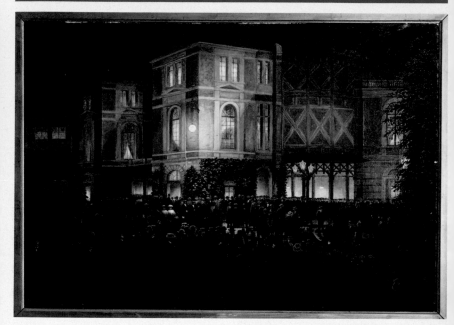

> *Designed for Richard Wagner, the 19th-century Festspielhaus is an architectural symphony.*

START Take bus no. 5 from the train station to the Festspielhaus.

① ★ **Festspielhaus.** The Holy Grail of Wagner performances, designed by Gottfried Semper to the specifications of the maestro himself, the Festival Theater opened in 1876 with the world premiere of *The Ring of the Nibelung* and still hosts a yearly festival of Wagner operas in July and August. The theater, with its concealed orchestra pit, is revolutionary in concept and an acoustic marvel, but not particularly attractive or comfortable—the seats have no padding, which can be a pain if you're sitting through a 5-hour opera. ⏲ 45 min. for guided tour. Festspielhügel. ☎ 0921/78780. Guided tour (German only, English leaflets available) 5€; tours Tues–Sun 10am, 10:45am, 2:15pm, 3pm (mornings only during festival). Closed Nov. Bus: 5.

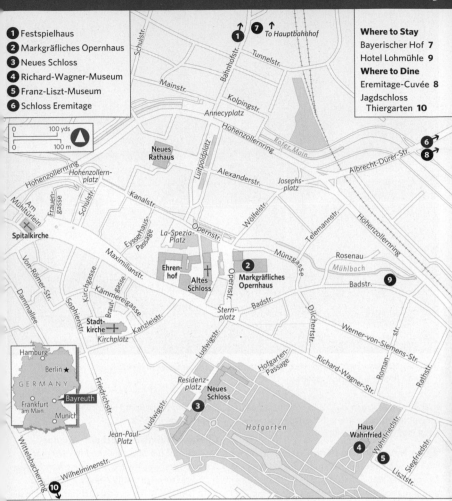

1 Festspielhaus
2 Markgräfliches Opernhaus
3 Neues Schloss
4 Richard-Wagner-Museum
5 Franz-Liszt-Museum
6 Schloss Eremitage

Where to Stay
Bayerischer Hof **7**
Hotel Lohmühle **9**
Where to Dine
Eremitage-Cuvée **8**
Jagdschloss
  Thiergarten **10**

Take bus no. 5 back to the Altstadt (Old Town) and continue the tour on foot.

2 ★★ **Markgräfliches Opernhaus (Margravial Opera House).** One of the finest and best-preserved baroque theaters in Europe, this old court opera house is stylistically the absolute antithesis of the Festspielhaus. Commissioned by Margravine Wilhelmine and built in the 1740s by Joseph Saint-Pierre, its ornate interior, constructed entirely of wood, glows with vivid reds and greens and is festooned with gilded stuccowork and chandeliers. The opera house was opened in 1748 by Wilhelmine's brother, Frederick the Great. Please note that the opera house is scheduled to close for a

Music in Bayreuth

Bayreuth's most eagerly awaited event is the **Richard-Wagner-Festspiele** (Richard Wagner Festival) in July and August. You have to apply for tickets at least a year in advance and prices are astronomical (tickets and info ☎ 0921/78780; www.bayreuther-festspiele.de). Bayreuth hosts another music festival in May that you might want to check out instead: **Musica Bayreuth** (tickets and info ☎ 0921/78780; www.musica-bayreuth.de).

> *Bayreuth's magnificent Markgräfliches Opernhaus was commissioned in the 1700s and remains one of the world's finest performance venues.*

major renovation in 2010 and will not reopen for public tours for some time. Opernstrasse 14. ☎ 0921/759-6922. Bus: 5.

3 ★★ Neues Schloss (New Castle). Commissioned by Margravine Wilhelmine and built by Joseph Saint-Pierre in 1753–54, this three-story, horseshoe-shaped structure combines classical lines with a rustic ground floor. The original baroque and rococo decor you'll see in nearly all the rooms was created by the Italian stucco-master Giovanni Battista Pedrozzi but greatly influenced by Wilhelmine, whose love of the airy, flowered rococo style is particularly evident in the Mirror Room, the Japanese Room, and the Music Room. On the ground floor there's a museum of Bayreuth porcelain. Wilhelmine, her husband, and her daughter are buried in the nearby Schlosskirche (Castle Church), a lovely single-aisle church painted rose pink and decorated with stuccowork. ⏲ 45 min. for guided tour. Ludwigstrasse 21. ☎ 0921/759-690. Guided tour (German only, English leaflets available) 5€. Apr–Sept Fri–Wed

9am–6pm (until 8pm Thurs); Oct–Mar Tues–Sun 10am–4pm. Bus: 14.

4 Haus Wahnfried/Richard-Wagner-Museum. This villa, designed for Wagner by Carl Wölfel, was destroyed during World War II and restored in the 1970s. Wagner lived here from 1874 onwards and it remained in his family until 1966. Collections in the museum include furniture, manuscripts, pianos, and Wagner's death mask, as well as items relating to the history of the Bayreuth Festival. Wagner and his formidable wife, Cosima (daughter of Franz Liszt), are buried in front of a small rotunda at the end of the garden. The museum is closed for renovation until at least 2013, but if you're a Wagnerite, you'll want to stop for a look at the exterior. ⏲ 15 min. Richard-Wagner-Strasse 48. ☎ 0921/757-280. www.wagnermuseum.de. Bus: 2.

5 Franz-Liszt-Museum. Franz Liszt (1811–86), the great Hungarian-born composer and piano virtuoso whose daughter Cosima married Wagner, died in this house in 1886. The

> *Schloss Eremitage served as a country palace for Margravine Wilhelmine, the sister of the 18th-century Prussian king Frederick the Great.*

museum shows the room where he died and displays memorabilia related to his life and work. No need to visit unless you're a fan. ⏱ 15 min. Waghnfriedstrasse 9. ☎ 0921/516-6488. Admission 1.60€. Daily Sept–June 10am–noon, 2–5pm; July–Aug 10am–5pm. Bus: 2 to Villa Wahnfried.

Take bus no. 22 or a taxi to reach Schloss Eremitage.

❻ Schloss Eremitage (Hermitage Castle). When Bayreuth's ebullient Margravine Wilhelmine was presented with a complex of buildings as a birthday present, she transformed the previous owner's faux-hermitage into a glamorous country palace with a grand English-style garden. Wilhelmine wrote her memoirs in the elaborately decorated Chinesisches Spiegelkabinett (Chinese Mirror Chamber); there's a curious grotto opening onto the inner courtyard and, in the elaborate gardens, the artificial ruins of a theater constructed in 1743. ⏱ 30 min. Eremitage 1, 4km (2½ miles) northeast of town. ☎ 0921/759-6937. Free admission to gardens, palace 3€. Apr–Sept Fri–Wed 9am–6pm, Thurs 9am–8pm; closed Oct–Mar. Bus: 22.

Where to Stay & Dine

★ Bayerischer Hof TOWN CENTER
Close to the train station and within walking distance of the Festspielhaus, this popular hotel has friendly service, pleasant rooms, a pool, a sauna, and a very good restaurant. Bahnhofstrasse 14. ☎ 0921/78600. www.bayerischer-hof.de. 50 units. Doubles 98€–120€. AE, DC, MC, V.

★★ Eremitage-Cuvée OUTSIDE BAYREUTH
FRANCONIAN/INTERNATIONAL Long revered as Bayreuth's finest restaurant—Cosima Wagner, Richard's notoriously hard-to-please wife, dined here—the Eremitage remains an elegant bastion of gastronomic excellence. Eremitage 6 (in Hotel Eremitage, about 4km/2½ miles northeast of town center). ☎ 0921/799-970. Entrees 14€–21€. MC, V. Lunch & dinner Tues–Sat.

★ Hotel Lohmühle TOWN CENTER
A cozy charm prevails in this hotel built in a traditional Franconian style beside the picturesque Mühlbach River; rooms are simply but comfortably furnished and the restaurant is one of the best in Bayreuth. Badstrasse 37. ☎ 0921/530-6469. www.hotel-lohmuehle.de. 42 units. Doubles 102€–172€ w/breakfast. AE, DC, MC, V.

★ Jagdschloss Thiergarten OUTSIDE BAYREUTH *CONTINENTAL/BAVARIAN* This former hunting lodge is home to two worthwhile restaurants, the upscale Schloss-Restaurant and the less expensive Jagdstübchen, which specializes in seasonal game dishes. Oberthiergärtner Strasse 36 (6km/4 miles south of Bayreuth). ☎ 09209/9840. Entrees 12€–26€. AE, MC, V. Lunch & dinner daily.

★★ Goldener Anker TOWN CENTER
This popular inn has hosted distinguished composers, singers, and conductors for more than 200 years. Rooms are furnished with fine antiques and Oriental rugs; each has a small bathroom. Opernstrasse 6. ☎ 0921/65051. www.anker-bayreuth.de. 42 units. Doubles 128€–198€ w/breakfast. AE, DC, MC, V.

Nuremberg

Nourenberc, as the city originally was known, dates back to about 1050. It was one of the wealthiest and most important cities in medieval Germany and the center of the German Renaissance. Then, after Hitler seized power in 1933, he made Nuremberg the Nazi Party's permanent convention and rally site, making it a prime target during World War II. Nearly all that is of interest to the visitor is found in Nuremberg's Altstadt (Old Town), one of the most successfully restored historic city centers in Germany. The entire Altstadt lies within a double wall of medieval fortifications, parts of which still remain. If you have only 1 day in Nuremberg, you'll have to pick and choose among the sights below.

> *A spectacular evening view of Nuremberg from the historic Kaiserburg.*

START Take the *U-Bahn* to the Opernhaus stop and walk north (about 5 min.) on Kartäusergasse to the Germanisches Nationalmuseum.

❶ ★★ **Germanisches Nationalmuseum.** Germany's largest and most important museum of German art and culture is Nuremberg's one must-see attraction. The German National Museum's collection covers the entire spectrum of German craftsmanship and fine arts from their beginnings to the present day, with extensive painting and sculpture sections that include works by Renaissance greats Albrecht Dürer and Veit Stoss and a self-portrait by Rembrandt. Everyday life in Germany through the ages is documented with domestic furnishings, folk objects, dollhouses, historic musical instruments, weapons, and the healing arts. ⏱ 2 hr. Kartäusergasse 1. ☎ 0911/13310. Admission 6€ adults, 4€ students/kids 6–16. Tues–Sun 10am–6pm (Wed until 9pm). *U-Bahn:* Opernhaus.

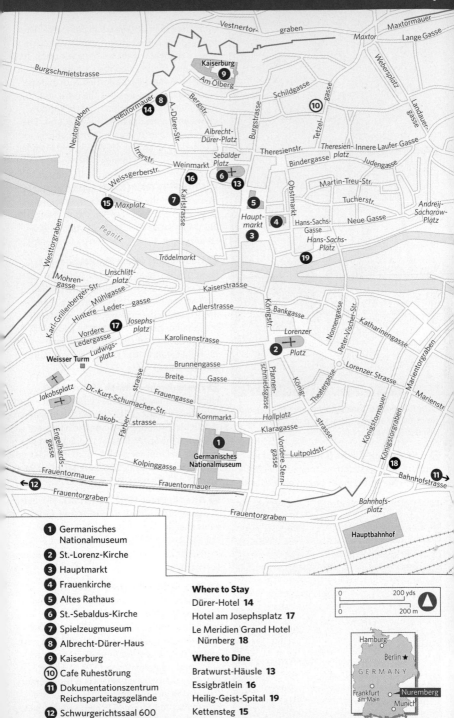

1 Germanisches
  Nationalmuseum
2 St.-Lorenz-Kirche
3 Hauptmarkt
4 Frauenkirche
5 Altes Rathaus
6 St.-Sebaldus-Kirche
7 Spielzeugmuseum
8 Albrecht-Dürer-Haus
9 Kaiserburg
10 Cafe Ruhestörung
11 Dokumentationszentrum
   Reichsparteitagsgelände
12 Schwurgerichtssaal 600

Where to Stay

Dürer-Hotel 14

Hotel am Josephsplatz 17

Le Meridien Grand Hotel
  Nürnberg 18

Where to Dine

Bratwurst-Häusle 13

Essigbrätlein 16

Heilig-Geist-Spital 19

Kettensteg 15

> *The towering St.-Lorenz-Kirche dates to 1270 and remains Nuremberg's largest and most ornate Gothic cathedral.*

took more than 200 years to complete. Twin towers flank the west portal with its sculptures depicting the theme of redemption, from Adam and Eve through the Last Judgment. Inside, soaring pillars adorned with expressive Gothic sculptures line the nave, and a magnificent stained-glass rosette window glows above the organ at the west end. The church contains two more remarkable works: *The Angelic Salutation* (1519), carved in linden wood by Veit Stoss, hangs over the entrance to the choir, and, to the left of the altar, a stone tabernacle by Adam Krafft (1496) presents likenesses of the sculptor and two apprentices. ⏱ 15 min. Lorenzer Platz 10. ☎ 0911/209-287. Mon–Sat 9am–5pm, Sun 1–4pm. *U-Bahn:* Lorenzkirche.

❸ **Hauptmarkt (Main Market Square).** Nuremberg's geographic and symbolic heart, this colorful, cobblestoned square is filled with flower, fruit, and vegetable stalls and a lively buzz. In the northwest corner stands the Schöner Brunnen (Beautiful Fountain), a pyramid-shaped stone fountain from 1396 that stands 18m (59 ft.) high. *U-Bahn:* Lorenzkirche.

❹ **Frauenkirche (Church of Our Lady).** Here, every day at noon, a gilded 16th-century mechanical clock called the Männleinlaufen (Little Men Running) chimes the hours as figures of the seven Electors appear and pay homage to Emperor Karl IV. ⏱ 10 min. East side of Marktplatz. ☎ 0911/206-560. Mon–Sat 9am–6pm, Sun 12:30–6pm. *U-Bahn:* Lorenzkirche.

❺ **Altes Rathaus (Old Town Hall).** The oldest part of the Altes Rathaus dates from 1340; a later section, completed in 1622, marks the architectural transition from Renaissance to baroque style. Rathausplatz. *U-Bahn:* Lorenzkirche.

❻ **St.-Sebaldus-Kirche (Church of St. Sebald).** Consecrated in 1273, this church (dedicated to Nuremberg's patron saint) represents the stylistic transition from late Romanesque to early Gothic styles. The nave and west choir are Romanesque; the larger east choir, consecrated in 1379, is Gothic. Between the two east pillars is a 16th-century Crucifixion group dominated by a life-size crucifix by Veit Stoss. ⏱ 15 min. Sebalderplatz.

❷ ★ **St.-Lorenz-Kirche (Church of St. Lawrence).** The largest and most beautiful Gothic church in Nuremberg was begun in 1270 and

Travel Tip

If you don't want to explore on your own, a guided 2½-hour walking tour (9€) of the city center departs daily from the tourist information office at the Hauptmarkt, and from mid-March through October a small sightseeing train (daily 10:30am–4pm; 6€) runs between the Hauptmarkt and all the major sights on a 40-minute tour (German commentary, English translations available). The Altstadt is easily walkable, but if you wish to explore beyond the old town you can buy a *Tages Ticket* (day ticket), good for one full day on Nuremberg's bus, tram, and *U-Bahn* (subway) system, for 3.80€.

> *The Spielzeugmuseum is a kid's dream come true, featuring dollhouses and train sets among its many exhibits.*

☎ 0911/214-2516. Daily Mar–May 9:30am–6pm, June–Sept 9:30am–8pm, Oct–Feb 9am–4pm. *U-Bahn:* Lorenzkirche.

⑦ ★★ kids Spielzeugmuseum (Toy Museum). Nuremberg is a major toy center, and toys—both hand- and machine-made—fill all three floors of this museum. Exhibits include a large collection of dolls and dollhouses, optical toys (such as peep shows, magic lanterns, and stereoscopes), and model trains and other miniature vehicles. Objects on the top floor illustrate the history of toys since 1945, including Barbie dolls and LEGO blocks. ⏱ 45 min. Karlstrasse 13–15. ☎ 0911/231-3164. Admission 5€ adults, 2.50€ students/kids 6–16. Tues–Fri 10am–5pm, Sat–Sun 10am–6pm. Bus: 36 to Hauptmarkt.

⑧ ★ Albrecht-Dürer-Haus. One of the great German artists of the Renaissance, Albrecht Dürer lived in this half-timber two-story house from 1509 to 1528. Built in 1420, it's the only completely preserved Gothic house left in Nuremberg. Exhibits are devoted to Dürer's life and works, original etchings and woodcuts, and copies of Dürer's paintings. ⏱ 15 min. Allbrecht-Dürer-Strasse 39. ☎ 0911/231-2568. Admission 5€, tour 2.50€. Tues–Sun

10am–5pm (Thurs until 8pm), Mon (July–Sept only) 10am–5pm; guided tour in English Sat 2pm. Tram: Tiergärtnertor.

⑨ ★ Kaiserburg (Imperial Castle). Looming above the city from its hilltop at the northern edge of the Altstadt, the Kaiserburg was the official residence of the German kings and emperors from 1050 to 1571. With their heavy oak beams, painted ceilings, and period Gothic furnishings, the great Rittersaal (Knights' Hall) and the Kaisersaal (Imperial Hall) look much as they did 500 years ago. A fine view of the roofs and towers of Nuremberg can be seen from its terraces. The Kaiserburg Museum contains antique weaponry, armor, and paintings. ⏱ 1 hr. Burgstrasse. ☎ 0911/244-6590. Admission: Combined ticket for all attractions 6€ adults, 5€ students, free for kids 15 and under. Daily Apr–Sept 9am–6pm, Oct–Mar 10am–4pm. Tram: Tiergärtnertor.

⑩ Cafe Ruhestörung. This popular spot has a pleasant patio where you can order coffee, a drink, a sandwich, or a light meal. Tetzelgasse 21. ☎ 0911/221-921. 4.50€–8€.

> *Nuremberg's vast Hauptmarkt is magically transformed into Christkindlesmarkt from Advent Sunday to Christmas Eve each year.*

⑪ ★★★ Dokumentationszentrum Reichsparteitagsgelände. I strongly recommend a visit to the Dokumentationszentrum Reichsparteitagsgelände (Nazi Party Rally Grounds Documentation Center) because it provides a chronological overview of the rise of Nazism and its subsequent horrors in a compelling format. A modern glass corridor now pierces the upper level of Albert Speer's Nazi Congress Hall and houses an exhibition that chronicles the ruthless misuse of power under National Socialism. Bayernstrasse 110. ☎ 0911/231-5666. Admission 5€ (includes audio-guide in English). Mon–Fri 9am–6pm, Sat–Sun 10am–6pm. Tram: 6 or 9 to Docu-Zentrum stop. Bus: 36, 55, or 65 to Docu-Zentrum.

⑫ Schwurgerichtssaal 600 (International Military Tribunal). Here, in room 600, a specially remodeled courtroom, 21 of the surviving leaders of the Third Reich stood trial in November 1945 for crimes against humanity. Afterward, ten were hanged. The building still serves as a courthouse, so tours are available on weekends only. Fürther Strasse 110. ☎ 0911/231-5421. Tour 2.50€. Tours (in German only) Sat–Sun 1–4pm. *U-Bahn:* Bärenschanze.

Nuremberg's Christmas Market

From Advent Sunday to December 24, Nuremberg's Hauptmarkt becomes the setting for the Christkindlesmarkt, the oldest Christmas fair in Germany, held here for some 400 years. The Christmas fair transforms Hauptmarkt into a small town of stalls selling tree ornaments, handicrafts, candies, fruitcakes, tinsel, and *Glühwein* (hot red wine spiced with cloves and cinnamon).

Nuremberg has been the capital of *Lebkuchen* since the early 15th century, when these delicious honey-and-spice cakes evolved into their round shape. Many consider Lebkuchen Schmidt, Zollhausstrasse 30 (☎ 0911/89660; www.lebkuchen-schmidt.com), to be the best Lebkuchen store in Nuremberg.

Franconian Fare

Nuremberg is in a region called Franconia, known for its hearty and relatively uncomplicated cuisine. The city is famous for its finger-size *Rostbratwurst* (roasted bratwurst), made of pork and various spices and then broiled on a charcoal grill. Your bratwursts may come with sauerkraut or rye bread with very hot mustard. Seasonal game and fish dishes also are staples in restaurants serving Franconian fare.

Where to Stay & Dine

> The Bratwurst-Häusle serves up its specialty on signature pewter plates.

★ **Bratwurst-Häusle** ALTSTADT FRANCONIAN The most famous bratwurst house in the city serves original, grilled Nürnberger Rostbratwurst (6, 8, 10, or 12 pieces) on pewter plates; Lederer Pils, a local beer, is a good accompaniment. Rathausplatz 1. ☎ 0911/227-695. www. die-nuernberger-bratwurst.de. Entrees 7€–12€. AE, MC, V. Lunch & dinner Mon–Sat. *U-Bahn:* Lorenzkirche.

Dürer-Hotel ALTSTADT This pleasant, modern hotel stands near the city wall and offers medium-size rooms with smallish, functional bathrooms; ask for a room overlooking the back garden. Neutormauer 32. ☎ 0911/214-6650. www.altstadthotels.com. 107 units. Doubles 140€–200€ w/breakfast. AE, DC, MC, V. *Tram:* Tiergärtnertor.

★★ **Essigbrätlein** ALTSTADT FRANCONIAN/ CONTINENTAL The city's most ancient restaurant, dating from 1550, serves an ever-changing, seasonally adjusted menu with many nouvelle recipes. The traditional specialty is *Essigbraten,* roast loin of beef marinated in vinegar. Weinmarkt 3. ☎ 0911/225-131. Reservations required. Entrees 24€–28€; fixed-price meals 42€–86€. AE, DC, MC, V. Lunch & dinner Tues–Fri, dinner Sat. Closed Jan 1–15, 2 weeks in Aug. *Bus:* 36 to Hauptmarkt.

★ kids **Heilig-Geist-Spital** ALTSTADT FRANCONIAN Carp, pork knuckles, *Sauerbraten,* and seasonal venison with noodles and berries are specialties at this historic wine house, in business for 650 years. More than 100 wines are available. Spitalgasse 16. ☎ 0911/221-761. www.heilig-geist-spital.de. Entrees 10€–14€. AE, DC, MC, V. Lunch & dinner daily. *Bus:* 46 or 47 to Spitalgasse.

★★★ **Hotel am Josephsplatz** ALTSTADT Small, reasonably priced, and ever so charming, this little gem is sophisticated and up-to-date with all its amenities yet old-fashioned and traditional in its decor and friendly, personalized service. Rooms are large and comfy and there's a charming roof terrace. Josephsplatz 30–32. ☎ 0911/214-470. www.hotel-am-josephsplatz.de. 36 units. Doubles 115€ w/breakfast. AE, MC, V. *U-Bahn:* Weisser Turm.

Kettensteg ALTSTADT FRANCONIAN/INTERNATIONAL This restaurant, bar, and beer garden beside the river in a romantic corner of the Altstadt has a limited menu (curried chicken, *Wiener Schnitzel,* bratwursts, salads) but a lively ambience. Maxplatz 35. ☎ 0911/221-081. Entrees 8€–13€. No credit cards. Lunch & dinner daily. *Bus:* 36 to Maxplatz.

★★ kids **Le Meridien Grand Hotel Nürnberg** ALTSTADT Built before World War I, this grand hotel retains much of its unique Art Nouveau atmosphere and boasts the largest guest rooms in the city. Bahnhofstrasse 1–3. ☎ 800/543-4300 in North America, or 0911/23220. www.starwoodhotels.com/ lemeridien. 186 units. Doubles 170€–400€. AE, DC, MC, V. *U-Bahn:* Hauptbahnhof.

Regensburg

One of Germany's best preserved medieval cities,
Regensburg started as a Celtic settlement called Radespona around 500 B.C. In
A.D. 79 the Romans conquered the Celts and turned the settlement into a major
Roman garrison town called Castra Regina that became their power base on
the upper Danube. In the 7th century, the town became the center from which
Christianity spread over southern Germany and into central Europe via the
Danube. Regensburg reached its zenith at the beginning of the Gothic era; its
most remarkable buildings date from that period.

> The nearly 900-year-old Steinerne Brücke spans the Danube River and rests on 16 imposing stone arches.

START Take any of the bright yellow buses
marked "Altstadt" found along
Maximilianstrasse next to the train station to
the city's medieval Altstadt (Old Town).

❶ ★★ Steinerne Brücke (Stone Bridge).
Built between 1135 and 1146, this stone span
over the Danube rests on 16 arches. Walk to
the middle for a wonderful view of the roofs
and church spires of the Altstadt. The 14th-
century gateway at the end of the bridge is
flanked by the huge roof of a 17th-century salt
loft. Thundorferstrasse on the Danube.

② 🍖 **Historische Wurstküche (Historic
Sausage Kitchen).** This famous wurst
stand at the end of Steinerne Brücke has
been in business for over 850 years and
is the best place in town for delicious
Regensburger sausages cooked over a
beechwood fire. Thundorferstrasse 3.
☎ 0941/466-210. 7€–10€.

❸ **Porta Praetoria.** The ancient, arched Prae-
torian Gate, now in fragments embedded in a
wall behind the cathedral, is the most

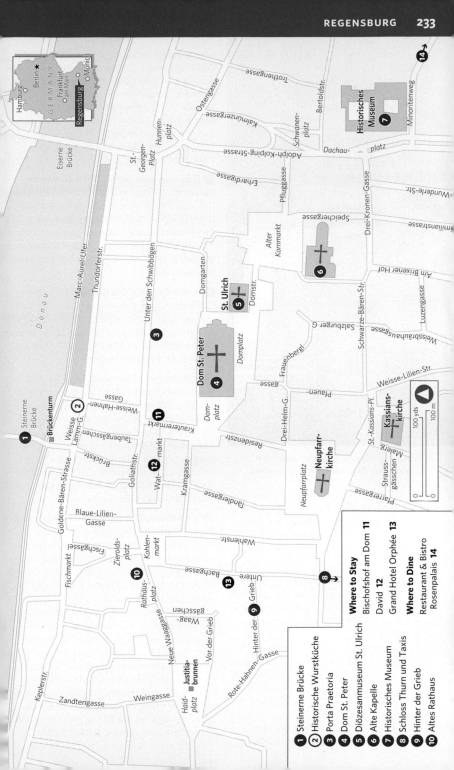

Where to Stay
Bischofshof am Dom 11
David 12
Grand Hotel Orphée 13

Where to Dine
Restaurant & Bistro
Rosenpalais 14

1 Steinerne Brücke
2 Historische Wurstküche
3 Porta Praetoria
4 Dom St. Peter
5 Diözesanmuseum St. Ulrich
6 Alte Kapelle
7 Historisches Museum
8 Schloss Thurn und Taxis
9 Hinter der Grieb
10 Altes Rathaus

> The Alte Kapelle was completely restored in rococo style in the 1700s but is actually about 1,000 years old.

impressive reminder of Regensburg's ancient past as a Roman garrison town called Castra Regrina. The Roman encampment covered an area of almost 25 hectares (62 acres). **Unter den Schwibbogen.**

④ ★★ Dom St. Peter (St. Peter's Cathedral). Regensburg's massive cathedral was begun in the 13th century on the site of an earlier Carolingian church. Special features include the richly decorated west front, 13th- and 14th-century stained-glass windows, and two Gothic statues—the Archangel Gabriel and Mary at the Annunciation—that stand in front of the west transept pillars. Join the 45-minute guided tour to visit the Kreuzgang (Cloister), with its Romanesque Aller Heiligenkapelle (All Saints' Chapel), and the 11th-century Sankt Stephan Kirche (St. Stephan's

Church), with an altar that connects to early Christian tombs. ⏱ 15 min. (without tour). Domplatz. ☎ 0941/586-500. Admission free to the cathedral; guided tour of cloister and St. Stephan's 3€. Cathedral May–Oct Mon–Sat 8am–6:30pm, Sun noon–6pm; Nov–April daily 8am–4pm. Tours in English of chapel and St. Stephan's Church May–Oct Mon–Sat 10am, 11am, 2pm, Sun 11am, noon, 3€.

⑤ Diözesanmuseum St. Ulrich (Diocesan Museum). Housed in an early Gothic church, this collection of religious art features sculptures, paintings, and gold and silver work (medieval reliquaries, bishops' crosses) from the 11th to 20th centuries. ⏱ 15 min. Domplatz 2. ☎ 0941/51688. Free admission. Apr–Oct Tues–Sun 10am–5pm.

⑥ ★ Alte Kapelle (Old Chapel). Originally Carolingian, Alte Kapelle was completely transformed in the rococo style in the 18th century by Anton Landes. ⏱ 15 min. Schwarz-Bären-Strasse 7 (Alter Kornmarkt). ☎ 0941/57973. Mon–Sat 10am–5pm, Sun noon–4pm.

⑦ ★ Historisches Museum. Displays in this small museum of local history, housed in a former Minorite monastery, focus on major developments in the cultural and artistic history of the region. Of special interest are the relics from Regensburg's Roman period and an exhibition of paintings by Albrecht Altdorfer and other masters of the Danube School. ⏱ 30 min. Dachauplatz 2–4. ☎ 0941/507-2448. Admission 2.20€. Daily 10am–4pm (Thurs until 8pm).

⑧ ★★ Schloss Thurn und Taxis (Thurn und Taxis Palace). When the ducal Thurn und Taxis family lost its monopoly on the German postal system in 1816, the family was given the buildings of St. Emmeram's Abbey in compensation. On guided tours, you can visit the state apartments, the library (with magnificent frescoes by Cosmas Damian Asam), and the Romanesque-Gothic cloisters, built between the 11th and 14th centuries. On your own you can visit the Carriage Museum, which houses an interesting collection of coaches, sleighs, and sedan chairs, and the Princely Treasure Chamber, which displays gold work, clocks, furniture, porcelain, and other valuables dating from the 17th to 19th centuries. ⏱ 1 hr. Emmeramsplatz 5. ☎ 0941/50481.

www.thurnundtaxis.de. Tours of palace/cloisters 11.50€, Treasure Chamber/Carriage Museum 4.50€. Palace/cloister tours Apr–Oct daily 11am, 2pm, 3pm, 4pm, also Sat–Sun 10am, 1pm; Nov–Mar Sat–Sun 10am, 11am, 2pm, 3pm. Carriage Museum/Treasure Chamber Mon–Fri 11am–5pm, Sat–Sun 10am–5pm.

9 ★ Hinter der Grieb. Stroll down this ancient lane with its old burghers' houses and you'll be wafted back to the Regensburg of the Middle Ages. Look back from the far end for a view of one of the cathedral spires.

10 ★★ Altes Rathaus (Old Town Hall). This Gothic structure, with its eight-story tower, gabled doorway, and charming oriel window, contains a richly decorated Reichsaal (Imperial Hall), where the parliament of the Holy Roman Empire sat from 1663 to 1806, and, in the basement, the original dungeons and torture chamber. ⏱ 15 min. Rathausplatz. ☎ 0941/507-3440. Guided tour 3€. Guided tours every 30 min. Mon–Sat 9:30am–noon and 2–4pm, Sun 10am–noon; guided tour in English daily 3:15pm.

Where to Stay & Dine

> Featuring elegant rooms with baroque styling, the Grand Hotel Orphée is one of Regensburg's most popular lodging options.

★★ Bischofshof am Dom ALTSTADT The rooms in this 200-year-old former ecclesiastical building have been refurbished in a rustic style that will appeal to traditionalists—as will the elegant restaurant. Krauterer Markt 3. ☎ 0941/58460. www.hotel-bischofshof.de. 55 units. Doubles 138€–148€ w/breakfast. AE, DC, MC, V.

★ David ALTSTADT BAVARIAN/INTERNATIONAL Located in a historic tower with wonderful views from its large roof garden, this exceptional restaurant serves artful regional cuisine in a charming setting. Watmarkt 5. ☎ 0941/561-858. Entrees 18€–27€. MC, V. Dinner only Tues–Sat.

★★ Grand Hotel Orphée ALTSTADT Three different buildings house three Orphée

hotels, but this one is my favorite because it's adjoined to the excellent Restaurant Orphée and has large, nicely decorated rooms with many special baroque features. Untere Bachgasse 8. ☎ 0941/5960-2300. www.hotel-orphee.de. 25 units. Doubles 125€–155€ w/breakfast. AE, DC, MC, V.

★★ Restaurant & Bistro Rosenpalais ALTSTADT INTERNATIONAL The menu at the elegant first-floor restaurant is inventive and full of seasonal surprises, while the casual street-level bistro serves up simpler pastas, soups, salads, and local dishes. Minoritenweg 20. ☎ 0941/599-7579. www.rosenpalais.de. Entrees 19€–28€; fixed-price menus 53€–69€. MC, V. Lunch & dinner Tues–Sat.

Rothenburg ob der Tauber

Of all the medieval cities in Bavaria and along the Romantic Road, Rothenburg ob der Tauber is the most famous. And justifiably so, since the entire town is one endless photo op. Thick medieval walls studded with fortified towers surround an urban core of cobblestoned streets, half-timber houses, and old churches—a townscape that has, in its essence, changed little in 400 years. After a period of prosperity in the Middle Ages as a Free Imperial City, Rothenberg lost its power and languished as a provincial backwater. That neglect, ironically, was what saved the Rothenburg that visitors enjoy today.

> *The impressive walls, cobblestone streets, and towers that greet visitors to Rothenburg ob der Tauber are landmarks of a fully preserved medieval city.*

START **From the train station, walk south on Steinweg, continue onto Schlacthofstrasse, and turn right on Spitalgasse, following it to the Spitalbastei (about a 15 min. walk).**

1 Spitalbastei. For a fun and fascinating introduction to Rothenburg, climb the stairs of this massive 16th-century tower and head north on the walkway that runs along the top of the town walls.

2 Klingenbastei. The introductory walk along the walls ends at this fortified gateway. Corner of Spitalgasse and Heilig Geist.

3 ★ Reichsstadtmuseum (City Museum). Housed in a 700-year-old Dominican nunnery with well-preserved cloisters, convent hall, and kitchen, this museum displays medieval panel paintings, a collection of gold coins, drinking vessels, armaments, and objects

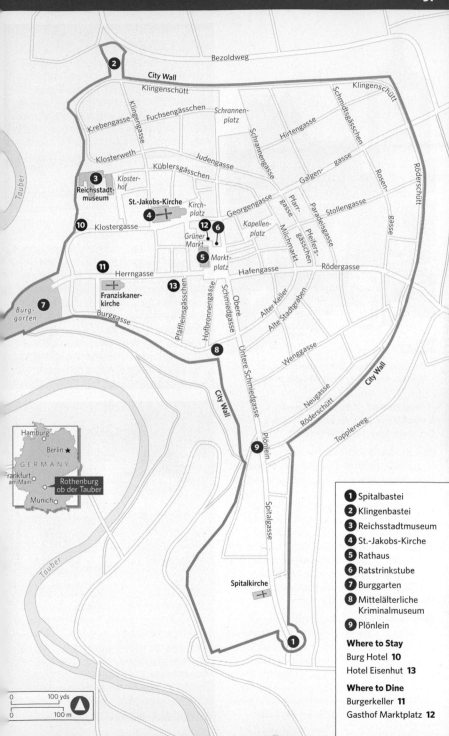

Bezoldweg

City Wall

Klingenschütt

Klingenschütt

Schmidsgässchen

Krebengasse

Klingengasse

Fuchsengässchen

Schrannen-platz

Hirtengasse

Klosterweth

Judengasse

Schrannengasse

Galgen-gasse

Rosen-gasse

Röderschütt

Reichsstadt-museum **3**

Kloster-hof

Küblersgässchen

St.-Jakobs-Kirche **4**

Kirch-platz

Georgengasse

Pfarr-gasse

Paradeisgasse

Pfeifers-gässchen

Stollengasse

gasse

10

Klostergasse

12 **6**

Grüner Markt

Kapellen-platz

Milchmarkt

11

Herrngasse

5

Markt-platz

Hafengasse

Rödergasse

Franziskaner-kirche

13

Pfäffleinsgässchen

Hofbronnengasse

Schmiedgasse

Obere

Alter Keller

Alte Stadtgraben

Burg-garten **7**

Burggasse

8

Unter Schmiedgasse

Wenggasse

City Wall

City Wall

Neugasse

Röderschütt

Topplerweg

9

Plönlein

Spitalgasse

Tauber

Tauber

Spitalkirche

1

GERMANY

Hamburg

Berlin ★

Frankfurt am Main

Rothenburg ob der Tauber

Munich

0   100 yds

0   100 m

1 Spitalbastei

2 Klingenbastei

3 Reichsstadtmuseum

4 St.-Jakobs-Kirche

5 Rathaus

6 Ratstrinkstube

7 Burggarten

8 Mittelälterliche Kriminalmuseum

9 Plönlein

Where to Stay

Burg Hotel **10**

Hotel Eisenhut **13**

Where to Dine

Burgerkeller **11**

Gasthof Marktplatz **12**

> One of Rothenburg's most picturesque locations is Plönlein, where two streets uniquely converge.

The Master Draught

In 1631, during the Thirty Years War, General Tilly, commander of the armies of the Catholic League, captured the Protestant city of Rothenburg and was given, as victor, a 3½-liter (7½-pint) tankard of wine. He said he would spare the town from destruction if one of the town burghers could down the huge tankard in one draught. Former mayor Nusch accepted the challenge and succeeded, thus saving Rothenburg and giving himself a 3-day hangover. This historical episode was first performed as a festival play, called *Die Meistertrunk* (The Master Draught), in 1881 and now forms the centerpiece of the **Historisches Festspiel** (History Festival), which takes place over a 4-day period every Whitsuntide (Pentecost, the seventh Sunday after Easter). Hundreds of citizens dress up in period costumes and re-create the period of the Master Draught. The play is also performed in early September and twice in October during the **Rothenburger Herbst,** an autumn celebration. For more details and yearly dates, visit www.rothenburg.de.

of local interest. ⏱ 30 min. Klosterhof 5. ☎ 09861/939-043. Admission 3€. Daily Apr–Oct 10am–5pm, Nov–Mar 1–4pm.

❹ ★ **St.-Jakobs-Kirche.** The Gothic Church of St. James is worth visiting primarily to see the *Heiliges-Blut-Altar* (Altar of the Holy Blood), a masterpiece created by the Würzburg sculptor Tilman Riemenschneider, whose work can also be seen in Würzburg, Creglingen, and Regensburg. The fine painted-glass windows in the church choir date from the late Gothic period. ⏱ 15 min. Klostergasse 15. ☎ 09861/700-620. Admission 1.50€. Daily Apr–Oct 9am–5:15pm; Dec 10am–4:45pm; Nov, Jan–Mar 10am–noon and 2–4pm.

❺ **Rathaus (Town Hall).** At the center of Rothenburg is the bustling Marktplatz (Market Square) dominated by the Rathaus, part 13th-century Gothic, part 16th-century Renaissance. From the top of its 50m (164-ft.) tower, you get a great view of the town. Marktplatz. ☎ 09861/40492. Admission to tower 1€. Tower open Apr–Oct 9:30am–12:30pm and 1–5pm.

Cuckoo Clocks and Christmas

Every day is Christmas at **Käthe Wohlfahrt's Weinachtsdorf** (Christmas Village), Herrngasse 1 (☎ 09861/4090), a Christmas-related emporium loaded with thousands upon thousands of Christmas ornaments. **Kunstwerke Friese,** Grüner Markt (☎ 09861/7166), specializes in cuckoo clocks and carries Hummel figurines, pewter beer steins, music boxes, and dolls.

⑥ Ratstrinkstube (Councilors' Tavern). This old inn with three clocks on its gabled facade, stands next to the Rathaus and now serves as the tourist information office. Windows on either side of the lowest clock open at 11am, noon, and 1, 2, 3, 9, and 10pm to reveal the figures of General Tilly and Herr Nusch, chief protagonists in the drinking bout that saved Rothenburg (see "The Master Draught"). Marktplatz. ☎ 09861/404-800.

⑦ Burggarten (Castle Gardens). This park and promenade occupy the site of the now-vanished imperial castle and offer lovely views over the Tauber Valley and the two-tier Doppelbrücke (Double Bridge) that crosses the Tauber River.

⑧ Mittelälterliche Kriminalmuseum (Medieval Crime Museum). A 14th-century hospital with Rothenburg's only 18th-century baroque facade houses this macabre museum dedicated to medieval crime and punishment. Here's your chance to see chastity belts, shame masks, a shame flute for bad musicians (there was apparently a whole lot of shaming going on in medieval Germany), a dunking basket, and an iron maiden. The displays are boringly prosaic, but your imagination will run wild. ⏰ 30 min. Burggasse 3-5. ☎ 09861/5359. Admission 3.80€. Daily Apr-Oct 9:30am-6pm; Nov, Jan-Feb 2-4pm; Dec-Mar 10am-4pm.

⑨ Plönlein. One of the most photographed spots in Rothenburg, this picturesque corner is formed by two diverging streets, one level and one descending, both of them ending at a fortified gateway. Junction of Untere Schmiedgasse and Kobolzellerseig.

Where to Stay & Dine

Burgerkeller ALTSTADT *BAVARIAN*
Housed in a 16th-century cellar (with tables outside in nice weather), the Burgerkeller is a pleasant spot to dine on local cooking, such as *Maultaschensuppe* (stuffed pasta in broth) and Nuremberg sausages on sauerkraut, and to sample local wines. Herrngasse 24. ☎ 09861/2126. Entrees 6€-10€. MC, V. Lunch & dinner Thurs-Tues.

★★★ Burg Hotel ALTSTADT
Everything about the Burg Hotel is picturesque, from its half-timber facade at the end of a cobblestoned cul-de-sac to its large, prettily decorated rooms with views out across the Tauber Valley. Klostergasse 1-3. ☎ 09861/94890. www.burghotel.eu. 15 units. Doubles 100€-170€ w/breakfast. AE, DC, MC, V.

Gasthof Marktplatz ALTSTADT *SWABIAN*
The food served at this simple inn isn't fancy; it's more like German comfort food. You'll find hearty, old-fashioned Swabian staples such as *Käsespätzle* (cheese-coated noodles) cooked with onions, and *Jägerschnitzel,* a pork schnitzel with cream sauce. Grüner Markt 10. ☎ 09861/6722. www.gasthof-marktplatz.de. Entrees 8.50€-14€. No credit cards. Lunch & dinner Wed-Sun.

> *The beautiful view from the Burg Hotel, which overlooks the sprawling Tauber Valley.*

★★★ Hotel Eisenhut ALTSTADT
Comprised of three interconnected medieval houses, Rothenburg's only luxury-oriented hotel has an old-fashioned ambience, the largest bedrooms and bathrooms in town, and fine dining. Herrngasse 3-7. ☎ 09861/7050. www.eisenhut.com. 78 units. Doubles 134€-225€. Closed Jan-Feb. AE, DC, MC, V.

Würzburg

Würzburg on the Main River is a lovely, lively university town surrounded by miles of vineyards. It grew up around a 7th-century Frankish duchy and grew to prominence under a series of powerful prince-bishops. The prince-bishops of the Schönborn family were responsible for building the Residenz, the city's most famous tourist attraction, and many baroque churches in the Altstadt (Old Town). Würzburg was almost entirely leveled in World War II, and the historic buildings you see today are mostly meticulous recreations.

> The majestic columns, chandeliers, and marble detail of the Emperor's Chamber in Würzburg's 18th-century baroque palace, the Residenz.

START From the train station, head south on Bahnhofstrasse, Textorstrasse, and Theaterstrasse to the Residenz, about a 15-minute walk.

① 🍷 **Weinstuben Juliusspital.** Before heading south to the Residenz, you may want to stop and sample a glass of Würzburg's white, fruity *Frankenwein* in the medieval wine cellar of the Juliusspital, a baroque complex built by the prince-bishop Julius Echter in 1575 as a hospital

with a courtyard and a church. The Juliusspital cultivates its own grapes and is the second largest winery in Germany. Juliuspromenade and corner of Barbarossa-platz. ☎ 0931/393-1400. www.juliusspital. de. Daily 10am–midnight. 5€–8€.

❷ ★★ **Residenz.** Considered one of the most important baroque palaces in Europe and now a UNESCO World Heritage site, the 345-room Residenz was completed in 1744 by architect Balthasar Neumann for Prince-Bishop Johann

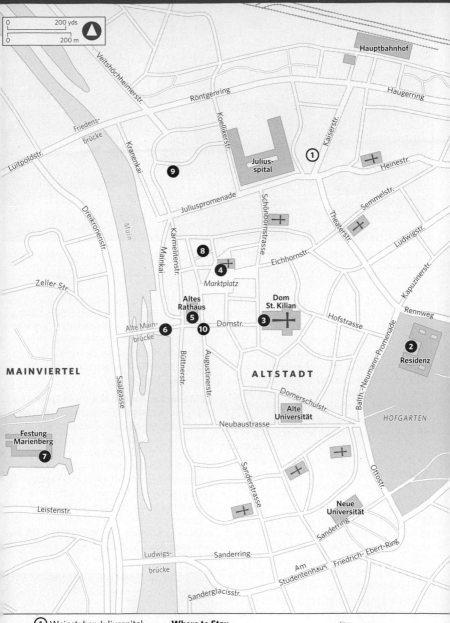

(1) Weinstuben Juliusspital

(2) Residenz

(3) Dom St. Kilian

(4) Marienkapelle

(5) Rathaus

(6) Alte Mainbrücke

(7) Festung Marienberg

Where to Stay

Greifensteiner Hof **8**

Maritim Hotel Würzburg **9**

Where to Dine

Fränkische Stuben **8**

Ratskeller Würzburg **10**

> *A view of Würzburg and the massive Romanesque cathedral, Dom St. Kilian, where the city's prince-bishops are entombed.*

von Schönborn. The most important areas to visit are the vaulted Treppenhaus, or stairwell, with a ceiling covered by a huge fresco with mythological allegories painted by Giovanni Battista Tiepolo; the Hofkirche, a court chapel with colored marble columns and two important altar paintings also by Tiepolo; and the Weisser Saal (White Hall) and Gartensaal (Garden Room), both slathered with a riot of fanciful stuccowork. Behind the palace, the formal and elegant Hofgarten, or court garden, also is worth visiting. ◷ 1 hr. Residenzplatz 2. ☎ 0931/355-170. www.residenz-wuerzburg. de. Admission 5€. Daily Apr–Oct 9am–6pm, Nov–Mar 10am–4pm. Guided tours in English daily 11am and 3pm.

❸ ★ **Dom (Cathedral) St. Kilian.** The fourth-largest Romanesque church in Germany was begun in 1045 on the site of a much earlier building and rebuilt after extensive damage in World War II. The interior of this four-towered basilica, where Würzburg's powerful prince-bishops once worshiped and were buried, shows the work of many centuries, from the simple, high-ceilinged Romanesque nave to the baroque stuccowork in the chancel and the Altar of the Apostles, created in 1967 as a resting place for three sandstone sculptures created by Tilman Riemenschneider in 1506. Funerary monuments to the prince-bishops, including two by Riemenschneider (against the seventh and eighth pillars), line the pillars of the nave. Between 1721 and 1736 Balthasar Neumann, architect of the Residenz, created the Schönborn Chapel for the tombs of the prince-bishops. ◷ 15 min. Domstrasse. ☎ 0931/321-1830. Free admission. Mon–Sat 10am–5pm, Sun 1–6pm.

❹ **Marienkapelle (St. Mary's Chapel).** This lovely red-and-white Gothic hall-church on Marktplatz, the city's liveliest square, was built in the 14th and 15th centuries by the citizens of Würzburg. Above the north doorway there is a 15th-century sculpture of the Annunciation; inside there is a tombstone carved by Tilman Riemenschneider and a 17th-century silver Madonna crafted by J. Killian, the silver master of Augsburg. ◷ 15 min. Domerpfarrgasse 10. ☎ 0931/372-335. Free admission. Mon–Sat 10am–4pm, Sun noon–3pm.

Mozart in Residenz

One of the annual highlights of Würzburg's cultural year is the **Mozartfest,** which begins at the end of May and continues to the first week in July. Many of the concerts by renowned musicians are performed in the beautiful baroque rooms of the Residenz. For more information call ☎ 0931/372-336 or visit www.mozartfest-wuerzburg.de.

5 **Rathaus (Town Hall).** Fronted by an 18th-century fountain, Würzburg's Rathaus was built in the 13th century as an episcopal residence; in 1659 the western part, known as the Roter Bau (Red Building), was added in Renaissance style. The building's painted facade dates from the 16th century. Have a look at the charming courtyard and admire the building from the outside; there's no need to go in. Rückermainstrasse 2.

6 ★ **Alte Mainbrücke (Old Main Bridge).** Twelve enormous baroque saints sculpted out of sandstone decorate this beautiful stone bridge built over the Main River between 1473 and 1543.

A marked footpath on the west side of the bridge leads up to Festung Marienberg, or take bus no. 9, which will drop you right at the gate.

7 ★★ **Festung Marienberg (Marienberg Fortress).** Now a UNESCO World Heritage site, Marienberg Fortress crowns the hilltop on the west side of the river. This huge complex of buildings, surrounded by vineyards, includes within its walls the 8th-century **Marienkirche** (St. Mary's Church), one of the oldest churches in Germany, and the **Prince's Building,** with recreated historic rooms once used by the prince-bishops of Würzburg. Focus your time and attention on the **Mainfränkisches Museum,** a local history museum

Würzburg's Master Sculptor

Tilman Riemenschneider (1460–1531), whose incredibly expressive wood sculptures are the highlight of the Mainfränkisches Museum (**7**), lived and worked in Würzburg for 48 years, serving as both a councilor and mayor. During the Peasants' Revolt of 1525, this master sculptor sided with the rebels and incurred the implacable wrath of the prince-bishops. As a result of his political views, Riemenschneider was imprisoned and tortured. He died shortly after being released from prison. You can see more work by this great artist at the Herrgottskirche near Creglingen (p. 208, **3**), St.-Jakobs-Kirche in Rothenburg ob der Tauber (p. 238, **4**), and Regensburg's cathedral (p. 234, **4**).

located in the fortress complex. Its must-see attraction is the room devoted to the carved wooden sculptures of Tilman Riemenschneider, the great Gothic master woodcarver and sculptor. ⏱ 1 hr. Marienberg 1. Fortress ☎ 09317/355-1750; museum ☎ 0931/205-940. Museum www.mainfraenkisches-museum. de. Admission: Prince's Building 4€, museum 3€. Tues–Sun 10am–5pm; fortress and Prince's Building closed Nov–Mar 15. Bus: 9.

Where to Stay & Dine

★ **Fränkische Stuben** ALTSTADT *FRANCONIAN* A lovely spot to sit outside on a warm evening and dine on local Franconian specialties. Try fresh fish in Riesling wine sauce or *Zwiebelkuchen* (an onion tart). Dettelbachergasse 2 (in the Greifensteiner Hof). ☎ 0931/87809. www.fraenkische-stuben.de. Entrees 8€–18€. AE, DC, MC, V. Lunch & dinner daily.

★ **Greifensteiner Hof** ALTSTADT Every room is different in this small, charming hotel in the heart of the Altstadt behind the Marienkirche. Bathrooms are on the small side, but there are nice designer touches throughout. Dettelbachergasse 2. ☎ 0931/35170. www. greifensteiner-hof.de. 40 units. Doubles 60€–90€ w/breakfast. AE, DC, MC, V.

★ **Maritim Hotel Würzburg** RIVERSIDE This modern chain-hotel next to the Main River features medium-size rooms decorated in an unobtrusive contemporary style. The good-size bathrooms have a tub and shower. Pleichortorstrasse 5. ☎ 0931/30530. www.maritim.de. 85 units. Doubles 100€–210€. AE, DC, MC, V.

kids **Ratskeller Würzburg** ALTSTADT *FRANCONIAN* Frankish foods with an occasional French twist are served at this atmospheric *Ratskeller,* but you may prefer simpler fare such as homemade sausage mixed with fried potatoes and eggs, or roast beef with fried onions; there's also a kids' menu. Langgasse 1. ☎ 0931/13021. www.wuerzburger-ratskeller.de. Entrees 6€–15€. AE, MC, V. Lunch & dinner daily.

Northern Bavaria & the Romantic Road Fast Facts

Accommodations Booking Services
Call **Hotel Reservation Service** (☎ 0870/ 243-0003; www.hrs.de) from anywhere in Germany. Tourist information centers in the major train stations and airports offer on-the-spot booking services for hotel rooms and pensions (B&Bs).

ATMs/Cashpoints
All the major cities and towns in this region—Würzburg, Rothenberg ob der Tauber, Augsburg, Nuremberg, Regensburg, and Passau—have banks and train stations with ATMs (*Geldautomaten*).

Dentists & Doctors
If you have a mild medical issue or dental problems while traveling in Germany, most hotels will be able to refer you to a local doctor (*Arzt*) or dentist (*Zahnarzt*) who speaks English. You will be expected to provide proof of either permanent or travel insurance (such as an EHIC card in the case of most residents of Europe), or you will be required to pay for treatment. In the event of minor injuries that require speedy treatment, go to the *Notaufnahme* (emergency) department of the nearest *Krankenhaus* (hospital). When the injuries are serious or life-threatening, call the doctor/ambulance emergency number (see "Emergencies," below).

Emergencies
To call the police (*Polizei),* dial ☎ **110.** To report a fire or to summon an emergency doctor (*Notarzt*) or an ambulance (*Krankenwagen),* dial ☎ **112.**

Getting There
The nearest international airports are in **Frankfurt** (see p. 494), and **Munich** (see p. 318). If you want to travel the Romantic Road from north to south, fly into Frankfurt, 119km (74 miles) north of Würzburg, the northern starting point. If you want to tour the Romantic Road from south to north, or tour northern Bavaria, fly into Munich, 132km (82 miles) northeast of Füssen, the southernmost town along the Romantic Road. The Frankfurt airport has a train station, so you can easily connect to any of the towns or cities covered in this chapter from there. For train schedules and information, call **Deutsche Bahn** (German Railways; ☎ 11861; www.bahn.de). Nuremberg has its own airport, **Airport Nürnberg** (☎ 0911/93700; www.airport-nuernberg.de), which serves European airlines and charter flights.

Getting Around
Germany is served by an excellent rail network and a car isn't necessary if you are sticking to the towns and cities covered in this chapter. Most rail service—and all InterCity trains, including the high-speed ICE (InterCity-Express) trains—are operated by **Deutsche Bahn** (German Railways; ☎ 11861; www.bahn. de). Some local and regional services are operated by private train companies. If, however, you want to explore the smaller sights along the Romantic Road and see the countryside of northern Bavaria, you must have a car. A detailed regional road map (Hallweg or Michelin) is essential; you can buy one at Frankfurt airport bookshops and most newsstands. Renting a car in Germany is fairly easy, but it's generally better price-wise if you book the car before your arrival. Most of the major international car-rental agencies have offices at the Frankfurt and Munich airports, including **Avis** (☎ 800/331-1212; www.avis.com), **Budget** (☎ 800/527-0700; www.budget. com) and **Hertz** (☎ 800/654-3001; www. hertz.com). You can also arrange to rent a car through **Rail Europe** (☎ 888/382-7245; www raileurope.com).

Internet Access
Almost all hotels in Germany, even in smaller towns, now offer Wi-Fi and/or broadband. If your hotel does not, ask your concierge or at the tourist office if there is an Internet cafe in the vicinity.

Pharmacies

At a German pharmacy, called an *Apotheke*, the trained staff can recommend over-the-counter medications for many common ailments. For cosmetics or toiletries, go to a *Drogerie*. German pharmacies are open regular business hours. They take turns staying open nights, on Sunday, and on holidays, and each *Apotheke* posts a list of those that are open off-hours.

Police

To report a lost or stolen article, such as a wallet or passport, visit the local police (*Polizei*) in your location. To call the police from anywhere in Germany, dial ☎ **110.**

Post Office

You'll recognize branches of **Deutsche Post** (☎ 01802/3333; www.deutschepost.de) by their yellow sign with a black horn. Post offices are open Monday to Friday 8am–6pm, Saturday 8am–noon.

Safety

This area of Germany is completely safe for tourists, but use common sense and don't leave valuables in plain sight when you park your car on a city street or parking lot near a scenic area.

Telephones

Call ☎ 11837 for information and ☎ 11834 for international information. Augsburg's area code is 0821; Bayreuth's is 0921; Nuremberg's is 0911; Regensburg's is 0941; Rothenburg's is 09861; and Würzburg's is 0931. Dial the area code when calling a town number from outside the town; you don't need to dial it when calling a town number from inside the town. There are public phones in many places—some accept coins and some take phone cards, available at post offices and newsstands.

Toilets

In some places you will find clean public toilets (*Toilette* in German; pronounced twah-*leh*-teh), many of them automatic and wheelchair-accessible; you need a .50€ coin to unlock the door. More convenient and widespread are toilets in cafes, bars, restaurants, hotels, malls, and some stores and at highway services and rest areas. Even if you are not obliged to pay, it is customary to leave the attendant .50€.

Visitor Information

The regional tourist board for Bavaria is **Bayern Tourismus Marketing,** Leopoldstrasse 146, 80804 Munich (☎ 089/212-3970; www.bayern.by). The **Romantic Road Association** can also provide additional information: Touristik Arbeitsgemeinschaft Romantische Strasse, Segringer Strasse 19, 91550 Dinkelsbühl (☎ 09851/551-387; www.romantischestrasse.de). In addition to those provided with the individual town listings, other key tourist offices are as follows: AUGSBURG Rathausplatz; ☎ 0821/502-070; www.augsburg-tourismus.de; Mon–Fri 9am–6pm, Sat 10am–1pm, Sun (summer only) 10am–1pm. BAYREUTH Luitpoldplatz 9; ☎ 092/88588; www.tourismus.bayreuth.de; Mon–Fri 9am–6pm, Sat 9am–2pm, Sun (May–Oct) 10am–2pm. NUREM-BERG Königstrasse 93 (☎ 0911/23360) and Hauptmarkt 18 (☎ 0911/233-6135); www.tourismus.nuernberg.de; Mon–Sat 9am–7pm, Sun 10am–4pm. REGENS-BURG Altes Rathaus; ☎ 0941/507-4410; www.regensburg.de; Mon–Fri 9am–6pm, Sat–Sun 9am–4pm (Sun Nov–Mar 9:30am–2:30pm). ROTHENBURG OB DER TAUBER Marktplatz; ☎ 09861/404-800; www.rothenburg.de; Mon–Fri 9am–6pm (Nov–Apr until 5pm), Sat–Sun 10am–3pm. WÜRZBURG Falkenhaus am Markt; ☎ 0931/372-335; www.wuerzburg.de; Mon–Fri 9am–6pm (Nov–Apr until 5pm), Sat–Sun 10am–3pm.

6
Munich

Our Favorite Munich Moments

Munich is a town that likes to celebrate. It's famous for throwing a big boisterous party called Oktoberfest, and if you walk through the Altstadt (Old Town) on a warm, sunny day or a balmy night, you see people sitting outside, in every square, drinking, eating, and enjoying life. The city is all about prosperity and *Gemütlichkeit,* one of those hard-to-translate words that means something like cozy and/or good-natured. It's no wonder that, according to polls, Munich is the Germans' first choice as a desirable place to live.

> PREVIOUS PAGE *Munich's Oktoberfest attracts millions of revelers each year.* THIS PAGE *The Neues Rathaus, on Marienplatz.*

1 Moseying through Marienplatz. To pick up on the buzz and beat of Munich, any time of the day, all you need do is wander through the city's best-loved square. See p. 252, **1**.

2 Visiting the Viktualienmarkt. There's just something wonderful about this great outdoor food market—it's colorful and intriguing, smells divine, and is full of excellent edible surprises. See p. 286, **5**.

3 Having ham hocks and a beer at Hofbräuhaus am Platzl. What could be more Munich than sitting at a communal table in the *Schwemme* (taproom) of the world's most famous beer hall and ordering a glass of Löwenbrau and a plate of *Schweineshaxe* (ham hocks)? See p. 283, **4**.

4 Assessing the Asamkirche. Munich has lots of lovely churches, but many of them had to be rebuilt after World War II, with interiors stripped of their original ornamentation. The

Asamkirche is a marvelous exception, florid to the point of dizziness. See p. 273, ❸.

❺ Tracking the model trains at the Deutsches Museum. Some people come to view the heavens in the observatory, others to gawk at the historic aircraft. But for a nostalgic reminder of your childhood, or at least of the days when kids played with model trains instead of video games, nothing beats the giant miniature choo-choo display at the Deutsches Museum. See p. 266, ❶.

❻ Coming face to face with Albrecht Dürer at the Alte Pinakothek. The Alte Pinakothek is hardly lacking in masterpieces, but coming across Albrecht Dürer's *Self-Portrait* of 1500 may stop you in your tracks. It's a brilliant and haunting work by a 29-year-old who was the first artist to paint himself as the subject. See p. 262, ❶.

❼ Browsing the showroom at BMW Welt. It's pure fantasy, but also quite a lot of fun. At the automaker's remarkable Munich showroom, the newest BMWs sit in perfectly trained spotlights like celebrity models, which is sort of what they are. But these are models you can touch, and if your credit line is good enough, there's no telling where the experience may take you. See p. 269, ❺.

❽ Baring it all in the Englischer Garten. The Germans aren't what you'd call prudish about their bodies. If it's a hot, sunny day, why not grin and bare it along with them in the Schönfeldwiese, a large meadow in the

> *Revelers share cold drinks and warm sentiments in Munich's massive, festive, and famous Hofbräuhaus am Platzl.*

Englischer Garten used for nude sunbathing. See p. 288, ❷.

❾ Going for bust at the Glyptothek. Lovers of antiquity have lots of treasures to discover in Munich. In the Glyptothek, the city's repository for ancient sculpture, the gallery devoted to Roman portrait busts introduces you to a marvelous world of marble faces, their personalities as sharp and vivid today as they were thousands of years ago. See p. 264, ❼.

❿ Marveling at Ludwig's coaches at Schloss Nymphenburg. There's so much to see and enjoy at Nymphenburg Palace that it's easy to spend half a day there. After visiting the palace, check out the nearby Marstallmuseum, where the collection of gilded sleighs and carriages used by King Ludwig II of Neuschwanstein fame will knock your socks off. See p. 274, ❷.

Fasching

Fasching, or Carnival, is a late winter, pre-Lenten festival. The first Fasching Ball in Munich dates back to 1829; nowadays there are thousands of events ranging from fancy-dress parties to extravagant balls. *München Harrisch* (Mad Munich), on the last Sunday before Shrove Tuesday, is one of the biggest events of the season, in which thousands of revelers dance and make their way through the streets to Marienplatz, where there are several stages as well as numerous food and drink stalls. Visit www.munich-tourist.de for more information.

Our Favorite Munich Moments

← To Nymphenburg (see inset)

Loristrasse
Linprun str.
Erzgiessereistr.
Dachauer Strasse
Schleissheimer Str.
Mässmann-str.
Theresienstr.
Hess-str.
Steinicke-weg
Emhuber-str.
Enhuber-str.
Augustenstr.
Theresienstrasse
Theresienstrasse

Neue Pinakothek

TECHNISCHE UNIVERSITÄT MÜNCHEN (TUM)

6 Alte Pinakothek

Nymphenburger Strasse
Blutenburgstr.
Pappenheimstr.
Rottmannstr.
Gabelsbergerstr.
Steinheilstr.
Wagner-Str.
Richard-
Luisenstr.
Barer str.

Stiglmaier-platz ⓤ
Stiglmaier-platz
Brienner Strasse
Lenbach-haus
9 Glyptothek
Arcisstr.

Karlstrasse
Augustenstr.
Propyläen
ⓤ Königsplatz

Karlstrasse
Spatenstr.
Marsstrasse
Seidlstrasse
Dachauer Strasse
Luisenstr.
Brienner
Karolinen-platz
Max-Joseph-Str.
Prinz-
Strasse

Wredestr.
Zirkus-Krone-Str.
Herbststr.
Hopfenstr.
Marsstrasse
Antiken-sammlungen
Meiserstr.
Barer-Strasse
Otto-

Arnulfstr.
Hirtenstr.
Lämmer-str.
Karlstrasse
Sophienstrasse
Arcostr.
Ottostrasse
Maximilians

Arnulfstr.
Elisenstrasse
Alter Botanischer Garten
Lenbach-platz
Pacellist

Starnberger Bahnhof
Hauptbahnhof ⓢ
Prielmayerstrasse
Maxburgstr.

Hauptbahnhof
Bahnhof-platz
Schützenstr.
Karls-platz
Kapellen-str.
Herzog-Max-Str.

Holzkirchner Bahnhof
Zollstr.
ⓘ
✉
Karlsplatz (Stachus) ⓢ
Michaels-kirche

Bayerstrasse
Martin-Greif-Str.
Hermann-Lingg-Str.
Mittererstr.
Bayerstrasse
Adolf-Kolping-Str.
Schlosserstr.
Zweigstr.
Senefelderstr.
Karlstor
Eisenmannstr.
Neuhauser Str.
Altheime Eck
Ettstr.

Bavariaring
Sankt-Pauls-platz
Paulskirche
Heyse-str.
Schwanthalerstrasse
Herzogspitalstr.
Hackenstr.
Hotterstr.

Theresienwiese (Festwiese) ⓤ
Sankt-Paul-Str.
Paul-Heyse-str.
Landwehr- strasse
Deutsches Theater
Josephspitalstr.
Herzog-Wilhelm-Str.
Brunn-str.
Kreuzstr.
Damen-stiftstr.
Sonnen-str.
Asam-kirche 4
Sendlinger Strasse
Oberanger

Theresienwiese
Georg-Hirth-Platz
Pettenkoferstr.
Schillerstrasse
strasse
Mathildenstrasse
Sommerstrasse
Josephspitalstr.

Rückertstr.
Heinrich-Strasse
Lessingstr.
Beethoven-platz
Nussbaumstrasse
Sendlinger Tor
Sendlinger-Tor-Pl.
Sendlinger Tor
An der Hauptfeuerwache
Unterer

Kaiser-Ludwig-Platz
Beethoven-strasse
Ziemssenstr.
Matthäus-kirche
Fliegenstr.
Blumenstr.
Müllerstr.
Anger-str.

Schubertstr.
Herzog-str.
Haydnstr.
Goethestrasse
Lindwurmstrasse
Reisingerstrasse
Augsburgerstr.
Thalkirchner Str.
Pestalozzistrasse
Holzstr.
Hans-Sachs-Str.

Mozartstr.
Goethe-platz
Goetheplatz ⓤ
Ringseisstr.
Maistrasse
Frauenlobstr.
Alter Südfriedhof

1 Marienplatz
2 Viktualienmarkt
3 Hofbräuhaus am Platzl
4 Asamkirche
5 Deutsches Museum
6 Alte Pinakothek
7 BMW Welt
8 Englischer Garten
9 Glyptothek
10 Schloss Nymphenburg

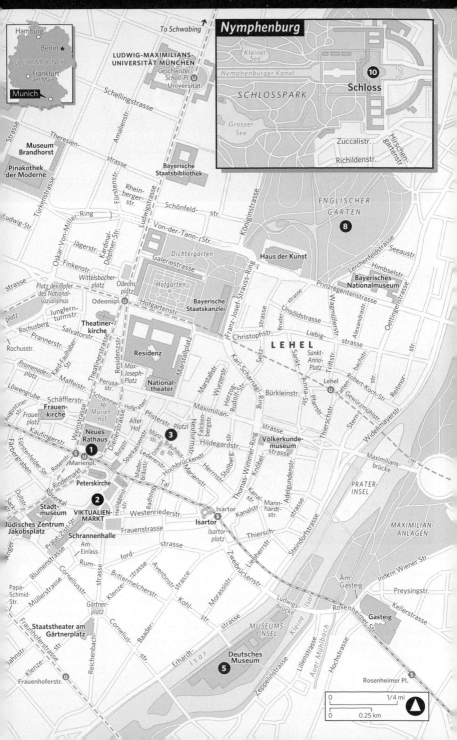

The Best of Munich in 1 Day

Munich is a rich, elegant, sophisticated city, with an unparalleled array of artistic and cultural treasures. Is it possible to see and do everything the capital of Bavaria has to offer in just A day? No. But this itinerary will let you sample a few of the city's many delights.

> *Frauenkirche's onion-domed towers have been city landmarks since they were added to the church in 1525.*

START **Take the *U-Bahn* or *S-Bahn* to Marienplatz.**

1 ★★★ **Marienplatz (St. Mary's Square).** This square in the heart of the Altstadt (Old City) is also the old heart of Munich. The monks who founded Munich built their abbey here; later, the square became Munich's market and the site for public gatherings and festivities. The **Mariensäule** (St. Mary's Column), the large column topped by a gilded statue of St. Mary in the center of the square, was erected in 1638 to celebrate the end of the Swedish invasion; four *putti,* one at each corner of the column's pedestal, are meant to symbolize Munich's triumph over war, pestilence, hunger, and heresy. ⏱ 30 min. In front of the Neues Rathaus (New Town Hall), btw. Weinstrasse and Dienerstrasse. *U-* or *S-Bahn:* Marienplatz.

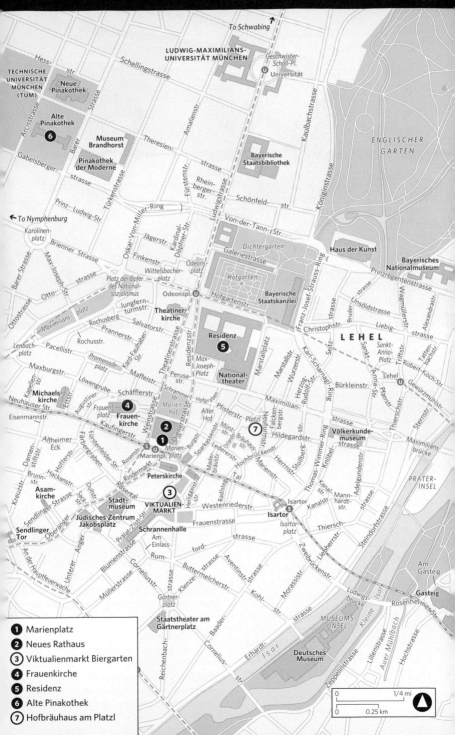

1 Marienplatz
2 Neues Rathaus
3 Viktualienmarkt Biergarten
4 Frauenkirche
5 Residenz
6 Alte Pinakothek
7 Hofbräuhaus am Platzl

> *Residents and visitors alike flood Munich's Viktualienmarkt to sample its wide variety of fresh fruits, vegetables, and other assorted food.*

② kids **Neues Rathaus (New Town Hall).** The best show on Marienplatz takes place at 11am, noon, and 5pm daily, when brightly painted mechanical figures emerge from the Glockenspiel (Carillon) on the central tower of the Neues Rathaus and reenact two famous events from Munich's history: the knights' tournament during the 1586 wedding feast of Wilhelm V and Renate of Lorraine, and the *Schäfflertanz* (Coopers' Dance), first performed in 1683 to express gratitude for the end of the plague. Take an elevator to the top of the 79m (259-ft.) tower for a good view of the city center. ☉ 30 min. Marienplatz. Tower open Mon–Fri 9am–7pm, Sat–Sun 10am–7pm; admission 1.50€. *U-* or *S-Bahn:* Marienplatz.

③ 🍴 ★★★ **Viktualienmarkt.** The hustle and bustle of Marienplatz flows into this big public market pulsing with the sights, sounds, and smells emanating from stalls and shops selling every kind of "victual," from fruit to nuts and everything in between. Browse until you find something to your taste—a sausage, a herring, a

sandwich, a cup of soup—and bring it with you to the **Biergarten.** It's perfectly okay to bring your own food there so long as you order a beer or other beverage from the drinks stand. See p. 286, **⑤**.

④ ★ **Frauenkirche.** By the end of World War II, Munich's largest church, completed in the late 15th century, was reduced to a pile of smoldering rubble. Only its landmark twin onion-domed towers remained standing. The rebuilt church is strikingly simple and dignified, and the view from the tower is spectacular. ☉ 15 min. Frauenplatz 12. ☎ 089/290-0820. Admission: church free; tower 3€ adults, 1.50€ students. Church Sat–Thurs 7am–7pm, Fri 7am–6pm; tower Apr–Oct daily 10am–5pm. *U-* or *S-Bahn:* Marienplatz.

⑤ ★★ **Residenz.** For centuries, right up until 1918, the kingdom of Bavaria was ruled by one family, the Wittelsbachs, who made the Residenz their primary royal residence. This enormous palace, begun in the 14th century and added to over the centuries, today houses

> *The immense and spectacularly ornate 14th-century palace, the Residenz, was home to the Bavarian royal family until 1918.*

a magnificent Treasury loaded with Wittelsbach riches; you can also visit the former royal apartments and state rooms. ⏱ 2 hr. See p. 274, ❶.

❻ ★★★ **Alte Pinakothek (Old Painting Gallery).** Munich has more than its share of great *Pinakotheken* (painting galleries), and this world-famous museum sits at the top of the list. Designed by Leo von Klenze, Munich's most famous neoclassical architect, the Alte Pinakothek opened in 1836 to house the royal collection of historic paintings. All the major artists of Germany, Holland, France, Spain, and Italy are represented, up to the 18th century. ⏱ 2 hr. See p. 262, ❶.

⑦ 🍺 ★ **Hofbräuhaus am Platzl.** It's big and boisterous and some might even call it a tourist-oriented cliché, but there's no denying the popularity of Munich's most famous beer hall. The beer is served in liter-size mugs, the food is hearty, and on the evenings when it's busiest, an oom-pah-pah band plays. See p. 283, ❹.

> *Brass players in the oom-pah-pah band in Munich's popular Hofbräuhaus am Platzl.*

The Best of Munich in 2 Days

This itinerary introduces you to an array of sights that highlight the diversity of Munich's great cultural treasures. Day 2 begins at the Deutsches Museum, one of Germany's most popular attractions, and goes from there to the robustly rococo Asamkirche. The tour then heads over to Munich's neoclassiest corner, Königsplatz, with its monumental trio of classically inspired buildings (two of them museums), and continues with a visit to the Neue Pinakothek gallery of 19th-century European paintings. The day's tour ends in the green, grassy meadows of the Englischer Garten, Europe's oldest public park.

> *The oldest public park in the world, the Englischer Garten is patterned after naturalistic English gardens of the 18th century, with meticulous lawns and tree-shaded paths.*

START Take *U-Bahn* line U4 or U5 to Schwanthalerhöhe—the Deutches Museum exit is marked in the station.

1 ★★★ **kids Deutsches Museum.** You don't have to be a science wizard or a techno-geek to enjoy at least some of the exhibits in the gigantic Deutsches Museum (German Museum of Science and Technology), which traces the history of science and technology from prehistoric times up to the present day. From rare historic treasures like a plane owned by the Wright brothers to demonstrations of glassblowing, the museum focuses on the ingenuity of humans to expand their knowledge and change the world. ⏲ 2 hr. See p. 266, **1**.

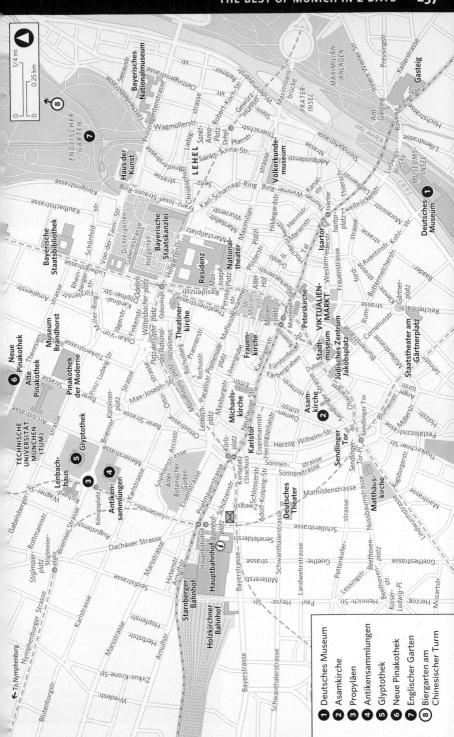

N
1/4 mi
0.25 km

Deutsches Museum
Asamkirche
Propyläen
Antikensammlungen
Glyptothek
Neue Pinakothek
Englischer Garten
Biergarten am Chinesischer Turm

> *The Propyläen gateway, one of the last works of classically inspired architect Leo von Klenze, has been a Munich landmark since 1862.*

> *The Deutsches Museum of Science and Technology is the largest technological museum in the world.*

2 ★★ **Asamkirche.** The swirling, whirling wonder of rococo is on full display in St. Johann Nepomuk, the official name of this small church dating from 1733. It's called the Asamkirche after the two Asam brothers who designed and built it (see "The Amazing Asam Brothers"). Step inside, sit down, and look around you. Every square inch seems to be decorated with paintings, gilding, and fanciful stuccowork. ⏲ 15 min. See p. 273, **3**.

3 Propyläen. What, you might ask, is a Greek temple doing in Munich? This monumental Doric-style gateway, dating from 1862, was one of the last works of Leo von Klenze, whose classically inspired buildings are found throughout Munich. Built as a memorial to Otto I Wittelsbach, who fought to overthrow the Turks from Greece and later became the first king of Greece, the structure served as a gateway to the new sections of Munich then being built to the west and as a centerpiece for two important antiquities museums. ⏲ 15 min. See p. 286, **9**.

4 ★ **Antikensammlungen.** If your schedule is really tight, visit either the Antikensammlungen (Antiquities Collection), devoted to Greek and Italian antiquities, or the Glyptothek (next stop). If you don't have any interest in either, head over to the Neue Pinakothek (**6**) instead. The Antikensammlungen has one of the world's greatest collections of Greek amphorae, and a fabulous collection of Etruscan jewelry. ⏲ 30 min. See p. 264, **6**.

The Amazing Asam Brothers

The "real" name of the Asamkirche is St. Johann Nepomuk, but it's always referred to locally by the last name of the two Bavarian brothers who designed and decorated it in a lavish but remarkably harmonious rococo style. Cosmas Damian Asam (1686–1739) specialized in the painting of frescoes, while his younger brother, Egid Quirin Asam (1692–1750), worked as a sculptor and stuccoist. Together they planned, executed, and supervised every detail of the church that now (unofficially) bears their name. Egid Quirin's house with its richly stuccoed baroque facade stands next door to the church at Sendlinger Strasse 61. The Asam boys learned their trades from their father, Hans Georg (1649–1711), who was known throughout Bavaria for his frescoes and stuccowork.

5 ★ **Glyptothek.** This is another neoclassical building by Leo von Klenze, architect of the Propyläen (**3**), and it contains a remarkable collection of Greek and Roman sculpture. Galleries VII–IX, devoted to Roman portrait busts, are my favorite rooms, but there are also on view memorable works from the Archaic to the Hellenistic periods in Greece. ⏱ 30 min. See p. 264, **7**.

6 ★★★ **Neue Pinakothek (New Painting Gallery).** Another day, another *Pinakothek*, this one crammed with luscious works from the 19th century. If the idea of looking at paintings by Goya, Van Gogh, Gauguin, Klimt, and other geniuses makes your mouth water, this is the place for you. The big works by the big names will keep you well occupied, but try to spare a few minutes to have a look at the works of the German Romantic painter Caspar David Friedrich. ⏱ 1 hr. See p. 263, **2**.

7 ★★★ kids **Englischer Garten.** Why, you ask, is Munich's largest and most beautiful park called the English Garden? The answer is because it's laid out in the kind of informal, "naturalistic" way characteristic of English gardens designed by Capability Brown in the 18th century. This is a place to enjoy with no preconceived notions of what you'll see or find—simply stroll along the winding paths and shady streamside walks and through the grassy meadows (where you can get in some nude sunbathing if the mood strikes and the weather's congenial). ⏱ 1 hr. See p. 288, **2**.

8 🍺 ★★★ **Biergarten Chinesischer Turm.** I can't think of a nicer way to end a day in Munich or a stroll in the Englischer Garten than by taking a seat at this vast outdoor beer garden and ordering a drink. It doesn't have to be beer. How about an *Apfelschörle* (half apple juice, half sparkling water)? If the place is full, you'll have about 7,000 people-watching opportunities. See p. 283, **6**.

> The enormous outdoor Biergarten Chinesisicher Turm sometimes plays host to as many as 7,000 thirsty revelers.

The Best of Munich in 3 Days

"Something old, something new" might be the motto for Day 3, which begins at a palace (Nymphenburg), ends at a villa (Stuck), and in between takes you to one of the most strikingly modern buildings in the world (BMW Welt). Nymphenburg Palace, the first stop, requires about half a day to visit if you want to see everything.

> *Many of the frescoes in Schloss Nymphenburg's Great Hall depict the nymph Flora, Roman goddess of flowers, for whom the palace was named.*

START **Schloss Nymphenburg is 8km (5 miles) from the city center. Take tram no. 12, 16, or 17 to Romanplatz; from there, it's about a 10-minute walk west to the palace entrance.**

❶ ★★★ **Schloss Nymphenburg.** Nymphenburg Palace was built so that the royal Wittelsbachs would have a place to chill in the hot summer months. This is a really fun place to explore, so give yourself half a day to wander through the palace rooms, visit the Marstallmuseum—where "Mad Ludwig's" gilded carriages give "four-wheel drive" a whole new meaning—and stroll through the beautiful grounds. See if you can find the 18th-century swimming pool. ◷ Half-day. See p. 274, ❷.

❷ ★ **BMW Welt.** Even if you don't give a rip about the history of Bavarian Motor Works, I suggest visiting BMW Welt (BMW World)—the company's showroom, museum, and factory—to see a stunning example of *new* architecture in Munich. And if you do, you'll also enjoy seeing the vintage Beemers in the museum—examples of German automotive design at its best. ◷ 1 hr. See p. 269, ❺.

❸ ★★ **Villa Stuck.** This charming house-museum was created and lived in by the artist Franz von Stuck. Built at the end of the 19th century, it is a perfect example of Jugendstil (Art Nouveau) design. ◷ 30 min. See p. 290, ❻.

Finish off your evening at either stop ❹ or ❺, depending on your preference.

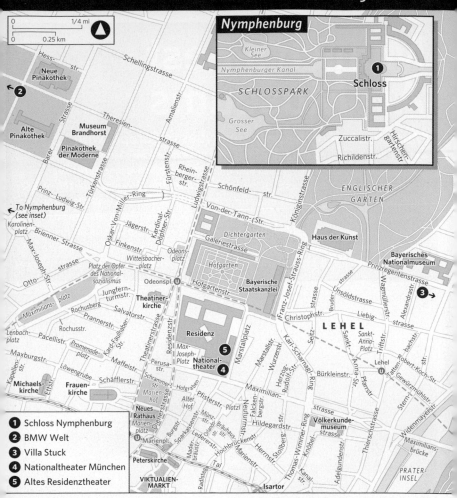

Nymphenburg

Kleiner
See

Nymphenburger Kanal

SCHLOSSPARK

Grosser
See

Schloss ❶

Zuccalistr.

Richildenstr.

---

0   1/4 mi
0   0.25 km

Hess-str.

Schellingstrasse

Neue
Pinakothek

❷

Theresien-
strasse

Museum
Brandhorst

Alte
Pinakothek

Pinakothek
der Moderne

Amalienstrasse

Rhein-
berger-
str.

Schönfeld- str.

ENGLISCHER
GARTEN

Prinz- Ludwig-Str.

Türkenstrasse

Fürstenstrasse

Ludwigstrasse

Von-der-Tann-(Str.

Königinstrasse

To Nymphenburg
(see inset)

Karolinen-
platz

Brienner Strasse

Jägerstr.

Kardinal-
Döpfner-Str.

Dichtergarten

Galeriestrasse

Haus der Kunst

Oskar-Von-Miller-Ring

Max-Joseph-
strasse

Finkenstr.

Wittelsbacher-
platz

Odeons-
platz

Hofgarten

Bayerisches
Nationalmuseum

Prinzregentenstrasse

Otto-
str.

Platz der Opfer
des National-
sozialismus

Odeonspl. Ⓤ

Hofgartenstr.

Bayerische
Staatskanzlei

Wagmüllerstr.

Maximilians-
platz

Jungfern-
turmstr.

Theatiner-
kirche

Franz-Josef-Strauss-Ring

strasse

Unsöldstrasse

Alexandrastr.

❸

Rochusberg

Salvatorstr.

Christophstr.

Bruder-
str.

Liebig-
strasse

LEHEL

Lenbach-
platz

Prannerstr.

Rochusstr.

Pacellistr.

Promenade-
platz

Theatinerstrasse

Residenzstr.

Residenz

Seitz-
str.

Karl-Scharnagl-Ring

Sankt-
Anna-
Platz

Triftstr.

Robert-Koch-Str.

Maxburgstr.

Kapellen-
str.

Löwengrube

Kard-Faulhaber- Str.

Maffeistr.

Max-
Joseph-
Platz

❺

National-
theater

❹

Marstallplatz

Marstallstr.

Herzog-
Rudolf-Str.

Sankt-Anna-Str.

Lehel Ⓤ

Gewürzmühlstr.

Michaels-
kirche

Eisstr.

Frauen-
kirche

Schäfflerstr.

Schrammer-
str.

Perusastr.

Maximilian-
straße

Wurzerstr.

Bürkleinstr.

Planstr.

Sternstr.

Widenmayerstr.

Marien-
hof

Hofgraben

Pfisterstr.

Platzl

Falcken-
bergstr.

Neuturmstr.

strasse

Thierschstrasse

Maximilians-
brücke

Neues
Rathaus

Marien-
platz

Ⓤ Marienpl.

Dienerstr.

Burgstr.

Alter
Hof

Münz-
str.

Sparkassenstr.

Ledererstr.

Münz-
str.

Bräuhaus-
str.

Hildegardstr.

Stollberg-

Knöbel-
str.

strasse

Völkerkunde-
museum

Adelgundenstr.

Maximilians-
brücke

Peterskirche

VIKTUALIEN-
MARKT

Radlsteg

Mader-
bräustr.

Heiliggeiststr.

Hochbrückenstr.

Tal

Herrnst.

Marienstr.

Thomas-Wimmer-Ring

Kanal-
str.

PRATER-
INSEL

Isartor

❶ Schloss Nymphenburg
❷ BMW Welt
❸ Villa Stuck
❹ Nationaltheater München
❺ Altes Residenztheater

---

❹ **Nationaltheater München.** If you're a fan of opera or ballet, I don't need to prod you—go to the National Theater and get a ticket for a performance by the world-class ★★★ **Bayerische Staatsoper** (Bavarian State Opera). Its opera and ballet companies both perform in the 2,100-seat theater. See p. 314.

❺ ★★★ **Altes Residenztheater.** If you love opera and/or theater (even if it's performed in German), book a seat to see whatever's playing at this stunning little rococo theater (also called the Cuvilliés Theater). In how many cities can you enjoy a performance in a plush, red, 18th-century royal court theater? See p. 314.

> BMW Welt's museum offers a spin through the proud history of one of the world's top auto companies.

Munich's Best Art Museums

Munich is one of the great art cities of Europe, with outstanding museums and collections that span the history of Western civilization. Four of the city's best and most comprehensive *Pinakotheken* (painting galleries) are clustered in one area called the Museum Quarter, or Art Park, with the two antiquities museums and the Lenbachhaus, with its early-20th-century German paintings, a short walk away. Even if you were racing through just to see the highlights, it would be impossible to visit all of these great museums in 1 day, so this is not so much a place-to-place tour as it is a directory of Munich's best art museums.

> The Neue Pinakothek houses a vast collection of 19th-century art, including this masterpiece by German Romantic landscape painter Caspar David Friedrich.

START **Take tram no. 27 to Pinakothek (the museum is across the street).**

SITE GUIDE
PAGE 265

❶ ★★★ **Alte Pinakothek (Old Painting Gallery).** The nearly 800 paintings on display in this world-famous museum represent the greatest German and European artists of the 14th through 18th centuries. The collection began with Wilhelm IV, Duke of Bavaria, who wanted to decorate his palace with historic paintings, and grew with each successive ruler. Housed in an immense Italian Renaissance–style building completed in 1836, the museum has two floors of exhibits. Pick up a map and audio-guide at the information desk to help you navigate through the many galleries, and hone in on the works that interest you.

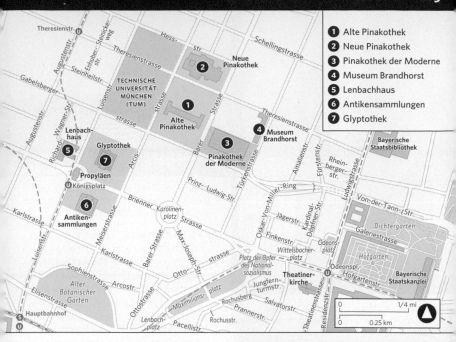

② ★★★ **Neue Pinakothek (New Painting Gallery).** This showcase for 19th-century art picks up where the Alte Pinakothek leaves off, with an outstanding collection of works by most of the major German and European artists and schools. The German paintings range from neoclassicism through Romanticism (note especially the haunting works of Caspar David Friedrich) to Secessionist works. British artists Thomas Gainsborough, Joshua Reynolds, and J. M. W. Turner are represented, as are the French realists and other greats such as Francisco Goya, Vincent van Gogh, Paul Gauguin, and Gustav Klimt. ⏱ 1–2 hr. Barer Strasse 27. ☎ 089/2380-5195. www.pinakothek. de/neue-pinakothek. Admission 9.50€ adults, 6€ students and seniors (Sun 1€ for all); audio tour free Wed–Sat, 4.50€ Sun. Wed–Mon 10am–6pm (Wed until 10pm). Closed major holidays. Tram: 27 to Pinakothek (the museum entrance is across the street).

③ ★★★ **Pinakothek der Moderne.** Devote most of your time at the Pinakothek der Moderne (Gallery of Modern Art, Architecture, and Design) to the **Staatsgalerie Moderner Kunst** (Gallery of Modern Art), which displays major 20th-century classics by internationally

> *The Alte Pinakothek displays works from 14th-century European artists, like this Self-Portrait in a Fur-Collared Robe by Albrecht Dürer.*

> Munich's most recent museum addition, the Brandhorst, features fascinating sculptures and art installations of the 20th century.

> This 1929 painting of Halle Church by Lyonel Feininger is displayed in the Pinakothek der Moderne.

known artists including Matisse, Picasso, Gris, Kandinsky, Kirchner, Ernst, and Giacometti. The other, more specialized collections include the **Neue Sammlung** (Craft and Design Collection), the **Museum of Architecture,** and the **Graphische Sammlung** (Graphics Collection). ⏱ 1–2 hr. Barer Strasse 40. ☎ 089/2380-5360. www.pinakothek.de/pinakothek-der-moderne. Admission 9.50€ adults, 6€ students 10–18, free for kids 9 and under (Sun 1€ for all). Tues–Sun 10am–6pm (Thurs until 8pm). Closed major holidays. Tram: 27 to Pinakothek (the museum is across the street).

4 ★★ **Museum Brandhorst.** Munich's newest museum opened in 2009 to showcase paintings, sculptures, works on paper, and art installations from the mid- to late 20th century. Featured are major works by American artists Cy Twombly, Andy Warhol, Jean-Michel Basquiat, and Alex Katz; the controversial British artist Damien Hirst; and the German painter Sigmar Polke. Plus, there's an unusual collection of books illustrated by Picasso. ⏱ 1 hr. Theresienstrasse 35a. ☎ 089/238-051-321. www.museum-brandhorst.de. Admission 7€ adults, 5€ seniors and students (Sun 1€ for all). Tues–Sun 10am–6pm (Thurs until 8pm). Tram: 27 to Pinakothek.

5 ★★ **Lenbachhaus.** The painter Franz von Lenbach built this Italianate villa between 1887 and 1891 to serve as his residence and atelier. It now houses an outstanding collection of works by the Blaue Reiter (Blue Rider) school of artists working in Munich before World War I. Bold colors and abstract forms characterize the work of Wasily Kandinsky, Paul Klee, Franz Marc, and Gabriele Münter. ⏱ 1 hr. Luisenstrasse 33. ☎ 089/2333-2000. www.lenbachhaus.de. Admission 6€ adults, 3€ students. Tues–Sun 10am–5pm. U-Bahn: Königsplatz.

6 ★ **Antikensammlungen (Antiquities Collection).** The Antikensammlungen is an essential stop for anyone interested in ancient art. The museum houses a collection of Greek, Etruscan, and Roman masterpieces of ornamental art, jewelry, small statues, and vases that range from a pre-Mycenaean version carved in 3000 B.C. from a mussel shell to large Greek and Etruscan models. The star attraction is a golden Greek necklace from the 4th century B.C. ⏱ 1 hr. Königsplatz 1. ☎ 089/5998-8830. www.antikem-am-koenigsplatz.mwn.de. Admission 3.50€ (Sun 1€); joint ticket with Glyptothek 6€. Tues–Sun 10am–5pm (Wed until 8pm). U-Bahn: Königsplatz (go to the south side of Königsplatz).

7 ★ **Glyptothek.** Germany's largest collection of ancient Greek and Roman sculpture is on view here, including 6th-century-B.C. *kouroi* (statues of youths), a colossal *Sleeping Satyr* from the Hellenistic period, and a haunting collection of Roman portraits. ⏱ 30 min. Königsplatz 3. ☎ 089/286-100. Admission 3.50€ (Sun 1€). Tues–Sun 10am–5pm (Thurs until 8pm). U-Bahn: Königsplatz.

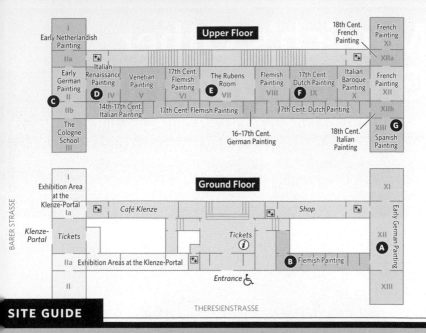

Upper Floor

I — Early Netherlandish Painting
IIa — Italian Renaissance Painting
II — Early German Painting
IIb
III — The Cologne School
14th–17th Cent. Italian Painting
IV — D
V — Venetian Painting
VI — 17th Cent. Flemish Painting
17th Cent. Flemish Painting
VII — The Rubens Room — E
16–17th Cent. German Painting
VIII — Flemish Painting
IX — 17th Cent. Dutch Painting — F
17th Cent. Dutch Painting
X — Italian Baroque Painting
18th Cent. Italian Painting
XI — French Painting
XII — 18th Cent. French Painting
XII — French Painting
XIIb
XIII — Spanish Painting — G

C

Ground Floor

BARER STRASSE

I — Exhibition Area at the Klenze-Portal
Ia — Café Klenze
Klenze-Portal — Tickets
IIa — Exhibition Areas at the Klenze-Portal
II
Shop
Tickets (i)
Flemish Painting — B
XI
XII — A
XIII — Early German Painting
Entrance
THERESIENSTRASSE

SITE GUIDE

1 Alte Pinakothek

Displayed on the ground floor in **A Galleries XI–XII** are 16th- and 17th-century works by such German Old Masters as Michael Pacher, Hans Holbein the Elder, Jan Polac, and Lucas Cranach the Elder (In particular look for his *Adam and Eve,* pictured). To the right of the main entrance, **B Rooms 16–23** are given over to a marvelous collection of canvases by the Brueghel family of painters.

Galleries on the first floor contain paintings by French, Italian, Spanish, German, Dutch, and Flemish artists. One of the museum's most fascinating paintings is the *Self-Portrait in a Fur-Collared Robe* by Albrecht Dürer in **C Gallery II.** Among the 15th- and 16th-century Italian paintings in **D Gallery IV** are *Lamentation over the Dead Christ,* a late work by the Florentine Sandro Botticelli; *Madonna and Child* by Leonardo da Vinci; and Giorgione's *Portrait of a Young Man.* All of **E Gallery VII** is devoted to works by the Flemish artist Peter Paul Rubens. Three works by Rembrandt—*Portrait of a Man in Oriental Costume* (1633), *The Holy Family* (1633), and *Sacrifice of Isaac* (1636)—are found in **F Gallery IX.** Striking

works by Spanish artists El Greco, Velázquez, and Murillo are found in **G Gallery XIII.** ⏱ 2–3 hr. Barer Strasse 27. ☎ 089/2380-5216. www. alte-pinakothek.de. 5.50€ adults, 4€ students, kids under 17 free (Sun 1€ for all); audio tour free Tues-Sat, 4.50€ Sun. Tues-Sun 10am–5pm (Tues until 10pm). Closed major holidays. Tram: 27 to Pinakothek (museum is across the street).

Munich's Other Great Museums

Munich is justly famous for its art museums, but it's also home to a fascinating array of great museums devoted to science and technology, transportation, and local and regional history. These museums are far more spread out over the city than the art museums, but all of them are easily accessible on public transportation. You can't hope to visit all of them in 1 day, so this isn't a museum-to-museum tour but a directory of the best "other" museums in Munich.

> The spectacularly modern design of BMW Welt is as riveting as the historical exhibits inside it.

START Take tram no. 18 to Deutsches Museum (the tram stops outside the museum).

SITE GUIDE
PAGE 270

❶ ★★★ kids Deutsches Museum (German Museum of Science and Technology). With some 16,000 exhibits in 50 departments, the German Museum of Science and Technology is the largest such museum in the world. Its huge trove of natural science and technological treasures includes rare historical objects, dioramas, and scale models that trace the history of science and technology from prehistoric times up to the present day and is augmented by demonstrations and interactive exhibits. Navigating your way around the four floors of this vast collection is daunting, and seeing everything in one visit is impossible. Pick up a map at the museum entrance and choose a few areas of special interest.

❷ ★ kids Münchner Stadtmuseum (Munich City Museum). Munich's history and the

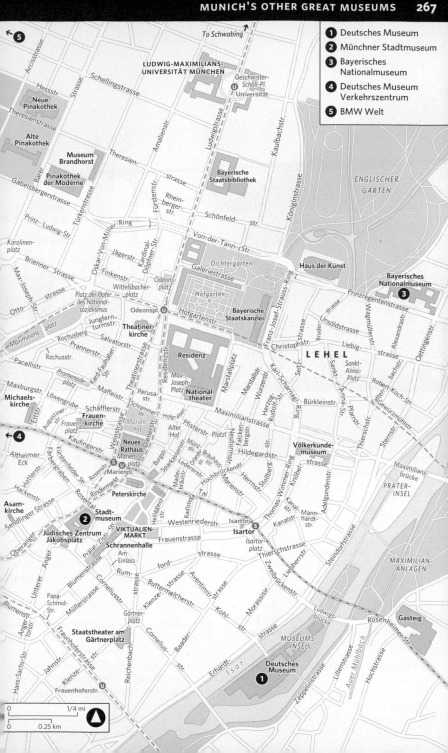

1 Deutsches Museum
2 Münchner Stadtmuseum
3 Bayerisches Nationalmuseum
4 Deutsches Museum Verkehrszentrum
5 BMW Welt

To Schwabing

LUDWIG-MAXIMILIANS-UNIVERSITÄT MÜNCHEN

Geschwister-Schöll-Pl.
Universität

Neue Pinakothek

Hessstr.

Arcisstrasse

Schellingstrasse

Theresienstrasse

Alte Pinakothek

Museum Brandhorst

Pinakothek der Moderne

Gabelsbergerstrasse

Barer str.

Türkenstrasse

Theresien- strasse

Amalienstr.

Fürstenstr.

Rhein- berger- str.

Ludwigstrasse

Bayerische Staatsbibliothek

Schönfeld- str.

Kaulbachstr.

Königinstrasse

ENGLISCHER GARTEN

Prinz- Ludwig-Str.

Oskar-Von-Miller-Ring

Kardinal- Döpfner-Str.

Von-der-Tann-(Str.

Karolinen- platz

Brienner Strasse

Max-Joseph-Str.

Otto-

strasse

Finkenstr.

Jägerstr.

Wittelsbacher- platz

Odeons- platz

Dichtergarten

Galeriestrasse

Hofgarten

Haus der Künst

Bayerisches Nationalmuseum **3**

Prinzregentenstrasse

Maximilians- platz

Rochusberg

Rochusstr.

Pacellistr.

Platz der Opfer des National- sozialismus

Jungfern- turmstr.

Salvatorstr.

Prannerstr.

Theatiner- kirche

Odeonspl.

Hofgartenstr.

Bayerische Staatskanzlei

Christophstr.

Franz-Josef-Strauss-Ring

LEHEL

Bruder- str.

Unsöldstrasse

Liebig- strasse

Seitz-

Sankt-Anna- Platz

Alexandrastr.

Oettingenstr.

Robert-Koch-Str.

Gewürzmühlstr.

Maxburgstr.

Michaels- kirche

Eisstr.

Promenade- platz

Löwengrube

Augustiner-str.

Kard.-Faulhaber-Str.

Maffeistr.

Schäfflerstr.

Residenz

Theatinerstrasse

Residenzstrasse

Perusa- str.

Max- Joseph- Platz

National- theater

Marstallplatz

Hofgraben

Maximilianstrasse

Marstallstr.

Wurzerstr.

Herzog-Rudolf-Str.

Karl-Scharnagl-Ring

Sankt-Anna-Str.

Thierschstr.

Sternstr.

Maximilians- brücke

PRATER- INSEL

Frauen- platz

Frauen- kirche

Schrammer- str.

Marien- hof

Dienerstr.

Alter Hof

Pfisterstr.

Platzl

Falcken- bergstr.

Neuturmstr.

Hildegardstr.

Völkerkunde- museum

Maximilians- brücke

Altheimer Eck

Hackenstr.

Färbergraben

Fürstenfelder Str.

Rosenstr.

Neues Rathaus

Marien- pl.

Marienpl.

Rindermarkt

Burgstr.

Sparkassenstr.

Ledererstr.

Münz- str.

Orlandostr.

Bräuhaus- str.

Madersträustr.

Hochbrückenstr.

Tal

Herrnstr.

Marienstr.

Stollbergstr.

Knöbelstr.

Thomas-Wimmer-Ring

Adelgundenstr.

Asam- kirche

Sendlinger Strasse

Hotterstr.

Rosental

Peterskirche

Heiliggeist- str.

Radlsteg

Westenriederstr.

Isartor

Isartor

Isartor- platz

Thierschstrasse

MAXIMILIAN- ANLAGEN

Oberanger

Anger

Jüdisches Zentrum Jakobsplatz

2 Stadt- museum

VIKTUALIEN- MARKT

Schrannenhalle

Am Einlass

Frauenstrasse

strasse

ford-

Kanalstr.

Kanal- str.

Thomas-Wimmer-Ring

Mann- hardtstr.

Unterer

Prälat-Zistl-Str.

Cornelius- strasse

Blumenstrasse

Rum-

Buttermelcherstr.

Aventinstr.

Kohl-

str.

Morassistr.

Zweibrückenstr.

Lieberherrstr.

Steindorfstrasse

MAXIMILIAN- ANLAGEN

Blumenstr.

Anger- torstr.

Papa- Schmid- Str.

Müllerstrasse

Klenze- str.

Gärtner- platz

Klenze-

Baader-

str.

strasse

Ludwigs- brücke

Auer Mühlbach

Rosenheimerstr.

Gasteig

Hans-Sachs-Str.

Jahnstr.

Staatstheater am Gärtnerplatz

Fraunhoferstrasse

Reichenbach-

Cornelius-

str.

Erhardt-

Isar

MÜSEUMS- INSEL

Zeppelinstr.

Lilienstrasse

Auer Mühlbach

Hochstrasse

Klenze-

Frauenhoferstr.

Deutsches Museum **1**

0 ___ 1/4 mi
0 ___ 0.25 km

> The Münchner Stadtmuseum, housed in a 15th-century arsenal, has a fascinating array of exhibits that document the history of life in the city.

everyday lives of its residents are chronicled in the Münchner Stadtmuseum. The one must-see exhibit is the *Moriskentanzer* (Moorish Dancers), featuring 10 carved and brightly painted 15th-century wooden figures. The second-floor photo museum traces the early history of the camera back to 1839. Children love the third-floor collection of marionettes and hand puppets and the gallery of fairground art, which includes the oldest-known carousel horses, dating from 1820. ⏱ 30–45 min. St.-Jakobs-Platz 1. ☎ 089/2332-2370. www.stadtmuseum-online.de. Admission 4€ adults, 2€ students/kids 6–15; free on Sun. Tues–Sun 10am–6pm. *U-* or *S-Bahn:* Marienplatz. Walk south on Rindermarkt and Oberanger to museum.

❸ ★★ **Bayerisches Nationalmuseum.** The objects on view in the vast Bavarian National Museum—sculptures, paintings, folk art, ceramics, furniture, textiles, clocks, and scientific instruments—rank among Bavaria's greatest historic and artistic treasures. A not-to-be-missed highlight is the **Riemenschneider Room,** which contains works in wood by the great sculptor Tilman Riemenschneider (1460–1531). The museum also contains a famous collection of Christmas Nativity cribs from Bavaria, Tyrol, and southern Italy. ⏱ 90 min. Prinzregentenstrasse 3. ☎ 089/211-2401. www.bayerisches-nationalmuseum.de. Admission 5€ adults, 3€ seniors and students (Sun 1€ for all). Tues–Sun 10am–5pm (Thurs until 8pm). *U-Bahn:* Lehel. Walk north on Wagmüllerstrasse and east on Prinzregentenstrasse to museum.

❹ ★★ kids **Deutsches Museum Verkehrszentrum.** How have people transported themselves for the last 200 years? You'll find out at the intriguing Transportation Museum, which deals with mobility and technology, travel and urban transport. There's a wonderful collection of horse-drawn carriages and bicycles, some of them 150 years old, and historic gems

> *Part of the Christmas Nativity crèche collection at the Bayerisches Nationalmuseum.*

like the "Puffing Billy" steam locomotive from 1814 and a passenger train from the late 19th century. These and a superlative collection of historic automobiles, including Daimlers, Opels, Mercedes, Tatas, Citroëns, and Bugattis, are displayed in three historic exhibition halls that opened in 1908 as venues for trade fairs. ⏱ 1 hr. Theresienhöhe 14a. ☎ 089/5008-6140. www. deutsches-museum.de. Admission 6€ adults, 4€ seniors, 12€ families. Daily 9am–5pm. Closed major holidays. *U-Bahn:* U4 or U5 to Schwanthalerhöhe (the Deutsches Museum exit is marked in the station).

❺ ★ **BMW Welt (BMW World).** If you have any interest in cars, it's worth the short trip out to Olympiapark to see the new BMW Welt showroom. Architecturally, this is a boldly dramatic structure with soaring lines. A glass-enclosed hourglass-shaped spiral ramp leads up to a sky bridge to the overpriced museum, which features a collection of motorcycles and cars dating from the company's beginning in 1929 up through to a hydrogen-powered roadster of the future. You can watch the assembly process in the factory buildings. ⏱ Showroom 15 min., museum 30 min., plant 45 min. Am Olympiapark 1. ☎ 0180/211-8822. www.bmw-welt. com. Free admission showroom; museum 12€ adults, 6€ seniors and kids under 16; plant tours 6€ adults, 3€ seniors and kids. Showroom and museum Tues–Fri 9am–6pm, Sat–Sun 10am–6pm. Plant guided tours Mon–Fri 8:30am–10pm. (reservations required). *U-Bahn:* Olympiapark (the station exit is almost in front of BMW Welt).

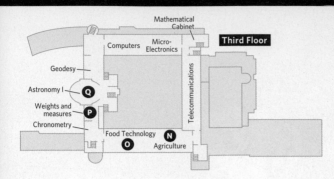

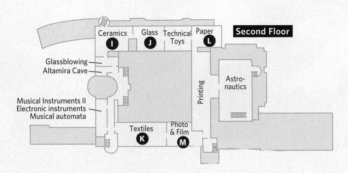

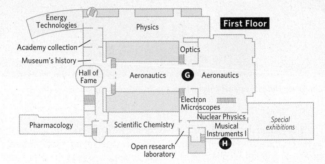

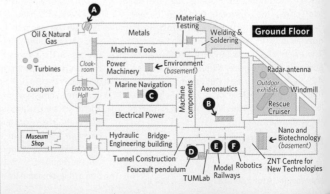

SITE GUIDE

1 Deutsches Museum

Highlights in the basement galleries include a **A Mining** section with a model salt mine, and the **B Kids' Kingdom** with lots of hands-on exhibits. The ground (main) floor has a **C Navigation** section with the first German submarine (1906) and a 1958 bathysphere, a reproduction of **D Foucault's Pendulum,** a huge collection of ★ **E Model Railways** set up and running in an elaborate landscape, and a fascinating section on **F Robotics.**

The most interesting section on the first floor is the impressive ★★ **G Aeronautics** hall, with a rare 1885 biplane, a 1909 plane owned by the Wright brothers, and a 1936 Messerschmitt. The gallery devoted to **H Musical Instruments** is also interesting.

Several intriguing exhibits having to do with the artistic and technical development of the decorative arts are found on the second floor.

Spend some time browsing the sections devoted to the manufacture of ★ **I Ceramics,** ★★ **J Glass** (with glassblowing demonstrations), ★ **K Textiles,** and ★ **L Paper** (with demonstrations), and the section that traces the development of ★ **M Film and Photography.**

Third floor galleries of particular interest include **N Agriculture, O Food Technology,** and ★ **P Weights and Measures,** with a collection of historic instruments used to measure time, weight, and distance. Explanations of the cosmos and a collection of the instruments used to explore outer space are exhibited in the ★★ **Q Astronomy** section. ⏲ 2–3 hr. Museumsinsel 1. ☎ 089/21791. www.deutsches-museum.de. Admission 8.50€ adults, 7€ seniors, 17€ families. Daily 9am–5pm. Closed major holidays. Tram: 18 to Deutsches Museum.

Steeples & Stucco: Munich's Churches

Munich's rich architectural legacy includes several notable churches dating from the 13th to the 18th centuries. You can visit all of these churches, which encompass Gothic, Renaissance, and baroque styles, on an easy 2-hour walking tour.

> The enormous interior of Michaelskirche is all the more impressive given the fact that the church was consecrated in 1597.

START **Frauenplatz is a 2-minute walk from Marienplatz. Take the *U-Bahn* or *S-Bahn* to Marienplatz, head west on Landschaftsstrasse, continue onto Filserbraugasse, and turn right at Frauenplatz.**

1 ★ **Frauenkirche.** Constructed from red brick in an unusually plain late Gothic style, this famous symbol of Munich—its full name is Dom zu Unserer Lieben Frau (Cathedral of Our Lady)—was completed in 1488 and has one of the largest church interiors in Germany, with room for 20,000 people. Because of

restrictions on building heights, the towers still dominate the city skyline. It's a hefty climb up the top, but the view extends all the way to the Alps. ⏱ 15 min. with tower. See p. 254, **4**.

2 **Michaelskirche (St. Michael's Church).** The first Jesuit church in northern Europe, St. Michael's was consecrated in 1597 and is notable for its vast interior and crypt containing the tombs of several Wittelsbach rulers, including Ludwig II, the builder of Neuschwanstein Castle (p. 338, **2**). ⏱ 15 min. Neuhauser Strasse

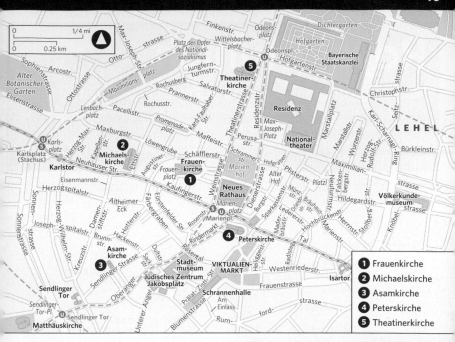

52. ☎ 089/231-7060. Free admission. Mon–Sat 8:30am–7pm, Sun 6:45am–10pm. *U-* or *S-Bahn:* Karlsplatz or Marienplatz.

❸ ★★ Asamkirche. This remarkable rococo church was built by the Asam brothers between 1733 and 1746 (see "The Amazing Asam Brothers," p. 258). Multicolored marbles, gold leaf, and silver cover every square inch of the interior of this small rectangular church with rounded ends. ⏱15 min. Sendlinger Strasse. ☎ 089/260-9357. Free admission. Daily 8am–5:30pm. *U-* or *S-Bahn:* Sendlinger Tor.

❹ Peterskirche (St. Peter's Church). The bell tower of this 13th-century Gothic church, remodeled during the baroque era, is known locally as Old Pete. There's a splendid view from the top, but you have to climb (and climb and climb) 306 steps to enjoy it. The interior of the church contains baroque-era sculptures, frescoes, and a bizarre relic in the second chapel on the left: the gem-studded skeleton of St. Mundita, who stares at you with the two false eyes in her skull. ⏱15 min. Rindermarkt 1. ☎ 089/260-4828. Free admission to church; tower 2.50€ adults, 1.50€ students. Mon–Sat 9am–6pm (Nov–Mar until 5pm), Sun 10am–7pm (Nov–Mar until 6pm). *U-* or *S-Bahn:* Marienplatz.

> The small, 18th-century Asamkirche may be modest on the outside, but the interior is a baroque fantasy.

❺ ★★ Theatinerkirche (Church of the Theatines). Munich's finest example of Italian baroque architecture was named for the Theatines, a Roman Catholic religious order. Begun by Italian architects in 1663 and completed by German court architects about a century later, it has fluted columns, an arched ceiling, and dollops of fanciful white stuccowork decorating every surface. ⏱15 min. Theatinerstrasse 22. ☎ 089/210-6960. Free admission. Mon–Fri 10am–1pm and 1:30–4:30pm, Sat 10am–3pm. *U-* or *S-Bahn:* Odeonsplatz.

Royal Munich

From the 12th century until 1918, Bavaria was ruled by the Wittelsbach family, whose two palaces, one in Munich's Altstadt and the other 8km (5 miles) northwest of the city center, are fascinating reminders of their royal lifestyle. You could visit both palaces in 1 day, but it would be an exhausting experience. Instead, break this tour up into 2 days and give each palace half a day.

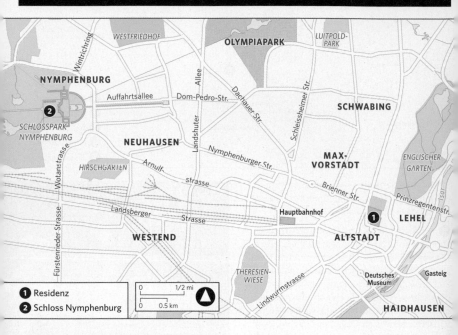

❶ Residenz
❷ Schloss Nymphenburg

START **Take tram no. 19 to Nationaltheater (the palace is on the same side as the theater), or the** *U-Bahn* **to Odeonsplatz (the palace is across the square).**

SITE GUIDE
PAGE 275

❶ ★★ **Residenz.** The official residence of the Wittelsbach family from 1385 to 1918, the enormous Royal Palace is a compendium of various architectural styles. Almost entirely destroyed in World War II, the Residenz was painstakingly reconstructed and today houses a number of museums and monuments. Unfortunately, there are no public guided tours, so choosing what to see in this huge and complex complex can be a challenge. To help navigate,

pick up a map and a free audio tour in the museum shop.

SITE GUIDE
PAGE 277

❷ ★★★ **Schloss Nymphenburg.** Nymphenburg Palace, the Wittelsbachs' summer residence, is one of the most sophisticated and beautiful palaces in Europe. Begun in 1664, it took more than 150 years to complete. In 1702, Elector Maximilian II Emanuel enlarged the original Italianate villa by adding four pavilions connected by arcaded passageways. Gradually the French style took over, and today the facade is a subdued baroque. The extensive palace grounds, with museums and historic buildings, should also be part of your visit.

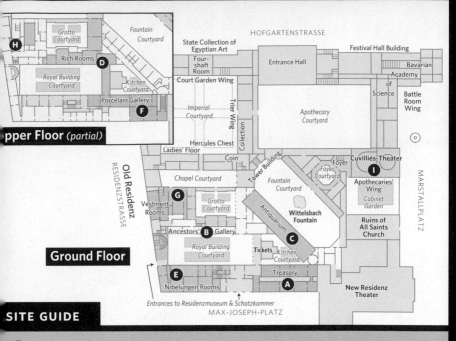

Upper Floor (partial)

Ground Floor

❶ Residenz

If you're pressed for time, head first for the ★★ **ⓐ Treasury** (entrance on Max-Joseph-Platz), filled with 3 centuries' worth of royal "collectibles," including superb gold work, precious gems, enamels, crystal, and the crown and scepter of the House of Bavaria.

In 1920 some 130 rooms of the Wittelsbach residence opened to the public as the ★★ **Residenz Museum.** It's impossible to list all the apartments, ceremonial rooms, and chapels in this vast and stylistically variable assemblage, but the following are worth looking at. The ★ **ⓑ Ancestors' Gallery** is embellished with gilded stuccowork and carvings. The oldest part of the palace is the enormous ★★ **ⓒ Antiquarium,** dating from 1570 and lined with antique busts. Completed in 1737, **ⓓ Die Reichen Zimmer** (State Rooms) are decorated in an early version of rococo style. The ★★ **ⓔ Königsbau** (King's Wing) houses the Royal Apartments, built between 1826 and 1835 and filled with original paintings, furniture, and sculpture.

German and French porcelain is displayed in the ★ **ⓕ Porcelain Rooms.** Near the sumptuously restored **ⓖ Hofkapelle** (Court Chapel)

is the **ⓗ Reliquienkammer** (Reliquary Room) with a collection of 16th- to 18th-century gold and silver plate. After touring the palace, head to Max-Joseph-Platz and visit the ★★ **ⓘ Altes Residenztheater** (also called the Cuvilliés-Theater), a stunning rococo theater dating from 1753. ⏱ 3–4 hr. Max-Joseph-Platz 3. ☎ 089/290-671. www.residenz-muenchen.de. Admission: Combined ticket museum and treasury 9€ adults, 8€ students/kids; Residenztheater 3€ adults, 2€ students/kids. Apr–Oct 15 daily 9am–6pm, Oct 16–Mar daily 10am–4pm. Tram: 19 to Nationaltheater; or *U-Bahn:* to Odeonsplatz.

> Ceiling of Schloss Nymphenburg's Festsaal.

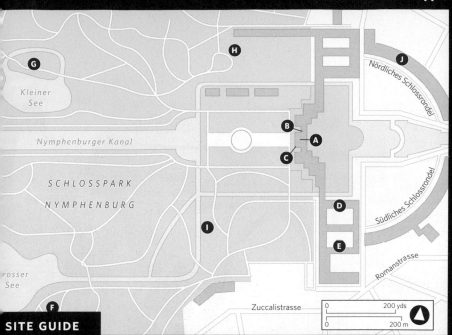

SITE GUIDE

2 Schloss Nymphenburg

Inside, you come first to the ★★ **A** **Festsaal** (Great Hall), embellished with 18th-century rococo stuccowork and frescoes devoted to the goddess Flora. In the south pavilion, Ludwig I's famous ★★★ **B** **Gallery of Beauties** displays paintings by J. Stieler (1827–50), including *Schöne Münchnerin* (Lovely Munich Girl) and a portrait of Lola Montez, the raven-haired dancer whose affair with Ludwig I forced his abdication. The colorful 18th-century ★ **C** **Chinesisches Lackkabinett** (Chinese Lacquer Cabinet) gets its name from its Chinese lacquer screens and panels.

The former court stables now house the ★★★ **D** **Marstallmuseum** with its dazzling collection of ornate gilded coaches and sleighs, including those used by Ludwig II. The adjacent ★ **E** **Porzellansammlung** (Porcelain Collection) contains superb pieces of 18th-century porcelain, including miniature porcelain copies of masterpieces in the Alte Pinakothek (p. 262, **1**).

Behind the palace, a canal runs through the 500-acre **Schlosspark** (Palace Park), an English-style park full of meadows and forested paths, to a fountain at the far end of formal, French-style gardens. The park contains the ★ **F** **Badenburg Pavilion,** with an 18th-century swimming pool; the **G** **Pagodenburg,** decorated in the Chinese style that was all the rage in the 18th century; and the **H** **Magdalenenklause** (Hermitage), meant to be a retreat for prayer and solitude. Prettiest of all the buildings in the park is ★★ **I** **Amalienburg,** built in 1734 as a hunting lodge for Electress Amalia; the interior salons are a riot of flamboyant colors, swirling stuccowork, and wall paintings.

One of the oldest porcelain factories in Europe, **J** **Porzellan-Manufaktur-Nymphenburg,** still produces and sells the famous Nymphenburg porcelain (Nördliches Schlossrondell 8, ☎ 089/179-1970, Mon–Fri 8:30am–5pm). ⏱ 3–4 hr. to visit palace and grounds. Schloss Nymphenburg 1 (8km/5 miles northwest of city center). ☎ 089/179-080. Admission to all attractions 10€ adults, 8€ seniors. Apr–Oct 15 daily 9am–6pm, Oct 16–Mar daily 10am–4pm. Badenburg and Magdalenenklause closed Oct 16–Mar. Tram: 12, 16, or 17 to Romanplatz.

OKTOBERFEST

The Original Kegger BY DONALD OLSON

THE WORLD'S GREATEST BEER FESTIVAL starts in late September and runs to the first Sunday in October. All the *trinken und essen* (drinking and eating) at this giant, 16-day party takes place at the **Theresienwiese** ("Wiesn" for short) festival grounds, where different beers are sold in 14 different tents, each with its own atmosphere, food, and musical entertainment. Though it's adults who do the chug-a-lugging (over 6 million liters of beer are sold every year), kids are very much a part of the Oktoberfest scene, with rides and different entertainment venues for families to enjoy.

Ludwig I, the Original Party Animal

In 1810, to celebrate his marriage to Princess Therese of Saxony-Hildburghausen, Prince Ludwig of Bavaria (later King Ludwig I) threw a big party and invited the people of Munich to attend.

Ludwig organized a horse race and provided copious amounts of beer and roast oxen.

The tradition of beer and food stands, begun in 1818, continues today at the site of the first Oktoberfest.

There is no charge to enter the Oktoberfest or any of the tents. If you want a seat in one of the tents, you must book in advance by contacting the tents as early as possible; after March there won't be any spaces left. If you are visiting without a seat reservation, arrive by 2:30pm weekdays or 11am weekends for your best chance at a seat.

> Beer and food are available only in the beer tents and you must have a seat or you won'tbe served a beer.

> The average cost for a Mass (1 liter) of beer is 8.50€.

> Oktoberfest beer has a 5% to 6% alcohol level, so pace yourself and drink plenty of water or you may find yourself on the floor, or otherwise embarrassing yourself.

The Best Tents

The beer tents range in size from 90 to 10,000 seats (with more seating outside). Here are a few of the best.

FISCHER-BRONI
(☎ 089/661-042): Forget the pig's knuckles and enjoy fish—pike, whitefish, salmon, trout—skewered and grilled in one of the most comfortable Oktoberfest tents.

SCHOTTENHAMEL
(☎ 089/5446-9319): The tapping of the first keg of Oktoberfest beer takes place inside this tent, now the largest of them all with seating for 10,000. This is the preferred hangout for the under-30s.

SCHÜTZEN-FESTZELT
(☎ 089/2318-1224): This midsize tent with seating for 4,442 is famous for its roast suckling pig, prepared in the traditional Bavarian style with malt-beer sauce and accompanied by warm potato salad.

AUGUSTINER-FESTHALLE
(☎ 089/2318-3266): The most family-friendly tent at Oktoberfest has a low-priced kids' day on Tuesdays and entertainment that's in full swing by midafternoon. There's seating for 6,000 inside, and 2,500 outside.

KÄFERS WIES'N-SCHÄNKE
(☎ 089/416-8356): Smallish and relatively cozy, this tent is considered to have the best food at Oktoberfest and attracts the most celebs.

OCHSENBRATEREI
(☎ 089/3838-1712): The sign, an ox slowly turning on a spit, says it all. This 6,000-seat tent is famous for its oxen dishes and offers traditional brass band music.

FEISINGER'S KAS- UND WEINSTUBEN
(☎ 089/892-9127): You're not a beer drinker and eating roast oxen is just not on your to-do list? At this little (92-seat) tent you can enjoy cheese and wine. Try Raclette, melted cheese over bread, or potatoes garnished with pickles or onions.

Munich's Best Beer Halls & Beer Gardens

The German *Biergarten* (beer garden) originated in Munich in the 19th century. To keep their beers cool, large breweries dug beer cellars in the banks of the Isar River, covering the banks in gravel and planting shady chestnut trees. Eventually, simple tables and benches were set up under the trees, and beer gardens became popular gathering spots. Beer gardens are usually attached to a beer hall (pub) or restaurant owned by a brewery. Oom-pah-pah bands, zither players, or accordionists sometimes add to the jovial atmosphere. The following tour will take you to Munich's biggest and best-known beer halls and beer gardens. Most are just a short walk apart, so you can try them all out or just sample a few, depending on your stamina.

> The Hofbräuhaus am Platzl is always spilling over with customers eager for refreshment and revelry.

START Neuhauser Strasse (at Kreuzstrasse). Take the *U-Bahn* to Karlsplatz/Stachus. From there, walk east on Neuhauser Strasse; Augustiner Grossgaststätte is about 5 minutes from the *U-Bahn* stop.

❶ ★★ **Augustiner Grossgaststätte.** The house beer, Augustiner Brau, comes from Munich's oldest brewery, with a tradition that

dates back to the 14th century, when Augustinian monks began brewing beer near the location of this famous beer hall, restaurant (p. 299), and hotel. The beer hall took on its current look (cavernous rooms, beer garden in the courtyard) in 1896. You can see the original beer-cellar architecture in the *Bierkeller*. Neuhauser Strasse 27. ☎ 089/2318-3257. Daily 9am–midnight. *U-Bahn:* Karlsplatz/Stachus.

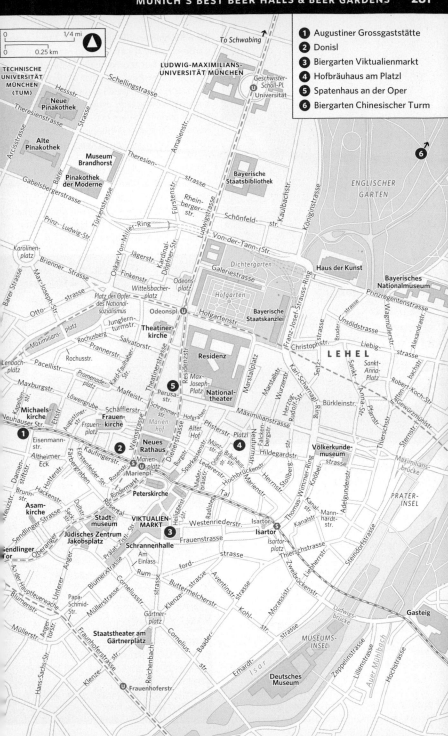

1 Augustiner Grossgaststätte
2 Donisl
3 Biergarten Viktualienmarkt
4 Hofbräuhaus am Platzl
5 Spatenhaus an der Oper
6 Biergarten Chinesischer Turm

> *Diners can bring their own food to Munich's Biergarten Viktualienmarkt, a favorite stop for weary shoppers in the square.*

❸ ★ Biergarten Viktualienmarkt. Many beer gardens today are attached to restaurants and serve food, but according to the Bayerische Biergartenverordnung (Bavarian Beer Garden Decree) beer gardens must allow their patrons to bring their own food. That's what lots of people do here in the beer garden in the middle of the always-hopping Viktualienmarkt (public market). If you're hungry, search the market stalls and food shops for a sandwich, sausage, or snack. You can bring it with you into the beer garden if you buy a beer or other beverage at the drinks stand. Viktualienmarkt 6. No phone. Summer daily 9am–10pm, winter 9am–6pm when weather is clear, closed Sun. *U-* or *S-Bahn:* Marienplatz.

Pretzels and Beer

Brezeln (pretzels) and large white *Radl* (radishes) are traditional accompaniments to the beer served in beer gardens and beer halls. If you choose to buy food, classic beer garden fare includes *Hoibe Hendl* (half a grilled chicken), *Hax'n* (pork knuckle), and *Steckerfisch* (grilled fish).

❷ ★ Donisl. Munich's oldest beer hall dates from 1715, when one of the owners of the wine tavern that stood here got a license to serve beer and established a beer tavern. From 1760 to 1775 the tavern was owned by Dionysius Haertl, who was such a congenial host that customers changed the tavern's name to "Zum Donisl" (a short form of Dionysius). Though you sit under umbrellas instead of chestnut trees, the beer garden out front is a great spot to sit and people-watch (and eat: most of the dishes are under 10€, see p. 302 for details). Inside, an accordion player provides music in the evening. Weinstrasse 1. ☎ 089/220-184. www.bayerischer-donisl.de. Daily 9am–midnight. *U-* or *S-Bahn:* Marienplatz.

④ ★ Hofbräuhaus am Platzl. The most famous beer hall in the world is housed in an 1896 neo-Renaissance building, but the brewery goes back to the 16th century. This is a huge place, with a Schwemme (taproom) that can hold 1,000 people and a summer beer garden that is always loaded with tourists. It's also the most commercialized of Munich's beer halls (a shop sells souvenirs) and a popular place to eat (p. 302). The Hofbräu beer is served by the *Mass* (equal to about a quart). Am Platzl 9. ☎ 089/290-1360. www.hofbraeuhaus.de. Daily 9am–midnight. *U-* or *S-Bahn:* Marienplatz.

⑤ ★★ Spatenhaus an der Oper. This upscale brewery restaurant near the Residenz and the National Theater doesn't get the tourist overload of the other beer halls and it serves better food (p. 303). There are several dining rooms to choose from and a terrace where you can sit under umbrellas. The Spaten brewery, now merged with Löwenbrau, recently celebrated its 600th anniversary; in 1872 it brewed the first Oktoberfest beer, and in 1894 it was the first brewery to brew a light lager using the Pilsner method: Spaten Münchner Hell. Residenzstrasse 12. ☎ 089/290-7060. www.spatenhaus.de. Daily 9:30am–12:30am. *U-* or *S-Bahn:* Marienplatz.

It's a 30-minute stroll to the final stop; if you don't want to walk, backtrack to Marienplatz, hop on the *U-Bahn* and take it to Giselastrasse, then take bus no. 54 or 154 to Chinesischer Turm.

⑥ ★★★ Biergarten Chinesischer Turm. This is one of the loveliest and liveliest places to have a beer that I know of. With seating for 4,000 people, this is Munich's second-largest summer beer garden and one of the most popular. It's located in the middle of the Englischer Garten park, surrounded by trees, at the foot of the Chinesischer Turm (Chinese Tower), a five-story wooden structure first constructed in 1790 (rebuilt in 1952) and modeled after the Great Pagoda in the Royal Botanic Gardens in London. Englischer Garten 3. ☎ 089/383-8720. May–Oct daily 11am–1am. *U-Bahn:* Giselastrasse, then bus 54 or 154 to Chinesischer Turm.

> *Located in the Englischer Garten, Biergarten Chinesischer Turm is the second-largest summer beer garden in Germany.*

The Cooks' Ball

In the late 19th century up to 5,000 servants, handworkers, soldiers, and students would come to the Chinese Tower early on Sunday mornings to dance to the music of a brass band. The dance began at 5am and ended at 8am so that servants could return to serve their employers breakfast or attend church. As a dance venue for servants it was known as the *Kocherlball* (cooks' ball). In 1904 the custom was forbidden by the police on moral grounds, but in 1989, to celebrate the 200th anniversary of the Englischer Garten, the early-morning dance was revived, and it's been celebrated in July every year since.

Marienplatz & the Altstadt

Munich's Altstadt, or Old Town, is an oval-shaped pedestrian-only district on the west bank of the Isar River. Over the past 200 years Munich has spread far beyond its old city walls, but this old quarter remains the city's throbbing center, jammed with churches, squares, museums, historic buildings, a food market, restaurants, beer halls, hotels, and endless shopping possibilities. The following walking tour takes about 3 hours to see the sights and stop in at a few churches; if you want to visit any of the museums along the way, budget your time accordingly.

> *The unparalleled detail and size of Munich's Neues Rathaus looms large in the city's historic Marienplatz.*

START Take the *U-Bahn* or *S-Bahn* to Marienplatz.

❶ ★★★ Marienplatz (St. Mary's Square).

When you're in Marienplatz you're in the busy, buzzing heart of Munich's Altstadt (Old Town) and the historic center of the city. Spend some time just wandering about, enjoying the atmosphere. Marienplatz itself is prime shopping territory, and the surrounding area is loaded with hotels, restaurants, cafes, beer halls, museums, and entertainment venues. ◷ 30 min. See p. 252, ❶.

❷ kids Neues Rathaus (New Town Hall).

Time your visit to Marienplatz so you can watch the famous Glockenspiel (Carillon), set in the tower of the 19th-century Town Hall, go through its paces. Every day at 11am, noon, and 5pm, mechanical figures emerge from beneath the clock and "reenact" episodes from Munich's past. After watching the Glockenspiel, take the elevator to the top of the tower for a panoramic view of the city. ◷ 30 min. See p. 254, ❷.

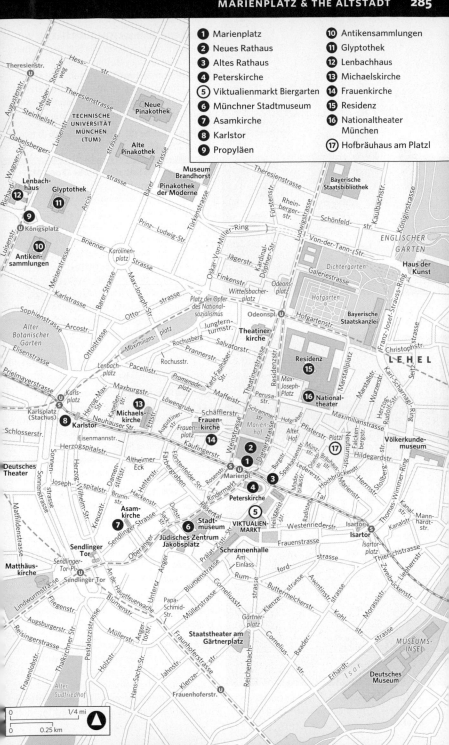

1 Marienplatz
2 Neues Rathaus
3 Altes Rathaus
4 Peterskirche
5 Viktualienmarkt Biergarten
6 Münchner Stadtmuseum
7 Asamkirche
8 Karlstor
9 Propyläen
10 Antikensammlungen
11 Glyptothek
12 Lenbachhaus
13 Michaelskirche
14 Frauenkirche
15 Residenz
16 Nationaltheater München
17 Hofbräuhaus am Platzl

> *The 15th-century Altes Rathaus serves as a monument to the city's proud past.*

> *Baroque-era sculptures such as Four Doctors of the Church, pictured here, adorn the interior of Peterskirche.*

❸ kids Altes Rathaus (Old Town Hall). You may want to step inside this building, with its plain, 15th-century Gothic tower, to visit the **Spielzeugmuseum** (Toy Museum), a collection of historic toys. ⏱ 30 min. Marienplatz. ☎ 089/294-001. Admission 3€ adults, 1€ kids. Daily 10am–5pm. *U-* or *S-Bahn:* Marienplatz.

❹ Peterskirche (St. Peter's Church). ⏱ 15 min. See p. 273, ❹.

❺   🍴 ★★★ Viktualienmarkt (Food Market). Munich's wonderfully lively Viktualienmarkt moved to this area in 1807 and today has about 140 stalls and shops selling meat, fowl, bread, honey, eggs, cheese, sausages, herbs, fruit, and vegetables, plus casual restaurants, snack stalls, and a beer garden. It's a great place to take a break. Browse the stalls and stands to find a snack, sausage, or sandwich to take away *(zum mitnehmen)*; you can bring your food into the **Biergarten** (Beer Garden) in the center of the market (Viktualienmarkt 6, no phone) as long as you order a drink. Most shops and stalls open 6am–6pm.

❻ ★ kids Münchner Stadtmuseum. A 15th-century arsenal building houses the Münchner Stadtmuseum (Munich City Museum), with its rich and fascinating collection of objects and exhibits that illustrate the lives of Munich citizens from all walks of life through the centuries. ⏱ 30–45 min. See p. 266, ❷.

❼ ★★ Asamkirche. Step inside and have a look at the amazing interior of this rococo church. ⏱ 15 min. See p. 273, ❸.

❽ Karlstor. Once part of Munich's medieval fortifications, the Karlstor (Karl's Gate) served as the western entrance into the city. Karlsplatz. *U-Bahn:* Karlsplatz.

The Propyläen is about 1km (about ½ mile) to the north, a 15-minute walk or 1 stop on the *U-Bahn.*

❾ ★ Propyläen. The architect Leo von Klenze (1784–1864) designed this monumental gateway with Doric columns and porticos as a symbolic entry point to the newer parts of Munich and as a memorial to Otto I Wittelsbach, who became king of Greece after that

> *The barrel-vaulted roof is a signature of Michaelskirche, which contains the tombs of several Wittelsbach rulers, including Ludwig II.*

country's liberation from the Turks. Inspired by the Propylaea of the Acropolis, the structure was completed in 1862. ⏲ 15 min. Königsplatz. *U-Bahn:* Königsplatz.

⑩ ★ **Antikensammlungen.** The Propyläen (❾), the Glyptothek (⑪), and the Antikensammlungen (Antiquities Collection), built in the Corinthian style and completed in 1848, form a monumental neoclassical grouping around Königsplatz. ⏲ At least 30 min. See p. 264, ❻.

⑪ ★ **Glyptothek.** Leo von Klenze, the architect who designed the Propyläen, built this museum between 1816 and 1830 to house the city's Greek and Roman sculpture collection. ⏲ 30 min. See p. 264, ❼.

⑫ ★★ **Lenbachhaus.** This 19th-century Italianate villa houses a brilliant collection of early-20th-century German paintings. ⏲ 1 hr. See p. 264, ❺.

Michaelskirche is 1.4km (just under a mile) southeast, another 15-minute walk. Or hop on the *U-Bahn*, take it 1 stop to Karlsplatz, and then head east on Neuhauser Strasse.

⑬ **Michaelskirche (St. Michael's Church).** Stop in for a brief look at this single-nave church with barrel-vaulted ceiling; Michaelskirche is the largest Renaissance church north of

the Alps and the final resting place of Ludwig II and many other Wittelsbachs. See p. 272, ❷.

⑭ **Frauenkirche (Church of Our Lady).** Spend a few minutes strolling through the interior of Munich's largest church, or climb the tower for a spectacular view all the way to the Alps. See p. 254, ❹.

⑮ ★★ **Residenz.** Exploring the enormous city palace of Bavaria's former rulers, the Wittelsbachs, can easily take half a day; if you don't have the time now, just stroll around the palace and have a look at the Hofgarten (Court Garden) behind it. See p. 274, ❶.

⑯ **Nationaltheater München.** The neoclassical National Theater is the home of the acclaimed Bavarian State opera and ballet companies. An earlier theater, built in 1825 by Leo von Klenze (architect of the Propyläen and Glyptothek), was destroyed in World War II, and this rebuilt, 2,100-seat theater opened in 1963. For information on the opera and ballet, see p. 314.

⑰ 🍺 **Hofbräuhaus am Platzl.** It's the most famous beer hall in the world. Head into the beer garden and toast your tour with a foaming mug. Am Platzl 9. See p.283, ❹.

The Englischer Garten & Vicinity

This tour around the Englischer Garten quarter introduces you to a diverse menu of outdoor and indoor delights. It takes you to three of Munich's great city parks and a trio of noteworthy museums, two of which are small gems that don't usually register on tourists' radar. (If you want to visit the museums, don't do this tour on a Monday.) You can do this tour in about half a day, including museum visits, or longer if you want to linger at any of the places along the way.

> *You could easily spend a few hours exploring Englischer Garten, Munich's largest and most popular park.*

START Hofgarten, behind the Residenz. Take tram no. 19 to Nationaltheater (the palace is on the same square as the theater) or the *U-Bahn* to Odeonsplatz (the palace is southeast across the square).

❶ Hofgarten (Court Gardens). The court garden of the Residenz (p. 274, ❶) belonged to the Wittelsbachs, who ruled Bavaria from 1180 until 1918. Laid out in a formal French style, the garden has a lovely fountain and a central pavilion dating from 1615 surrounded by parterres, hedges, lawns, and flower beds.

🕐 15 min. Max-Joseph-Platz 3. Tram: 19 to Nationaltheater; or *U-Bahn:* to Odeonsplatz.

SITE GUIDE PAGE 291

❷ ★★★ Englischer Garten (English Garden). How you want to explore Munich's largest (5 sq. km/1,236 acres) and most famous park is up to you. Established in 1789 by Count Rumford, an American (born Benjamin Thompson) who served as Bavaria's Minister of War, this is also the oldest public park in the world, with tree-shaded walks, streams, and a lake.

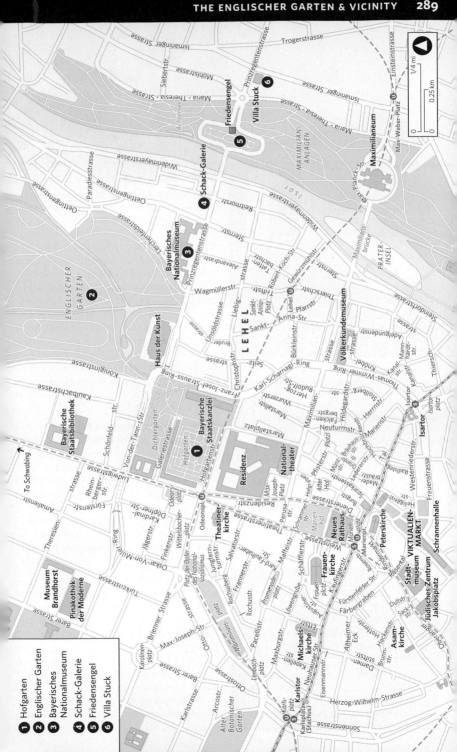

> *Originally laid out for members of the royal court in 1613, the Hofgarten was opened to the public in 1780.*

> *The beautiful Bayerisches Nationalmuseum offers a wide array of arts and crafts from the Romanesque period to the Renaissance.*

❸ ★★ **Bayerisches Nationalmuseum.** The enormous Bavarian National Museum was created in 1885 to preserve and display Bavaria's artistic heritage. If your time is limited, confine yourself to the ground-floor displays of Bavarian arts and crafts from the Romanesque period to the Renaissance, especially the Tilman Riemenschneider sculptures, and have a look at the enormous collection of Christmas crèches in the basement. ⏱ 90 min. See p. 268, ❸.

T. S. Eliot Hits the Hofgarten

The Hofgarten (p. 288, ❶) is the first place to be named in T. S. Eliot's canonical poem *The Waste Land* (1922), where it's used to symbolize the dying courts of Old Europe and the empty charms of aristocratic life: "Summer surprised us, coming over the Starnbergersee / With a shower of rain; we stopped in the colonnade, / And went on in sunlight, into the Hofgarten, / And drank coffee, and talked for an hour."

❹ ★ **Schack-Galerie.** When Count Adolf Friedrich von Schack of Schwerin (1815–94) settled in Munich in 1855 he became a patron of German artists and began to buy their works. He built this small villa to show his unusually comprehensive collection, which contains numerous masterpieces of German Romanticism by the greatest painters of the period: Anselm Feuerbach, Moritz von Schwind, Arnold Böcklin, Franz von Lenbach, Carl Spitzweg, and Carl Rottmann. ⏱ 30–45 min. Prinzregentenstrasse 9. ☎ 089/2380-5224. Admission 3€. Wed–Sun 10am–5pm. *U-Bahn:* Lehel.

❺ **Friedensengel (Angel of Peace).** The stone figures on the Luitpoldbrücke (Luitpold Bridge) personify Bavaria's four historic regions and population groups: Bavarians, Swabians, Franconians, and the people of the Palatinate. At the far end of the bridge, the Friedensengel monument commemorates the 25 years of peace that followed the war of 1870–71. If the mood strikes you, stroll along the riverside promenade or explore **Maximilian-Anlage,** the park around the Friedensengel.

❻ ★★ **Villa Stuck.** If you like house museums, this magnificent 1898 Jugendstil (Art Nouveau) villa is a must. It was designed and lived in by the Symbolist artist Franz von Stuck (1863–1928) and contains his most famous painting (*Die Sünde,* or The Sin) and sculpture (*Amazon*). Stuck made all the furniture, paneling, bas-reliefs, and coffered ceilings. ⏱ 30 min. Prinzregentenstrasse 60. ☎ 089/455-5510. www.villastuck.de. Admission 9€ adults, 4.50€ seniors/students. Tues–Sun 11am–6pm. *U-Bahn:* Prinzregentenplatz.

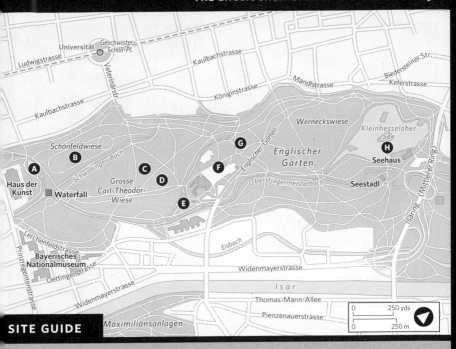

② Englischer Garten

In April 1972, to celebrate the Munich Summer Olympics, the **Ⓐ Japanisches Teehaus** (Japanese Teahouse), used for traditional Japanese tea ceremonies, and a Japanese garden were created on a small island at the south end of the park. Just to the north is **Ⓑ Schönfeldwiese,** a large meadow used since the 1960s for nude sunbathing. The oldest construction in the park, the **Ⓒ Burgfriedsäule,** a boundary marker from 1724, stands in a grove of trees below the **Ⓓ Monopteros,** a small round Ionic temple designed by Leo von Klenze, the architect of the Propyläen (p. 286, ⑨) and the Glyptothek (p. 264, ⑦); built on a man-made hill, the temple was completed in 1836. Von Klenze also designed the commemorative **Ⓔ Steinerne Bank** (Stone Bench) on the site of an earlier wooden temple; the inscription on the bench reads "Hier wo Ihr wallet, da war sonst Wald nur und Sumpf" (Here where you meander was once only wood and marsh). A giant beer garden (p. 283, ⑥) occupies the plaza near the **Ⓕ Chinesischer Turm** (Chinese Tower), first built in 1790 to resemble the Great Pagoda in the Royal Botanic Gardens in London. A little to

the north stands the **Ⓖ Rumford-Saal** (Rumford Hall), a small Palladian building built in 1791 as an officers' mess hall and renamed to honor Count Rumford, the creator of the Englischer Garten. The **Ⓗ Kleinhesseloher See** (lake) was created between 1800 and 1812 between the districts of Schwabing and Kleinhesselohe, the original northern limit of the park. ☺ At least 90 min. Bounded on the south by Von-der-Tann Strasse and Prinzregentenstrasse, on the west by Königinstrasse, on the east by Lerchenfeldstrasse. Free admission. Open 24/7. *U*- or *S-Bahn:* Marienplatz or Odeonsplatz.

Munich Shopping Best Bets

Best All-Round Department Store
Ludwig Beck am Rathauseck, Marienplatz 11
(p. 293)

Best Bavarian Porcelain
Porzellan-Manufaktur-Nymphenburg, Dienerstrasse 17 (p. 296)

Best Contemporary Crafts Gallery
Bayerischer Kunstgewerbe-Verein, Pacellistrasse 6–8 (p. 293)

Best Food Emporium
Alois Dallmayr, Dienerstrasse 14–15 (p. 296)

Best Men's and Women's Outerwear
Loden-Frey, Maffeistrasse 7–9 (p. 296)

Best Jewelry
Hemmerle, Maximilianstrasse 14 (p. 296)

Best Shopping Mall
Fünf Höfe, Theatinerstrasse (p. 297)

Best Traditional Bavarian Clothing
Frankonia, Maximiliansplatz 10 (p. 297)

Most Historic Toy Shop
**Münchner Puppenstuben und Zinnfiguren-
Kabinett,** Maxbugstrasse 4 (p. 297)

Best Market
Viktualienmarket (p. 296)

Marienplatz at Christmas

Marienplatz, the main square of the inner
city, is the scene of a famous **Christkindl
Markt** (Christmas Market). From late
November through December, the plaza
overflows with stalls selling toys, tree ornaments, handicrafts, and a mouthwatering
array of traditional snacks and sweets, including gingerbread, sugarcoated almonds,
and piping-hot *Glühwein,* a spiced red wine.

> *Munich is a great place to sample Bavarian cuisine,
> including the many different types of sausages the
> region has to offer.*

Munich Shopping A to Z

Arts & Crafts
★★★ Bayerischer Kunstgewerbe-Verein
KARLSPLATZ The work of more than 400 local artists and artisans is showcased and sold at this historic art gallery and browsable showroom. Pacellistrasse 6–8. ☎ 089/290-1370. www.kunsthandwerk-bkv.de. *U-Bahn:* Karlsplatz.

Books
★★ Hugendubel MARIENPLATZ
Munich's largest bookstore carries English-language titles, travel guides, and maps. Marienplatz 22. ☎ 089/290-1470. www.hugendubel.de. *U-* or *S-Bahn:* Marienplatz.

Department Stores
Karstadt NEAR TRAIN STATION
This all-purpose, less-expensive department store is right across from the main train

station. Bahnhofplatz 7. ☎ 089/55120. *U-Bahn:* Hauptbahnhof.

★★★ Ludwig Beck am Rathauseck MARIENPLATZ
Sometimes called "the Bloomingdale's of Germany," this is Munich's best department store and a good place for handmade crafts from all across Germany. Marienplatz 11. ☎ 089/236-910. www.ludwigbeck.de. *U-* and *S-Bahn:* Marienplatz.

Eyeglasses
★★ Pupille NEAR RESIDENZ
If you want your specs to be spectacular, or at least highly fashionable, this is the place

> ### Made in Munich
> Munich is the fashion capital of Germany, and when the topic is shopping, Munich ranks right up there with Paris and London. Specialty items include *Tracht* (traditional Bavarian costumes such as dirndls, lederhosen, and Alpine and hunting garb) and Bavarian-made porcelain.

> *If you're seeking traditional Bavarian costumes, crafts, and folk art, there is no better destination than Dirndl-Ecke.*

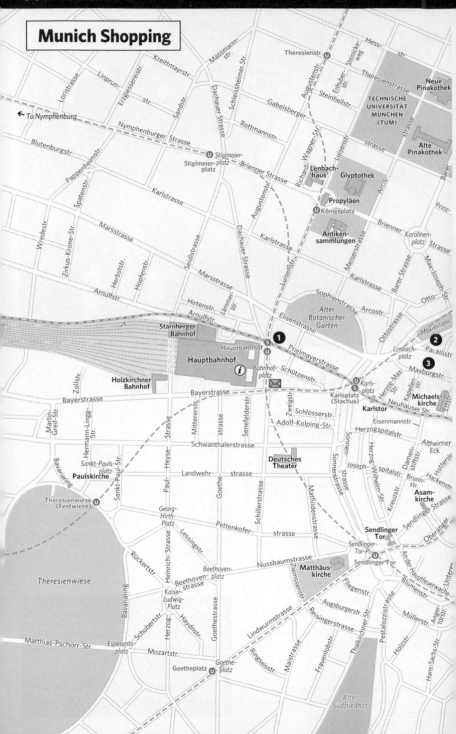

Munich Shopping

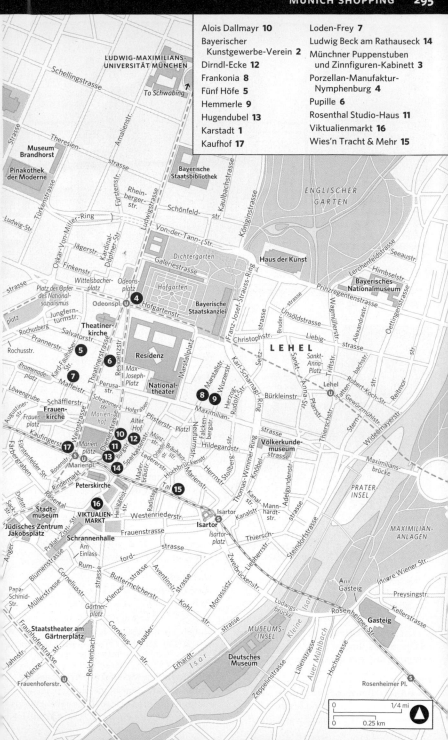

Alois Dallmayr **10**

Bayerischer
 Kunstgewerbe-Verein **2**

Dirndl-Ecke **12**

Frankonia **8**

Fünf Höfe **5**

Hemmerle **9**

Hugendubel **13**

Karstadt **1**

Kaufhof **17**

Loden-Frey **7**

Ludwig Beck am Rathauseck **14**

Münchner Puppenstuben
 und Zinnfiguren-Kabinett **3**

Porzellan-Manufaktur-
 Nymphenburg **4**

Pupille **6**

Rosenthal Studio-Haus **11**

Viktualienmarkt **16**

Wies'n Tracht & Mehr **15**

> *The popular Alois Dallmayr on Dienerstrasse is packed daily with hungry diners seeking the best in traditional Bavarian dishes.*

> *The ultimate shopping destination for outerwear is Loden-Frey, which also features a full line of traditional German clothing.*

to shop; German eyewear is remarkably cool and the optics superb. Theatinerstrasse 8. ☎ 089/2424-3838. www.pupille.de. Tram: 19.

Food

★★★ **Alois Dallmayr** NEAR MARIENPLATZ A fabulous delicatessen and restaurant (p. 299), Dallmayr's is also a wonderful if pricey place to browse for food gifts and goodies. Dienerstrasse 14–15. ☎ 089/21350. www.dallmayr.de. *U-Bahn:* Marienplatz.

★★★ **Viktualienmarkt** NEAR MARIENPLATZ Munich's great public market has dozens of stalls selling fresh foodstuffs, but you can also find honey, spices, candy, cookies, and other local goodies to take home with you. See p. 286, ⑤. *U-* or *S-Bahn:* Marienplatz.

Jewelry

★★★ **Hemmerle** NEAR MARIENPLATZ Former jewelry designers for the Bavarian monarchy, this company designs limited-edition pieces handcrafted in the store and sells its own status-symbol watch. Maximilianstrasse 14. ☎ 089/242-2600. www.hemmerle.de. *U-Bahn:* Marienplatz.

Outerwear

★★★ **Loden-Frey** MARIENPLATZ Founded in 1842, this is *the* place for high-quality loden (a waterproof wool) wear, including coats, jackets, and hats. Maffeistrasse 7–9. ☎ 089/210-390. *U-* or *S-Bahn:* Marienplatz

Porcelain

★★★ **Porzellan-Manufaktur-Nymphenburg** ODEONSPLATZ One of the oldest porcelain factories in Europe is located on the grounds of Nymphenburg Palace (p. 274, ❷) and has a

> The bustling outdoor Viktualienmarkt is regularly lined with shoppers and diners seeking treats inside its many crowded stalls.

second showroom on Odeonsplatz, in central Munich. Odeonsplatz 1. ☎ 089/179-1970. www. nymphenburg.com. *U-Bahn:* Odeonsplatz.

★★★ Rosenthal Studio-Haus MARIENPLATZ

Come to this factory outlet store for the widest selection of Bavarian-made Rosenthal china, glass, and cutlery (but don't expect rock-bottom prices). Dienerstrasse 17. ☎ 089/222-617. www.rosenthal.de. *U-* or *S-Bahn:* Marienplatz.

Shopping Mall

★★★ Fünf Höfe NEAR MARIENPLATZ

The name translates as "Five Courtyards," and that's exactly what Munich's newest and most attractive shopping mall is: five separate courtyards surrounded by upscale shops, cafes, bars, restaurants, galleries, and two museums. Dolce & Gabbana, Zara, and Armani are among the designers who have boutiques here. Bounded by and with entrances on Theatinerstrasse, Salvatorstrasse, Maffeistrasse, and Kardinal-Faulhaber-Strasse. *U-* or *S-Bahn:* Marienplatz.

Toys

★★★ Münchner Puppenstuben und Zinnfiguren-Kabinett KARLSPLATZ

Established in 1796, this is Germany's oldest miniature pewter foundry, and it still sells traditional Christmas decorations and dollhouse-size pewter miniatures from 150-year-old

molds. Maxburgstrasse 4. ☎ 089/293-797. www.mini-kabi.net. *U-Bahn:* Karlsplatz.

Traditional Bavarian Clothing

★ Dirndl-Ecke NEAR MARIENPLATZ

This store carries a large selection of dirndls, folk art, and handicrafts. Am Platzl 1/Sparkassenstrasse 10. ☎ 089/220-163. *U-* or *S-Bahn:* Marienplatz.

★★★ Frankonia MAXIMILIANSPLATZ

Munich's most prestigious collection of *Tracht* (traditional Bavarian costumes), including wool cardigan jackets with silver buttons, is sold at this venerable store that opened in 1908. Maximiliansplatz 10. ☎ 089/290-0020. *U-Bahn:* Odeonsplatz.

★ Kaufhof MARIENPLATZ

You can find just about anything at this large department store, including lederhosen and dirndls (at least around Oktoberfest time). Marienplatz. ☎ 089/231-851. *U-* or *S-Bahn:* Marienplatz.

★★ Wies'n Tracht & Mehr MARIENPLATZ

Call it a dirndl outlet, but don't call it cheap—prices start at 400€; vintage dirndls are also sold here. Tal 19 (btw. Marienplatz and Isartor). No phone. www.wiesn-tracht-mehr.de. *U-* or *S-Bahn:* Marienplatz.

Munich Restaurant Best Bets

Best Beer Hall Food
Spatenhaus an der Oper, Residenzstrasse 12
(p. 303)

Best Deli Nosh
Alois Dallmayr, Dienerstrasse 14–15 (p. 299)

Best Italian
Brenner, Maximilianstrasse 15 (p. 302)

Best Modern European
Gasthaus Glockenbach, Kapuzinerstrasse 29
(p. 302)

Best Neighborhood Bistro
Gandl, St.-Anna Platz 1 (p. 302)

Best Sausages
Nürnberger Bratwurst Glöckl am Dom, Frauenplatz 9 (p. 303)

Best Seafood
Austernkeller, Stollbergstrasse 11 (p. 299)

Best Vegetarian
Prinz Myshkin, Hackenstrasse 2 (p. 303)

Beer Gardens

If you're in Munich between the first sunny
spring day and the last fading light of a
Bavarian-style autumn, be sure to dine at
one of the city's celebrated Biergärten.
Traditionally, beer gardens were simply
tables placed under chestnut trees planted
above the storage cellars to keep beer cool
in summer. (Lids on beer steins, inciden-
tally, were meant to keep out flies.) It's
estimated that today Munich has at least
400 beer gardens and cellars. For descrip-
tions of our favorites, see "Munich's Best
Beer Halls & Beer Gardens," p. 280.

> *Renowned for its atmosphere and authentic dishes,
> the Nürnberger Bratwurst Glöckl am Dom is one of
> Munich's friendliest dining destinations.*

Munich Restaurants A to Z

★★ **Alois Dallmayr** ALTSTADT *DELICATESSEN/ CONTINENTAL* In the casual Café-Bistro or classier Restaurant sections of Munich's oldest and most elegant delicatessen you can order a tempting array of dishes, including herring, sausages, smoked fish, soups, and, of course, *Kaffee und Kuchen* (coffee and cake). **Dienerstrasse 14–15.** ☎ 089/213-5100. www.dallmayr.de. Café-Bistro entrees 15€–38€; Restaurant fixed-price menus 59€–123€. AE, DC, MC, V. Lunch Mon–Sat, early dinner Mon–Fri. *U- or S-Bahn:* Marienplatz.

★★ **Augustiner Grossgaststätte** ALTSTADT *BAVARIAN/GERMAN* This famous beer hall and restaurant, with cavernous rooms and *gemütlich* (cozy) atmosphere, serves up such specialties as dumpling soup and roast duck with red cabbage. The house beer, Augustiner Bräu, comes from one of Munich's oldest breweries, which owns the restaurant.

Neuhauser Strasse 27. ☎ 089/2318-3257. Entrees 10€–20€. MC, V. Lunch & dinner daily. *U-Bahn:* Karlsplatz/Stachus.

★★ **Austernkeller** ALTSTADT *SEAFOOD* This "oyster cellar" has the largest selection of oysters in town, served raw or in dishes such as oysters Rockefeller, plus fish soup, fresh fish, and popular favorites such as lobster Thermidor and shrimp grilled in the shell. A less expensive and lighter menu is available at lunchtime. Stollbergstrasse 11. ☎ 089/298-787. www.austernkeller.de. Reservations required. Entrees 12.50€–24€. AE, DC, MC, V. Lunch Mon–Fri, dinner daily. *U-Bahn:* Isartor.

★★ **Boettners** ALTSTADT *INTERNATIONAL* The cooking is light and refined, with a French influence, but several traditional Bavarian dishes fill out the menu. Special offerings include herb-crusted lamb, beef filet,

> *At Alois Dallmayr you can dine in the cafe or pick up an elegant dish at the bustling deli counters.*

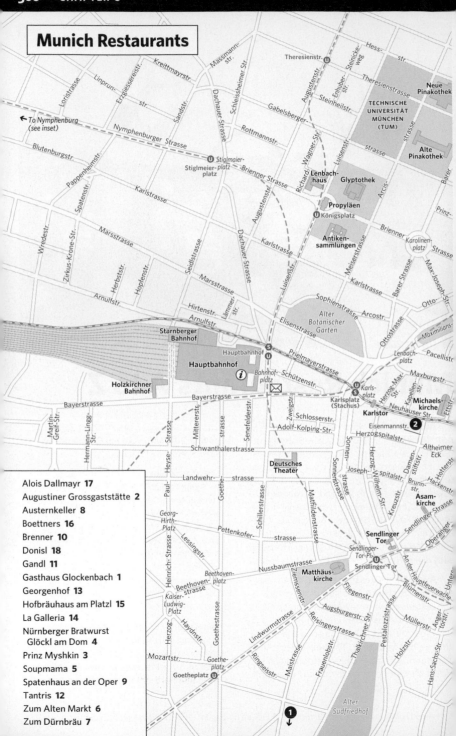

Munich Restaurants

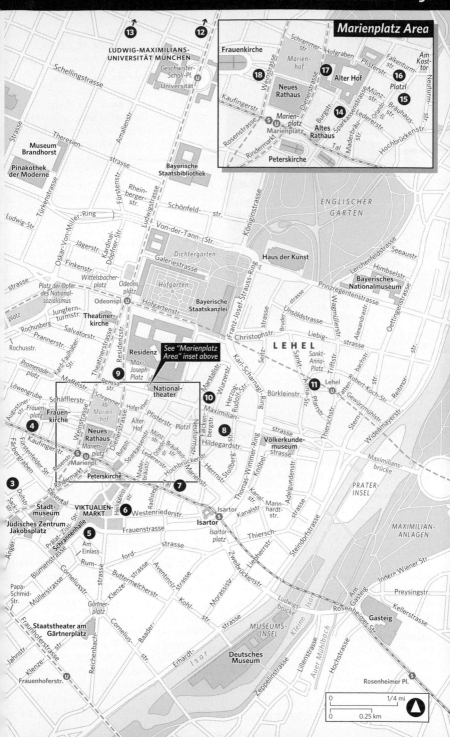

Marienplatz Area

Frauenkirche
Schrammer-str.
Hofgraben
Marien-hof
Falkenturm-str.
Am Kost-tor
17 Alter Hof
Pfisterstr.
16
Neut_m-str.
18
Weinstr.
Dienerstr.
Neues Rathaus
Kaufingerstr.
Münz-str.
Bräuhaus-str.
Platzl
15
Rosenstrasse
Marien-platz
Marienplatz
Burgstr.
Sparkassenstrasse
Ledererstr.
14 Altes Rathaus
Tal
Rindermarkt
Maderbräu-str.
Hochbrückenstr.
Peterskirche

LUDWIG-MAXIMILIANS-UNIVERSITÄT MÜNCHEN

13
12

Geschwister-Scholl-Pl.
Universität

Schellingstrasse

Amalienstr.

Theresien-strasse

Museum Brandhorst

Pinakothek der Moderne

Türkenstr.

Bayerische Staatsbibliothek

Rhein-berger-str.

Schönfeld-str.

Ludwigstrasse

Ludwig-Str.

Von-der-Tann-(Str.

ENGLISCHER GARTEN

Oskar-Von-Miller-Ring

Jägerstr.

Kardinal-Döpfner-Str.

Wittelsbacher-platz

Galeriestrasse

Dichtergarten

Haus der Kunst

Königinstrasse

Platz der Opfer des National-sozialismus

Jungfern-turmstr.

Odeons-platz

Hofgarten

Bayerische Staatskanzlei

Lerchenfeldstrasse
Seeaustr.

Bayerisches Nationalmuseum

Prinzregentenstrasse

Rochusberg

Salvatorstr.

Odeonspl.

Hofgartenstr.

Franz-Josef-Strauss-Ring

Christophstr.

Unsöldstrasse

Wagmüllerstr.

Alexandrastr.

Oettingenstrasse

Rochusstr.

Prannerstr.

Theatiner-kirche

LEHEL

Liebig-strasse

Promenade-platz

Karl-Faulhaber-Str.

Maffeistr.

Theatinerstr.

Residenzstr.

Residenz

Max-Joseph-Platz

See "Marienplatz Area" inset above

Seitz-str.

Bruder-str.

Karl-Scharnagl-Ring

Sankt-Anna-Platz

Sankt-Anna-Str.

Triftstr.

Robert-Koch-Str.

Reitmor-

Löwengrube

9

Berdal-str.

National-theater

Marstallstr.

Wurzerstr.

Herzog-Rudolf-Str.

Bürkleinstr.

11 Lehel

Gewürzmühlstr.

Wildenmayerstr.

Augustiner-str.

Frauen-platz

Schäfflerstr.

Schrammer-str.

Hofgraben

10

Maximilian-straße

Frauen-kirche

Weinstr.

Marien-hof

Pfisterstr.

Platzl

Falken-bergstr.

Thomas-Wimmer-Ring

Knöbel-

Adelgundenstr.

Maximilians-brücke

4

Kaufingerstr.

Dienerstr.

Alter Hof

8

Hildegardstr.

Völkerkunde-museum

strasse

PRATER-INSEL

Fürstenfelder Str.

Rosenstr.

Neues Rathaus

Münz-str.

Ohm-str.

Neuturm-

Herrnstr.

Kanal-str.

Mann-hardt-str.

3

Marienpl.

Burgstr.

Sparkassenstr.

Ledererstr.

Maderbräu-str.

Hochbrückenstr.

Marienstr.

Stollberg-

MAXIMILIAN-ANLAGEN

Peterskirche

Tal

7

Stadtmuseum

Jüdisches Zentrum Jakobsplatz

VIKTUALIEN-MARKT

6

Westenriederstr.

Isartor

Isartor-platz

Am Gasteig

Innere Wiener Str.

5

Schrannenhalle

Prälat-Zistl-Str.

Frauenstrasse

Thierschstr.

Preysingstr.

Am Einlass

strasse

Zweibrückenstr.

Steindorfstrasse

Rosenheimer Str.

Kellerstrasse

Anger-

Blumenstrasse

Corneliusstrasse

Müllerstrasse

Rum-

ford-

Buttermelcherstr.

Aventinstrasse

Kohl-str.

Morassistr.

Ludwig-brücke

Isar

Gasteig

Papa-Schmid-Str.

Gärtner-platz

Klenze-str.

Kleine

MUSEUMS-INSEL

Staatstheater am Gärtnerplatz

Cornelius-str.

Baader-str.

Erhardt-str.

Deutsches Museum

Isar

Auer Mühlbach

Hochstrasse

Jahnstr.

Reichenbach-str.

Lilienstrasse

Zeppelinstrasse

Rosenheimer Pl.

Frauenhoferstrasse

Klenze-str.

Frauenhoferstr.

0   1/4 mi
0   0.25 km

> Dine on Italian, French, and German cuisine at Gandl, a popular neighborhood bistro.

www.bayerischer-donisl.de. Reservations recommended. Entrees 8€–15€. AE, DC, MC, V. Lunch & dinner daily. *U-* or *S-Bahn:* Marienplatz.

★ **Gandl** ALTSTADT *ITALIAN/FRENCH*
The lunch menu at this popular neighborhood bistro leans toward Italian, but at night the cooking becomes more traditionally French and German with offerings such as *entrecôte* (steak) with arugula salad, grilled filet of salmon in saffron sauce, and lamb in red-wine sauce. Eat on the terrace if the weather's nice. St.-Anna Platz 1. ☎ 089/2916-2525. www.gandl. de. Entrees 8€–18€; fixed-price menu 17€–19€. Only EU credit cards accepted. Lunch & dinner Mon–Sat. *U-Bahn:* Lehel.

★★★ **Gasthaus Glockenbach** SOUTH OF TRAIN STATION *MODERN EUROPEAN* Menu offerings at this elegant but unpretentious Michelin-starred restaurant change with the seasons and typically include venison and pheasant in autumn, lamb and veal dishes in spring, and locally sourced vegetables. Kapuzinerstrasse 29. ☎ 089/534-043. Reservations recommended. Entrees 23€–30€, fixed-price menus 20€–45€ lunch, 35€–70€ dinner. AE, MC, V. Lunch & dinner Tues-Sat. *U-Bahn:* Goetheplatz.

Georgenhof SCHWABING *GERMAN/INTERNATIONAL* This casual eatery and wine bar has a seasonally inspired menu that includes *Spargel* (asparagus) in May and June, Bavarian game dishes such as *Rehpfeffer* (venison) with egg *Spätzle* or tagliatelle with venison ragout, and a wood-fired stove for grilled lamb and steak. Fredrichstrasse 1. ☎ 089/393-101. www.georgenhof-muenchen. de. Entrees 11€–22€. MC, V. Lunch & dinner daily. *U-Bahn:* Universität.

★ **Hofbräuhaus am Platzl** ALTSTADT *GERMAN* The experience may be more memorable than the food in Munich's world-famous beer hall and summer beer garden. The menu includes *Weisswürste* and several other sausages, *Schweinbraten* (roasted pork), *Spanferkel* (roast suckling pig), and the big favorite, *Schweineshaxe* (ham hocks). Am Platzl 9. ☎ 089/290-1360 www.hofbraeuhaus.de. Entrees 5€–10€. No credit cards. Lunch & dinner daily. *U-* or *S-Bahn:* Marienplatz (then a 5-min. walk north on Sparkassenstrasse and east on Bräuhausstrasse).

lobster stew, and seasonal dishes with white truffles. Pfisterstrasse 9. ☎ 089/221-210. www. boettners.de. Reservations required. Entrees 18€–42€; fixed-price menu 84€. AE, DC, MC, V. Lunch & dinner daily. *U-Bahn:* Marienplatz.

★★★ **Brenner** ALTSTADT *ITALIAN*
The vibe's as good as the food at this Italian restaurant with lots of indoor and outdoor spaces and moods, a grill in the middle of the dining room, and pasta, meat, and fish dishes for every size appetite. Maximilianstrasse 15. ☎ 089/452-2880. www.brennergrill.de. Entrees 12.50€–26€. AE, MC, V. Lunch & dinner Mon–Thurs 8:30am–1am, Fri-Sat 8:30am–2am, Sun 11:30am–midnight. Tram: 14.

★ **Donisl** ALTSTADT *BAVARIAN/INTERNATIONAL*
Munich's oldest beer hall dates from 1715 and offers traditional Bavarian specialties such as *Weisswürste,* Munich's famous little white sausages. An accordion player provides music in the evening and there's a summer beer garden. Weinstrasse 1. ☎ 089/220-184.

★ La Galleria ALTSTADT *ITALIAN*

The roster of dishes at this appealing Italian restaurant changes seasonally, but you may find entrees such as mushroom tartar, homemade gnocchi with duck and figs, veal with arugula, roast duck with lentils, or braised crab with polenta. Sparkassenstrasse 11. ☎ 089/297-995. Reservations recommended. Entrees 21€–24€, fixed-price lunch 16€–24€, fixed-price dinner 48€–54€. AE, DC, MC, V. Lunch & dinner daily. Closed Aug 10–30. *U-* or *S-Bahn:* Marienplatz.

★ Nürnberger Bratwurst Glöckl am Dom

ALTSTADT *BAVARIAN* The coziest and friendliest of Munich's local restaurants features specialties from Nuremberg; *Nürnberger Schweinwurstl mit Kraut* (pork sausages with cabbage) is the dish to try. Frauenplatz 9. ☎ 089/295-264. www.bratwurst-gloeckl.de. Entrees: 8€–16€. No credit cards. Lunch & dinner daily. *U-* or *S-Bahn:* Marienplatz.

★ Prinz Myshkin ALTSTADT *VEGETARIAN*

The menu at this bright, popular vegetarian restaurant includes freshly made salads, macrobiotic dishes, Asian-inspired vegetarian entrees, and vegetarian *involtini* (stuffed roll-ups). The casseroles, soups, and pizzas are excellent. Hackenstrasse 2. ☎ 089/265-596. www.prinzmyshkin.com. Reservations recommended. Entrees 10€–16€. AE, MC, V. Lunch & dinner daily. *U-* or *S-Bahn:* Marienplatz.

Soupmama ALTSTADT *SOUPS & SALADS*

If it's a bowl of hot, homemade soup you want, or a nice fresh pasta or salad, head to this little restaurant with two counters for eating in, or take-away service if you want to eat elsewhere. Soups change daily but might include Berlin potato soup with wurst, Greek lentil soup, or Moroccan carrot soup. Frauenstrasse 2. ☎ 089/2307-7645. Soups and salads 4€–6.50€. No credit cards. Lunch & early dinner Mon–Sat. *U-* or *S-Bahn:* Marienplatz.

★★ Spatenhaus an der Oper ALTSTADT

BAVARIAN/INTERNATIONAL This brewery restaurant serves Bavarian specialties, with fewer tourists and better food than most Munich beer restaurants. Try the *Bayerische Teller* (Bavarian plate), which comes loaded with various meats, including pork and sausages. The first-floor dining room is more casual than the

> *Thin Nuremberg-style bratwurst is traditionally served with sauerkraut or potato salad and horseradish.*

room upstairs. Residenzstrasse 12. ☎ 089/290-7060. www.spatenhaus.de. Reservations recommended. Entrees 9.50€–28€. AE, MC, V. Lunch & dinner daily. *U-Bahn:* Marienplatz.

★★★ Tantris SCHWABING *INTERNATIONAL*

A famed culinary mecca since 1972, this sophisticated Michelin-starred restaurant offers fixed-price multicourse menus. A typical meal might look something like this: tuna salad with avocado and tomato; sautéed mussels with asparagus; quail confit with goose liver; and hazelnut soufflé with marinated figs. Johann-Fichte-Strasse 7. ☎ 089/361-9590. www.tantris.de. Reservations required. Fixed-price menus 105€–200€. AE, DC, MC, V. Lunch & dinner Tues–Sat. Closed for annual holidays in Jan and May. *U-Bahn:* Dietlindenstrasse.

★ Zum Alten Markt ALTSTADT *BAVARIAN/*

INTERNATIONAL The chef at this friendly eatery makes a great *Tafelspitz* (boiled beef) and classic dishes such as roast duck with applesauce or roast suckling pig. Dreifaltigkeitsplatz 3. ☎ 089/299-995. www.zumaltenmarkt.de. Entrees 12.50€–17€. No credit cards. Lunch & dinner Mon–Sat. *U-* or *S-Bahn:* Marienplatz.

★ Zum Dürnbräu ALTSTADT *BAVARIAN*

Specialties at this charmingly traditional Bavarian restaurant, which has a lovely garden out back, include several beef dishes (tongue, *Tafelspitz,* filet), goose in season, and pork. Dürngräugasse 2. ☎ 089/222-195. Entrees 6.50€–18€. No credit cards. Lunch & dinner daily. *U-* or *S-Bahn:* Marienplatz.

Munich Hotel Best Bets

Best Bavarian Style
Platzl Hotel, Sparkassenstrasse 10 (p. 309)

Best Boutique Hotel
Mandarin Oriental, Neuturmstrasse 1 (p. 309)

Most Glamorous Hotel
Bayerischer Hof & Palais Montgelas, Promenadeplatz 2-6 (p. 305)

Best Guesthouse
Gästehaus Englischer Garten, Liebergesellstrasse 8 (p. 305)

Best Historic Hotel
Kempinski Hotel Vier Jahreszeiten München, Maximilianstrasse 17 (p. 309)

Best Value
Hotel am Markt, Heiliggeiststrasse 6 (p. 308)

Best for Families
Hotel Jedermann, Bayerstrasse 95 (p. 308)

> *Munich's upscale and leading edge Bayerischer Hof offers rooftop relaxation at the health club with a pool and sauna.*

Munich Hotels A to Z

★ **Advokat Hotel** ALTSTADT
This streamlined hotel in a 1930s apartment building is strictly minimalist in approach and has an understated elegance, with medium-size rooms, clean, simple furnishings, and compact bathrooms. Baaderstrasse 1. ☎ 089/216-310. www.hotel-advokat.de. 50 units. Doubles 165€–285€ w/breakfast. MC, V. S-Bahn: Isartor.

★★★ **Bayerischer Hof & Palais Montgelas** ALTSTADT This full-service luxury hotel dates from 1841 and has individually decorated rooms with large ballrooms, plus a health club with pool and sauna. Promenadeplatz 2–6. ☎ 800/223-6800 in North America or 089/21200. www.bayerischerhof.de. 395 units. Doubles 270€–460€. AE, DC, MC, V. Tram: 19.

kids **Eden-Hotel-Wolff** NEAR TRAIN STATION
Most of the rooms in this pleasant hotel across from the train station are fairly large, and all are decorated in a comfortable, un-obtrusive style with larger-than-average bathrooms. Arnulfstrasse 4. ☎ 089/551-150. www.ehw.de. 211 units. Doubles 148€–316€ w/breakfast. AE, DC, MC, V. U- or S-Bahn: Hauptbahnhof.

★ **Gästehaus Englischer Garten** SCHWABING
This quiet, charming guesthouse has small- to medium-size rooms decorated with a homey mixture of antiques, old-fashioned beds, and Oriental rugs; an annex across the street has 15 small apartments. Liebergesellstrasse 8. ☎ 089/383-9410. www.hotelenglischergarten. de. 25 units. Doubles 71€–120€ w/o bathroom, 120€–180 w/bathroom. AE, MC, V. U-Bahn: Münchener Freiheit.

The elegant Eden-Hotel-Wolff, just across the street from the train station, welcomes travelers with comfortable and affordable rooms.

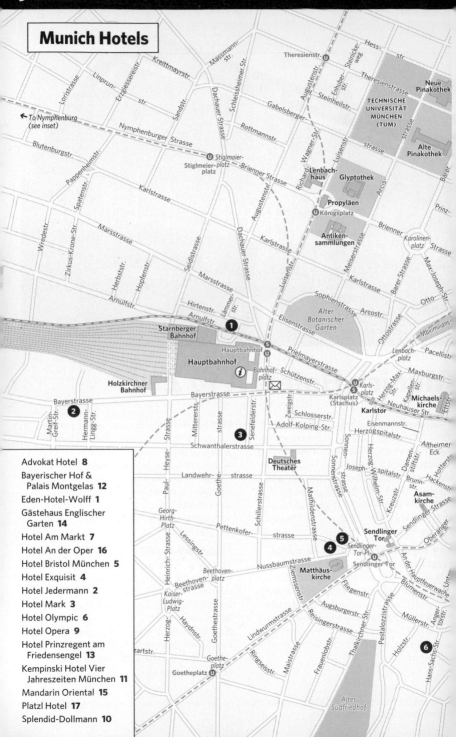

Munich Hotels

To Nymphenburg
(see inset)

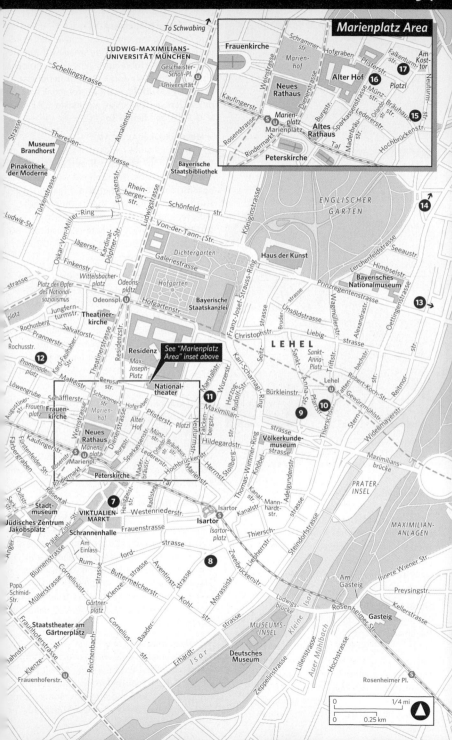

> *The rooftop restaurant at the Mandarin Oriental hotel offers spectacular city views and quality meals that have earned it a Michelin star.*

Hotel am Markt ALTSTADT

This popular budget hotel has small, neat rooms, many of which share bathrooms, and offers clean, no-frills comfort in a wonderful central location. Heiliggeistrasse 6. ☎ 089/225-014. www.hotel-am-markt.eu. 32 units. Doubles 109€–149€. AE, MC, V. *U-* or *S-Bahn:* Marienplatz.

Hotel an der Oper ALTSTADT

The bedrooms in this five-story hotel are on the small side and the decor is basic modern without being particularly distinguished, but the location is wonderful for sightseeing and shopping. Falkenturmstrasse 11 (just off Maximilianstrasse, near Marienplatz). ☎ 089/290-0270. www.hotelanderoper.com. 68 units. Doubles 180€–270€. AE, MC, V. *Tram:* 19.

Hotel Bristol München ALTSTADT

The rooms in this congenial, convenient hotel in central Munich are fairly small, with simple, serene, comfortable furnishings and compact, shower-only bathrooms. Pettenkoferstrasse 2. ☎ 089/5434-8880. www.bristol-munich.de. 55 units. Doubles 99€–150€ w/breakfast. AE, MC, V. *U-Bahn:* Sendlinger Tor.

★ Hotel Exquisit ALTSTADT

Located on a quiet residential street in the heart of Munich, this small, appealing hotel with unusually helpful staff has large rooms comfortably furnished in an old-fashioned German style, some of them overlooking a pretty garden. Pettenkoferstrasse 3. ☎ 089/551-9900. www.hotel-exquisit.com. 50 units. Doubles 175€ w/breakfast. AE, DC, MC, V. *U-Bahn:* Sendlinger Tor.

kids Hotel Jedermann NEAR TRAIN STATION

This pleasant, family-run hotel offers clean, comfortable rooms, most with roomy, shower-only bathrooms at affordable, family-friendly prices (cribs and cots, adjoining rooms, and baby-sitting available). Bayerstrasse 95. ☎ 089/543-240. www.hotel-jedermann.de. 55 units. Doubles 65€–189€ w/breakfast. MC, V. *U-* or *S-Bahn:* Hauptbahnhof.

Hotel Mark NEAR TRAIN STATION

This hotel might not be fancy, but it is clean, convenient, well maintained, and moderately priced. Senefelderstrasse 12. ☎ 089/559-820. www.hotel-mark.de. 95 units. Doubles 92€–262€ w/breakfast. AE, DC, MC, V. *U-* or *S-Bahn:* Hauptbahnhof.

★ Hotel Olympic ALTSTADT

The public areas in this small, stylish, gay-friendly hotel, built as a private villa around 1900, retain much of their original detailing, but the midsize rooms are minimalist and modern and have shower-only bathrooms. Hans-Sachs-Strasse 4. ☎ 089/231-890. www.hotel-olympic.de. 38 units. Doubles 155€–200€ w/breakfast. AE, DC, MC, V. *U-Bahn:* Sendlinger Tor.

★ Hotel Opera ALTSTADT

An Italianate building with a courtyard and garden houses this boutique hotel with distinctively decorated rooms that feature antiques or a cool, modern look; some rooms have small balconies. St.-Anna-Strasse 10.

> The cozy, chestnut and alder wood–adorned rooms of the Platzl Hotel offer Bavarian ambience in a convenient location across from the Hofbräuhaus.

☎ 089/210-4940. www.hotel-opera.de. 25 units. Doubles 195€–275€ w/breakfast. AE, MC, V. *U-Bahn:* Lehel.

★ Hotel Prinzregent am Friedensengel

BOGENHAUSEN The guest rooms at this quietly charming boutique hotel are nicely decorated in a Bavarian-chalet style with big, comfy beds and lots of wood; the level of service is exceptional. Ismaninger Strasse 42–44. ☎ 089/416-050. Fax 089/4160-5466. www.prinzregent.de. 64 units. Doubles 325€–425€ w/breakfast. AE, MC, V. *U-Bahn:* Prinzregenten-Platz.

★★★ Kempinski Hotel Vier Jahreszeiten

München ALTSTADT Founded in 1858, the Vier Jahreszeiten exudes a subdued, old-fashioned self-assurance that carries over into the large, richly appointed rooms, luxurious bathrooms, and on-site health club with pool. Maximilianstrasse 17. ☎ 800/426-3135 in North America, or 089/21250. www.kempinski-vierjahreszeiten.de. 308 units. Doubles 246€–450€. AE, DC, MC, V. Tram: 19.

★★ Mandarin Oriental ALTSTADT

Munich's loveliest small hotel enjoys a fabulous Altstadt location and features sumptuously comfortable rooms equipped with every modern amenity you can think of. The staff at this full-service charmer with seasonal rooftop pool provide outstanding service. Neuturmstrasse 1. ☎ 089/290-980. www.mandarinoriental.com. 73 units. Doubles 395€–520€. AE, DC, MC, V. *U-* or *S-Bahn:* Marienplatz.

★★ Platzl Hotel ALTSTADT

If you're looking for a taste of old-fashioned Bavarian ambience, this hotel located across from the Hofbräuhaus (p. 302) is one of the best choices in Munich. The rooms tend to be small, but they're paneled in chestnut and alderwood and furnished with 19th-century reproduction antiques. Sparkassenstrasse 10. ☎ 089/237-030. Fax 089/2370-3800. www.platzl.de. 167 units. Doubles 190€–240€ w/breakfast. AE, DC, MC, V. *U-Bahn:* Marienplatz.

★★ Splendid-Dollmann ALTSTADT

No two rooms are the same, and some are on the small side, but the overall ambience in this smartly done boutique hotel is hard to beat. Thierschstrasse 49. ☎ 089/238-080. www.splendid-dollmann.de. 36 units. Doubles 160€–200€. AE, DC, DISC, MC, V. *U-Bahn:* Lehel.

Munich Nightlife & Entertainment Best Bets

Best Bar
Master's Home, Frauenstrasse 11 (p. 311)

Best Beer Hall
Augustiner Grossgaststätte, Neuhauser Strasse 27 (p. 280, **❶**)

Best Cafe
Café Arzmiller, Salvatorstrasse 2 (p. 311)

Best Jazz Club
Jazzclub Unterfahrt, Einsteinstrasse 42 (p. 314)

Best (Mostly) Gay Club
Nachtgalerie, Arnulfstrasse 17 (p. 314)

Best Opera & Ballet
Bayerische Staatsoper, Max-Joseph-Platz 2 (p. 314)

Best Symphony Orchestra
Münchner Philharmoniker, Rosenheimerstrasse 5 (p. 315)

Starkbierzeit: Munich's Other Beer Festival

Munich has another beer-themed festival that takes place in the spring. *Starkbierzeit* (literally, "strong beer time") is a local neighborhood affair that happens at all the city's beer gardens and brewery restaurants. The 1-liter servings of malty Starkbier that help Munich residents say *auf wiedersehen* to winter were originally intended to sustain brew-brewing monks during their Lenten fast. One of the best places to celebrate *Starkbierzeit* is the brewery-restaurant-beer garden **Paulaner am Nockherberg,** 77 Hoch Strasse (☎ 089/14599-130), in southeast Munich. Paulaner serves the original Starkbier, a sweet, strong brew called Salvator, and pairs it with a traditional dish of crisp-skinned ham hocks served with sharp mustard.

> *Jazz artists from all over Europe and the U.S. perform 6 nights a week at Munich's renowned Jazzclub Unterfahrt, in Haidhausen.*

Munich Nightlife & Entertainment A to Z

Bars

Havana Club ALTSTADT
This lively singles bar fueled by rum-based cocktails starts hoppin' around 11pm. Herrnstrasse 30. ☎ 089/291-884. www.havanaclub-muenchen.de. *S-Bahn:* Isartor.

★ **Master's Home** NEAR MARIENPLATZ
Done up like an Edwardian-era London club, his bar-restaurant attracts an eclectic assortment of locals and tourists and stays open until 3am. Frauenstrasse 11. ☎ 089/229-909. www.mastershome-muenchen.de. *U- or S-Bahn:* Marienplatz.

★ **Nachtcafé** ALTSTADT
One of the most happening all-night nightspots in Munich attracts soccer celebs, movie stars, writers, and waves of "ordinary" patrons

to its bar, restaurant, and 11pm stage shows of jazz, blues, and soul. Maximiliansplatz 5. ☎ 089/595-900. Tram: 49.

Schumanns American Bar ALTSTADT
This chic spot offers expensive cocktails mixed and/or invented by the owner, Charles Schumann, and a well-heeled crowd that can afford them. Odeonsplatz 6. ☎ 089/229-060. Tram: 19.

Beer Halls & Beer Gardens
See our "Munich's Best Beer Halls & Beer Gardens" tour on p. 280.

Cafes
★★ **Café Arzmiller** ALTSTADT
One of the last classic coffeehouses in Munich, Arzmiller has a sunny, almost Mediterranean atmosphere and features changing art

The famed Munich Philharmonic orchestra regularly wows audiences at Munich's modern Gasteig Kulturzentrum, on the river's east bank.

Munich Nightlife & Entertainment

To Nymphenburg (see inset)

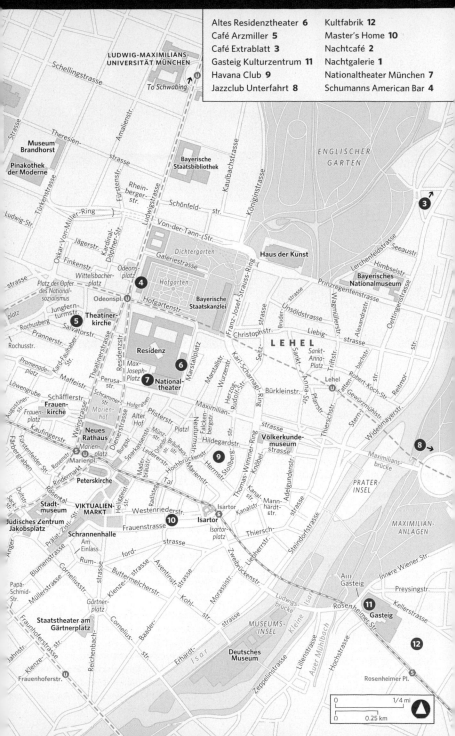

Altes Residenztheater **6**
Café Arzmiller **5**
Café Extrablatt **3**
Gasteig Kulturzentrum **11**
Havana Club **9**
Jazzclub Unterfahrt **8**

Kultfabrik **12**
Master's Home **10**
Nachtcafé **2**
Nachtgalerie **1**
Nationaltheater München **7**
Schumanns American Bar **4**

> *There's much to admire at the beautiful rococo Altes Residenztheater before the show even starts.*

exhibitions. Salvatorstrasse 2. ☎ 089/294-273. *U-* or *S-Bahn:* Marienplatz.

Café Extrablatt SCHWABING
This is a sprawling hangout for writers, artists, students, and the occasional celeb. Leopoldstrasse 7. ☎ 089/333-333. *U-Bahn:* Universität.

Clubs & Discos
★ Kultfabrik ALTSTADT
Wander from venue to venue as your mood dictates at this complex of bars, restaurants, and dance clubs. For bar-hopping don't show up before 8pm; for dancing wait until at least 10:30pm. Grafingerstrasse 6. ☎ 089/4900-2730. Cover varies. *S-Bahn:* Ostbahnhof.

Nachtgalerie ALTSTADT
Two dance halls and a rocking mix of party music in all genres draws a mostly under-30 and often sloshed metrosexual crowd. Arnulfstrasse 17. ☎ 089/324-5595. www.nachtgalerie. de. Cover 10€. *S-Bahn:* Hackerbrücke (at the end of the bridge, turn right and descend the steps).

Jazz
★★ Jazzclub Unterfahrt HAIDHAUSEN
Jazz artists from the U.S. and Europe perform nightly except Monday at Munich's leading jazz venue. Einsteinstrasse 42. ☎ 089/448-2794. www.unterfahrt.de. Cover 10€–14€. *U-Bahn:* Max-Weber-Platz.

Opera & Ballet
★★★ Altes Residenztheater (Cuvilliés Theater)
IN RESIDENZ This jewel-box rococo theater in the Residenz (p. 274, ❶) is a gorgeous performance venue for plays and operas. Residenzstrasse 1. ☎ 089/2185-1940. www. bayerischesstaatsschauspiel.de. Ticket prices vary. Tram: 19.

Nationaltheater München NEAR RESIDENZ
The National Theater is the performance venue for two world-class companies—the ★★★ **Bayerische Staatsoper** (Bavarian State Opera) and the **Bayerisches Staatsballett** (Bavarian State Ballet). Max-Joseph-Platz 2. ☎ 089/2185-1920. www.bayerische.staatsoper. de. Ticket prices vary. Tram: 19.

> *Devotees of opera, symphony, or ballet won't want to miss a performance at the Nationaltheater München.*

Symphony Concerts

Gasteig Kulturzentrum HAIDHAUSEN

The world-famous ★★★ **Münchner Philhar-moniker** (Munich Philharmonic) orchestra performs from mid-September to July in the Philharmonic Hall at the Cultural Center, on the east bank of the river. Rosenheimerstrasse 5. ☎ 089/5481-8181. www.mphil.de. *S-Bahn:* Rosenheimerplatz.

Entertainment Tips

As southern Germany's cultural capital, Munich is renowned for its opera, symphony concerts, and theater. To find out what's going on culturally, pick up a copy of *Monatsprogramm* from one of the tourist offices. The best way to purchase tickets is to go directly to the venue's box office, called a *Kasse;* box offices are generally open during the day and reopen an hour before the performance. The tourist information office in the Hauptbahnhof (main train station) also sells tickets.

More informally, you can chill out in a leafy beer garden or beer hall, catch the local scene in a cafe, or check out bars and dance clubs for late-night partying. Cafes are quiet in the afternoon but pick up steam as the evening wears on. Nightclubs tend to get going around 11pm or midnight.

Dachau

Visiting the former concentration camp at Dachau is an

intense emotional experience on many different levels. It brings into sharp focus the most horrific chapter in modern German history and puts a human face on the sufferings endured by millions of "undesirables" living in Nazi-controlled Germany and Europe from 1933 to 1945. There is a grim irony in the fact that Dachau, before the Nazis took control, was one of the leading artists' colonies in Germany, noted for its progressive attitudes and school of landscape painters. Allow at least half a day for this trip.

> *The International Memorial at Dachau was designed by artist Nandor Glid, a concentration camp survivor, and includes this arresting bronze sculpture of skeletons arranged to look like a barbed-wire fence.*

START Dachau is 19km (12 miles) northwest of Munich. Take *S-Bahn* line S2 from Munich's main train station to Dachau (direction: Petershausen), about a 25-minute ride. At the Dachau train station transfer to bus no. 726 (direction: Saubachsiedlung), which will take you to the camp entrance.

❶ ★★★ KZ-Gedenkstätte Dachau (Dachau Concentration Camp Memorial). In 1933, shortly after Hitler became German chancellor, Himmler ordered the first German concentration camp to be set up in Dachau. Between 1933 and 1945, more than 206,000 prisoners arrived (the exact number is unknown), and more than 32,000 died. The first to arrive were political prisoners (Communists and Social Democrats), followed soon after by "beggars," "antisocial elements," homosexuals,

Jehovah's Witnesses, and, after 1938, growing numbers of Jews.

Dachau did not have gas chambers. Prisoners were forced to become slave laborers and died of overwork, starvation, disease, beatings, hangings, torture, lethal injections, and mass executions by shooting. When U.S. Army soldiers liberated the camp on April 29, 1945, they discovered some 67,000 prisoners on the verge of death.

In 2002, parts of the memorial were redesigned to focus on the fate of the prisoners and to integrate the still-existing historic buildings into the reworked permanent exhibition. Visitors now follow the route of the prisoners, enter rooms in which citizens were stripped of all their belongings and rights, and where, after disinfecting, they were given a striped prison uniform. Inscribed boards show the rooms'

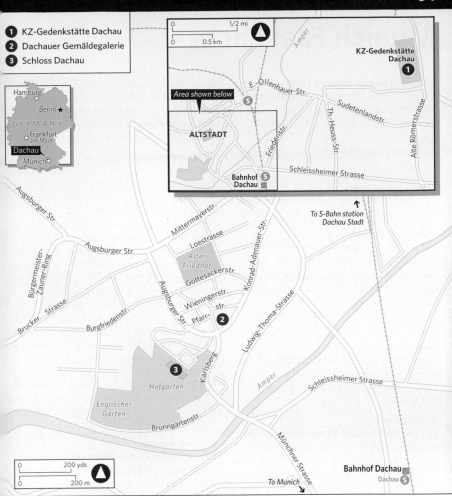

1. KZ-Gedenkstätte Dachau
2. Dachauer Gemäldegalerie
3. Schloss Dachau

original conditions and functions. The names of many of the dead are not known, but displays showing prisoners' faces and videos of survivor interviews put a very human face on the horrific pain and suffering endured by ordinary citizens at the hands of a murderous political machine. ⏱ 1½–2 hr. Alte-Römerstrasse 75. ☎ 08131/1741. www.kz-gedenkstaette-dachau.de. Free admission. Audio tour 3€. Tues–Sun 9am–5pm. Guided tours in English daily 11am and 1pm.

❷ **Dachauer Gemäldegalerie (Painting Gallery).** In the 19th century, Dachau was an artists' colony, and the quiet beauty of its countryside inspired an entire school of landscape painting. Many of those works are on view in this museum. ⏱ 30 min. Konrad-Adenauer-Strasse 3. ☎ 08131/567-516. www.dachauer-galerien-museen.de. Admission 4€. Tues–Fri 11am–5pm, Sat–Sun 1–5pm.

❸ **Schloss Dachau (Dachau Castle).** All that's left of this hilltop castle, once a summer residence of the Wittelsbachs, was built in 1715 in the western wing of the former fortress. In the early 19th century the castle housed an artists' colony. Stop by to take in the view of Munich from the terrace, or spend a few minutes visiting the grand Renaissance hall. ⏱ 15 min. Schlossstrasse 7. ☎ 0813/87923. Admission 2€. Tues–Sun Apr–Sept 9am–6pm, Oct–Mar 10am–4pm.

Munich Fast Facts

Accommodations Booking Services
You can book a hotel room at the **Munich tourist office** in the main train station, open Mon–Sat 9am–8:30pm and Sun 10am–6pm.

ATMs
You'll find bank ATMs (called *Geldautomaten*) all over Munich.

Currency Exchange
Currency exchange windows in the train station are open daily from 6am to 11:30pm.

Dentists & Doctors
If you have a mild medical issue or dental problems while traveling in Germany, most hotels will be able to refer you to a local doctor (*Arzt*) or dentist (*Zahnarzt*) who speaks English. If a medical condition is serious, ask your hotel concierge for help getting to the nearest hospital (*Krankenhaus*) emergency room.

Emergencies
To call the police (*Polizei*), dial ☎ **110.** To report a fire or to summon an emergency doctor (*Notarzt*) or an ambulance (*Krankenwagen*), dial ☎ **112.**

Getting There
BY PLANE **Franz Josef Strauss International Airport** (☎ 089/9752-1313; www.munich-airport.com) is 29km (18 miles) northeast of the city center; you can fly direct from the U.S., the U.K., or anywhere in Germany or Europe. The *S-Bahn* S-8 train connects the airport with the Hauptbahnhof (main train station) in downtown Munich; the fare for the 40-minute trip is 9.20€ adults, 1.20€ kids. The **Lufthansa Airport Bus** (☎ 0180/583-8426) also runs between the airport and Munich's main train station; the 40-minute trip costs 10€ adults, 5€ kids. A taxi to the city center costs about 70€. BY TRAIN You can reach Munich by train from any city in Germany or Europe. Munich's Hauptbahnhof (main train station) on Bahnhofplatz has a tourist information center and a train information office; **Deitsche Bahn** (German Railways; ☎ 11861; www.bahn.de) provides information and schedules. BY CAR Most of downtown Munich is a pedestrian-only area, traffic jams are frequent, and parking spaces are elusive and costly. For excursions into the countryside, **Avis** (☎ 089/126-0000; www.avis.com), **Hertz** (☎ 089/129-5001; www.hertz.com), and **Sixt Autovermietung** (☎ 089/550-2447; www.sixt.com) have desks at the airport and train station.

Getting Around
Subways (*U-Bahn*), trams (*Strassenbahn*), buses, and light-rail lines (*S-Bahn*) make getting around the city easy. For information, call the public-transportation authority, **MVV** (☎ 089/4142-4344; www.mvv-muenchen.de). The same ticket entitles you to ride the *U-Bahn, S-Bahn,* trams, and buses. Purchase tickets from vending machines marked *Fahrkarten* in *U-Bahn* and *S-Bahn* stations; machines display instructions in English. You can also buy tickets in a tram or from a bus driver. Tickets must then be validated in the machines found on platforms and in buses and trams; a validated ticket is good for 2 hours. You can transfer as often as you like to any public transportation as long as you travel in the same direction. Munich has four concentric fare zones. Most, if not all, of your sightseeing will take place in Zone 1, which includes the city center. A day ticket (*Tageskarte*) good for travel within the city limits costs 5€ for adults.

Internet Access
Times Square Online Bistro (☎ 089/5508-8000; www.times-square.net) in the train station has computer workstations, a bistro, and a bar and is open daily from 7:30am to 1am. A growing number of hotels, cafes, and bars offer Wi-Fi.

Pharmacies
In German, a pharmacy is an *Apotheke*. For cosmetics or toiletries, go to a *Drogerie*. Most pharmacies operate during normal business and shopping hours but post details of the nearest 24-hour pharmacy. **International Ludwig's Apotheke,** Neuhauserstrasse 11 (☎ 089/260-3021; *U-* and *S-Bahn:* Marienplatz), a drugstore where English is spoken, is open Mon–Fri 9am–8pm and Sat 9am–4pm.

Police
To report a lost or stolen article, such as a wallet or passport, visit the local police (*Polizei*)

in your location. To call the police from any-where in Germany, dial ☎ **110.**

Post Office

You'll recognize branches of **Deutsche Post** (☎ 01802/3333; www.deutschepost.de), of which there are many around the city, by their yellow sign with a black horn. The **Postamt München** (main post office), Bahnhofplatz 1 (☎ 089/599-0870), across from the train station, is open Mon–Fri 7am–8pm, Sat 8am–4pm, Sun 9am–3pm.

Safety

Munich, like all big cities, has its share of crime, especially pickpocketing and purse- and camera-snatching, but it is generally a safe city. Most robberies occur in the much-frequented tourist areas, such as Marienplatz and the train station.

Taxis

Taxis are cream-colored, plentiful, and expen-sive. Find one at the taxi stands located across the city, or hail a cab on the street if its rooftop light is illuminated. Fares begin at 2.70€; each additional kilometer costs 1.25€ to 1.60€. To order a cab call **Taxizentrale,** ☎ 089/21610.

Telephones

Call ☎ 11837 for information and ☎ 11834 for international information. Munich's area code is 089; use 89 if you're calling Munich from out-side Germany, 089 if you're within Germany but not in Munich. You don't need to dial the area code when calling a number from within Mu-nich. There are public phones in many places—some accept coins and some take phone cards, available at post offices and newsstands.

Toilets

In some places you will find clean public toilets (*Toilette* in German; pronounced twah-*leh*-teh), many of them automatic and wheelchair-acces-sible; you need a .50€ coin to unlock the door. More convenient and widespread are toilets in cafes, bars, restaurants, hotels, malls, and some stores and at highway services and rest areas. Even if you are not obliged to pay, it is custom-ary to leave the attendant .50€.

Tours

You can see Munich by bus, on a bike, or by walking. **BUS TOURS Panorama Tours** (☎ 089-5490-7560; www.autobusoberbayern.de) has

> *Munich's commuters gather at the Odeonsplatz U-Bahn station to travel the vast underground system throughout the city.*

daily 1-hour bus tours every 20 minutes (13€, kids half-price) from in front of the train sta-tion; buy your ticket onboard. **BIKE TOURS** The English-speaking expats at **Mike's Bike Tours** (☎ 089/2554-3988 or 0172/852-0660; www.mikesbiketours.com)offer a 4-hour tour (24€) that spins around the sights of central Munich (including 45 min. in a beer garden), departing daily Mar–Apr 14 and Sept–Nov 10 at 12:30pm; Apr 15–Aug daily at 11:30am and 4pm. Tours meet 15 minutes before setting off, under the tower of the Altes Rathaus on Marienplatz. No need to reserve, just show up. Price includes bike rental and helmet. **WALK-ING TOURS Munich Walk Tours** (☎ 0171/274-0204; www.munichwalktours.de), conducted in English, include a City Walk tour daily at 10:45am (also 2:45pm during high season) and a 2½-hour Hitler's Munich tour (Nov–Mar daily 10:30am). Tours cost 10€ adults, 9€ under 26, kids under 14 free. They meet at the New Rathaus directly under the Glockenspiel on Marienplatz. No need to reserve; you pay the guide (identifiable by a yellow sign).

Visitor Information

Munich's tourist office, **Fremdenverkehrs-amt München** (☎ 089/2339-6500; www.muenchen.de), operates a tourist information center in the main train station, open Mon–Sat 9am–8:30pm, Sun 10am–6pm. Another branch at Marienplatz in the Neues Rathaus (New Town Hall) is open Mon–Fri 10am–8pm, Sat 10am–4pm.

7
Southern Bavaria & the Bavarian Alps

The Best of Southern Bavaria & the Alps in 3 Days

Upper Bavaria *(Oberbayern)*, the southeastern part of Germany, gently rises through foothills covered with verdant pastures, lake-splashed countryside, and groves of evergreens to the dramatic heights of the Alps that divide Germany and western Austria. Many visitors to this region come primarily to see the fairy-tale castles built by Ludwig II, but southern Bavaria also abounds with romantic villages, rococo churches, houses with fancifully painted facades, world-class ski resorts, and nature on a grand scale. This itinerary includes Munich, Bavaria's capital city; Neuschwanstein, the most famous castle in Germany; and the Zugspitze, the highest peak in Germany.

> PREVIOUS PAGE *Known for its ski resort, Garmish-Partenkirchen offers beautiful Alpine views in summer.*
> THIS PAGE *Iconic Schloss Neuschwanstein.*

START Munich. TRIP LENGTH 155km (96 miles).

1 ★★★ **Munich.** Whether you want beer and oom-pah-pah, champagne and opera, or a mixture of the two with some great sightseeing and shopping thrown in for good measure, you can't visit southern Bavaria without spending at least a day in Munich. Sample Munich's urban delights by strolling through **Marienplatz** (St. Mary's Square), the heart of the city, and the adjacent **Viktualienmarkt,** Munich's great outdoor food market. The cultural riches of Munich are boundless, but a stop to see the remarkable painting collection in the **Alte Pinakothek** (Old

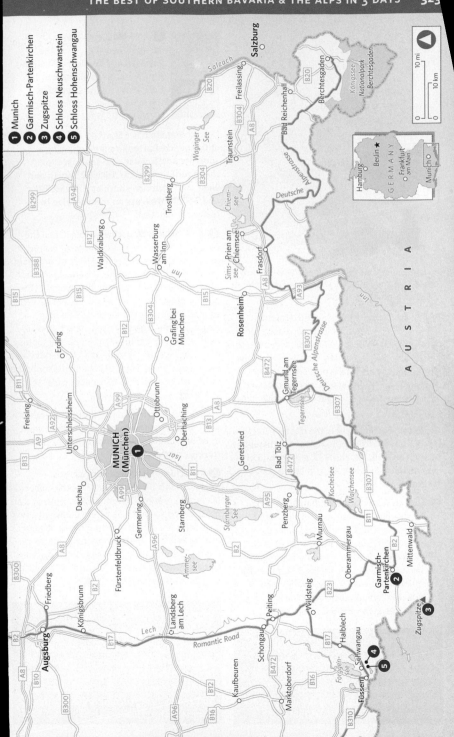

1 Munich
2 Garmisch-Partenkirchen
3 Zugspitze
4 Schloss Neuschwanstein
5 Schloss Hohenschwangau

GERMANY
Hamburg
Berlin ★
Frankfurt am Main
Munich

A U S T R I A

10 mi
10 km

Salzburg
Salzach
Freilassing
Bad Reichenhall
Berchtesgaden
Königssee Nationalpark Berchtesgaden

B20
B304
B20
A8
B8
Traunstein
Deutsche Alpenstrasse
Waginger See
B299
Trostberg
B304
B299
A94
Wasserburg am Inn
Waldkraiburg
B12
B388
B15
B15
B304
B15
Grafing bei München
Chiem-See
Sims-Prien am see Chiemsee
Frasdorf
A8
A93
Rosenheim
Inn
B472
B307
Deutsche Alpenstrasse
Erding
B12
Gmund am Tegernsee
Tegernsee
B307
Freising
B11
Unterschleissheim
A92
A9
B13
Ottobrunn
Oberhaching
A8
B13
MUNICH (München) 1
Isar
Geretsried
Bad Tölz
B472
Kochelsee
Walchensee
B307
Dachau
A99
A96
Germering
Starnberg
B11
Penzberg
A95
Starnberger See
B2
Murnau
Kochel
B11
Mittenwald
B2
Fürstenfeldbruck
Ammer-see
Oberammergau
Garmisch-Partenkirchen 2
Friedberg
B300
Königsbrunn
B2
Landsberg am Lech
Lech
Schongau
Peiting
Wildsteig
B23
Zugspitze 3
Augsburg
A8
B17
Romantic Road
Halblech
B17
Schwangau
4
5
Forggen-see
Füssen
A8
B10
Kaufbeuren
B472
Marktoberdorf
B16
B12
A96
B300
B16
B310

> *The imposing and beautiful Zugspitze is Germany's tallest mountain, offering panoramic views of the Austrian and Bavarian Alps.*

Painting Gallery) is essential, and I'd also recommend a spin through the royal palace called the **Residenz.** Round out your visit with a trip to a beer hall or a beer garden—the world famous **Hofbräuhaus am Platzl** is only one of many possibilities. ⏱ 1 day. For full coverage of Munich, including hotel and restaurant recommendations, see chapter 6.

Garmisch-Partenkirchen, the destination for Day 2, is about 90km (56 miles) southwest of Munich on A95, B2, and B23, a drive of a little over an hour. By train, the trip takes about 1½ hours.

② ★★ **Garmisch-Partenkirchen.** One of Europe's preeminent winter ski and all-season sports resorts, Garmisch-Partenkirchen beguiles with its Alpine setting and range of outdoor activities. Make this your overnight stay for Day 2 and make a trip up the Zugspitze (**③**) your primary activity. ⏱ 1 day. For information on Garmisch-Partenkirchen, including hotel and restaurant recommendations, see p. 348.

SITE GUIDE PAGE 325

③ ★★★ 🧒 **Zugspitze.** For spectacular views of the Bavarian and Tyrolean (Austrian) Alps, you can go all the way to the summit of the Zugspitze, Germany's tallest mountain (2,960m/9,711 ft.).

Neuschwanstein is 65km (40 miles) west of Garmisch-Partenkirchen, following a wide arc north, west, and south around the mountains; by car, take B23 north and west, and continue south on St2059, B17, and St2016 (there is no train service to Neuschwanstein).

④ ★★★ **Schloss Neuschwanstein.** Of all the castles in Germany, this is the most visited. In fact, it's the most popular tourist attraction in the country. That's not necessarily because visitors know anything about Ludwig II, who built it, but because Neuschwanstein served as a prototype for Disneyland's Sleeping Beauty Castle. The setting is superb, the castle itself a 19th-century faux-medieval fantasy. This place can be packed, so if you're not there early, your timed-entry ticket may be for hours after your arrival. ⏱ 35 min. once inside. See p. 338, **②**.

From Neuschwanstein it's about a 20-minute walk to Hohenschwangau. If you don't want to walk, a shuttle bus service runs between the two castles.

⑤ ★★ **Schloss Hohenschwangau.** You might call this ponderous neo-Gothic pile Neuschwanstein's "parent castle," since it's almost next door and was where Ludwig II spent part of his childhood. Architecturally it's not as interesting as Neuschwanstein, but it's certainly worth a visit to see the taste and style of German royalty in the 1830s and 1840s. ⏱ 35 min. once inside. See p. 340, **④**.

Greetings from Bavaria

In Bavaria, people generally use the greeting *Grüss Gott* (pronounced *grease* got) rather than *Guten Morgen* (good morning) or *Guten Tag* (good day). The saying means, roughly, "God greets you." Goodbye is *Für Gott* (for God; pronounced *fear* got) or *Für dich* (for you; pronounced *fear* deek).

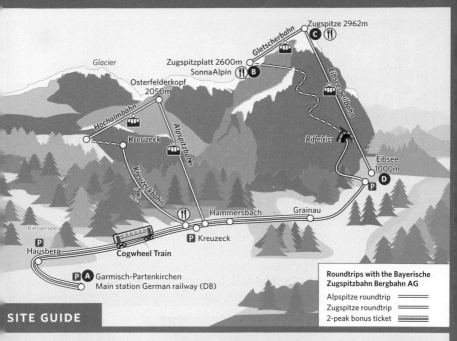

Roundtrips with the Bayerische
Zugspitzbahn Bergbahn AG

Alpsitze roundtrip ═══════
Zugspitze roundtrip ═══════
2-peak bonus ticket ═══════

③ Zugspitze

There are two different ways to reach the
Zugspitze from the center of Garmisch-
Partenkirchen, both beginning with a trip on
the Zugspitzbahn (cog railway), which departs
from in back of the Ⓐ **main railway station**
(Olympiastrasse 27). On the first route, stay
on the Zugspitzbahn as it travels uphill, past
giant boulders and rushing streams, to the
Ⓑ **Zugspitzplatt,** a high plateau with sweeping views. At the Zugspitzplatt, transfer onto
a cable car, the Gletscherbahn, for a 4-minute
ride uphill to the Ⓒ **Zugspitzgipfel** (summit),
where you find extraordinary panoramas, a
cafe and restaurant, a gift shop, and many
Alpine trails. Total travel time to the top is
about 55 minutes.

    The second way to get to the summit of
the Zugspitze is to take the Zugspitzbahn for
a shorter trip, disembarking 14km (9 miles)
southwest of Garmisch at the lower station of
the Ⓓ **Eibsee Sielbahn** (Eibsee Cable Car).
The stop is next to an Alpine lake and is clearly
marked. From here, the cable car carries you
to the Zugspitzgipfel. Total travel time to the
top is about 40 minutes. A round-trip ticket

enables you to ascend one way and descend
the other for the widest range of spectacular
views. ⏱ 3–4 hr. Bayerische Zugspitzbahn,
Olympiastrasse 27, Garmisch-Partenkirchen.
☎ 08821/797-900. www.zugspitze.de. Cog railway operates daily hourly 8:35am–2:35pm; cable
cars half-hourly 8:30am–4:30pm (until 5:30pm
July–Aug). Round-trip fare 36€ adults, 25.50€
teens 16–17, 20€ kids 6–15, 83€ families.

The Best of Southern Bavaria & the Alps in 5 Days

With 5 days you can see all the highlights of southern Bavaria and the Bavarian Alps. Spend your first 2 days in Munich—you don't need a car while there but will need one for the last 3 days of this itinerary. From Munich, the tour heads south into the Bavarian countryside to Füssen with stops at Landsberg am Lech and the rococo Wieskirche along the way. Füssen, your overnight for Day 3, is near Neuschwanstein and Hohenschwangau castles. The Alpine resort of Garmisch-Partenkirchen is your destination for Day 4, with a trip up the Zugspitze, and the tour ends in the mountain town of Berchtesgaden.

> *Beautiful Bavarian buildings line Ludwigstrasse on a sun-drenched day in Garmisch-Partenkirchen.*

START Munich. **TRIP LENGTH** 344km (214 miles).

1 ★★★ **Munich.** For suggestions on how to spend your first day in Munich, see the 3-day tour (p. 322, **1**). On Day 2, take half a day to visit **Schloss Nymphenberg** (Nymphenberg Palace), which you can easily reach by streetcar. After that, spend some afternoon time in the science-and-technology-oriented **Deutsches Museum** or one of Munich's great art museums: the **Neue Pinakothek** (New Painting Gallery), **Pinakothek der Moderne** (Modern Art Gallery), or **Museum Brandhorst.** Round out your day with a stroll in Munich's fabulous park, the **Englischer Garten** (English Garden). ☺ 2 days. For full coverage of Munich, including hotel and restaurant recommendations, see chapter 6.

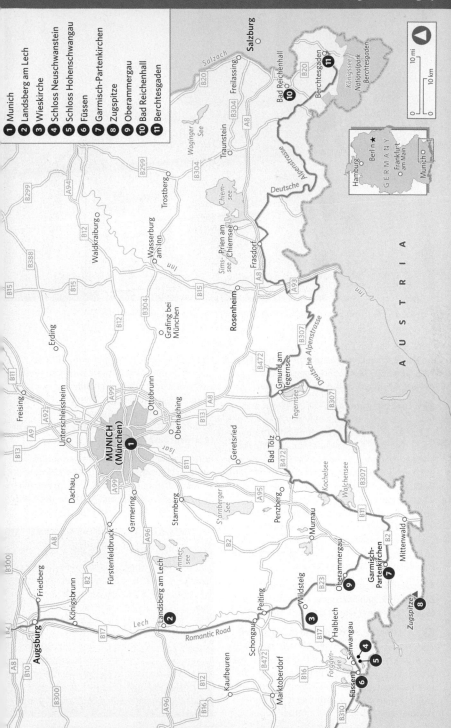

> It took 8 years to complete the cupola in the interior of the 18th-century Wieskirche.

On Day 3, travel west from Munich on B2R, A96, and St2054 to Landsberg am Lech (59km/37 miles), about an hour's drive.

2 ★ **Landsberg am Lech.** The medieval and baroque charms of this lovely Bavarian town are hidden behind a perimeter wall with towers and gates. The triangular-shaped **Markt-platz,** surrounded by painted townhouses, has a charming fountain in the center. The elegant **Rathaus** (Town Hall) with its finely worked stucco gable by Dominikus Zimmermann, designer of the Wieskirche (**3**), is also note-worthy (Hauptplatz 52), as is the **Bayertor** (Bavarian Gate) with its turrets and sculptures (Alte Bergstrasse). ⏱ 1 hr. Tourist information: Hauptplatz 152. ☎ 08191/128-247.

Take St2054 south and continue south on B17, St2059, and St2559 to the Wieskirche (51km/32 miles), about a 45-minute drive.

3 ★★★ **Wieskirche (Church in the Meadow).** This remarkable pilgrimage church in a beauti-ful Alpine meadow is one of the world's most exuberantly decorated buildings. Dominikus Zimmermann (1685–1766) spent 8 years creating this rococo masterpiece, which was completed in 1754. Behind a rather sober

facade, the light-flooded interior with its enormous cupola shimmers with a superabun-dance of woodcarvings, gilded stucco, col-umns, statues, and bright frescoes. ⏱ 30 min. Wies (6km/4 miles southeast of Steingaden). ☎ 08862/501. Free admission. Daily 8am–5pm (Apr–Sept until 7pm).

Retrace your route to B17, and continue south to Neuschwanstein (24km/15 miles), about a 30-minute drive. As you approach Schwangau, turn left on St2016 to the castle.

Travel Tip

The Romantische Strasse (Romantic Road) scenic driving tour (p. 206) starts in northern Bavaria and makes stops at several Bavarian towns before ending in Füssen. You might want to consider ending this tour at Füssen (**6**), skipping Garmisch-Partenkirchen and Berchtes-gaden, and driving the Romantic Road tour in reverse, starting in Füssen and heading north to Würzburg. If you opt for this plan you'll need at least 2 days for the Romantic Road portion of the trip.

> *Maximilian II restored beautiful Schloss Hohen-schwangau and his son Ludwig II hosted such luminaries as composer Richard Wagner here.*

4 ★★★ **Schloss Neuschwanstein.** Cultivate some patience before stopping at Neuschwanstein Castle. It's the most popular tourist attraction in Germany, and the wait to get in can be a long one (ordering tickets online before your trip can save you time). The castle's cafe is a good place to get lunch. ⏱ 35 min. once inside. See p. 338, **2** and p. 339 **3**.

Hohenschwangau, the neighboring Wittelsbach castle, is a 20-minute walk downhill from Neuschwanstein.

5 ★★ **Schloss Hohenschwangau.** Ludwig II's father, King Maximilian II of Bavaria, was responsible for turning an 800-year-old ruin into this neo-Gothic castle, used mostly as a summer retreat. Ludwig II didn't have many happy memories of his childhood here, but he did get to invite the composer Richard Wagner to visit and played duets with him on the piano. The tour takes you into the main rooms of the castle, decorated in the Troubadour style fashionable in the 1830s and 1840s. ⏱ 35 min. once inside. See p. 340, **4**.

From Hohenschwangau and Neuschwanstein, take St2016 south, then drive northwest on St2008, B17, and B16 to Füssen (4.5km/2¾ miles).

Shopping for Woodcarvings in Oberammergau

To view a selection of the craft arts unique to the region, visit **Pilatushaus,** where you can watch woodcarvers, potters, sculptors, and practitioners of *Hinterglas,* painting done directly on glass, in reverse (Ludwig-Thoma-Strasse 10, ☎ 08822/949-511, June–Oct Mon–Fri 1–6pm, Sat 10am–12:30pm). Competition is fierce for sales of local woodcarvings—mostly religious, drinking, or hunting scenes—but know before you buy that even some of the most expensive "handmade" pieces may have been roughed in by machine prior to being finished off by hand. Two reliable shops with a wide range of carvings are **Holzschnitzerei Franz Barthels,** Schnitzlergasse 4 (☎ 08822/4271), and **Tony Baur,** Dorfstrasse 27 (☎ 08822/821), which has the most sophisticated inventory of woodcarvings crafted from maple, pine, and linden.

> *The Oberammergau Passion Play was first performed in 1634, in thanks for being spared from the plague.*

6 ★ **Füssen.** Make this town in the foothills of the Bavarian Alps your Day 3 overnight. The sights here can be seen in a couple of hours and include the late-Gothic **Hohes Schloss** (High Castle), the **Staatsgalerie** art collection, the **Kloster St.-Mang** (Monastery of St. Magnus), the **Museum der Stadt Füssen** (City Museum), and the **Lechfall,** a nearby waterfall. ⏱ 2 hr. See p. 204, **6**; for hotel and restaurant recommendations, see p. 205.

On Day 4, travel east from Füssen to Garmisch-Partenkirchen via B16, B17, B179, B187, and B23 (58km/36 miles), about an hour's drive.

7 ★★ **Garmisch-Partenkirchen.** Your overnight stay for Day 4 is a famed sports and ski resort lying beneath the Wetterstein mountain range of the Bavarian Alps. If you like hiking, there are many opportunities here to get out and enjoy the *frische Luft* (fresh air) on mountain trails. You can also easily while away part of the day just wandering around the two towns. I'd recommend that you take half a day and visit the Zugspitze **8**. ⏱ 1 day for both

the town and the Zugspitze. For information on Garmisch-Partenkirchen, including hotel and restaurant recommendations, see p. 348.

8 ★★★ **Zugspitze.** The observation deck atop Germany's highest peak offers spectacular views of the Alps. To reach it, you take a cog railway and a cable car. See p. 324, **3**.

Oberammergau's Passion Play

Actors first performed the famous Oberammergau *Passionspiele* (Passion Play) in 1634, when the town's citizens took a vow to give thanks for being spared from the plague. Locals have performed the 5½-hour, 16-act drama depicting Christ's journey to the Cross every decade since 1680 (the next will be in 2020). Over 2,000 villagers make up the cast for this religious epic. Actors must be natives of the town or have lived there for at least 20 years. Performances take place from mid-May to early October in the **Passionspiel Theater,** Passionswiese 1 (☎ 08822/92310).

> *Idyllic Berchtesgaden is spectacularly framed by the impressive Bavarian Alps towering over the horizon.*

Day 5 begins with a drive to Oberammergau, 20km (12 miles) north of Garmisch-Partenkirchen via B23, about 20 minutes away.

9 Oberammergau. This village in the Ammergau Alps has been famous for its woodcarvers since the 15th century, and more particularly for its *Passionspiele* (Passion Play), performed by the villagers every 10 years. Though the town is now very commercialized, it's pleasant to spend some time browsing in the folk-art shops, visiting the rococo **Church of St. Peter and St. Paul** (Dorfstrasse), and admiring the many examples of *Luftmalerei* (fresco painting on building facades). ⏱ 1 hr. Tourist information: Eugen-Pabst-Strasse 9A. ☎ 08822/92310.

From Oberammergau, head east on B23, B2, A95, B472, B13, St2073, B318, and B20 to Bad Reichenhall (180km/112 miles), a drive of a little over 2 hours.

10 Bad Reichenhall. For about 2,400 years, the prosperity of this Alpine town—one of Germany's top-rated health spas—has been based on salt (in the form of saline springs).

To learn about the history of salt extraction, visit the **Bad Reichenhaller Salzmuseum** (Salt Museum), housed in an old salt works building from the 1830s (Alte Saline Reichenhall, Salienstrasse; ☎ 08651/700-2146; admission 6€ adults, 4€ kids; tours daily May–Oct 10–11:30am and 2–4pm, Nov–Apr Tues and Fri 2–4pm). Also visit **St. Zeno,** an impressive 12th-century Gothic church with later baroque additions and a frescoed interior (Salzburger Strasse 30). ⏱ 1 hr. Tourist information: Wittelsbacherstrasse 15. ☎ 08651/6060.

From Bad Reichenhall, take B20 south to Berchtesgaden (19km/12 miles), about a 25-minute drive.

11 ★ Berchtesgaden. Spectacular Alpine scenery is what makes this town worth an overnight stay. Enclosed on three sides by snow-covered peaks, Berchtesgaden is a mountain-lover's dream and a good place to headquarter for excursions. ⏱ 3 hr. to explore the town and nearby attractions. For information on Berchtesgaden, including hotel and restaurant recommendations, see p. 344.

The German Alpine Road

Lovers of mountains and mountain scenery will love the Deutsche Alpenstrasse (German Alpine Road), which runs for some 500km (310 miles) from Lindau on the Bodensee (Lake Constance) through the Allgäu region of the Bavarian Alps to Berchtesgaden and the Königssee. Be prepared for mountain roads with many bends and curves.

> *Bucolic beauty and impressive vistas line the 500-kilometer (300-mile) journey along the Alpine Road from Lindau to Berchtesgaden.*

START Lindau is 183km (114 miles) southwest of Munich and 417km (259 miles) southeast of Frankfurt. You can arrive by train (2–3 hr. or 4–4½ hr., respectively), or by car: From Munich, take A96 west and south (about 2 hr.); from Frankfurt, take A3 and A7 south (about 4 hr.). If you've come south along the Romantic Road, it will be easier to begin this tour from Füssen (start from stop ❺). **TRIP LENGTH** 488km (303 miles) and at least 3 days.

❶ ★★ **Lindau.** ◷ At least 1 hr. See p. 390.

Give yourself about half a day to drive from Lindau to Füssen (❺) so you have time in the afternoon to visit Hohenschwangau and Neuschwanstein castles. From Lindau, the Alpine Road runs northeast along B308 into the Allgäu, a region known for its dairy products, climbing steadily with many bends. Beyond Oberreute, 32km (20 miles) east of Lindau, watch for signs indicating the Paradies viewpoint.

> *One of Füssen's many picturesque squares.*

② ★★★ **Paradies.** Situated on a curve of the mountain road, the "Paradise" viewpoint offers a sweeping panorama southwest to the distant Appenzell Alps in Switzerland.

From Paradies, continue east on B308 to Oberstaufen (10km/6¼ miles).

③ Oberstaufen. Lying at the foot of the 1,834m-high (6,017-ft.) Hochgrat massif, this resort has an Alpine charm with hiking in the summer and good ski slopes in the winter.

Travel Tip

The Deutsche Alpenstrasse is not one long seamless highway but a series of connected public roads. These road segments are in good condition but you may become confused by the number of roads that make up the route and their numbering. In general, you will be following roads with a B (for *Bundestrasse*) designation, regardless of whether the segment is signposted DEUTSCHE ALPENSTRASSE. B roads are identified by black numbers on a yellow background.

Tourist information: Hugo-Königsegg-Strasse 8. ☎ 08386/193-000. www.oberstaufen.de.

From Oberstaufen, the Alpine Road continues east on B308 through Immenstadt and Sonthofen to Hindelang, a total distance of about 32km (20 miles), and about 35 minutes by car.

④ ★ **Hindelang.** Decked out with summer flowers, this Alpine village is both a recreation/vacation center and a health spa. Climb (or drive) up Jochstrasse, the continuation of B308 just east of Hindelang, for magnificent views of the craggy peaks of the Allgäu Alps. Oberjoch, 6km (3¾ miles) farther east on winding B308, claims to be Germany's highest mountain village and attracts hikers in the summer and skiers in the winter. Continue on for a little over 1km (about ½ mile) until you come to the Kanzel viewpoint almost on the mountain's summit; from here you have a wonderful panorama of the Ostrach Valley and the mountains that surround it. **Tourist information: Am Bauernmarkt 1; ☎ 08324-8920. www.bad-hindeland.info.**

1 Lindau
2 Paradies
3 Oberstaufen
4 Hindelang
5 Füssen
6 Schloss Neuschwanstein
7 Schloss Hohenschwangau
8 Wieskirche

> *The spectacularly ornate throne room of Schloss Neuschwanstein.*

The German Alpine Road (Deutsche Alpenstrasse)

9 Rottenbuch	**13** Kloster-Bräustüberl	**17** Mittenwald
10 Echelsbacher-Brücke	**14** Schloss Linderhof	**18** Schliersee
11 Oberammergau	**15** Garmisch-Partenkirchen	**19** Tatzelwurm-Wasserfall
12 Kloster Ettal	**16** Zugspitze	**20** Berchtesgaden

From Hindelang, continue east on B308 and B310 to Füssen (37km/23 miles), about a 45-minute drive. Beyond Wertach, the Alpine Road skirts beautiful Grüntensee (Grünten Lake), and beyond Pfronten, it runs close to the Austrian frontier to Füssen, where you might want to spend your first night.

5 ★ **Füssen.** This town on the Lech River has lovely squares and narrow cobblestoned streets flanked by medieval stone houses. Füssen's main attractions are the **Hohes Schloss** (High Castle), **Kloster St.-Mang** (Monastery of St. Magnus), and the **Lechfall,** a nearby waterfall. Neuschwanstein and Hohenschwangau castles are close by. ⏱ At least 1 hr. See p. 204, **6**; for hotel and restaurant recommendations, see p. 205.

To reach Hohenschwangau and Neuschwanstein castles from Füssen, drive southeast on B16, B17, and St2008 (signposts will be for Hohenschwangau) for 4.5km (2¾ miles).

6 ★★ **Schloss Neuschwanstein.** ⏱ 35 min. once inside. See p. 338, **2**.

7 ★ **Schloss Hohenschwangau.** ⏱ 35 min. once inside. See p. 340, **4**.

On Day 2 you'll be driving from Füssen to Garmisch-Partenkirchen, a total distance of 95km (59 miles). Give yourself at least half a day for this drive, including stops along the way. The first stop, the Wieskirche, is about 27km (17 miles) north of Füssen on B17, B16, and St2059, a 30-minute drive.

8 ★★★ **Wieskirche (Church in the Meadow).** A masterpiece of the rococo, the interior of this delightful church is a frothy confection that must be seen to be believed. See p. 328, **3**.

Travel Tip

If it takes you about half a day to reach Füssen, you can visit Ludwig's fairy-tale castles—about 10 minutes away—during the afternoon of Day 1. The castles are immensely popular tourist attractions and can only be seen on guided tours with timed-entry tickets, so it's wise to book online in advance. If you can't get a ticket for an afternoon tour, return as early as you can on the morning of Day 2.

> *Transformed from a royal hunting lodge to a palatial chateau, lavish Schloss Linderhof is known as "Little Versailles."*

From the Wieskirche, take St2059 and St2058 northeast to Rottenbuch (12km/7 miles), about a 20-minute drive.

9 Rottenbuch. What you want to see in this tiny village is the **Maria-Geburts-Kirche** (Church of the Nativity of the Virgin), a former Augustinian monastery remodeled in the 18th

---

Travel Tip

Füssen and the castles of Neuschwanstein and Hohenschwangau mark the end of the Romantische Strasse (Romantic Road) scenic drive that begins in northern Bavaria. If you'd like to combine the two tours, end your tour of the German Alpine Road at Füssen (stop **5**) and from there, drive the Romantic Road route northward. See the Romantic Road tour on p. 206—that tour travels southward, ending in Füssen, so you'll be following it backwards. If you opt for this plan you'll need at least 3 days to reach Würzburg, which will be the last stop on your tour of the Romantic Road.

---

century in a sumptuous rococo style similar to that of the Wieskirche.

Continue south via St2058 and B23 for 3km (about 2 miles) to Echelsbacher-Brücke.

10 ★ Echelsbacher-Brücke (Echelsbach Bridge). This famous single-arch span, made of reinforced concrete and completed in 1929, offers another photo-op stop. Park your car and walk to the middle of the bridge for a breathtaking view of the Ammer River and its pine-covered gorge some 76m (249 ft.) below.

Oberammergau is 17km (10 miles) south of the bridge on B23, a 20-minute drive.

11 Oberammergau. ⏱ 1 hr. See p. 331, **9**.

Continue south on B23 to Ettal (4.4km/2¾ miles).

12 ★ Kloster Ettal (Ettal Abbey). Located in a high, narrow Alpine valley, the vast Benedictine monastery of Ettal was founded in 1330 by Holy Roman Emperor Ludwig IV of Bavaria. In the 18th century the original Gothic structure was given a baroque makeover with a prominent dome by Italian architect Enrico Zucalli. Spend a few minutes exploring the church with its richly decorated interior. Kaiser-Ludwig-Platz 1, ☎ 08822/740. www.kloster-ettal.de. Free admission. Daily 8am–5pm.

13 🍺 Kloster-Bräustüberl. The monks at Ettal have been producing a much-loved liqueur and beer (Ettaler) for some 400 years. You can sample it here, or have a coffee and get a snack for the road. Daily 8am–5pm. 5€–8€.

A short but worthwhile detour from the Alpine Road takes you to another castle built by Ludwig II. Head west from Ettal on St2060 for 11km (7 miles), about 15 minutes by car.

14 ★★★ Schloss Linderhof. Inspired by the Petit Trianon at Versailles, Ludwig II's "little Versailles" is considerably smaller than Neuschwanstein Castle but has some special effects that you won't want to miss. ⏱ 1 hr. for palace tour and a stroll in the gardens. See p. 340, **5**.

From Linderhof, take St2060 east then B23 south 23km (14 miles) to Garmisch-Partenkirchen, a 20-minute drive.

15 ★ **Garmisch-Partenkirchen.** This famous winter sports resort is a good option for your Day 2 overnight. You might want to check into your hotel before ascending the Zugspitze, your last adventure of the day. For information on Garmisch-Partenkirchen, including hotel and restaurant recommendations, see p. 348.

16 ★★★ **kids Zugspitze.** A two-pronged trip by cog railway and cable car lifts you from the town to the observation platform near the top of Germany's highest peak. ⏱ 3–4 hr. See p. 324, **3**.

The itinerary on Day 3 takes you from Garmisch-Partenkirchen to Berchtesgaden, a distance of some 256km (159 miles). Mittenwald is 18km (11 miles) south of Garmisch-Partenkirchen via St2541, B2, and St2042, about a 20-minute drive.

17 ★ **Mittenwald.** Johann Wolfgang von Goethe called Mittenwald "a living picture-book," a description that still holds true today. If you're in a hurry, simply stroll down the main street and have a look at the marvelous painted houses with their steep gabled roofs. The town is an internationally known center for violin making, a tradition that dates back to the 17th century and is explained in the **Geigenbau- und Heimatmuseum** (Violin Building and Local History Museum), full of beautiful examples of the violin-makers' art (Ballenhausgasse 3; ☎ 08823/2511; admission 4€; Tues–Fri 10am–noon and 1–5pm, Sat–Sun 10am–noon, closed Nov 6–Dec 16). ⏱ 1 hr. Tourist information: Dammkarstrasse 3. ☎ 08823/33981. www.mittenwald.de.

From Mittenwald, head northeast for a little over 33km (21 miles) on St2042, B11, and B307 to Sylvenstein-Staudamm (Sylvestein Dam) and reservoir. From here, continue north on B307 for 48km (30 miles) to Bad Weissee, a spa-resort on the Tegernsee, one of southern Bavaria's many beautiful mountain lakes. Along the way, the Alpine Road dips briefly into Austria. From Bad Weissee it's 16km (10 miles) to Schliersee via B307 and St2076.

> *Scenic Mittenwald in Upper Bavaria was referred to as a "living picture-book" by renowned German writer Johann Wolfgang von Goethe.*

18 ★ **Schliersee.** Stop in this mountain hamlet for a few minutes to visit the lovely **St.-Sixtus-Kirche** (Church of St. Sixtus), a medieval church rebuilt between 1712 and 1715 in the baroque style. Johann-Baptist Zimmermann (brother of Dominikus Zimmerman, architect of the Wieskirche), was responsible for the swirling stuccowork and frescoes.

From Schliersee, the Alpine Road continues on B307 to Tatzelwurm, about 28km (17 miles) southeast, a 30-minute drive.

19 **Tatzelwurm-Wasserfall.** Park in the lot signposted NATURDENKMAL TATZELWURM and follow the pathway to this mountain waterfall (about a 15-min. walk there and back).

Berchtesgaden is 113km (70 miles) east of Tatzelwurm, about a 2-hour drive via B307, B472, and the A8 Autobahn. Along the way, the Alpine Road descends into the Inn Valley and skirts along the southern shore of the Chiemsee (Chiem Lake). The Alpine Road comes to an end in the extreme southeastern corner of Germany at Berchtesgaden.

20 ★ **Berchtesgaden.** For information on Berchtesgaden, including hotel and restaurant recommendations, see p. 344.

Ludwig's Fairy-Tale Castles

With some advance planning and a car, the three castles most associated with Ludwig II—Neuschwanstein, Hohenschwangau, and Linderhof—can be visited in 1 day. Füssen, the town closest to the castles, would be a good overnight choice at the start of the tour, Garmisch-Partenkirchen a good overnight choice at the end. With a very early start, you could also make this a 1-day tour from Munich. Another option is to take the Romantic Road scenic driving tour (p. 206) and add Neuschwanstein and Hohenschwangau to the end of your itinerary.

> Schloss Linderhof's ornate exterior is only surpassed by its fabulous interior, which features crystal chandeliers, gold leaf, and a disappearing dining table.

START Füssen is located 132km (82 miles) southwest of Munich, about 1¾ hours via A8 and B16. **TRIP LENGTH** 77km (48 miles) and 1 day.

❶ ★ Füssen. See p. 204, **❻**; for hotel and restaurant recommendations, see p. 205.

To reach Neuschwanstein and Hohenschwangau castles from Füssen, drive southeast on B16, B17, and St2008 (signposts will read HOHENSCHWANGAU) for 4.5km (2¾ miles).

SITE GUIDE
PAGE 341

❷ ★★★ Schloss Neuschwanstein. Was he "Mad King Ludwig," as some assert, or the "Dream King"? However you interpret the personality of Ludwig II of Bavaria, what's true is that he built fantastic—in the sense of "fantasy"—castles like Neuschwanstein. You can see the castle's interior only on a guided tour with a timed-entry ticket, so you may have to wait around a bit to enter Germany's most popular tourist attraction. You can't drive up to the castle; be prepared to walk, take the shuttle bus, or ride in a horse-drawn carriage.

① Füssen
② Schloss Neuschwanstein
③ Café & Bistro
④ Schloss Hohenschwangau
⑤ Schloss Linderhof
⑥ Garmisch-Partenkirchen

③ 🍴 **Café & Bistro.** On the 2nd floor of Schloss Neuschwanstein you can enjoy sandwiches, desserts, and beverages with a memorable view of the Allgäu Alps. ☎ 08362/81110. Open same hours as castle.

Castle Visiting Tips

Neuschwanstein and Hohenschwangau castles are the most popular tourist attractions in Germany, and you'll be spared a potentially long wait by booking your tickets online at www.ticket-center-hohenschwangau.de (tickets for Linderhof cannot be booked online). You can see the castles only on guided, timed-entry tours. A special Königsschlösser (King's Palaces) ticket for 18€ admits you to all three castles and is valid for 6 months. Information about the castles is available at the tourist office in the Rathaus in Schwangau, Münchenerstrasse 2, ☎ 08362/81980 (from Schloss Neuschwanstein, backtrack to B17, then go north on B17 to Schwangau).

> You get the best view of Schloss Neuschwanstein from the Marienbrücke, about a 10-minute walk from the castle.

> Schloss Hohenschwangau, which was rescued from ruin in the 19th century by Maximilian II.

Hohenschwangau Castle is a 20-minute walk downhill from Neuschwanstein. You can also take a shuttle bus or horse-drawn carriage.

❹ ★★ **Schloss Hohenschwangau.** Hohenschwangau Castle was an 800-year-old ruin when Ludwig's father bought it in 1832 and built the neo-Gothic castle you see today. The rooms of Hohenschwangau were designed and furnished in the Troubador style fashionable in the 1830s and 1840s. One of the castle's most attractive chambers is the Hall of the Swan Knight, named for the wall paintings depicting the saga of Lohengrin, a Germanic hero associated with the swan (and with whom, as swan and hero, Ludwig identified). The music room on the second floor contains copies of letters between Ludwig II and his musical idol, Richard Wagner, and the grand piano on which the two played duets. ⏱ 35 min. once inside; arrive at ticket office (8am–5:30pm summer, 9am–3:30pm winter) as early as possible to avoid tour-bus groups, or order tickets online. Hohenschwangau, Alpseestrasse. ☎ 08362/81127.

www.hohenschwangau.de. Guided tours every half-hour daily Apr–Sept 9am–6pm, Oct–Mar 10am–4pm; tours in English available at different times throughout the day. Tours 9€ adults, 8€ students, free for kids 13 and under. Closed Nov 1; Dec 24, 25, 31; Jan 1.

Linderhof is about 46km (29 miles) northeast of Hohenschwangau, about a 45-minute drive. Head south on St2016, turn right onto St2008, and then follow B179 and B198 north. In the village of Ammerwald, turn right onto St2060 and follow signs to Linderhof.

❺ ★★★ **Schloss Linderhof.** In 1869, King Ludwig II transformed this former royal hunting lodge into a small, dazzling-white château meant to resemble the Petit Trianon at Versailles. Linderhof Castle's ornate exterior is restrained when compared to the interior, which is a riot of neo-rococo flashiness, glittering with gold leaf, mirrors, crystal chandeliers, and such contrivances as a dining table designed to rise from the kitchens

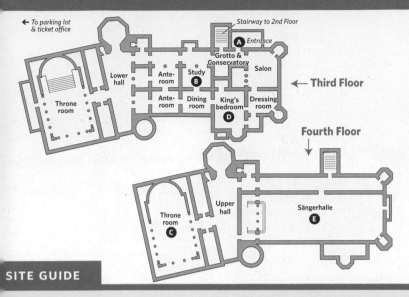

To parking lot & ticket office →

Stairway to 2nd Floor

A Entrance

Grotto & Conservatory

Salon

Lower hall

Ante-room

Study **B**

Throne room

Ante-room

Dining room

King's bedroom **D**

Dressing room

← **Third Floor**

Fourth Floor ↓

Throne room **C**

Upper hall

Sängerhalle **E**

SITE GUIDE

② Schloss Neuschwanstein

Getting from the parking lot to the **A** **castle entrance** involves a steep, 800m (½-mile), 30-minute climb; a horse-drawn carriage ride from the ticket office; or a bus to Marienbrücke, a bridge that crosses over the Pöllat Gorge. From Marienbrücke, the walk to the castle entrance includes a 170-step stairway.

Construction of the castle began in 1869 and continued for some 17 years, stopping only when Ludwig died in 1886. The king lived here on and off for only 170 days. Ludwig's **B** **study** is decorated with painted scenes from the medieval legend of Tannhäuser, and everything from curtains to chair coverings is made of silk embroidered with the Bavarian coat of arms. The **C** **throne room,** designed to look like a Romanesque basilica with columns of red porphyry and a mosaic floor, was never completed. The intricate woodcarving in the **D** **king's bedroom** took 4½ years to complete; through the balcony window you can see the waterfall in the Pöllat Gorge and the Allgäuer Alps in the distance.

Decorated with marble columns and frescoes depicting the life of Parsifal, a mythical medieval knight, the **E** **Sängerhalle** (Singer's Hall) takes up almost the entire fourth floor of the castle and was modeled after Wartburg Castle

in Eisenach (p. 178, **④**), the site of song contests in the Middle Ages. You can also visit the castle's enormous kitchens on the second floor and watch a 20-minute film about Ludwig II. ⏱ 35 min. once inside; arrive at ticket office (8am–5:30pm summer, 9am–3:30pm winter) as early as possible to avoid tour bus groups, or order tickets online. Neuschwansteinstrasse 20. ☎ 08362/81035. www.neuschwanstein.de. Guided tours every half-hour daily Apr–Sept 9am–6pm, Oct–Mar 10am–4pm; tours in English available at different times throughout the day. Tours 9€ adults, 8€ students, free for kids 13 and under. Closed Nov 1; Dec 24, 25, 31; Jan 1. Shuttle bus from Schlosshotel Lisl near parking lot, 1.80€ up, 1€ down. Carriage ride from the ticket office, 5€ up, 2.50€ down.

> *Visitors are carried by quaint horse-drawn carriage to Schloss Neuschwanstein, the most photographed site in Germany.*

> *Ludwig II had the Venus grotto from Wagner's opera* Tannhaüser *recreated at Schloss Linderhof.*

at mealtimes so the king would not have to deal with servants. The park, with its formal French gardens, contains several fanciful buildings, including the Grotte (Grotto), an artificial cave with stalagmites and stalactites, a waterfall, and a lake where Ludwig kept two swans and a swan-shaped boat in which he was rowed about in front of a backdrop scene from Wagner's opera *Tannhäuser.* ⏲ 1 hr. for palace tour and stroll in the gardens. Linderhof 12. ☎ 08822/92030. www.schlosslinderhof.de. Guided tours of palace daily Apr–Oct 15 9am–6pm, Oct 16–March 10am–4pm; tours in English available throughout the day. Tours 7€ adults, 6€ seniors/students (1€ less in winter). Parking 2€. Closed Nov 1; Dec 24, 25, 31; Jan 1; park buildings closed Oct 16–Mar.

From Linderhof, head southeast via St2060 and B23 to Garmisch-Partenkirchen (26km/16 miles), about a 30-minute drive.

❻ ★★ Garmisch-Partenkirchen. For information on Garmisch-Partenkirchen, including hotel and restaurant recommendations, see p. 348.

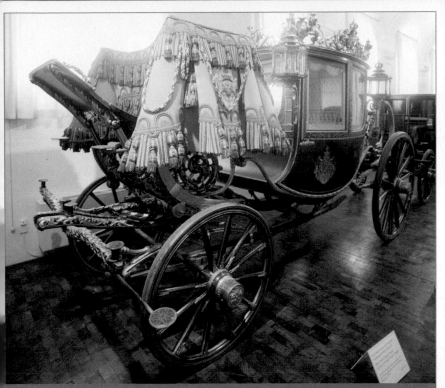

Ludwig II: Crazy for Castles

For some, Ludwig II is the "Mad King." For others, he is the "Dream King," and for still others he is the "Swan King." This strange, self-obsessed monarch has become one of the legendary figures in Bavarian history. Biographies, films, plays, and even a musical have been written about him.

Born in Munich in 1845 to King Maximilian II of Bavaria and Marie of Prussia, Ludwig II spent part of his childhood in Hohenschwangau Castle (p. 340, ❹). At age 18 he was crowned king of Bavaria. Tall, handsome, spoiled, and melancholic, Ludwig grew bored with the affairs of state and eventually became more and more obsessed with acting out his extravagant fantasies. Some of the gilded sleighs and carriages he rode in are on display in the Marstallmuseum at Schloss Nymphenburg (p. 274, ❷) in Munich. A patron of the composer Richard Wagner, Ludwig often had Wagner's operas performed for his own solitary pleasure. At Linderhof (p. 340, ❺), the first palace that he built, Ludwig went so far as to reconstruct the Venus grotto from Wagner's opera *Tannhäuser* and would be rowed around the artificial lake in a swan-shaped boat. An elaborate Moorish theme prevails in Königshaus am Schachen (p. 350, ❹), Ludwig's mountain hunting-lodge near Garmisch-Partenkirchen. The most famous of Ludwig's design efforts is the turreted castle of Neuschwanstein (p. 338, ❷), perched on a crag high above the town of Schwangau.

Ludwig's excesses eventually threatened to bankrupt the kingdom, and in 1886, at age 41, he was declared insane. Three days later, he was found drowned in Lake Starnberg on the outskirts of Munich, along with the physician who had declared him insane. Was he murdered or did he commit suicide? No one knows. Ludwig's remains rest in the crypt of the Michaelskirche (p. 272, ❷) in Munich along with those of other Wittelsbach royals.

Berchtesgaden

The mountain town of Berchtesgaden is the capital of a
highly scenic region called the Berchtesgadener Land, an area of the Berchtesgaden Alps in the southeastern corner of Germany. The town, enclosed by mountains on three sides, is dominated by the massive massif called the Watzmann
(2,712m/8,897 ft.), the third-highest peak in Germany. Berchtesgaden marks the
end of the Deutsche Alpenstrasse (German Alpine Road, p. 332) and serves as a
base for many Alpine excursions, so the summer traffic here can be very heavy.

> *The picturesque Alpine town of Berchtesgaden and the majestic lake Königssee are focal points of
> Berchtesgaden National Park.*

START **From the Berchtesgaden train
station, head northeast along Salinenplatz,
Bahnhofweg, and Maximilianstrasse to
Schlossplatz, a 15-minute walk.**

❶ **Schlossplatz (Castle Square).** The heart of
Berchtesgaden and its most attractive square
is bordered by a 16th-century arcade, the front
of the **Stiftskirche** (❷), and the old Augustinian priory, now called the **Schloss** (castle; ❸).

❷ **Stiftskirche St. Peter und Johannes (Collegiate Church of Saints Peter and John).** The
alternating bands of colored stone on the
facade of this twin-spired abbey church show
an Italian Lombard influence similar to that of

St. Zeno in Bad Reichenhall (p. 331, ❿). Step
in for a quick look at the interior. Founded in
the 12th century by Augustinian monks, the
church has a 13th-century Gothic chancel,
16th-century vaulting, and some interesting
works of art, including a small silver altar donated by Empress Maria Theresa of Austria.
Schlossplatz.

❸ ★★ **Königliches Schloss Berchtesgaden
(Royal Castle).** Over the centuries, as the Augustinian monks became wealthier and more
independent from the grasping archbishops
of Salzburg, what had been a fairly simple
monks' priory became a rather sumptuous

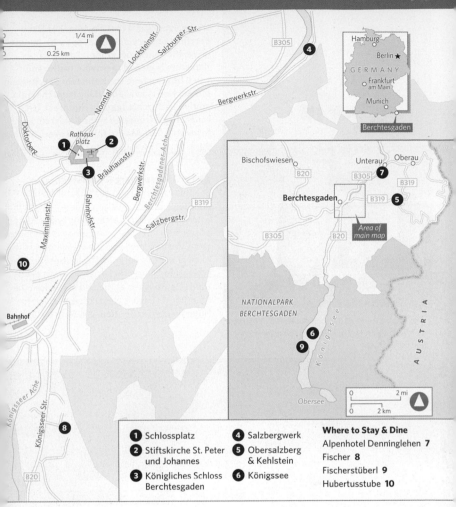

1 Schlossplatz

2 Stiftskirche St. Peter
und Johannes

3 Königliches Schloss
Berchtesgaden

4 Salzbergwerk

5 Obersalzberg
& Kehlstein

6 Königssee

Where to Stay & Dine

Alpenhotel Denninglehen **7**

Fischer **8**

Fischerstüberl **9**

Hubertusstube **10**

alace. Prince Ruprecht Wittelsbach, who
took over the palace in 1929 and lived here
until 1955, filled it with his collections of his-
oric weapons, furniture, tapestries, porcelain,
nd medieval wood sculptures, including two
ieces by Tilman Riemenschneider, the mas-
er carver of Würzburg. ⏱ 50 min. with guided
our. Schlossplatz 2. ☎ 08652/947-980. Tours
€ adults, 3.50€ students, 3€ kids 6–17. May 16–
ct 15 tours daily 10am, noon, 2pm, 4pm; Oct
6–May 15 tours Sun–Fri 11am, noon.

❸ ★★ kids **Salzbergwerk (Salt Mines).** The min-
g of salt, or "white gold" as it was once called,

began in Berchtesgaden in the 16th century and
brought wealth to what had been a poor region.
The brine created here by washing the salt rock
is piped to Bad Reichenhall (p. 331, **10**) for pro-
cessing. Donning miner's garb, visitors tour the
salt mines and caves in a small train and cross
an underground lake in a raft. ⏱ 90-min. tour.
Bergwerkstrasse 83. ☎ 08652/60020. www.
salzzeitreise.de. Tours 14€ adults, 9€ students
and kids 4–16. Daily May–Oct 9am–5pm, Nov–Apr
11:30am–3pm. Located 2km (1¼ miles) from train
station—about a 20-min. walk, or take bus no.
840 to Salzbergwerk stop.

> *The historic heart of Berchtesgaden is Schlossplatz, bordered by several medieval buildings, including the Stiftskirche.*

Obersalzberg is 4km (2½ miles) east of Berchtesgaden via B319, about a 10-minute drive; the road from Obersalzberg to Kehlstein is closed to private traffic and you'll have to take the Kehlstein bus. Regular bus service is available daily from the train station to Berchtesgaden-Hintereck (6€ round-trip); from there, the Kehlstein bus (operates mid-May to mid-Oct every 20 min 9am–5pm, 18€ round-trip) continues uphill to Kehlstein.

❺ ★★ **Obersalzberg & Kehlstein.** Such beautiful scenery and such nasty Nazi connotations. In Obersalzberg, the Alpine hamlet where Hitler settled after being released from prison and where he completed his autobiography, *Mein Kampf,* you can walk around the ruins of Hitler's Berghof, the house where he entertained Nazi officials and foreign politicians. Demolished at the end of the war, the Adlerhorst (Eagle's Nest) retreat, given to Hitler by Martin Borman as a 50th birthday

> *Visitors cross an underground lake in Berchtesgaden's salt mines, which were opened in the 16th century.*

gift, is perched at a higher elevation in Kehlstein, reached by a spectacular mountain road blasted through the rock and then an elevator access only via shuttle bus or on a guided tour). The on-site Kehlsteinhaus restaurant (open daily mid-June to mid-Oct, corresponding to Kehlstein bus schedule) provides a magnificent panorama of the neighboring mountains. ⏱ 3 hr., including travel time.

Königssee is about 7km (4½ miles) south of Berchtesgaden via B305, about a 15-minute drive. You can also take a local train or an RVO bus (marked "Königssee") from the train station to Schönau at the northern tip of the lake.

❻ ★★ Königssee. The emerald-green waters of this long, narrow Alpine lake gleam within the towering rock walls of the surrounding mountains, filling the entire valley between the Watzmann, Jenner, and Gotzenberg peaks. The lake is the centerpiece of the Nationalpark Berchtesgaden, formed in 1978 to protect the natural beauty of this entire region. Because it is surrounded by mountains, the only way to explore it is by boat. At Schönau, on the lake's northern tip, excursion boats head out on 2-hour excursions around the 8km-long (5-mile) lake, stopping at the picturesque Kirche St. Bartholomä (St. Bartholomew's Church) and at Salet. You can disembark at Salet and take a 15-minute walk to the Obersee, a lake once part of the Königssee but separated from it 800 years ago by an avalanche, and the 400m-high (1,312-ft.) Röthbach falls. ⏱ 4 hr. Boat excursions year-round by Bayerische Seenschifffahrt, Schönau. ☎ 08652/96360. www.seenschiffahrt.de. Fares 15€ adults, 7.50€ kids 5–15. Departures every 15 min. in summer 8am–5:15pm, every 45 min. in winter 9:45–3:45pm.

Where to Stay & Dine

> *The Alpenhotel Denninglehen offers a spectacular view of the mountains, along with a beautiful indoor pool.*

★ Alpenhotel Denninglehen OUTSIDE BERCHTESGADEN This modern Alpine-chalet hotel enjoys a spectacular location and has a heated indoor pool, and the rooms aren't bad, either, although the bathrooms are small. Am Priesterstein 7 (6km/30 miles east of Berchtesgaden via B305 and B319). ☎ 08652/97890. www.denninglehen.de. 25 units. Doubles 70€–96€ w/breakfast. MC, V.

★ kids Fischer OUTSIDE BERCHTESGADEN This comfortable, well-maintained, chalet-style holiday hotel on the road to Königssee is a good choice for families. Königsseer Strasse 51. ☎ 08652/9550. www.alpenhotel-fischer.de. 54 units. Doubles 108€–132€ w/breakfast. MC, V.

Fischerstüberl KÖNIGSSEE *BAVARIAN* Seasonal specialties such as fresh trout from the Königssee and local venison are on the menu at this popular lakeside restaurant. St. Bartholomä 3. ☎ 08652/3119. Entrees 15€–27€. MC, V. Lunch & dinner daily mid-Apr–Oct. Accessible by excursion boat from Schönau, St. Bartholomä stop.

Hubertusstube BERCHTESGADEN *INTERNATIONAL* The food is good and the view of the Alps is spectacular at this old-fashioned hotel restaurant. Maximilianstrasse 20 (in Hotel Vier Jahreszeiten). ☎ 08652/9520. Reservations recommended. Entrees 13€–26€. AE, MC, V. Lunch & dinner daily.

Garmisch-Partenkirchen

Given its stunning location at the foot of the Wetterstein range of the Bavarian Alps, it's no wonder that Garmisch-Partenkirchen enjoys a reputation as Germany's top winter-sports resort. In 1936, the 4th Winter Olympics took place here, and in 1978 the town played host to the World Alpine Ski Championships. The town is also a center for summer hiking, mountain climbing, and year-round ice-skating. If you haven't come specifically to ski, hike, skate, or climb, the best way to explore this international resort is simply to stroll around the conjoined towns, enjoying the panoramic views of the Alps and the colorful buildings that line the side streets.

> A competitor flies from a ski jump built for the 1936 Olympics.

START It's a 10-minute walk from the train station to the Olympic Ice Stadium; head north on Bahnhofstrasse, turn left at Olympiastrasse, and follow this street to Olympia-Eissport-Zentrum.

❶ **Olympia-Eissport-Zentrum (Olympic Ice Stadium).** Built for the 1936 Winter Olympics, this winter-sports arena in Garmisch contains three giant skating rinks open to the public. Adlerstrasse 25. ☎ 08821/753-291. Admission 4.20€ adults, 2.40€ kids 6–15. Public skating daily July to mid-May 11am–4pm.

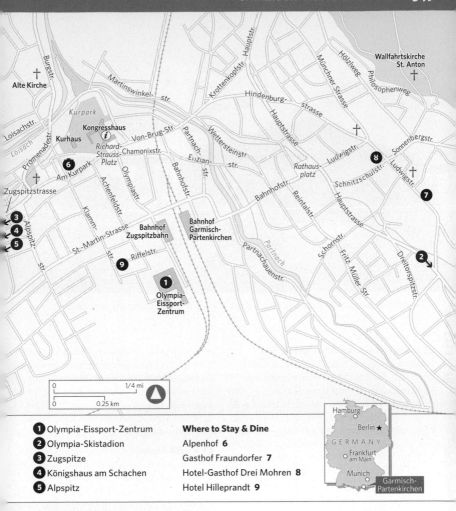

① Olympia-Eissport-Zentrum
② Olympia-Skistadion
③ Zugspitze
④ Königshaus am Schachen
⑤ Alpspitz

Where to Stay & Dine

Alpenhof **6**
Gasthof Fraundorfer **7**
Hotel-Gasthof Drei Mohren **8**
Hotel Hilleprandt **9**

GERMANY

Hamburg
Berlin ★
Frankfurt
am Main
Munich
Garmisch-Partenkirchen

② **Olympia-Skistadion (Olympic Ski Stadium).** Another iconic remnant of the 1936 Winter Olympics, and still integral to the skiing-life of Garmisch, this stadium on the slopes at the edge of town has two ski jumps and a slalom course. The World Cup Ski Jump takes place here every January 1. Unless you're a ski buff, however, you won't find much of interest at the site. About 1km (½ mile) south of train station, a 10-min. walk south on Bahnhofstrasse, Lagerhausstrasse, Gehfeldstrasse, and Kochelbergstrasse.

③ ★★★ kids **Zugspitze.** Heading up to the top of Germany's highest mountain via cog railway and cable car is the one must-do activity in Garmisch-Partenkirchen. ⏱ At least 3 hr. See p. 324, ③.

Getting Around

You don't need a car, but having one makes getting around a little easier. A free municipal bus runs every 15 minutes between the Bahnhof (train station) and Marienplatz, Garmisch's main square. A network of 10 funiculars and cable cars departing from the train station and the borders of the town carry visitors up local peaks.

> The dramatic peaks of the Zugspitze attract skiers in winter and hikers when the snow melts.

④ ★ Königshaus am Schachen (Royal Hunting Lodge). In the mountains above Garmisch-Partenkirchen, at an elevation of 1,688m (5,538 ft.) and accessible only by foot (the climb is strenuous, and you'll need a good map), this excursion to a site associated with King Ludwig II (see "Ludwig II: Crazy for Castles," p. 343) is not for everyone but rewarding for those who make the effort. Built by Ludwig II in 1872, the exterior of Königs-haus am Schachen looks like a cross between a Swiss chalet and a Greek temple, and the "Dream King" insisted that the interior be decorated in an elaborately fanciful Moorish style. The only way to see the lodge is by guided tour (in German only). ⏱ 4 hr. (including travel time). 8246 Garmisch-Partenkirchen. ☎ 08821/92030. www.schachenhaus.de. June–early Oct (exact dates depend on weather). Tours 11am, 1pm, 2pm, and 3pm. Admission 4€ adults, free for kids 13 and under.

❺ ★★ kids Alpspitz. Getting there is half the fun, and the mountain hiking trails at the top offer wonderful views. The Kreuzeckbahn

Excursions from Garmisch-Partenkirchen

Alpine hiking is a major summertime attraction in Garmisch-Partenkirchen. People come from around the world to roam the mountain paths (called *Hohenwege*, or "high ways"), enjoy nature, and watch animals in the forest. The tourist office in Garmisch-Partenkirchen (see "Fast Facts," p. 353) will provide you with a brochure on the area's best-known trails, from easy rambles to difficult climbs.

Garmisch-Partenkirchen Entertainment

From mid-May through September, Bavarian folk music and dancing take place every Saturday night in the Bayernhalle, Brauhausstrasse 19, and the Garmisch park bandstand plays host to classical concerts Saturday through Thursday. On Friday, these concerts move to the Partenkirchen bandstand. A Folklore Week takes place in early August and a 5-day Richard Strauss Festival in June (the composer lived in Garmisch from 1908 until 1949). Check with the tourist office (see "Fast Facts," p. 353) for details.

arries you up and across a rugged landscape
o the lowest station of the Hochalm cable car,
vhich then takes you up to a 2,050m-high
6,725-ft.) summit called Osterfelderkopf.
Here you can enjoy the panoramic views,
or set off on hiking trails that skirt areas of
vildflowers, unusual geologic features, and
ush Alpine meadows. Return to Garmisch on
he Alpspitzbahn, a scenic 10-minute descent
above gorges, cliffs, and grassy meadows.
⏱ 2 hr., more if you're going to hike. Kreuzeck-
bahn/Alpspitzbahn cable-car terminus, Olympiastrasse 27 (1.6km/1 mile south of Garmisch).
Cable cars run year-round approx. every ½ hr.
8:30am–4:30pm (Mar–June until 5pm, July–Aug
until 5:30pm). Round-trip fare 21€ adults, 16€
kids 6–15.

> *Many of the buildings in charming Garmisch-
Partenkirchen have colorful painted facades.*

Where to Stay & Dine

Alpenhof GARMISCH *BAVARIAN/MEDITER-
ANEAN* Regarded as one of the best res-
aurants in Garmisch, the Alpenhof serves
raditional Bavarian and Mediterranean spe-
ialties, including fresh trout, grilled salmon,
nd ragout of venison; vegetarian dishes are
lso available. Am Kurpark 10. ☎ 08821/59055.
www.alpenhof-garmisch.de. Reservations rec-
mmended. Entrees 9€–20€. MC, V. Lunch &
inner daily. Closed 3 weeks in Nov.

Gasthof Fraundorfer PARTENKIRCHEN *BAVAR-
AN* At this large, tourist-friendly restaurant,
he food is hearty and uncomplicated (sau-
age, ham hocks with sauerkraut) and yodel-
rs, musicians, and dancers provide Bavarian
ntertainment nightly. Ludwigstrasse 24.
☎ 08821/9270. www.gasthof-fraundorfer.de.
eservations recommended. Entrees 8€–14€.
E, MC, V. Lunch & dinner Wed–Mon.

Hotel-Gasthof Drei Mohren PARTENKIRCHEN
his family-owned and -operated hotel of-
ers cozy accommodations at moderate
rices; rooms are comfortable without a lot
f frills. Ludwigstrasse 65. ☎ 08821/9130. Fax
08821/18974. www.dreimohren.de. 29 units.
oubles 70€–110€ w/breakfast. AE, DC, MC, V.

> *Diners are treated to traditional German meals
and festive entertainment at the popular Gasthof
Fraundorfer on Ludwigstrasse.*

kids **Hotel Hilleprandt** GARMISCH
This chalet, with pleasant rooms, wooden
balconies, a pretty garden, and a backdrop of
forest-covered mountains, is close to the Zugspitze Bahnhof (train station) and the Olympic
Ice Stadium. Riffelstrasse 17. ☎ 08821/943-
040. www.hotel-hilleprandt.de. 13 units. Doubles 84€–120€ w/ breakfast. MC, V.

Southern Bavaria & the Bavarian Alps Fast Facts

> Cable cars offer unparalleled views to the visitors they carry to the top of the Zugspitze and other Alpine mountains.

Accommodations Booking Services

Call **Hotel Reservation Service** (☎ 0870/243-0003; www.hrs.de) from anywhere in Germany. Tourist information centers in the train stations and in the larger towns (Munich, Lindau, Füssen, Garmisch-Partenkirchen, Berchtesgaden) offer on-the-spot booking services for hotel rooms and B&Bs.

ATMs

All the major cities and towns in this region—Munich, Lindau, Füssen, Garmisch-Partenkirchen, Berchtesgaden—have banks and train stations with ATMs (Geldautomaten).

Dentists & Doctors

If you have a mild medical issue or dental problems while traveling in Germany, most hotels will be able to refer you to a local doctor (Arzt) or dentist (Zahnarzt) who speaks English. You will be expected to provide proof of either permanent or travel insurance (such as an EHIC card in the case of most residents of Europe), or you will be required to pay for treatment. In the event of minor injuries that require speedy treatment, go to the Notaufnahme (emergency) department of the nearest Krankenhaus (hospital). When the injuries are serious or life-threatening, call the doctor/ambulance emergency number (see "Emergencies," below).

Emergencies

To call the police (Polizei), dial ☎ 110. To report a fire or to summon an emergency doctor (Notarzt) or an ambulance (Krankenwagen), dial ☎ 112.

Getting There

The nearest international airport is Munich's **Franz Josef Strauss International Airport** (☎ 089/9752-1313; www.munich-airport.com); you can fly there direct from cities in the U.S., the U.K., Germany, and Europe. Munich is 179km (111 miles) northeast of Lindau, the westernmost town along the German Alpine Road.

Getting Around

Germany is served by an excellent rail network and a car isn't necessary if you are sticking to the principal towns covered in this chapter (Munich, Lindau, Füssen, Garmisch-Partenkirchen, Berchtesgaden). If, however, you want to explore this region and see the countryside of southern Bavaria and the Bavarian Alps, having a car is essential. You'll also need a detailed regional road map (Hallweg or Michelin); you can buy one at Munich airport bookshops and most newsstands. Most of the major international car-rental agencies have offices at Munich airport, including **Avis** (☎ 800/331-1212; www.avis.com), **Budget** (☎ 800/527-0700; www.budget.com) and **Hertz** (☎ 800/654-3001; www.hertz.com). You can also arrange to rent a car through **Rail Europe** (☎ 888/382-7245; www.raileurope.com).

Internet Access

Almost all hotels in Germany, even in smaller towns, now offer Wi-Fi and/or broadband. If yours does not, ask your concierge or at the tourist office if there is an Internet cafe in the vicinity.

Pharmacies

At a German pharmacy, called an Apotheke, the trained staff can recommend over-the-counter medications for many common ailments. For cosmetics or toiletries, go to a *Drogerie*. German pharmacies are open regular business hours. They take turns staying open nights, on Sunday, and on holidays, and each *Apotheke* posts a list of those that are open off-hours.

Police

To report a lost or stolen article, such as a wallet or passport, visit the local police (*Polizei*) in your location. To call the police from anywhere in Germany, dial ☎ **110.**

Post Office

You'll recognize branches of **Deutsche Post** (☎ 01802/3333; www.deutschepost.de) by their yellow sign with a black horn. Post offices are open Monday to Friday 8am–6pm, Saturday 8am–noon.

Safety

This area of Germany is completely safe for tourists, but use common sense and don't leave valuables in sight when you park your car near a scenic area, church, or historic site.

Telephones

Call ☎ 11837 for information and ☎ 11834 for international information. Berchtesgaden's area code is 08652; Garmisch-Partenkirchen's is 08821. Dial the area code when calling a town number from outside the town; you don't need to dial it when calling a town number from inside the town. There are public phones in many places—some accept coins and some take phone cards, available at post offices and newsstands.

Toilets

In some places you will find clean public toilets (*Toilette* in German; pronounced twah-*leh*-teh), many of them automatic and wheelchair-accessible; you need a .50€ coin to unlock the door. More convenient and widespread are toilets in cafes, bars, restaurants, hotels, malls, and some stores and at highway services and rest areas.

Even if you are not obliged to pay, it is customary to leave the attendant .50€.

Tours

Panorama Tours (☎ 89/5490-7560; www.autobusoberbayern.de), based in Munich, offers bus tours to attractions throughout southern Bavaria. Guided tours of Ludwig's castles and the Bavarian lakes can be arranged through **European Castles Tours,** Astrid Baur Travel, Hoehenstrasse 8, 87629 Hopfen am See (☎ 202/580-8732 in the U.S., or ☎ 171/546-6839 in Germany; www.europeancastlestours.com). Private car tours of the castles and the entire region are available through **John's Bavarian Tours,** Auerfeldstrasse 20, 81541 Munich (☎ 162/320-7323; www.johns-bavarian-tours.com).

Visitor Information

For additional information on Bavaria, you may want to contact the regional tourist board: **Bayern Tourismus Marketing,** Leopoldstrasse 146, 80804 Munich (☎ 089/212-3970; www.bayern.by). More information on the German Alpine Road is available from **Touristikverein Deutsche Alpenstrasse,** c/o Tourismusverband München-Oberbayern, Radolfzeller Strasse 15, 81243 München (☎ 089/829-2180; www.deutsche-alpenstrasse.de). Information about the Nationalpark Berchtesgaden is available from **Nationalparkverwaltung Berchtesgaden,** Doktorberg 6, 83471 Berchtesgaden (☎ 08652/968-640, www.nationalpark-berchtesgaden.bayern.de).

In addition to those provided with the individual town listings, other key tourist offices are as follows: BERCHTESGADEN Königsseestrasse 2; ☎ 08652/964-960; www.berchtesgaden.de; Mon–Fri 8:30am–5pm, Sat 9am–noon. GARMISCH-PARTENKIRCHEN Richard-Strauss-Platz 2; ☎ 08821/180-700; www.gapa.de; Mon–Sat 8am–6pm, Sun 10am–noon.

8
The Black Forest & the Bodensee

The Black Forest & the Bodensee in 3 Days

The southwestern corner of Germany is defined by the legendary Schwarzwald, or Black Forest, and the Bodensee (Lake Constance), one of Europe's great lakes. Vineyards and fruit orchards thrive in the region's mild, sunny climate. This tour takes in scenic Black Forest viewpoints, as well as glamorous Baden-Baden, a spa resort with thermal waters and an elegant casino; Freiburg im Breisgau, a medieval university town; and Lindau, a lovely resort town on the Bodensee that basks in an almost Mediterranean balminess. Spend a night in each and you'll get a nice feel for the charms this corner of Germany has to offer.

> *PREVIOUS PAGE Lichtentaler Allee is an elegant, plant-covered park promenade that runs along the Oosbach River in Baden-Baden. THIS PAGE Freiburg im Breisgau's Rathausplatz is known for its chestnut trees.*

START **Baden-Baden is 182km (113 miles) south of Frankfurt on A5 (about a 2-hr. drive); and 320km (199 miles) west of Munich on A8 (3 hr.). It is easily accessible by train from anywhere in Germany (it's a 4-hr. ride from Munich, 3 hr. from Frankfurt). TRIP LENGTH 407km (253 miles), including the excursion from Freiburg.**

❶ ★★ **Baden-Baden.** The most glamorous spa resort in the Black Forest came to prominence in the 19th century, but people have been getting into hot water here as far back as the Roman era, when the emperor Caracalla came to soak his arthritic bones in the thermal pools. You can experience this unique aspect of Baden-Baden health culture yourself at

the giant **Friedrichsbad** or **Caracalla Therme** bathing complexes. Then spend a couple of hours promenading down time-honored **Lichtentaler Allee,** sip the famous waters in the **Trinkhalle,** and have a look at the famous casino set amid landscaped gardens. The new

Traveling by Train

You can reach all three towns in this tour by train, but if you want to explore the countryside—the itinerary includes a scenic excursion from Freiburg—having a car will open up more of the region.

Museum Frieder Burda houses a marvelous collection of modern paintings and sculptures. ⏲ 1 day. For information on Baden-Baden, including hotel and restaurant recommendations, see p. 380.

Take A5 south to Freiburg im Breisgau (115km/71 miles), a 75-minute drive; or, if you have the time (at least 5 hr.) and want to see more of the Black Forest, take the highly scenic Black Forest Crest Road (p. 362).

❷ ★★ **Freiburg im Breisgau.** The largest city in the Black Forest, Freiburg has about 200,000 inhabitants and 30,000 students

> *Friedrichsbad's giant, lush Roman-Irish steam and freshwater bath complex in Baden-Baden was built in the 1840s.*

attending its famous university. Because of its protected location on a plain surrounded by mountains, Freiburg is at the center of one of Germany's oldest wine-growing regions (see the "Black Forest Vineyards" tour on p. 370). Freiburg is a city to enjoy simply by spending a couple of hours wandering through its medieval Altstadt (Old Town), where little streams called *Bächle* rush in channels alongside the sidewalks. Admire the Gothic Münster (Cathedral) and, if you're in a museum mood, visit the **Augustinermuseum** (Augustinian Friars Museum) with its collections of religious art and medieval wooden sculpture. You can also hike or take a funicular up to a panoramic viewpoint called the **Schlossberg**. ◷ Half-day. For information on Freiburg im Breisgau, including hotel and restaurant recommendations, see p. 384.

From Freiburg im Breisgau, head south on Günterstalstrasse/L124 and follow the narrow, twisting road to Schauinsland (18km/11 miles), a drive of about 25 minutes.

❸ Schauinsland. Here, from the parking lot, you can climb the 91 steps to an observation tower for a panoramic view toward Feldberg, which you will visit later (**❻**) during this excursion from Freiburg. This area also has easy hiking trails. ◷ 15 min.

Continue south on L124 and B317 to the hamlet of Todtnau (14km/8¾ miles), about a 15-minute drive.

❹ ★ Todtnau. This Black Forest village is a regional sports center and a base for hikers. A marked 1.6km-long (1-mile) footpath leads from the village to an impressive series of waterfalls. ◷ 1 hr. to get to the falls and back.

Continue south on B317 to Utzenfeld and follow L142 northwest to the Belchen (17km/11 miles), about a 25-minute drive.

❺ ★★ Belchen. An enclosed gondola, the Belchen Seilbahn, takes you to the top of this famous, mile-high peak for one of the most spectacular views in the Black Forest. From the grassy summit you can see the Feldberg and other nearby mountains, green hillside pastures, tile roofs in small villages, and the vast Rhine plain to the west. ◷ 90 min. for gondola ride and stroll on summit. Belchenstrasse 13. ☎ 07673/888-280. Gondola 6€. Daily 9:30am–5pm.

From the Belchen, backtrack on L142 and B317 to Todtnau and continue northeast on B317 to Feldberg (18km/11 miles), about a 35-minute drive.

❻ ★ Feldberg. Another enclosed gondola, the Feldbergbahn, takes visitors to the 1,450m (4,760-ft.) summit of a peak called Seebuck and a panorama that takes in the highest peaks of the Alps to the south. ◷ 1 hr. for gondola and stroll at summit. ☎ 07655/8019. Gondola 6.80€. Daily 9am–4:30pm.

Continue east on B317 and turn south on B500 to Schluchsee (17km/10 miles), about a 20-minute drive.

❼ Schluchsee. Schluchsee is one of the loveliest of the Black Forest lakes. It is also the

> The Belchen Seilbahn gondolas take visitors on a mile-long climb to spectacular views at the mountain's peak.

largest expanse of water in the Black Forest and a center for water sports of all kinds.

From Schluchsee, head back north along B500 and K4962 to Titisee (17km/11 miles), about a 20-minute drive. Along the way you'll pass through Naturpark Schwarzwald, a protected area that encapsulates some of the most scenic qualities of the Black Forest.

8 ★ **Titisee.** Set like a jewel within the low, forested hills of the southern Black Forest, this lake is popular with swimmers, boaters, and hikers.

Return to Freiburg im Breisgau for the night by heading northwest along B31/ B500 (29km/18 miles, about a 30-minute drive); or drive southeast on B31 to Lindau (147km/91 miles, about a 2-hour drive) and spend the night there. B31 is also the best route to take if you are driving from Freiburg to Lindau.

9 ★★ **Lindau.** Lindau is not a place that requires strenuous sightseeing. Swim, bike, stroll, and enjoy the almost Mediterranean languor of this little island-resort in the Bodensee. You can see everything on a 2-hour walk around the lovely Altstadt (Old Town). ⊕ Half-day. For information on Lindau, including hotel and restaurant recommendations, see p. 390.

High Points of the Black Forest

If you want to see more of the countryside, you can make an easy 145km (90-mile) circuit (stops **3**–**8** on this tour) through a scenic part of the Black Forest and be back in Freiburg in time for dinner. Along the way, you pass waterfalls, two of the forest's highest peaks (both with cable cars), and two of its most beautiful lakes. Give yourself a full afternoon, or at least 5 hours, to make this excursion. If you don't have time, head straight to Lindau, stop **9** on this tour.

The Black Forest & the Bodensee in 5 Days

The Black Forest and the Bodensee offer numerous opportunities for sightseeing and discovery. This itinerary expands on the 3-day highlights tour by adding a daylong tour from Freiburg im Breisgau to some picturesque villages where cuckoo clocks are still made, and another daylong tour from Lindau to the magical garden island of Mainau. You will also have the opportunity to spend some extra time in Freiburg and Lindau, and perhaps spend the night at a guesthouse in the scenic countryside.

> *Mainau, a semitropical island in the Bodensee, features a baroque castle, orange trees, and flowers that bloom year-round.*

START **Baden-Baden is 182km (113 miles) south of Frankfurt on A5 (about a 2-hr. drive); and 320km (199 miles) west of Munich on A8 (3 hr.). It is easily accessible by train from anywhere in Germany (4-hr. from Munich, 3 hr. from Frankfurt).** TRIP LENGTH **553km (344 miles).**

① ★★ **Baden-Baden.** ⏲ 1 day. For information on Baden-Baden, including hotel and restaurant recommendations, see p. 380.

Take A5 south to Freiburg im Breisgau (115km/71 miles), a 75-minute drive; or, if you have more time (at least 5 hr.) and want to see more of the Black Forest, take the scenic Black Forest Crest Road (p. 362).

② ★★ **Freiburg im Breisgau.** ⏲ 1 day. For information on Freiburg im Breisgau, including hotel and restaurant recommendations, see p. 384.

Take B31 southeast to Titisee-Neustadt and the start of the German Clock Road (35km/22 miles), about a 35-minute drive.

③ ★★ **The German Clock Road.** Give yourself a full day to explore the Black Forest countryside, where the clockmaking tradition dates back to the mid-19th century and continues today. You'll want to leave yourself enough time at the end of the day for the 2¼-hour drive from Gütenbach (the end of the German Clock Road) to Lindau. ⏲ 1 day. See "Keeping Time: The German Clock Road," p. 366.

Lindau is 155km (96 miles) southeast of Gütenbach on B31, a drive of about 2¼ hours.

④ **Lindau.** ⏲ 1 day. For information on Lindau, including hotel and restaurant recommendations, see p. 390.

1 Baden-Baden
2 Freiburg im Breisgau
3 The German Clock Road
4 Lindau
5 Mainau

The island of Mainau, about 52km (32 miles) west of Lindau, makes a great day trip via ferry.

5 ★★ **Mainau.** The centerpiece of this semi-tropical island, where palms and orange trees grow and fragrant flowers bloom year round, is a baroque castle. In 1853, Grand Duke Friedrich I of Baden purchased the island as a summer residence. A passionate plant lover, he laid the foundations for the Arboretum, the Rose Garden, and the Orangery, gardens that his great-grandchild, Count Lennart Bernadotte, would later develop. Palms, citrus and fruit trees, orchids, azaleas, rhododendrons, tens of thousands of tulips (in spring), and roses (in summer) fill the gardens of this 110-acre

(45-hectare) botanical wonderland. Butterflies from throughout the world flit and flutter through the Butterfly House. The island has a Mediterranean luxuriance that invites leisurely strolling and cafes and a restaurant where you can dine or enjoy a drink. ⏱ 5 hr. including roundtrip ferry from Lindau. ☎ 07531/3030. www.mainau.de. Admission 16€. Daily mid-Mar to mid-Oct 7am–8pm, winter 9am–dusk. Daily ferry service from Lindau by Bodensee-Schiffsbetriebe, Schützingerweg 2. ☎ 08382/275-4810. www.bsb-online.com. 35€ roundtrip Kombiticket includes ferry and admission at Mainau.

The Black Forest Crest Road

One of the most scenic and popular car trips in Germany, the Schwarzwaldhochstrasse (Black Forest Crest Road) runs almost the entire length of the forest, from Baden-Baden to Freiburg im Breisgau. Much of the 232km (144-mile) route follows the mountaintops (hence the name) at heights of around 1,000m (3,250 ft.). You can drive the Crest Road in 1 day, using it as your point-to-point route from Baden-Baden to Freiburg, but you may want to break the trip and stop for the night at Triberg or one of the other picturesque villages. The Crest Road is loaded with viewpoints that show off the fabled natural beauty of the northern and central portions of the Black Forest.

> The beautiful rococo high altar of St. Peter in the Black Forest is the burial place of the dukes of Zähringen.

START Baden-Baden is 182km (113 miles) south of Frankfurt on A5 (about a 2-hr. drive); and 320km (199 miles) west of Munich on A8 (3 hr.). It is easily accessible by train from anywhere in Germany (4-hr. from Munich, 3 hr. from Frankfurt). TRIP LENGTH 267km (166 miles) and 1 or 2 days.

① ★★ **Baden-Baden.** For information on Baden-Baden, including hotel and restaurant recommendations, see p. 380.

From Baden-Baden, take B500 south to Mummelsee (28km/17 miles), about a 30-minute drive.

② **Mummelsee.** Located below the Hornisgrinde, at 1,164m (3,819 ft.) the highest point in the northern Black Forest, this small, picturesque, spruce- and pine-fringed lake is named after the legendary *Mümmeln* (water sprites) once believed to inhabit its dark, icy depths.

Continue south on B500 to Ruhestein (15km/9 miles), where a left turn onto L401 takes you down into the Allerheiligen Valley. Allerheiligen is about 17km (11 miles) south of Ruhestein.

③ ★ **Allerheiligen.** All that's left of this late-13th-century monastery church are the vaulted porch, transept walls, and polygonal Gothic chapel. About 2km (1¼ miles) beyond the abbey ruins, a steep footpath along rock

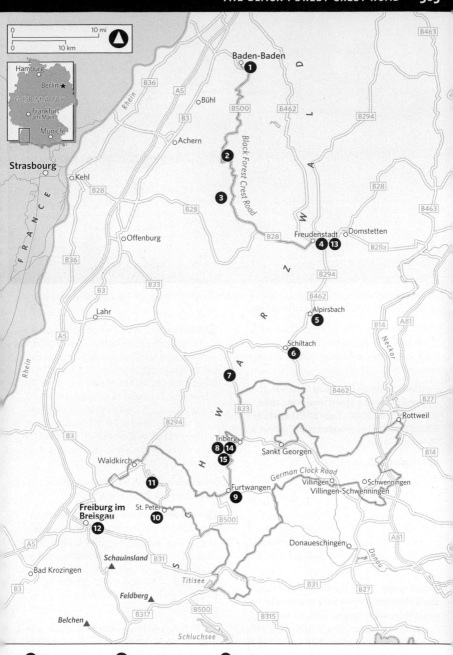

1 Baden-Baden
2 Mummelsee
3 Allerheiligen
4 Freudenstadt
5 Alpirsbach
6 Schiltach
7 Schwarzwälder Freilichtmuseum Vogtsbauernhof
8 Triberg
9 Furtwangen
10 St. Peter
11 Kandel
12 Freiburg im Breisgau

Where to Stay & Dine
Jägerstüble **13**
Romantik Parkhotel Wehrle **14**
Römischer Kaiser **15**

> *The beautiful Black Forest Crest Road runs from Baden-Baden to Freiburg im Breisgau along mountain ridges, rolling hills, lush forests, and meadows.*

walls overhung with giant trees leads to the Allerheiligen Wasserfälle (waterfall). ⏱ 1 hr. including the 45-min. walk to and from the waterfall).

Continue south on L401 and turn left at Oppenau, where a steep mountain road climbs back to B500. Take B500 east for 31km (19 miles) to Freudenstadt, about a 35-minute drive.

❹ **Freudenstadt.** Built by order of the Duke of Württemberg in the 17th century, Freudenstadt was destroyed by fire in 1945 but by 1950 had been rebuilt according to its original plan. Spend a few minutes viewing the arcaded houses and the 17th-century Stadtkirche (City Church) that surround the town's huge Marktplatz (Market Square), reputedly the largest in Europe.

From Freudenstadt, the Crest Road runs along the foot of the Kinzig and Elt valleys, passing through several villages before reaching Alpirsbach, about 60km (37 miles) south of Freudenstadt on B294 and B462.

❺ **Alpirsbach.** Stop in this pretty village and take a few minutes to look at the church (Karlstrasse 12), a rare three-aisle Romanesque pier basilica built between 1125 and 1135 and joined to the buildings of a former Benedictine monastery. The basilica still has its 12th-century apse, unusual buttresses that stand on columns instead of on the floor, and traces of 12th-century wall paintings; the vault tracery and bays in the adjoining cloisters were built in the Gothic Flamboyant style.

Schiltach is 9km (5½ miles) southwest of Alpirsbach on B294 and B462.

❻ ★★ **Schiltach.** Spend a little time strolling around this idyllic Black Forest village. The setting, in a double valley formed by the confluence of the Schiltach and Kinzig rivers, and the unusually complete collection of well-preserved half-timber buildings around the steeply sloping Marktplatz (Market Square), make for a picturesque scene. ⏱ 30 min.

The Schwarzwälder Freilichtmuseum is in Gutach, 16km (10 miles) west of Schiltach on B294.

❼ ★★ **Schwarzwälder Freilichtmuseum Vogtsbauernhof.** The open-air Schwarzwälder Freilichtmuseum Vogtsbauernhof (Black Forest Open-Air Museum) provides a wonderful

Travel Tip

You need a car for this route and should be prepared for some steep, twisting roads.

introduction to the domestic and agricultural history of the Black Forest. The Vogtsbauern farm, still in its original 1570 state, is showcased along with five other historic farmhouses and outbuildings moved here from other locations. Each farmhouse is different: One is a two-story building with a threshing floor that separates the living quarters and the animals' stalls; in another, the living quarters, stalls, and workshops are all under one roof. Crafts, furniture, and farm implements are on display in the various buildings. ⊙ 2 hr. for unhurried visit. Wählenhöfe (on B33 btw. Hausach and Gutach). ☎ 07831/93560. Admission 6€. Apr–Oct 9am–6pm (Aug until 7pm).

From the museum, take B33 and B500 south to Triberg (18km/11 miles), about a 20-minute drive.

8 Triberg. ⊙ 30 min. See p. 368, **6**.

Continue south on B500 to Furtwangen (16km/10 miles), about a 20-minute drive.

9 Furtwangen. The highlight of this small clockmaking town is the Deutsches Uhrenmuseum (German Clock Museum) with its superlative collection of Black Forest timepieces. ⊙ 30–45 min. See p. 369, **8**.

Continue south on B500 along the Hexenloch, a deep, steeply wooded gorge laced with waterfalls. Turn right (north) on L128 and L127. Between St. Märgen and St. Peter the twists and turns of the road allow plenty of great views. St. Peter is 31km (19 miles) from Furtwangen; this stretch should take about 40 minutes to drive.

10 ★ St. Peter. This village is worth a stop to visit **St. Peter auf dem Schwarzwald** (St. Peter in the Black Forest), a fine baroque church attached to a former Benedictine monastery. The abbey church is the burial place of the dukes of Zähringen, the founders of Freiburg im Breisgau, and contains statues by the great sculptor J. A. Feuchtmayer. The extravagance of the late rococo–style interior is exemplified in the high altar, ceiling paintings, and an elegant library decorated with delicate stuccowork. ⊙ 15 min.

From St. Peter, take L112 northwest to Kandel (12km/7½ miles).

11 ★★ Kandel. This is one of the few mountains in the Black Forest whose summit offers an open view of the surrounding countryside. From the viewing platform a splendid panorama takes in the Vosges, the Feldberg, the Belchen, and the vineyard-clad Kaiserstühl massif near Freiburg. ⊙ 30 min. on foot from parking lot to viewpoint and back.

Freiburg im Breisgau is 15km (9 miles) southwest of Kandel via L112 and B3, about a 20-minute drive.

12 ★★ Freiburg im Breisgau. See p. 384.

Where to Stay & Dine

Jägerstüble FREUDENSTADT *GERMAN/SWABIAN* Hearty local dishes like *Eisbein* (veal shank) with sauerkraut and venison goulash are on the menu at this popular re-creation of an old Black Forest inn. Marktplatz 12. ☎ 0744/2387. www. jaegerstueble-fds.de. Entrees 12€–18€. MC, V. Breakfast, lunch & dinner daily.

★ Romantik Parkhotel Wehrle TRIBERG The area's finest traditional inn dates back to the 17th century and offers upscale comfort in its main building. There's also a newer resort-type chalet with pool and balconied rooms. Gartenstrasse 24. ☎ 07722/86020. www.parkhotel-wehrle.de. 50 units. Doubles 149€–210€ w/breakfast. AE, DC, MC, V.

Römischer Kaiser TRIBERG Owned by the same family since 1840, this old-fashioned guesthouse offers a pleasant assortment of rooms that vary in size and shape but provide a cozy, comfortable ambience at a reasonable price. Sommerauerstrasse 35 (1.5km/1 mile outside Triberg). ☎ 07722/96940. www.roemischer-kaiser. com. 27 units. 72€–88€ w/breakfast. AE, MC, V (add'l 4% charge if paying with credit card).

Keeping Time: The German Clock Road

Since 1667, when the first wooden clock was made in Waldau, clocks have been produced in the Black Forest. The cuckoo clock was invented in this part of Germany, and timepieces of all shapes and sizes have been and are still being produced here. The scenic Deutsche Uhrenstrasse (German Clock Road) showcases museums, factories, shops, and sights related to clocks as well as delightful villages, picturesque shingle-roofed houses, and lush mountain meadows. The itinerary given here takes in the most interesting stops along the route. You could drive it in a long day, but give yourself 2 days if you want to fully enjoy the sights, including the often-gorgeous landscapes.

> *Gremmelsbach's Haus der 1000 Uhren features on its exterior what may be the world's largest cuckoo clock.*

START **Titisee-Neustadt is 35km (22 miles) southeast of Freiburg im Breisgau on B31, about 35 minutes by car. TRIP LENGTH 106km (66 miles) and 1 or 2 days.**

❶ **Titisee-Neustadt.** The lake brings holidaymakers and sports enthusiasts, but clock aficionados come to visit **Clock Factory "Hönes,"** Bahnhofstrasse 12 (☎ 0765/1496;

Mon–Fri 7:30am–noon and 1–3:30pm), which still produces and sells handmade Black Forest cuckoo clocks and shield clocks. ⏱ 1 hr.

From Titisee-Neustadt, take L172 northeast to Eisenbach (8.5km/5¼ miles), about a 10-minute drive.

❷ **Eisenbach.** Make a quick stop in this small resort town to see the display of old clocks

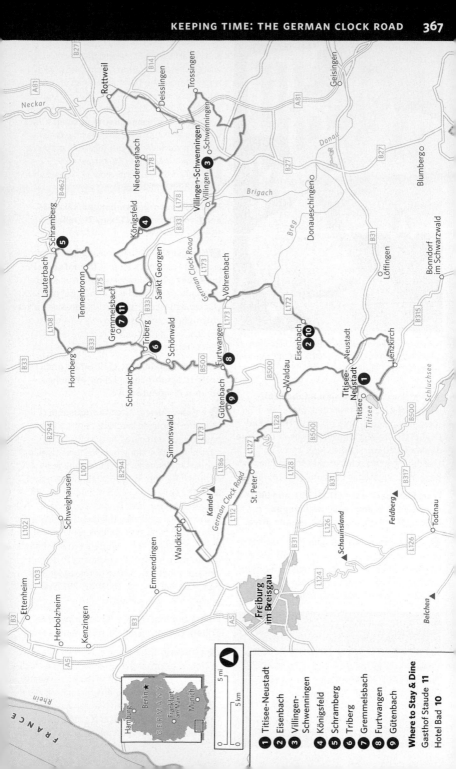

1 Titisee-Neustadt
2 Eisenbach
3 Villingen-Schwenningen
4 Königsfeld
5 Schramberg
6 Triberg
7 Gremmelsbach
8 Furtwangen
9 Gütenbach

Where to Stay & Dine

Gasthof Staude 11
Hotel Bad 10

> *A costumed local makes a traditional Black Forest hat called a Bollenhut at Triberg's popular open-air Schwarzwald Museum.*

and clock dials in the **Heimatstube Wolf-winkelhalle,** (Bei der Kirche 1; Mon, Wed–Fri 10am–noon and 2–4pm). Stop by **Hotel Bad** (Hauptstrasse 55) for a quick look at the large, double-faced world time clock from 1865, created by master clockmaker Johann Baptist Beha and mounted in the hotel's restaurant.

From Eisenbach, take L172, L180, and L181 northeast to Villingen-Schwenningen (25km/16 miles), about a 30-minute drive.

❸ ★ **Villingen-Schwenningen.** The first watch factory in this town was set up in 1858, and that long history is reflected in two museums, both of which you can breeze through in a few minutes. The **Uhren- und Heimatmuseum** (Clock

---

Shopping Tip

If you're looking for a traditional Black Forest timepiece but don't have the time or interest to drive the entire Clock Road, you can drive to Triberg (stop ❻), 55km (34 miles) northeast of Freiburg im Breisgau on B294 and B33, and find shops selling cuckoo clocks, woodcarvings, music boxes, and other traditional crafts.

---

and Local History Museum) displays sundials, wall clocks, grandfather clocks, and pocket watches from the 17th to the 19th centuries (Kronenstrasse 16; ☎ 07720/822-371; admission 2€; Sun–Fri 10am–noon and 2–6pm, Sat 2–6pm). The **Uhrenindustriemuseum** (Clock Industry Museum) documents how the city earned a worldwide reputation as a maker of industrial timepieces (Burkstrasse 39; ☎ 07720/38044; admission 3€; Tues–Sun 10am–noon and 2–6pm).

From Villingen-Schwenningen, take B33 north to Königsfeld (12km/7½ miles), a 15-minute drive.

❹ **Königsfeld.** If you're looking for an antique clock, make a quick stop at **UhrenFabrik Peter Auber** (Clock Factory Peter Auber), the only factory in the Black Forest that produces clocks with lacquered shields patterned after old originals; there's a showroom and shop that sells original clocks from the last 200 years (Friedrichstrasse 12; ☎ 07725/3105).

From Königsfeld, take L177, L420, and L175 north to Schramberg (12km/7½ miles), about a 15-minute drive.

❺ ★ **Schramberg.** The **Stadtmuseum** (City Museum), housed in a 19th-century villa, has exhibits dedicated to the city's long-standing clockmaking industry and displays a rare Art Nouveau "Art Clock" made by Arthur Junghans in 1896 (Bahnhofstrasse 1; ☎ 07422/29268; free admission; Tues–Fri 2–6pm, Sat–Sun 10am–noon and 2–5pm). Ask at the tourist office for the free *Geschichtspfad Zeitreise* (history trail walking tour) leaflet that describes the most interesting buildings in the town, most of them having to do with clock production. ⏲ 30 min. Tourist information: Hauptstrasse 25. ☎ 07422/29215. www.typisch-schwarzwald.de.

From Schramberg, take B33 southwest to Triberg (24km/15 miles), a 30-minute drive.

❻ ★ **Triberg.** Triberg has long been a center of clockmaking, and its main street is a clock-shopper's paradise, lined with shops selling every kind of timepiece imaginable. Visitors also come to walk a trail that follows the Gutach rapids along a scenic pathway to a series of waterfalls cascading 160m (525 ft.)

> The Deutsches Uhrenmuseum gallery has the world's largest collection of Black Forest Clocks, as well as timepieces from all over the world.

hrough the forest. (The walk takes about an ₁our, roundtrip.) Traditional Black Forest cos-₁umes and local craftwork are exhibited in the **;chwarzwald Museum** (Wallfahrtstrasse 4; ☎ 07722/4434; admission 4.50€; daily ₁0am–5pm), and the nearby **Wallfahrtskirche ₁laria in der Tanne** (Pilgrimage Church of Our ₁ady of the Firs, Clemens-Maria-Hofbauer-₅trasse) has a display of exuberantly carved ₁nd painted rustic baroque furnishings. ⏲ 30 ₁in. For hotel recommendations in Triberg, see ₁. 365.

;o north from Triberg on B33 and K5726 to ₃remmelsbach (5.5km/3½ miles), about a ₁0-minute drive.

⑦ Gremmelsbach. It's worth a brief stop here ₂ check out the selection of classic wooden ₁uckoo clocks at **Haus der 1000 Uhren** ‹House of 1,000 Clocks) with its giant cuckoo ₁lock—reputedly the largest in the world—out ₁nt (Hauptstrasse 8; ☎ 07722/96300; ₁lon-Sat 9am–5). Josef Weisser, a painter of ₁lock faces, launched the business in 1824; his ₁reat-great-grandson is the current owner.

From Gremmelsbach, take L175 south to Furt-wangen (23km/14 miles), a 30-minute drive.

⑧ ★ Furtwangen. This town sits in a high mountain valley and is home to one of the more interesting museums on the route. In addition to the world's largest collection of Black Forest clocks, the **Deutsches Uhrenmuseum** (German Clock Museum) showcases timepieces from all around the world and all epochs (Robert-Gerwig-Platz 1, ☎ 07723/920-117; admission 4€; daily Apr–Oct 9am–6pm, Nov–Mar 10am–5pm). ⏲ 30 min.

From Furtwangen, take L173 west to Güten-bach (7km/4¼ miles), a 10-minute drive.

⑨ Gütenbach. This village was one of the historic centers of home-based clockmaking. Take a quick look at exhibits in the **Dorf- und Uhrenmuseum** (Village and Clock Museum), which document the world of Black Forest village life and clockmaking in the days before the Industrial Revolution, and include a fine collection of rare and unusual clocks (Dorerhof 2, ☎ 0723/2526; admission 2.50€; mid-June to Sept Wed 2–5pm, Sat 11am–1pm).

From Gütenbach, head back to Freiburg im Breisgau on L128, a distance of 44km (27 miles) and about an hour's drive.

Where to Stay & Dine

Gasthof Staude GREMMELSBACH
This Black Forest inn sits at 900m (2,950 ft.) and has quiet, comfortable guestrooms and a good-value restaurant that serves regional specialties. Obertal 20. ☎ 07722/4802. www.gasthaus-staude.de. 14 units. Doubles 66€–84€. MC, V.

kids Hotel Bad EISENBACH
Popular with hikers and outdoor enthusiasts, this hotel offers comfortable modern rooms, a good restaurant, and a pool and sauna. Hauptstrasse 55. ☎ 07657/1505. www.bogensporthotel.de. 32 units. Doubles 66€ w/ breakfast. MC, V.

Black Forest Vineyards

If you'd like to tour some local vineyards, the Kaiserstuhl near Freiburg im Breisgau is a good place to visit on a 1-day wine-tour by car. This small enclave of volcanic outcrops sandwiched between the Basel-Freiburg Autobahn and the Rhine is where you'll find some of the Baden wine region's finest wines, grown in terraced vineyards. The Kaiserstuhl also has plenty of options for eating out, from rustic country inns to elegant Michelin-starred restaurants. *Note: Weingut* means winery, or wine estate.

> *The picturesque vineyards of Oberrotweil.*

START Endingen is 26km (16 miles) north of Freiburg im Breisgau on A5, about a 25-minute drive. TRIP LENGTH 38km (24 miles) and 1 day.

1 Weingut Schneider. This winery in Endingen was founded in 1981. It has earned a strong reputation for whites, including *Weissburgunder* (Pinot Blanc) and *Grauburgunder* (Pinot Gris), but also produces a red *Spätburgunder* (Pinot Noir). Königschaffhauserstrasse 2, Endingen am Kaiserstuhl. ☎ 07642/5278. www.weingutschneider.com. Fri 3–6pm, Sat 9am–2pm.

From Endingen, take L113, K4923, and K5128 west to Bischoffingen (10km/6 miles), about a 10-minute drive.

2 Weingut Karl-Heinz Johner. The vintner's aim at this vineyard in Bischoffingen is to make wines that best express the unique *terroir* of the Kaiserstuhl. The benchmarks here are Burgundy-style reds, especially racy *Spätburgunder*s, and a mouth-filling *Weissburgunder* that some say is better than its Pinot Blanc cousins across the Rhine in Alsace. Gartenstrasse 20, Vogtsburg-Bischoffingen. ☎ 07662/604. www.johner.de. Mon–Sat 2–5pm.

From Bischoffingen, take K4925, K5128, and L115 south to Oberrotweil (3km/2 miles).

3 Weingut Salwey. This family-owned and -run estate in Oberrotweil produces floral and fruity *Weissburgunder*s and fine *Grauburgunder*s as well as some finely aromatic *Spätburgunder*s. Hauptstrasse 2, Oberrotweil am Kaiserstuhl. ☎ 07662/384. www.salwey.de. Mon–Sat 9am–noon and 2–5pm (Sat until 4pm).

Freiburg im Breisgau is 24km (15 miles) southeast of Oberrotweil on L115, a 30-minute drive.

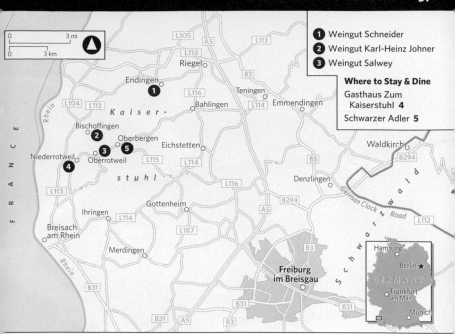

1 Weingut Schneider
2 Weingut Karl-Heinz Johner
3 Weingut Salwey

Where to Stay & Dine
Gasthaus Zum
Kaiserstuhl **4**
Schwarzer Adler **5**

> A Cabernet Sauvignon grape harvester at work in a vineyard in the Black Forest's wine-rich region of Kaiserstuhl.

Where to Stay & Dine

★ **Gasthaus Zum Kaiserstuhl** NIEDERROTWEIL The small dining room at this appealing guest-house with its flowery curtains and formica decor offers locally sourced game and fish enlivened with fresh herbs and edible flowers. Rooms are comfortable and unpretentious. Niederrotweil 4. ☎ 07662/237. www.gasthaus-zum-kaiserstuhl.de. 3 units. Doubles 38€–68€ w/breakfast. Lunch Tues–Sun, dinner Tues–Sat. Entrees 15€–20€. MC, V.

★★ **Schwarzer Adler** VOGTSBURG-OBERBER-GEN *FRENCH* The classic French cuisine served at this cozy wood-paneled *Gasthof* (guest-house) has earned a Michelin star since 1969. The wine list is as spectacular as the food and includes the best wines of Baden. Bad-bergstrasse 23. ☎ 07662/933-010. www.franz-keller.de. Reservations recommended. Mar–Oct lunch & dinner daily, Nov–Feb dinner Wed–Fri, lunch & dinner Sat–Sun. Entrees 17€–28€. MC, V.

A GRAPE GUIDE

Germany's Wine Regions BY DONALD OLSON

PEOPLE TEND TO ASSOCIATE GERMANY WITH BEER RATHER THAN WINE,
but wine has been produced and enjoyed in Germany since the Romans planted
the first vineyards some 2 millennia ago. Though German wine is overshadowed
by the vintages from France and Italy, you'll find interesting regional German wines
at almost every restaurant. Under the German wine law, there are two categories of quality, *Tafelwein* (table wine) and *Qualitätswein* (quality wine). If the word
"Deutscher" doesn't precede the category, the wine is not made solely from
German grapes. For more on German wine, see p. 632.

Wine-growing Regions

Germany has 13 designated wine-growing regions ranging in size from a few hundred to several thousand acres. The most famous vineyards, and the ones of most appeal to travelers, are found in the western and southwestern parts of the country.

AHR Despite its northerly location near Bonn, the 1,300-acre Ahr is the main producer of red wines (such as Spätburgunder) in Germany.

BADEN Some 41,000 acres in size, Germany's most southerly wine region includes the famous Kaiserstuhl near Freiburg and produces red and white wines with a reputation for intensity and lower acidity than elsewhere in Germany.

FRANKEN Würzburg (p. 240) is the center of this 15,000-acre region along the Main River, famous for the *Bocksbeutel* (a flask-shaped bottle) and the best Silvaner in Germany.

HESSISCHE BERGSTRASSE At just 1,000 acres, this is one of the smallest wine-growing areas with some surprisingly good Rieslings.

MITTELRHEIN Rieslings do extremely well in the slate soils on the steep slopes along the Rhine between Bingen and Koblenz (p. 454, **7**), but this region has shrunk considerably as more impassible sites have been abandoned.

MOSEL-SAAR-RUWER The Riesling rules on these 32,000 acres along the Mosel River and its tributaries between Luxembourg and Koblenz. There are four distinct regions and microclimates, and the combination of slate and steep vineyards produces vibrant and elegant wines with a fine acidity.

NAHE Wines produced in this 12,000-acre region range from racy to robust. White varieties include Riesling, Silvaner, and Müller-Thurgau.

PFALZ Rich wines reflect the warm climate of southern Germany in this 59,000-acre region extending to the Alsatian border. The most famous vineyards are located in Mittelhardt, the northern half of the region.

RHEINGAU Classic and substantial Rieslings are produced on these 7,700 acres along the northern side of the Rhine between Wiesbaden and Rüdesheim. This region is the home of Hock (derived from Hochenheim), the traditional English term for wines from the Rhine.

RHEINHESSEN The largest wine-growing region in Germany (65,000 acres) produces often underrated Rieslings and is the home of the original Liebraumilch. The best vineyards are close to the Rhine, where the soil imparts more complexity and interest to the wines.

SAALE-UNSTRUT Six vineyards line the Saale and Unstrut rivers in this 1,000-acre region west of Leipzig in the former East Germany; Müller-Thurgau and Silvaner are the most widely planted varieties.

SACHSEN The smallest wine-growing region in Germany is 750 acres along the Elbe River around Meissen and Dresden (p. 166); the vineyards include Müller-Thurgau and Traminer, which has an avid local following.

WÜRTTEMBERG This 27,000-acre area along the Neckar River extends from the Tauber river valley to south of Stuttgart (p. 430) and produces both red and white wines, including Riesling, Müller-Thurgau, and Silvaner.

GO FOR GRAPE: The Main German Varietals

RIESLING: The most important of the German grape varieties, Riesling (*ree*-sling) is considered by many to be the world's premier white wine grape.

MÜLLER-THURGAU: Originally thought to be a cross between Riesling and Silvaner, and now believed to be a cross between two Riesling clones, these grapes produce dry to semi-dry and aromatic wines.

SPÄTBURGUNDER: Spätburgunder (*shpate*-bur-*gun*-der) grapes produce light, pale wines that have received more attention from growers and the public in recent years.

SILVANER: The low-yielding Silvaner (sill-*von*-er) grape produces dry neutral wines that benefit most from a drier style of winemaking.

GEWÜRZTRAMINER: People either love or hate spicy, aromatic, and distinctive Gewürztraminers (guh-*wurtz*-trah-min-er); the best versions come from the Pfalz and Baden.

Around the Bodensee by Car, Boat & Train

German-speakers call this enormous body of water the Bodensee, but elsewhere in Europe it's known as Lake Constance. Whatever you call it, it is the largest lake in Germany, and, because of its mild, generally sunny climate and natural beauty, it's considered by the Germans to be a kind of inland Riviera. In the summer, holidaymakers descend on the historic towns that line the shores of the Bodensee. The itinerary below follows an easy route along the German shoreline, from the city of Konstanz to the island-city of Lindau, stopping at smaller towns, villages, and attractions along the way.

> *Germany's largest lake, the Bodensee, is called the "Inland Riviera" due to the region's temperate climate.*

START Konstanz is 263km (163 miles) south of Baden-Baden on A81 (about a 3-hr. drive); and 125km (78 miles) east of Freiburg im Breisgau on B31 (about 2 hr.). Konstanz is easily accessible by train from all the major cities in Germany, about 3 hours by train from either Baden-Baden or Freiburg. TRIP LENGTH 135km (84 miles) and 2 days.

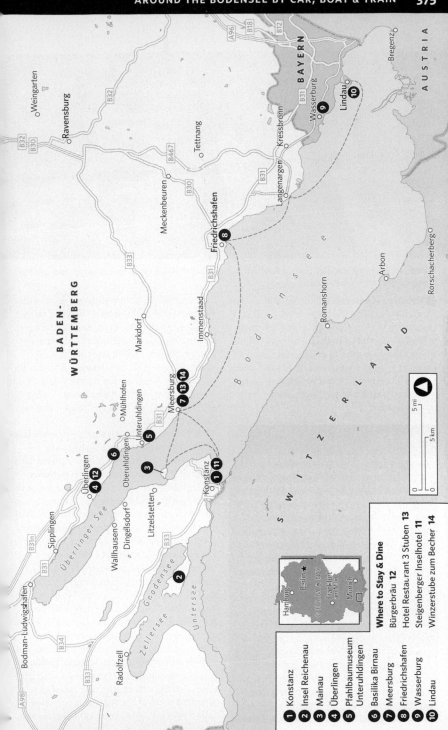

Where to Stay & Dine
Bürgerbräu **12**
Hotel Restaurant 3 Stuben **13**
Steigenberger Inselhotel **11**
Winzerstube zum Becher **14**

1 Konstanz
2 Insel Reichenau
3 Mainau
4 Überlingen
5 Pfahlbaumuseum Unteruhldingen
6 Basilika Birnau
7 Meersburg
8 Friedrichshafen
9 Wasserburg
10 Lindau

> *Visitors come to the medieval town of Konstanz to enjoy the shops, the largest beach in the area, and the magical beauty of nearby Mainau island.*

❶ Konstanz (Constance). Situated at the tip of a peninsula right on the border with Switzerland, Konstanz—or Constance, as it's known in English—straddles both banks of the Rhine, which flows beneath the bridge that connects the northern and southern parts of town. With 81,000 inhabitants it's the largest town in the region and a busy and bustling summer holiday destination.

Travel Tip

With a car this is an easy 2-day trip, but you don't need a car for this itinerary. It's fun and easy to tour the Bodensee's towns and attractions by boat. Bodensee-Schiffsbetriebe (Schützingerweg 2, Lindau; ☎ 08382/275-4810; www.bsb-online.com) provides daily ferry service between Konstanz, Mainau, Lindau, and nearly all the other lakeside towns on this itinerary. You can also follow this itinerary by train, since all the towns mentioned are served by Deutsche Bahn (German Railways) regional and local lines (☎ 01805/996-633 or www.bahn.de for schedules). The Bodensee is perfect for biking, too, and you could bike this entire itinerary in 3 or 4 days. In Konstanz, bikes can be rented at Velotours (Ernst-Sachs-Strasse 1; ☎ 07531/98280; www.velotours.de); the company also offers customized bike tours.

Spend half an hour wandering around the **Altstadt** (Old Town) with its twisting streets, attractive shops, churches, and two Rhineside towers that are remnants of the town's medieval walls. The Altstadt is unusually intact because Konstanz managed to escape bombing by Allied Forces during World War II. How? It simply left all its lights on at night, a ploy that made the bombers think it was neutral Switzerland.

Chief among Altstadt sights is the **Münster** (Cathedral; Münsterplatz 4), begun in the 11th century and not completed until the 17th. South of the Münster stands the **Rathaus** (Town Hall; Hussenstrasse 15), a Renaissance building with a painted facade that illustrates the history of Konstanz. Spend about 15 minutes touring the nearby **Rosgartenmuseum,** a regional museum that contains a famous Paleolithic wall carving of a reindeer and a collection of artifacts from the Middle Ages to the 19th century (Rosgartenstrasse 3–5; ☎ 07531/900-246; admission 3€; daily 10am–5pm). From here, head toward the harbor and stroll along the **Seeufer** (Lake Shore), an attractive promenade that passes the port, public gardens, a casino, dozens of cafes and restaurants, and the historic **Konzilgebäude** (Council Building; Hafenstrasse 2), where the Council of Constance, the only papal conclave ever held north of the Alps, was convened between 1414 and 1418. You might also want to spend half an hour at the ★ **Archäologisches Landesmuseum** (Local Archaeology Museum), housed in an old convent building on the north bank of the Rhine and exhibiting Stone Age, Bronze Age, Roman, and Celtic artifacts (Benediktinerplatz 5; ☎ 07531/98040; admission 4€; Tues–Sun 10am–6pm). ⏱ 2 hr. Tourist information: Bahnhofplatz 13. ☎ 07531/133-030. www.konstanz.de.

The islands of Reichenau and Mainau make delightful day trips from Konstanz, but traveling to either of them will add half a day or more to this itinerary. If you don't have time, skip to stop ④ on this tour. Reichenau is 7km (4½ miles) west of Konstanz in the Untersee, a southern arm of the lake. Mainau, the same distance but to the northwest, lies in the waters of the Überlingensee. Ferries leave from the harbor at Konstanz daily for Mainau, or you can cross over to the island via a bridge just north of the city. Excursion boats travel to Reichenau throughout the season, but you can also get there by train from Konstanz.

③ ★ Insel Reichenau (Reichenau Island). In 724 St. Pirmin founded the first Benedictine monastery east of the Rhine on this island, which later became a center for the production of illuminated manuscripts. Three churches are the main attraction here, and since the island is only 5 sq. km (2 sq. miles), you can walk to all of them. The late-9th-century **St. Georgskirche** (Church of St. George) in Oberzell is remarkable for its harmonious design and wall paintings from about A.D. 1000. The oak roof frame of the **Münster St. Maria and Markus** (Church of Saints Mary and Mark) in Mittelzell, the chief town on the island, is believed to have the oldest roof frame in Germany, created from oaks that were felled around 1236. The **Stiftskirche (College Church) St. Peter** in Niederzell on the western tip of the island has wall paintings from the 12th century. ⏱ 2 hr.

② ★★ Mainau. ⏱ 5 hr. See p. 361, ⑤.

Überlingen is 42km (25 miles) from Konstanz via B31, about 1 hour by car. By ferry the trip takes about 2 hours. You can also easily reach Überlingen by train in about 1 hour 20 minutes; a transfer at Radolfzell is required.

> *Many visitors to Lindau take in the gardens of Mainau as a day trip.*

④ Überlingen. Founded in the 12th century by Holy Roman Emperor Frederick Barbarossa, this former Free Imperial City on the northwest arm of the Bodensee is a pleasant spot to stop for a stroll along the **Seepromenade** (Lakeside Walk) and have a look at the town's Gothic **Münster** (Cathedral) and **Rathaus** (Town Hall) and the Renaissance-era **Alte Kanzlei** (Old Municipal Chancellery), all grouped around **Münsterplatz** (Cathedral Square). ⏱ At least 30 min.

The Pfahlbaumuseum is 7km (4 miles) southeast of Überlingen via the Seepromenade. You can also reach the museum by ferry from Überlingen, a 10- to 20-minute ride.

Bodensee Facts

The Bodensee is 15km (9 miles) across at its widest point, 74km (46 miles) long, and has 258km (160 miles) of shoreline. The northern shore of the Bodensee is German; Switzerland and Austria share the western and southern portions of the lake. The Rhine flows into the lake from the Swiss Alps, which rise up in majestic splendor along the southern shore, and flows out at Konstanz, continuing on from there to the North Sea.

> *The Zeppelin Museum in Friedrichshafen chronicles the history of the airship in the city in which it was born*

⑤ ★ Pfahlbaumuseum Unteruhldingen.
The interesting, open-air Pfahlbaumuseum Unteruhldingen (Lake Dwellings Museum) re-creates a Bronze Age village with reconstructions of prehistoric lakeside dwellings on stilts modeled on local artifacts dating from 975 to 850 B.C. Costumed interpreters in the dwellings illustrate the life of the lake dwellers some 3,000 years ago. ⏱ 45 min. Strandpromenade 6, Unteruhldingen. ☎ 07556/8543. www. pfahlbauten.com. Admission 7€. Daily Apr–Sept 9am–7pm, Oct 9am–5pm, Nov–Mar 10am–4pm.

The town of Birnau is 8.5km (5¼ miles) southeast of Überlingen, about a 10-minute drive via L200 north, B31, and K7762 south. By train you can reach Birnau from Überlingen in less than 10 minutes. There is no ferry service to Birnau.

⑥ ★ Basilika Birnau. Set on a terrace above the lake with vineyards all around it, this pink basilica is an arresting sight and worth a stop. Built for the Cistercians between 1746 and 1750, the church is Southern German rococo at its most charming, its jewelbox interior exuberantly decorated with paintings, cartouches, and stuccowork. ⏱ 15 min. Birnau. ☎ 07556/92030. Daily 7:30am–7pm.

Meersburg is 8km (5 miles) southeast of Birnau on L201, a 10-minute drive. By train, it's 30 minutes from Birnau to Meersburg.

⑦ ★ Meersburg. One of the prettiest towns along the Bodensee, flower-filled Meersburg is a delightful place to spend a relaxing morning or afternoon, and it's charming enough that you might want to stay overnight. Built in terraces that cascade down to the lakeshore, the town has a lovely, car-free ★ **Oberstadt**

(Upper Town) filled with narrow streets, half-timber houses, and stylish shops. While here, visit the museum and period rooms in the massive ★ **Altes Schloss** (Old Castle), the oldest intact castle in Germany (Steigstrasse; ☎ 07532/80000; admission 6.50€; daily Mar–Oct 9:30am–6:30pm, Nov–Feb 10am–5pm). The **Neues Schloss** (New Castle), with its elegant 18th-century baroque interiors, is also worth visiting (Schlossplatz; ☎ 07532/440-4900; admission 4.50€; daily Apr–Oct 10am–1pm and 2–6pm). ⏲ At least 1 hr. to see both castles.

Friedrichshafen is 20km (12 miles) southeast of Meersburg on B31, a 25-minute drive. It's a 50-minute journey by train and about 1 hour by ferry.

8 **Friedrichshafen.** This busy port—the second-largest town on the Bodensee after Konstanz—is where Count Ferdinand von Zeppelin (1838–1917) created the dirigibles that bear his name. His work is recounted in the **Zeppelin Museum,** which also contains a partial reconstruction of the legendary *Hindenburg,* which exploded over Lakehurst, New Jersey, in 1937 (Seestrasse 22; ☎ 07541/38010; admission 7.50€; Tues–Sun

May–Oct 9am–5pm, Nov–Apr 10am–5pm). ⏲ 30 min. for the museum.

Wasserburg is 17km (11 miles) southeast of Friedrichshafen via B31. The train takes only 20 minutes; by ferry, the trip takes 70 minutes.

9 **Wasserburg.** This small, picturesque Bavarian village—once owned by the Fugger family of Augsburg (see "Meet the Fuggers," p. 220) is squeezed onto a narrow peninsula jutting out into the Bodensee. It's now something of a boutique health and tourist resort, a place to relax and unwind but without any major or must-see sights. To appreciate it, simply take a leisurely stroll out to the tip of the promontory and enjoy the view toward the mountains of Switzerland, Liechtenstein, and Austria. ⏲ 30 min.

Lindau is 5km (3 miles) southeast of Wasserburg, a 10-minute drive via Friedrichshafener Strasse and L116. Going by train also takes 10 minutes; by ferry it's a 20-minute journey.

10 ★★ **Lindau.** ⏲ Half-day. For information on Lindau, including hotel and restaurant recommendations, see p. 390.

Where to Stay & Dine

★ **Bürgerbräu** ÜBERLINGEN
Comfortable rooms, a fine restaurant, and a 200-year tradition of hospitality make this beautiful half-timber guesthouse a standout. Aufkircher Strasse 20. ☎ 07551/92740. www.buergerbraeu-ueberlingen.de. 12 units. Doubles 92€ w/breakfast. AE, MC, V.

★★ **Hotel Restaurant 3 Stuben** MEERSBURG
This restored half-timber house with modern furnishings offers wonderful ambience and a noteworthy restaurant in the heart of the old town. Kirchstrasse 7. ☎ 07534/80090. www.3stuben.de. 14 units. Doubles 128€–158€ w/breakfast. AE, MC, V.

★★★ **Steigenberger Inselhotel** KONSTANZ
Occupying its own little island, this former Dominican monastery is now the best full-service hotel on the Bodensee. Auf der Insel 1. ☎ 07531/1250. www.konstanz.steigenberger.com. 102 units. Doubles 310€–400€ w/breakfast. AE, DC, MC, V.

★ **Winzerstube zum Becher** MEERSBURG
SWABIAN Charming and unpretentious, this little *Weinstube* (wine restaurant) serves Swabian specialties like *Zwiebelrostbraten* (beef with onions) and local delicacies such as fish from the Bodensee and wine from its own winery. Höllgasse 4 (near Altes Schloss). ☎ 07532/9009. Entrees 12€–28€. AE, MC, V. Lunch & dinner Tues–Sat.

Baden-Baden

Baden-Baden is one of the world's most famous spa resorts. Its thermal springs have been healing aches and pains since before the Romans arrived some 1,800 years ago. In the 19th century, European nobility gave the town a glamorous new cachet as the most elegant and sophisticated playground in Germany, an aura that lives on today. People still flock here to take *die Kur* (the cure) and to try their luck in the casino. Baden-Baden isn't a demanding town with important historic sights that you must see. The pace is relaxed and the streets are geared toward pleasurable strolls and upscale shopping. Its many fine hotels and restaurants make it an excellent base for exploring the Black Forest.

> *The Kurhaus and elegantly landscaped Kurgarten have been a place for formal gatherings since the 1820s.*

START From the railway station, take bus no. 201 to Leopoldsplatz and then no. 243, which takes you to the southern end of Lichtentaler Allee.

❶ ★★ **Lichtentaler Allee.** The time-honored center of activity is an elegant park promenade lined with rhododendrons, azaleas, roses, and trees set along the bank of the narrow Oosbach River, often called the Oos.

❷ **Staatliche Kunsthalle (State Art Gallery).** This building, dating from 1909, is now a showcase for visiting contemporary art exhibits. ☻ Varies, depending on the exhibition.

Lichtentaler Allee 8a. ☎ 07221/300-763. www.kunsthalle-baden-baden.de. See next entry for opening times and admission price.

❸ ★★ **Museum Frieder Burda.** This building designed by Richard Meier opened in 2005 and houses an impressive collection of modern paintings and sculptures by German expressionists, American abstract expressionists, and late works by Picasso bequeathed by Baden-Baden collector Frieder Burda. ☻ 1 hr. Lichtentaler Allee 8. ☎ 07221/398-980. www.sammlung-frieder-burda.de. Admission 12€, ticket good for both museums. Tues–Sun 10am–6pm.

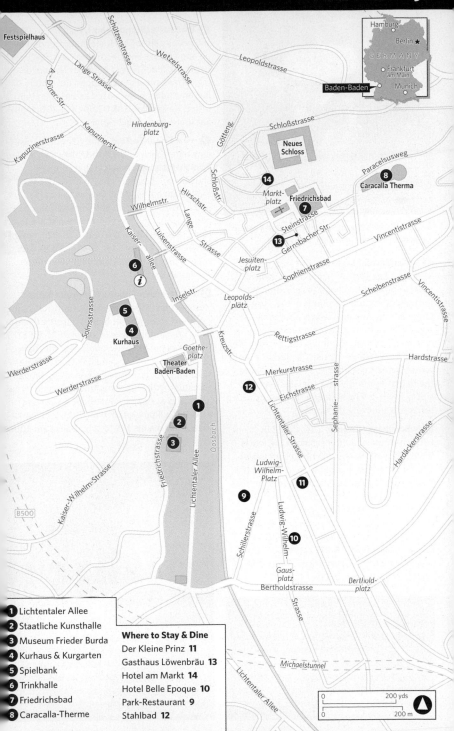

1 Lichtentaler Allee
2 Staatliche Kunsthalle
3 Museum Frieder Burda
4 Kurhaus & Kurgarten
5 Spielbank
6 Trinkhalle
7 Friedrichsbad
8 Caracalla-Therme

Where to Stay & Dine
Der Kleine Prinz **11**
Gasthaus Löwenbräu **13**
Hotel am Markt **14**
Hotel Belle Epoque **10**
Park-Restaurant **9**
Stahlbad **12**

> *Baden-Baden's elegant, popular Spielbank casino has been open for more than 200 years.*

❹ ★ Kurhaus & Kurgarten. The neoclassical Kurhaus (Kaiserallee 1), one of the town's most important buildings, is set within the formally landscaped grounds of the Kurgarten. Originally, the building was a "Promenade House," where the rich and prominent came to see and be seen. In the 1820s, it was turned into a "Conversation House," a place for more formal gatherings, and the site has remained the hub of Baden-Baden's social scene ever since. The left wing houses a restaurant with a terrace overlooking the gardens.

❺ ★ Spielbank (Casino). Considered by many to be the most beautiful casino in the world, Baden-Baden's famous gaming room is also Germany's oldest, in operation for more than 200 years. The various casino rooms, in the right wing of the Kurhaus, were designed in the style of an elegant French château. If you don't want to gamble, you can take a guided tour of the historic gaming rooms. ⏱ 30 min. for tour. Kaiserallee 1. ☎ 07221/21060. Admission 3€, tour 4€. Daily 2pm–2am. Tours daily every 30 min. 9:30am–noon.

❻ Trinkhalle (Pump Room). Built in the 1840s, the neoclassical Trinkhalle is surrounded by an open loggia and decorated with frescoes depicting Black Forest legends. The building, where guests once sipped the waters of Baden-Baden, now is used as the main tourist office. Kaiserallee 3. ☎ 07221/275-200. Mon–Sat 10am–5pm, Sun 2–5pm.

❼ ★★★ Friedrichsbad. This giant bath complex dates back to 1877 and follows an ancient Roman-Irish bath method that involves a shower, two saunas, a brush massage, thermal steam baths, three freshwater baths, and a 30-minute rest. Bathing suits may not be worn, and women and men share the pools. Römerplatz 1. ☎ 07221/275-920. www.carasana.de. 21€ for 3 hr., 29€ for 3½ hr. with soap-brush massage. Daily 9am–10pm (last admission 8pm).

❽ ★★ Caracalla Therme (Caracalla Baths). Here, you decide on your own bath and sauna regimen. The water bubbles up from artesian wells at a temperature of about 70°C (158°F). Bathers begin in cooler pools, working up to the warmer ones. You must wear a bathing suit in the pools, but the scene in the saunas is au naturel. Medicinal treatments include mud baths and massages, and there's a bar and a cafeteria. Römerplatz 1. ☎ 07221/275-940. www.carasana.de. 13€ for 2 hr. Daily 8am–10pm

Getting Around Baden-Baden

Bus no. 201, which runs at 10-minute intervals, connects the railway station to most of the sites in town (one-way fare 2€). Once in town, you can walk everywhere or take the sightseeing train City-Bahn, which runs daily from 9:30am to 5:30pm and makes stops at all of the major attractions (5€).

The Festspielhaus

Baden-Baden's 2,500-seat Festspielhaus (Festival Hall) opened in 1998 and is the second-largest opera and concert hall in Europe, with a year-round program of classical music concerts, operas, and ballets (Beim Alten Bahnhof 2; ☎ 07221/301-3101; www.festspielhaus.de).

Where to Stay & Dine

★★★ Der Kleine Prinz CITY CENTER

This full-service boutique hotel with a gourmet restaurant occupies two turn-of-the-20th-century mansions and is consistently ranked as one of the best hotels in Germany. Each of the large, high-ceilinged rooms is furnished differently, with hand-chosen furniture and accessories. Lichtentaler Strasse 36. ☎ 07221/346-600. www.derkleineprinz.de. 45 units. Doubles 175€–299€ w/breakfast. AE, MC, V.

Gasthaus Löwenbräu CITY CENTER GERMAN/BAVARIAN

This popular spot in the Altstadt is good for simple, affordable, well-prepared food and has a summer beer garden. Gernsbacher Strasse 9. ☎ 07221/22311. Entrees 5.50€–18€. AE, DC, V. Lunch & dinner daily.

Hotel am Markt CITY CENTER

Clean, modest, and inexpensive, this small family-run hotel is neither grand nor glamorous, but the rooms are comfortable and the location is convenient. Marktplatz 18. ☎ 07221/27040. www.hotel-am-markt-baden.de. 27 units. Doubles 55€–83€ w/breakfast. AE, MC, V.

★★★ Hotel Belle Epoque CITY CENTER

Impeccably high standards and a commitment to service and comfort prevail in this small, sumptuous hotel housed in a villa built in 1870. Maria-Victoria-Strasse 2C. ☎ 07221/300-660. www.hotel-belle-epoque.de. 16 units. Doubles 215€–299€ w/breakfast. AE, MC, V.

> Built in a 19th-century villa, the Hotel Belle Epoque is renowned for impeccable service and commitment to excellence.

★★★ Park-Restaurant CITY CENTER INTERNATIONAL/RHINELAND

The menu at this renowned dining room emphasizes classic French cooking, seafood, and regional Rhine Valley foods. Specialties include sautéed goose liver, roast saddle of venison or lamb, and grilled lobster and fish. In Brenner's Park Hotel, Schillerstrasse 4. ☎ 07221/9000. www.brenners.com. Reservations required. Entrees 32€–48€. AE, DC, MC, V. Lunch & dinner daily.

★ Stahlbad CITY CENTER CONTINENTAL/ALSATIAN

This charming restaurant with a garden terrace offers specialties like pepper steak, seasonal game dishes, and fresh fish. Augustaplatz 2. ☎ 07221/24569. www.stahlbad.com. Reservations required. Entrees 15€–30€, fixed-price menu 19.50€. AE, DC, MC, V. Lunch & dinner Tues–Sun.

Shopping in Baden-Baden

Pedestrian-only Sophienstrasse and Gernsbacher Strasse are lined with some of the most expensive boutiques in Germany. For women's wear, try Escada Boutique (Sophienstrasse 18; ☎ 07221/390-448) and Münchner Moden (Lichtentaler Strasse 13; ☎ 07221/31090). The best men's store is Herrenkommode (Sophienstrasse 16; ☎ 07221/29292). Cuckoo clocks, puppets, and other locally produced items can be found at Boulevard (Lichtentaler Strasse 21; ☎ 07221/24495).

Freiburg im Breisgau

The largest city in the Black Forest, picturesque Freiburg with its medieval Altstadt (Old Town) and important university, nestles in a plain surrounded by mountain peaks and 1,600 acres of vineyards, more than you find near any other city in Germany (see the "Black Forest Vineyards" tour on p. 370). If you're traveling in the Black Forest, Freiburg makes for an atmospheric overnight stay. Although the town was heavily damaged during World War II, Freiburg's medieval charm has been preserved, and exploring its ancient streets is a pleasure. The large student presence adds a lively, youthful edge to the old city. Most of what you want to see lies within the Altstadt, an area bounded by the Hauptbahnhof (main train station) on the west side of the inner city, the Dreisam River on the south, and a wooded hill called the Schlossberg on the east. This part of town is medieval Freiburg at its most appealing.

> *Freiburg im Breisgau, from the mountain peaks on one side to its boat-lined harbor on the other, has maintained much of its medieval charm.*

START **It's an easy 10-minute walk from the train station to Rathausplatz. From the station, head southeast on Bismarckstrasse and Bertoldstrasse, turn left at Universitätsstrasse, and right at Turmstrasse.**

❶ **Rathausplatz (Town Hall Square).** Chestnut trees and a fountain add to the charm of Rathausplatz, a busy square just west of the cathedral. On the west side of the square is the **Neues Rathaus** (New Town Hall),

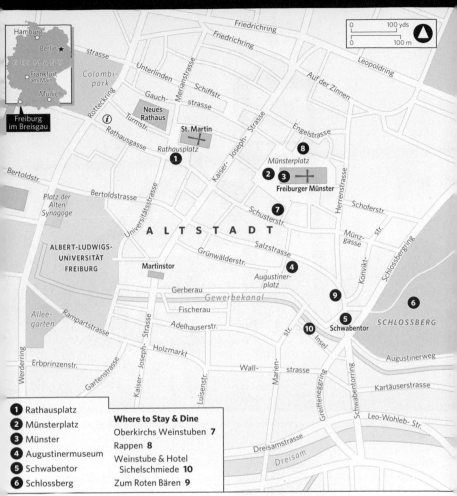

1 Rathausplatz	**Where to Stay & Dine**
2 Münsterplatz	Oberkirchs Weinstuben **7**
3 Münster	Rappen **8**
4 Augustinermuseum	Weinstube & Hotel
5 Schwabentor	Sichelschmiede **10**
6 Schlossberg	Zum Roten Bären **9**

comprised of two highly decorated 16th-century merchants' houses connected by an arcade.

2 ★ **Münsterplatz (Cathedral Square).** A trio of historic buildings along the south side of the town's main square offer a glimpse of what Freiburg looked like before World War II. The

Getting Around Freiburg

The Altstadt, where you find all the major attractions, is easily walkable and car-free. The small kiosk marked "Plus-Punkt" has bus and tram information (Salzstrasse 3; ☎ 0761/451-1500).

> The bustling Rathausplatz is bordered by the Neues Rathaus.

> *The imposing Schwabentor, which stands in one of Freiburg's most picturesque neighborhoods, dates from the Middle Ages.*

mid-18th-century **Erzbischöflisches Palais** (Archbishop's Palace) has a pale-yellow facade and an ornate wrought-iron balcony. The oxblood-colored **Historisches Kaufhaus** (Merchants' Hall), a Gothic customs and financial administration center with protruding, pointed-roof watchtowers and a 16th-century gallery decorated with the statues of four Hapsburg emperors, is still used as the town's official reception hall. The third building to the left of the Historisches Kaufhaus is the baroque **Wentzingerhaus,** built in 1761 for a local painter and sculptor.

❸ ★★ **Münster (Cathedral).** One of Germany's masterpieces of Gothic architecture, Freiburg's rose-colored cathedral was begun in 1200 in the Romanesque style, but by the time the structure was completed in 1620, Gothic elements had been incorporated into the design.

The cathedral contains some superb stained-glass windows, the earliest dating from the 13th century. For a wonderful view of Freiburg and the distant mountains, climb to the top of the famous West Tower, a magnificent openwork spire atop an open octagonal belfry. One of the gargoyles peering down from the tower's roof has its backside turned toward the archbishop's house across the square, supposedly a sign of the architect's contempt for the city fathers. ⏱ 30 min. Münsterplatz. ☎ 0761/202-790. Cathedral free admission, tower 2€. Cathedral Mon–Sat 10am–6pm, Sun 1–6pm; tower Mon–Sat 9:30am–5pm, Sun 1–5pm (closed Mon Nov–Mar).

❹ ★ **Augustinermuseum (Augustinian Friars Museum).** A 14th-century Augustinian monastery with a yellow baroque front houses the Augustinermuseum. The collection includes religious art (Gothic sculptures, original

> *A view of the spectacular Gothic cathedral, the Münster, from the Schlossberg, which can be accessed by cable car.*

stained glass from the cathedral), paintings (the most noteworthy are works by the Renaissance artists Mathias Grünewald and Hans Baldung Grien), and Art Nouveau glass. ⓧ 30 min. Augustinerplatz. ☎ 0761/201-2531. Free admission. Tues–Sun 10am–5pm.

❺ **Schwabentor (Swabian Gate).** One of two surviving gates from the Middle Ages, when Freiburg was a walled city, the Schwabentor dates from around 1200. Paintings on the tower include one of St. George, the city's patron saint. The neighborhood around the Schwabentor is called the Insel (Island) because rushing streams, called *Bächle,* surround it. The Insel is the most picturesque quarter in Freiburg, with narrow cobblestoned streets and restored houses once used by fishermen and tanneries.

❻ **Schlossberg (Castle Hill).** From the Schwabentor, a pathway climbs up Castle Hill, which provides good views of the cathedral. You can also ascend the Schlossberg from the Stadtgarten (City Gardens) by cable car (☎ 0761/39855; roundtrip fare 3€; operates Jun–Sept 10am–7pm, Oct–Jan 11:30am–6pm).

The *Bächle* of Freiburg

Freiburg's Altstadt has many lovely old fountains and a unique system of streams called *Bächle* (little brooks) that date back to the 12th century. First devised to keep the city clean and to help fight fires, the brooks channel water from the Dreisam River through the old university town and help to keep it cool in the hot summer months. You can see the *Bächle* running alongside many Altstadt streets. According to local folklore, if you step in one, you will marry a person from Freiburg.

> *The spires of the Gothic Münster tower over Freiburg's rooftops.*

Festivals in Freiburg

Festivals are a year-round part of life in Freiburg. On the last weekend in June, a 4-day public wine-tasting festival (Weinkost, pictured) takes place in the Münsterplatz. Freiburg's pre-Lenten carnival, called Fasnet, is one of the best in Germany, with bonfires and parades. The Frühlingsmess (Spring Fair), in May, and the Herbstmesse (Autumn Fair), in October, both last 10 days. Weinkost is a long wine-tasting event in July or August. And in June the city plays host to the 2-week-long Zelt-Musik-Festival (Tent Music Festival), with performances in giant outdoor tents. Anything from beach volleyball to circus acts accompany the main lineup.

Where to Stay & Dine

> *Oberkirchs Weinstuben is a landmark destination for food and wine lovers and also offers rooms upstairs for lodgers.*

Oberkirchs Weinstuben ALTSTADT *GERMAN*
This historic *Weinstube* (wine tavern) serves hearty portions of good, old-fashioned food: tasty soups, pork and veal standards, and seasonal dishes like venison. Above the *Weinstube,* 25 rooms all have private bathrooms or showers (doubles 146€–176€ w/breakfast). Münsterplatz 22. ☎ 0761/202-6868. www. hotel-oberkirch.de. Entrees 12€–23€, fixed-price menus 18€–21€. AE, MC, V. Lunch & dinner Mon–Sat. Closed Jan.

Freiburg Nightlife

With some 30,000 university students, Freiburg has a thriving bar and club scene. Two clubs in one, Crash (Schnewlinstrasse 3; ☎ 0761/32475; www.crash-freiburg. de; Wed–Sat 10pm–3:30am) serves drinks and plays background punk, house, and funk; in the basement, Drifler's Club plays house and techno for dancers. Neither club charges a cover. Hausbrauerei Feierling (Gerberau 46; ☎ 0761/26678; www. feierling.de; daily 11am–midnight) is a brewpub with a popular beer garden.

★ **Rappen** ALTSTADT
The best rooms in this charming, low-key inn have smack-dab views of Freiburg's mighty cathedral. Rooms are generally on the small side and simply but comfortably furnished. Münsterplatz 13. ☎ 0761/31353.www.hotelrappen. de. 20 units. Doubles 104€–115€ w/ breakfast. AE, DC, MC, V.

★ **Weinstube & Hotel Sichelschmiede**
ALTSTADT *REGIONAL* For outdoor summer dining, this wine tavern on a small square flanked by a rushing *Bächle* (little brook) is the most picturesque spot in Freiburg. Try the *Zwiebel* (onion) dishes, a specialty of the region. Insel 1. ☎ 0761/35037. www.sichelschmiede.de. Entrees 8€–15€. MC, V. Lunch & dinner daily.

★★ **Zum Roten Bären** ALTSTADT
Reputedly the oldest inn in Germany, "At the Red Bear," with its pretty painted facade and noteworthy restaurant, is an atmospheric place to stay and a wonderful spot to dine. Rooms in the older section have more charm; those in the modern wing have little balconies overlooking leafy gardens and red-tiled rooftops. Oberlinden 12. ☎ 0761/387-870. www. roter-baeren.de. 25 units. Doubles 149€–169€ w/breakfast. AE, DC, MC, V.

Lindau

With pretty, flower-bedecked squares, a lively harbor, and a charming harborside promenade, Lindau has all the ingredients of a popular tourist destination. This is not a place that requires strenuous sightseeing; go for a leisurely stroll, swim, and take a turn at the tables in the casino. Founded in the 9th century, Lindau was for hundreds of years a center of trade between Bavaria, Italy, and Switzerland. Today, so many historic buildings line the narrow streets of the Altstadt (Old Town) that the entire town is a protected landmark. The itinerary below will take you past the most attractive parts of the town.

> *Lindau offers beautiful squares, elegant Old-World architecture, and a picturesque harbor on the lovely Bodensee, Germany's largest lake.*

START **Lindau Harbor.** A road bridge for cars and a causeway for walkers and trains connects the Altstadt (Old Town) to the mainland. The train station is right in the Altstadt, across from the harbor. If you're coming by car, cross the causeway and park in one of the large car parks outside the Altstadt, because you won't be able to drive into the historic center.

❶ ★★★ **Hafen (Harbor).** Completed in 1856, Lindau's famous harbor is the most attractive on the whole of the Bodensee. Ferries and pleasure boats ply the waters against a shimmering backdrop created by the Swiss and Austrian Alps. At night, thousands of lights create a magical atmosphere around the harbor.

❷ **Mangturm (Tower).** Rising from the See-promenade (Lake Promenade) that runs around the harbor is the 13th-century tower called the Mangturm. The name derives from the laundry, or "mangle house," that once stood beside the tower. It's a reminder of the heavy fortifications that once surrounded the city, and also marks where Lindau was once divided into two islands.

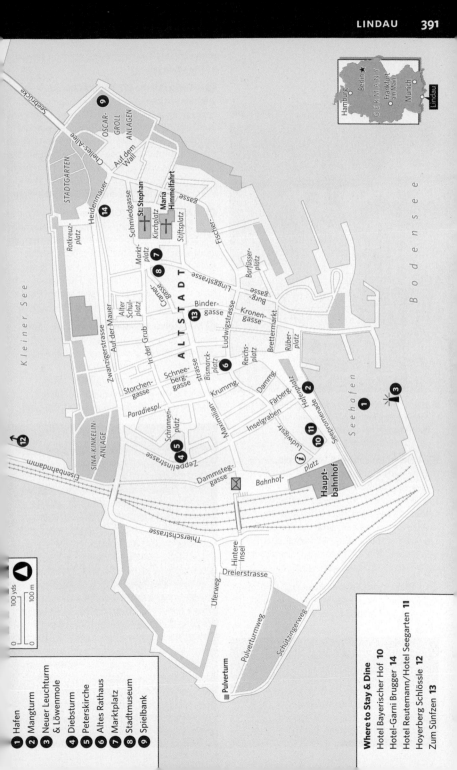

Where to Stay & Dine
Hotel Bayerischer Hof **10**
Hotel-Garni Brugger **14**
Hotel Reutemann/Hotel Seegarten **11**
Hoyerberg Schlössle **12**
Zum Sünfzen **13**

1 Hafen
2 Mangturm
3 Neuer Leuchtturm & Löwenmole
4 Diebsturm
5 Peterskirche
6 Altes Rathaus
7 Marktplatz
8 Stadtmuseum
9 Spielbank

GERMANY

Hamburg
Berlin ★
Frankfurt am Main
Munich
Lindau

> *Built in the 13th century and once a Lindau fortification on the Bodensee, the Mangturm was also a lighthouse for many years.*

❸ ★ **Neuer Leuchtturm & Löwenmole.** Flanking the harbor entrance are the 19th-century Neuer Leuchtturm (New Lighthouse) and the Löwenmole (Lion Tower), a pillar whose sculpted lion, the symbol of Bavaria, looks out over the lake. You can climb the narrow spiral staircase of the lighthouse (daily 9:30am–5pm; admission 1.75€) for a panoramic vista of the Alps across the water. ⏱ **15 min.**

❹ ★ **Diebsturm (Thieves' Tower).** Built around 1370 at the most westerly point of the old town wall, this round tower with projecting

Getting Around Lindau

From Lindau, you can make day trips by boat to towns in Austria and Switzerland and to most of the German towns on the northern shore of the Bodensee. If you need a taxi, call Taxi-Ring-Zentrale (☎ 0800-6006-6666).

upper turrets and oriel windows once served as the town jail.

❺ ★ **Peterskirche (St. Peter's Church).** A rectangular structure with a flat wooden ceiling and a tall, square tower, St. Peter's Church was built around A.D. 1000 and is Lindau's oldest building. It's worth a quick peek inside to see the 15th-century frescoes by Hans Holbein the Elder on the interior walls. In 1928, the church became a memorial for the soldiers of World War I. **Oberer Schrannenplatz. Daily 9am–5pm.**

❻ ★ **Altes Rathaus (Old Town Hall).** Erected in 1422 and notable for its grandly painted facade of a princely procession, the town hall's stepped gables are typical of the 15th-century Gothic style, but in the 16th century the building received a Renaissance face-lift. The interior is the town library. Frescoes represent scenes from a session of the 1496 Imperial Diet. **Reichsplatz.**

❼ **Marktplatz (Market Square).** Take a few minutes to see the Lutheran and Catholic churches standing side-by-side on the east side of this picturesque square, with its flower-bedecked central fountain. **St. Stephan,** the Lutheran church on the left, has a barrel-vaulted ceiling and a fairly bare

Outdoor Recreation in Lindau

The shores of the Bodensee around Lindau are perfect for cycling, and the water is clean enough to swim in. You can rent bikes in the train station at **Fahrrad-Station-Lindau** (☎ 08382/21261; Mon–Fri 9am–6pm, Sat–Sun 9:30am–7pm). **Lindenhofpark,** on the mainland, is the most scenic area for biking. Three lakeside beaches are open in the summer from 10:30am to 7:30pm and charge 2.50€ to 3€ admission. The biggest is **Strandbad Eichwald,** with a grassy lakeside area and three heated swimming pools (☎ 08283/5539; half-hour walk east along Uferweg on the mainland, or take bus no. 3 to Karmelbuckel). The **Römerschanze** is a smaller in-town beach popular with families (next to Lindau harbor in the Altstadt; ☎ 08283/6830). **Strandbad Lindenhofbad** in Lindenhof Park on the mainland is farther from the city and less of a scene (☎ 08283/6637; bus no. 1 or 2 to Anheggerstrasse, then bus no. 4 to Alwind).

interior; **Maria Himmelfahrt** (Church of the Ascension), the Catholic church on the right, is full of baroque decoration and has a frescoed ceiling (both generally open 8am–5pm).

8 Stadtmuseum (City Museum). This museum, located in a stately 18th-century baroque town house, displays a large collection of furniture (ranging from Gothic to Art Nouveau), silverware, glassware, tin and ceramic objects, historical toys, paintings, sculptures, and a noteworthy collection of mechanical musical instruments. ⏱ 15 min. Marktplatz 6. ☎ 08382/944-073. Admission 2.50€. Apr–Sept Tues–Fri 11am–5pm, Sat 2–5pm, Sun 11am–5pm.

9 Spielbank (Casino). The waterside Stadtpark (City Park) is the setting for Lindau's glitzy casino, where you can play slot machines (daily noon–2am) and/or blackjack and roulette (daily 3pm–2am); men must wear a jacket and tie. Chelles Allee 1. ☎ 08382/27740. Admission 2.50€. Must be 21 with valid passport to enter.

Where to Stay & Dine

★★★ **Hotel Bayerischer Hof** ALTSTADT The Bayerischer Hof offers Old World charm and service, and large, luxurious rooms (book one with a lake view). It's adjacent to Hotel Reutemann/Hotel Seegarten (see below) and shares their outdoor pool and fitness areas, but it has its own spa. Seepromenade. ☎ 08382/9150. www.bayerischerhof-lindau.de. 97 units. Doubles 175€–314€. AE, DC, MC, V.

★ **Hotel-Garni Brugger** ALTSTADT This small, welcoming hotel is the best affordable choice in Lindau. The rooms are up to date and furnished in a functional, comfortable, modern style with lots of light. The location is an easy walk from the lake and casino. Bei der Heidenmauer 11. ☎ 08382/93410. www.hotel-garni-brugger.de. 23 units. Doubles 85€–98€ w/breakfast. AE, DC, MC, V.

★★ kids **Hotel Reutemann/Hotel Seegarten** ALTSTADT These upscale, interconnected lakeside hotels on the harbor promenade have large rooms, some with lake views and flower-filled balconies. There's a lakefront garden with sunbathing areas, outdoor pool, fitness center, and sauna. Children younger than 9 stay free. Seepromenade. ☎ 08382/9150. www.bayerischerhof-lindau.de. 64 units. Doubles 125€–226€. AE, DC, MC, V.

★★ **Hoyerberg Schlössle** LINDAU-AESCHACH CONTINENTAL Located on the mainland about a 15-minute drive from the Altstadt, this hotel restaurant with views of the mountains and lake has few rivals on the Bodensee. Menu offerings vary seasonally but may typically include cream

> *Hotel Seegarten offers large rooms with beautiful balconies overlooking the lake.*

of scampi soup, local perch stuffed with herbs, and saddle of venison with flour dumplings and French beans. Hoyerbergstrasse 64, at Lindau-Aeschach (from the causeway, take Langenweg and Friedrichshafener Strasse northwest to Hoyerbergstrasse). ☎ 08382/25295. Reservations required. Entrees 22€–35€, fixed-price menus 64€–80€. AE, DC, MC, V. Lunch Wed–Sun, dinner Tues–Sun. Closed Feb.

Zum Sünfzen ALTSTADT GERMAN/BAVARIAN This restaurant serves good, dependable food at reasonable prices. Dishes range from schnitzels to pepper steaks to roast pork with homemade *Spätzle*. Fresh fish from the Bodensee is a specialty. Maximilianstrasse 1. ☎ 08382/5865. www.suenfzen.de. Reservations recommended. Entrees 10€–20€. AE, DC, MC, V. Lunch & dinner daily.

The Black Forest & the Bodensee Fast Facts

> *Passenger ferries bring visitors to and from Lindau and offer tours of the beautiful Bodensee.*

Accommodations Booking Services

Call **Hotel Reservation Service** (☎ 0870/243-0003; www.hrs.de) from anywhere in Germany. Tourist information centers in the major train stations and airports offer on-the-spot booking services for hotel rooms and B&Bs.

ATMs

All the major cities and towns in this region—Baden-Baden, Freiburg, and Lindau—have banks and train stations with ATMs *(Geldautomaten)*.

Dentists & Doctors

If you have a mild medical issue or dental problems while traveling in Germany, most hotels will be able to refer you to a local doctor *(Arzt)* or dentist *(Zahnarzt)* who speaks English. You will be expected to provide proof of either permanent or travel insurance (such as an EHIC card in the case of most residents of Europe), or you will be required to pay for treatment. In the event of minor injuries that require speedy treatment, go to the *Notaufnahme* (emergency) department of the nearest *Krankenhaus* (hospital). When the injuries are serious, call the doctor/ambulance emergency number (see "Emergencies," below).

Emergencies

To call the police *(Polizei)*, dial ☎ 110. To report a fire or to summon an emergency doctor *(Notarzt)* or an ambulance *(Krankenwagen)*, dial ☎ 112.

Getting There

The nearest international airport is **Frankfurt** (see p. 494), 174km (108 miles) north of Baden-Baden and 280km (174 miles) north of Freiburg. The Frankfurt airport also has a train station, so you can easily connect to Baden-Baden (1½ hr.), Freiburg (1½ hr.), and other towns covered in this chapter. For train schedules and information, call **Deutsche Bahn** (German Railways; ☎ 11861; www.bahn.de).

Getting Around

Germany is served by an excellent rail network and a car isn't necessary if you are sticking to the towns and cities covered in this chapter. If, however, you want to tour the countryside of the Black Forest or around the Bodensee, having a car is essential. A detailed regional road map (Hallweg or Michelin) is also essential; you can buy one at Frankfurt airport bookshops and most newsstands. Renting a car in Germany is fairly easy, but it's generally better price-wise if you book the car before your arrival. Most of the major international car-rental agencies have offices at Frankfurt Airport, including **Avis** (☎ 800/331-1212; www.avis.com), **Budget** (☎ 800/527-0700; www.budget.com), and **Hertz** (☎ 800/654-3001; www.hertz.com). You can also arrange to rent a car through **Rail Europe** (☎ 888/382-7245; www.raileurope.com).

Touring the Bodensee (Lake Constance) by boat is fun, but you have to pay attention to ferry schedules and won't be able to see as much of the countryside around the lake in as short a time as you would in a car. If you want to take a scenic day trip on the lake, **Bodensee-Schiffsbetriebe,** Schützingerweg 2, Lindau (☎ 08382/275-4810; www.bsb-online.com), provides daily passenger service between Lindau and Mainau. You can also drive west from Lindau to Meersburg and catch the car ferry to Mainau operated by **Autofähre Konstanz-Meersburg** (☎ 07531/803-666).

Internet Access

Almost all hotels in Germany, even in smaller towns, now offer Wi-Fi and/or broadband. If they don't, ask your concierge or at the tourist office if there is an Internet cafe in the vicinity.

Pharmacies

At a German pharmacy, called an *Apotheke,* the trained staff can recommend over-the-counter medications for many common ailments. For cosmetics or toiletries, go to a *Drogerie.* German pharmacies are open regular business hours. They take turns staying open nights, on Sunday, and on holidays, and each *Apotheke* posts a list of those that are open off-hours.

Police

To report a lost or stolen article, such as a wallet or passport, visit the local police (*Polizei*) in your location. To call the police from anywhere in Germany, dial ☎ **110.**

Post Office

You'll recognize branches of **Deutsche Post** (☎ 01802/3333; www.deutschepost.de) by their yellow sign with a black horn. Post offices are open Monday to Friday 8am–6pm, Saturday 8am–noon.

Safety

This area of Germany is completely safe for tourists, but use common sense and don't leave valuables in plain sight when you park your car on a city street or parking lot near a scenic area.

Telephones

Call ☎ 11837 for information and ☎ 11834 for international information. Baden-Baden's area code is 07221; Freiburg's is 0761; Lindau's is 008382. Dial the area code when calling a town number from outside the town; you don't need to dial it when calling a town number from inside the town. There are public phones in many places—some accept coins and some take phone cards, which are available at post offices and newsstands.

Toilets

In some places you will find clean public toilets (*Toilette* in German; pronounced twah-*leh*-teh), many of them automatic and wheelchair-accessible; you need a .50€ coin to unlock the door. More convenient and widespread are toilets in cafes, bars, restaurants, hotels, malls, and some stores and at highway services and rest areas. Even if you are not obliged to pay, it is customary to leave the attendant .50€.

Visitor Information

The regional tourist board for the Bodensee is **Internationale Bodensee-Tourismus,** Hafenstrasse 6, 78462 Konstanz (☎ 07531/90940; www.bodensee.de). For the Black Forest it's **Black Forest Tourism,** Hauptgeschäftsstelle Freiburg, Ludwigstrasse 23, 79104 Freiburg (☎ 0761/896-4670; www.blackforest-tourism.com). In addition to those provided with the individual town listings, other key tourist offices are as follows: BADEN-BADEN Trinkhalle, Kaiser Allee 3 and Schwarzwaldstrasse 52 (the B500 road into town); ☎ 07221/275-200; www.baden-baden.com; Mon-Sat 10am–5pm, Sun 2–5pm. FREIBURG Rotteckring 14; ☎ 0761/388-1880; www.freiburg.de; Mon-Fri 8am–8pm (until 6pm Oct–May), Sat 9:30am–5:30pm (until 2:30pm Oct–May), Sun 10am–noon. LINDAU Ludwigstrasse 68 (across from the train station); ☎ 08382/260-031; www.lindau-tourismus.de; Mon–Fri 9am–6pm, Sat 2–6pm, Sun 10am–2pm.

Heidelberg, Stuttgart & the Swabian Alb

Heidelberg, Stuttgart & the Swabian Alb in 3 Days

This part of southern Germany, east of the Black Forest, is noteworthy for its historic university towns of Heidelberg and Tübingen, both on the Neckar River, and the big, buzzy city of Stuttgart that lies between them. On a 3-day tour you can easily visit all three, see the giant baroque palace at Ludwigsburg, and get a feel for the different landscapes they all inhabit, including the Neckar Valley and a bit of the Swabian Alb around Tübingen.

> *PREVIOUS PAGE A panoramic view of Heidelberg from Schloss Heidelberg. THIS PAGE Tübingen's Altstadt escaped World War II with many of its historic buildings intact.*

START Heidelberg is 94km (58 miles) south of Frankfurt on A5, about a 1-hour drive. It is easily accessible by train from all major cities in Germany and Europe (a 1-hr. trip from Frankfurt). TRIP LENGTH 164km (102 miles).

1 ★★ **Heidelberg.** Its reputation as an enchanted purveyor of wine and romance, song and student life, fun and frivolity, has drawn people to Heidelberg for well over 150 years. Discovered by the 19th-century German

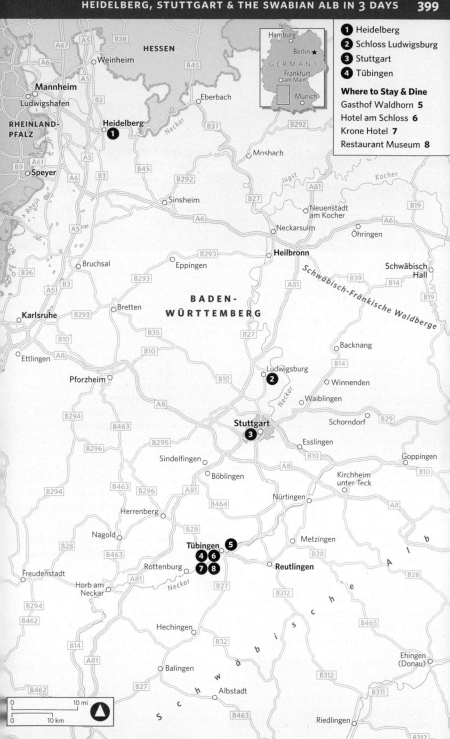

1 Heidelberg
2 Schloss Ludwigsburg
3 Stuttgart
4 Tübingen

Where to Stay & Dine
Gasthof Waldhorn 5
Hotel am Schloss 6
Krone Hotel 7
Restaurant Museum 8

HESSEN

Weinheim

Mannheim
Ludwigshafen

RHEINLAND-
PFALZ

Speyer

Eberbach

Heidelberg
1

Mosbach

Neckar

GERMANY
Hamburg
Berlin ★
Frankfurt
am Main
Munich

Kocher

Sinsheim

Neuenstadt
am Kocher

Öhringen

Neckarsulm

Heilbronn

Bruchsal

Eppingen

Schwäbisch
Hall

Karlsruhe

Bretten

BADEN-
WÜRTTEMBERG

Schwäbisch-Fränkische Waldberge

Ettlingen

Backnang

Pforzheim

Ludwigsburg
2

Winnenden

Neckar

Waiblingen

Stuttgart
3

Schorndorf

Goppingen

Sindelfingen

Esslingen

Böblingen

Kirchheim
unter Teck

Herrenberg

Nürtingen

Nagold

Metzingen

Tübingen
4 6
5

7 8

Reutlingen

Rottenburg

Horb am
Neckar

Neckar

Freudenstadt

A l b

Hechingen

S c h w ä b i s c h e

Ehingen
(Donau)

Balingen

Albstadt

Riedlingen

0   10 mi
0   10 km

> *The imposing and romantic Schloss Heidelberg, while mostly in ruins, still stands majestically over the city.*

Romantics, who praised and painted it, this ancient university town on the Neckar River came to a wider public attention with the 1924 musical *The Student Prince,* and, in a less saccharine light, as a U.S. army base after World War II. What makes Heidelberg unique today is that, unlike scores of other German towns and cities, it was relatively undamaged in the war and thus offers visitors the chance to see a small and in some ways quintessential German city (135,000 inhabitants, of whom 28,000 are students) whose Altstadt (Old Town) looks much as it did a century ago, with a mixture of architectural styles ranging from the Gothic to the neoclassical. There's a newer, postwar section of Heidelberg, too, but it's quite separate from the Altstadt and you won't be spending much if any time there, unless you're shopping or on business.

Heidelberg is a city for strolling, and you can see everything on foot in a leisurely day (though on this itinerary, if you want to visit Schloss Ludwigsburg, the next stop, you'll need to keep it to half a day). The most famous attraction is **Schloss Heidelberg** (Heidelberg Castle), the epitome of a romantic hilltop ruin with a classic view down to the tiled roofs of

the Altstadt nestled alongside the river. Visit the **Kurpfälzisches Museum** (Museum of the Palatinate) to see Tilman Riemenschneider's masterful wooden altarpiece of Christ and the Apostles, dating from 1509. Universitätsplatz (University Square) marks the old center of Heidelberg University and is near Marktplatz, the Altstadt's main square, dominated by the Gothic **Heiliggeistkirche** (Church of the Holy Spirit). Cross the **Alte Brücke** (Old Bridge) and stroll along **Philosophenweg** (Philosopher's Way), a 250-year-old promenade that provides a view of romantic Heidelberg from the other side of the Neckar. You can also, depending on your schedule, take a short or longer cruise along the Neckar River. ⊙ At least a half-day. For information on Heidelberg, see p. 424.

From Heidelberg, take A6 southeast and A81 south to Ludwigsburg (103km/64 miles), about a 70-minute drive.

② ★★ kids **Schloss Ludwigsburg.** Ludwigsburg Palace is the largest preserved baroque palace in Germany (475 rooms). Known as "the Swabian Versailles," it was built between 1704 and 1744 for Duke Eberhard Ludwig and is surrounded by a unique park landscape that includes an enchanting *Märchengarten* (fairy-tale garden), with mechanical figures activated by the sound of voices, and Schloss Favorite, which was used as a hunting lodge. Both can be visited only on a guided tour. A

Traveling by Train

You can visit all three of these cities by train and explore them on foot or by using public transportation once you arrive.

> Built between 1704 and 1744, and with 475 rooms, Schloss Ludwigsburg is the largest preserved baroque palace in Germany.

...eisurely stroll through the town of Ludwigs-burg, with its lovely baroque market square, is also pleasant. ⏱ 3 hr. to tour palaces and gardens and stroll through town. Schlossstrasse 30. ☎ 07141/182-004. www.schloss-ludwigsburg. de. Admission to both palaces 8€, to gardens 7.50€. Daily 10am–5pm, tours every 30 min., tours in English Mon–Fri 1:30pm, Sat–Sun 11am, 1:30pm, 3:15pm (varies seasonally).

From Ludwigsburg, take B27 south to Stutt-**gart (17km/11 miles and about a 25-minute drive), your destination for Night 1.**

❸ ★★ **Stuttgart.** Stuttgart is the undisputed arts capital of southwestern Germany, with several museums that will make a full day spent here a rewarding one. Unlike Heidelberg and Tübingen, Stuttgart suffered massive destruction during World War II. It's something of a case history for postwar German reconstruction, in that it rebuilt the palaces and opera house in its old central core but didn't attempt to replicate the rest of the destroyed city. New housing and new buildings went up, new highways were built, and modern Stuttgart was born. Today it's Germany's sixth-largest city, with about 600,000 residents.

> Otto Dix's 1927 painting Le Salon hangs in the Kunstmuseum Stuttgart, the city's collection of 19th- and 20th-century art.

And though it's an industrial powerhouse, manufacturing cars and optical equipment, Stuttgart is one of the greenest big cities in Germany, with lots of parks and even vineyards right in the city. It's big enough to have buzz, small enough to navigate easily on foot or using public transportation.

Devote your day in Stuttgart to museum-hopping and maybe shopping (the area around the train station is a new retail mecca).

> *Rows of beautiful riverfront homes backed by impressive mountains line the Neckar River in Tübingen.*

If you're interested in viewing an excellent collection of German painting, from Old Masters to Modern Masters, visit the **Staatsgalerie** (State Art Gallery) or the outstanding collection of 19th- and 20th-century German art in the new **Kunstmuseum Stuttgart** (Stuttgart Art Museum). You'll find a treasure trove of regional art and objects in the **Landesmuseum Württemberg** (Regional History Museum). Car lovers won't want to miss the Mercedes-Benz Museum or the Porsche Museum, both filled with dazzling arrays of vintage automobiles. ⏲1 day. For information on Stuttgart, including hotel and restaurant recommendations, see p. 430.

Spend another night in Stuttgart, or continue on to Tübingen, south on B27 and B28 (44km/27 miles and a 50-minute drive), and spend your second night there.

❹ ★★ **Tübingen.** This delightfully atmospheric town on the banks of the Neckar and Ammer rivers was one of the few towns in Germany to remain completely untouched

by the bombs and battalions of World War II. The town's history is so closely linked with its famous university, founded in 1477, that there is a saying: Rather than *having* a university, Tübingen *is* a university. Today, some 25,000 students study here.

You can explore Tübingen's remarkable **Altstadt** (Old Town), with its twisting lanes, magnificent half-timber houses, and quiet little squares, in about 2 hours, but if you really want to soak up its ancient atmosphere, spend the night. Start your excursion with a scenic view of the town and the willow-fringed Neckar River from the **Eberhardsbrücke** (Eberhard Bridge), then stroll along the **Platanenallee,** a popular promenade created on an island in the river. Once part of the town's fortifications, the **Hölderlinturm** (Hölderlin's Tower) was later turned into a residence where the poet Friedrich Hölderlin lived from 1807 to 1843 (Bursagasse 6). A Renaissance fountain with a statue of Neptune graces **Am Markt,** especially lively on Mondays,

Wednesdays, and Fridays, when a traditional outdoor market is held. Facing the square is the **Rathaus** (Town Hall), a 15th-century structure with 19th-century painted designs on its facade. A plaque on **Judengasse,** a quiet residential street below the Rathaus, commemorates the fate of Tübingen's Jews, who lived in this area until they were expelled from the town in 1477. The Gothic **Stiftskirche** (Collegiate Church) is worth a quick visit to see the tombs of the dukes of Württemburg and the 15th-century carved wooden pulpit and rood screen; climb the tower for a panoramic view of the town (Holzmarkt; church daily 9am–5pm; tower admission 2€, open Tues–Fri 10:30am–5pm, Sat–Sun 2–5pm). A magnificent Renaissance portal gives access to **Schloss Hohentübingen,** a four-wing castle complex built by the arch-dukes of Tübingen and today housing an intriguing antiquities museum; give yourself half an hour here to explore (Burgsteige 11; ☎ 07071/297-7384; admission 4€; Wed–Sun May–Sept 10am–6pm, Oct–Apr 10am–4pm). ⏱ 1 day. Tourist information: An der Neckarbrücke 1. ☎ 07071/91360. www.tuebingen.de.

Where to Stay & Dine

> Three gabled houses dating to 1491 contribute to the elegant Old-World charm of Tübingen's Hotel am Schloss.

★ Gasthof Waldhorn NEAR TÜBINGEN FRENCH/GERMAN The area's best restaurant, located 6km (3¾ miles) from Tübingen's town center, features inventively prepared French and German specialties created with locally sourced ingredients and backed up with an impressive wine list. Schönbuchstrasse 49 (drive north on Am Stadtgraben, turn left on Wilhelmstrasse, left on Bebenhauser Strasse, left on Schönbuchstrasse). ☎ 07071/61270. www.waldhorn-bebenhausen.de. Reservations required. Entrees 24€–36€, fixed-price menu 78€. No credit cards. Lunch & dinner Wed–Sun. Closed 2 weeks in Aug.

★ Hotel am Schloss TÜBINGEN This romantic charmer near Tübingen's castle consists of three steep-gabled houses, the oldest dating from 1491, that have been simply but comfortably renovated but lack an elevator. The hotel's restaurant serves good, traditional Swabian food. Burgsteige 18. ☎ 07071/92940. www.hotelamschloss.de. 35 units. Doubles 108€–135€ w/breakfast. AE, DC, MC, V.

★ Krone Hotel TÜBINGEN If you want to stay on the Neckar River in the heart of town, this quiet, well-respected hotel is your best choice. The rooms are comfortable but not fussy, and the hotel's restaurant is one of the best in town. Uhlandstrasse 1. ☎ 07 071/13310. www.krone-tuebingen.de. 47 units. Doubles 139€–159€ w/breakfast. AE, DC, MC, V.

★ Restaurant Museum TÜBINGEN SWABIAN Join the students who know this restaurant as a good place for tasty and reasonably priced lunches, or come for dinner when Swabian specialties like medallions of veal tempt the taste buds. Wilhelmstrasse 3. ☎ 07071/22828. www.restaurant-museum.de. Entrees 9€–22€, fixed-price menus 16€–19€. AE, MC, V. Lunch & dinner daily.

Heidelberg, Stuttgart & the Swabian Alb in 4 Days

Swabia (*Schwaben* in German) is the name for a medieval duchy now contained within the federal state of Baden-Württemberg. Swabia has been a leader of German industry for decades, but the region also is renowned for its scenic countryside. To the north, the Schwäbische Wald (Swabian Forest) stretches to the Schwäbische Alb, a wedge of limestone upland south of Stuttgart and between Tübingen and Ulm. Forests sweep south to the Bodensee and west to the Danube River. The smaller Neckar River flows past Heidelberg and Tübingen through a vineyard-covered valley. This 4-day itinerary introduces you to Swabia's major attractions.

> Picturesque Abtei Blaubeuren was founded as a Benedictine monastery but now houses a Protestant seminary school.

START Heidelberg is 94km (58 miles) south of Frankfurt on A5, about a 1-hour drive. It is easily accessible by train from all major cities in Germany and Europe (a 1-hr. trip from Frankfurt). TRIP LENGTH 292km (181 miles).

❶ ★★ **Heidelberg.** Give yourself at least half a day to explore Heidelberg. If you do your sightseeing in the morning, you can spend the afternoon visiting the castles in Neckarsteinach (p. 410, ❷), in the Neckar Valley, and

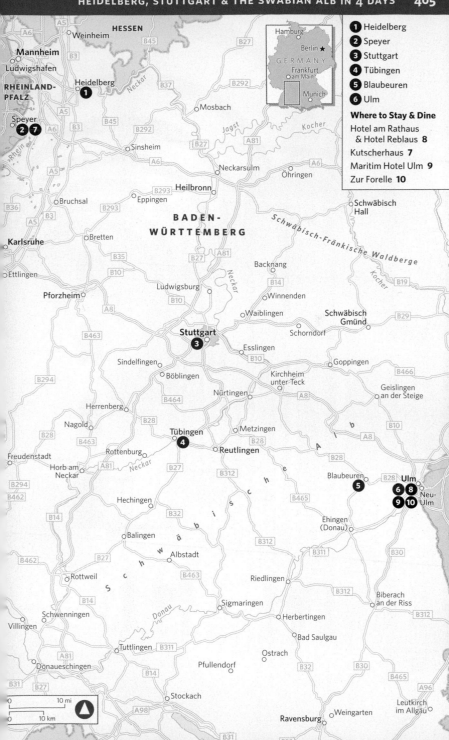

1 Heidelberg
2 Speyer
3 Stuttgart
4 Tübingen
5 Blaubeuren
6 Ulm

Where to Stay & Dine

Hotel am Rathaus
 & Hotel Reblaus 8
Kutscherhaus 7
Maritim Hotel Ulm 9
Zur Forelle 10

> The interior of Speyer's enormous 11th-century Romanesque cathedral.

return to spend the night. ⏱ 1 day. For information on Heidelberg, including hotel and restaurant recommendations, see p. 424.

On Day 2, head southwest on A5 to Speyer (36km/22 miles), about a 30-minute drive.

❷ ★ **Speyer.** This Free Imperial City lays claim to being over 2,000 years old and has the largest intact Romanesque building in Europe. Speyer is worth visiting just to see the ★★ **Kaiserdom** (Imperial Cathedral), a superlative example of 11th-century Romanesque architecture and a UNESCO World Heritage site. This enormous triple-nave cross-vaulted basilica, built of red sandstone between 1025 and 1061, has a magnificent crypt with the tombs of several emperors, kings, and queens of the Holy Roman Empire (Edith-Stein-Platz; ☎ 06232/1020; Apr–Oct Mon–Fri 9am–7pm, Sat 10am–6pm, Sun 1:30–6pm, Nov–Mar daily 9am–5pm). The ★ **Historisches Museum der Pfalz** (Palatinate Historical Museum) displays several collections devoted to the history and culture of the region, the most important being the Domschatz (Cathedral Treasury), the Wine Museum (which has the oldest bottle of wine in existence, dating from A.D. 300), and the Prehistoric Collection, whose star attraction is the Golden Hat of Schifferstadt, a solid-gold cone-shaped ritual object from the Bronze Age (Domplatz; ☎ 06232/13250; admission 4€; Tues–Sun 10am–6pm). Also worth visiting is the **Technik-Museum** (Museum of Technology), with its assortment of historic airplanes, automobiles, locomotives, and a 20-ton World War II U-boat (Geibstrasse 2; ☎ 06232/67080; admission 13€; Mon–Fri 9am–6pm, Sat–Sun 9am–9pm). A rare glimpse into medieval Jewish culture is the 12th-century **Judenbad**, or *Mikwe*, a ritual bathing place for women (Judengasse; admission 3€; Apr–Oct daily 10am–5pm). Also have a look at the early-18th-century **Dreifaltigkeitskirche** (Church of the Holy Trinity), an architectural masterpiece with a riotous rococo interior (Grosse Himmelgasse, Wed

> *One of the many vintage automobiles at the popular Mercedes-Benz Museum in Stuttgart.*

10:30am–4pm, Sun 2–5pm). ⏱ At least 3 hr. Tourist information: Maximilianstrasse 13. ☎ 06232/142-392. www.speyer.de.

Make Stuttgart, 124km (77 miles) southeast of Speyer on A5 and A8, your overnight destination for Day 2; try to visit one museum during the afternoon you arrive and another the next morning.

❸ ★★ **Stuttgart.** ⏱ 1 day. For information on Stuttgart, including hotel and restaurant recommendations, see p. 430.

From Stuttgart, head south via B27 and B28 to Tübingen (44km/27 miles), and make this ancient and atmospheric university town your overnight stay for Day 3.

❹ ★★ **Tübingen.** Tübingen presents the visitor with a glimpse of a "real"—not rebuilt—German town, with buildings that date from the Middle Ages up to the 19th century crowded into a labyrinth of narrow, sloping streets that run down to the Neckar, where students oar visitors up and down the river in slim punts called *Stocherkähne*. ⏱ At least a half-day. See p. 402, ❹; for hotel and restaurant recommendations, see p. 403.

From Tübingen, drive east on B28, entering the scenic region of the Swabian Alb, to Blaubeuren (68km/42 miles), a drive of just over an hour. (If you're doing this itinerary by train, you'll need to skip Blaubeuren and go on directly to Ulm, ❻.)

Traveling by Train

It's faster and easier to follow this itinerary by car, but it's not essential. You can easily get to every place mentioned, except for Blaubeuren in the Swabian Alb, by train.

> *Historic buildings provide a beautiful backdrop to Tübingen's bustling Altstadt.*

5 ★ **Blaubeuren.** Stop in this scenic village in the Swabian Alb for some quick sightseeing. A short, signposted walk will take you to the **Blautopf,** a small, deep, shimmering blue lake (the name means "blue bowl"). Then follow the HOCHALTAR signs to visit **Abtei Blaubeuren** (Blaubeuren Abbey), which includes a photogenic group of half-timber buildings and the **Klosterkirche** (Abbey Church) with its magnificent 14th-century altarpiece (the *Hochaltar*). ⏱ 1 hr.

Ulm, your afternoon and overnight destination for Day 4, is 20km (12 miles) east of Blaubeuren via B28, about a 30-minute drive.

A Day Trip into the Swabian Alb

If you want to add an extra day to your itinerary, you can easily make a day trip by car from either Stuttgart or Tübingen into the Swabian Alb, a highly scenic area characterized by low mountains and stark rock outcroppings (see "The Swabian Alb," p. 416).

6 ★★ **Ulm.** Located on the Danube River and surrounded by the forests and hills of the Swabian Alb, Ulm was one of Europe's richest and most important cities in the Middle Ages, thanks to its textile industry and its location on several important trade routes. Its prosperity and political power declined as a result of the Thirty Years War and the War of the Spanish Succession, and it suffered more devastation during World War II. Yet this city of 170,000 inhabitants, the birthplace of Albert Einstein, remains an appealing and quietly intriguing place to explore, with a mixture of old and new architecture and a central location that makes it a good choice for an overnight stay. From Ulm it's easy to get to the nearby Swabian Alb, the Black Forest, the Bodensee, or Bavaria.

The city's chief glory is its enormous ★★★ **Münster** (Cathedral), a masterpiece of Gothic architecture and famous for having the tallest (161m/528 ft.) church spire in the world. Give yourself at least 30 minutes to explore this massive, five-nave basilica, and pay particular attention to the intricately carved 15th-century choir stalls, pulpit, and altar, as well as the 15th-century frescoes in the chancel; if you climb the 768 steps of the tower you'll be rewarded with an unforgettable view all the way to the Alps (Münsterplatz; ☎ 0731/967-5023; cathedral free admission, tower 2.50€; daily 9am–dusk). Standing on Münsterplatz adjacent to the cathedral is the **Stadthaus,** a contemporary building by American architect Richard Meier dating from 1993 and used as a tourist office and arts center. Marktplatz, Ulm's ancient market square, is the site of the Gothic-Renaissance **Rathaus** (Town Hall), its facade decorated with frescoes and crowned by an astronomical clock, and the **Fischkastenbrunnen** (Fish Crate Fountain), dating from 1482 and once used by market vendors to keep their fish cool. Next to the Rathaus is Gottfried Böhm's **Stadtsbibliothek** (Public Library), a vigorously modern building shaped like a glass pyramid. The collections of the noteworthy ★ **Ulmer**

Museum, housed in four historic 15th-, 16th-, and 17th-century buildings, include luminous works by 15th-century Ulm masters such as Hans Multscher and 20th-century paintings by Picasso, Klee, Stella, and Rothko (Marktplatz 9; ☎ 0731/161-4330; admission 3.50€; Tues–Sun 11am–5pm). Exhibits in the unique ★ **Museum der Brotkultur** (Bread Museum) chronicle 8,000 years of the cultural and social history of bread and include paintings by artists from Brueghel to Picasso (Salzstadelgasse 10; ☎ 0731/69955; admission 3.50€; daily 10am–5pm, Wed until 8:30pm). After visiting the museums, spend some time wandering through the old ★ **Fischerviertel** (Fishermen's Quarter) south of the Münster along the Blau River. With its narrow lanes, half-timber medieval houses, cobblestoned streets, and little footbridges, this is Ulm's most picturesque area. ⏱ 4 hr. to see the main sights. Tourist information: Münsterplatz. ☎ 0731/161-2830. www.tourismus.ulm.de.

Where to Stay & Dine

★ **Hotel am Rathaus & Hotel Reblaus** ULM
If you're looking for historic ambience and atmosphere, these two antiques-filled hotels located behind the Rathaus in Ulm's old town are the best places to stay. Book a room with windows facing out onto Ulm's amazing cathedral. Kronengasse 8-10. ☎ 0731/968-90. www.rathausulm.de. 34 units. Doubles 88€–120€ w/breakfast. AE, DC, MC, V.

★ **Kutscherhaus** SPEYER RHINELAND
This atmospheric restaurant and beer garden, housed in a gabled, half-timber one-time stagecoach depot, specializes in regional Rhineland dishes. Fischmarkt 5A. ☎ 06232/0592. www.kutscherhaus-speyer.de. Entrees 13€–18€. AE, DC, MC, V. Lunch & dinner Fri-Tues.

★ kids **Maritim Hotel Ulm** ULM
With large rooms, a heated pool, and babysitting services, this full-service high-rise hotel on the Danube is Ulm's family-friendliest. Basteistrasse 40. ☎ 0731/9230. www.maritim. de. 287 units. 153€–215€. AE, DC, MC, V.

> *This 400-year-old building houses the popular Zur Forelle restaurant in Ulm's Fishermen's Quarter.*

★★ **Zur Forelle** ULM SWABIAN
Housed in a 400-year-old building in Ulm's historic Fishermen's Quarter, this atmospheric restaurant specializes in regional cooking and offers dishes such as Ulm-style salmon-and-herb soup and beef and liver stew with roasted potatoes. Fischergasse 25. ☎ 0731/63924. www. zurforelle.com. Reservations recommended. Entrees 12€–24€. AE, MC, V. Lunch & dinner daily.

Castles Along the Neckar Valley

The Neckar River rises in the Black Forest and flows north and west for some 367km (228 miles) before emptying into the Rhine at Mannheim. One of the prettiest stretches of the Neckartal, or Neckar Valley, lies east of Heidelberg, an area where the valley is steep and windy, the castles (or castle ruins) are plentiful, and the towns are small and charming.

> Forested slopes dotted with castles make the Neckar Valley a storybook landscape.

START Heidelberg is 94km (58 miles) south of Frankfurt on A5, about a 1-hour drive. It is easily accessible by train from all major cities in Germany and Europe (a 1-hr. trip from Frankfurt). **TRIP LENGTH 164km (102 miles) and 1 day.**

1 ★★ **Schloss Heidelberg (Heidelberg Castle).** ⏱ At least 1 hr. See p. 427, **8**.

Neckarsteinach is 14km (8¾ miles) east of Heidelberg, about a 20-minute drive on B37. From the castle, take Schlossstrasse east and follow the signs to B37, which parallels the Neckar River.

2 **Neckarsteinach.** This town is famous for its four castles, which stand on a narrow ridge overlooking the village and were built between 1100 and 1250. The Vorderburg and Mittelburg castles are privately owned, but spend a few minutes visiting the ruins of **Hinterburg,** the oldest of the four, and **Burg Schadeck,** nick-named the *Schwalbennest* (Swallow's Nest), for impressive views over the Neckar Valley (both castles free admission; open daily 9am–dusk).

From Neckarsteinach, backtrack to the town of Neckargemünd and watch for the signs to Dilsberg, 4.5km (2¾ miles) to the south.

3 **Dilsberg.** This small hamlet with its steep cobblestoned streets and pretty churches is crowned by **Festung Dilsberg** (Dilsberg Fortress), a walled compound with a wonderful panoramic view from its restored tower (admission 1€; daily 9am–dusk). ⏱ 15 min.

Take B37 and B45 northeast to Hirschhorn (18km/11 miles), about a 25-minute drive.

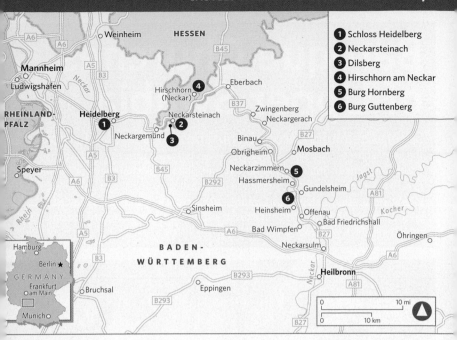

4 ★ Hirschhorn am Neckar. This medieval village stretches along the right bank of the Neckar, which here loops around in a horseshoe bend. From the 14th-century tower of **Burg Hirschhorn** (Hirschhorn Castle), perched on a fortified promontory above the village, you'll have an unparalleled view of the river and its wooded slopes (admission 1€; daily 9am–dusk). ⏱ 15 min.

From Hirschhorn, retrace your route to B37 and drive southeast 38km (24 miles) to Burg Hornberg, about a 35-minute drive, and 1.5km (1 mile) above the town of Neckarzimmern.

5 ★ Burg Hornberg. This massive 16th-century castle with its tall keep is surrounded by vineyards that are at least 1,500 years old. Spend a few minutes in the castle museum, which exhibits the armor of Götz von Berlichingen, a medieval knight immortalized in a play by Johann Wolfgang von Goethe. The parts of the castle open to the public are mostly bare, but it's fun to climb to the tops of the various towers and look out over the Neckar River and Valley. ☎ 06261/5001. Admission 3€. Daily 10am–4pm. ⏱ 15 min.

Burg Guttenberg is 10km (6 miles) south of Burg Hornberg, about a 15-minute drive via B27, L588, and K3948.

6 ★ kids Burg Guttenberg. A rare example of a completely intact medieval castle, Guttenberg Castle was constructed in typical German fortress form with a massive defense wall and moat protecting an inner courtyard with living apartments. The castle is a popular family destination because it houses the German Raptor Research Center, which presents daily falcon demonstrations. The castle museum displays family artifacts and works of art, and an installation called "Living in a Knight's Castle" interprets life in the castle from medieval times to the present. ⏱ At least 30 min. Burgstrasse. ☎ 06266/228. Admission 5€. Apr–Oct daily 10am–6pm.

The fastest return route to Heidelberg from Burg Guttenberg is via A6 north, a distance of 61km (38 miles) and about a 50-minute drive.

Baroque Churches of Upper Swabia

Several beautiful baroque churches are scattered among the gentle hills of the Upper Swabian Plateau between Ulm and the Bodensee (Lake Constance). They are Roman Catholic pilgrimage churches, for the most part, whose sober pastel facades hide an amazing world of color and almost gleeful decoration inside. If you want to see all these churches in a day, plan to spend no more than 30 to 45 minutes at each. You might also want to consider bringing a lunch with you.

> *Kloster Schussenried mixes Romanesque, Gothic, and baroque styles.*

START Obermarchtal is 40km (25 miles) southwest of Ulm on B311, about a 45-minute drive. **TRIP LENGTH** 240km (149 miles) and 1 full day.

❶ Kloster Obermarchtal (Obermachtal Monastery). The old abbey church in this small town, dating from 1686, serves as a primer on the beginnings of baroque style. The architecture here is rigid and the furnishings add a

heaviness that is lightened only by the stucco-work. Klosteranlage 2. ☎ 07375/95020. Daily 8am–6pm.

Zweifalten is 10km (6 miles) west of Obermarchtal via L249, B311, L271, and B312, about a 15-minute drive.

❷ ★★ Kloster Zweifalten (Zweifalten Abbey). The sober facade of the monastery church in the village of Zweifalten, on the Danube side

1 Kloster Obermarchtal
2 Kloster Zwiefalten
3 Kloster Schussenried
4 Wallfahrtskirche Steinhausen
5 Kloster Weingarten
6 Kloster Wiblingen

of the Swabian Alb, hides a lavishly decorated baroque interior. Built between 1739 and 1753 for the Benedictine order, it glows with a profusion of luminous colors, fanciful shapes, and exuberant stucco decoration that includes angels and cherubs everywhere you look and confessionals built to resemble grottoes. Zwiefalten. No phone. Daily 8am–5pm.

Continue southeast on B312, and then follow L275 and L284 to Bad Schussenried (35km/22 miles), about a 35-minute drive.

3 Kloster Schussenried (Schussenried Abbey). The intricately carved choir stalls in this sumptuously decorated church date from 1718

and are separated by statuettes representing men and women who founded religious orders. The library has a huge painted ceiling and a rococo balustrade supported by twin columns embellished with vivacious cherubim and effigies of Fathers of the Church. Klosterhof. ☎ 07583/2541. Apr–Oct Tues–Fri 10am–1pm and 2–5pm, Sat–Sun 10am–5pm; Nov–Mar Sat–Sun 1–4pm.

From Bad Schussenried, take L306 east to Steinhausen (27km/17 miles), a 35-minute drive.

4 ★ Wallfahrtskirche Steinhausen (Pilgrimage Church of Steinhausen). This church was

> *OPPOSITE PAGE For centuries, visitors have sought out the beautiful Wallfahrtskirche Steinhausen, seen here gleaming in the sunset. ABOVE Elaborate painting and stuccowork decorate the raised dome of Kloster Weingarten.*

on the pilgrimage route to Santiago de Compostela in Spain. Dominikus Zimmermann, master of the baroque in Swabia, gave the nave and chancel an oval shape and encircled them with carved and colored pillars, cornices, and window embrasures adorned with birds, insects, and flowers. **Ingoldinger Strasse 5.** ☎ **07583/2541. Daily 9am-5pm.**

From Steinhausen, take K7573 and L306 west to B30, then head south to Weingarten (46km/27½ miles), about a 50-minute drive.

5 ★★ **Kloster Weingarten (Weingarten Abbey).** Consecrated in 1724, this Benedictine abbey church with its fine sandstone facade is 102m (335 ft.) long and 44m (144 ft.) wide, making it one of the largest baroque sanctuaries in Germany. The rounded west front, framed by two elegant towers, and the raised dome, with wide windows, show Italian influences. The interior painting and stuccowork are relatively restrained but the scenes on the

ceiling, painted by Cosmas Damien Asam, are full of life and virtuosity. **Kirchplatz 3.** ☎ **0751/ 50960. Daily 7am-7pm.**

From Weingarten, take B30 north to Kloster Wiblingen (78km/48 miles).

6 **Kloster Wiblingen (Wiblingen Abbey).** Although its foundation dates back to the 11th century, the final touches were not put to the abbey church until the 18th century. The abbey library, completed in 1760, is one of the finest examples of the rococo in Swabia. Its gallery, supported by 32 rhythmically placed columns painted in alternating shades of pink and blue, projects into the center of the room and combines with a large false-relief frescoed ceiling to create an ensemble rich in color and movement. **Schlossstrasse 38.** ☎ **0751/502-8975. Daily summer 9am-6pm, winter 9am-5pm.**

Ulm is 5km (3 miles) north of Kloster Wiblingen via Wiblinger Strasse.

The Swabian Alb

The Swabian Alb—also called the Swabian Jura—is the central portion of a chain of highlands that stretches from France and Switzerland into southwestern Germany. Some 220km (136 miles) long and 80km (50 miles) wide, the Swabian Alb was formed by volcanic activity during the Jurassic Period; the area's bizarre cliffs were once the sponge and coral reefs of the Jurassic Sea. This ancient uplifted area forms the dividing line between water flowing into the North Sea via the Rhine and water flowing into the Black Sea via the Danube. Majestic castles and baroque churches perch dramatically on craggy summits, but the landscape also includes broad plains, beech woods, juniper scrubland, and sleepy villages.

> The Burgruine Reussenstein, castle ruins dating from 1270, are a magnet for visitors to the spectacular Swabian Alb.

START Kirchheim unter Teck is 37km (23 miles) southeast of Stuttgart on A8, about a 35-minute drive. **TRIP LENGTH** 214km (133 miles) and 2 days. You will need a car for this trip.

❶ Kirchheim unter Teck. Stop and spend a few minutes looking around this attractive town nestled beneath the ruins of Teck Castle, built in 1538, along the small Lauter River, a tributary of the Neckar. Kirchheim is the most important wool market in southern Germany and still has wool-spinning establishments. The pinnacled, half-timber **Rathaus** (Town Hall) overlooking the main crossroads is the most ornately decorated building in town.

From Kirchheim unter Teck, take L1200 southeast to Holzmaden (5.5km/3½ miles), and follow the arrows to Urwelt-Museum Hauff.

❷ ★ Urwelt-Museum Hauff. This museum houses a fascinating assembly of fossil skeletons found in local shale quarries, including ichthyosaurs, plesiosaurs, crocodiles, pterosaurs, fish, sea lilies, and ammonites dating back almost 160 million years. Life-size models of saurians and dioramas, videos, and animations provide information about life in the Jurassic Sea. ⏱ 15 min. Aiechelberger Strasse 90. ☎ 07023/2873. www.urweltmuseum.de. Admission 4€. Tues–Sun 9am–5pm.

Continue south on L1200 to Burgruine Reussenstein (9km/5½ miles).

❸ ★ Burgruine Reussenstein (Castle Ruins). Built in 1270 atop a 760m-high (2,500-ft.) escarpment, this castle—today an impressive

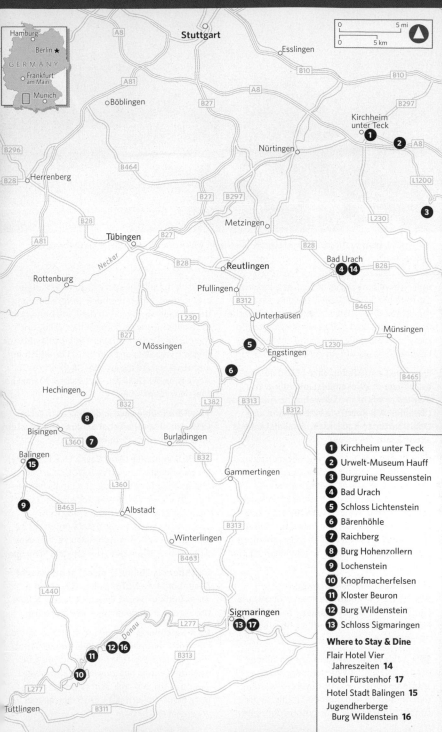

1 Kirchheim unter Teck
2 Urwelt-Museum Hauff
3 Burgruine Reussenstein
4 Bad Urach
5 Schloss Lichtenstein
6 Bärenhöhle
7 Raichberg
8 Burg Hohenzollern
9 Lochenstein
10 Knopfmacherfelsen
11 Kloster Beuron
12 Burg Wildenstein
13 Schloss Sigmaringen

Where to Stay & Dine

Flair Hotel Vier
 Jahreszeiten 14
Hotel Fürstenhof 17
Hotel Stadt Balingen 15
Jugendherberge
 Burg Wildenstein 16

> *A winding stone path leads visitors to Uracher Wasserfall, which cascades through the lush wilderness.*

ruin—served the dukes of Teck as a lookout over the Neidlingen Valley, the only pass into the Swabian Alb. Park in the lot and follow the trail to the lookout point built into the castle ruins for a dramatic view of the entire valley beyond the plain of Teck. ⏲ 30 min.

From the Castle Ruins, take L1200 east to the village of Wiesensteig and follow the marked roads of the Schwäbische Albstrasse (Swabian Alb Road) via Westerheim and Donnstetten to Bad Urach. Total distance is about 23km (14 miles).

④ ★ Bad Urach. This delightfully picturesque town with its half-timber houses clustered around the central Marktplatz (Market Square) is enclosed deep in the Erms Valley. Leave your car in the parking area marked AUSSICHT (viewpoint) and follow the path to **Uracher Wasserfall** (Urach Falls), an impressive cascade hidden in a forest glen ⏲ 20 min. to and from the waterfall.

Follow the signposted Schwäbische Albstrasse (Swabian Alb Road, K6708) via Ohnastetten and Holzelfingen to Schloss Lichtenstein (22km/14 miles), about a 25-minute drive.

⑤ ★ Schloss Lichtenstein. Duke Wilhelm of Urach, Count of Württemberg, was so smitten by the Romantic novel *Lichtenstein* that in 1840 he had this neo-Gothic castle constructed on a high rocky spur, decorated

it in the then-fashionable Troubadour style, and named it after the book. Before crossing the entrance bridge, turn right and head over to take in the views of the Echaz Valley and the castle, which contains a large collection of historic weapons and armor. ⏲ 1 hr. with tour and stroll around the grounds. ☎ 07129/4102. Admission 5€. Daily Apr–Oct 9am–5:30pm; Feb, Mar, Nov 10am–4pm.

The Bärenhöhle cave in Erpfingen is 12km (7½ miles) southwest of Schloss Lichtenstein on B313, about a 15-minute drive.

⑥ kids Bärenhöhle (Bear Cave). Used as a shelter by prehistoric peoples 8,000 years ago, and as a lair for now-extinct animals before that, this large cave was discovered 50 years ago. The biggest cavern contains well-preserved stalactites and stalagmites. ⏲ 30 min. ☎ 07128/92518. Admission 5€. Apr–Nov daily 9am–5:30pm; Mar, Nov Sat–Sun 9am–5pm.

Raichberg is 28km (17 miles) southwest of Bärenhöhle via K6767 and L382, about a 40-minute drive. At Onstmettingen, follow the signs for Nädelehaus and Raichberg.

⑦ ★ Raichberg. Walk to the lip of the plateau or climb the *Aussichtsturm* (view tower) atop this 956m (3,136-ft.) summit and you'll be rewarded with a fine view of the downward sweep of the Alb and, 3km (2 miles) away, Burg Hohenzollern (⑧). ⏲ 30 min. on foot to viewpoint and back.

> *Burg Hohenzollern sits imperially on its hilltop far above the Neckar Valley.*

From Raichberg, head north via K7103, L360, and K7111 to Burg Hohenzollern (about 15km/9 miles), a 20-minute drive.

8 ★★ Burg Hohenzollern. Rising majestically from a rocky outcrop above the upper Neckar Valley and bristling with turrets, Hohenzollern Castle looks like a fortress out of a fairy tale. The ancestral seat of the Hohenzollern dynasty, which eventually ruled Prussia and the entire German empire until 1918 (p. 422), the castle has an ancient lineage but was reconstructed from the original plans between 1850 and 1867. In 1952 the tombs of Friedrich Wilhelm I and Friedrich der Grosse (Frederick the Great) of Prussia were moved here from Potsdam. The Schatzkammer (Treasury) contains a collection of Hohenzollern mementoes. From the castle ramparts you have a stunning panorama. ⏱ 90 min. with tour. ☎ 07471/920-787. Grounds and castle tour 8€. Daily Mar 15–Oct 9am–5:30pm, Nov–Mar 15 10am–4:30pm. Tours every 15 to 30 min., in German only.

After visiting Burg Hohenzollern you'll want to think about where to spend the night. You can stay in the vicinity, or you can head back to Stuttgart (p. 430), 67km (42 miles) north via B27, about an hour's drive. Tübingen (p. 402, ❹; hotel and restaurant recommendations on p. 403), another overnight possibility, is only 28km (17 miles) north via B27, about a 30-minute drive. The next part of

> *Duke Wilhelm of Urach had Schloss Lichtenstein, with its panoramic view of the Echaz Valley, constructed in the Troubadour style.*

the tour heads southwest from Burg Hohenzollern to Lochenstein, 22km (14 miles) via B27 and B463, about a 20-minute drive.

> *The Gnadenkapelle (Chapel of Mercy) at Kloster Beuron.*

9 ★ **Lochenstein.** Another photo op. Leave the car at the parking lot and climb to the 963m (3,159 ft.) summit (surmounted by a cross) for a sweeping view that includes Hohenzollern Castle. ⏱ 30 min. on foot there and back.

Beyond Lochenstein the road sweeps downhill in tight curves and then crosses the bare, rolling uplands of the Grosser Heuberg plateau. Follow L440, L433, K5908, K8277, and L277 south to Knopfmacherfelsen, 26km (16 miles) south of Lochenstein.

10 ★ **Knopfmacherfelsen.** Below the car park, make your way to a viewpoint for a view of the Danube Valley as far as Beuron Abbey (**11**). ⏱ 15 min. there and back.

Retrace your route northward on L277 to K8278 east, and take K8278 east to Kloster Beuron (5.5km/3½ miles).

11 ★★ **Kloster Beuron (Beuron Abbey).** A flourishing Benedictine congregation at Beuron contributed greatly to the revival of monastic life and the use of the Gregorian chant, and the monks here are among the world's greatest executants of that ethereally beautiful music. The Frauenkapelle on the north side of the baroque abbey church was built in the "Beuron style" based on the simpler forms of Byzantine and Romanesque architecture. ⏱ 30 min. to look around the monastery buildings open to the public. Abteistrasse 2. ☎ 07466/170. Mass and vespers with Gregorian chant Mon–Sat 11:15am and 6pm, Sun 10am and 3pm.

Below Beuron, the road follows the Danube Valley toward the fortress of Wildenstein, 7km (4½ miles) east of Beuron via K8278, K8217, and K8216.

12 **Burg Wildenstein.** Stop and have a quick look at the view from this fortified citadel commanding the Danube Gap. Wildenstein Fortress was built between 1200 and 1300 with two moats and two towers linked by a long wall. Today it functions as a youth hostel.

From Burg Wildenstein, follow L277 east to Sigmaringen (26km/16 miles), about a 30-minute drive. Between Thiergarten and

Gutenstein the cliffs give way to fantastically shaped rock needles.

⓭ ★ Schloss Sigmaringen. Strategically built on a rocky spur rising from the valley at the mouth of the Upper Danube Gap, the town of Sigmaringen once served as the capital of a principality ruled by the Swabian (Catholic) branch of the Hohenzollern clan. Dominating the town's skyline is this castle, founded in the 11th century but reconstructed in a pastiche of historical styles between 1895 and 1905 following a fire. Use your time here to visit the State Apartments, the church (decorated with rococo stuccowork), and the museums, which display 15th- and 16th-century Swabian Primitive paintings, historic vehicles, and an enormous collection of arms and armor. ⏱ 1 hr. Karl Anton Platz 8. ☎ 07571/729-230. www.hohenzollern.com. Admission 6€. Daily Nov–Feb 10am–3:30pm, Mar–Apr 9:30am–4:30pm, May–Oct 9am–5pm.

From Sigmaringen, Tübingen is 65km (40 miles) north on B27, a drive of about 75 minutes. Stuttgart is 97km (60 miles) north on B27, a drive of about 1 hour 40 minutes. If you want to go on to the Bodensee, Lindau (p. 390) is 94km (58 miles) south on L286, about 90 minutes by car. The cathedral

> *Spectacular Schloss Sigmaringen perches on a rocky bluff above the Upper Danube Gap.*

town of Ulm (p. 408, **❻**) is 78km (48 miles) northeast via B311, also a 90-minute drive.

Where to Stay & Dine

★ Flair Hotel Vier Jahreszeiten BAD URACH
This attractive, well-run hotel in the center of the historic town center occupies a half-timber building with an annex across the street. The rooms are comfy, the restaurant a good place to dine on local specialties after a day of sightseeing. Stuttgarterstrasse 5. ☎ 07125/943-494. www.flairhotel-vierjahreszeiten.de. 48 units. Doubles 98€–125€ w/breakfast. MC, V.

Hotel Fürstenhof SIGMARINGEN
A reliable, somewhat generic hotel that caters to tourist groups, the Fürstenhof offers clean, comfortable, unfussy rooms, some with balconies, and has the best restaurant in town. Zeppelinstrasse 14. ☎ 07571/72060. www.fuerstenhof-sig.de. 34 units. Doubles 75€–85€ w/breakfast. MC, V.

★ Hotel Stadt Balingen BALINGEN
This modern hotel has more contemporary oomph and style than most hotels in the region. Rooms are bright and comfortable, the service is friendly, and there's a good restaurant. Hirschbergstrasse 48. ☎ 07433/260-070. www.hotel-stadt-balingen.de. 60 units. Doubles 77€–97€ w/breakfast. AE, MC, V.

Jugendherberge Burg Wildenstein LEIBERTINGEN If you're traveling on a budget but still want to sleep in a castle overlooking the Danube Valley, the hostel in Wildenstein Castle is just the place. Bathrooms are shared, meals are available, and bed linens are included in the price. 88637 Leibertingen-Wildenstein. ☎ 07466/411. www.leibertingen-wildenstein.jugendherberge-bw.de. 37 units. Dorm beds 19.10€ for guests under 27, 22.10€ for guests over 27. MC, V.

MEET THE HOHENZOLLERNS

Germany's Royal Family BY DONALD OLSON

WHO WERE THE HOHENZOLLERNS? Until the demise of the Holy Roman Empire in 1806, Germany remained a collection of free cities and small principalities ruled by a bewildering assortment of princes, dukes, margraves, burgraves, electors, and prince-bishops. The Wittelsbach family controlled Bavaria (where Ludwig built all those fairy-tale castles). But it was the Hohenzollerns who became the most powerful royal dynasty in Germany. Early on, the Hohenzollerns split into two branches. The Swabian branch remained relatively unimportant, but the Franconian branch expanded into the Brandenburg and Prussian regions of Germany, and the consolidation of their holdings ultimately led to the unification of Germany and the creation of the German Empire in 1871, at which time the title of German Emperor was established. When the Weimar Republic was formed in 1918, at the end of World War I, the Hohenzollerns were forced to abdicate and the German monarchy came to an end.

The First Hohenzollern

COUNT FREDERICK III OF ZOLLERN (1171–1200), a retainer of two Holy Roman Emperors, married the daughter of Conrad II, Burgrave of Nuremberg, and had two sons. When his wife's father died without male heirs, Frederick III was granted the burgraviate of Nuremberg. The family name became Hohenzollern at this time. The name derived from their castle, Burg Hohenzollern, in the Swabian Alb (p. 419, **8**).

THE SWABIAN HOHENZOLLERNS
In 1200 Frederick III's elder son, Frederick IV, received the county of Zollern and burgraviate of Nuremberg and founded the Swabian branch of the House of Hohenzollern. This southern branch remained Catholic and eventually split into three branches. By 1850 the Swabian principalities had been incorporated as the Prussian province of Hohenzollern, and by 1869 the Swabian branch became extinct.

THE FRANCONIAN HOHENZOLLERNS
In 1218 Frederick IV gave the burgraviate of Nuremberg to his younger brother, Conrad III, who founded the Franconian branch of the Hohenzollern dynasty. In the 16th century, the Franconian branch became Protestant and expanded its power through marriage and the purchase of surrounding lands.

Dukes, Electors & Kings of Prussia

FREDERICK WILLIAM (1620–1688), known as the Great Elector, steered Brandenburg-Prussia from obscurity to become one of Europe's greatest powers.

FREDERICK II THE GREAT (1712–1786), one of Germany's most enlightened rulers, became king of Prussia in 1740. In addition to his military training he studied literature and music, composing his own musical pieces and promoting the arts at his palace, Sanssouci (p. 130, **1**). As king, he doubled the area of Prussia and made his kingdom the most powerful state in Germany.

The Last German Emperor

WILHELM II (1859–1941), son of Prince Frederick Wilhelm of Prussia and Victoria, daughter of Queen Victoria, became the ninth king of Prussia in 1888 and the third emperor of Germany. He supported German imperialism, pursuing an anti-British policy (even though he was Queen Victoria's grandson) and encouraging Austro-Hungarian aggression after the assassination of Archduke Franz Ferdinand, a conflict that developed into the First World War. Forced to abdicate in 1918, Wilhelm fled the country with his family and lived in Holland for the rest of his life.

Reaching into Romania

In 1866, disguised as a salesman and traveling second-class, **Charles Eitel** (1839–1914), a member of the Swabian Hohenzollern-Sigmaringen family, made his way eastward to accept the throne of Romania. He had been invited to become prince of Romania and later became its first king. Hohenzollerns continued to rule in Romania until 1947 when the Kingdom of Romania was abolished and replaced with the Communist-led People's Republic of Romania.

Heidelberg

Heidelberg, on the Neckar River, is renowned for its castle, its university (the oldest in Germany), and its romantic charm. One of the few German cities not to be leveled in World War II, it has a full array of buildings from the Middle Ages, the Renaissance, and the baroque and neoclassical eras. The looming ruins of the ancient castle, the old lanes and squares, and the leafy hills and woodlands along the Neckar all had great appeal to the German Romantics, who "discovered" Heidelberg in the early 19th century and popularized it in their writings, music, and paintings. Wandering through the Altstadt (Old Town) is as essential a part of any tour as visiting the attractions.

> *A panoramic view of the streets and rooftops of the city from Schloss Heidelberg.*

START From the Hauptbahnhof (main train station), take streetcar no. 1 or 2 to Bismarckplatz. From here you can get around the Altstadt on foot.

❶ Hauptstrasse. Cross over from Bismarckplatz and walk east along this wide, busy pedestrian street lined with shops and restaurants and crossed by the narrow medieval lanes of Heidelberg's compact Altstadt.

❷ ★ Kurpfälzisches Museum. The Museum of the Palatinate, Heidelberg's most noteworthy museum, contains a large collection of regional painting and sculpture. The one masterpiece on display is Tilman Riemenschneider's 1509 wooden altarpiece of Christ and the Apostles. You can also see an archaeological collection with a cast of the jawbone of 600,000-year-old *Homo heidelbergensis* (Heidelberg Man), discovered in the vicinity nearly 100 years ago. ⏱ 45 min. Hauptstrasse 97. ☎ 06221/583-402. www.museum-heidelberg.de. Admission 3€. Tues–Sun 10am–6pm.

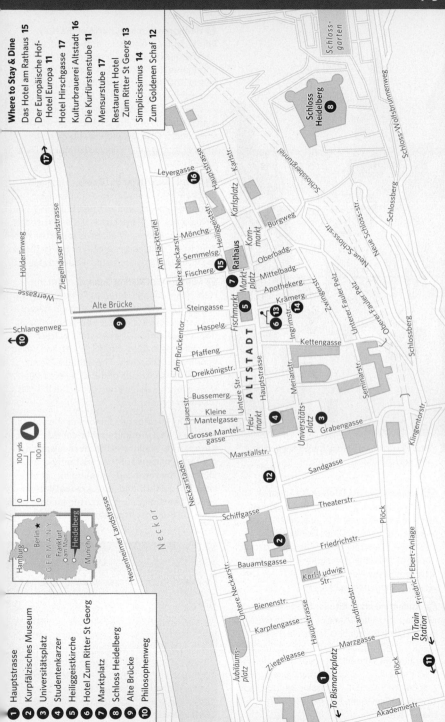

Where to Stay & Dine

Das Hotel am Rathaus 15
Der Europäische Hof-
Hotel Europa 11
Hotel Hirschgasse 17
Kulturbrauerei Altstadt 16
Die Kurfürstenstube 11
Mensurstube 17
Restaurant Hotel
Zum Ritter St Georg 13
Simplicissimus 14
Zum Goldenen Schaf 12

1 Hauptstrasse
2 Kurpfälzisches Museum
3 Universitätsplatz
4 Studentenkarzer
5 Heiliggeistkirche
6 Hotel Zum Ritter St Georg
7 Marktplatz
8 Schloss Heidelberg
9 Alte Brücke
10 Philosophenweg

> *Heidelberg's Hauptstrasse is a vibrant and busy center of activity.*

❸ Universitätsplatz (University Square). This charming square, graced by the Löwenbrunnen (Lion's Fountain), has long been a focal point of student life. On its northeastern side is the Alte Universität (Old University), a building from the 18th century, and at the south end is the Neue Universität (New University), completed in 1932.

❹ Studentenkarzer (Students' Prison). From 1778 to 1914 generations of students were incarcerated for minor offenses in these cramped cells. Graffiti and drawings, including portraits and silhouettes, cover the walls and even the ceilings. ⏱ 15 min. Augustinerstrasse 2. ☎ 06221/543-554. Admission 3€. Apr–Oct Tues-Sun 10am-6pm, Nov–Mar Tues-Sat 10am-4pm.

❺ Heiliggeistkirche (Church of the Holy Spirit). Make a brief stop at the imposing, late-Gothic church, built around 1400, that dominates the west end of Marktplatz. For nearly 300 years, the church was the burial place of the Palatinate Electors. In 1706, a wall was erected to divide the church between Roman Catholics and Protestants. The wall has since been removed and the church restored to its original plan. Heiliggeiststrasse 17. Daily 8am-6pm.

❻ Hotel Zum Ritter St. Georg. This highly decorated Renaissance mansion with a stepped-gable facade was erected in 1592 for a Huguenot cloth merchant. It's been used as a guesthouse since 1701 and is today the Hotel Zum Ritter St. Georg, named for the statue of the *Ritter* (knight) at the top. Hauptstrasse 178.

❼ Marktplatz (Market Square). With the Herkulesbrunnen (Hercules Fountain) at its center, the Altstadt's main square is always a busy spot. It becomes even busier on market days (Wed and Sat), when stalls of fresh flowers, fish, vegetables, cheese, meat, and baked goods draw shoppers. The Rathaus (Town Hall) on the east side of the square is an early-18th-century building reconstructed in 1908 following a fire.

To reach Heidelberg's famous castle you can walk or take a 2-minute cable-car ride from Kornmarkt. Walking is the more rewarding approach because of the constantly changing views of the town and surrounding countryside. The easiest and most gradual path begins at the Klingentor; a shorter, steeper path leads up Burgweg from Kornmarkt.

A Heidelberg Christmas

At Heidelberg's famous Christmas Market, some 140 stalls selling handcrafted gifts and tasty treats are spread across six different squares. The market is inaugurated at the Rathaus with traditional European Christmas music. Throughout this festive season, classical and carol concerts enliven the churches, a skating rink is set up at the foot of Heidelberg Castle, and a kids' petting zoo with live donkeys, goats, and rabbits appears in the Kornmarkt.

Heidelberg Nightlife

The large student population keeps Heidelberg humming after dark. Heidelberg's most famous student tavern, **Zum Roten Ochsen** (Red Ox Inn), Hauptstrasse 217 (☎ 06221/20977; www.roterochsen.de), opened in 1703. **Zum Sepp'l**, next door at Hauptstrasse 213 (☎ 06221/23085), dates from 1634.

❽ ★★ Schloss Heidelberg. In the 19th century, the enormous ruins of Heidelberg Castle became a symbol for the German Romantics and a mecca for tourists. Built between 1400 and 1620, the castle served as the residence of the Prince Electors until French troops sacked and destroyed it in the late 17th century. Entering the main gate, you come first to the Pulverturm (Gun Tower) and then the Elizabethentor (Elizabeth's Gate), erected by Friedrich V in 1615 for his teenage wife Elizabeth Stuart, daughter of the English king James I. A bridge across the former moat leads to a courtyard terrace with a magnificent view of Heidelberg, the Neckar Valley, and the Friedrichsbau (Palace of Friedrich IV), erected from 1601 to 1607. The Grosse Fass (Great Cask), one of the largest wine barrels in the world, built in 1751 to hold more than 208,000 liters (about 55,000 gallons) of wine, can be seen in the castle's cellars. The Apothekenmuseum (Pharmacy Museum) re-creates a baroque-era chemist's shop. The Hortus Palatinus (Castle Gardens), laid out in the 17th century, contain the remains of a grotto and a sandstone sculpture of Father Rhine. ⏱ At least 1 hr. Schlossberg. ☎ 06221/872-7000. www.schloss-heidelberg.de. Admission 3€; 1-hr. guided tours in English 4€, audio tour 4€. Daily 8am–5:30pm.

❾ Alte Brücke (Old Bridge). This handsome stone bridge across the Neckar River was built between 1786 and 1788 by Elector Karl Theodor. Destroyed in 1944 by German troops trying to halt the advance of the Allied army, it was rebuilt 2 years later. Near the twin-towered bridge gate on the town side are statues of Karl Theodor; Minerva, the Roman goddess of wisdom; and the charming *Brückenaffe* (Bridge Ape).

If you want to continue your walking tour of Heidelberg, cross over the Alte Brücke and turn left, following Neuenheimer Landstrasse along the north bank of the Neckar. Turn right at Bergstrasse and right again on the Philosophenweg. This portion of the tour covers an additional 4km (2½ miles).

❿ ★ Philosophenweg (Philosophers' Way). Now some 250 years old, this popular 2km (1¼-mile) walking trail on the north bank of the Neckar provides memorable views of the castle, the river, and Heidelberg's Altstadt. Thanks to a unique microclimate, Japanese cherries, cypresses, lemons, bamboos, rhododendrons, gingkos, yucca trees, and several other plants from the Mediterranean, North Africa, and Asia flourish in the Philosophengärtchen (Philosophers' Garden) at the end of walk. ⏱ 90 min. to reach the path and stroll to the garden and back.

> *The lushly planted walking trail known as Philosophenweg runs along the beautiful north bank of the Neckar River.*

Where to Stay & Dine

> *Mensurstube serves traditional fare at the historic Hotel Hirschgasse, which dates back to 1472.*

★ **kids Das Hotel am Rathaus** ALTSTADT
One of Heidelberg's nicest and most affordable small hotels has a great location, simple modern furnishings, and some larger rooms suitable for families. The one potential drawback is the lack of an elevator. Heiliggeiststrasse 1. ☎ 06221/14730. www.hotels-in-heidelberg.de. 17 units. Doubles 99€–154€ w/ breakfast. AE, DC, MC, V.

★★★ **Der Europäische Hof-Hotel Europa**
CITY CENTER The only 5-star hotel in the Rhine-Neckar region, this impeccable, family-owned and -operated hotel feels more like a palatial resort than a hotel that's only a couple of minutes' walk from the Altstadt. The large, traditionally furnished rooms have luxuriously appointed bathrooms and the rooftop

pool and sauna area is beautifully designed. Friedrich-Ebert-Anlage 1. ☎ 800/223-4541 in North America, or 06221/5150. www. europaeischerhof.com. Doubles 358€–374€. AE, DC, MC, V.

★★★ **Die Kurfürstenstube** ALTSTADT *FRENCH*
The best dining spot in Heidelberg features elegant and creative culinary delights such as artichoke and grilled scallop salad with tangerine essence, pheasant with bacon, and filet of turbot with celery on saffron foam with coriander tortellini. In Der Europäische Hof-Hotel Europa, Friedrich-Ebert-Anlage 1. ☎ 06221/5150. www.kurfuerstenstube.de. Reservations required. Entrees 28€–32€, fixed-price menus 75€–84€. AE, DC, MC, V. Lunch & dinner daily.

★★ Hotel Hirschgasse NORTH SIDE OF RIVER
This historic hotel dates from 1472 and enjoys
a tranquil and romantic setting. The rooms are
all sumptuously comfortable suites. Hirschgasse 3. ☎ 06221/4540. www.hirschgasse.de.
20 units. Doubles 150€–335€. AE, DC, MC, V.

Kulturbrauerei Altstadt ALTSTADT This small,
hip hotel near the river has medium-size
rooms furnished in a cool, minimalist style.
The hotel is connected to a microbrewery with
a summer beer garden and has a good, moderately priced restaurant that serves regional
specialties. Leyergasse 6. ☎ 06221/90000.
www.heidelberger-kulturbrauerei.de. 21 units.
Doubles 121€–160€ w/breakfast. AE, MC, V.

★★ Mensurstube NORTH SIDE OF RIVER GER-
MAN/REGIONAL No other place in Heidelberg
captures bygone days quite like this rustic
and cozy spot in the ancient Hotel Hirschgasse. The limited menu sticks to traditional
dishes made with fresh ingredients and often
includes *Rinderfilet* (filet of beef) served with
bone marrow and a red-wine sauce. In the Hotel Hirschgasse, Hirschgasse 3. ☎ 06221/4540.
www.hirschgasse.de. Reservations recommended. Entrees 18€–29€. AE, DC, MC, V. Lunch
& dinner daily.

kids **Restaurant Hotel Zum Ritter St. Georg**
ALTSTADT GERMAN/INTERNATIONAL
Locals flock here when the house specialty,
saddle of venison, is on the menu. Other menu
offerings include staples such as pork loin with
sauerkraut and roast salmon in a basil-cream
sauce. A children's menu includes dishes
such as *Wiener Würstchen* (small Vienna-style
sausages). Hauptstrasse 178. ☎ 06221/1350.
www.ritter-heidelberg.de. Reservations recommended. Entrees 10€–16€, fixed-price menus
34€–57€. AE, DC, MC, V. Lunch & dinner daily.

★★★ Simplicissimus ALTSTADT FRENCH
The menu changes often at this elegant
gourmet restaurant known for its *cuisine moderne*, but expect dishes such as lamb with a
red-wine and onion purée, fresh mushrooms
in cream sauce with homemade noodles,

> *The beautifully appointed Hotel Zum Ritter St.
Georg's restaurant serves German and international cuisine.*

duck breast with asparagus, or crayfish with
fresh melon and herb-flavored cream sauce.
Ingrimstrasse 16. ☎ 06221/183-336. www.
restaurant-simplicissimus.de. Reservations
required. Entrees 19€–45€, fixed-price menu
35€–65€. V. Dinner Wed–Sat. Closed 2 weeks in
Mar and Aug.

Zum Güldenen Schaf ALTSTADT GERMAN/
REGIONAL This historic pub-restaurant offers a
menu emphasizing regional dishes from Swabia
and the Pfalz. Stick with the seasonal specialties
like venison or goose, or try the house specialty,
rack of lamb. Hauptstrasse 115. ☎ 06221/20879.
www.schaf-heidelberg.de. Entrees 8€–23€. AE,
DC, MC, V. Lunch & dinner daily.

Stuttgart

For more than a century Stuttgart has been a center of German industry—Mercedes-Benz, Porsche, and Zeiss optics all have plants here—yet the city remains surprisingly verdant, nestled in gently rolling hills with woods and vineyards, and with a big park, the Schlossgarten, right in the historic core. As a cultural center, Stuttgart boasts museums and performing arts venues that are among the best in Germany. Over half the city was destroyed in World War II and then rebuilt, and contemporary structures have been incorporated into the urban fabric. You might not find Stuttgart particularly beautiful, but it is an interesting city and with its many urban amenities it makes for a good overnight stop. Depending on your interests, it could easily take a couple of days to see all the sights listed here.

> The 16-day Stuttgart Beer Festival in late September features rides, food, and tents, as well as beer for five million visitors.

START Hauptbahnhof (main train station); from here you can reach all the major attractions in the city center on foot.

❶ **Hauptbahnhof.** A great deal of work has been done in recent years to make Stuttgart's main train station and the surrounding area more up-to-date and retail-savvy.

❷ **Schlossgarten (Castle Garden).** Established in the 19th century, this fountain- and flower-filled park stretches from the **Neues Schloss** (New Castle), an impressive 18th-century building (rebuilt 1958) that houses

Getting Around Stuttgart

You can easily navigate the city center on foot. The Mercedes-Benz and Porsche museums, Wilhelma (the zoo), and some other sights require the use of public transportation or taxi. Stuttgart has a comprehensive *S-Bahn* (light rail) system that links up with the *U-Bahn* (subway). A 1-day ticket (*Einzel Tageskarte*) costs 5.60€ and can be purchased from machines in *U-Bahn* stations or from bus drivers.

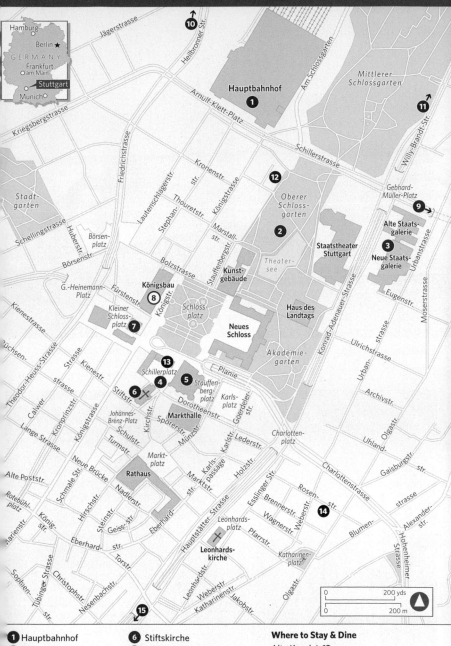

1 Hauptbahnhof
2 Schlossgarten
3 Staatsgalerie
4 Schillerplatz
5 Landesmuseum Württemberg
6 Stiftskirche
7 Kunstmuseum Stuttgart
8 Café Königsbau
9 Mercedes-Benz Museum
10 Porsche Museum
11 Wilhelma

Where to Stay & Dine

Alte Kanzlei 13
Der Zauberlehrling 14
Hotel am Schlossgarten 12
Wielandshöhe 15

> *You'll find an incredible collection of 19th- and 20th-century art at Stuttgart's famed Kunstmuseum.*

Stuttgart Festivals

A visit to Stuttgart can be even more enjoyable when you time your trip to coincide with one of the city's major festivals. At the **Stuttgart Wine Festival** in late August, wine lovers converge to taste a selection of more than 350 Württemberg wines. The 16-day **Stuttgart Beer Festival,** the second largest in Germany, begins in late September and features food, rides, and tents for thirsty beer drinkers. Some 5 million people attend the festival. Starting in late November, Stuttgart plays host to a lively **Weihnachtsmarkt** (Christmas Market), one of the oldest and largest in Europe, with about 230 decorated stalls selling gifts and holiday food specialties.

> *Café Königsbau on Königstrasse is one of Germany's most famed destinations for pastry, cake, and coffee.*

state government offices, north to Schiller-strasse. At the park's eastern edge stands the **Staatstheater** (State Theater), dating from 1912 and today home to Stuttgart's renowned opera and ballet companies. Schlossplatz (Palace Square), on the park's western side, is dominated by the **Jubiläumssäule** (Jubilee Column), erected in 1846 to celebrate the 25-year anniversary of Wilhelm I, King of Würt-emberg's ascension and his 60th birthday. The square is enlivened with sculptures by Alexander Calder and other famous artists.

❸ ★★★ **Staatsgalerie (State Art Gallery).** Stuttgart's finest art museum exhibits works spanning some 600 years. Spend part of your time in the German Old Masters section, which highlights Swabian paintings and sculpture from the 14th through the 16th centuries. The post-modern Neue Staatsgalerie (New State Gallery), wing designed by the British architect James Stirling and completed in 1984, contains a marvelous collection of 19th- and 20th-century works by the German expressionists (Ernst Kirchner, Ernst Barlach, Max Beckmann), in addition to seminal works from the artists of the Bauhaus school and Blaue Reiter (Blue Rider) group. ⊕ 2 hr. Konrad-Adenauer-Strasse 30–32. ☎ 0711/470-400. www.staatsgalerie.de. Admission 4.50€ (free Wed). Tues–Sun 10am–6pm. *U-Bahn:* Staatsgalerie.

❹ **Schillerplatz.** A memorial to the German dramatist Friedrich Schiller, erected in 1839 by the Danish sculptor Bertel Thorvaldsen, stands in the center of this cobblestoned square, scene of a twice-weekly street market and also used for major events such as the Christmas Market.

❺ ★★ **Landesmuseum Württemberg.** Rebuilt after World War II, the Altes Schloss (Old Castle) houses this regional history museum that traces the art and culture of Swabia and Württemberg from the Stone Age to the present. On display are prehistoric stone sculptures, the Württemberg crown jewels, a large collection of Swabian sculptures, and treasures found in the tomb of a Celtic prince (c. A.D. 530). The museum's noteworthy

> *The Mercedes-Benz Museum honors Karl Benz and Gottlieb Daimler with displays of nearly 75 historical vintage vehicles.*

collection of musical instruments and clocks is housed in a separate building in a corner of Schillerplatz. ⏱ 1 hr. to see the highlights. Schillerplatz 6. ☎ 0711/279-3400. www. landesmuseum-stuttgart.de. Admission 4.50€. Tues–Sun 10am–5pm. *U-Bahn:* Schlossplatz.

⑥ Stiftskirche (Collegiate Church). Dating from the mid-15th century, this church was restored, and its interior altered, after World War II damage. Step inside for a quick look at the chancel, where a 16th-century monument depicts 11 armored dukes of Württemberg. Stiftstrasse 12. Mon–Thurs 10am–7pm, Fri–Sat 10am–4pm.

⑦ ★★★ Kunstmuseum Stuttgart (Stuttgart Art Museum). Opened in spring 2005, this beautiful new museum—a filigreed glass cube surrounding a rough-hewn limestone inner core—houses the city's collection of 19th- and 20th-century works by artists from southern Germany, including the most important collection of Otto Dix paintings in the world. ⏱ 1 hr. Kleiner Schlossplatz 1. ☎ 0711/216-2188. www.kunstmuseum-stuttgart.com. Admission 5€. Tues–Sun 10am–6pm (Wed, Fri until 9pm). *U-Bahn:* Schlossplatz.

Stuttgart Performing Arts

Staatstheater (State Theater), Oberer Schlossgarten (☎ 0711/202-090; *S-Bahn:* Hauptbahnhof), is home to the highly regarded Stuttgart Ballet and Staatsoper (State Opera). Classical and other concerts are given in the **Liederhalle,** Berliner Platz 1–3 (☎ 0711/216-7110; *U-Bahn:* Liederhalle/Berlinerplatz), home to the Stuttgart Philharmonic and the Radio Symphony Orchestra. Tickets for all concerts are on sale at the tourist information office.

Stuttgart Shopping

For a special food-shopping experience, head to the **Markthalle** (Market Hall), Dorotheenstrasse 4, a 1914 Art Nouveau building just off Marktplatz and full of stalls selling local and foreign delicacies.

⑧ 🍴 **Café Königsbau.** Coffee, cake, and light meals are served at this old-fashioned *Konditorei* (pastry shop) in the colonnade of the Königsbau next to the new art museum. Königstrasse 28. ☎ 0711/290-787. 4€–8€.

You'll need to use public transport to reach the last three stops on this tour.

⑨ ★★ **Mercedes-Benz Museum.** This museum in the Cannstatt district honors the invention of the motorcar by Karl Benz and Gottlieb Daimler. Nearly 75 historical vehicles are shown, including the first motorcycle (built in 1885) and the first Mercedes (1902), but Mercedes' role in World War II is glossed over. ⏱ 1 hr. Mercedesstrasse 100. ☎ 0711/173-0000. www.mercedes-benz-classic.com. Admission 8€, includes audio tour in English. Tues–Sun 9am–5pm. *S-Bahn:* S1 from main train station to Neckarpark (Mercedes-Benz); follow signs to the museum (about a 10-min. walk).

⑩ ★ **Porsche Museum.** The museum, which opened in 2008, displays a choice collection of sleek, stylish Porsche racing and sports cars, the oldest from 1948. ⏱ 1 hr. Porsche-platz 1. ☎ 0711/9112-0911. www.porsche.com/international/aboutporsche/porschemuseum/. Admission 8€ adults, 4€ kids over 14, free for kids 14 and under. Tues–Sun 9am–6pm. *S-Bahn:* S6 from main train station to Neuwirtshaus/Porscheplatz.

⑪ ★ **kids Wilhelma.** Home to more than 9,000 animals and plants from around the world, Wilhelma is the largest zoo and botanical garden in Europe. The park was laid out in 1848 and contains a collection of historical buildings in the Moorish style. ⏱ 2 hr. Neck-artalstrasse. ☎ 0711/54020. www.wilhelma. de. Admission 11.40€ adults, 5.70€ kids 16 and under. Daily 8:15am–5pm (Nov–May until 4pm). *U-Bahn:* 14 to Wilhelma stop.

Where to Stay & Dine

★ **Alte Kanzlei** ALTSTADT *SWABIAN* This restaurant specializes in traditional Swabian dishes such as *Maultaschen* (pasta stuffed with ham, egg, spinach, or other fillings) and *Zwie-belrostbraten* (roast beef topped with onions). There's a cafe section where you can get lighter meals, or you can sit out on the terrace and have an ice cream. Schillerplatz 5A. ☎ 0711/294-457. www.alte-kanzlei-stuttgart.de. Entrees 10€–20€. AE, DC, MC, V. Lunch & dinner daily.

★ **Der Zauberlehrling** CITY CENTER Quirkiness is not always charming, but it is here, in this small guesthouse with themed bedrooms furnished in an imaginative and sometimes humorous way. Rosenstrasse 38. ☎ 0711/237-7770. www.zauberlehrling.de. 9 units. Doubles 145€–280€. AE, MC, V.

★★ **Hotel am Schlossgarten** CITY CENTER Stuttgart's finest full-service hotel features elegant rooms and suites with upscale bathrooms and boasts one of the city's top restaurants. Schillerstrasse 23. ☎ 0711/202-6888. www.hotelschlossgarten.com. 116 units. Doubles 275€–305€. AE, DC, MC, V.

> *If you have the budget for it, Hotel am Schloss-garten is hard to beat.*

★★★ **Wielandshöhe** OUTSIDE CITY CENTER *INTERNATIONAL* Vincent Klink, one of Germany's top chefs, prepares imaginative and mouth-watering dishes using only organic ingredients. The set menus change every month based on what's in season. Alte Weinsteige 71 (about 4.5km/2½ miles southwest of city center). ☎ 0711/640-8848. www.wielandshoehe. de. Set menus 74€–98€. AE, DC, MC, V. Lunch & dinner Wed–Sat.

Heidelberg, Stuttgart & the Swabian Alb Fast Facts

> Germany has an excellent rail network, as these people at Stuttgart's Central Station can attest.

Accommodations Booking Services

Call **Hotel Reservation Service** (☎ 0870/243-0003; www.hrs.de) from anywhere in Germany. Tourist information centers in the major train stations and airports offer on-the-spot booking services for hotel rooms and B&Bs.

ATMs

All the major cities and towns in this region—Heidelberg, Stuttgart, Speyer, Ulm, and Tübingen—have banks and train stations with ATMs (*Geldautomaten*).

Dentists & Doctors

If you have a mild medical issue or dental problems while traveling in Germany, most hotels will be able to refer you to a local doctor (*Arzt*) or dentist (*Zahnarzt*) who speaks English. You will be expected to provide proof of either permanent or travel insurance (such as an EHIC card in the case of most residents of Europe), or you will be required to pay for treatment. In the event of minor injuries that require speedy treatment, go to the *Notaufnahme* (emergency) department of the nearest *Krankenhaus* (hospital). When the injuries are serious or life-threatening, call the doctor/ambulance emergency number (see "Emergencies," below).

Emergencies

To call the police (*Polizei*), dial ☎ **110.** To report a fire or to summon an emergency doctor (*Notarzt*) or an ambulance (*Krankenwagen*), dial ☎ **112.**

Getting There

The nearest international airport is **Frankfurt** (p. 494), 88km (55 miles) north of Heidelberg and 230 km (143 miles) northwest of Stuttgart. The Frankfurt airport also has a train station, so you can easily connect to Heidelberg (1 hr.), Stuttgart (1 hr. 40 min.), and other towns covered in this chapter. For train schedules and information, call **Deutsche Bahn** (German Railways; ☎ 11861; www.bahn.de). Stuttgart has a smaller, regional airport, **Flughafen Stuttgart** (☎ 01805/948-444; www.flughafen-stuttgart. de), which is served by Lufthansa and connecting flights of other European carriers.

Getting Around

Germany is served by an excellent rail network and a car isn't necessary if you are sticking to the towns and cities covered in this chapter. If, however, you want to tour the Swabian Alb or the Neckar Valley, you'll need a car. A detailed regional road map (Hallweg or Michelin) is essential; you can buy one at Frankfurt airport bookshops and most newsstands. Renting a car in Germany is fairly easy, but it's generally better price-wise if you book the car before your arrival. Most of the major international car-rental agencies have offices at Frankfurt Airport, including **Avis** (☎ 800/331-1212; www.avis.com), **Budget** (☎ 800/527-0700; www.budget.com), and **Hertz** (☎ 800/654-3001; www.hertz.com). You can also arrange to rent a car through **Rail Europe** (☎ 888/382-7245; www.raileurope.com).

Internet Access

Almost all hotels in Germany, even in smaller towns, now offer Wi-Fi and/or broadband. If yours does not, ask your concierge if there is an Internet cafe in the vicinity.

Pharmacies

At a German pharmacy, called an *Apotheke,* the trained staff can recommend over-the-counter medications for many common ailments. For cosmetics or toiletries, go to a *Drogerie.* German pharmacies are open regular business hours. They take turns staying open nights, on Sunday, and on holidays, and each *Apotheke* posts a list of those that are open off-hours.

Police

To report a lost or stolen article, such as a wallet or passport, visit the local police (*Polizei*) in your location. To call the police from anywhere in Germany, dial ☎ **110.**

Post Office

You'll recognize branches of **Deutsche Post** (☎ 01802/3333; www.deutschepost.de) by their yellow sign with a black horn. Post offices are open Monday to Friday 8am–6pm, Saturday 8am–noon.

Safety

This area of Germany is completely safe for tourists, but use common sense and don't leave valuables in plain sight when you park your car on a city street or parking lot near a scenic area.

Taxis

If you need a taxi in Heidelberg, call **Taxi Hdi-ekt** (☎ 06221/739-090), or **Taxizentrale** ☎ 06621/181-021). For a taxi in Stuttgart, call **Lasten-Taxi** (☎ 0711/814-004) or **Taxi-Auto-Zentrale** (☎ 0711/553-980).

Telephones

Call ☎ 11837 for information and ☎ 11834 for international information. Heidelberg's area code is 06221; Stuttgart's is 0711. Dial the area code when calling a town number from outside the town; you don't need to dial t when calling a town number from inside the town. There are public phones in many places—some accept coins and some take phone cards, available at post offices and newsstands.

Toilets

In some places you will find clean public toilets (*Toilette* in German; pronounced twah-*leh*-teh), many of them automatic and wheelchair-accessible; you need a .50€ coin to unlock the door. More convenient and widespread are toilets in cafes, bars, restaurants, hotels, malls, and some stores and at highway services and rest areas. Even if you are not obliged to pay, it is customary to leave the attendant .50€.

Tours

If you want to take a boat trip on the Neckar River, **Rhein-Neckar-Fahrgastschiffahrt** (☎ 06221/20181; www.rnf-schifffahrt.de) offers daily guided boat tours (commentary in German and English) between Heidelberg and Neckarsteinach from April through October. The round-trip tour lasts about 3 hours and costs 10€; boats depart from the landing stage between the Theodor-Heuss-Brücke (bridge) and the Alte Brücke (Old Bridge). There's also a shorter, 40-minute trip that departs daily at 4pm.

Visitor Information

The regional tourist board for southwestern Germany is **Tourismus-Marketing Baden-Württemberg,** Esslinger Strasse 8, 70181 Stuttgart (☎ 0711/238-580; www.tourismus-bw.de). In addition to those provided with the individual town listings, other key tourist offices are as follows: **HEIDELBERG** Willy-Brandt-Plaza 1 (outside the train station); ☎ 06221/19433; www.cvb-heidelberg.de; Mon–Sat 9am–7pm (6pm Nov–Mar), Sun (Apr–Oct only) 10am–6pm. **STUTTGART** Königstrasse 1A; ☎ 0711/22280; www.stuttgart-tourist.de; Mon–Fri 9am–8pm, Sat 9am–6pm, Sun 11am–6pm.

10
Frankfurt, the Rhineland & the Ruhr

The Best of Frankfurt, the Rhineland & the Ruhr in 3 Days

The distances between key points in this central part of western Germany are relatively short, and the Autobahn (highway) network is among Germany's best, so getting to and fro is a snap. However, with two large cities (Frankfurt and Cologne), one small city (Aachen), and two small towns (Limburg and Monschau) on the to-do list, there's not much spare time for hanging around.

> PREVIOUS PAGE *Frankfurt's financial district is a gleaming, modern center of business and commerce.*
THIS PAGE *The towering Kölner Dom dominates the skyline in Cologne.*

START Frankfurt is 545km (339 miles) southwest of Berlin on A115, A9, and A4; and 390km (242 miles) northwest of Munich on A9 and A3. TRIP LENGTH 307km (191 miles).

❶ ★ **Frankfurt.** Assuming you arrive in Frankfurt on the morning of Day 1, spend a few hours in the nearby city. Good options include admiring the half-timber houses in the **Römerberg,** Frankfurt's historic core, or visiting the **Städel Museum,** which showcases a wide range of paintings by European masters. ☺ At least a half-day. For information on Frankfurt, including hotel and restaurant recommendations, see p. 474.

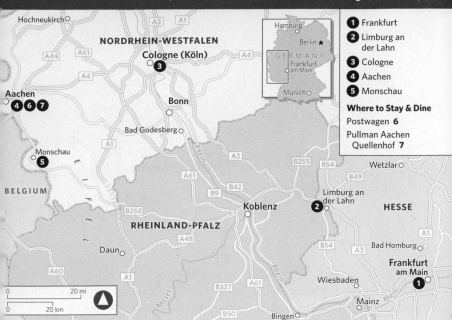

From Frankfurt, take A648 and A66 west to the intersection with A3, and go north on A3 to Limburg an der Lahn (74km/46 miles).

2 ★ Limburg an der Lahn. Limburg stands on the Lahn River, a tributary of the Rhine, just off Autobahn A3. It's a short diversion from the highway on the way to Cologne, and a worthwhile one to make. The town (pop. 34,000) holds one of Germany's finest cathedrals, the 13th-century, many-colored, twin-towered ★★ **Limburger Dom** (☎ 06431/929-983; www. dom.bistumlimburg.de), a well-nigh perfect example of late Romanesque architectural style. The cathedral is sited on a high hill close to Limburger Schloss (Limburg Palace), from the same period. This is the literal high point of Limburg's Altstadt (Old Town), which retains to a considerable degree the look of a medieval town, with an astounding array of intact timber-frame buildings. One of these is Germany's oldest such freestanding house, a Gothic creation from 1289 (at Römer 2-4-6). ⏱ 2 hr. Tourist information: Hospitalstrasse 2; www.limburg.de.

Continue north on A3 to Cologne (Köln; 120km/75 miles). Try to drive this at the end of your first day and spend the night in Cologne, in order to have as much time there the next day as possible.

3 ★★ Cologne. Given the option of spending time in either Frankfurt or Cologne, but not both, Cologne is the better bet for those who like after-dark action. In terms of cultural attractions like museums and other sightseeing possibilities, the cities are about equal. ⏱ 1 day. For information on Cologne, including hotel and restaurant recommendations, see p. 482.

Spend another night in Cologne, or take A4 west to Aachen (79km/49 miles) and spend the night there.

4 ★ Aachen. A spa town squeezed up against Germany's borders with the Netherlands and Belgium, Aachen (pop. 260,000) was known by the end of the 17th century as the "Spa of Kings," due to all the European bluebloods who poured in to take the waters. Further back, it

Traveling by Train

For those riding the rails, there are frequent high-speed ICE (InterCity-Express) trains going between Frankfurt and Limburg (30 min.), Limburg and Cologne (45 min.), and Cologne and Aachen (36 min.). From Aachen to Monschau by bus takes around 1 hour.

> *Aachen's 14th-century Rathaus was built on the original site of Charlemagne's palace.*

was capital of the Franks under Charlemagne in the 8th and 9th centuries (see "Charlemagne"). Aachen today has a breezy contemporary style,

Carnival in Cologne

The Germans are a dull, earnest, stolid lot, whose sense of humor is surgically removed at birth, right? Try maintaining that fiction after a visit to Cologne's annual Karneval (Carnival). The good burghers dress up in colorfully outlandish costumes, attend street parades and stage shows, imbibe non-trivial amounts of Kölsch beer, and in general go totally loopy during the "crazy days" between Thursday's *Weiberfastnacht* (Women's Carnival Day) and *Rosenmontag* (Rose Monday, or Shrove Monday), when every one of Cologne's one million inhabitants takes to the streets. The cry of *Kölle Alaaf!* (Cologne Lives!) resounds through the city and, by way of television, across the land. By Ash Wednesday, which begins the fasting season of Lent in the 40 days preceding Easter, it's all over for another year. Düsseldorf, Mainz, and Bonn are among other Rhineland cities with their own vibrant carnival traditions.

culturally enlivened by its tri-country location. The ★★ **Aachener Dom** (Aachen Cathedral), also known as the Kaiserdom (Imperial Cathedral), Klosterplatz (☎ 0241/4770-9127; www.aachendom.de), dates from 800. It contains Charlemagne's throne, his Parian marble sarcophagus, and a treasury of ecclesiastical objects once belonging to the many Holy Roman emperors who were crowned here from 936 to 1531.

The magnificent 14th-century ★ **Rathaus** (Town Hall; Markt) was built on the original site of Charlemagne's palace, part of which can be seen in the Granusturm, a tower at the east side of the hall. The richly decorated facade is adorned with statues of 50 German rulers, 31 of them crowned in Aachen. In the center are reliefs of Charlemagne and Pope Leo III. On the second floor the grand Imperial Hall, where coronation banquets took place, contains exact replicas of the Holy Roman Empire's crown jewels. ⏱ 2 hr.

From Aachen, take L233 and B258 south through the Naturpark Hohes Venn-Eifel (p. 464, ❺)—you'll briefly cross into and out of Belgium on this scenic road—to Monschau (34km/21 miles).

> *Locals and visitors gather daily among the timber-frame buildings in Monschau's Marktplatz.*

5 ★★ **Monschau.** Don't pass up the chance to visit this supremely picturesque small town (pop. 13,000). Monschau's old timber-frame, slate-roofed buildings and cobblestoned streets are clustered along the lower slopes of a deep gorge on the upper Rur River, close to the Belgian border. Burg Monschau, a partly ruined 13th-century castle that now hosts a youth hostel and an outdoor performance venue, affords grand views of the town. Housed in the fine patrician Rotes Haus (Red House, 1752), the **Scheibler-Museum,** Laufenstrasse 10 (☎ 02472/5071; admission 2.50€ adults, 1.50€ students), tells the tale of Monschau's history as a wealthy cloth town. ⏱ 2 hr.

Charlemagne

Aachen was for a time a city of power and importance. It was the capital of King of the Franks Karl der Grosse (Charles the Great, or Charlemagne; 742–814), who conquered a vast empire in western Europe. He did pretty much the usual stuff for justifying that royal moniker "the Great"— subjugating, annihilating, and fostering a bit of a cultural upswing, the Carolingian Renaissance, while his sword was down at the repair shop. In 800, Charlemagne was crowned emperor of the Romans by the pope, in a doomed effort to re-create the centuries-dead Roman Empire in the west.

Where to Stay & Dine

Postwagen AACHEN *CONTINENTAL* Perched seemingly precariously on a corner of the Rathaus (Town Hall), this 17th-century setting is worth visiting even if you're not hungry. Main-menu dishes are served from the kitchen of the equally atmospheric Ratskeller restaurant. Markt 40. ☎ 0241/35001. Entrees 10€–21€. AE, DC, MC, V. Bus: 4.

★★ **Pullman Aachen Quellenhof** AACHEN This elegant hotel (with spa) blends antique and conservatively modern decor in both the public and the private rooms. The brasserie serves regional cuisine. Monheimsallee 52. ☎ 0241/91320. www.accorhotels.com. 185 units. Doubles 190€–365€. AE, DC, MC, V. Bus: 3A, 3B, 13A, 13B, or 57.

The Best of Frankfurt, the Rhineland & the Ruhr in 1 Week

With a week at your disposal you can see a great deal of the Rhineland and the Ruhr. Still, you'll have to make some choices, since many of the star attractions are substantial cities in their own right. The aim here is to achieve a mix of urban and country experiences, while keeping at the back—or at the front—of your mind the region's tradition as a place of vineyards and wines.

> *The vineyards of the Mosel Valley are a big attraction to wine lovers.*

START **Frankfurt** is 545km (339 miles) southwest of Berlin on A115, A9, and A4; and 390km (242 miles) northwest of Munich on A9 and A3. TRIP LENGTH 1,031km (641 miles).

❶ ★ **Frankfurt.** ⏱ 1 day. For information on Frankfurt, including hotel and restaurant recommendations, see p. 474.

On Day 2, take A66 southwest from Frankfurt to Mainz (43km/27 miles).

❷ ★ **Mainz.** Standing at the intersection of the Rheingau and Rheinhessen wine regions, Mainz is naturally a wine town, fortified by a proud imperial history and a bustling, commercial present. ⏱ 3 hr. See p. 450, ❶.

> *The farmers' market on the Marktplatz in Mainz is a popular shopping venue.*

From Mainz, take A60, A67, and A672 south and east to Darmstadt (42km/26 miles).

❸ Darmstadt. It's worth stopping off briefly at this town to visit the Mathildenhöhe artists' colony, northeast of the center of town.

This gives Darmstadt (pop. 142,000) part of its justification for dubbing itself the "center of Jugendstil (Art Nouveau)." The colony was founded in 1899 by *Grossherzog* (grand duke) of Hessen Ernst Ludwig and encompasses houses designed by and for Jugendstil artists

Spa Side Trips from Frankfurt

An alternative, or complement, to touring in the city is to visit ★ **Wiesbaden** (pop. 278,000), a 45-minute ride on the *S-Bahn* train from Frankfurt. There's been a spa here since Roman times. Today, hotel spas are complemented by the traditional (on a Roman foundation) **Kaiser Friedrich Therme,** Langgasse 38–40 (☎ 0611/172-9660; pictured), and the modern **Thermalbad Aukammtal,** Leibnizstrasse 7 (☎ 0611/172-9880). Wiesbaden's **Kurhaus,** Kurhausplatz 1 (☎ 0611/172-9290), centered on a cupola-crowned hall and a casino, hosts concerts, plays, ballets, conferences, congresses, exhibitions, and trade shows.

Even closer to Frankfurt is **Bad Homburg** (pop. 52,000), just 20 minutes on the *S-Bahn* and still basking in the grandeur left over from turn-of-the-20th-century Europe. The spa facilities are in the **Kaiser-Wilhelms-Bad,** in the Kurpark (☎ 06172/178-178; www.kur-royal. de). The Kurpark's immaculately tended gardens are filled with brooks, ponds, arbors, and seasonal flowers.

and architects. It is dominated by the **Hochzeitsturm** (Wedding Tower, 1908), 48m (157 ft.) high, at Olbrichweg 13. ⏱ 1 hr.

From Darmstadt, backtrack to A67 and head south, then go west on B47 to Worms (45km/28 miles).

④ **Worms.** The town (pop. 82,000) in which the Diet of Worms in 1521 declared would-be reformer of the Catholic church Martin Luther a heretic and an outlaw—at the same time giving the English language one of its least delectable puns—makes a good starting point for touring the Deutsche Weinstrasse (German Wine Route; see p. 456). The Luther-bashing

diet (imperial assembly) took place in the 14th-century Chapel of St. Nicholas, inside Worms's majestic cathedral, the ★ **Dom St. Peter** (Lutherring 9; ☎ 06241/6151), built in 1181 and a fine example of the late Romanesque style. ⏱ 2 hr.

From Worms, take A61 south to Speyer (47km/29 miles), where you'll spend the night.

⑤ **Speyer.** The old imperial town is the location of one of Germany's finest cathedrals, the **Kaiserdom.** ⏱ 2 hr. For information on Speyer, including hotel and restaurant recommendations, see p. 488.

Rhine & Mosel Wines

Of Germany's 13 designated wine regions, six—Ahr, Mittelrhein, Mosel, Nahe, Rheingau, and Rheinhessen—lie in the triangle formed by the Mittelrhein (Middle Rhine) from south of Bonn upstream to Worms, and along the Mosel River from Trier downstream to Koblenz. This traditional wine country, a classic scenery of imposing castle ruins, elegant spas, and old villages with church spires and timber-frame houses, is among the most charming parts of the country. Vineyards flourish on steep hillsides, protected from harsh winds by wooded neighboring hills. This is especially so along the Rhine, the Mosel, and their tributaries, where the grapes soak up warmth reflected off sunlit water.

The slow maturing of these grapes gives them their typical fresh, fruity acidity. Though the Ahr, Rheingau, and Rheinhessen regions produce quality *Spätburgunder* reds, and there are a few blush/rosé wines, most wines from these regions are whites, with special emphasis on clear, aromatic Rieslings and *Weissburgunder*s. Even Liebfraumilch, which in its cheap, mass produced guise had become an international *persona non grata* among wines, still has its admirers when produced by capable wineries under its original German name, *Liebfrauenmilch*. In fact, the local viticulture has many smaller producers that create excellent wines.

For more on Germany's wine regions, see our "Grape Guide" on p. 372.

The Bloody Huertgen

In September 1944, the advancing U.S. army drew close to the German frontier at Aachen and launched an attack into the Hürtgenwald (Huertgen Forest) south of the city. The German defenders had prepared a dense network of fortified positions in the large, trackless forest, backed up by artillery, mortars, and machine guns. During subsequent months one American division after another was fed into the Hürtgenwald mincing machine and chewed up. To exhausted troops assaulting a dug-in and determined foe in miserable weather, facing hidden mines and snipers at every step, and taking hundreds of casualties for the gain of a few trees, the battle took on the character of an unending nightmare. Not until February 1945 were they able to fight their way out of the forest to the clear ground beyond, at a cost of 32,000 killed, wounded (or otherwise disabled), and missing.

> *The ancient Roman city of Trier is Germany's oldest and also contains the country's oldest cathedral, Trierer Dom.*

From Speyer on Day 3, go west through the Naturpark Pfälzer Wald on B39 and B37 to Kaiserslautern, then northwest on B270 and B41 to Idar-Oberstein, and then west through the Naturpark Saar-Hunsrück on B422 and local roads to Trier. This is a scenic but perhaps tiring drive of 192km (119 miles), for which you should allow 3–4 hours.

6 ★★★ **Trier.** Use the afternoon when you arrive, and then the morning of Day 4, to visit as much as you can reasonably fit in of historic Trier, Germany's oldest city. ⏲ About 1 day total. For information on Trier, including hotel and restaurant recommendations, see p. 490.

On the afternoon of Day 4, follow the road (B53 and B59) that runs along the Mosel River to Koblenz (part of this road forms the Moselweinstrasse, or Mosel Wine Route), a distance of 182km (113 miles).

7 ★★ **Mosel Valley.** Notable stops in the valley are **Piesport** (p. 459, **11**), **Bernkastel-Kues** (p. 459, **12**), **Traben-Trarbach** (p. 460, **13**), and **Cochem** (p. 460, **14**). The day ends at **Koblenz** (p. 454, **7**). ⏲ Half-day.

Spend the night in Koblenz (see p. 455 for hotel and restaurant recommendations). Begin Day 5 on the riverside road (B9) along the Rhine to Bonn (64km/40 miles).

8 ★★ **Rhine Valley.** The scenic riverside route is easily its own reward, but if you have time, stop for a look around in **Remagen** (p. 454, **8**). ⏲ 2 hr.

9 **Bonn.** ⏲ 4 hr. See p. 454, **9**.

From Bonn, take B56 and B266 generally west through Euskirchen and into the Eifel at Mechernich, and then via Gemünd and Einruhr to Monschau, a total distance of 86km (53 miles).

10 ★ **Eifel.** The Eifel is a region of highlands between Aachen, Cologne, Koblenz, and Trier. A good spot to break the journey through this hilly, forested region is at Einruhr, a village on the shore of the Obersee lake. If you can spare

Hitler's Headquarters

Two once-secret locations in this region served Nazi dictator Adolf Hitler as headquarters during key events in World War II. Outside Wiesental, on the eastern edge of what is now the Naturpark Hoch-Taunus, was the Führerhauptquartier Adlerhorst (Eagle's Nest). From this disguised underground bunker complex, Hitler directed the Ardennes Offensive—the Battle of the Bulge—against the U.S. army in Belgium and Luxembourg in December 1944 and January 1945. The Führerhauptquartier Felsennest (Rocky Nest), at Rodert, outside the Eifel spa town of Bad Münstereifel, was where Hitler planned and launched the invasion of France in May 1940 and later planned the invasion of Britain, which was subsequently called off. Both complexes were destroyed after the war.

the time, step aboard an electric-powered tour boat operated by Rursee-Schifffahrt (☎ 02446/479; www.rurseeschifffahrt.de) for a leisurely cruise that seems a little like sailing through some remote wilderness. ⏲ 2 hr.

From Einruhr, continue on into Monschau, then take B258 and L233 north into Aachen (33km/21 miles), where you'll spend the night.

⑪ ★ **Aachen.** ⏲ 2 hr. See p. 441, ❹. For hotel and restaurant recommendations, see p. 443.

From Aachen on Day 6, take A544, A44, A61, A46, and A57, traveling generally northeast, to Düsseldorf (85km/53 miles).

⑫ ★ **Düsseldorf.** ⏲ 6 hr. See p. 468, ❶.

In the late afternoon, take A57 south from Düsseldorf to Cologne (Köln), a distance of just 38km (24 miles). This should give you time to experience Cologne's notable nightlife scene.

⑬ ★★ **Cologne.** Enjoy Cologne's nightlife, then explore the city's highlights in the morning. ⏲ Half-day. For information on Cologne, including hotel and restaurant recommendations, see p. 482.

At midday of Day 7, take A3 southeast from Cologne to Limburg an der Lahn (120km/75 miles).

> A cruise along the Rhine is a great way to take in the region's beauty.

⑭ ★ **Limburg an der Lahn.** ⏲ 2 hr. See p. 441, ❷.

From Limburg, take B274 southwest through the scenic gap between Naturpark Nassau and Naturpark Rhein-Taunus, to hit the Rhine at Lorch. Then, go south along the river on B42 (the Rheingauer-Riesling Route), to Assmannshausen, for a total distance of 65km (40 miles).

⑮ ★★ **Rheingau.** Assmannshausen is the starting point for a drive through the Rheingau wine district (p. 452, ❸). Go east on B42 along the north bank of the Rhine through a succession of wine villages including Rüdesheim, Oestrich, and Erbach. ⏲ 3 hr.

Continue east on B42 and A66, through Wiesbaden (see "Spa Side Trips from Frankfurt, p. 446), to Frankfurt (71km/44 miles from Assmannshausen).

Cologne Water

Sweet-smelling *Kölnisch Wasser—eau de cologne,* or simply cologne—was developed by Italian chemist and Cologne resident Giovanni Maria Farina in 1708. "I have discovered a scent that reminds me of a spring morning in Italy, of mountain narcissus, orange blossom just after the rain. It gives me great refreshment, strengthens my senses and imagination," wrote Farina in a letter to his brother. Launched in 1709, the scented water was employed to hide the stench of aristocrats who rarely bathed, and it proved an instant hit. This original cologne, based on a secret formula, is still sold at ★ **Johann Maria Farina,** Obenmarspforten 21 (☎ 0221/294-1709; www.farina1709.com). The smallest bottles (4 milliliters / ¼ U.S. fluid ounce) cost between 5€ and 50€.

Along the Rhine from Mainz to Bonn

Starting out near Frankfurt and finishing up near Cologne, this itinerary courses along the Rhine as it flows downstream through two emblematic German regions. On Day 1 you'll see Mainz and the Rheingau wine district, along the east-west stretch of the river between Wiesbaden and Bingen. On Days 2 and 3 you'll explore the Mittelrhein (Middle Rhine). Day 4 is devoted to Bonn. If your time is limited, you could easily skip a few stops along the way and complete this tour in 3 days. Speckled with historic castles (many of them in ruins) and wine villages, the route is both a trip down Germany's memory lane and an introduction to a buoyant part of the country.

> *The Benedictine Abbey of St. Hildegard (which produces and sells its own wine) sits above the charming town of Rüdesheim.*

START Mainz is 43km (27 miles) southwest of Frankfurt on A66. **TRIP LENGTH** 3 or 4 days and 197km (122 miles).

1 ★ **Mainz.** Pronounced *Mine*-ts, the city (pop. 198,000) lies on the west bank of the Rhine, at its confluence with the Main River. It was founded as Moguntiacum at this strategic spot by the Romans around 13 B.C. and housed a legionary fortress that was a key part of the empire's Rhine defenses. There's an annual wine festival the first week in August and the first week in September. In the Altstadt (Old Town), stands the 11th-century ★★ **Mainzer Dom** (Mainz Cathedral; Marktplatz; ☎ 06131/253-344; www.bistummainz.de), a veritable red-sandstone mountain, dedicated to St. Martin of Tours. Close to the Dom, the **Stephanskirche** (Church of St. Stephen) has stained-glass windows (1978)

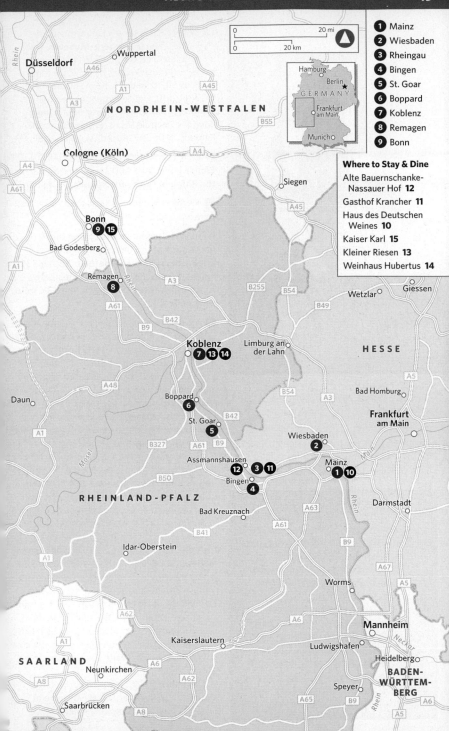

1	Mainz
2	Wiesbaden
3	Rheingau
4	Bingen
5	St. Goar
6	Boppard
7	Koblenz
8	Remagen
9	Bonn

Where to Stay & Dine

Alte Bauernschanke-
Nassauer Hof **12**

Gasthof Krancher **11**

Haus des Deutschen
Weines **10**

Kaiser Karl **15**

Kleiner Riesen **13**

Weinhaus Hubertus **14**

> The 11th-century Mainzer Dom is the most important Catholic cathedral in the country after Cologne's.

by Marc Chagall. For the city's Roman history, visit the ★ **Landesmuseum Mainz** (Mainz Regional Museum), Grosse Bleiche 49–51

The Lorelei

If truth be told, there's not much to distinguish the Loreleyfelsen (Lorelei Rock) from many another rock along the Rhine. It's 120m (394 ft.) high and rises clifflike out of the water, forming a granite promontory that considerably narrows the river at a bend just upstream from St. Goarshausen. It's a pretty enough scene, but it's likely the legend of the Lorelei that draws the crowds, who jostle both here and across the river for the best view. It's said that the siren song of this *Rheintochter* (Rhine Maiden), or river nymph, lures unwitting sailors into the rock and to their deaths in the deep, dark, swirling waters.

(☎ 06131/28570; www.landesmuseum-mainz.de). The **Gutenberg-Museum,** Liebfrauenplatz 5 (☎ 06131/1226-4044; www.gutenbergmuseum.de), displays the innovations of Mainz native Johannes Gutenberg (1398–1468), who invented the mechanical printing press. ⏱ 4 hr. Tourist information: Touristik Zentrale Mainz, Brückenturm am Rathaus. ☎ 06131/286-210. www.touristik-mainz.de.

From Mainz, take A60 and then A643 across the Rhine to Wiesbaden (21km/13 miles).

2 ★★ **Wiesbaden.** ⏱ 3 hr. See "Spa Side Trips from Frankfurt," p. 446.

From Wiesbaden, go west along the north bank of the Rhine, through the Rheingau region, to Rüdesheim (50km/31 miles). Spend the night here or in nearby Assmannshausen (another 5.5km/3½ miles west on A42).

3 ★★ **Rheingau.** Between the Taunus Mountains and the Rhine lies one of Germany's main wine-producing regions, the Rheingau. Nearly every town and village from Wiesbaden west to Assmannshausen is associated with wine, and vineyards crowd the sunny, south-facing slopes. Take the riverside road through Walluf, Eltville, and Erbach, where you can divert inland to the Hessian State Winery at ★ **Kloster Eberbach,** a Cistercian monastery founded in 1136. Scenes from the 1986 movie *The Name of the Rose* were filmed here. Eberbach, in 1712, first used the classification *Kabinett* to denote quality in German wines. Return to the river at Hattenheim and continue through Oestrich and Winkel. Divert inland at Winkel to Johannisberg on K631 (Schillerstrasse), to where an 18th-century baroque palace, **Schloss Johannisberg** (☎ 06722/70090; www.schloss-johannisberg.de; free admission; wine tastings Mon–Fri 10am–1pm and 2–6pm, Sat–Sun 11am–5pm), reached along Schlossallee from the village's southern edge, stands proudly above its retinue of vineyards. It's worth getting out for a stroll around the palace, which now houses a restaurant, a wine shop, and wine cellars.

Continue through Johannisberg village, and return to the riverside at Geisenheim on L3272, before going west on B42 to

★ **Rüdesheim.** With its old courtyards and winding alleyways lined with timber-frame houses, Rüdesheim is the epitome of a Rhine wine town. Riesling is produced here, as well as *Sekt* (sparkling wine) and brandy. During Rüdesheim's annual wine festival in August, the old taverns on Drosselgasse are crowded with visitors. The history of Rheingau wines from Roman times to the present is outlined at the **Rheingauer Weinmuseum** (Rheingau Wine Museum), Rheinstrasse 2 (☎ 06722/2348; www.rheingauer-weinmuseum.de; admission 5€ adults, 3€ kids 6–18; Mar–Oct daily 10am–6pm), housed in a 12th-century castle, the Brömserburg. On a hill between Rüdesheim and Assmannshausen—reached by cable car from either town—is the **Niederwalddenkmal,** a colossal statue of Germania (a mythical female figure representing Germany) erected in 1883 as a monument to German unification.

Go west into ★ **Assmannshausen,** known for its Burgundy-style wine. The old village's timber-frame houses and vineyards perch on steep hillsides, which afford fine views of the Rhine. From here, loop back eastward along the river to Rüdesheim. Along the way, you pass the ruined 13th-century castle **Burg Ehrenfels.** ⏱ 4 hr.

Cross over the Rhine on the small car ferry from Rüdesheim to Bingen.

④ **Bingen.** Just offshore from this town (pop. 26,000) is a tiny island on which stands the **Mäuseturm** (Mouse Tower). According to medieval legend, the greedy Bishop Hatto of Mainz was devoured by hungry mice there. ⏱ 1 hr.

From Bingen, go north on riverside B9 to St. Goar (30km/19 miles).

⑤ ★ **St. Goar.** Just before you enter this small town (pop. 3,000), you come to a busy viewing-point looking across the river to the famous ★ **Loreleyfelsen** (Lorelei Rock; see "The Lorelei"). You can cross over on the ferry to neighboring St. Goarshausen for a close-up view of the rock. In addition, St. Goar holds the ruins of massive 13th-century ★★ **Burg Rheinfels** (☎ 06741/7753), the largest castle along the Rhine Valley. ⏱ 2 hr.

> *Burg Rheinfels, the largest castle in the Rhine Valley, was partially destroyed by French invaders in 1797.*

> In Bonn, Beethoven's personal possessions, musical instruments, and manuscripts are on display at Beethoven-Haus, where the great composer was born in 1770.

From St. Goar, stay on B9 along the riverbank, northwest to Boppard (14km/9 miles).

❻ Boppard. Sited at a sweeping bend in the river, Boppard (pop. 16,000) seems to encapsulate the low-key virtues of the scenic stretch of the Rhine between Bingen and Bonn. It's a popular tourism center in summer, set in a landscape of vineyards, forests, and farms and possessing timber-frame houses and a graceful late-Romanesque church, St.-Severus-Kirche (1236). ⏱1 hr.

Continue on B9 along the riverbank, north to Koblenz (21km/13 miles), where you can spend your second night.

❼ ★ Koblenz. Surrounded by vine-covered hills dotted with castles and fortresses, Koblenz (pop. 107,000) has stood at the confluence of the Rhine and Mosel rivers since the Roman general Drusus established a fort at strategic Ad Confluentes in 8 B.C. The point where the two rivers meet, the Deutsches Eck (German Corner), is marked by a colossal equestrian statue of Kaiser Wilhelm I. At the edge of the Altstadt (Old Town), near the

Deutsches Eck, is Koblenz's oldest church, the **Kastorkirche** (St. Castor's), originally built in 836, though in its present form it dates mostly from the 12th century. Across the Rhine from Koblenz stands a powerful fortress, 19th-century ★ **Festung Ehrenbreitstein** (☎ 0261/974-2441; www.burgen-rlp.de), which can be reached by chairlift between April and October. The fortress, constructed on a rock, towers 120m (394 ft.) above the Rhine. Koblenz hosts the **Mittelrhein Museum,** Florinsmarkt 15–17 (☎ 0261/129-2520; www.mittelrhein-museum.de; admission 2.50€, free for students), which contains art related to the Middle Rhine. ⏱4 hr. Tourist information: Bahnhofplatz 17. ☎ 0261/303-8849. www.koblenz-touristik.de.

From Koblenz, stay on B9 along the riverbank, northwest to Remagen (40km/25 miles).

❽ Remagen. This handsome river resort town (pop. 16,000) has a military distinction that goes beyond its founding as a Roman fortification. On March 7, 1945, during the closing weeks of World War II in Europe, soldiers from the U.S. 9th Armored Division captured the damaged but still standing Ludendorff railway bridge across the Rhine. This unexpected coup allowed the Allies to pour troops across and establish a bridgehead on the river's east bank. Four German officers were executed for permitting the bridge to be taken. The bridge subsequently collapsed and was never rebuilt. Its two standing towers now house the **Friedensmuseum Brücke von Remagen** (Bridge at Remagen Peace Museum; ☎ 02642/20159; www.bruecke-remagen.de; admission 3.50€ adults; 1€ kids 6–18; early Mar–Apr and first 2 weeks Nov daily 10am–5pm; May–Oct daily 10am–6pm). ⏱2 hr.

Continue along the riverbank on A9 north to Bonn (21km/13 miles), where you can spend your third night.

❾ ★ Bonn. A sleepy provincial town best known for being the birthplace of composer Ludwig van Beethoven (1770–1827), Bonn (pop. 320,000) had "greatness" thrust upon it in 1949, when it was made capital of the old West Germany. That lasted until Berlin regained its place as the national capital in 1991, after Germany's reunification. Beethoven is (unsurprisingly) still a big deal in his home-town, as you can see in the ★ **Beethoven-Haus,** Bonngasse 18–26 (☎ 0228/981-750; www.beethoven-haus-bonn.de; admission 5€ adults; 4€ kids 6–18; Apr–Oct Mon–Sat 10am–6pm, Sun 11am–6pm; Nov–Mar Mon–Sat 10am–5pm, Sun 11am–5pm); the second-floor room where he was born is decorated with a simple marble bust of the great composer. Many of Beethoven's personal possessions are in the house, among them manuscripts and musical instruments that include his last piano, a custom-made instrument with a special sounding board to amplify sound for the hearing-impaired composer.

Bonner Münster (Bonn Minster; ☎ 0228/985-880; www.bonner-muenster.de), a Romanesque basilica constructed between the 11th and 13th centuries, has five spires and is dedicated to two Roman soldiers, Cassius and Florentius, who were executed for being Christian. You can trace German history since 1945 at the **Haus der Geschichte der Bundesrepublik Deutschland** (House of the History of the Federal Republic of Germany), Willy-Brandt-Allee 14 (☎ 0228/91650; www.hdg.de; free admission; Tues–Sun 9am–7pm). The **Kunstmuseum Bonn** (Bonn Art Museum), Friedrich-Ebert-Allee 2 (☎ 0228/776-260; www.kunstmuseum-bonn.de; admission 7€ adults, 3.50€ kids 6–18; Tues and Thurs–Sun 11am–6pm, Wed 11am–9pm) and has a collection of works by expressionist artist August Macke (1887–1914), whose promising career was cut tragically short when he was killed in action in World War I. ⏱ 1 day. Tourist information: Windeckstrasse 1 (at Münsterplatz). ☎ 0228/775-000. www.bonn.de.

Where to Stay & Dine

★★ **Alte Bauernschanke-Nassauer Hof**
ASSMANNSHAUSEN The wine-grower owners have turned two of the oldest mansions in town into this fine hotel and restaurant. Rooms are beautifully furnished in a refined contemporary style. Niederwaldstrasse 23. ☎ 06722/49990. www.altebauernschaenke.de. 53 units. Doubles 85€–115€ w/breakfast. AE, MC, V.

★ **Gasthof Krancher** RÜDESHEIM
In this family-run hotel next to the Kranchers' own vineyards, everything is decorated in a regional motif. Rooms are a bit cramped but reasonably comfortable, and the restaurant serves Rhineland specialties. Eibinger-Oberstrasse 4. ☎ 06722/2762. www.gasthof-krancher.de. 62 units. Doubles 56€–76€ w/breakfast. MC, V.

★★ **Haus des Deutschen Weines** MAINZ GERMAN The Rhineland has no lack of traditional old eateries that serve mostly local wines, so a place that serves a light, modern variation in a contemporary setting is something of a welcome change. Gutenbergplatz 3–5. ☎ 06131/221-300. www.hdw-gaststaetten.de. Entrees 8€–17€. AE, MC, V. Lunch & dinner daily. Tram: 50, 51, or 52.

★★ **Kaiser Karl** BONN
A town house from 1905 has been converted into this stylish four-story hotel. The decor includes lacquered Japanese screens, English antiques, Oriental carpets, Venetian mirrors, and Edwardian potted palms. Vorgebirgsstrasse 56. ☎ 0228/985-570. www.kaiser-karl-hotel-bonn.de. 42 units. Doubles 140€–420€. AE, DC, MC, V. *U-Bahn:* Bonn West.

★ **Kleiner Riesen** KOBLENZ
The "Little Giant," a large, modern, informal chalet, sits away from town traffic, directly on the banks of the Rhine, its rooms close enough to afford views of passing boats. Kaiserin-Augusta-Anlagen 18. ☎ 0261/303-460. www.hotel-kleinerriesen.de. 28 units. Double 88€ w/breakfast. AE, DC, MC, V. Bus: 571 or 573.

Weinhaus Hubertus KOBLENZ GERMAN
The oldest wine tavern in town, dating from 1696, the Hubertus looks like a timbered country inn and offers German wines accompanied by homemade dishes—soups, sandwiches, and light platters—to complement the wines. Florinsmarkt 6. ☎ 0261/31177. www.weinhaus-hubertus.de. Entrees 8€–15€. MC, V. Dinner Wed–Mon. Bus: 1.

The Rhineland & Mosel Valley for Wine Lovers

The valleys of the Rhine and Mosel rivers comprise one of Europe's classic wine regions, with a tradition that dates back to Roman times. This is a land of wine towns and villages, castles (many in ruins), vineyards, old inns, and wine taverns serving hearty Rhineland-Palatinate specialties like *Sauerbraten* (beef marinated in wine vinegar).

> *Thanks to its central location on the Mosel, Traben-Trarbach has become the wine capital of the Mosel Valley.*

START Bockenheim an der Weinstrasse is 38km (24 miles) northwest of Mannheim on A650, A61, A6, and B271. **TRIP LENGTH** 525km (326 miles) and 4 days.

❶ Bockenheim an der Weinstrasse. At this village, you enter the Deutsche Weinstrasse (German Wine Route), a scenic route that runs south for almost 80km (50 miles) to Schweigen-Rechtenbach **❽** on the French border. ⏱ 1 hr.

From Bockenheim, take B271 south through Grünstadt to Bad Dürkheim (18km/11 miles).

❷ ★ **Bad Dürkheim.** In this spa town (pop. 19,000) stands the **Dürkheimer Riesenfass** (Dürkheim's Giant Barrel, 1934), Sankt-Michaels-Allee 1 (☎ 06322/2143; www. duerkheimer-fass.de). It's said to be the world's largest wine barrel, capable of holding 1.7 million liters (449,000 U.S. gallons), though it was never filled. Today it's an

1 Bockenheim
2 Bad Dürkheim
3 Wachenheim
4 Deidesheim
5 Neustadt-an-der-Weinstrasse

6 Annweiler am Trifels
7 Klingenmünster
8 Schweigen-Rechtenbach
9 Saarbrücken

10 Trier
11 Piesport
12 Bernkastel-Kues
13 Traben-Trarbach
14 Cochem
15 Burg Eltz

Where to Stay & Dine
Alte Thorschenke 21
Beim Weinbauer 21
Deidesheimer Hof 16
Hotel Zur Post 19
Jugendstilhotel Bellevue 20
Schweigener Hof 18
St. Martiner Castell 17

> *Bad Dürkheim's wine festival is one of the most popular in Germany.*

atmospheric restaurant. Dürkheim's annual Wurstmarkt (Sausage Market) attracts 600,000 visitors and takes place on the second and third weekends in September; despite its name, it's a wine festival. ⏱ 1 hr.

From Bad Dürkheim, a drive of 5km (3 miles) south on B271 leads to Wachenheim.

❸ **Wachenheim.** The small town (pop. 5,000) is overlooked by a ruined 12th-century castle, the **Wachtenburg,** that's a focal point of Wachenheim's annual Burg- und Weinfest (Castle and Wine Festival; on two consecutive weekends in June). ⏱ 1 hr.

Continue south on B271 to Deidesheim (3.5km/2¼ miles).

❹ ★ **Deidesheim.** Some of the German Wine Route's most engaging timber-frame buildings are found here on the main square, Marktplatz. A good choice for wine tasting in the town (pop. 4,000) is **Weingut Geheimer Rat von Dr. Bassermann-Jordan,** Kirchgasse 10 (☎ 06326/6006; www.bassermann-jordan.de), dating from 1718. ⏱ 1 hr.

Continue south on B271 to Neustadt-an-der-Weinstrasse (9km/5½ miles).

❺ **Neustadt-an-der-Weinstrasse.** The largest town (pop. 54,000) on the German Wine Route lies at the foot of the Haardt hills and has 2,000 hectares (5,000 acres)

of vineyards lying within the town limits. In the Altstadt (Old Town) are narrow, crooked streets, taverns, and wine shops. For wine tastings, visit **Weingut Probsthof,** Probstgasse 7 (☎ 06321/6315).

In Hambach, 5km (3 miles) south on L512, visit the historic castle ★ **Hambacher Schloss** (☎ 06321/30881; www.hambacher-schloss.de; admission 4.50€). The castle has been dubbed the "Cradle of German Democracy" for its role in the 1832 democracy movement. ⏱ 1 hr.

Another 20km (12 miles) south on L512, through a succession of pretty villages and small towns—Diedesfeld, Maikammer, Edenkoben, Rhodt unter Rietburg, Gleisweiler, and Frankweiler—leads to Siebeldingen. From Siebeldingen, a diversion of 9km (5½ miles) west along B10 leads to Annweiler am Trifels. If you'd sooner save a couple of hours by skipping the diversion and staying on the Wine Route, simply go south on L508 from Siebeldingen to Klingenmünster (❼), a distance of 11km (7 miles).

❻ ★ **Annweiler am Trifels.** Set among forested hills, this town (pop. 7,000) is the site of 11th-century ★ **Reichsburg Trifels** (☎ 06346/8470; admission 4€), the Rhineland's most fabled castle. In 1193, England's King Richard the Lionheart was imprisoned here until he was bailed out with a huge ransom. ⏱ 2 hr.

Regain the German Wine Route by going southeast on B48 to Klingenmünster (13km/8 miles).

7 Klingenmünster. From here, a sign points the way to the ruins of **Burg Landeck** (Landeck Castle), reached after a stroll of 2km (1¼ miles) up through a chestnut-tree forest. At the end, the castle ruins command magnificent views. ⏱ 2 hr.

From Klingenmünster, the German Wine Route goes 5km (3 miles) south on B48 to Bad Bergzabern, an old spa town noted for its timber-frame houses. From here, drive south on B38 to Schweigen-Rechtenbach (5km/3 miles).

8 ★ Schweigen-Rechtenbach. In this village (pop. 1,500) at the French frontier stands a stone arch, the Deutsches Weintor (German Wine Gate, 1935), that marks the Wine Route's southern end. From a gallery on the gate, you can view miles of vineyards. Then, follow a didactic nature trail, the Weinlehrpfad, for 1.5km (1 mile), until you reach the hamlet of Sonnenberg, a short way from the border. ⏱ 2 hr.

From Schweigen-Rechtenbach on the afternoon of Day 2, backtrack to Bad Bergzabern, then go west on B427, B10, A8, and A6 to Saarbrücken (110km/68 miles).

9 ★ Saarbrücken. Saarland's state capital (pop. 178,000) doesn't have as much to commend it as this status might suggest, though it is a pleasant enough place. Its location on the French border, and periods of French ownership, have given it a certain Gallic twinkle as well as some fine restaurants. Stroll through the central zone around Rathausplatz and down to the Berliner Promenade along the Saar River, then cross over the river to view baroque **Saarbrücker Schloss** (Saarbrücken Palace, 1748). A visit to the **Historisches Museum Saar,** Schlossplatz 15 (☎ 0681/506-4510; www.historisches-museum.org; admission 5€ adults, 3€ kids 6–18; Tues-Wed, Fri, and Sun 10am–6pm, Thurs 10am–8pm, Sat noon–6pm), affords an insight into the region's tangled Franco-German history since 1870. ⏱ 4 hr. Tourist information: Rathaus St. Johann, Rathausplatz 1. ☎ 0681/938-090. www.saarbruecken.de.

> *A colorful mural in Traban-Trabach celebrates the city's reputation as a major wine destination.*

From Saarbrücken on Day 3, take A620 and A8 north through the forested Naturpark Saar-Hünsruck to intersection 5. Switch to B51 north, through Mettlach, home to ceramics maker Villeroy & Boch, then follow the Saar northward on B51 to the Mosel River at Konz and finally into Trier, for a total distance of 95km (59 miles).

10 ★★★ Trier. This ancient Roman city is the highlight of the Mosel Valley and the center of the Mosel wine trade. ⏱ 1 day. For information on Trier, including hotel and restaurant recommendations, see p. 490.

From Trier on Day 4, cross to the north (left) bank of the Mosel, and hug the riverbank on B53 all the way into Piesport (46km/29 miles).

11 Piesport. A pretty wine village tucked into a loop of the Mosel, Piesport (pop. 2,000) is best known for its Riesling wines and a steep, vineyard-speckled riverbank, the Moselloreley. ⏱ At least 1 hr.

Continue on B53 to Kues (16km/10 miles).

12 ★ Bernkastel-Kues. This wine town (pop. 7,000) straddles the Mosel. Colorful old timber-frame buildings—one of them, the Spitzhäuschen, dates from 1416—surround the Markt. In the center of the square stands the **St. Michaelsbrunnen** (St. Michael's Fountain, 1606), which flows with wine during the

> *Burg Eltz is a fully preserved medieval castle impressively perched on the Mosel between Trier and Koblenz.*

annual September wine festival. At nearby Wehlen (north on B50/B53 about 5km/3 miles), **Weingut S.A. Prüm,** Uferallee 25-26 (☎ 06531/3110; www.sapruem.com), a winery the Prüm family has operated since 1156, offers wine-tasting. ⊕ At least 1 hr.

Continue on B53 downriver to Traben-Trarbach (27km/17 miles).

⑬ ★★ Traben-Trarbach. The annual wine festival in July in this town (pop. 6,000) attracts visitors from all over Europe to the old wine cellars. Above Trarbach are the ruins of a 14th-century castle, the **Grevenburg.** ⊕ At least 1 hr. Tourist information: Am Bahnhof 5. ☎ 06541/83980. www.traben-trarbach.de.

From Traben-Trarbach, follow B53, and then B49 downriver, through Zell, to Cochem (55km/34 miles).

⑭ ★★ Cochem. Squeezed against the Mosel's left bank by a vineyard-covered hill, Cochem (pop. 5,000) is a stage for wine tastings and wine festivals. Its biggest attraction is **★ Reichsburg Cochem** (☎ 02671/255). The original 12th-century castle, destroyed in 1689, has been restored from the original ground plans, and its ramparts and turrets create a dramatic backdrop for the town. To reach the castle, follow steep Schlossstrasse

from the center of Cochem; the walk of 700m (½ mile) is worth it for the rewarding views of the town and the Mosel. ⊕ At least 1 hr.

From Cochem, take B49 and B416 downstream to Moselkern, where you turn inland, through Wierschem, to Burg Eltz (29km/18 miles).

⑮ ★ Burg Eltz. One of the few intact medieval castles in the region, stately Burg Eltz is set above the village of Moselkern, on the Mosel's left bank, and surrounded by woodlands. The original structure, built from the 12th century to the 17th century, has been preserved in all its glory—the romance of the Middle Ages really comes alive here—and the medieval furnishings include old paintings and tapestries. A treasury contains works by goldsmiths and silversmiths, armor, weapons, and other objects acquired by the family over the centuries.

Unspoiled Beilstein

At Ellenz, between Traben-Trarbach and Cochem, a tiny vehicle-carrying ferry shuttles back and forth across the Mosel to Beilstein on the right bank. This idyllic medieval wine village has an unusual Markt (market square) hewn into the rocky hillside. Above the town stand the ruins of a 12th-century castle, Burg Metternich.

🕐 1 hr. ☎ 02672/950-500. www.burg-cochem. de. Admission 5€ adults, 3€ kids 6–17, 14.50€ families. Mid-Mar to Oct daily 9am–5pm; first 2 weeks Nov daily 10am–3pm; mid-Nov to late Dec daily 11am–1pm; Christmas and New Year 10am–3pm; early Jan to mid-Mar Wed and Sat–Sun 11am–1pm.

From Burg Eltz, return to the Mosel at Hatzenport and follow the river downstream on B416 all the way into Koblenz (p. 454, ❼), a total of 39km (24 miles).

Wine-Tasting

Be sure to take some time out for a spot of wine-tasting as you go along the river (not if you are driving, of course). Just before Cochem, at the riverside village of Ediger-Eller, the winery **Weingut Schlosskellerei Freiherr von Landenberg,** Moselweinstrasse 60 (☎ 02675/277; www.mosel-weinproben.de), located in a 5-centuries-old cellar, is worth visiting.

Where to Stay & Dine

★ **Alte Thorschenke** COCHEM
Atmosphere is guaranteed in an inn that traces its origins back to 1332. Wines served in the hunting-themed German restaurant come from the hotel's own winery. Brückenstrasse 3. ☎ 02671/7059. www.castle-thorschenke.com. 35 units. Doubles 89€–130€ w/breakfast. AE, DC, MC, V.

★ **Beim Weinbauer** COCHEM
The oldest building in Cochem, a 16th-century affair ornamented with both a step gable and a bell gable, has plain guest rooms and small apartments, a traditional restaurant, and a program of wine-tasting. Mosel Promenade 11–12. ☎ 02671/7448. www.beim-weinbauer.de. 8 units. Doubles 60€–80€ w/breakfast. AE, MC, V.

★★ **Deidesheimer Hof** DEIDESHEIM
At this graceful and central hotel, housed in a medieval building, are two fine restaurants, the sophisticated Schwarzer Hahn and the artfully rustic St. Urban. Am Marktplatz 1. ☎ 06326/96870. www.deidesheimerhof.de. 31 units. Doubles 125€–255€. AE, DC, MC, V.

★ **Hotel Zur Post** BERNKASTEL-KUES
Modest yet authentic, this hotel along the river was founded in 1827 as an inn on the Mosel Valley mail route. Regional dishes are served in the bright, timber-beamed restaurant. Gestade 17. ☎ 06531/96700. www.hotel-zur-post-bernkastel.com. 42 units. Doubles 90€–110€ w/breakfast. DC, MC, V.

★★ **Jugendstilhotel Bellevue** TRABEN-TRAR-BACH An Art Nouveau mansion from 1903 facing the tour-boat dock houses one of the Mosel Valley's finest hotels, and its elegant Continental restaurant Clauss-Feiss. An der Mosel 11. ☎ 06541/7030. www.bellevue-hotel.de. 60 units. Doubles 135€–170€ w/breakfast. AE, DC, MC, V.

★ **Schweigener Hof** SCHWEIGEN-RECHTENBACH
This family-run lodging on the eastern edge of the village has contemporary style, vineyard views, and a distinctive take on a wellness theme—"WellVINess"—that combines health-enhancing treatments with wine tastings. Traditional Franco-German Alsace cuisine is served in the restaurant. Hauptstrasse 2. ☎ 06342/9250. www.schweigener-hof.com. 35 units. Doubles 55€–99€ w/breakfast. AE, MC, V.

★ **St. Martiner Castell** ST. MARTIN
An old house in this pretty village just west of Maikammer (and about 9km/5½ miles south of Neustadt an der Weinstrasse) hosts this fine hotel. The restaurant serves regional German cuisine ably supported by a cast of French dishes. Maikammerer Strasse 2. ☎ 06323/9510. www.hotelcastell.de. 26 units. Doubles 90€–98€ w/breakfast. MC, V.

Cruising on the Mosel

Multiple boat tour options on the Mosel River are available. Some of these are multiday cruises departing from Koblenz, but shorter excursions are available from Trier, going downriver as far as Bernkastel-Kues. Tours are operated by **Personenschifffahrt Gebrüder Kolb,** Georg-Schmitt-Platz 2 (☎ 0651/26666; www.kolb-mosel.com).

The Best of the Rhineland & the Ruhr Outdoors

Much of the Rhineland and the Ruhr is densely populated, urban, and industrial. But the region does have a dozen or so nature parks and a single national park that give locals and visitors a welcome chance to get away from the crowds and enjoy Mother Nature. This short itinerary loops north and then south through the region, taking in the most notable nature parks and finishing up in the Eifel district's national park.

> *The parks of the Rhineland are natural wonderlands with mountains, streams, and lakes.*

START From Frankfurt, take A45 east and north to intersection 38, where you switch to B275, B457, and finally B455 north to Schotten. **TRIP LENGTH** 4 days and 292km (181 miles).

1 ★ **Naturpark Hoher Vogelsberg.** The Upper Vogelsberg Nature Park protects 883 sq. km (341 sq. miles) of central Europe's largest volcanic landscape, comprised of low mountains, forests, moors, and lakes. Visitors to these mountains flow up a "shield" volcano's shallow incline to the summit of the Vogelsberg (Bird Mountain), 773m (2,536 ft.) high, from where millions of years ago lava flowed downward to form vast basalt layers. Recreation activities

Where to Stay & Dine
Carat Hotel Resort **10**
Graf Leopold **9**
Hotel im Hagen **8**
Landgasthaus Waldschenke **6**
Landhotel & Gasthaus Velte **7**

1 Naturpark Hoher Vogelsberg
2 Naturpark Hochtaunus
3 Naturpark Rhein-Taunus
4 Naturpark Siebengebirge
5 Nationalpark Eifel

include hiking, horseback riding, and fishing. The Eurasian lynx, once locally extinct, is being reintroduced. ⏱ Half-day. Visitor center: Informationszentrum Hoherodskopf. ☎ 06044/966-9330. www.hoherodskopf.eu. Free admission. May–Oct daily 10am–5pm; Nov–Apr Mon–Fri 11am–5pm, Sat–Sun 10am–5pm.

From Schotten, take B455 and B456, traveling generally southwest, about 74km (46 miles) to Anspach.

2 Naturpark Hochtaunus. As applies to all German mountain ranges north of the Alps, the name "High" Taunus has to be taken with a pinch of basalt. In the High Taunus Nature

Travel Tip

Ideally, you would spend a full day at each of these five parks, to allow plenty of time for off-road hiking. This tour takes a less ambitious approach, involving more driving than walking, and fits the Naturpark Hoher Vogelsberg and the Naturpark Hochtaunus into Day 1, the Naturpark Rhein-Taunus and the Naturpark Siebengebirge into Day 2, and the Nationalpark Eifel into Days 3 and 4.

Park, the highest mountain is the Grosser Feldsberg—at 878m (2,881 ft.) not too shabby, and head and shoulders higher than the neighboring Vogelsberg. The park covers 1,350 sq. km (521 sq. miles) of low mountains, forest, and meadowland. A unique attraction in this area is the **★★ Römerkastell Saalburg** (☎ 06175/93740; www.saalburgmuseum.de; admission 5€ adults, 3€ kids 6–18, kids 5 and under free; Mar–Oct daily 9am–6pm, Nov–Feb Tues–Sun 9am–4pm), a reconstructed Roman fortress from the 2nd century A.D. Stationed at this exposed outpost of the empire was a cohort (a roughly 600-man battalion) of auxiliary infantry and cavalry. The reconstruction affords fascinating insights into life on the military frontier in Germania close to 2,000 years ago, and the on-site museum has some impressive finds. ⏱ Half-day. Park HQ: Brandholz 1, Neu-Anspach. ☎ 06081/442-130. www.naturpark-hochtaunus.de.

From Anspach, drive northwest to pick up B275 heading southwest to Idstein (29km/18 miles).

3 Naturpark Rhein-Taunus. An alternative way of getting here from Naturpark Hochtaunus (**2**) would be to simply roll downhill. Most of the Rhine-Taunus Nature Park's low

> *With its elegant spires, Schloss Drachenburg, built in 1884, is as much a fairy-tale castle as anything in Disneyland.*

volcanoes on the east bank of the Rhine, the park lies between Ittenbach and Königswinter and covers just 48 sq. km (19 sq. miles). The highest mountain is the Grosser Ölberg, at 460m (1,509 ft.). Partway up one mountain is the Drachenfels (Dragon's Rock, 321m/1,053 ft.). **Schloss Drachenburg** (Drachenburg Palace), with its spires, turrets, and towers, dates from 1884 and should not be confused with the ruined medieval castle atop the Drachenfels. ⏱ Half-day. Park HQ: Königswinterer Strasse 409, Margaretenhöhe, Ittenbach. ☎ 02223/909-494. www.naturpark-siebengebirge.de.

From Königswinter, go north on A59, skirt the southern edge of Cologne on A559, then switch to the interchange for Düren and go south on B56 to Düren, for a total distance of 87km (54 miles).

❺ ★★ **Nationalpark Eifel.** Düren is a convenient access point to the Eifel region. The Eifel National Park protects 110 sq. km (42 sq. miles) in the central zone of this forested region, which additionally comprises two nature

hills, covering 810 sq. km (313 sq. miles) of scenic landscape descending to the Rhine, are forested, and they make for tolerably easy hiking and mountain-biking. The handsome park headquarters town of Idstein contains the **Residenzschloss** (1634), a Renaissance-style palace, and the 15th-century **Hexenturm** (Witches' Tower). ⏱ Half-day. Park HQ: Weitenmühlweg 5, Idstein. ☎ 06126/4379. www.naturpark-rhein-taunus.de.

From Idstein, take A3 northwest to Königswinter (110km/68 miles).

❹ ★ **Naturpark Siebengebirge.** Blink too often, and you might miss Naturpark Siebengebirge (Seven Mountains Nature Park) altogether. Part of a cluster of around 50 extinct

Heartbreak Ridge

A green U.S. 106th Infantry Division took up positions along the forested Schneifel (or Schnee Eifel) ridge, just inside Germany, in the "quiet" Ardennes sector, on December 11, 1944. Five days later, the massive surprise German offensive in the Ardennes, dubbed the Battle of the Bulge, erupted. Attacked around both ends of the ridge and cut off by the enemy's capture of the bridge across the Our River to their rear, the Americans attempted to break out of the encirclement and were cut to pieces. On December 19, the survivors of two full regiments, along with their supporting artillery and engineering corps and other troops, surrendered. American losses in men killed, wounded, and taken prisoner likely exceeded 7,000. In his book *A Time for Trumpets: The Untold Story of the Battle of the Bulge* (1984), Ardennes veteran Charles B. MacDonald described the fight for the Schneifel ridge as "the most costly defeat for American arms during the course of the war in Europe."

parks: the **Naturpark Hohes Venn-Eifel** (a trans-border park shared with Belgium) and the **Naturpark Südeifel** (Southern Eifel). The landscape varies from rolling meadows and forest-covered ridges to lakes and moderately sized mountains, including the Eifel's highest, Höhe Acht (747m/2,451 ft.), near the Nürburgring Formula 1 racing circuit, and the Schneifel (697m/2,287 ft.), a dark green mass looming against the Belgian border. A far-from-exhaustive alphabetical list of outdoor activities in this fresh-air fanatic's paradise includes ballooning, canoeing, fishing, hang gliding, horseback riding, hiking, hunting, mountain biking, rock climbing, sailing, skiing (both downhill and cross-country), and swimming. The Eifel was a great place to be during the Devonian Period, 380 million years ago. It was a lot warmer then, for one thing, and mostly covered by the shallow Eifel Coral Sea, which boasted genuine coral reefs and was rich in marine plant and animal life. The Devonian layer is now fertile ground for fossil hunters. ⏲ 2 days. Park HQ: Urftseestrasse 34, Schleiden-Gemünd (33km/21 miles south of Düren on B265). ☎ 02444/95100. www. nationalpark-eifel.de.

Where to Stay & Dine

★★ **Carat Hotel Resort** MONSCHAU Just a few minutes' walk from the heart of this most beautiful of old Eifel towns, the modern Carat has space to indulge its guests with a spa and a well-regarded restaurant. Laufenstrasse 82. ☎ 02472/860. www.carathotel.de. 100 units. Doubles 104€–154€ w/breakfast. AE, DC, MC, V.

★★ **Graf Leopold** DAUN *FRENCH* A venerable castle, the Dauner Burg, in the tiny "capital" of the Vulkaneifel, is a romantic setting for refined Franco-Mediterranean cuisine. Romantik Schloss-Hotel Kurfürstliches Amtshaus, Burgfriedstrasse 28. ☎ 06592/9250. www.daunerburg.de. Entrees 27€–30€. AE, MC, V. Lunch & dinner Sun, dinner Mon–Sat.

★ **Hotel im Hagen** MARGARETHENHÖHE This small country hotel near Königswinter, in the heart of the Siebengebirge mountains, has family values, Bavarian-style charm, and a decent Hessian restaurant. Ölbergringweg 45. ☎ 02223/92130. www.hotel-im-hagen.de. 20 units. Doubles 70€–98€ w/breakfast. AE, DC, MC, V.

★★ **Landgasthaus Waldschenke** FREIENSEEN (LAUBACH) *CONTINENTAL* The seasonal cuisine at this country-house restaurant absorbs German, Belgian, and French influences, and there are grand views from the garden terrace. Tunnelstrasse 42. ☎ 06405/6110. Entrees 14€–23€. AE, MC, V. Lunch Thurs–Tues, dinner Mon–Tues and Thurs–Sat.

★ **Landhotel & Gasthaus Velte** WESTERFELD The rooms in this family-run country hotel in a village just outside Neu Anspach are outfitted in a modern, unremarkable way, though they don't lack for much. You dine on traditional Hessian fare in the rustic restaurant. Usinger Strasse 38. ☎ 06081/917-900. www.landhotel-velte.de. 15 units. Doubles 88€–112€ w/breakfast. AE, MC, V.

Volcanoes of the Eifel

The southern Eifel is a volcanic zone, the Vulkaneifel, which geologists judge to still be active, although the last eruption was 11,000 years ago and the last cataclysmic eruption 40,000 years ago. There are some 70 circular crater lakes, called *Maaren*, in the region, along with fields of solidified lava and ash. A myriad of volcanic springs has made the southern Eifel a spa-zone today. If you have a strong enough interest in the topic to justify a drive of around an hour (through a ruggedly scenic landscape), visit the **Eifel-Vulkanmuseum,** Leopoldstrasse 9 (☎ 06592/985-353; www.vulkaneifel.de), in Daun, 95km (59 miles) southeast of Nationalpark Eifel, to learn more about this fascinating geology.

THE BUILDING
OF BAUHAUS

Germany's Modernist Masters BY DONALD OLSON

FOUNDED IN WEIMAR IN 1919, the Bauhaus School of Art and Architecture was forced to move to Dessau in 1925 and finally to Berlin before it was shut down by the Nazis in 1933 for being "too modernist." But in its brief and beleaguered 14 years of existence, the Bauhaus had a profound impact on architecture and design in Germany and the Western world. The school sought to sweep away the heavy-handed historicism of 19th- and early-20th-century European architecture and the kitschy overdecoration of everyday objects, replacing them with unadorned exteriors and clear forms that focused on the utility and functionality of the building and the furnishings within it. Everything from houses to factories and cradles to teapots was radically reimagined, and the Bauhaus creations that emerged have become icons of modern design.

Teachers and Artists

The Bauhaus was staffed by a roster of versatile artists, many of whom were forced to leave Germany and later became internationally famous. (See also "Express Yourself: The Great German Expressionists," p. 628.)

WALTER GROPIUS (1883–1969)

A Berlin-born architect, Gropius founded the Bauhaus and saw it through its first years in Weimar and Dessau. Forced by the Nazis to leave Germany, he emigrated to the U.S. where he became Dean of the Harvard Graduate School of Design. Gropius pioneered a screen wall system that allowed external glass walls to continue without interruption. He designed the **New Bauhaus School** building in Dessau, completed in 1926.

MIES VAN DER ROHE (1886–1969)

Aachen-born Mies came to prominence in 1927 when he designed the German Pavilion for the International Exposition in Barcelona, shown above (and the famous chrome-and-leather Barcelona chair), a flat-roofed building with movable internal walls of glass and marble.

From 1930 until it was shut down by the Nazis, he was director of the Bauhaus school. In 1937 he moved to the U.S., where he served as head of the architecture department at the Armour Institute of Technology in Chicago and designed a series of glass skyscrapers, culminating in the Seagram Building in New York. His last work was the **Neue Nationalgalerie (New National Gallery)** in Berlin (p. 75, **6**), constructed in 1962.

ANNI ALBERS (1899–1994)

Though she became the most famous textile artist of the 20th

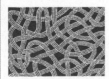

century, Albers began weaving only because the male-dominated Bauhaus barred women from certain disciplines. In 1925, when the Bauhaus moved to Dessau, she began to develop her functionally unique textiles with

minimalist, gridlike patterns. In 1933 she and her husband, Josef Albers, were invited to teach in the U.S, where they remained for the rest of their lives. Anni Albers's weavings were shown throughout the country and in a 1949 show at the Museum of Modern Art.

VASSILY KANDINSKY (1866–1944)

A Russian painter and art theorist, Kandinsky is credited with painting the first modern abstract works of art.

He taught at the Bauhaus from 1922 until the Nazis closed it in 1933, during which time geometrical elements and planes rich in colors took on increasing importance in his painting. Above, students in Weilhelm reproduce Kandinsky's *Weilhelm-Marienplatz* (1909) in the eponymous square (2008).

Visiting Bauhaus Sites

▲ **DESSAU** Home to the **Bauhausgebäude,** a masterpiece of modern architecture designed by Walter Gropius, completed in 1926. Nearby, on Ebertallee, are the **"Master Houses,"** three modernist semidetached villas that served as the living quarters and studios for Bauhaus Masters (teachers).
BERLIN Bauhaus-Archiv/Museum of Design. Completed in 1979, this building is one of the last works of Walter Gropius. See p. 87, **14**.
WEIMAR The Bauhaus Museum (see "Bauhaus in Weimar," p. 191) displays original Bauhaus furniture, kitchenware, textiles, and artwork from the school's Weimar years. The first Bauhaus building ever constructed (1923).

Industrial History in the Ruhr

Since the time of industrialization in the 19th century, Germany's industrial heartland, the Ruhrgebiet (Ruhr District), with its coal mines, steel plants, and other heavy industries, has been among the country's most valuable economic resources. To a large degree, the period of the great smokestack industries now belongs to the past. Today, there's a surprising amount of green in what was once dubbed Germany's "Black Country." But when it comes to industrial archaeology, the Ruhr still rules. Allot 1 day of this tour to Düsseldorf, 1 day to Duisburg and Essen, and 1 day to Bocum and Dortmund.

> *Zeche Zollverein in Essen, formerly a coal mine, now houses a design museum and hosts cultural events.*

START Düsseldorf is 42km (26 miles) north of Cologne on A57 and A46; and 228km (142 miles) northwest of Frankfurt on A66, A3, and A46. **TRIP LENGTH** 3 days and 100km (62 miles).

SITE GUIDE
PAGE 472

❶ ★ Düsseldorf. Big, commercial, and fashion-conscious today, Düsseldorf (pop. 585,000) was founded in the 8th century as a humble fishing village along the Rhine.

On Day 2, travel north on A52 and A3 to Duisburg (35km/22 miles).

❷ Duisburg. This industrial town (pop. 495,000) is Europe's largest inland port and a powerful pump for the continent's commercial arteries. That makes a visit to the **Museum der Deutschen Binnenschifffahrt** (Museum of German Inland Shipping), Apostelstrasse 84 (☎ 0203/808-8940; www.binnen-schifffahrtsmuseum.de; admission 3€ adults, 2€ kids 6–18; Tues–Sun 10am–5pm), in the harbor zone, a worthwhile experience for anyone moved by old sail and steam-powered river and canal barges. And if you want to tour this monster of a port, what better way than to go by boat? Harbor tours run by **Weisse Flotte Duisburg** (☎ 0203/7139-667; www.wf-duisburg.de

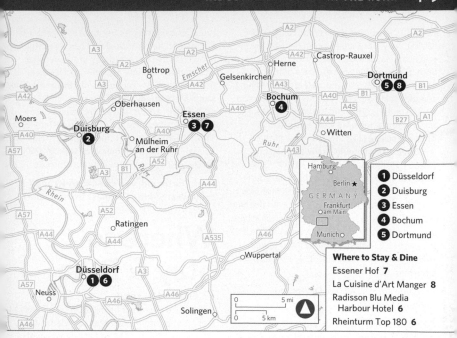

1	Düsseldorf
2	Duisburg
3	Essen
4	Bochum
5	Dortmund

Where to Stay & Dine

Essener Hof **7**

La Cuisine d'Art Manger **8**

Radisson Blu Media
Harbour Hotel **6**

Rheinturm Top 180 **6**

depart from the Schwanentor Bridge.
🕑 Half-day. Tourist information: Königstrasse 86.
☎ 0203/285-440. www.duisburgnonstop.de.

From Duisburg, take A40 east to Essen (25km/16 miles).

3 ★ Essen. Formerly a hive of heavy industry, Essen (pop. 580,000) has been busy reinventing itself as a cultural and shopping center. Still, the city has much in the way of industrial archaeology, nowhere more so than at the massive ★ **Zeche Zollverein** (☎ 0201/830-360; www.zollverein.de; guided tours 8€ adults, 5€ kids 6–18; Apr–Oct daily 10am–7pm; Nov–Mar Sat–Thurs 9am–5pm, Fri 9am–7pm), a former coal mine and coking plant in the northeast of the city that's now a UNESCO World Heritage site. A part of the complex, Shaft 12 (1932), was built in the Bauhaus style and now houses the **Red Dot Design Museum**

(☎ 0201/301-040; www.red-dot.de; admission 5€ adults, 3€ kids 6–18; Tues–Thurs 11am–6pm, Fri–Sun 11am–8pm). 🕑 Half-day. Tourist information: Touristikzentrale, Handelshof (mall), Hauptbahnhof 2 (main train station). ☎ 0201/887-2048. www.essen.de.

On Day 3, take A40 east to Bochum (18km/11 miles).

4 Bochum. If you're up for some more heavy industrial archaeology, Bochum (pop. 380,000) can oblige. Head to the ★ **Deutsches Bergbau-Museum Bochum** (German Mining Museum of

Getting Around Düsseldorf

Düsseldorf is served by *U-Bahn* (underground) and *S-Bahn* (suburban) railways, along with *Strassenbahn* (tram) and bus lines, all operated by VRR (☎ 01803/504-034; www.vrr.de).

Boat Tours in the Ruhr District

Between Duisburg and Essen lies the city of Mülheim an der Ruhr, a center of light industry. Based here are the "White Fleet" tour boats of the **Weisse Flotte** (☎ 0208/960-9996; www.mhvg.de), which cruise the Ruhr region's rivers and canals. Boats depart from the Wasserbahnhof (Water Station) at the Alte Schleuse (Old Lock) on the Ruhr River. There's a variety of cruise options to choose from, costing from 22€ to 70€ for adults and around 60% of the adult price for kids.

Bochum), Am Bergbaumuseum 28 (☎ 0234/58770; www.bergbaumuseum.de; admission 6.50€ adults, 3€ kids 6–18; Tues–Fri 8:30am–5pm, Sat–Sun 10am–5pm), north of the city center. The museum is housed in a coal mining complex that dates back to the 1860s; you can also go underground into the mine. Some of the coal extracted here went into the fires of steam engines like those on view in the ★★ **Eisenbahnmuseum** (Railway Museum), Dr.-C.-Otto-Strasse 191 (☎ 0234/492-516; www.eisenbahnmuseum-bochum.de; admission 6€ adults, 3€ kids 6–14; Mar to mid-Nov Tues–Fri and Sun 10am–5pm), in an old depot in the southwestern suburb of Dahlhausen, where you can ride trains hauled by a Prussian steam locomotive. ◷ Half-day. Tourist information: Huestrasse 9. ☎ 01805/260-234. www.bochum-tourismus.de.

Continue east on A40 to Dortmund (22km/14 miles).

❺ ★ **Dortmund.** The Ruhr's largest city (pop. 590,000) presents a remarkably green face

today, considering its heritage as a center of mining and heavy industry. The city is still known for its beer, made by breweries like Dortmunder Actien-Brauerei and featured in the local brewery museum, the **Brauerei-Museum Dortmund,** Steigerstrasse 16 (☎ 0231/840-0200; admission 2.50€ adults, 1.25€ kids 6–14; Tues, Wed, Fri, and Sun 10am–5pm, Thurs 10am–8pm, Sat noon–5pm). ◷ Half-day. Tourist information: Königswall 18A. ☎ 0231/1899-9222. www.dortmund-tourismus.de.

From Dortmund, you can take A40 and A52 southwest 69km (43 miles) to Düsseldorf.

Where to Stay & Dine

★★ **Essener Hof** ESSEN
Just across the street from Essen's main railway station, this family-run hotel, founded in 1883, is a fount of tranquillity and good taste, with a country-style Continental restaurant. Am Handelshof 5. ☎ 0201/24250. www.essener-hof.com. 127 units. Doubles 105€–185€ w/breakfast. AE, DC, MC, V. Tram: 101, 105, 106, or 107.

★★ **La Cuisine d'Art Manger** DORTMUND
FRENCH/MEDITERRANEAN Housed in a former tennis-club villa in the leafy Gartenstadt district east of the city center, this place exudes both class and quality, and it has a garden terrace. Lübkestrasse 21. ☎ 0231/531-6197. www.artmanger.com. Entrees 30€–38€. No credit cards. Dinner Tues–Sat. U-Bahn: Lübkestrasse.

★ **Radisson Blu Media Harbour Hotel** DÜSSELDORF In the center of the ultramodern, waterfront MedienHafen district, this V-shaped hotel offers contemporary luxury. Dine on Italian food at restaurant Amano. Hammer Strasse 23. ☎ 800/333-3333 in North America, or 0211/3111910. www.radissonblu.com. 135 units. Doubles 169€–370€. AE, DC, MC, V. Tram: 708.

★ **Rheinturm Top 180** DÜSSELDORF *FRENCH* Gently revolving atop the Rhine Tower (172m/564 ft.), this restaurant has grand views and well-prepared food—grills, game dishes, and soups. Stromstrasse 20. ☎ 0211/863-2000. Entrees 23€–31€. AE, DC, MC, V. Lunch & dinner daily. Tram: 704, 709, or 719.

Neanderthal Man

A stroll through the pleasant Neandertal (Neander Valley) between Düsseldorf and Wuppertal takes you in the footsteps of a vanished people. Some 40,000 years ago, our distant biological cousin *Homo neanderthalensis,* or Neanderthal Man, no doubt accompanied by Neanderthal Woman, passed this way. That was 10,000 years before the species exited history's stage, dying out after an evolutionary run lasting 200 millennia. In 1856, quarry workers made what was later recognized to be the first-ever discovery of Neandertal bones in a cave in the valley. But the Neandertal was a valuable source of limestone for the Ruhr's ravenous steel industry, and the cave was dynamited before its value was understood. German scientists pinpointed the cave's former location in 1999 and unearthed more Neanderthal bones at the spot. The hands-on ★ **Neanderthal Museum,** Talstrasse 300 (☎ 02104/979-715; www.neanderthal.de; admission 9€ adults, 5.50€ kids 6–16; Tues–Sun 10am–6pm), at Erkrath, near Mettmann, in the valley, is a great experience for both adults and kids.

> Brauerei-Museum Dortmund.

SITE GUIDE

① Düsseldorf

Start out in the Altstadt (Old Town) to view Marktplatz (Market Square) and the 16th-century Gothic Ⓐ ★ **Rathaus** (Town Hall); like much of historic Düsseldorf, it was destroyed in the war but the facade was carefully restored. Also in the Altstadt is Ⓑ **St.-Lambertus Basilika** (St. Lambert's Basilica) and the Ⓒ **Schlossturm** (Castle Tower), both of 13th-century origin. Ⓓ ★ **Königsallee,** or the "Kö," flanks an ornamental canal, one bank of which is lined with office buildings and the other with elegant shops, cafes, and restaurants. The Kö is a major European shopping destination, with such names as Armani, Burberry, Chanel, Ferragamo, Luis Vuitton, Prada, Cartier, and Tiffany gracing the storefronts. At the canal's northern end is the rambling Ⓔ **Hofgarten** park, laced with walking paths and dotted with ponds that are home to a number of white and black swans.

The once-dilapidated, now trendy waterfront Ⓕ ★★ **MedienHafen** district was a flourishing warehouse sector in the 19th century. Today it is a showcase for modern architecture, especially in the buildings of Frank Gehry. The

most striking example of Gehry's work is a trio of "organic" high rises with wavy lines at Neuer Zollhof (New Customs House). For the best view, walk down the riverside promenade Am Handelshafen, beginning at the Rheinturm (Rhine Tower) and heading toward Franzius-strasse. Also sure to catch your eye are the Colorium, a colorful skyscraper designed to evoke the works of dutch painter Piet Mondrian, and the Roggendorf-Haus, not so much for the building itself but the colorful plastic sculptures crawling all over it. The figures are called "Flossis" for their webbed hands and fee (*Flosse* is German for fin).

The painting collection at the Ⓖ ★ **Museum Kunst Palast** (Art Palace Museum), Ehren-hof 4–5 (☎ 0211/899-0200 Mon–Fri, or 0211/8992460 Sat–Sun; www.museum-kunst-palast.de; admission 2.50€ adults, 1€ kids 6–18 Tues–Wed and Fri–Sun 11am–6pm, Thurs 11am 9pm), has works by Rubens, Caspar David Friedrich, and the Die Brücke and Blaue Reiter schools, plus sculpture, prints, and drawings; early Persian bronzes and ceramics; textiles from late antiquity to the present; and a desig

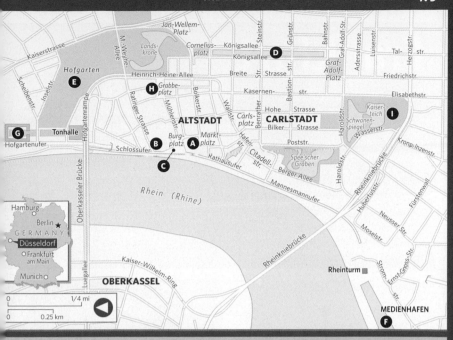

collection. It also includes the Glasmuseum Hentrich, one of the largest glass collections in Europe, with pieces ranging from 1st-century vessels to Art Nouveau Tiffany vases to modern works by Chihuly. Across Hofgarten, the black-glass edifice of the ❤ ★ **K20** museum of modern art, Grabbeplatz 5 (☎ 0211/838-1130; www.kunstsammlung.de; admision 6.50€ adults, 4.50€ kids 6–18; Tues–Fri 10am–6pm, Sat–Sun 11am–6pm), recently reopened after a major renovation, contains 100 paintings by Paul Klee along with works by Dalí, Picasso,

Matisse, Bonnard, Léger, Johns, and Pollock. Sister museum ❶ **K21,** Ständehausstrasse 1 (☎ 0211/838-1600; www.kunstsammlung. de; admission 6.50€ adults, 4.50€ kids 6–18; Tues–Fri 10am–6pm, Sat–Sun 11am–6pm), hosts international art that dates from 1980 to the present, including paintings, photography, and moving images on film and video. Spend an evening in Düsseldorf if you can to experience the "longest bar in the world," the city's nickname for the some 260 bars, restaurants, and clubs within a 1km sq. radius in the Altstadt. The district is an extremely popular destination for hen and stag parties (you're sure to see several groups of them if you're there on the weekend) but even on weekdays you'll find crowds along the winding cobblestoned streets into the wee hours. If you're looking for a somewhat more sedate atmosphere, head to one of the outdoor restaurants along the river promenade. ⊙ 1 day. Tourist information offices are located at the Hauptbahnhof (main train station; Immermannstrasse 65B; ☎ 0211/1720-2844) and in the Altstadt (Old Town; intersection of Marktstrasse and Rheinstrasse; ☎ 0211/1720-2840). www.duesseldorf-tourismus.de.

Frankfurt

Since many international flights land at Frankfurt Airport, the thriving metropolis of Frankfurt am Main (pop. 650,000) is likely to afford your first impression of Germany. Where Frankish tribes settled in the 3rd century around a *Furt* (ford) on the Main River is now the country's leading banking and financial center, home to the Bundesbank (Germany's central bank), the European Central Bank, and the Frankfurt Stock Exchange. Though it doesn't have monuments or museums to equal Berlin's or Munich's, the city is a worthy tourist destination with a distinct personality. You'll need the best part of 2 days to take in Frankfurt's main attractions. If you want to allocate just 1 day to the city, as seems likely for many visitors, passing on some of the museum recommendations should do the trick.

> *A mix of modern architecture, half-timber houses, and landscaped parks, busy Frankfurt is both beautiful and thriving.*

START **There's no better place to start out than in the heart of the Old Town, the Römerberg, served by the *U-Bahn* station Dom/Römer.**

❶ ★ **Altstadt (Old Town).** Frankfurt's Altstadt was among Germany's greatest and most historic until World War II bombing leveled it. This is where you will find the Römerberg, the Römer, the Kaiserdom, and the Goethe-Haus

(all described in this tour). At the northern edge of the Altstadt is the Hauptwache, a square named for the baroque guardhouse (1730) that stands there. *U-Bahn:* Dom/Römer *U-* or *S-Bahn:* Hauptwache.

❷ ★★★ **Römerberg.** The Altstadt's historic core is famous for its magnificent half-timber houses. It centers on a trio of Gothic patrician houses with stepped gables, known

The magnificent 13th- and 14th-century gabled houses of the Römerberg offer a beautiful backdrop for Frankfurt's market square.

collectively as the ★★ **Römer.** They were built between 1288 and 1305 and bought by the city a century later for use as the Rathaus (Town Hall). This is still the official seat of Frankfurt's lord mayor. The second floor of the center house is the **Kaisersaal** (Imperial Hall), lined with romanticized 19th-century portraits of 52 emperors, 13 of whom celebrated their

Getting Around Frankfurt

Frankfurt is linked by a fast, modern *U-Bahn* (subway), *S-Bahn* (city rail), *Strassenbahn* (tram), and bus network, run by VGF (☎ 069/19449; www.vgf-ffm.de). Tickets start out at 1.50€. Except for bus travel (where you have the option of paying the driver, be sure to buy your ticket before boarding. Consider purchasing a Frankfurt Card from either of the city's tourist offices (p. 495). This allows unlimited travel on public transportation anywhere within the greater Frankfurt area, including on the airport shuttle, plus half-price admission to city museums. It costs 9€ for 1 day and 13€ for 2 days; children 14 and under go free when traveling with an adult.

Anne Frank in Frankfurt

A moving alternative to mainstream sightseeing in Frankfurt is to visit a couple of sites associated with Anne Frank. Although Anne is best known for the time she spent living in hiding in Amsterdam during World War II, Germany provided the bookends to the young Jewish diarist's short life. She was born in Frankfurt in 1929 and died at **Bergen-Belsen Concentration Camp** (see the box on p. 528) in 1945. You can view from the outside the houses where Anne lived with her family, first at Marbachweg 307 (*U-Bahn:* Dornbusch) and later at Ganghoferstrasse 24 (*U-Bahn:* Hügelstrasse), in the north of Frankfurt, before she, her father Otto, mother Edith, and elder sister Margot were forced to flee from the Nazis to Amsterdam in 1934. In addition, there's a nearby memorial youth center, the **Jugendbegegnungsstätte Anne Frank,** Hansaallee 150 (☎ 069/560-0020; www.jbs-anne-frank.de; *U-Bahn:* Dornbusch), that contains an interactive exhibit about her life, *Anne Frank: Ein Mädchen aus Deutschland* (*Anne Frank: A Girl from Germany*).

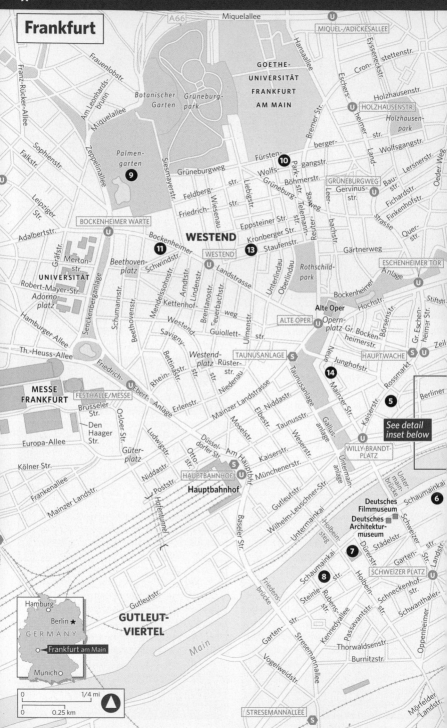

Frankfurt

A66

Miquelallee

MIQUEL-/ADICKESALLEE

GOETHE-
UNIVERSITÄT
FRANKFURT
AM MAIN

HOLZHAUSENSTR.

Holzhausenstr.

Holzhausen-
park

Botanischer
Garten

Grüneburg-
park

Frauenlobstr.

Am Leonhards-
brunn

Miquelallee

Zeppelinallee

Franz-Rücker-Allee

Sophienstr.

Falkstr.

Palmen-
garten

9

Fürsten-

Wolfs-

10

Böhmerstr.

Grüneburg-

Park str.

Bremer Str.

berger-

gangstr.

Wolfsgangstr.

Land str.

GRÜNEBURGWEG

Gervinus-
str.

Bau- str.

Fichardstr.

Finkenhofstr.

Lersnerstr.

Oeder Weg

Quer- strasse

Grüneburgweg

Feldberg- str.

Liebigstr.

Wiesenau

Friedrich-

Eppsteiner Str.

Kronberger Str.

Staufenstr.

13

Gärtnerweg

BOCKENHEIMER WARTE

Bockenheimer

WESTEND

WESTEND

ESCHENHEIMER TOR

Anlage

Leipziger
Str.

Adalbertstr.

Gräfstr.

Merton-
str.

UNIVERSITÄT

Robert-Mayer-Str.

Adorno-
platz

Hamburger Allee

Th.-Heuss-Allee

**MESSE
FRANKFURT**

FESTHALLE/MESSE

Brüsseler
Str.

Den
Haager
Str.

Europa-Allee

Kölner Str.

Frankenallee

Mainzer Landstr.

Beethoven-
platz

Schwindstr.

Arndtstr.

Lindenstr.

Brentanostr.

Feuerbachstr.

Landstrasse

Unterlindau

Oberlindau

Rothschild-
park

Bockenheimer

Hochstr.

Börsenstr.

Gr. Eschenheimer Str.

Stiftstr.

Zeil

Schumannstr.

Mendelssohnstr.

Kettenhof-

weg

Westend-

Savigny-

Guiollett-

str.

Ulmenstr.

Alte Oper

ALTE OPER

Opern-
platz

Gr. Bocken-
heimerstr.

HAUPTWACHE

Senckenberganlage

Beethovenstr.

Bettinastr.

Rhein-

Westend-
platz

Rüster-
str.

Niedenau

Taunusanlage

TAUNUSANLAGE

Neue

Junghofstr.

Mainzer Str.

Kaiserstr.

Rossmarkt

5

Berliner

See detail
inset below

Friedrich-
Ebert- Anlage

Erlenstr.

Mainzer Landstrasse

Niddastr.

Elbestr.

Taunusstr.

Weserstr.

Gallus- anlage

WILLY-BRANDT-
PLATZ

Ludwigstr.

Osloer Str.

Güter-
platz

Niddastr.

Poststr.

Otto-

Düssel-
dorfer Str.

Am Hauptbhf.

Moselstr.

Kaiserstr.

Münchenerstr.

Untermain- anlage

HAUPTBAHNHOF

Hauptbahnhof

Hafentunnel

Baseler Str.

Gutleutstr.

Wilhelm-Leuschner-Str.

Untermainkai

Holbein-
steg

Untermain-
brücke

Schaumainkai

6

**Deutsches
Filmmuseum**

**Deutsches
Architektur-
museum**

Schaumainkai

Schweizer Str.

Städelstr.

Dürerstr.

Garten- str.

Landstr.

7

SCHWEIZER PLATZ

Gartenstr.

GUTLEUT-
VIERTEL

Gutleutstr.

Friedens-
brücke

Main

Schaumainkai

Steinlestr.

Rubensstr.

8

Kennedyallee

Passavantstr.

Holbeinstr.

Schweizer str.

Schneckenhof-
str.

Schwanthaler-
str.

Oppenheimer Str.

Thorwaldsenstr.

Burnitzstr.

Mörfelder
Landstr.

Vogelweidstr.

Stresemannallee

STRESEMANNALLEE

GERMANY

Hamburg

Berlin ★

Frankfurt am Main

Munich

0   1/4 mi
0   0.25 km

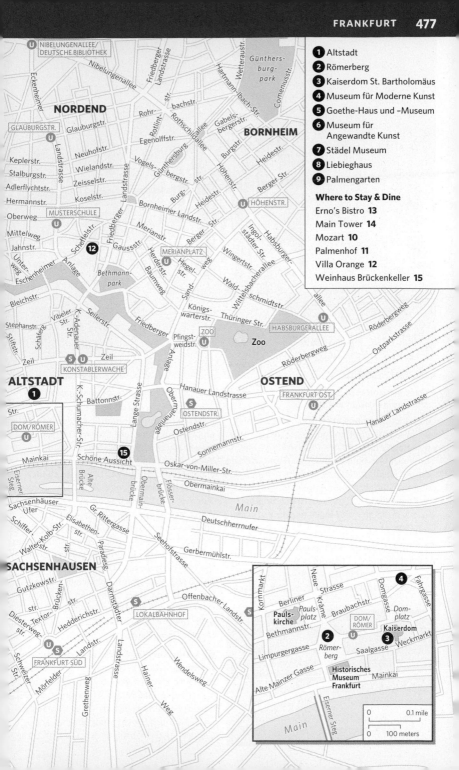

1 Altstadt
2 Römerberg
3 Kaiserdom St. Bartholomäus
4 Museum für Moderne Kunst
5 Goethe-Haus und –Museum
6 Museum für Angewandte Kunst
7 Städel Museum
8 Liebieghaus
9 Palmengarten

Where to Stay & Dine
Erno's Bistro 13
Main Tower 14
Mozart 10
Palmenhof 11
Villa Orange 12
Weinhaus Brückenkeller 15

> *Constructed between the 13th and 15th centuries, Kaiserdom St. Bartholomäus is the most impressive structure in Frankfurt's Altstadt.*

coronation banquets here. You can visit this hall daily from 10am to 1pm and 2 to 5pm only on an hourly tour (☎ 069/2123-4920; tours 2€, available in both English and German). The Römer's elaborate facade, with its ornate balcony and statues of four emperors, overlooks ★★ **Römerplatz** and the **Justitia-Brunnen** (Justice Fountain). ⏱ 2 hr. Römerplatz. *U-Bahn:* Dom/Römer.

❸ ★ **Kaiserdom St. Bartholomäus.** The Altstadt's dominant feature is Kaiserdom St. Bartholomäus (Imperial Cathedral of St. Bartholomew, 13th–15th centuries), in which

rulers of the Holy Roman Empire were elected and crowned for more than 400 years. Note the greatly ornamented, red-sandstone Westturm (West Tower), topped by both a lantern and a dome. In the north chancel, look for the *Maria-Schlaf-Altar* (Altar of Mary Sleeping, 1438), portraying a dying mother of Jesus and the only altar remaining from the church's original interior. Among other things, the Dom-Museum exhibits sumptuous robes worn by imperial Electors at coronations from the 1400s onward. ⏱ 1 hr. Domplatz. ☎ 069/297-0320. www.dom-frankfurt.de. Cathedral: free admission. Daily 9am–noon and 2–6pm. Dom-Museum: admission 2€ adults, 1€ kids 5–16. Tues–Fri 10am–5pm, Sat–Sun 11am–5pm. *U-Bahn:* Dom/Römer.

❹ ★ **Museum für Moderne Kunst (Museum for Modern Art).** In the center of the Altstadt, this museum opened in 1991 in a structure designed like a boat. Major artists since the 1950s are displayed here, including Roy Lichtenstein (view his *Brush Stroke*), Andy Warhol, and George Segal (look for his *Jazz Combo*). ⏱ 1 hr.

Sailing the Main

The easiest way to take in Frankfurt's skyline is on the Main River aboard one of the cruise vessels operated by **Primus-Linie,** Mainkai 36 (☎ 069/133-8370; www.primus-linie.de). Boats depart from the Main's north bank at Mainkai, offering a 50-minute tour for 7.20€ and a 100-minute tour for 9.40€; kids are 3.70€ on either tour.

Domstrasse 10. ☎ 069/2123-0447. www.mmk-frankfurt.de. Admission 8€ adults, 4€ kids 7–18, free last Sat of month. Tues and Thurs–Sun 10am–6pm; Wed 10am–8pm. *U-Bahn:* Dom/Römer.

❺ Goethe-Haus und -Museum. The house in which the writer and philosopher Johann Wolfgang von Goethe (1749–1832) was born is decorated in various 18th-century styles: neoclassical, baroque, rococo. You can view the library and one of Goethe's most important childhood possessions, a puppet theater. On the second floor is an astronomical clock built around 1749. The picture gallery contains paintings, mainly by Frankfurt artists of the period. In an annex, the museum has a library of volumes, manuscripts, graphic artworks, and paintings associated with Goethe. ⌚ 1 hr. Grosser Hirschgraben 23–25. ☎ 069/138-800. www.goethehaus-frankfurt.de. Admission 5€ adults, 1.50€ kids 7–18. Mon–Sat 10am–6pm, Sun 10am–5:30pm. *U-* or *S-Bahn:* Hauptwache.

> The works of Andy Warhol and other recent masters are on display at the city's sprawling Museum für Moderne Kunst.

❻ ★ Museum für Angewandte Kunst. More than 30,000 objects from Europe and Asia are exhibited in the Museum für Angewandte Kunst (Museum for Applied Arts), housed in a 19th-century villa and a 1985 white Rationalist structure designed by American architect Richard Meier. Among the collections are *Mainzer Meistermöbel* (rococo furnishings created in Mainz), 15th-century Venetian glassware, fine porcelain, and Persian carpets and faience. ⌚ 1 hr. Schaumainkai 17. ☎ 069/2123-4037. www.angewandtekunst-frankfurt.de. Admission 8€ adults, 4€ kids 7–18. Tues and Thurs–Sun 10am–5pm, Wed 10am–9pm. *U-Bahn:* Schweizer Platz.

Frankfurt Shopping

The best English-language bookstore in town is **British Bookshop,** Börsenstrasse 17 (☎ 069/280-492; www.british-bookshop.de). For a piece of a Merc, head over to the **Mercedes-Benz Store** (pictured), Kaiserstrasse 19–21 (☎ 069/2648-8731; www.mein-mercedes-benz.de), where everything from key rings to luggage is up for grabs. Fine Höchst porcelain has been a coveted product since 1746; pick up some at ★ **Höchster Porzellan-Manufaktur,** Palleskestrasse 32 (☎ 069/3009-0240; www.hoechster-porzellan.de). The weekly **Frankfurter Flohmarkt** (Flea Market), Schaumainkai, on Saturdays from 8am to 2pm along the Main River in the south-side Alt-Sachsenhausen district, is known for its art and antiques dealers.

Frankfurt Nightlife

Despite its name, the ★ **Alte Oper,** Opernplatz (☎ 069/13400; www.alteoper.de), Frankfurt's grand Old Opera, no longer hosts opera but rather classical music. In contrast, **Oper Frankfurt,** Willy-Brandt-Platz (☎ 069/134-0400; www.oper-frankfurt.de), has both opera and ballet performances. Theater and musical theater in English are performed at (where else?) the **English Theatre,** Gallusanlage 7 (☎ 069/2423-1620; www.english-theatre.org), just outside the western Altstadt. For a glamorous spectacle that's fun for all the family, take in a variety show at ★ **Tiger-palast,** Heiligkreuzgasse 16–20 (☎ 069/920-0220; www.tigerpalast.de).

> *You'll find works by French Impressionists, Dutch masters, and more on display at Frankfurt's Städel Museum.*

❼ ★★★ Städel Museum. Most European schools of painting are represented in this art gallery. On the first floor are French Impressionists such as Renoir and Monet, along with German painters of the 19th and 20th centuries. Note in particular Ernst Ludwig Kirchner's *Standing Nude with Hat* (1910). Also on the first floor are Johann Heinrich Wilhelm Tischbein's *Goethe in the Campagna* (1787) and Jean-Antoine Watteau's *Embarkation for Cythera* (1710). The second floor has an outstanding collection of Flemish Primitives, 16th-century German masters, and 17th-century Dutch masters, featuring works such as Jan van Eyck's *Madonna* (1433) and Lucas Cranach the Elder's impish *Venus* (1532). In the Department of Modern Art are works by Bacon, Dubuffet, Tàpies, Yves Klein, and others. ⏱ 2 hr. Schaumainkai 63. ☎ 069/605-0980. www.staedelmuseum.de. Admission 10€ adults, 8€ kids 12–16, 18€ families. Tues, Fri, and Sun 10am–6pm, Wed–Thurs 10am–9pm. *U-Bahn:* Schweizer Platz.

❽ ★ Liebieghaus. Housed in an 1896 villa, the city's sculpture collection includes objects from ancient Egypt, classical Greece and Rome, and medieval and Renaissance Europe. Highlights include a small bronze horse from the 8th century B.C. and Roman copies of Polykleitos's *Torso*, Praxiteles's *Satyr*, and Myron's *Athena*. The medieval section has a *Virgin and Child* created in Trier in the 11th century; the *Head of Barbel von Ottenheim*, attributed to Lucas van Leyden (1462); Tilman Riemenschneider's *Virgin and Child on a Crescent Moon;* Andrea della Robbia's altarpiece of the Assumption; and the 16th-century *Black Venus with Mirror*. ⏱ 2 hr. Schaumainkai 71. ☎ 069/650-0490. www.liebieghaus.de. Admission 8€ adults, free for kids 11 and under, 14€ families. Tues and Fri–Sun 10am–6pm, Wed–Thurs 10am–9pm. Tram: 15 or 16 to Otto-Hahn-Platz.

❾ Palmengarten. In the Palm Garden, a park and botanical garden laid out around a palm house from 1869, you can admire a perennial garden, a rock garden, and a rose garden. The Tropicarium is a complex for tropical vegetation; the Sub-Antarctic House displays plants from southern Chile, Argentina, and New Zealand; and the Entrance Conservatory houses insectivorous plants and bromeliads. Collections of orchids, palms, succulents, water lilies, and many other plants are displayed. In the park, there's a small lake with boats to rent in summer. ⏱ 1 hr. Siesmayerstrasse 61. ☎ 069/2123-3939. www.palmengarten.frankfurt.de. Admission 5€ adults, 2€ kids 5–15, 9.50€ families. Feb–Oct daily 9am–6pm, Nov–Jan daily 9–4pm. *U-Bahn:* Westend.

Where to Stay & Dine

> You can eat up the scenery 53 floors above Frankfurt at the Main Tower restaurant.

★★★ **Erno's Bistro** WESTEND-SÜD *FRENCH*
A chic midtown rendezvous despite being cramped and claustrophobic, Erno's serves both *cuisine moderne* and what is known as *cuisine formidable* with theatrical flair. Liebigstrasse 15. ☎ 069/721-997. www.ernosbistro.de. Entrees 42€–46€. AE, MC, V. Lunch & dinner Mon–Fri. *U-Bahn:* Westend.

★ **Main Tower** INNENSTADT *CONTINENTAL*
Set on the semicircular 53rd floor of one of Frankfurt's tallest buildings, this starkly modern restaurant offers reliable cuisine backed up with grand views. Neue Mainzer Strasse 52–58. ☎ 069/3650-4777. www.maintower-restaurant.de. Entrees 18€–30€. AE, MC, V. Dinner Tues–Sat. *S-Bahn:* Taunusanlage.

★ **Mozart** WESTEND-SÜD
Everything inside this excellent small hotel—walls, furniture, bed coverings—is white or pink. The breakfast room could pass for an 18th-century salon. Parkstrasse 17. ☎ 069/5050-0050. www.mozart-frankfurt.de. 35 units. Doubles 95€–185€ w/continental breakfast. AE, DC, MC, V. *U-Bahn:* Holzhausenstrasse.

★ **Palmenhof** WESTEND-SÜD
A short walk from the Palmengarten, this five-story Art Nouveau building from 1890 has architectural flourishes and well-kept rooms with somewhat fussy furnishings and high ceilings. Bockenheimer Landstrasse 89–91. ☎ 069/753-0060. www.palmenhof.com. 46 units. Doubles 85€–240€. AE, DC, MC, V. *U-Bahn:* Westend.

★★ **Villa Orange** NORDEND-OST
Radical renovation of a century-old building with lots of architectural character resulted in a cozy nest of a hotel that's comfortable, intimate, tasteful, and well mannered. Hebelstrasse 1. ☎ 069/405-840. www.villa-orange.de. 38 units. Doubles 90€–255€. AE, MC, V. *U-Bahn:* Musterschule.

★ **Weinhaus Brückenkeller** ALTSTADT *GERMAN*
Candlelit tables, wooden wine barrels, and low arched ceilings create an Old World atmosphere in this cellar eatery, and a setting for light, imaginative food. Schützenstrasse 6. ☎ 069/298-0070. www.brueckenkeller.de. Entrees 22€–32€. AE, DC, MC, V. Lunch & dinner daily. Tram: 14.

Cologne

Though historically known as a religious center for its
cathedral, churches, shrines, and relics of the saints, Cologne (pop. 1,000,000)
shares the general Rhineland passion for a rollicking good time. This lifestyle
approach is best exemplified by the "crazy days" during the annual Carnival, as
well as the presence in town of rather more bars and taverns than would seem
strictly justified by the population figure. Still, Cologne (German: Köln) doesn't
neglect its cultural side, even if it has to get by with far fewer world-class
highlights than Berlin and Munich. You could, just about, do a quick run-through
of the city's highlights in 1 day; an additional day will allow you time to soak up
some atmosphere in what's among Germany's most vibrant cities.

> *The Hohenzollernbrücke connects Cologne by rail with European cities on the other side of the Rhine, and is flanked at both ends by statues of Hohenzollern royalty.*

START **The city's main railway station, Köln
Hauptbahnhof, is right in the heart of the city.**

① ★★★ **Kölner Dom (Cologne Cathedral).**
Germany's largest Gothic cathedral, with
twin spires rising 157m (515 ft.) high, couldn't
be more convenient for anyone arriving in
the city by train—just step out of the Hauptbahnhof (main train station) and you're there.
Construction began in 1248 on what was to
be an awe-inspiring setting for the supposed
bones and other relics of the Magi (the Three

Kings, or Three Wise Men, of the Christian
Nativity story), brought to the city in 1164. The
relics were later placed inside a magnificent
reliquary, the ★★ **Dreikönigenschrein** (Three
Kings Shrine). This elaborate container in the
shape of a triple-nave basilica, made from gold
and silver and decorated with precious stones
and images of Christ, the Apostles, and the
Prophets, remains the most important and
valuable object in the cathedral and can be
seen behind the high altar. Close by is a side
chapel that contains an ★ **altarpiece** (1451)

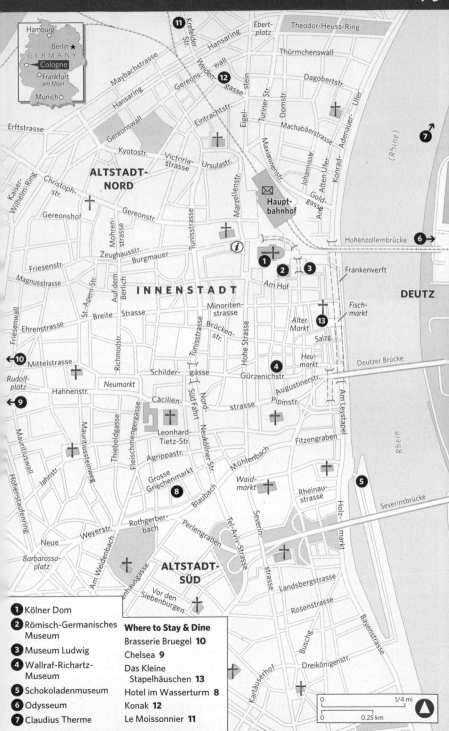

1 Kölner Dom

2 Römisch-Germanisches Museum

3 Museum Ludwig

4 Wallraf-Richartz-Museum

5 Schokoladenmuseum

6 Odysseum

7 Claudius Therme

Where to Stay & Dine

Brasserie Bruegel **10**

Chelsea **9**

Das Kleine Stapelhäuschen **13**

Hotel im Wasserturm **8**

Konak **12**

Le Moissonnier **11**

> *Kölner Dom contains stained-glass windows from many time periods; the Bavarian Windows (detail pictured), along the south side of the church, were donated by King Ludwig I of Bavaria.*

that depicts the Magi, who are patrons of the city (their three crowns appear on its coat of arms). Other venerable sights around the cathedral—a UNESCO World Heritage site—include the ★ **Gero-Kreuz** (Gero Cross, c. 960), a crucifix that adorns the tomb of Archbishop Gero; the choir (1310); and the stained-glass windows (1507–09). A range of guided tours is available. ⊙ 1 hr. Domkloster. ☎ 0221/9258-4720. www.koelner-dom.de. Cathedral: free admission; Tower: 2.50€ adults, 1€ kids 6–18, 5€ families; Treasury: 4€ adults, 2€ kids 6–18,

8€ families; combination Tower/Treasury 5€ adults, 2.50€ kids 6–18. Mon–Fri 10am–6:30pm, Sat 10am–5pm, Sun 1–5pm. *U-Bahn:* Dom/Hauptbahnhof; *S-Bahn:* Hauptbahnhof.

❷ ★★ **Römisch-Germanisches Museum.**
Cologne got its moniker courtesy of the ancient Romans, whose emperor Claudius named it Colonia Claudia Ara Agrippinensium in honor of his wife (and niece) Agrippina. The city was chosen to be the capital of the province of Germania Inferior (Lower Germany). In the Römisch-Germanisches Museum (Roman-Germanic Museum) just behind the Dom are many objects from Cologne's Roman period, which ran from the 1st century B.C. to the 5th century A.D. Pride of place goes to the magnificent Dionysos Mosaic (3rd century), an elaborate floor decoration from a Roman villa that stood on this very spot. It depicts the Greek god of wine in a variety of louche settings. In addition, there's Roman glassware, pottery, funerary monuments, sculptured heads, and a lot of other stuff. ⊙ 1 hr. Roncalliplatz 4. ☎ 0221/2212-4438. www.museenkoeln.de. Admission 8€ adults, 5€ kids 6–18. Tues–Sun 10am–5pm (until 10pm first Thurs in month). *U-Bahn:* Dom/Hauptbahnhof; *S-Bahn:* Hauptbahnhof.

Getting Around Cologne

One-way tickets on Cologne's excellent bus, tram, *U-Bahn,* and *S-Bahn* connections cost from 1.60€ to 9.80€. A day ticket, the *Kölner Tageskarte,* allows you to travel throughout the city's public transportation network from 9am to 3am for 5.60€. The Köln WelcomeCard, available from the city's tourist office (p. 495), allows unlimited travel on public transportation and reduced admission to city museums and other attractions. Depending on your choice of transportation option, for 24 hours the card costs 9€, 12€, or 22€.

> Female Head, *by Pablo Picasso, is one of the works on display in Cologne's Museum Ludwig.*

❹ ★★ **Wallraf-Richartz-Museum.** A representative selection from 7 centuries' worth of European art is packed into the halls of the city's finest art gallery. The museum reckons its finest piece is Stefan Lochner's *Madonna in the Rose Bower* (c. 1450). This luminous work has competition from an array of Dutch, Flemish, and Italian Old Masters, French Impressionists, Vincent van Gogh, James Ensor, and many more. Look out for more works from Lochner and from other German artists, including Albrecht Dürer's *Piper and Drummer* (1504). ⏱ 2 hr. Obenmarspforten. ☎ 0221/2212-1119. www.wallraf.museum. Admission 5.80€ adults, 3.30€ kids 5–16. Tues–Fri 10am–6pm (until 10pm Thurs), Sat–Sun 11am–6pm. *U-Bahn:* Heumarkt.

❸ ★ **Museum Ludwig.** If you're a fan of modern art in general and of Picasso in particular, you'll love this gallery, which has literally hundreds of Picassos in addition to works by the likes of Marc Chagall, Salvador Dalí, Roy Lichtenstein, Kasimir Malevich, and Andy Warhol. ⏱ 1 hr. Heinrich-Böll-Platz. ☎ 0221/2212-6165. www.museum-ludwig.de. Admission 9€ adults, 6€ kids 6–13, 18€ families. Tues–Sun 10am–6pm (until 10pm first Thurs in month). *U-Bahn:* Dom/Hauptbahnhof.

Tours of Cologne

Three tour-boat lines in Cologne offer short cruises on the Rhine, taking in the city's riverfront and places of interest both upstream and down. Tour fares begin at 6.80€ for adults and 3.40€ for kids 4–13. Boats depart from docks on the river's west (left) bank, in the central zone between the Hohenzollernbrücke and Deutzer Brücke bridges.

A great way to get a high view of the city and its location on the Rhine, is to ride the ★ **Kölner Seilbahn** (Cologne Cable Car; ☎ 0221/547-4180; www.koelner-seilbahn. de), which departs from a point close to the Zoologischer Garten (Zoo), north of the city center, and crosses the river to the Rheinpark (Rhine Park) on the east bank.

Cologne Nightlife

Home to two orchestras, the Gürzenich-Orchester and the WDR Sinfonieorchester, the **Kölner Philharmonie,** Bischofsgartenstrasse 1 (☎ 0221/204-080; www.koelner-philharmonie.de), is a 1980s architectural showcase, with a soaring roof and enviable acoustics. The Rhineland's leading opera house, **Oper Köln,** Offenbachplatz (☎ 0221/2212-8400; www.operkoeln. com), is known for its innovative repertory of both classical and contemporary works. Dance programs are also presented.

The daily jazz is hot at **Jazzlokal Em Streckstrump,** Buttermarkt 37 (☎ 0221/257-7931; www.papajoes.de). Several times a week, **Underground,** Vogelsanger Strasse 200 (☎ 0221/542-326; www.underground-cologne.de), hosts alternative rock bands. **Luxor,** Luxemburger Strasse 40 (☎ 0221/924-460; www.luxor-koeln. de), offers live music most nights, generally from inexperienced bands that show promise.

One of the city's most dramatic and surreal nightlife options is ★ **E-Werk,** Schanzenstrasse 28 (☎ 0221/96790; www.e-werk-cologne.com), a combination of a dance club and a large concert hall. It's housed within what used to be an electrical power plant. Recorded music alternates with live acts.

> Madonna in the Rose Bower, *by Stefan Lochner, one of the Wallraf-Richartz-Museum's most highly prized pieces.*

5 kids **Schokoladenmuseum (Chocolate Museum).** Chocolate has been doing its psychoactive stuff on humans for at least 3,000 years, and the Schokoladenmuseum on the Rhine bank has the skinny—well, maybe that's not the right word in this case—on the how's, why's, and wherefore's. A production line shows you how it all comes together, and you get to taste the final product. ⏱1 hr. Am Schokoladenmuseum 1A. ☎0221/931-8880. www.schokoladenmuseum. de. Admission 7.50€ adults, 5€ kids 6–16, 21€ families. Tues–Fri 10am–6pm, Sat–Sun 11am–7pm. *U-Bahn:* Severinsbrücke.

6 kids **Odysseum.** The Odysseum science center is an "educational experience," yes, but a fun one! All the old favorites are here—and you don't get much older than the formation

Cologne's Traditional Beer Taverns

Order a beer in Cologne and you're sure to get a *Kölsch* (pictured above). That's both the name of the local beer—by which any true-born Cologne native means the *only* beer—and the name for the local dialect. Indeed, it is quipped that *Kölsch* is the only language you can drink. In traditional brew houses, this light, top-fermented beer will be served by a blue-shirted, invariably sardonic waiter known as a *Köbe*, a name that dates back to medieval pilgrims on the Jakobusweg, or the pilgrimage route to Santiago de Compostela, in Spain. Among the most atmospheric taverns in Cologne's Altstadt (Old Town) where you can down a local beer (and scarf a hot meal) are these:

- **Alt-Köln am Dom,** Trankgasse 7–9 (☎0221/137-471).

- **Ausschank der Paffen Brauerei Max Päffgen,** Heumarkt 62 (☎0221/257-7765; www.max-paeffgen.de).

- **Brauhaus Sion,** Unter Taschenmacher 5–7 (☎0221/257-8540; www.brauhaus-sion.de).

- **Früh am Dom,** Am Hof 12–18 (☎0221/2613-2111; www.frueh.de).

- **Haus Töller,** Weyerstrasse 96 (☎0221/258-9316; www.haus-toeller.de).

- **Päffgen Brauhaus,** Friesenstrasse 64–66 (☎0221/135-461; www.paeffgen-koelsch.de).

of the planet and the career of the dinosaurs. These are backed up by some newbies, like robots and virtual space adventures. It's all hands-on, heads up, and buttons down. Language may be a barrier at some stations, but at others the lingo is universal. ⏱ 4 hr. Corintostrasse 1, Köln-Kalk. ☎ 0221/6906-8111. www.odysseum.de. Admission 14€ adults, 9.50€ kids 13–17, 7.50€ kids 4–12, 34.50€ families. Daily usually 9am–6pm or 10am–7pm; times vary, so check before going. *S-Bahn:* Köln Trimbornstrasse. Tram: 1 or 9.

❼ Claudius Therme. A modern take on the Roman baths so beloved in the time of emperor Claudius, this facility in the Rheinpark has multiple indoor and outdoor pools, along with spa, sauna, massage, and other wellness services. ⏱ At least 2 hr. Sachsenbergstrasse 1. ☎ 0221/981-440. www.claudius-therme.de. Admission Mon–Fri 2 hr. 14€, 4 hr. 20€; Sat–Sun and holidays 2 hr. 16€, 4 hr. 22€. Daily 9am–midnight. *S-Bahn:* Köln Messe/Deutz, and then bus 150.

Where to Stay & Dine

> A medieval structure that escaped the ravages of World War II houses the traditional wine tavern and restaurant Das Kleine Stapelhäuschen.

★★ **Brasserie Bruegel** BELGISCHES VIERTEL *CONTINENTAL* Cologne has its share of Belgian-style Bruegelian flair, typified by this split-level place with modish good looks and live music after 10pm. Hohenzollernring 17. ☎ 0221/252-579. www.bruegel.de. Entrees 15€–25€. AE, MC, V. Lunch & dinner Mon–Fri, dinner Sat–Sun. *U-Bahn:* Westend.

★ **Chelsea** BELGISCHES VIERTEL Original art fills this chic boutique hotel, with its glamorously contemporary rooms and huge, beautifully maintained bathrooms. The on-site restaurant is a sophisticated rendezvous point. Jülicherstrasse 1. ☎ 0221/207-150. www.hotel-chelsea.de. 35 units. Doubles 91€–164€. AE, DC, MC, V. *U-Bahn:* Rudolfplatz.

★★ **Das Kleine Stapelhäuschen** ALTSTADT-NORD Housed in a rare medieval building that survived World War II, this Fish Market fixture has period atmosphere and a traditional wine tavern and restaurant. Fischmarkt 1–3. ☎ 0221/272-7777. www.koeln-altstadt.de/stapelhaeuschen. 32 units. Doubles 64€–141€ w/breakfast. AE, MC, V. *U-Bahn:* Heumarkt.

★★★ **Hotel im Wasserturm** ALTSTADT-SÜD A daringly reinvented 19th-century round water tower southwest of the city center is now an 11-story deluxe hotel, with ingenious contemporary design and decor. Kaygasse 2. ☎ 0221/20080. www.hotel-im-wasserturm.de. 88 units. Doubles 175€–385€. AE, DC, MC, V. *U-Bahn:* Poststrasse.

★ **Konak** NEUSTADT-NORD *TURKISH* This unassuming restaurant, popular with locals and visiting Turks alike, focuses on putting the flavorful tastes of Anatolia on the plate instead of wearing its ethnic heritage on its sleeve. Weidengasse 42–44. ☎ 0221/121-385. www.konak-koeln.de. Entrees 7€–20€. AE, DC, MC, V. Dinner Tues–Sun. *U-* or *S-Bahn:* Hansaring.

★★ **Le Moissonnier** NEUSTADT-NORD *FRENCH* A picture of the early 20th century, this brasserie has mirrors, cove moldings, dark paneling, bentwood chairs, and tiled floors. Menu items change according to how inspiration moves the chef. Krefelder Strasse 25. ☎ 0221/729-479. www.lemoissonnier.de. Entrees 30€–40€. V. Lunch & dinner Tues–Sat. *U-* or *S-Bahn:* Hansaring.

Speyer

Founded around 10 B.C. as a Roman military outpost on the Rhine and later expanded as the minor town of Civitas Nemetum, Speyer grew from these unpromising beginnings to be one of Germany's most prestigious medieval towns, a place of kings, emperors, and imperial assemblies and a seat of powerful bishops. It is primarily this medieval significance that makes Speyer (pop. 50,000) worth visiting today.

> Speyer's enormous and ornate Kaiserdom has two massive domes and four spires and houses the tombs of four emperors.

START Bus no. 573 goes from the Speyer train station to Domplatz (for the Kaiserdom) in around 10 minutes. It's a walk of about 1.6km (1 mile) from the train station, going south on Bahnhofstrasse, and then east on Maximilianstrasse. You can easily walk to all other sights featured here.

1 ★★★ **Kaiserdom (Imperial Cathedral).** Consecrated in 1030 and dedicated to the Virgin Mary and St. Stephen (and with the Archangel Michael, John the Baptist, and St. Bernard of Clairvaux as additional patrons), Speyer's Kaiserdom is the largest Romanesque edifice in Germany. When you enter the medieval church you seem lost in a vast space; the whole length of the nave and east chancel opens up, lit by muted daylight from above. The cathedral has two domes and four

spires and contains the tombs of four German emperors, three empresses, four kings, and a host of bishops. ⏱ 1 hr. Domplatz. ☎ 06232/1020. www.dom-speyer.de. Cathedral: free admission; Crypt: 2€ adults, 1€ kids 6–16. Apr–Oct Mon–Sat 9am–7pm, Sun noon–5pm; Nov–Mar Mon–Sat 9am–5pm, Sun noon–5pm.

2 **Domgarten.** The cathedral's extensive garden extends all the way to the Rhine. These leafy acres host an annual open-air festival of live music, theater, and dance in September. ⏱ 30 min. Free admission. Open 24/7.

3 ★★ **Historisches Museum der Pfalz.** The castlelike building (1908) next to the cathedral that houses the Historisches Museum der Pfalz (Palatinate Historical Museum) provides much-needed space for the museum's million-object catalog. Exhibits date from prehistoric

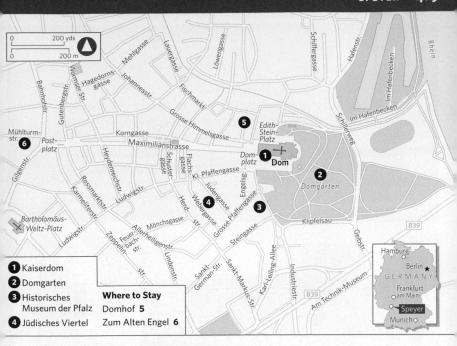

1 Kaiserdom
2 Domgarten
3 Historisches
Museum der Pfalz
4 Jüdisches Viertel

Where to Stay
Domhof **5**
Zum Alten Engel **6**

times, though the Roman and medieval periods make the strongest showing. The Weinmuseum (Wine Museum) shows how the Romans produced their vino and has the world's oldest bottle of wine (c. A.D. 300)—containing an unappetizing-looking liquid. Objects found in the tombs of emperors under the Dom are exhibited in the Domschatz (Treasury). Among the most celebrated exhibits here are the remarkably plain crown of Holy Roman Emperor Konrad II from 1027, and a page written in silver from the 5th-century *Codex Argenteus* (a replica, sadly—the original is too fragile to be displayed). ⏱ 2 hr. Domplatz. ☎ 06232/13250. www.museum.speyer.de. Admission 4€ adults, 3€ kids 6–16, 10€ families. Tues–Sun 10am–6pm.

4 Jüdisches Viertel (Jewish Quarter).
Speyer was once a center of Jewish culture. Ruins from the old Jewish Quarter can be seen behind the Palatinate Historical Museum. The synagogue's east wall is the *Judenbad* (*mikveh* in Hebrew), a 12th-century purification bathhouse, the oldest and best-preserved relic of its kind in the country. ⏱ 45 min. Judengasse. ☎ 06232/291-971. Admission 2€ adults, 1€ kids 6–16 (for access to both the ruins and bathhouse). Apr–Oct daily 10am–5pm.

Where to Stay & Dine

★★ Domhof ZENTRUM
Right across the street from the cathedral, this hotel has location, a garden ambience enhanced by wall-climbing plants, and a moderately Old World style. Check out the adjoining house-brewery and restaurant. Bauhof 3. ☎ 06232/13290. www.domhof.de. 49 units. Doubles 83€–125€ w/breakfast. MC, V.

★★ Zum Alten Engel ZENTRUM *RHINELAND*
To reach this convivial spot, you descend antique masonry steps to a century-old, brick-vaulted cellar, flickering with candles and awash with antiques. The hearty regional cuisine includes such dishes as fried sausages, liver dumplings, sauerbraten, and pepper steak. An extensive wine list includes some 180 choices. Mühlturmstrasse 7. ☎ 06232/70914. www.zumaltenengel.de. Entrees 11€–22€. MC, V. Apr–Sept dinner Mon–Sat; Oct–Mar dinner daily.

Trier

Despite being tucked away in an outlying corner of the country, scarcely reached by the beaten track, lively, alluring Trier (pop. 105,000) sports an enviable list of accomplishments and attractions. Historically, it looks back proudly on its time as an ancient Roman city and onetime imperial capital. Culturally, due to proximity to Luxembourg and France, it has more than a whiff of francophone style. And in the eats and drinks department, it's a center of Mosel viticulture and sustains a roster of regional, national, and international restaurants. Try to devote a full day to Trier.

> The ancient monument of Porta Nigra was once a heavily armed gate for the Romans who founded Trier.

START The Porta Nigra is the ideal place to start out. The tourist information office is here, and for those traveling by train, it's a walk of just 600m (⅓ mile) along Bahnhofstrasse and Christophstrasse from Trier's Hauptbahnhof (main train station). Most city buses also stop at the gate.

❶ ★★ Porta Nigra (Black Gate). The multi-story, gray sandstone Black Gate (c. A.D. 200) was the fortified north gate in the ancient Roman city's defensive walls. Trier was founded by the Romans as Augusta Treverorum on the lands of the conquered Treveri tribe in 30 B.C.,

making this Germany's oldest city, and in the early 4th century it served as the empire's capital in the west during Constantine the Great's ascent to supreme power. After the fall of the empire, the Porta Nigra was saved for posterity by being made a Christian church; today, it and the rest of the city's Roman remains are a UNESCO World Heritage site. Tours of the gate are led by a guide wearing the full armor and regalia of a Roman army centurion. ⏱1 hr. Porta-Nigra-Platz. ☎ 0651/75424. Admission 2.10€ adults, 1€ kids 6–18, 5.10€ families. Apr–Sept daily 9am–6pm; Mar and Oct daily 9am–5pm; Nov–Feb daily 9am–4pm.

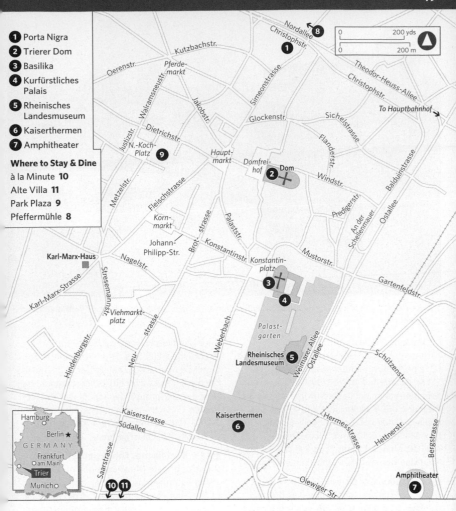

Map Legend

1. Porta Nigra
2. Trierer Dom
3. Basilika
4. Kurfürstliches Palais
5. Rheinisches Landesmuseum
6. Kaiserthermen
7. Amphitheater

Where to Stay & Dine

à la Minute **10**
Alte Villa **11**
Park Plaza **9**
Pfeffermühle **8**

2 ★★ Trierer Dom (Cathedral). Trier's vast cathedral, dedicated to St. Peter, shares its parent town's own distinction as being the oldest in Germany. It developed from a church built around 320 on the site of a patrician's residence, possibly the house of Constantine's mother, the empress Helena (St. Helen). Over the next 17 centuries, the cathedral was variously extended, redesigned, and repaired, though most of it is in the Romanesque style and made from the same gray local sandstone as the Porta Nigra. The Domschatz (Treasury) contains many historically important

> The ancient Trierer Dom has its origins in a church built on the site circa 320.

> *Kaiserthermen, an amazing labyrinth of ancient Roman bath ruins, was built by Emperor Constantine in the 4th century.*

ecclesiastical objects, among them the 10th-century, gold-and-ivory Andreas-Tragaltar, a portable altar named for St. Andrew. ⏱ 1 hr. Domfreihof. ☎ 0651/979-0790. www.dominformation.de. Cathedral: free admission; Treasury: 1.50€ adults, .50€ kids 4-16, 3.50€ families. Cathedral: Apr-Oct daily 6:30am-6pm; Nov-Mar daily 6:30am-5:30pm. Treasury: Apr-Oct Mon-Sat 10am-5pm, Sun 12:30-5pm; Nov-Mar Mon-Sat 11am-4pm, Sun 2-4pm.

❸ ★ **Basilika.** Constantine had this impressively large basilica constructed as the *aula palatina,* or audience hall (throne room), of his palace in around 310. It is said to be the second-largest roofed building to have survived from the Roman Empire, surpassed only by the Pantheon in Rome. Even though most of the palace was subsequently dismantled, the basilica, like the Porta Nigra, escaped this fate by being transformed into a Christian church. ⏱ 30 min. Konstantinplatz. ☎ 0651/72468. Free admission (except during organ recitals and other concerts). Apr-Oct Mon-Sat 10am-6pm, Sun noon-6pm; Nov-Mar Tues-Sat 11am-noon and 3-4pm, Sun noon-1pm.

❹ **Kurfürstliches Palais.** Next to the Basilika stands the 17th-century rococo Kurfürstliches Palais (Electoral Palace), built in the German Renaissance style as a residence for the Archbishop-Electors, Trier's governors. You won't be able to see the interior of the palace because it's used for city offices, but you can take a stroll through the adjoining ★ **Palastgarten** (Palace Garden; free admission, open 24/7), full of ponds, flowers, and statues. ⏱ 30 min. Am Palastgarten.

❺ ★★ **Rheinisches Landesmuseum.** The Rhineland State Museum is one of the outstanding museums of Roman antiquities north of the Alps. Numerous reliefs from funerary monuments show daily life in Roman times. The museum's most popular exhibit is the *Neumagener Weinschiff* (Neumagen Wine Ship), a sculpture of a wine-bearing vessel of the 3rd century A.D. Also to be seen are mosaics and frescoes, ceramics, glassware, a 2,700-year-old Egyptian casket with a mummified occupant, an outstanding coin collection, and prehistoric and medieval art and sculpture. ⏱ 1 hr. Weimarer Allee 1. ☎ 0651/97740. www.landesmuseum-trier.de. Admission 6€ adults, 4€ kids 6-18, 12€ families. Tues-Sun 10am-5pm.

❻ **Kaiserthermen (Imperial Baths).** At the southern end of the Palastgarten stand the ruins of the magnificent Kaiserthermen, built by Constantine in the early 4th century. This was among the entire empire's largest bath complexes, though evidence from the labyrinthine network of underground support facilities suggests it was never brought fully into use. In addition to viewing what remains on the surface, you get to go underground in the company of a guide reenacting the role of an imperial secret agent. ⊙ 1 hr. Palastgarten. ☎ 0651/44262. Admission 2.10€ adults, 1€ kids 6–18, 5.10€ families. Apr–Sept daily 9am–6pm; Mar and Oct daily 9am–5pm; Nov–Feb daily 9am–4pm.

➐ Amphitheater. In addition to baths and patrician dwellings, a well-appointed Roman city needed an amphitheater, where gladiators engaged in hand-to-hand combat, animals fought, and Christians were thrown to the lions, all for the gratification of the crowd. Trier's dates from A.D. 100 (it's the oldest Roman structure in Trier), and could hold around 20,000 spectators. You can tour both the aboveground and underground remains with a guide dressed as a gladiator. ⊙ 1 hr. Amphitheaterplatz. ☎ 0651/73010. Admission 2.10€ adults, 1€ kids 6–18, 5.10€ families. A collective ticket to the amphitheater, baths, and Porta Nigra is available from the tourist office. Apr–Sept daily 9am–6pm; Mar and Oct daily 9am–5pm; Nov–Feb daily 9am–4pm.

The Revolutionary Next Door

Trier's most famous son is not Constantine the Great—who in any case was not a native of the city—but someone of whom the Roman emperor might not have entirely approved: Karl Marx (1818–83). The founder of scientific socialism, who wrote with relish of the "specter" of Communism that was haunting Europe, was born in the **Karl-Marx-Haus,** Brückenstrasse 10 (☎ 0651/970-680; www.fes.de/marx; admission 3€), a solid burgher's house built in 1727 that's now a museum. It contains exhibits on Marx's personal history, volumes of poetry, original letters, and photographs with personal dedications. There's also a collection of rare editions of his works.

Where to Stay & Dine

★★★ **à la Minute** TRIER-SÜD *MEDITERRANEAN*
Trier's old Südbahnhof (South Station) has been turned into an airy and spacious platform for delectable dining. The menu is limited in extent but not in ambition. Leoplatz 1. ☎ 0651/650-2285. www.a-la-minute-trier.de. Entrees 13€–21€. AE, MC, V. Lunch & dinner Sun–Fri, dinner Sat. Bus: 3, 9, 15, or 83.

★★ **Alte Villa** TRIER-SÜD
This 1743 baroque villa in the south of the city has been transformed into a tasteful lodging, with breakfast served in the garden in warm weather. Saarstrasse 133. ☎ 0651/938-120. www.hotelaltevilla.de. 20 units. Doubles 85€–130€ w/breakfast. AE, MC, V. Bus: 3, 9, 15, or 83.

★ **Park Plaza** ZENTRUM
There won't be any unpleasant surprises at this sleek chain hotel just steps from the center of town. Rooms are contemporary but in a cozy rather than a cool way. Nikolaus-Koch-Platz 1. ☎ 0651/99930. www.parkplaza-trier.de. 150 units. Doubles 115€–175€. AE, MC, V. Bus: 3, 4, 6, 7, 8, 11, 16, 40, 81, 82, or 83.

★★ **Pfeffermühle** MOSEL *FRENCH*
The "Pepper Mill" occupies two elegant and restrained pale-pink-and-white dining rooms in a 19th-century house with windows overlooking the Mosel. In summer, you can dine on the terrace. Zurlaubener Ufer 76. ☎ 0651/26133. www.pfeffermuehle-trier.de. Entrees 22€–28€. MC, V. Dinner Mon, lunch & dinner Tues–Sat. Bus: 2, 6, 7, 12, or 87.

Frankfurt, the Rhineland & the Ruhr Fast Facts

Accommodations Booking Services
Call **Hotel Reservation Service** (☎ 0870/243-0003) from anywhere in Germany. Tourist info points at major train stations and airports can assist with last-minute local hotel bookings. Tourist offices also arrange accommodation.

ATMs/Cashpoints
The main towns in the region have multiple ATMs from a range of banks.

Dentists & Doctors
If you have a mild medical issue or dental problem, most hotels will be able to refer you to a doctor (*Arzt*) or dentist (*Zahnarzt*) who speaks English. You will need to provide proof of permanent or travel insurance (an EHIC card in the case of most residents of Europe), or to pay for treatment. For a minor injury that requires speedy treatment, go to the *Notaufnahme* (emergency) department of the nearest *Krankenhaus* (hospital). For a serious injury, call the doctor/ambulance emergency number (see "Emergencies," below). To contact an English-speaking dentist or doctor in Frankfurt, call ☎ 069/19292.

Emergencies
To call the police (*Polizei*), dial ☎ **110.** To report a fire or to summon an emergency doctor (*Notarzt*) or an ambulance (*Krankenwagen*), dial ☎ **112.**

Getting There
This region is served primarily by **Frankfurt am Main** (FRA) in the east, and by a number of regional airports, including **Saarbrücken** (SCN) in the south, **Cologne Bonn** (CGN) in the center, and **Düsseldorf** (DUS) in the north. Plenty of international and national flights are available to all of these airports. All cities and most towns are well served by train. International highways enter the region from the Netherlands, Belgium, Luxembourg, and France to the west and southwest, and important German highways enter from Berlin, Hannover, Dresden, and Stuttgart. **Eurolines** (www.eurolines.com) international buses stop at Aachen, Cologne, Dortmund, Duisburg, Düsseldorf, Essen, and Frankfurt.

Getting Around
In much of the region you can travel fast on the Autobahn (A) roads and *Bundesstrasse* (B) roads—many of these two categories, in particular the A roads, also have a European (E) designation. Using the comprehensive and efficient train network is undoubtedly the best way to get around by public transportation. Most rail service—and all InterCity trains, including the high-speed ICE (InterCity-Express) trains—are operated by **Deutsche Bahn** (German Railways; www.bahn.com). Some local and regional services are operated by private train companies. Regional bus service is not great, and is likely to be slow. Cologne, Dortmund, Düsseldorf, Essen, and Frankfurt have integrated public transportation networks of light-rail (*S-Bahn*) and underground (*U-Bahn*) trains, trams, buses, and trains.

Internet Access
Many hotels have one or more terminals for the use of their guests. Wi-Fi and/or broadband is often available, either free or for an hourly or daily charge. Most towns of any size are likely to have at least one internet cafe. In Frankfurt, there's **CyberRyder,** Töngesgasse 31 (☎ 069/9139-6754; www.cyberyder.de).

Pharmacies
In German, a pharmacy is an *Apotheke*. For cosmetics and toiletries, go to a *Drogerie*. Most pharmacies operate during normal shopping hours and post details of the nearest 24-hour pharmacy.

Police
To report a lost or stolen article, such as a wallet or passport, visit the local police (*Polizei*) in your location. To call the police from anywhere in Germany, dial ☎ **110.**

Post Office
You'll recognize branches of **Deutsche Post** (☎ 01802/3333; www.deutschepost.de) by their yellow sign with a black horn. Some

centrally located post offices in towns and cities are as follows: **Cologne:** Trankgasse 11 (Altstadt-Nord); **Düsseldorf:** Heinrich-Heine-Allee 23 (Altstadt); **Frankfurt:** Hauptbahnhof (main train station) and Zeil 90 (both Innenstadt); **Trier:** Fleischstrasse 56–60 (Innenstadt). Post offices are open Monday to Friday 8am–6pm, Saturday 8am–noon.

Safety

The risk of being a crime victim in this region is not great, although slightly higher in the larger cities. Frankfurt is relatively safe, but it's best to stay out of the area around the Hauptbahnhof (main train station) at night.

Taxis

In Cologne, call **TAXI RUF Köln** (☎ 0221/2882); in Frankfurt, **Taxi Frankfurt** (☎ 069/230-001); in Düsseldorf, **Taxi Düsseldorf** (☎ 0211/33333); and in Trier, **Taxi-Zentrale-Trier** (☎ 0651/12012).

Telephones

Call ☎ 11837 for information and ☎ 11834 for international information. Cologne's area code is 0221; Frankfurt's is 069; Düsseldorf's is 0211; Saarbrücken's is 0681; and Trier's is 0651. Dial the area code when calling a town number from outside the town; you don't need to dial it when calling a town number from inside the town. There are public phones in many places—some accept coins and some take phone cards, available at post offices and newsstands.

Toilets

In some places you will find clean public toilets, many of them automatic and wheelchair-accessible; you need a .50€ coin to unlock the door. More convenient and widespread are toilets in cafes, bars, restaurants, hotels, malls, and some stores, and at highway services and rest areas. Even if you are not obliged to pay, it is customary to leave the attendant .50€. There are many decent public toilets in central Frankfurt, especially in the Altstadt (Old Town).

Tours

Wine tours are the classic kinds of tours in an area that counts six of Germany's 13 officially recognized wine regions, with those along the Rhine and Mosel (p. 456), and through the Rheingau (p. 452, **3**) being the most popular. The Rhine and Mosel rivers are equally noted for boat tours, both short hops and full-fledged multiday cruises. Industrial archaeology tours are available in cities like Dortmund (p. 470, **5**) and Essen (p. 469, **3**). The Roman Empire's frontier along the Rhine has left behind a huge number of places worth visiting—ruins, archaeological sites, and museums. The later medieval period has bequeathed the area a great many romantic and ruined castles. The U.S. army fought a series of hard battles in this region during World War II. The battle for the Schneifel ridge, which kicked off the Battle of the Bulge, was an out-and-out defeat; the Battle of the Huertgen Forest could be considered a pyrrhic victory, with heavy casualties incurred; and the capture of the bridge at Remagen and the breakout across the Rhine were decisive victories. Military tours of these areas are available.

Visitor Information

Tourist offices are ubiquitous. They range from big-city branches in Cologne, Düsseldorf, and Frankfurt, all the way down to tiny offices in some villages. In addition to those provided with the individual town listings, other key tourist offices are as follows: **AACHEN** Tourist Info Elisenbrunnen, Friedrich-Wilhelm-Platz; ☎ 0241/180-2960; www.aachen.de; Easter to Dec Mon–Fri 9am–6pm, Sat 9am–3pm, Sun 10am–2pm; Jan to Easter Mon–Fri 9am–6pm, Sat 9am–2pm. **COLOGNE** Service Center, Kardinal-Höffner-Platz 1; ☎ 0221/2213-0400; www.koelntourismus.de; Mon–Sat 9am–8pm, Sun 10am–5pm. **FRANKFURT** There are two branches, one at the Hauptbahnhof (main train station, main entrance; ☎ 069/2123-8800; Mon–Fri 8am–9pm, Sat–Sun 9am–6pm) and the other in Römerberg (Römerberg 27; ☎ 069/2123-8800; Mon–Fri 9:30am–5:30pm, Sat–Sun 9:30am–4pm). The website for both is www.frankfurt-tourismus.de. **SPEYER** Maximilianstrasse 13; ☎ 06232/142-392; www.speyer.de; Apr–Oct Mon–Fri 9am–5pm, Sat 10am–3pm, Sun 10am–2pm; Nov–Mar Mon–Fri 9am–5pm, Sat 10am–noon. **TRIER** Porta Nigra; ☎ 0651/978-080; www.trier.de; Jan–Feb Mon–Sat 10am–5pm, Sun 10am–1pm; Mar–Apr & Nov–Dec Mon–Sat 9am–6pm, Sun 10am–3pm; May–Oct Mon–Sat 9am–6pm, Sun 10am–5pm.

11

Sauerland, Niedersachsen & Bremen

The Best of Sauerland, Niedersachsen & Bremen in 3 Days

Niedersachsen (Lower Saxony) is a large region that lies between the industrial Ruhr district and the North Sea. In just 3 days, it's not easy to fit in the kind of touring that lets you get off the beaten path. Mixing towns with a varied character and segments of scenic roads adds up to a fair introduction. On the first day, you visit Kassel and tour through the Fulda and Weser river valleys to iconic Hameln. The second day has you touring around Hameln before heading to Hannover to visit the royal gardens there. Bremen, a historic port city, takes up Day 3.

> **PREVIOUS PAGE** *This whimsical statue depicts the animal characters of the "Bremen City Musicians" fairy tale by the Brothers Grimm.* **THIS PAGE** *Bergpark Wilhelmshöhe, outside Kassel, is a wonderland of parks, gardens, and palaces.*

START Kassel is 144km (89 miles) east of Dortmund on A44; and 145km (90 miles) north of Frankfurt on A5 and A7. By ICE train, it's about a 1 hour 45 minute trip from Frankfurt to Kassel. **TRIP LENGTH** 531km (330 miles).

1 ★★ **Kassel.** A location 70km (43 miles) as the crow flies northwest of Germany's geographical midpoint makes Kassel a good springboard for reaching into northern Germany by car. Reconstruction after World

> *Some of the hundreds of timber-frame houses that line the streets of the Altstadt in charming Hann. Münden.*

War II left little of historical worth in a city where in the early 19th century the Brothers Grimm collected and wrote down their classic fairy tales. The city's scenic setting straddling the Fulda River at the eastern end of Sauerland is Kassel's primary attribute. There is also the world-class quinquennial Kassel dOCUMENTA modern-art show—the next one is in 2012 (see "A Date for Your Diary").

Multiple green zones lie within leisurely reach of Kassel by car, from the ★★★ **Sauerland** (wooded, hilly country in North Rhineland-Westphalia) to the west and the ★★ **Weserbergland** (the rugged hill country that flanks the river north from Hann. Münden to beyond Hameln) to the north. You can pick up information on exploring these regions at Kassel's tourist information office. Closer to the city, and worthwhile if you have time to investigate them, are the forested **Habichtswald** and **Meissner-Kaufunger Wald** nature parks. Still closer, and easy to get to by public transportation, are antique parks that stand a chance of being chosen for UNESCO World Heritage status. Along the Fulda's left bank, ★ **Staatspark Karlsaue** is a baroque garden with an impressive Orangerie (1710) as its focus and a small lake, the Aueteich, at its heart. An even better choice is ★★ **Bergpark Wilhelmshöhe,** a stunning arrangement of baroque parks, gardens, palaces,

Traveling by Train

If you're traveling by train, Kassel isn't as good a starting point as it is for those going around by car. Train riders should consider basing themselves for 2 or 3 nights in centrally located Hannover, visiting both that city and Hameln (45 min. away) from there and then either moving on to Bremen (1 hr.) for the third night or staying 1 more night in Hannover and visiting Bremen from there.

A Date for Your Diary

Kassel's dOCUMENTA modern-art show (www.documenta.de) is one of Europe's most eagerly awaited. Since it comes around but once every 5 years, there can be quite a lot of eager waiting involved. It started out in 1955 as a way of showcasing works by artists the Nazis had considered "degenerate." Nowadays, most art displayed at dOCUMENTA is created especially for the show. The most recent show, in 2007, attracted more than 750,000 visitors to Kassel during its 3-month run; the next dOCUMENTA is in 2012 (June 9–Sept 16).

> The 587-foot Herkules monument in Kassel's Bergpark Wilhelmshöhe features a statue atop a pyramid and an octagonal base with cascading water.

and monuments on a hill 6km (3¾ miles) west of Kassel. Construction on the park began in 1696 but wasn't completed until 1866. At this baroque garden's heart is a neoclassical palace ★★ **Schloss Wilhelmshöhe.** The grandiose pile was built by Elector of Hesse Wilhelm I, and between 1891 and 1918 it served another Wilhelm, Kaiser Wilhelm II, as his summer residence. In addition to visiting the restored period rooms, you'll likely want to view a fine gallery of paintings by German, Dutch, and Italian Old Masters ☎ 0561/316-800; www.museum-kassel. de; admission 6€ adults, free for kids 17 and under; Apr–Oct Tues–Wed and Fri–Sun 10am–5pm, Thurs 10am–8pm; Nov–Mar Tues–Sun 10am–5pm).

Farther up the hill is one of those follies that fruitcake European bluebloods liked to construct—with a little help from the peasantry's taxes. The **Herkules** (Hercules Monument, 1717) consists of a statue of the Greek-Roman demigod standing atop a pyramid, which itself stands on a giant octagonal base from which descend long, stepped water cascades. The total height of the thing is 179m (587 ft.). No doubt it was just what Kassel was short of at the time.

In the town, be sure to visit the **Brüder Grimm-Museum** (Brothers Grimm Museum;

☎ 0561/787-2033; www.grimms.de) in its handsome villa, the Palais Bellevue (1714). ⏱ 4 hr. for one of the parks and the museum; you'll need more time if you want to explore the regions around Kassel. Tourist information: Rathaus, Obere Königsstrasse 8. ☎ 0561/707-707. www.kassel.de.

The plan now is to spend the rest of the day on a pleasant jaunt from Kassel along the Fulda and Weser river valleys, making brief stops at pretty riverside towns, to iconic Hameln, for a total distance of 143km (89 miles). The first stop, Hann. Münden, is 27km (17 miles) northeast of Kassel on riverside B3, along the winding Fuldatal (Fulda Valley).

❷ ★ **Hann Münden.** The town (its name is sometimes written as Hannoversch Münden in places) stands where the Fulda and Werra rivers flow together to form the Weser—or as a romantic poem (1899) inscribed on the Weserstein puts it, where the rivers kiss and become one. In the ★ **Altstadt** (Old Town) are hundreds of timber-frame houses dating from the 16th to the 18th centuries. Also take some time to see the central ★ **Rathaus** (Town Hall, 1618), built in the local style known as the *Weserrenaissance* (Weser Renaissance), along with the riverfront scene around the venerable stone **Alte Werrabrücke** (Old Werra Bridge, 1329). Hann. Münden is the southern entry point to the Weserbergland. ⏱ 2 hr. Tourist information: Rathaus, Lotzestrasse 2. ☎ 05541/75313. www.hann.muenden.de.

From Hann. Münden, take B80 north to Bad Karlshafen (40km/25 miles).

③ ★★ Bad Karlshafen. The many handsome white baroque buildings here are a

The Totally Awesome Baron von Münchhausen

You won't be surprised to learn that the German nobleman Karl Friedrich Hieronymous, Freiherr (Baron) von Münchhausen (1720–97), suffered from Munchausen syndrome. He invented it, after all—or at any rate, he would surely claim he did. His many tall tales are recounted in Rodolf Erich Raspe's 1888 book *The Travels and Surprising Adventures of Baron Munchausen*. In dinky little Bodenwerder, you'll find street sculptures depicting the blowhard baron sitting on a flying cannonball, riding the front half of a horse, and engaging in other highly unlikely feats of derring-do. There's the Münchhausen Museum (p. 515, ⑦), too, for anyone who wants to know more about the baron.

consequence of the town's foundation in 1699 as a refuge for Protestant French Huguenots fleeing religious persecution in their homeland. If you have enough time (a half-day at a minimum), if you are visiting during the tourist season (spring–fall), if the weather is good, and if you enjoy river cruises—admittedly a long string of *ifs*—you might want to take a boat tour from here down or up the Weser and back. ⏱ 3 hr. (not including riverboat tour). For information on Bad Karlshafen, see p. 514, ④.

Hameln, your destination for Night 1, is 76km (47 miles) north of Bad Karlshafen on B83. On the way, you pass through pretty riverside towns and villages. The most notable of these, worth at least a brief pause each, are Höxter, Holzminden (on the east bank), and Bodenwerder, hometown of that famous teller of tall tales, Baron von Münchhausen (see "The Totally Awesome Baron von Münchhausen").

④ ★★★ Hameln. Even if there were nothing more to Hameln (often written as Hamelin in English) than its association with the Pied Piper of Hamelin, it would still be worth visiting. There is more to Hameln, however, in its many handsome *Fachwerkhäuser* (timber-frame buildings) dating from the 16th and 17th centuries in a distinctive local style known as Weser Renaissance. Strolling around the town is the business for the morning of the second day. ⏱ Half-day. See p. 515, ⑧. For hotel and restaurant recommendations, see p. 517.

After lunch, head out of Hameln northeast on B217 for Hannover (48km/30 miles).

⑤ ★★★ Hannover. The state capital of Niedersachsen, Hannover (often written as Hanover in English) was once a royal city, the seat of an ambitious ducal family whose heirs inherited the throne of England and founded that country's Hanoverian dynasty. This status is reflected in the regal ★★ **Herrenhäuser Gärten** (Herrenhausen Gardens) in the north of the city. There are four interrelated gardens in this complex. If you have time for only one, make it the baroque ★★★ **Grosser Garten** (Great Garden), which dates back to 1638, though it was subsequently modified several times down to 1710.

Another grand open space in the city is ★ **Maschsee** (1936), an artificial lake created

> *The fountains in Hannover's beautifully landscaped Herrenhäuser Gärten.*

by a Nazi-era engineering project to divert the Leine River. Today it is the centerpiece of Hannover's most popular leisure zone; in summer there are boat tours on the lake. ⊕ **Half-day.** For information on Hannover, including hotel and restaurant recommendations, see p. 546.

On the morning of Day 3, take A7 north out of Hannover, and then switch to A27 northwest to Bremen (125km/78 miles).

⑥ ★★★ Bremen. Along with Hamburg, the proud *Freie Hansestadt Bremen* (Free and Hanseatic City of Bremen) is one of Germany's most important port cities (see the box on p. 578 for more on the Hanseatic League). In this case, however, the medieval Hanseatic League trading-town on the Weser River has lost much of its blue-water harbor business to Bremerhaven, 54km (34 miles) downstream as the crow flies, at the mouth of the Weser. Bremen is large enough that it'll take most of a day to visit its main sights.

Your first port of call should be ★★★ **Marktplatz.** In centuries past, the central Market square was the mercantile city's civic pride and joy (indeed it still is), lined with grand buildings and monuments that proclaimed Bremen's wealth and importance to the world. These include the 15th/17th-century ★★ **Rathaus** (Town Hall, originally built in 1410); the ★ **St.-Petri Dom** (St. Peter's Cathedral), founded in the 13th century; the merchants' 16th-century former guild hall, the **Schütting;** a statue of

the chivalrous medieval knight Roland; and a sculpture of the four animals from the Brothers Grimm fairy tale *Bremer Stadtmusikanten* (Bremen City Musicians). From here, you can stay with the days-of-yore theme by visiting the restored ★★ **Schnoorviertel,** a quaint old fishermen's district down by the Weser that's now a hive of artisanal stores, small galleries, and chic cafes. ⊕ 1 day, including Bremerhaven (**⑦**). For information on Bremen, including hotel and restaurant recommendations, see p. 538.

It's 72km (45 miles) from Bremen to Bremerhaven on the slow, minor roads along the Weser. The return journey on A27 is 66km (41 miles) by fast Autobahn (expressway).

⑦ ★ Bremerhaven. On a long summer evening, or if you have time in hand due to sticking to only a few of Bremen's main sights, you might want to consider visiting Bremen's harbor town, by car or public transportation or on a boat tour downriver on the Weser. Bremerhaven hosts two fine marine-themed museums: the ★★ **Deutsches Auswandererhaus** (German Emigration Center) and the ★ **Deutsches Schiffahrtsmuseum** (German Maritime Museum), but unless you've been a very fast mover, or passed on Bremen, it's unlikely you'll have time to visit them. In that case, the trip to Bremerhaven and back, combined with maybe a brief waterfront stroll, will have to be its own attraction. See p. 542, **⑨**.

The Best of Sauerland, Niedersachsen & Bremen in 1 Week

A week buys you plenty of variation in this large region, with its mix of cities like Hannover and Bremen, rugged landscapes and riverscapes, seacoast, and islands. I recommend ambling along on country roads for some segments, and then for others zipping along on the fast and ubiquitous Autobahn net.

> White-painted baroque buildings lend beauty to the elegant town of Bad Karlshafen on the Weser River.

START Kassel is 144km (89 miles) east of Dortmund on A44; and 145km (90 miles) north of Frankfurt on A5 and A7. By ICE train, it's about a 1 hour 45 minute trip from Frankfurt to Kassel. TRIP LENGTH 974km (605 miles).

1 ★★ **Kassel.** ☺ 3 hr. See p. 498, **1**.

Take B3 northeast out of Kassel to Simmershausen, where it hits the Fulda River and then follows its winding course downstream on the left bank, to Hann. Münden (23km/14 miles).

2 ★ **Hann. Münden.** A brief stroll around the ★ **Altstadt** (Old Town) to view some of the more than 700-centuries-old timber-frame houses concentrated here can just about cover it for Hann. Münden. ☺ 1 hr. See p. 501, **2**.

Continue on B3 to Göttingen, a distance of 32km (20 miles), through the Naturpark Hannoversch Münden's delightful forest and agricultural country.

0   20 mi
0   20 km

NORTH SEA

Nationalpark
Niedersächsisches Wattenmeer

Wattenmeer **12**

Neumünster

**SCHLESWIG-
HOLSTEIN**

Lübeck

Brunsbüttel

Itzehoe

Cuxhaven

Elbe

Stade

Hamburg

Buxtehude

Bremerhaven

Bremervörde

Wilhelmshaven
11 *Jade-
busen*

Sittensen

Elbe

Lüneburg

Westerstede

*Naturpark
Lüneburger Heide*

Oldenburg

Bremen
10

Rotenburg
(Wümme)

Uelzen

Weser

Soltau

Cloppenburg

Bassum

*Naturpark
Südheide*

Vechta

NIEDERSACHSEN

Eschede

Sulingen

Fairy Tale Road

Diepholz

Nienburg

Celle

Elbe-Seitenkanal

*Naturpark
Steinhuder
Meer*

*Steinhuder
Meer*

Mittellandkanal

Osnabrück
13

Minden

Hannover
9

Mittellandkanal

Braunschweig
8

Herford

Hildesheim
7

Salzgitter

Bielefeld

Hameln
6

Weser

Goslar

Münster
14

Gütersloh

5

*Nationalpark
Harz*

**NORDRHEIN-
WESTFALEN**

Paderborn

Fairy Tale Road

Northeim

Hamm

Lippstadt

Bad Karlshafen
4

Soest

Göttingen
3

THÜRINGEN

Hann. Münden
2

Weser

Werra

HESSEN

Kassel
1

*Nationalpark
Kellerwald-
Edersee*

Eder

Fulda

Hamburg
Berlin ★
G E R M A N Y
Frankfurt
am Main
Munich

> *Although most of Hildesheim was destroyed during World War II, this preserved area offers a glimpse of the town's historic beauty.*

3 Göttingen. With its prestigious university that dates back to 1743 and a bunch of research departments from the famed Max Planck Institute, Göttingen is very much of a student town. Having miraculously escaped serious bombing and ground combat in World War II, the ★★ **Altstadt** (Old Town) is largely original and intact. After what seems like an interminable ride through unprepossessing suburbs and outer districts, you get to experience this historical treasure around the central **Altes Rathaus** (Old Town Hall, 1443). Nearby is the famous bronze ★ **Gänseliesel-Brunnen** (Goose Girl Fountain), a copy of an original bronze sculpture (1901) of a young girl carrying geese. It's a tradition for male students to kiss the "girl" upon receiving their doctorates (there's a law against it, but it's not strictly enforced). ⏲ 2 hr.

From Göttingen, cut west across country to Bad Karlshafen on B3, L559, L561, and B80—through Dransfeld, Niemetal, Oberweser, and Gieselwerder—a scenic route 49km (30 miles) long.

4 ★★ Bad Karlshafen. This graceful town of white-painted baroque buildings on the Weser River is an entry point to the Weserbergland (Weser Hill Country) and the Deutsche Märchenstrasse (German Fairy-Tale Road; p. 512). One of the focal points for tourism in this area, it has a decent range of hotels and restaurants for your first night's stay. ⏲ 2 hr. See p. 514, **4**; for hotel and restaurant recommendations, see p. 517.

On Day 2, follow the course of the Weser River north on B83 to Hameln (79km/49 miles), a drive that takes in part of the Fairy-Tale Road (on the way to Hameln, visit stops **5**–**7** and **9** of that tour, p. 512). Your first stop is Höxter (23km/14 miles).

5 Fairy-Tale Road. Stops along this section of the Fairy-Tale Road include Höxter, Fürstenberg, and Bodenwerder. ⏲ Half-day. See p. 514, **5**–**7**.

From Bodenwerder, your last stop on the Fairy-Tale Road, take B83 north 23km (14 miles) to Hameln.

6 ★★★ **Hameln.** Touring this iconic old town should take up the afternoon of Day 2. The town has made this easy for you by painting rat symbols on the sidewalk—all you need do is follow the rats for a circular walking tour that should take around an hour to do and that takes in most of the salient points of interest in the ★★ **Altstadt** (Old Town). In addition to exploring the center of town, set aside a little time for a stroll along the Weser River. End the day with dinner at the atmospheric, if somewhat touristy, ★ **Rattenfängerhaus** (p. 517), or at one of the many other *gemütlich* (cozy) restaurants in the town. ☉ Half-day. See p. 515, **8**; for hotel and restaurant recommendations, see p. 517.

On the morning of Day 3, go east on B1, through the **Hildesheimer Wald (Hildesheim Forest),** to the county town of Hildesheim **(48km/30 miles).**

7 ★★ **Hildesheim.** This 12-centuries-old ecclesiastical center could have been one of the standout highlights of your tour. Sadly, in the closing weeks of World War II, virtually all of the timber-frame buildings in what until then had been numbered among Germany's best-preserved medieval towns were destroyed in a single Allied air raid. A surviving small zone on the southern fringe of the Altstadt (Old Town) affords a faint idea of what was lost. So, too, do the reconstructed buildings around the historic ★ **Markt:** the all-timber ★★ **Kochenhaueramtshaus** (Butchers' Guildhouse, 529), now a tolerably decent traditional restaurant that's well worth experiencing; the 13th-century Gothic **Rathaus** (Town Hall); the **Wedekindhaus** (1598); and the **Tempelhaus** (Templars' House, 1350).

Two Romanesque medieval churches, the ★★ **Dom** (Cathedral) and the ★ **Michaeliskirche** (St. Michael's Church), which trace their histories back to the 9th and 11th centuries, respectively, are UNESCO World Heritage sites. Climb the tower of the 12th-century Gothic ★ **Andreaskirche** (St. Andrew's Church) for fine views over Hildesheim.

All these points of interest are in and around the center of town. South of the center, Johnsensee is a small artificial lake on the Leine River. Stroll around the lake to get some fresh air, and if you're hungry, there's a pretty

> The 12th-century tomb of Henry the Lion stands regally beside the magnificent Dom in Braunschweig.

good cafe-restaurant, **Noah,** Hohnsen 28 (☎ 05121/691-530; www.noah-cafe.de), with a lakeside terrace. ☉ Half-day. **Tourist information:** Rathausstrasse 18–20. ☎05121/17980. www.hildesheim.de.

Continue on B1 northeast to Braunschweig (45km/28 miles).

8 ★★ **Braunschweig (Brunswick).** Founded around 900, Braunschweig took a heavy beating in World War II. Those few pieces of a once grand medieval and Renaissance heritage to have been reconstructed are clustered together in five separate *Traditionsinseln* (traditional "islands"), speckled around the ★★ **Altstadt** (Old Town). Pick up a town map from the tourist office to be able to identify and get around the *Traditionsinseln*.

The old market square, ★★ **Altstadtmarkt,** is lined by the Renaissance **Gewandhaus** (Cloth Hall, 1591), the 14th-century **Altes Rathaus** (Old Town Hall), and the **Martinikirche** (St. Martin's Church, 12th–14th centuries). To the east, on ★ **Burgplatz,** the great ★★ **Dom** (Cathedral) contains the 12th-century tombs of Duke of Saxony Heinrich der Löwe (Henry the Lion) and his wife, Mathilde. A homier historical vestige is the **Magniviertel** (Magnus Quarter), where timber-frame houses, or *Fachwerkhäuser,* shelter in the shadow of the 13th-century **Magnikirche** (St. Magnus's Church).

There are two easy and interesting side trips from Braunschweig. One is to Wolfsburg (33km/21 miles northeast on A39), a stronghold of the Volkswagen automobile corporation (think VW, Porsche, Audi, Bentley, Bugatti, Lamborghini, SEAT, and Scania). Here, the spectacular ★★ **Autostadt,** VW-Mittelstrasse (☎ 0800/288-678-238; www. autostadt.de), a visitor attraction and promotional installation rolled into one, should appeal to fans of European automotive engineering. There's a museum section of vintage autos, a hands-on section where kids get to "drive" and even design their own cars, an ear-splitting sound-and-light show starring a Lamborghini Murciélago supercar, and more. Those who prefer a good book should head instead to ★ **Wolfenbüttel** (13km/8 miles south on A395). Peruse the rare and antique volumes in the **Herzog-August-Bibliothek** (1886), based on a collection established in the town by Duke August the Younger in 1644, and then stroll among the centuries-old *Fachwerkhäuser* (timber-frame houses) in Wolfenbüttel's Altstadt (Old Town). ☉ Half-day. Tourist information: Vor der Burg 1. ☎ 0531/470-2040.

> *Hannover's Neues Rathaus.*

At the end of Day 3, take A2 west from Braunschweig to Hannover (69km/43 miles), where you can spend the night.

❾ ★★★ **Hannover.** In addition to the sites mentioned on p. 502, **❺**, visit the spectacular **Neues Rathaus** (New Town Hall, 1913), just north of Maschsee. Inside the building, which evokes imperial Germany's self-regard on the eve of World War I, are a group of models of the city at four periods in its existence (or, in the case of 1945's bomb-shattered wasteland, its nonexistence).

A neat little side trip from Hannover (you could perhaps fit it in as a detour on the way to Bremen) is ★ **Steinhuder Meer,** a lake 33km (21 miles) along B441 northwest from Hannover that's at the heart of a nature park. The small lakeside resort of Steinhude has a dock for boat trips, and local restaurants there serve smoked eel from the lake's waters. ☉ Half-day. For information on Hannover, including hotel and restaurant recommendations, see p. 546.

Head northwest from Hannover on A7 and A27 to Bremen (129km/80 miles).

❿ kids ★★★ **Bremen.** In addition to the suggestions for visiting Bremen on p. 503, **❿**, if you are traveling with kids a must-see is the hands-on science center ★★ **Universum Bremen** (p. 523, **❼**). Adult beer-lovers, on the other hand, might find that staying away from the brewery tours at **Becks-Brauerei,** Am Deich 18–19, is more than their self-control can attain (☎ 0421/5094-5555; www.becks. de/besucherzentrum; guided tours 9.50€; Jan–Apr Thurs–Fri 12:30 and 3:30pm, Sat 12:30, 2 (in English), 3:30, and 5pm; May–Dec 11am, 12:30, 2 (in English), 3:30, and 5pm, Sat 9:30 and 11am, 12:30, 2 (in English), 3:30, and 5pm). Have dinner at a decent restaurant and maybe a drink in an atmospheric bar in the restored medieval Schnoorviertel district. Stay the night in Bremen, as well as the morning of the next day. ☉ 1 day (an afternoon and the next morning). For information on Bremen, including hotel and restaurant recommendations, see p. 538.

After lunch on Day 5, take A28 westward from Bremen, and then go north on A29 to Wilhelmshaven (102km/63 miles).

> *The beautiful and popular beach on Borkum is one of seven barrier islands in the Wadden Sea off the Ostfriesland coast.*

11 kids **Wilhelmshaven.** This port town, which has long hosted one of the Germany's two main fleet bases (the other is at Kiel, on the Baltic coast; see p. 574, **9**), was effectively obliterated during World War II, then rebuilt after the war without much in the way of charm. Compensate for this with a seafood dinner before turning in at your hotel. During both world wars, warships sortied from here on operations into the North Sea and Atlantic Ocean. Today the town hosts the German navy's largest and most capable surface combatants, its guided-missile frigates, along with a significant merchant marine trade. With a pair of binoculars, you can observe ships coming and going on the Jadebusen (Jade Bay). Consider a visit on the afternoon of Day 5 or first thing the next morning to one of two marine-themed attractions, both likely to be of great interest to children: ★★ **Oceanis,** a virtual underwater research station (p. 537, **9**); and the ★ **Deutsches Marine-museum** (German Navy Museum), Südstrand 125 (☎ 04421/41061; www.marinemuseum.de; admission 8.50€ adults, 5€ kids 6–14; Apr–Oct daily 10am–6pm; Nov–Mar daily 10am–5pm). ⏱ 2 hr. For hotel and restaurant recommendations for Wilhelmshaven, see p. 537.

Ideally, you'll get away from Wilhelmshaven early on Day 6, for the tour along the Ostfriesland seacoast from east to west, all the way to Emden, a road distance of 136km (85 miles). For most of its length, the road that more or less hugs the seacoast is designated successively L6, L5, L4, and L3.

12 ★ **Ostfriesland coast.** The tour takes you through small harbor towns, most of which have their own fishing boats and an elegant sufficiency of great seafood restaurants. In addition, you can gaze offshore across the Wattenmeer (Wadden Sea) to the ★★★ **Ostfriesische Inseln** (East Frisian Islands), a line of seven low-lying barrier islands: ★★ **Wangerooge,** ★★★ **Spiekeroog,** ★★★ **Langeoog,** ★ **Baltrum,** ★★ **Norderney,** ★★ **Juist,** and ★ **Borkum.** Ferries depart for the islands from multiple harbors along the mainland coast. Together, this coastline, the shallow sea, and the islands comprise a national seashore, the ★★★ **Nationalpark Niedersächsisches Wattenmeer** (Lower Saxony Wadden Sea National Park), a popular vacation playground in summer. Ideally, you'd want to sail across to one of the islands, even if you have time enough only to take the ferry straight back again—a good bet is from Neuharlingersiel across to Spiekeroog (see "Friesland Ferries," p. 510).

Astonishingly, you can even make expeditions on foot on the seabed from the mainland to the islands (when the tide is out, naturally). This fascinating activity, known as ★ **Watt-wandern** (mudflat hiking), carries an element of risk—you could be caught by a fast-incoming tide—and should only be done in the company of an official guide (see "Walking Across a Sea," p. 535).

Although it's a natural finishing point of an east-west itinerary along the Frisian coast, Emden (p. 532, **1**) is a not hugely fetching port city but has some decent hotels and sea-food restaurants and an attractive waterfront along Am Delft, close to the Rathaus (Town Hall). Still, it's at the start of Autobahn A31, which makes it convenient for a fast getaway on your 7th and final day. (Lodging and dining recommendations for Emden appear on p. 537.) ⏱1 day.

Take A31 south, and then A30 east to Osnabrück. This is a distance of 205km (127 miles), so you should aim to get an early start on Day 7.

⑬ ★ **Osnabrück.** Along with Münster (⑭), Osnabrück was a setting for the Peace of Westphalia (1648), a treaty that brought to an end two terrible European wars, the Thirty Years War and the Eighty Years War. Taking its cue from this, and notwithstanding the many subsequent wars that have scourged Europe (and Germany's role in more than a few of them), Osnabrück has declared itself a *Friedenstadt* (City of Peace). An additional point of peaceful persuasion is that this is the hometown of author Erich Maria Remarque (1898–1970), whose 1929 novel *All Quiet on the Western Front,* set during World War I, is an

Friesland Ferries

A trip, be it ever so brief, from the mainland across to one of the ★★★ **Ostfriesische Inseln** (East Frisian Islands) is worth doing. Be aware, though, that the Wattenmeer is a very shallow sea—so shallow it disappears almost entirely at low tide! By necessity, the island ferries are dependent on the tides, so you'll need to check out the timetables to be sure you have enough time for the trip. The following information should help you to plan. Note that the ferries to Borkum and Norderney carry cars; the others will not.

ISLAND	MAINLAND HARBOR	FERRY COMPANY	TRAVEL TIME
Baltrum	**Nessmersiel**	**Baltrum Linie** ☎ 4933/99166 www.baltrum-linie.de	**30 min.** jetboat 15 min.
Borkum	**Emden**	**AG Ems** ☎ 0185/180-182 www.ag-ems.de	**130 min.** jet-catamaran 60 min.
Juist	**Norddeich**	**AG Reederei Norden Frisia** ☎ 04931/9870 www.reederei-frisia.de	**90 min.**
Langeoog	**Bensersiel**	**Schiffahrt der Inselgemeinde Langeoog** ☎ 04972/693-260 www.schiffahrt-langeoog.de	**50 min.**
Norderney	**Norddeich**	**AG Reederei Norden Frisia** 04932/9130 www.reederei-frisia.de	**55 min.**
Spiekeroog	**Neuharlingersiel**	**Fähre Spiekeroog** ☎ 04974/214 www.spiekeroog.de	**60 min.**
Wangerooge	**Harlesiel**	**Schifffahrt und Inselbahn Wangerooge** ☎ 04464/949-414 www.siw-wangerooge.de	**90 min.**

> *The 14th-century Gothic Rathaus and Lambertikirche are two of the most impressive landmarks in Münster's Prinzipalmarkt.*

antiwar classic. Head for the central Altstadt (Old Town) to visit the Rathaus (Town Hall), where the Peace of Westphalia was signed, and the central square, the Markt. The German-Jewish surrealist painter Felix Nussbaum (1904–44), who was murdered at Auschwitz, was born in Osnabrück. His hometown now has a museum, the ★ **Felix-Nussbaum-Museum,** Lotter Strasse 2 (☎ 0541/323-2064; admission 5€ adults, 3€ kids 6–16; Tues–Fri 11am–6pm, Sat–Sun 10am–6pm), dedicated to his life and work. The museum is in a striking modern building (1998) designed by Polish-American architect Daniel Libeskind.

Ironically, in view of Osnabrück's contemporary peaceful proclivities, the town is close to the scene of one of history's most famous, dramatic, and mysterious battles. Take B61, A1, and L218 northeast for 22km (14 miles) to Kalkriese and its ★★ **Varusschlacht Museum und Park,** Venner Strasse 69 (☎ 05468/920-4200; www.kalkriese-varusschlacht.de; admission 7€ adults, 4€ kids 6–16; Apr–Oct daily 10am–6pm; Nov–Mar Tues–Sun 10am–5pm). Archaeologists believe the land around the village to have been a key scene of action at the Battle of the Teutoburger Wald, in A.D. 9, in which rebel German tribes lured three full Roman legions commanded by Publius Quinctilius Varus into a trap and annihilated them. You can tour the museum and walk the battleground. ⏱ 4 hr. Tourist information: Bierstrasse 22-23. ☎ 0541/323-2202. www.osnabrueck.de.

You can either speed south on A1 to Münster (57km/35 miles) or take a scenic route through Teutoburger Wald (Teutoburg Forest) on B51 that's a tad shorter in distance but takes longer to do.

⑭ **Münster.** This is a university town with plenty of laid-back bars and other student haunts (and it shares co-honors with Osnabrück for the Treaty of Westphalia). Watch out for students and faculty zipping around on bicycles. Head for the city center around Prinzipalmarkt to view the 14th-century Gothic **Rathaus** (Town Hall) and **Lambertikirche** (St Lambert's Church); on nearby Domplatz stands the 13th-century **St.-Paulus-Dom** (St. Paul's Cathedral). South of the train station, part of the old mercantile district, the **Hansaviertel** (Hanseatic Quarter), around the Dortmund–Ems Canal harbor, is being redeveloped as a cultural hub, the **Kreativkai** (Creative Wharf). ⏱ 3 hr. Tourist information: Heinrich-Brüning-Strasse 9. ☎ 0251/492-2710. www.muenster.de.

From Münster, you can easily get to Dortmund, Düsseldorf, Cologne, and other cities in western Germany on Autobahn A1.

The Fairy-Tale Road

This itinerary covers around a quarter of the Deutsche Märchenstrasse (German Fairy-Tale Road), a tourist route 600km (373 miles) long. What the segment between Kassel and Hameln (155km/96 miles) lacks in distance, it more than makes up for with a scenic route along the Weser River through the Weserbergland (Weser Hill Country). The Brothers Grimm, Baron von Münchhausen, and the Pied Piper of Hamelin are your driving companions along the way.

> Beautiful 16th-century timber-frame homes greet visitors to Marktstrasse in the historic village of Höxter.

START **Kassel** is 232km (144 miles) east of Düsseldorf on A44; and 196km (122 miles) north of Frankfurt on A5 and A7. TRIP LENGTH 155km (96 miles) and 3 days.

1 ★★ **Kassel.** The Brothers Grimm, who lived in Kassel (pop. 195,000) in the late 18th and early 19th centuries, were inspired by local tales of sleeping princesses, witches, and magic spells to compile their collection of fairy tales. Fitting right in with the fairy-tale theme of this tour is ★ **Löwenburg** (Lion Castle;

☎ 0561/3168-0244; admission 4€, free for kids 17 and under), a faux-medieval panoply of turrets and towers that dates from 1800 and was designed to look like a ruin. ⏱ 4 hr. See p. 498, **1**.

From Kassel, take B3 northeast to Hann. Münden (27km/17 miles).

2 ★ **Hann Münden.** This attractive small town (pop. 25,000) is located at a scenic spot where the Werra and Fulda rivers combine to form the Weser. With the help of a little

Minden

To Hannover

A2

A2

Fairy Tale Road

B83

Hildesheim

Hameln
8 **12**

N I E D E R S A C H S E N

Hämelschenberg
9

Bad Pyrmont

B83

Bodenwerder
7

Weser

**N O R D R H E I N -
W E S T F A L E N**

Holzminden

B83

Höxter
5

Fürstenberg
6

A7

Paderborn

Northeim

B83

Bad Karlshafen
4 **11**

Fairy Tale Road

Sababurg
3

Göttingen

A44

B83

Weser

A7

B80

Hann. Münden
2

Werra

H E S S E N

A44

A38

Hamburg

Berlin ★

THÜRINGEN

Fairy Tale Road

Kassel
1 **10**

G E R M A N Y

Frankfurt
am Main

A49

Munich

A7

| 0 | | 10 mi |

| 0 | | 10 km |

1 Kassel

2 Hann. Münden

3 Sababurg

4 Bad Karlshafen

5 Höxter

6 Fürstenberg

7 Bodenwerder

8 Hameln

9 Schloss
    Hämelschenburg

Where to Stay & Dine

Christinenhof **12**

Hessischer Hof **11**

Hotel am Kurpark **11**

Hotel zur Krone **12**

Kartoffelhaus im
    Bürgerhaus **12**

Rattenfängerhaus **12**

Schlosshotel Bad
    Wilhelmshöhe **10**

imagination, its 700 *Fachwerkhäuser* (timber-frame houses), dating from the 16th to the 18th centuries, create the air of a fairy-tale setting. ⏱ 2 hr. See p. 501, **2**.

From Hann. Münden, take B80 north along the Weser to Rheinhardshagen, then go west on L3229, before following signs to Sababurg (24km/15 miles). Depending on how quickly you got through stops **1** and **2**, you may have to choose just one of Sababurg's attractions.

3 ★★ kids **Sababurg.** The route to here takes you through the Rheinhardswald, a forest

that's reputed to be enchanted and has a romantic castle at its heart. Sababurg's main attraction is ★★ **Dornröschenschloss** (Sleeping Beauty Castle, 1334), Sababurgerstrasse (☎ 05671/8080; www.sababurg.de; admission: gardens 2.50€ adults, 1€ kids 6–15, castle 3.50€ adults, 2.50€ kids; guided tours Apr–Oct Wed 2:30pm, Sun 11am and 2:30pm). Local legend tells of how the castle, surrounded by a forest grove containing oak trees 650 years old, is where the famous Brothers Grimm fairy tale was set. Reenactments of the tale take place at the castle. Separate guided tours of the castle and its

> *Bodenwerder boasts several sculptures that honor Germany's literary (and real-life) boastful folk hero, Baron von Münchhausen.*

fine gardens are available. Nearby **Tierpark Sababurg** (Sababurg Animal Park; ☎ 05671/766-4990; www.tierpark-sababurg.de; admission 4€ adults, 2.30€ kids 4–15; Mar daily 9am–5pm, Apr–Sept daily 8am–7pm, Oct daily 9am–6pm, Nov–Feb daily 10am–4pm) was established as an aristocratic hunting reserve in 1571. Nowadays, the 450 animals from 80 different species can still be shot—with cameras. ⏱ 4 hr. for both the castle and Animal Park.

From Sababurg, go north on K55 to Gottsbüren, then east on L763 to Gieselwerder, on the Weser River, and then north on riverside B80 to Bad Karlshafen (17km/11 miles), where you'll spend your first night.

❹ ★★ **Bad Karlshafen.** Dubbed the *Weisse Stadt* (White Town) for its many white-painted 18th-century baroque buildings, Bad Karlshafen (pop. 4,000) is an almost unreasonably handsome place. Stroll along the spa town's waterfront Kurpromenade and through the streets around central Hafenplatz to soak up sights and atmosphere. Then, visit the **Deutsches Hugenotten-Museum** (German Huguenot Museum; Hafenplatz 9;

☎ 05672/1410; www.hugenottenmuseum.de; admission 4€ adults, 2€ kids 6–16; mid-Mar to Oct Tues–Sun 10am–5pm, Nov–Dec Sat–Sun 2–5pm), housed in a former tobacco factory, to learn the story of the French Protestant Huguenot refugees for whom the town was founded in 1699. If you have time, consider a riverboat cruise on the Weser, sailing with either **Linie 2000** (☎ 05672/999-923; www.weserschiff-hessen.de) or **Flotte Weser** (☎ 05151/939-999; www.flotte-weser.de). Cruises depart from a dock on the south (left) bank, off Weserstrasse. ⏱ At least 2 hr. (not including riverboat tour). Tourist information: Kur- und Touristik-Information, Rathaus, Hafenplatz 8. ☎ 05672/999-922. www.bad-karlshafen.de.

From Bad Karlshafen, follow the course of the Weser north on B83 to Höxter (23km/14 miles).

❺ Höxter. It's worth investing an hour or so in a stroll around Höxter. The center of the Weser River town (pop. 16,000), around Marktstrasse, has impressive *Fachwerkhäuser* (timber-frame houses) and buildings in the Weser Renaissance style dating from the 16th and 17th centuries. Just 2km (1¼ miles) east of the town stands spectacular ★ **Schloss Corvey** (Corvey Palace; ☎ 05271/694-010; www.schloss-corvey.de; admission 5€ adults, 2.50€ kids 6–18; Apr and Oct Tues–Sun 10am–5pm, May–Sept daily 10am–6pm), which occupies the much-transformed buildings and gardens of a celebrated Carolingian imperial monastery founded in 815. There are regular guided tours of the palace and, at Christmas, special events—a market, a Nativity play, and concerts. ⏱ 1 hr. (not including Corvey). Tourist information: Weserstrasse 11. ☎ 05271/19433. www.hoexter.de.

At Höxter, a bridge over the Weser gives you a chance to make a rewarding side trip to Fürstenberg on the river's right (east) bank, by going south on L550 (7km/4½ miles). You can also get to Fürstenberg by river steamer from Bad Karlshafen (❹) or other docks served by the Flotte Weser line.

❻ **Fürstenberg.** This hilltop village (pop. 1,200) overlooking the river is notable for its Renaissance palace, ★ **Jagdschloss Fürstenberg** (1590), which is home to Porzellanmanufaktur Fürstenberg (☎ 05271/4010; www.fuerstenberg-porzellan.com; admission 5€ adults, 3€ kids 7–18; Apr–Oct Tues–Sun 10am–5pm, Nov–Mar Sat–Sun 10am–5pm), a manufacturer of fine white porcelain, established here in 1747. You can visit the company's museum, and children can get hands-on experience by making their own porcelain. ⏱ 2 hr. Tourist information: Meinbrexener Strasse 2. ☎ 05271/694-717. www.gemeinde-fuerstenberg.de.

Return to Höxter, and continue to follow the Weser north on B83 to Bodenwerder (41km/25 miles).

❼ ★ **kids** **Bodenwerder.** Although it's a pretty little riverside town, Bodenwerder (pop. 6,000) might not entirely justify a visit—except that it's the hometown of Baron von Münchhausen (see "The Totally Awesome Baron von Münchhausen," p. 502), whose tall tales continue to tickle funny bones around the world centuries after he lived. Naturally, there's a **Münchhausen Museum** (☎ 05533/40541), on Münchhausenplatz, and a bunch of sculptures around town that illustrate some of his many remarkable . . . well, unbelievable, really . . . feats. ⏱ 2 hr.

Continue north on B83 to Hameln (23km/14 miles), where you'll spend the night.

❽ ★★★ **kids** **Hameln.** Not only does Hameln "own" one of the best-known and most disquieting fairy tales of all, that of the Pied Piper of Hamelin (see the box, below), but it looks the part, too. The town (pop. 58,000), better known in English as Hamelin, has a magnificent ★★ **Altstadt** (Old Town). This is not filled with vast monumental buildings but is built to a human scale, with row upon row of delightful 16th- and 17th-century *Fachwerkhäuser* (timber-frame houses), many of them with painted and carved decorations on their facades. Thanks to those fabled rats, Hameln is a commercial success story, with a large roster of craft and souvenir stores, hotels, and restaurants and cafes with sidewalk terraces. It carries this off with

The Pied Piper of Hamelin

He who doesn't pay the piper may later pay a terrible price. According to legend, the good burghers of Hameln were forced to learn this lesson in 1284, when they engaged a traveling rat-catcher to rid the town of a plague of rats. With a price in gold agreed, the Pied Piper played his enchanted pipe, and the rats followed him down to the Weser River, where they drowned. The townsfolk refused to pay up, though, so he played his pipe once more, and this time 130 of the town's children followed him and disappeared from human ken.

If today's citizens feel any remorse about being descended from swindlers, they do a good job of disguising it. For Hameln, the rat-catcher's tale is the gift that keeps on giving, right down to the present day. The simplest explanation behind the legend may be that emigrants—who were likely to have been the young and adventurous—may have been enticed to leave Hameln in the 13th century for scantly populated lands in eastern Europe.

Whatever the truth, if any, kids love the delightful shivers the Pied Piper fairy tale imparts, and the engaging thought that their own parents, too, would be ever so sad if their little darlings were no longer around.

> *Sundays at noon, Hameln actors recreate the local legend of the Pied Piper in a costumed children's play.*

considerable charm. Head first to the central ★★ **Hochzeitshaus** (Wedding House, 1617), a civic hall in the Weser Renaissance style. Several times a day, the building's *Glockenspiel* (carillon) chimes out, and mechanical figures emerge to reenact the Pied Piper tale. Every Sunday at noon from mid-May to mid-September a free open-air performance of the fairy tale takes place on a stage in front of the Hochzeitshaus. On a self-guided walking tour of the main sights—easily done by following the rat icons on the sidewalk—you'll see points of interest that include the Gothic **Marktkirche St.-Nicolai** (St. Nicholas's Market Church, c. 1200); the ★ **Rattenfängerhaus** (Rat-Catcher's House, 1603), a not entirely appetizing name for what's now a restaurant (p. 517); the **Dempterhaus** (1608); and the 19th-century **Pfortmühle** (mill), down by the Weser. Finally, visit ★ **Museum Hameln,** Osterstrasse 8–9 (☎ 05151/202-1215; www.museum-hameln.de; at this writing the museum was closed for refurbishment and was provisionally expected to reopen in January 2011), housed in a pair of side-by-side Weser Renaissance jewels, the **Leisthaus** (1589) and the

★ **Stiftsherrenhaus** (Canon's House, 1558). ⏲ 6 hr. Tourist information: Hameln Marketing und Tourismus, Deisterallee 1, Bürgergarten. ☎ 05151/957-823. www.hameln.de.

From Hameln, go south on B83 to Emmerthal (about midway between Bodenwerder and Hameln), and go right (west) at Emmerthal on L431 for 2.5km (1½ miles) to Hämelschenburg, for a total distance of 11km (7 miles).

❾ ★ **Schloss Hämelschenburg.** If you can tear yourself away from iconic Hameln, a visit to magnificent Hämelschenburg Palace (1588), a masterpiece of the local Weser Renaissance architectural style, makes for a worthwhile short side trip. You can either just stroll around the grounds or take a tour of the opulent interior and visit the palace museum. ⏲ At least 1 hr. Schlossstrasse 1, Emmerthal (Hämelschenburg). ☎ 05155/951-690. www.schloss-haemelschenburg.de. Admission 5.50€ adults, 3.50€ kids 5–18, 16.50€ families. Apr and Oct Tues–Sun 11am–5pm; May–Sept Tues–Sun 10am–6pm; also Mon on national holidays.

Where to Stay & Dine

> Hameln's Rattenfängerhaus is a popular favorite for its traditional food and Pied Piper frescoes.

★★ Christinenhof HAMELN
Set in a beautifully modernized, 3-centuries-old timber-frame building in the Old Town, the Christinenhof offers loads of traditional style and even runs to a heated indoor pool. Alte Marktstrasse 18. ☎ 05151/95080. www.christinenhof-hameln.de. 30 units. Doubles 99€ w/breakfast. MC, V.

★ Hessischer Hof BAD KARLSHAFEN
On a quiet street a little way back from the riverfront, this hotel fits right in with the "White Town's" elegance; its well-regarded restaurant serves German and Continental cuisine. Carlstrasse 13-15. ☎ 05672/1059. www.hess-hof.de. 19 units. Doubles 78€ w/breakfast. AE, MC, V.

★★ Hotel am Kurpark BAD KARLSHAFEN
A waterside location at the bridge over the Weser, close to the river tours dock, adds scenic attraction to a family-run hotel with small, homey rooms. The restaurant serves regional cuisine with a strong line in fish. Brückenstrasse 1. ☎ 05672/1850. www.hotel-am-kurpark.com. 36 units. Doubles 70€–76€ w/breakfast. MC.

★★ Hotel zur Krone HAMELN
Though housed in an antique, timber-frame building on a pedestrians-only street on the edge of the Altstadt, the rooms here are bright and contemporary. Similarly, the in-house German restaurant has more of a modern ambiance than the popular Rattenfängerhaus (see below) next door. Osterstrasse 30. ☎ 05151/9070. www.hotelzurkrone.de. 32 units. Doubles 95€–99€ w/breakfast. AE, MC, V.

★★ Kartoffelhaus im Bürgerhaus HAMELN
GERMAN Just off the Weser River, in a timber-frame house dating from 1530, this atmospheric place specializes in traditional German potato-based menus. Kupferschmiedestrasse 13. ☎ 05151/22383. www.kartoffelhaus-hameln.de. Entrees 10€–21€. AE, MC, V. Lunch & dinner Tues–Sun.

★ Rattenfängerhaus HAMELN GERMAN
The "Rat-Catcher's House," dating from 1603, is inevitably a tourist favorite—justifiably so, for its bustling air and consistently good traditional cooking. Osterstrasse 28. ☎ 05151/3888. www.rattenfaengerhaus.de. Entrees 9€–20€. AE, DC, MC, V. Morning coffee (from 10am), lunch & dinner daily.

★★ Schlosshotel Bad Wilhelmshöhe KASSEL
You'll likely leave thinking this hotel is really not so "bad" after all—its ultramodern looks are a refreshing contrast to the nearby old palaces and monuments in Bergpark Wilhelmshöhe. Schlosspark 8. ☎ 0561/30880. www.schlosshotel-kassel.de. 105 units. Doubles 84€–129€ w/breakfast. AE, MC, V.

FAIRY TALES

German Legends and the Brothers Grimm

BY GEORGE MCDONALD

THE BROTHERS Jacob (1785–1863) and Wilhelm (1786–1859) Grimm traveled around Germany in the early 19th century to gather local folklore tales. They published these in their compendium, *Kinder-und Hausmärchen,* the famous *Grimm's Fairy Tales.* Although not purely morality tales, the stories were instructive and had strict rules of reward and punishment. Their enduring appeal lies in their giving a voice to childhood anxieties while affording children a safe vantage point from which to observe and explore the adult world.

German Fairy-tale Road (Deutsche Märchenstrasse)

From Hanau, on the Main River just east of Frankfurt, where the Brothers Grimm were born, this tourist route stretches northward along the Weser River for 600km (373 miles), past gnarled forests, and timber-frame cottages, cobblestone streets, medieval villages, and castles, to end in Bremen. Your ideal reading companion for the trip is a copy of *Grimm's Fairy Tales.* Little Red Riding Hood, the Big Bad Wolf, the Pied Piper of Hamelin, Hansel and Gretel, Rumpelstiltskin, Cinderella, fairies, wizards, dwarfs, goblins, and wicked witches are all associated with the Fairy-tale Road. Some stops along the way include:

HAMELN (HAMELIN) The Weser River town is the setting for the famous tale of the Pied Piper, recalled in a weekly open-air theater performance in summer.

KASSEL The Waldeck region and the Reinhardswald forest around Kassel were the birthplace of many legends about witches, sleeping princesses, strange beasts, and magic spells. These tales had a profound influence on the Grimm brothers, who lived in Kassel from 1798 to 1830.

NEUSTADT A circular tower here is said to be the one from which Rapunzel let down her golden tresses.

HÖXTER Noted for its timber-frame buildings and a crooked old tower, this Weser River town lays claim to having inspired *Hansel and Gretel;* it presents the drama on the first Saturday of each month from May to September.

SABABURG The Dornröschenschloss, a castle near Hann. Münden, is a persuasive setting for the Sleeping Beauty (Dornröschen) legend. Briar roses bloom in the courtyard.

SCHWALM RIVER Germans have dubbed the route along this river *Rotkäppchenland,* or Little Red Riding Hood country.

A Twist in the Tale

You might not recognize some plot elements of early versions of these famous fairy tales.

◀**HANSEL AND GRETEL** (*Hänsel und Gretel*). Early versions of the story were sanitized to make it more child-friendly, with the evil mother being changed to a stepmother, thus creating the evil-stepmother trope.

CINDERELLA (*Aschenputtel*). In the Grimm version, there is no fairy godmother. It is the beautiful tree she planted on her mother's grave that comes to her aid in attending the ball. Cinderella is a passive heroine, rescued from a life of drudgery by the handsome prince.

RAPUNZEL. In early versions of this tale, Rapunzel asks why her dress is getting so tight, thus naively revealing to her wicked stepmother that she is pregnant following a dalliance with the prince.

LITTLE RED RIDING HOOD (*Rotkäppchen*). In the French oral version, the hunter doesn't save Little Red Riding Hood from the Big Bad Wolf—she distracts the predatory beast herself by performing a striptease, and then escapes. The Grimms sanitized the tale into a warning to children not to stray from the approved path.

Sauerland, Niedersachsen & Bremen for Families

A combination of Niedersachsen's landscapes—from the Lüneburger Heide's extensive heathland to the North Sea coastline—provides the setting for a wealth of kid-oriented attractions. This isn't meant to be a point-to-point tour so much as a roundup of family-friendly spots you can visit as side trips from other towns in the region.

> *The Zoo am Meer on the Weser River in Bremerhaven is home to more than 200 northern ocean animals.*

START Hameln is 47km (29 miles) southwest of Hannover on B217; and 48km (30 miles) west of Hildesheim on B1. From Hameln, follow B1 east for 25km (16 miles) to Rasti-Land.

❶ Rasti-Land. Should Hameln's (p. 515, ❽) rats lose their charm, this modestly adventurous adventure-park, just off B1, has rides and water-rides—none of them white-knuckle affairs—and other attractions best suited to kids up to around 10. ☉ 6 hr. Quanthofer Strasse 9, Salzhemmendorf (Oldendorf). ☎ 05153/94070. www.rasti-land.de. Admission 18.50€ ages 12 and up, 16.50€ kids 3–11. June–Aug daily 10am–6pm, Apr–May and Sept–Oct intermittently 10 or 10:30am to 5pm. Train: Osterwald, then follow signs to Rasti-Land (2km/1¼ miles).

❷ Familienpark-Sottrum. Family-oriented Sottrum is a good bet for kids up to around 12. It's educational in a fun kind of way, with sections covering dinosaurs and prehistoric peoples. There's a children's farm, a petting zoo, pony-riding, a small circus, pedal-boats, playgrounds, and other low-stress stuff. Sottrum is within easy reach of Hildesheim (p. 507, ❼). ☉ 4–8 hr. Ziegeleistrasse 28, Sottrum (southern edge of village). ☎ 05062/8860. www.familienpark-sottrum.de. Admission 8.50€ adults, 7.50€ kids 2–14. Apr to mid-Oct daily

0   20 mi
0   20 km

NORTH SEA

Nationalpark
Niedersächsisches Wattenmeer

Wattenmeer

Neumünster

SCHLESWIG-
HOLSTEIN

Lübeck

Brunsbüttel

Itzehoe

Cuxhaven

Stade

Hamburg

Buxtehude

Wilhelmshaven

8 Bremerhaven

9 Jade-
busen

Bremervörde

Westerstede

Oldenburg

Bremen **7**

Sittensen

Naturpark
Lüneburger Heide

Lüneburg

Rotenburg
(Wümme)

6

Soltau

Uelzen

Cloppenburg

Bassum

Weser

5

Naturpark
Südheide

Eschede

NIEDERSACHSEN

Vechta

Sulingen

4

Celle

Diepholz

Nienburg

Naturpark
Steinhuder
Meer

Steinhuder
Meer

3

Hannover

Braunschweig

Mittellandkanal

Osnabrück

Minden

Hildesheim

Salzgitter

Herford

Hameln

1

Bielefeld

2

Münster

Gütersloh

Goslar

NORDRHEIN-
WESTFALEN

Paderborn

Nationalpark
Harz

Hamm

Lippstadt

Northeim

Bad Karlshafen

Göttingen

THÜRINGEN

1 Rasti-Land
2 Familienpark-Sottrum
3 Dinopark
4 Serengeti-Park
5 Weltvogelpark Walsrode
6 Heide-Park Soltau
7 Universum Bremen
8 Zoo am Meer
9 Oceanis

Naturpark
Rothaar-
gebirge

Hann. Münden

Kassel

HESSEN

Hamburg

Berlin
★

GERMANY

Frankfurt
am Main

Nationalpark
Kellerwald-
Edersee

Munich

10am–6pm. Train: Derneburg, then bus 461. From Hildesheim, go southeast on B243 to Nette, and northeast on L493 to Sottrum (24km/15 miles).

❸ ★ **Dinopark.** Just west of Steinhuder Meer, Niedersachsen's largest lake, and an easy drive from Hannover (p. 546), Dinopark is set on a historic site, the Naturdenkmal Saurierfährten (Dinosaur Tracks Natural Monument). This fascinating scene contains more than 250 preserved dinosaur footprints from the Cretaceous Period, 140 million years ago. In addition, the park has a fun educational trail that leads past large models of dinosaurs from various periods. Kids get to make their own (much smaller) models in a workshop area. ⏲ 4 hr. Alte Zollstrasse 5, Münchehagen (off Hannoversche Strasse). ☎ 05037/2075. www.dinopark.de. Admission 9.50€ ages 13 and up, 8€ kids 4–12. Mar–Oct daily 10am–6pm, Nov Sat–Sun 10am–5pm, Dec two weekends 10am–5pm, Jan one weekend 10am–5pm. Train: Wunstorf, then bus 716. From Hannover, go north on B6 and west on A2 and B441, through Wunstorf and Hagenburg, to Münchehagen (43km/27 miles).

❹ ★★ **Serengeti-Park.** You can ride through this safari park—it covers about 200 hectares (490 acres)—in your own car, as most visitors do, or board one of the park's tour buses to observe lions, tigers, giraffes, elephants, antelope, camels, and the rest of the park's 1,500 exotic creatures of land, sea, and sky. In addition, there's an area with low-intensity rides, a lake with duck-shaped pedal-boats, and shows for younger kids. You could easily make this a side trip from Hannover (p. 546) or Bremen (p. 538). ⏲ At least 4 hr. Am Safaripark 1, Hodenhagen (off Bahnhostrasse). ☎ 05164/97990. www.serengeti-park.de. Admission 23€ adults, 19€ kids 3–12; bus tour 3.50€. Apr–Oct daily 10am–6pm. From Hannover, go north on A352 and A7, then west on L191 to Serengeti-Park (54km/33 miles). Or take a train to Hodenhagen, then follow the signs to the park (a walk of 4km/2½ miles), or take a taxi (8€) from outside the train station.

❺ ★ **Weltvogelpark Walsrode.** Birds flit here, there, and seemingly everywhere at Weltvogelpark Walsrode (Walsrode World Bird Park), through a space that covers 24

hectares (59 acres). This is enough to allow natural-seeming habitats for many of the 4,000 colorful inhabitants, representing 700 different bird species from around the world. Among them are toucans, pelicans, peacocks, and penguins. The park is most convenient to Hannover (p. 546). ⏲ 4 hr. Ahrsener Strasse 1, Walsrode (off Ebbinger Strasse). ☎ 05161/60440. www.vogelpark-walsrode.de. Admission 16€ adults, 11€ kids 4–17, 32 € families with 1 adult, and 48€ families with 2 adults. Late Mar–Sept daily 9am–7pm; Oct daily 9am–6pm. From Hannover, go north on A352, A7, and A27, then north on B209 and L161 (67km/42 miles). Or take a train to Walsrode, then take bus 511 or walk 3km (2 miles) to the park (follow the signs).

❻ ★★★ **Heide-Park Soltau.** This is the place for thrills. There's plenty to northern Germany's largest theme park—it covers 85 hectares (210 acres) and has close to 50 rides. A half-dozen rides—with names like Big Loop, Desert Race, and Indy Blitz—fall into the white-knuckle class, but there are sedate rides for less-adventurous kids and positively calm ones for the tiniest tots, along with many other visitor attractions. The park is also convenient

Kid-Friendly Breaks & Dining

Rasti-Land, Familienpark-Sottrum, Serengeti-Park, Weltvogelpark Walsrode, Heide-Park Soltau, Zoo am Meer, and Oceanis all have snack bars and/or cafeterias serving burgers and fries, pizzas, and other light fare.

Serengeti-Park's ★ **Restaurant Zanzibar** has a Continental menu and outdoor tables along diminutive Viktoriasee (Lake Victoria). Traditional German dishes are served at Weltvogelpark Walsrode's timber-frame ★ **Rosencafé,** and plainer, inexpensive food at Gasthof zum Kranich.

Heide-Park Soltau has reed-roofed ★ **Panorama** for regional German cuisine; a U.S.-style diner, Capitol, shaped like the Capitol in Washington, D.C.; and Brauhaus, a beer garden with a Continental menu. In the park's 4-star hotel, the ★ **Port Royal** (☎ 08105/919-101; www.hotelportroyal. de), both ★★ **Schatzinsel** and plainer ★ **La Tortuga** serve Continental cuisine.

> With more than 250 dinosaur footprints from the Cretaceous Period and an educational trail, Münchehagen's Dinopark is a family favorite.

to Hannover (p. 546). ⏱ 1 day. Heidenhof, Soltau (at Hambostel). ☎ 01805/919-101. www. heide-park.de. Admission 33€ ages 12 and up, 26€ kids 4–11. Apr–Oct daily 9am–6pm. From Hannover, go north on A352 and A7, then west on B71, K9, and K2 (90km/56 miles).

7 ★★ **Universum Bremen.** This science center on the northern edge of Bremen (p. 538) looks like either a flying saucer that's made a dodgy landing or a stainless-steel mussel (take your pick). Inside are hundreds of hands-on exhibits in multiple fields of science and technology, grouped under broad headings, like Expedition Mankind, Expedition Earth, and Expedition Cosmos. Outside, in the EntdeckerPark (*Entdecker* is German for "discoverer"), are installations for investigating wind, water, and more. ⏱ 4 hr. Wiener Strasse 2 (off Universitätsallee), Bremen. ☎ 0421/33460. www.universum-bremen.de. Admission 15.50€ adults, 10.50€ kids 6–18, 39.50€ families. Mon–Fri 9am–6pm, Sat–Sun 10am–7pm. Tram: 6 to the Universität/NW1 stop.

8 ★ **Zoo am Meer.** Bremerhaven's Sea Zoo, on the north (right) bank of the Weser River, takes both its inspiration and most of its 200 or so creatures from the northern ocean. Polar bears, sea lions, and (from the southern ocean) Humboldt penguins, as well as other marine and sea-related mammals and birds like gannets and eider ducks, disport in pools and clamber around on rocks. The Nordseeaquarium tanks hold North Sea fish, crustaceans, and more. ⏱ 4 hr. H.-H.-Meier-Strasse 5 (off Columbus-strasse), Bremerhaven. ☎ 0471/308-410. www. zoo-am-meer-bremerhaven.de. Admission 6.50€ adults, 3.50€ kids 4–14; Mon 5€ adults, 2.50€ kids. Apr–Sept daily 9am–7pm; Mar and Oct 9am–6pm; Nov–Feb 9am–4:30pm. Bus: 501, 502, 505, 506, 508, or 509. From Bremen, go north on A27, then west on B212 (Grimsbystrasse and Lloyd-strasse) to Bremerhaven's Neuer Hafen (New Harbor), for Zoo am Meer (67km/42 miles).

9 ★ **Oceanis.** One of a cluster of marine-related attractions at Wilhelmshaven's harbor, within easy reach of Bremen (p. 538), Oceanis takes you on an interactive journey to a virtual underwater research station (so you don't get your feet wet). It ends with a virtual submarine ride. ⏱ At least 3 hr. Bontekai 63 (at Weser-strasse), Wilhelmshaven. ☎ 04421/755-055. Admission 8.90€ adults, 5.90€ kids 6–14, 21.90€ families. Mid-Mar to mid-Nov daily 10am–6pm; mid-Nov to mid-Mar Sat–Sun 10am–6pm. From Bremen, go northwest on A28 and A29, then east on B210 (Oldenburgerstrasse), then follow signs for Maritime Meile Wilhelmshaven, for Oceanis (103km/64 miles).

Sauerland, Niedersachsen & Bremen Outdoors

A constellation of national parks, nature parks, and a national seashore sparks green and blue on the landscape between the industrial Ruhr District and the North Sea. These may be small by some international comparisons, but they are no less treasured for that. Your options are so varied—forested landscapes, a mountain range, a lake of Ice Age provenance, heathland and moors, the shores of a shallow sea—that it would be difficult to see everything on one trip. What follows is a list of highlights, with information on how to reach each park as a side trip as you make your way through the region.

> At low tide, take a walk along the shallow tidal mudflats of the Wattenmeer (Wadden Sea) at Nationalpark Niedersächsisches Wattenmeer.

START Winterberg is 94km (58 miles) from Kassel (p. 498, ❶), going south on A49, west on A44, B251, L3083, and L740, and south on B480.

❶ ★ **Naturpark Rothaargebirge.** Covering 1,355 sq. km (523 sq. miles) of western Sauerland, this nature park protects primarily the extensive spruce and beech forests in the Rothaargebirge mountains. A good starting point for hiking into the park is Winterberg, a winter sports resort just east of ★★ **Kahler Asten,** the low mountain range's second

NORTH SEA

Nationalpark Niedersächsisches Wattenmeer **7**

Wattenmeer

SCHLESWIG-HOLSTEIN

Neumünster
Itzehoe
Brunsbüttel
Cuxhaven
Stade
Hamburg
Bremerhaven
Bremervörde
Lüneburg
Wilhelmshaven
Jadebusen
Westerstede
Sittensen
Naturpark Lüneburger Heide **6**
Oldenburg
Rotenburg (Wümme)
Bremen
Uelzen
Soltau
Cloppenburg
Bassum
NIEDERSACHSEN
Gedenkstätte Bergen-Belsen
Naturpark Südheide **5**
Eschede
Vechta
Sulingen
Nienburg
Celle
Diepholz
Naturpark Steinhuder Meer **4** **11**
Steinhuder Meer
Wolfsburg
Osnabrück
Minden
Hannover
Braunschweig
Herford
Hildesheim
Salzgitter
Bielefeld
Hameln
Gütersloh
Goslar
NORDRHEIN-WESTFALEN
Nationalpark Harz **10**
Hamm
Lippstadt
Paderborn
3
Northeim
Bad Karlshafen
Göttingen
Hamburg
Berlin
GERMANY
Frankfurt am Main
Munich
Hann. Münden
9
HESSEN
Kassel
8
Naturpark Rothaargebirge
2
Nationalpark Kellerwald-Edersee
1

1 Naturpark Rothaargebirge
2 Nationalpark Kellerwald-Edersee
3 Nationalpark Harz
4 Naturpark Steinhuder Meer
5 Naturpark Südheide
6 Naturpark Lüneburger Heide
7 Nationalpark Niedersächsisches Wattenmeer

> *The Harz Mountains near Goslar are the traditional home of Walpurgisnacht, an annual event held to banish witches from the region.*

of the nature park's 406 sq. km (157 sq. miles). Hiking and bicycling trails snake through the hilly, forested landscape in which beech and oak trees predominate. Along the national park's northern fringe lies the ★★ **Edersee,** an artificial lake created by the construction in 1914 of a dam on the Eder River. This was one of several dams in the region hit by British air force bombers during the famous Dam Busters raid in 1943. The planes dropped specially developed "bouncing bombs" that skipped across the lake before exploding and breaching the dam, causing considerable death and destruction downstream (the dam was rebuilt within months). Boat tours on the lake, operated by **Personenschiffahrt Edersee** (☎ 05623/5415; www.personenschiffahrt-edersee.de), depart from a dock at Waldeck-Strandbad on the north shore and call at up to seven small harbors around the lake. The park makes a good day trip from Kassel (p. 498, ❶). ☉ 1 day. Visitor Center: NationalparkZentrum Kellerwald, Weg zur Wildnis 1, Herzhausen (western end of Edersee, on B252). ☎ 05635/992-781. www.nationalpark-kellerwald-edersee.de and www.nationalparkzentrum-kellerwald.de. Admission 6€ adults, 4€ kids 6–18, 16€ families. Apr–Oct daily 9am–6pm; Nov–Mar 10am–4:30pm. From Kassel, take B83 and A49 south, then A44 and B251 west, then L3084 and B252 south to Herzhausen, a total of 66km (41 miles).

Witching Hours

Witches are big in the Harz Mountains. On Walpurgisnacht (Walpurgis Night; Apr 30–May 1), revelers dressed as witches gather on the Brocken, northern Germany's highest mountain, to dance with the devil to the light of burning torches. The folk festival, also know as Hexennacht (Witches Night), is a melding of pagan and Christian traditions. Walpurgis refers to St. Walpurga, an 8th-century English nun and missionary to the pagan Franks of continental Europe. Her feast day (May 1) marks the arrival of spring, and with the dawn the witches and other creatures of darkness are banished. In addition to the witches' dance on the Brocken, many villages in the Harz have folk festivals on this night.

highest peak (841m/2,759 ft.). The *Infozentrum* (visitor center) on Kahler Asten has information about hiking trails, weather, and other useful stuff. ☉ At least a half-day. Park HQ: Heinrich-Jansen-Weg 14, Brilon. ☎ 02961/943-223. www.naturpark-rothaargebirge.de.

❷ ★★ **Nationalpark Kellerwald-Edersee.** Established in 2004 as a more stringently protected zone within a larger nature park—★ **Naturpark Kellerwald-Edersee**—this national park covers 57 sq. km (22 sq. miles) out

> *Naturpark Steinhuder Meer attracts boaters, kayakers, swimmers, and bird-watchers.*

3 ★★★ kids **Nationalpark Harz.** The Harz National Park was created in 2006 by combining two national parks, one in the former West Germany and the other in the former East Germany (during the Cold War, the Iron Curtain ran through the Harz Mountains). The unified park extends across 247 sq. km (95 sq. miles) and protects around 10% of the Harz, a forested range that tops out at 1,141m (3,743 ft.) at the summit of the ★★ **Brocken,** northern Germany's highest mountain. It's close to Goslar (p. 544) but could also be visited as a day trip from Hildesheim (p. 507, **7**) or Hannover (p. 546). Visitors enjoy hiking that is considerably less strenuous than in the Alps, though not as spectacular. There's grand wining and dining in the main mountain towns, places like ★★ **Goslar** (p. 544), Clausthal-Zellerfeld, Bad Harzburg, Schierke, and ★★ **Wernigerode,** and in any number of pretty villages. Kids might enjoy a ride to the Brocken summit aboard a narrow-gauge train operated by **Harzer Schmalspurbahn** (☎ 03943/5580; www.hsb-wr.de), departing from Wernigerode, Drei Annen Hohne, and other stations. In winter, break out your snow gear for downhill skiing, *Langlauf* (cross-country skiing), and a variety of other winter sports. ⏱ 1 day. Visitor Center: Nationalpark-Besucherzentrum

TorfHaus, Torfhaus, 8km (5 miles) east of Altenau on L504. ☎ 05320/331-790. www.nationalpark-harz.de. Apr–Oct daily 9am–5pm; Nov–Mar daily 10am–4pm. From Goslar, take B6 east then B4 south to Torfhaus, a total of 25km (16 miles). You can also reach the park via train to Bad Harzburg, Goslar, or Wernigerode.

4 ★★ kids **Naturpark Steinhuder Meer.** Northwestern Germany's largest lake, shallow Steinhuder Meer is a relic of the last Ice Age set in a relatively flat landscape and covering a surface of 30 sq. km (12 sq. miles). This is not quite one-tenth of the nature park's total area, but the lake's attractiveness as a center for sailboating, kayaking, windsurfing, swimming, and other water recreation makes it a major draw. Bird-watchers get much to observe, both on the water and in the internationally important wetlands around the lakeshore. ★ **Boat tours,** aboard small wooden launches or larger cruisers, depart from Steinhude on the south shore and are operated by **Steinhuder Personenschifffahrt** (☎ 05033/1721; www.steinhuder-personenschifffahrt.de). A good boat trip takes you to **Insel Wilhelmstein,** a tiny island on which stands an 18th-century fortification. Visit the nature park's Steinhude information center for details

> *The sprawling Lüneburger Heide is a vast, open moor dotted with thatched-roof houses.*

park HQ is along the way in Celle, just off the B3. You can also reach the park by train to Eschede or Unterlüss.

⑥ ★★ Naturpark Lüneburger Heide. Open heathland, moor and bog, meadows, and patches of coniferous forest occupy a landscape that once was heavily forested. Over centuries, the trees were felled for agriculture and industry. In an ironic example of what now constitutes a natural landscape, Naturpark Lüneburger Heide (Lüneburg Heath Nature Park) preserves 1,070 sq. km (413 sq. miles)

about the moors and meadows beyond the lake, which make for easy-going bicycling country. The park is a little more than a half-hour's drive from Hannover (p. 546). ⊕ 1 day. Tourist information: Informationszentrum, Am Graben 3–4, Steinhude. ☎ 0533/939-134. www.naturpark-steinhuder-meer.de. May–Oct daily 10am–1pm and 2–6pm; Nov–Apr Wed–Sun 11am–1pm and 2–5pm. From Hannover, go north on B6, west on A2 and B441, and then north on K41 to Steinhude, a total of 33km (21 miles). Or take a train to Wunstorf, then bus 710, 711, 716, or (July–Aug) 835 to Steinhude.

⑤ ★ Naturpark Südheide. The Southern Heath Nature Park covers 480 sq. km (185 sq. miles) and has a flat landscape of heath, moor, and forest similar to that of its larger cousin, the Naturpark Lüneburger Heide (⑥). It likewise has an extensive net of hiking, bicycling, and horseback-riding trails. The park is within easy reach of Hannover (p. 546). ⊕ At least a half-day. Park HQ: Trift 26, Celle. ☎ 05141/916-469. www.region-celle.de. From Hannover, take the B3 and B191 northeast 61km (38 miles) to Eschede, on the southern edge of the park. The

Bergen-Belsen Concentration Camp

Even among such monstrous company as Auschwitz, Ravensbrück, and Treblinka, the Nazi Bergen-Belsen *Konzentrationslager* has a malign distinction. Though it was not an extermination camp in the strict sense—there were no gas chambers—an estimated 100,000 inmates died of maltreatment, malnutrition, disease, and execution between 1940 and 1945. Among them was Anne Frank (1929–45), author of one of the world's most-read books, *The Diary of a Young Girl.* The young Jewish diarist's short life began in Frankfurt (p. 474), continued in exile and hiding in Amsterdam, and ended here from the effects of typhus a few weeks before British troops liberated the camp in April 1945.

The Allies destroyed the camp soon after the survivors were removed. On the site, west of Naturpark Südheide (⑤), roughly between Hannover (p. 546) and Lüneburg (p. 550), now stands the memorial and documentation center **★ Gedenkstätte Bergen-Belsen**. In the center, you learn about the camp's history. On the grounds, a simple stone memorial honors Anne Frank and her sister Margot, who were buried in a mass grave. ⊕ 2 hr. Anne-Frank-Platz, Lohheide (5km/3 miles southwest of Bergen on L298). ☎ 05051/475-9112. www.bergenbelsen.de. Free admission. Apr–Sept daily 10am–6pm; Oct–Mar daily 10am–5pm. Train: Celle, then by bus no. 3 (up to six buses daily; the bus ride from the station to the camp takes 72 min.).

of this fair scenery and as much as possible of the human culture that grew up on it. Flocks of grazing *Heidschnucke,* a breed of North German moorland sheep, maintain the heath in its "natural" state. Strict laws enforce the maintenance of the thatch-roofed houses and rural atmosphere. This low, undulating terrain—the highest point, Wilseder Berg, close to the park's center, is 169m (554 ft.) above sea level—has long, open vistas and is crisscrossed by hiking, bicycling, and horseback-riding trails. Much of the heath is a gorgeous purple carpet when the heather blooms in August and September. A dozen villages ringing the Lüneburger Heide are resources for hotels, restaurants, visitor information, bicycle rentals, and tours by traditional horse-and-carriage. You can easily make this a day trip from Bremen (p. 538) or use the charming city of Lüneburg (p. 550) as a jumping-off point. ⏱ At least a half-day. Park HQ: Schlossplatz 6, Winsen. ☎ 04171/693-139. www.naturpark-lueneburger-heide.de. From Bremen, take A1 and B75 80km (50 miles) east to Schneverdingen, a good jumping-off point at the western edge of the park. Or go by train to Schneverdingen or Wintermoor.

❼ ★★★ Nationalpark Niedersächsisches Wattenmeer. The Lower Saxony Wadden Sea National Park is one part of a UNESCO Biosphere Reserve established in 2009. This stretches among the islands and sandbanks and along mainland seacoast of the shallow Wattenmeer (Wadden Sea) on either side of the Elbe estuary from the Dutch to the Danish border. By German standards, it is a large national park, covering 278 sq. km (107 sq. miles), and it encompasses both heavily touristed islands and seacoast resorts and stringently protected wildlife reserves. The area is a resting place for many species of Northern European birds, and seals can be spotted here as well. For more on this national seashore, see the "Frisian Island-Hopping" tour (p. 530). Bremen (p. 538) is the closest large city; for more on Wilhelmshaven, where the park HQ is located, see p. 536, ⓭. ⏱ 1 day. Park HQ: Virchow-strasse 1, Wilhelmshaven. ☎ 04421/9110. www.nationalpark-wattenmeer.niedersachsen. de. From Bremen, take A28 west and A29 north to Wilhelmshaven for the park HQ, then follow B210 and local roads to Esens, at the edge of the park. Total distance to Esens is 132km (82 miles).

Where to Stay & Dine

★★ Alter Winkel STEINHUDE
Lake views are guaranteed at this rustic, waterfront hotel with bright pinewood furnishings in the rooms, a nautical-themed restaurant, and a beer garden at the water's edge. Alter Winkel 8. ☎ 05033/8447. www.alterwinkel.de. 5 units. Doubles 74€–95€ w/ breakfast. MC, V.

★ Drei Annen DREI ANNEN-HOHNE
Modernized since its time as a Communist-era guesthouse, this large, rambling hotel on the eastern edge of Nationalpark Harz has plainly furnished rooms, a small indoor pool, and a wellness area, and its restaurant serves traditional German food. Drei Annen-Hohne 110. ☎ 039455/5700. www.drei-annen.de. 69 units. Doubles 88€ w/breakfast. No credit cards.

★★★ Hotel Schloss Waldeck WALDECK
It's tough to beat a 12th-century castle that's been fitted out as a deluxe hotel; its fine restaurant and the grand view over the Edersee are like icing on the cake. It's just northeast of Nationalpark Kellerwald-Edersee. Am Schlossberg. ☎ 05623/5890. www.schloss-hotel-waldeck.de. 40 units. Doubles 106€–246€ w/ breakfast. AE, MC, V.

★★ Landgasthof Gilsbach LANGEWIESE
Close to the center of the Rothaargebirge, the timber-frame Gilsbach hotel and restaurant has a touch of Tyrol about it, but with rooms furnished in contemporary style. Bundesstrasse 25. ☎ 02758/98420. www.landgasthof-gilsbach.de. 10 units. Doubles 62€–76€ w/breakfast. AE, MC, V.

Frisian Island-Hopping

The Ostfriesische Inseln (East Frisian Islands) are a chain of seven islands separated from the German mainland by the shallow Wattenmeer (Wadden Sea). Bathed by the warm waters of the Gulf Stream, the islands—from west to east, Borkum, Juist, Norderney, Baltrum, Langeoog, Spiekeroog, and Wangerooge—have a temperate maritime climate. In summer they are vacation hotspots; when winter storms hit, it's a different story. Together, the sea, the coastline, and the islands comprise the Nationalpark Niedersächsisches Wattenmeer (Lower Saxony Wadden Sea National Park; p. 529, ❼). This route takes you from south to north; pick and choose what to see along the way. Budget about 1 day per island to take into account ferry rides and time to see the sights.

> *The beautiful beaches of Borkum, the biggest of the East Frisian Islands, draw sunbathers from all over Europe.*

START **Emden is 251km (156 miles) northwest of Hannover; and 131km (81 miles) northwest of Bremen by the shortest and fastest route. For information on ferry service to** the islands, see "Friesland Ferries," p. 510.
TRIP LENGTH **From a few days to 2 weeks, depending on how many islands you decide to visit.**

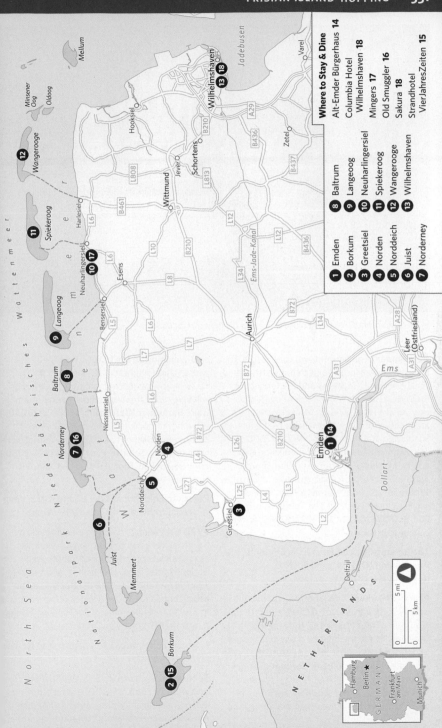

Where to Stay & Dine
Alt-Emder Bürgerhaus **14**
Columbia Hotel
Wilhelmshaven **18**
Mingers **17**
Old Smuggler **16**
Sakura **18**
Strandhotel
VierJahresZeiten **15**

8 Baltrum
9 Langeoog
10 Neuharlingersiel
11 Spiekeroog
12 Wangerooge
13 Wilhelmshaven

1 Emden
2 Borkum
3 Greetsiel
4 Norden
5 Norddeich
6 Juist
7 Norderney

> *The pastoral harbor town of Emden is home to the ferry port for Borkum.*

❶ ★ Emden. The harbor town (pop. 52,000) is the western access point to the Ostfriesland (East Friesland) seacoast and the ferry port for Borkum. A noteworthy dab of contemporary culture is to be found inside the modern architecture of the ★ **Kunsthalle** (Art Gallery), Hinter dem Rahmen 13 (☎ 04921/97500; www.kunsthalle-emden.de; admission 8€ adults, 6€ kids 6–18; Tues–Fri 10am–5pm, Sat–Sun 11am–6pm). Among works of German expressionism here is Emil Nolde's *Dancer in a Red Dress* (1910). ⏱ 3 hr. Tourist information: Bahnhofsplatz 11. ☎ 04921/97400. www.emden-touristik.de.

The Borkum ferry departs from Emden's **Ausenhafen (Outer Harbor),** off Nesserlander Strasse.

❷ ★★ kids Borkum. The largest East Frisian island (36 sq. km/14 sq. miles) is the busiest in summer. Needless to say, the long North Sea beaches are the biggest draw, but there's a sophisticated tourist infrastructure that even runs to a casino, **Spielbank Borkum,** Georg-Schütte-Platz 6 (☎ 04922/91800; www.casinoland.de). Other outdoors activities include hiking on the dunes, bird-watching, and seal-watching. In the harbor, visit the red-and-white-painted lightship *Borkumriff* (☎ 04922/2030; www.feuerschiff-borkumriff.de). Kids will love riding the old narrow-gauge steam train, **Borkumer Kleinbahn** (☎ 04922/3090; www.borkumer-kleinbahn.de), between the harbor and Borkum town. ⏱ 1 day. Tourist information: Georg-Schütte-Platz 5. ☎ 04922/9330. www.borkum.de. Mon–Fri 9am–5:30pm, Sat–Sun 10am–noon.

Return to Emden and take L2 and K233 along the coast to Greetsiel (30km/19 miles).

❸ kids Greetsiel. A handsome fishing village, Greetsiel has a pair of Dutch-style windmills along a canal, a candy-striped lighthouse, wetlands good for bird-watching, and a ship-in-a-bottle museum, the **Greetsieler Museumshaus,** containing 800 examples of the craft. ⏱ 2 hr. Tourist information: Zur Hauener Hooge 11. ☎ 04926/91880. www.greetsiel.de.

From Greetsiel, take L27 northeast to Norden (17km/11 miles).

❹ Norden. Founded in 1255, the bustling market town (pop. 25,000) is a resource for lodging, eating, shopping, and bar-hopping. Around the central Markt (Market Square) are

> *Norddeich's renowned Seehundstation provides a home for dozens of orphaned seals.*

the 13th-century **Ludgerikirche** (St. Ludger's Church), with an Arp Schnitger organ (1692), and, since drinking tea is an East Friesland tradition, the **Ostfriesische Teemuseum** (East Frisian Tea Museum; ☎ 04931/12100; www. teemuseum.de; admission 4€ adults, 1.50€ kids 6–16, 9€ families; daily 10am–5pm). ☺ 1 hr. Tourist information: Am Markt. ☎ 04931/ 986-201. www.norden.de.

From Norden, take B72 northwest to the ferry dock at Norddeich (5km/3 miles).

5 🧒 **Norddeich.** Here, visit the national park's seal research and recovery center, ★ **Seehundstation,** Dörper Weg 22 (☎ 04931/8919; www. seehundstation-norddeich.de; admission 5€

adults, 3€ kids 4–18; Mar–Apr Tues–Sun 11am–4pm, May–June and Sept–Oct Tues–Sun 10am–5pm, July–Aug daily 10am–5pm, Nov–Feb Wed and Sat 11am–4pm). ☺ 2 hr. Tourist information: Dörper Weg 22. ☎ 04931/986-200. www. norddeich.de.

From Norddeich, take the ferry to Juist.

6 ★ 🧒 **Juist.** The virtually car-free island (16 sq. km/6 sq. miles) is good for anyone who wants to breathe healthy sea air and build

The Cruise Begins Here

If you should notice a massive ship, painted in bright Caribbean colors, being maneuvered delicately down the Ems River to the sea at Emden, don't be surprised. It's just the latest product of Meyer Werft, a shipyard that constructs the world's largest cruise liners, at Papenburg, 36km (22 miles) upriver.

The Riddle of the Sands

Some visitors to the East Frisian Islands carry with them a book considered to be the first-ever spy novel. Anglo-Irish author Erskine Childers wrote *The Riddle of the Sands* (1903) as a warning to Great Britain that war with Germany was coming. In the book, two friends sailing a small sailboat among the islands are slowly drawn deeper into a mystery with explosive international implications. Winston Churchill credited the novel with prompting a literal sea-change in Britain's naval strategy to counter a rising imperial Germany.

> *Windsurfers descend like seagulls on the inviting tidal basin beaches of beautiful Langeoog.*

sandcastles on the beach, with dunes-hiking and sea sports by way of variation. Bright lights are pretty much confined to the one emanating from the Memmert lighthouse. A small museum, the **Küstenmuseum** (Seacoast Museum), Loogster Pad 29 (☎ 04935/1488; www.kuestenmuseum-juist.de; admission 2.50€ adults, 1.50€ kids 6–18; Apr–Oct Tues–Fri 9:30am–1pm and 2:30–5pm; Nov–Mar Tues and Sat 2:30–5pm), in the hamlet of Loog, covers island history, geology, and wildlife biology. ☼ 1 day. Tourist information: Kurverwaltung, Strandstrasse 5. ☎ 04935/809-120. www.juist.de. July–Aug Mon–Fri 9am–12:30pm and 2–5pm, Sat–Sun 9am–12:30pm; Sept–June Mon–Thurs 9am–12:30pm and 2–5pm, Fri 9am–12:30pm.

Take the ferry back to Norddeich, then hop on the ferry to Norderney.

❼ ★★ kids **Norderney.** Car use is restricted, as is visitor access to half of its area of 26 sq. km (10 sq. miles), in the national park. Yet Norderney is a bustling vacation island in summer and has been since the 19th century. There are great beaches, plenty of restaurants and bars, and a casino, **Spielbank Norderney** (☎ 04935/91100; www.casinoland.de), at the Conversationshaus on Kurplatz. ☼ 1 day. Tourist information: Am Kurplatz 3. ☎ 04932/8910. www.norderney.de.

Return to Norddeich and take L5 east to Nessmersiel (17km/11 miles). Leave your car at the ferry dock car park, 2km (1¼ miles) to the north, and take the ferry to Baltrum.

❽ ★ kids **Baltrum.** Covering an area of just 7 sq. km (3 sq. miles), sleepy little Baltrum is the smallest island of the chain, affording tranquillity, isolation, and simple seaside pleasures in summer. ☼ 1 day. Tourist information: Kurverwaltung, Rathaus (Town Hall). ☎ 04939/800. www.baltrum.de.

Return to Nessmersiel and continue east on L5 to Bensersiel to catch the ferry to Langeoog (16km/10 miles).

❾ ★★ kids **Langeoog.** The car-free island (20 sq. km/8 sq. miles) has its own narrow-gauge railway, the Inselbahn, which runs between the ferry dock and the town (1km/½ mile). In addition to its beaches, dunes, and a restricted zone of the national park, Langeoog has a small marine museum and North Sea aquarium, the

Schiffahrtsmuseum/Nordsee-Aquarium
(☎ 04972/693-211; admission 3€ adults,
1.50€ kids 6–18; Easter school holidays to Fall
school holidays Mon–Thurs 10am–noon and
3–5pm, Fri–Sat 10am–noon). ⊕ 1 day. Tourist
information: Kurverwaltung, Hauptstrasse 28.
☎ 04972/6930. www.langeoog.de.

**Return to Benserseil and take L5 and L6 east
to Neuharlingersiel (10km/6 miles).**

🔟 **Neuharlingersiel.** The pretty old fishing village and modern seacoast resort and boating
center is the ferry port for Spiekeroog. There
are good small hotels and seafood restaurants
around the harbor. ⊕ 1 hr. Tourist information:
Edo-Edzards-Strasse 1. ☎ 04974/1880. www.
neuharlingersiel.de.

**Catch the ferry at Neuharlingersiel to
Spiekeroog.**

Walking Across a Sea

At low tide, the Wattenmeer (Wadden Sea)
virtually disappears, the seabed becomes
visible, seabirds feast on mollusks in the
sand, and seals soak up rays on sandbars.
If you feel like walking the mud flats, from
May to October you can join a *Wattwandern*
(mudflat-hiking) trip and plow across to one
of the islands through a salty mire that tries
to suck your feet in deeper with every step.
Warning: Do not attempt this without an
official guide. There is a real danger of being
caught by a fast incoming tide.

The unusual landscape you're walking on is
the bottom of a sea, and in a few hours all this
will disappear under water again. When you
reach the island, you need to wait for high tide
to be able to go back by boat. Mudflat-hiking
is available from Nessmersiel to both Norderney and Baltrum, from Neuharlingersiel to
Langeoog, and from Harlesiel to Spiekeroog;

to the other islands it is either forbidden or
impossible. The distances range from 6km
(3¾ miles) to 10km (6 miles). Tours cost
around 24€ for adults and 12€ for kids 8–16
(this includes the cost of returning by island
ferry or by small boat), and take up to 8 hours
(special 2-hr. tours are available for families
with kids 7 and under). Participants need to
be fit and in good health (halfway across to
the islands is not a good time to discover the
contrary).

Because this activity carries an element
of risk (though not a large one), you should
inform yourself fully at local tourist offices
along the Wattenmeer coast. For information (in German) from the licensed guides
covering the East Frisian Islands, go to
www.wattwandern.de; for the North Frisian
Islands of Schleswig-Holstein, go to www.
wattenloepers.de.

⓫ ★ kids Spiekeroog. Considering that the beach on the North Sea shore is 14km (9 miles) long, on an island that covers just 18 sq. km (7 sq. miles), kids likely won't have much difficulty finding something to do. When the beach palls, there are horse-and-carriage tours, the national park reserve, and a handful of small museums. ⏱ 1 day. Tourist information: Kurverwaltung and Schifffahrt, Noorderpad 25. ☎ 04976/919-3101. www.spiekeroog.de.

Return by ferry to Neuharlingersiel and take L6 east to Carolinensiel, then go north on local roads to the Harlesiel ferry dock (a total of 9km/5½ miles). Take the ferry to Wangerooge.

⓬ ★ kids Wangerooge. The chain's second-smallest island (8 sq. km/3 sq. miles) is a summer paradise for beach-going, sailing, bird-watching, and other open-air activities. A narrow-gauge train, the Inselbahn, runs on a track that's just 1km (½ mile) long. Housed in the old lighthouse, the **Inselmuseum Alte Leuchtturm,** Zedeliusstrasse 3 (☎ 04469/8324; www.leuchtturm-wangerooge.de; admission 2€ adults, 1€ kids 6–18; Apr–Oct Wed–Mon 10am–1pm and 2–5pm), is a museum of island history and culture. ⏱ 1 day. Tourist information: Westturm, Bahnhofsvorplatz ☎ 04469/94880. www.wangerooge.de and www.westturm.de.

Return to Harlesiel and take K86, K87, and L810 east and south along the coast to Wilhelmshaven (43km/27miles).

⓭ ★★ kids Wilhelmshaven. The harbor town (pop. 82,000) on Jadebusen (Jade Bay) hosted major German navy fleet units during both world wars. A part of the old base is now the **★★ Maritime Meile** (Maritime Mile), a cluster of marine attractions, including **★★ Oceanis,** a virtual underwater research station (p. 523, ➒); and the **★ Deutsches Marinemuseum** (German Navy Museum). The visitor center for **★★★ Nationalpark Niedersächsisches Wattenmeer** (p. 529, ➐) is also here. ⏱ 4 hr. For information on Wilhelmshaven, see p. 509, ⓫.

> *An old lighthouse on Wangerooge houses the Inselmuseum Alte Leuchtterm.*

Where to Stay & Dine

> The Columbia offers views of Wilhelmshaven's port and a location convenient to both the beach and town.

★★ **Alt-Emder Bürgerhaus** EMDEN
In an Altstadt (Old Town) building dating from 1875, with Art Nouveau decor, this family-run hotel has small but smart rooms and an excellent seafood restaurant as well. Friedrich-Ebert-Strasse 33. ☎ 04921/97610. 12 units. Doubles 156€–178€ w/breakfast. AE, DC, MC, V.

★★★ **Columbia Hotel Wilhelmshaven**
WILHELMSHAVEN Looking like a superior Mediterranean resort hotel, the Columbia has spacious rooms, an indoor pool and spa, and restaurants serving seafood and regional cuisine. Jadeallee 50. ☎ 04421/773-380. www.columbia-hotels.com. 145 units. Doubles 125€–155€. AE, MC, V.

★ **Mingers** NEUHARLINGERSIEL
The bright rooms overlooking the fishing boats in the harbor have contemporary furnishings, and the in-house restaurant serves great seafood and Frisian cuisine. Am Hafen West 1–2. ☎ 04974/9130. www.mingers-hotel.net. 32 units. Doubles 100€–120€ w/breakfast. MC, V.

★★ **Old Smuggler** NORDERNEY SEAFOOD/GER-MAN One of the best-loved and longest-lasting eateries on any of the islands, this homespun place takes an old-fashioned pride in itself and in its plain but tasty fare. Birkenweg 24. ☎ 04932/3568. www.oldsmuggler-norderney. de. Entrees 12€–24€. No credit cards. Lunch & dinner Thurs–Tues.

★★ **Sakura** WILHELMSHAVEN JAPANESE
Why not try the seacoast's natural specialty in a different guise at this excellent sushi restaurant? There's no sea view or harbor view, just straight-on sushi and helpful advice for beginners. Gökerstrasse 104. ☎ 04421/771-205. Entrees 6€–14€. MC, V. Lunch & dinner daily.

★★ **Strandhotel VierJahresZeiten** BORKUM
A grand position right on the island's western shore marks out this ultramodern resort hotel, which has an indoor pool and spa and a fine Continental restaurant. Bismarckstrasse 40. ☎ 04922/9220. www.strand-hotel.com. 60 units. Doubles 144€–192€ w/breakfast. MC, V.

Bremen

Once a powerhouse of the medieval Hanseatic League maritime trading federation, the city on the Weser River is now, together with its downriver seaport Bremerhaven, a German federal state. The "Free Hanseatic City of Bremen" (pop. 548,000; see "The Hanseatic League," p. 578) has a proud heritage that is confirmed every bit as much by the restored fishermen's cottages in the Schnoorviertel as by the grand historic buildings on Marktplatz. It's unlikely you'll be able to see everything Bremen has to offer in a single day, so if that's all the time you have you'll have to pick and choose from the list below.

> *Bremen's impressive Rathaus is the heart of the city's political and commercial activities.*

START From Bremen's Hauptbahnhof (main train station), take tram no. 4, 5, 6, or 8, or bus no. 24 or 25 to Domsheide (3 stops), for Marktplatz. Or walk to Marktplatz along Herdentorsteinweg (1.6km/1 mile).

❶ ★★★ Marktplatz (Market Square). All roads in Bremen lead to this monumental square, the old Hanseatic town's political and commercial heart. The highlights here are the magnificent Rathaus (**❷**), closely followed by St.-Petri Dom (**❸**). A statue of the knight Roland, a medieval symbol of civic freedom, stands on the square. In addition, Marktplatz has the elegant Schütting (1538), a Flemish Renaissance building by Antwerp

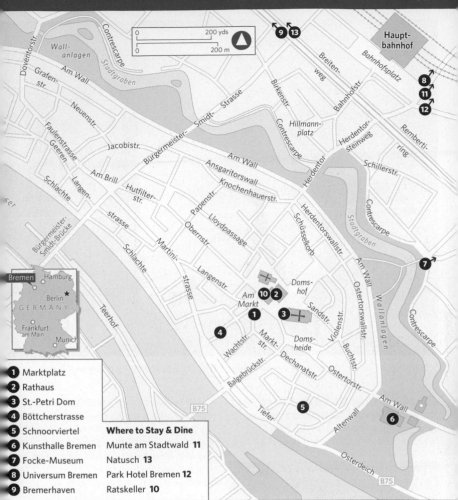

0 | 200 yds
0 | 200 m

1 Marktplatz
2 Rathaus
3 St.-Petri Dom
4 Böttcherstrasse
5 Schnoorviertel
6 Kunsthalle Bremen
7 Focke-Museum
8 Universum Bremen
9 Bremerhaven

Where to Stay & Dine

Munte am Stadtwald **11**
Natusch **13**
Park Hotel Bremen **12**
Ratskeller **10**

architect Johann den Buschener, that was originally the Merchants Guild House and now houses the Chamber of Commerce. On the square's western face is a row of gabled houses. By contrast, Bremen's Parliament, the Haus der Bürgerschaft (1966), looks like the modern interloper it is. ⏱ 1 hr. Tram: 2, 3, 4, 5, 6, or 8.

2 ★★ kids **Rathaus (Town Hall).** The Rathaus is all you would expect of a trading city that was among medieval Europe's wealthiest. Its basic Gothic layout dates from 1410, though most of the embellished Weser-Renaissance

facade was added 2 centuries later, and it's just as ornate on the inside as on the outside. Should the kids get fidgety, point out to them, at the hall's west end, the sculpture of the *Bremer Stadtmusikanten,* four fairy-tale animals who wanted to become Bremen City Musicians (see "The *Bremer Stadtmusikanten,*" p. 540). ⏱ 45 min. Am Markt 21. ☎ 01805/ 101-030. www.rathaus-bremen.de. Admission 5€ adults, free for kids 12 and under. Guided tours: Mon–Sat 11am, noon, 3pm, and 4pm; Sun 11am and noon (actual times may vary due to official business). Tram: 2, 3, 4, 5, 6, or 8.

> *St.-Petri Dom, on the Marktplatz, is a massive marvel of sandstone construction dating back to 1219.*

❸ ★ St.-Petri Dom (St. Peter's Cathedral). Bremen's Protestant cathedral is a massive sandstone pile, with twin towers 99m (325 ft.) high, constructed over centuries beginning in 1219 in a succession of architectural styles. Like the Rathaus across the way, the church is a statement of the city's medieval wealth and power. Amid all the splendor, a grisly sight that should be good for a few nightmares is a bunch of mummified medieval corpses in the Bleikeller, a lead-lined crypt. ⏱ 30 min. Sandstrasse 10–12. ☎ 0421/365-040. www. stpetridom.de. Cathedral: free admission; Tower: 3€ adults, 1€ kids 6–18; Bleikeller: 1.40€ adults, 1€ kids. Apr to mid-May and mid-Oct to mid-Nov Tues–Sat 10am–noon and 2–4pm, Sun 11am–noon and 2–4pm; mid-Nov to Mar daily 11am–noon and 2–3pm. Tram: 2, 3, 4, 5, 6, or 8.

❹ ★ Böttcherstrasse. "Coopers' Street," leading southwest from Marktplatz to the Weser, is a 1930s faux-medieval re-creation of a block of buildings that had gone to rack and ruin. Its gabled brick buildings house handicraft and pottery stores and art galleries. ⏱ 30 min. Tram: 2, 3, 4, 5, 6, or 8.

❺ ★★ Schnoorviertel. The restored fishermen's district along the Weser, east of

---

The *Bremer Stadtmusikanten*

Bremen has taken four ill-treated animals to its heart. As told in a Brothers Grimm fairy tale, the *Bremer Stadtmusikanten* (Bremen City Musicians) were a donkey, a dog, a cat, and a rooster, all of them past their prime. Being of no further use to their masters, they were awaiting their fate. Instead, one after another, they lit out and joined up on the road to Bremen, intending to live out their days in clover as musicians in that fair city.

Fate intervened. They surprised a gang of robbers in a cottage, chased them away, and lived there . . . you know, happily ever after. They never did get to Bremen. So why is there a bronze sculpture of the four unlikely friends, one atop the other, outside Bremen Town Hall? Well, once upon a time . . .

> *Bremen's Schnoorviertel district offers shops, galleries, restaurants, and charming historical atmosphere.*

Marktplatz, is loaded with historical atmosphere. The oldest cottages in the conservation zone date from the 15th century, though most are of later provenance. Many of them now house small galleries, offbeat and artisanal stores, and casual small restaurants and bars. ⏱ 2 hr. Tram: 2, 3, 4, 5, 6, or 8.

❻ ★★ **Kunsthalle Bremen (Bremen Art Gallery).** This noteworthy museum was closed for

Bremen Nightlife

For classical music, there's **Die Glocke,** Domsheide 4–5 (☎ 0421/33699; www. glocke.de), and for opera, dance, theater, and more, there's **Theater Bremen,** Goetheplatz 1–3 (☎ 0421/365-3333; www.theaterbremen.de). Try your luck at **Casino Bremen,** Böttcherstrasse 3–5 (☎ 0421/329-000; www.casino-bremen. de). Live music, DJs, party evenings, and musical theater are on the agenda at **Aladin,** Hannoversche Strasse 11 (☎ 0421/ 435-150; www.aladin-bremen.de). Good bars are to be found in the **Schnoorviertel** district (p. 540, ❺).

Bremen's Free Market

When the cry "Ischa Freimaak!" resounds in the city, it means that the annual **Bremer Freimarkt** (☎ 0421/565-1722; www. freimarkt.de) has begun. Northern Germany's largest festival, often compared to Munich's Oktoberfest, traces its history all the way back to an imperial proclamation of 1035. It consists of hundreds of market stalls, plus beer tents, rides and other fairground attractions, music and dance performances, and more. The Freimarkt attracts up to four million visitors during its 17-day run at the end of October, in two main locations: the Bürgerweide, close to Bremen's Hauptbahnhof (main train station), and on the central main square, Marktplatz. On the second Saturday, the Freimarktsumzug, a folk procession with around 5,000 participants, takes place.

refurbishment at this writing; call or check the website to see if it will be open when you visit. Am Wall 207. ☎ 0421/329-080. www.kunsthalle-bremen.de. Tram: 2, 3, 4, 6, or 8.

❼ ★ Focke-Museum. Set in a park and housed in a variety of old and modern buildings, this regional museum of art and cultural history is an amazingly eclectic trip down Bremen's memory lane. Exhibits and artworks range from finds that recall Roman fleets patrolling the Weser to paintings of portly Hanseatic merchants and photographs of German emigrants departing for America. ⏲ 2 hr. Schwachhauser Heerstrasse 240. ☎ 0421/699-6000. www.focke-museum.de. Admission 4€ adults,

2€ kids 6–18, 7€ families. Tues 10am–9pm, Wed–Sun 10am–5pm. Tram: 4 or 5 to the Focke-Museum stop.

❽ ★★ kids Universum Bremen. ⏲ 4 hr. See p. 523, ❼.

SITE GUIDE PAGE 543

❾ ★ Bremerhaven. Downriver from Bremen—a drive of 66km (41 miles) on Autobahn A27 (or a short train ride to Bremerhaven Hauptbahnhof)—Bremen's smaller sister city (pop. 115,000) handles much of the combined port's deep-water traffic. Maritime heritage is, naturally, a big deal here.

Where to Stay & Dine

> *The large but comfortable Park Hotel Bremen overlooks the city's park and offers many recreational amenities.*

★★ Munte am Stadtwald BÜRGERPARK
Big but not impersonal, this family-run hotel fronts the city park and offers multiple dining options and a wellness area with pool, sauna, and solarium. Parkallee 299. ☎ 0421/22020. www.hotel-munte.de. 134 units. Doubles 127€–170€ w/breakfast. AE, DC, MC, V. Bus: 22.

★★ Natusch BREMERHAVEN SEAFOOD
Head to the Fischereihafen (Fishing Harbor) for fish straight off the nearby boats, in a multiroom restaurant with decor ranging from elegant to fishermen's kitsch. Am Fischbahnhof 1. ☎ 0471/71021. www.natusch.de. Entrees 17€–27€. AE, MC, V. Lunch & dinner Tues–Sun. Bus: 504, 505, or 506.

★★★ Park Hotel Bremen BÜRGERPARK
Like a palatial residence with its own grounds and lake, the spa hotel offers elegance and fine dining in a countrylike setting in Bürgerpark, near the Altstadt. Im Bürgerpark. ☎ 0421/34080. www.park-hotel-bremen.de. 177 units. Doubles 230€–350€ w/breakfast. AE, DC, MC, V. Bus: 26 or 27.

★★ Ratskeller ALTSTADT GERMAN
It may see a tad obvious, and you won't be alone down there, yet dining on North German fare in the Town Hall wine cellar (1405) has an unbeatable medieval vibe. Rathaus, Am Markt. ☎ 0421/321-676. www.ratskeller-bremen.de. Entrees 10€–21€. AE, DC, MC, V. Lunch & dinner daily. Tram: 2, 3, 4, 5, 6, or 8.

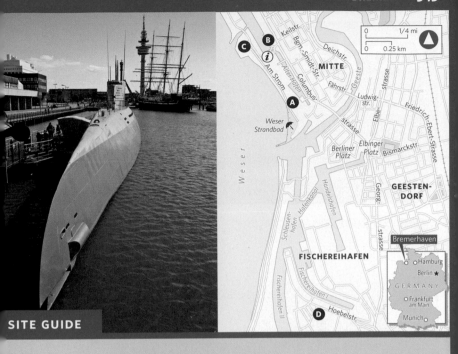

SITE GUIDE

⑨ Bremerhaven

The Ⓐ ★ **Deutsches Schiffahrtsmuseum** (German Maritime Museum, pictured above and right), Hans-Scharoun-Platz 1 (☎ 0471/482-070; www.dsm.museum; admission 6€ adults, 4€ kids 5–18), has some superb exhibits. Among these are a salvaged World War II-vintage U-boat, the *Wilhelm Bauer* (U-2540), out on the water, and, inside, a recovered *Hansekogge* (Hanseatic cog sailing ship) from 1380. Just along the dock is the Ⓑ ★★ **Deutsches Auswandererhaus** (German Emigration Center), Columbusstrasse 65 (☎ 0471/902-200; www.dah-bremerhaven. de; admission 11€ adults, 6€ kids 4–14), a superb evocation of Germany's long history of emigration to the United States. Closer to the river, Ⓒ ★ **Zoo am Meer** (Sea Zoo; p. 523, ⑧) is a treat for the kids. Dine on fresh fish at Ⓓ **Natusch** (p. 542). ⊙ Half-day. Tourist information: Tourist-Info Hafeninsel, H.H.-Meier-Strasse 6. ☎ 0471/414-141. www.bremerhaven.de. Apr–Oct daily 9:30am–6pm; Nov–Mar Mon–Fri 9:30am–5pm, Sat–Sun 10am–4pm.

Goslar

For going back in time to the Middle Ages, in spirit at least, Goslar, founded in 922, is hard to beat. A bustling town (pop. 42,000) in the northwest foothills of the Harz Mountains, it is both a gateway to the mountains and a resort town in its own right. The entire marvelously preserved Altstadt (Old Town) is a UNESCO World Heritage site, a status that reflects Goslar's history as an imperial residence of the Holy Roman Empire and a wealthy silver-mining town.

> The beautiful mountain town of Goslar is a bustling destination for tourists and a former imperial vacation spot.

START **From Goslar station to Marktplatz, at the heart of the Altstadt, walk a bit less than 1km (½ mile) south on Rosentorstrasse and Hokenstrasse.**

❶ ★★ **Altstadt (Old Town).** The Altstadt's beautifully preserved mix of monumental medieval Gothic buildings, defense towers, water mills, patrician mansions, churches, abbeys, almshouses, and Renaissance *Fachwerkhäuser*

(timber-frame houses) covers a thousand years of history and repays long strolls and detailed study. ★ **Schuhhof,** a square a couple of blocks northwest of central Marktplatz, is a neat ensemble of Renaissance-period timber-frame houses. Behind Marktplatz, the 12th-century ★ **Marktkirche St.-Cosmas-und-Damian** (Market Church of Saints Cosmas and Damian) has two high towers, each with a differently designed bronze pinnacle. Facing

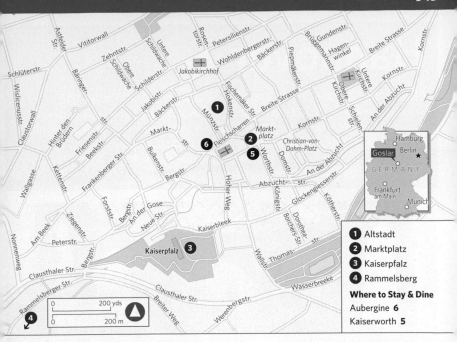

1 Altstadt
2 Marktplatz
3 Kaiserpfalz
4 Rammelsberg

Where to Stay & Dine
Aubergine 6
Kaiserworth 5

the church, at Hoher Weg 1, the elegant **Brust-tuch** mansion (1526) was built for a wealthy mine-owner (it's now a hotel). ⏱ 4 hr.

2 ★★★ kids **Marktplatz (Market Square).** On this square stands the 15th-century Gothic Rathaus (Town Hall), with its street-level arcades and a roof of Harz slate. A comical imperial eagle stands atop the **Marktbrunnen** (Market Fountain, 1230). Four times a day—at 9am, noon, 3pm, and 6pm—*Glockenspiel* (carillon) bells ring out and animated figures emerge from the gable of the slate-clad **Käm-mereigebäude** (Treasury Building; now the Kaiserring foundation and Henry's restaurant), to present different aspects of Goslar's history. The **Kaiserworth,** a Gothic guild house dating from 1494, is now a fine hotel and restaurant (see below), with a cafe terrace out on the cobblestones in summer. ⏱ 45 min.

3 ★★ **Kaiserpfalz.** A UNESCO World Heritage site, the Imperial Palace stands at the top of a grassy slope south of Marktplatz. It dates from the Salian Dynasty of German kings and Holy Roman Emperors, with its earliest elements traceable to 1005, though most of the structure is a 19th-century reconstruction. In the 12th-century chapel is buried the heart of

Kaiser Heinrich III, who died in 1056. ⏱ 2 hr. Kaiserbleek 6. ☎ 05321/311-9693. Admission 4.50€ adults, 2.50€ kids 6–18. Apr–Oct daily 10am–5pm, Nov–Mar daily 10am–4pm.

4 ★ kids **Rammelsberg.** The third of Goslar's UNESCO sites, the old Rammelsberg silver mine was the source both of Goslar's prosperity and its importance to Germany's medieval rulers, who built an imperial residence in the town. Admission includes a guided tour (it's chilly in the mine, so dress warmly). ⏱ 2 hr. Bergtal 19. ☎ 05321/7500. www.rammelsberg. de. Admission 12€ adults, 7€ kids 6–18. Daily 9am–6pm (last mine tour 4:30pm).

Spending the Night in Goslar

★★ **Kaiserworth,** Markt 3 (☎ 05321/7090; www.kaiserworth.de), housed in a transformed Gothic guild house, retains its historic ambience while adding contemporary elegance. Doubles go for 122€–207€ with breakfast. For lunch or dinner, enjoy southern European cuisine in a modern, cozy dining room at ★★ **Aubergine,** Marktstrasse 4 (☎ 05321/42136).

Hannover

Niedersachsen's state capital (pop. 525,000) was the principle residence of the Hanoverians, whose scions became kings of Great Britain during the 17th century. Sadly, much of Hannover's former aristocratic grace was lost due to heavy bombing in World War II. The modern city has many parks and is a center of commerce, culture, and nightlife. If you only have a day in Hannover, you'll have to cut some stops from the list below.

> *Hannover's Herrenhäuser Gärten offers a wealth of plant life, statuary, and fountains.*

START From Hannover's Hauptbahnhof (main train station), walk 400m (¼ mile) along Bahnhofstrasse to the below-ground Kröpcke tram stop, and take tram no. 4 or 5 to the Herrenhäuser Gärten stop (about 10 min.).

❶ ★★ **Herrenhäuser Gärten.** The Herrenhaus Gardens, four magnificent 17th- and 18th-century gardens, offer quite different experiences. There's the grand baroque ★★★ **Grosser Garten** (Great Garden), a medley of flowers, trees, plants, statuary, fountains, and pavilions; the ★ **Berggarten** (Hill Garden), with its botanical

garden and hothouse; the English-landscape Georgengarten (Georgian Garden); and the Welfengarten (Guelph Garden), which now belongs to the University of Hannover. ⏱ 3 hr. Herrenhäuser Strasse 4. ☎ 0511/1684-7743. www.hannover.de/herrenhausen. Apr–Sept: admission 4€ adults, free for kids 14 and under; Oct–Mar: Grosser Garten free admission, Berggarten 2€ adults, free for kids 14 and under. May–Aug daily 9am–8pm, Sept daily 9am–7pm, Oct daily 9am–6pm, Nov–Jan daily 9am–4:30pm, Feb daily 9am–5:30pm. Tram: 4 or 5.

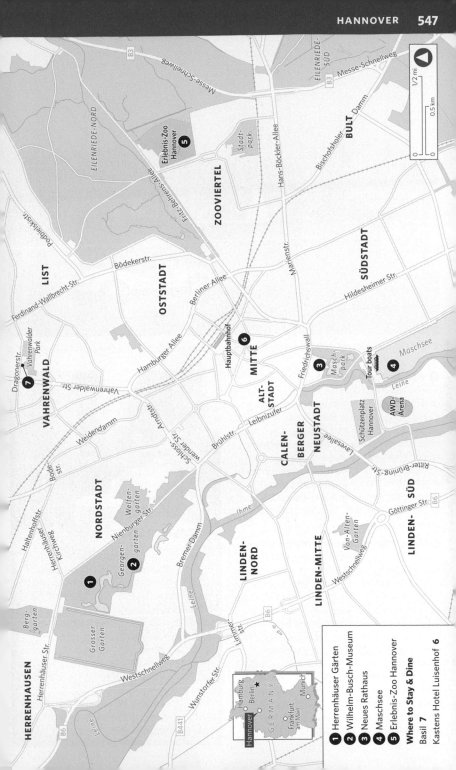

EILENRIEDE SÜD

B3 Messe-Schnellweg

BULT

Damm

1/2 mi

0.5 km

Messe-Schnellweg

EILENRIEDE NORD

Erlebnis-Zoo Hannover ⑤

Stadt-park

ZOOVIERTEL

Hans-Böckler-Allee

Bischofsholer

SÜDSTADT

Marienstr.

Bödekerstr.

LIST

OSTSTADT

Berliner Allee

Hildesheimer Str.

Ferdinand-Wallbrecht-Str.

Podbielskistr.

Dragonerstr.

Vahrenwalder Park

Hamburger Allee

Hauptbahnhof

⑥

MITTE

Friedrichswall

Masch-park

Maschsee

③

Tour boats ④

Leine

VAHRENWALD ⑦

Vahrenwalder Str.

Arndtstr.

Weidendamm

Brühlstr.

Leibnizufer

ALT-STADT

CALEN-BERGER

Schützenplatz Hannover

AWD-Arena

Bode str.

Schloss-str.

Wender Str.

NEUSTADT

Lavesallee

Haltenhoffstr.

NORDSTADT

Welfen-garten

Nienburger Str.

Georgen-garten

②

Bremer Damm

Ihme

LINDEN-NORD

LINDEN-MITTE

Von-Alten-Garten

Ritter-Brüning-Str.

Göttinger Str.

B6

LINDEN-SÜD

Herrenhäuser Kirchweg

Herrenhäuser

①

Leine

Westschnellweg

Berg-garten

HERRENHAUSEN

Grosser Garten

Herrenhäuser Str.

Limmer-str.

Westschnellweg

Wunstorfer Str.

B6

B441

Leine

Where to Stay & Dine

Basil **7**

Kastens Hotel Luisenhof **6**

① Herrenhäuser Gärten
② Wilhelm-Busch-Museum
③ Neues Rathaus
④ Maschsee
⑤ Erlebnis-Zoo Hannover

GERMANY

Hamburg

Berlin ★

Hannover

Frankfurt am Main

Munich

> *The Maschsee was artificially created by a Nazi engineering project that diverted the Leine River.*

② **Wilhelm-Busch-Museum.** Wilhelm Busch (1832–1908) was among the earliest comic-strip creators. His book *Max und Moritz* (1865), a humorous moralizing tale about two bad boys, established many genre conventions. A large exhibit of Busch memorabilia is housed in this museum at the Herrenhäuser Gärten. ⏱ 45 min. Georgengarten 1. ☎ 0511/1699-9916. www.wilhelm-busch-museum.de. Admission 4.50€ adults, 2.50€ kids 6-18, 10€ families. Tues–Sun 11am–6pm. Tram: 4 or 5.

③ **Neues Rathaus (New Town Hall).** This extravagant monument of imperial Germany was completed in 1913, just before the outbreak of World War I. Hannover's destruction in World War II is depicted in one of four models of the city at various times in its history. Take an elevator ride up to the domed cupola for great views. The elegant restaurant Gartensaal, at the back, has a patio with outdoor seating (in summer) and steps leading down to a pond. ⏱ 1 hr. Trammplatz 2. ☎ 0511/1684-5333. Town Hall: free admission; Dome elevator: 2.50€ adults, 2€ kids 6-18. Mar–Oct Mon–Fri 9:30am–6pm, Sat–Sun 10am–6:30pm; Nov–Feb daily 11am–4:30pm. Bus: 100, 120, or 200.

Old Town Flea Market

The stalls belonging to what is said to be Germany's oldest flea market take up position each Saturday on the riverside street Am Hohen Ufer, on the east bank of the Leine River, as they have done at this location since the 1960s. They are joined these days on the edge of Hannover's Altstadt (Old Town) by art, antiques, handcraft, and curio traders. On the flea-market side of things, old comics, secondhand books, toys, ornaments, and, truth be told, a considerable amount of junk it's hard to imagine selling at any price, are the stock in trade. The market is on Saturday from 7am to 4pm.

4 ★ kids **Maschsee.** A 1930s public-works project diverted the Leine River to create this long artificial lake located just south of the Neues Rathaus. Maschsee's shore is a magnet for joggers and in-line skaters. There's a beach at the southern end, cafes on the banks, and sailboats and rowboats. In summer, there are tour boats on the water. ⏲ 2 hr. Rudolf-von-Bennigsen-Ufer. Bus: 100 or 200.

5 ★ kids **Erlebnis-Zoo Hannover.** This is among Germany's top zoos, home to a broad range of land and marine animals and birds from around the world. These are combined with "Experience" zones—Yukon Bay, a Yukon Trail experience, opened in 2010. ⏲ 4 hr. Adenauerallee 3. ☎ 0511/2807-4163. www.zoo-hannover. de. Admission: Mar–Oct 19.50€ adults, 13.50€ kids 3–17; Nov–Feb 12€ adults, 10€ kids 3–17. Mar–Oct daily 9am–6pm, Nov–Feb daily 10am–4pm. Tram: 11.

Where to Stay & Dine

> The vaulted ceilings and a wide range of reasonably priced dishes make Basil one of Hannover's prime dining destinations.

★★ **Basil** VAHRENWALDER *FUSION*
The columns, vaulted ceiling, and bare brick walls of a 19th-century cavalry riding hall house a chic restaurant that "charges" moderate prices for inventive menu dishes that range from the coasts of the Mediterranean to Asia. Dragonerstrasse 30A. ☎ 0511/622-636. www.basil. de. Entrees 19€–25€. AE, MC, V. Dinner Mon–Sat (Sun during big conventions). Tram: 1 or 2.

★★ **Kastens Hotel Luisenhof** MITTE
Just minutes from the Hauptbahnhof, Hannover's top hotel has kept up with the times, adding a spa to a list of positives that includes two sophisticated restaurants. Spacious rooms are stylishly furnished. Luisenstrasse 1–3. ☎ 0511/30440. www.kastens-luisenhof.de. 146 units. Doubles 127€–387€. AE, DC, MC, V. Tram: 1, 2, 3, 4, 5, 6, 8, 11, or 16.

Lüneburg

The town (pop. 73,000) on the Ilmenau River owes its tourist-attraction status to past centuries as a wealthy member of the Hanseatic League (see "The Hanseatic League," p. 578) and to the happy fact that it was not bombed in World War II. Many of its historical treasures are intact to delight the eye today. Lüneburg's Altstadt (Old Town) is picturesque and has a pronounced medieval air, yet there's too much going on for it to be an open-air museum.

> Spared by World War II's bombs, historic Lüneburg's preserved baroque medieval architecture transports visitors centuries into the past.

START From Lüneburg station, it's about a 1.2km (¾-mile) walk to the Altes Rathaus, west across the Ilmenau River, on Lüner Torstrasse and Lüner Strasse.

❶ ★★ Altes Rathaus (Old Town Hall). The 17th-century baroque facade of the Altes Rathaus reaches up to a central bell tower that contains a *Glockenspiel* (carillon) of bells made from Meissen porcelain. Inside, elements of the building date from as far back as 1230. The ornate Grosser Ratsstube (Great Council Hall) was embellished over 2 centuries, culminating in the intricate woodwork (1566–84) of local sculptor Albert von Soest. ⏲ 1 hr. Am Markt 1. ☎ 0800/220-5005. Admission 4.50€ adults, 3.50€ kids 7–18, 11€ families. Guided tours Tues–Sat 11am, 2pm, and 3pm; Sun 11am and 2pm.

❷ ★★ Altstadt (Old Town). The Altstadt is filled with historical buildings, though few rise to the level of historic. South of the Markt, on Grosse Bäckerstrasse, is the Raths-Apotheke (1598), a pharmacy with an ornamented facade Follow Grosse Bäckerstrasse to a large square, Am Sande, around which is an array of gabled old *Backstein* (brick) buildings. Even in such company, the 16th-century Schwarzes Haus (Black House), a former brewery, stands out (it now holds the town's chamber of commerce). ⏲ 2 hr.

❸ St.-Johanniskirche (Church of St. John). Jus off Am Sande, this church traces its history back to 927. Most of it was constructed later, with the tower dating from the 15th century— this leans by a few degrees from vertical, yet

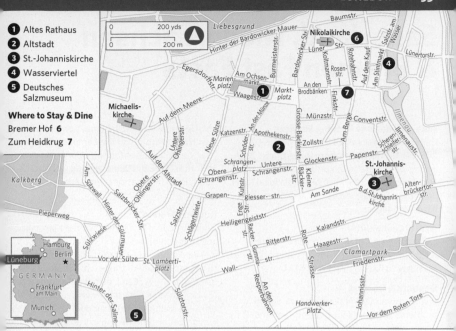

1 Altes Rathaus
2 Altstadt
3 St.-Johanniskirche
4 Wasserviertel
5 Deutsches Salzmuseum

Where to Stay & Dine
Bremer Hof **6**
Zum Heidkrug **7**

---

there's no talk of a "Leaning Tower of Lüneburg." ⏱ 30 min. Bei der St.-Johanniskirche. ☎ 04131/44542. Free admission. Apr–Oct Sun–Thurs 10am–5pm, Sat–Sun 10am–6pm; Nov–Mar Mon–Fri noon–2pm, Sat 1–6pm, Sun 11:30am–4pm.

4 ★★ **Wasserviertel (Water District).** The Wasserviertel began to be developed in the 13th century as the town's harbor on the Ilmenau River. Some parts of this area may have been a bit too pristinely restored, but student bars in the area help to keep things lively. The wooden Alter Kran (Old Crane), used for loading salt onto boats, actually dates from the 14th century, though it was "modernized" in the 18th. ⏱ 1 hr.

5 **Deutsches Salzmuseum.** Lüneburg's prosperity during the Middle Ages was built on its monopoly on salt, extracted in great quantity from works in the town, then shipped along the Ilmenau River to the Elbe, and from there on to Lübeck (p. 606) and other Hanseatic towns. Exhibits in the Deutsches Salzmuseum (German Salt Museum) take you on a trip through the centuries to view the social, commercial, and industrial implications of sitting on a rich deposit of "white gold."

⏱ 45 min. Sülfmeisterstrasse 1. ☎ 04131/45065. www.salzmuseum.de. Admission 6€ adults, 4€ kids 6–18, 18.50€ families. May–Sept Mon–Fri 9am–5pm, Sat–Sun 10am–5pm; Oct–Apr daily 10am–5pm.

Where to Stay & Dine

★ **Bremer Hof** ALTSTADT

This old merchant's house in a quiet corner of town features bright contemporary decor in the rooms. The timber-frame in-house restaurant serves North German cuisine. Lüner Strasse 12–13. ☎ 04131/2240. www.bremer-hof. de. 40 units. Doubles 93€–135€ w/breakfast. AE, DC, MC, V.

★★★ **Zum Heidkrug** WASSERVIERTEL *CONTINENTAL* In its antique setting, the restaurant of the same-name hotel sports a Michelin star for master chef Michael Röhm's mélange of Mediterranean and light German *neue Küche* (nouvelle cuisine). Am Berge 5. ☎ 04131/24160. www.zum-heidkrug.de. Entrees 20€–38€. AE, MC, V. Lunch & dinner Wed–Sat.

Sauerland, Niedersachsen & Bremen Fast Facts

Accommodations Booking Services
Call **Hotel Reservation Service** (☎ 0870/ 243-0003) from anywhere in Germany. Tourist info points at the major train stations and airports can assist with last-minute local hotel bookings. Tourist offices can also arrange accommodation.

ATMs/Cashpoints
The main towns in the region have multiple ATMs from a range of banks. Even small towns are likely to have at least one ATM.

Dentists & Doctors
If you have a mild medical issue or dental problems while traveling in Germany, most hotels will be able to refer you to a local doctor (*Arzt*) or dentist (*Zahnarzt*) who speaks English—large hotels in busy tourist or business areas are more likely to be able to do this. You will be expected to provide proof of either permanent or travel insurance (such as an EHIC card in the case of most residents of Europe), or you will be required to pay for treatment. In the event of minor injuries that require speedy treatment, go to the *Notaufnahme* (emergency) department of the nearest *Krankenhaus* (hospital). When the injuries are serious or life-threatening, call the doctor/ ambulance emergency number (see "Emergencies," below).

Emergencies
To call the police (*Polizei*), dial ☎ **110.** To report a fire or to summon an emergency doctor (*Notarzt*) or an ambulance (*Krankenwagen*), dial ☎ **112.**

Getting There
Frankfurt am Main (FRA), **Düsseldorf** (DUS), **Hamburg-Fuhlsbüttel** (HAM), **Bremen** (BRE), and, to a lesser degree, **Hannover** (HAJ) are the main airports serving this region. Plenty of international and national flights are available to all five airports. All cities and most towns are well served by train. Multiple European and German national highways enter the region from all points of the compass. **Eurolines** (www.eurolines.com) international buses stop at Braunschweig, Hannover, and Osnabrück. There is no international ferry service to the region.

Getting Around
Going by car affords the maximum flexibility, and in much of the region you can travel fast on the Autobahn (A) roads and *Bundesstrasse* (B) roads—many of these two categories, in particular the A roads, also have a European (E) designation. Using the comprehensive and efficient train network is undoubtedly the best way to get around by public transportation. Most rail service—and all InterCity trains, including the high-speed ICE (InterCity-Express) trains—are operated by **Deutsche Bahn** (German Railways; www.bahn.com). Some local and regional services are operated by private train companies. Regional bus service is not great, except in areas not well served by train—Sauerland, the Lüneburger Heide, the Harz Mountains, and the Ostfriesland seacoast, for instance—and is likely to be slow. Ferries connect the mainland to the Ostfriesische Inseln (East Frisian Islands) and Helgoland (see "High Seas Helgoland," p. 565).

Internet Access
Many hotels have one or more terminals for the use of their guests. Wi-Fi and/or broadband is often available, either free or for an hourly or daily charge. Most towns of any size are likely to have at least one Internet cafe.

Pharmacies
In German, a pharmacy is an *Apotheke*. For cosmetics or toiletries, go to a *Drogerie*. Pharmacies operate during normal shopping hours and post details of the nearest 24-hour pharmacy. There are pharmacies in even the smallest towns; towns and cities like Bremen, Kassel, Hannover, Osnabrück, Münster, and Hildesheim have many.

Police

To report a lost or stolen article, such as a wallet or passport, visit the local police (*Polizei*) in your location. To call the police from anywhere in Germany, dial ☎ **110.**

Post Office

You'll recognize branches of **Deutsche Post** (☎ 01802/3333; www.deutschepost.de) by their yellow sign with a black horn. Some centrally located post offices in towns and cities are as follows: **Bremen:** Am Markt (Marktplatz); **Hannover:** Ernst-August-Platz 1–2 (Hauptbahnhof/main train station); **Hildesheim:** Hindenburgplatz 16 (Altstadt); **Kassel:** Königsplatz 6 (Mitte). Post offices are open Monday to Friday 8am–6pm, Saturday 8am–noon.

Safety

There are few if any safety concerns in this region. In big cities like Bremen and Hannover, there may be a modest risk in places, but this is not a significant concern. The areas around the main train stations in the larger towns and cities can seem a bit creepy after dark.

Taxis

In Bremen, call **Taxi-Ruf Bremen** (☎ 14014); in Hannover, **Taxi Hannover** (☎ 3811); and in Kassel, **Taxi-Service-Zentrale Kassel** (☎ 88111).

Telephones

Call ☎ 11837 for information and ☎ 11834 for international information. Bremen's area code is 0421; Hannover's is 0511; Hameln's is 05151; Osnabrück's is 0541; and Kassel's is 0561. Dial the area code when calling a town number from outside the town; you don't need to dial it when calling a town number from inside the town. There are public phones in many places—some accept coins and some take phone cards, available at post offices and newsstands.

Toilets

In some places you will find clean public toilets, many of them automatic and wheelchair-accessible; you need a .50€ coin to unlock the door. More convenient and widespread are toilets in cafes, bars, restaurants, hotels, malls, and some stores, and at highway services and rest areas. Even if you are not obliged to pay, it is customary to leave the attendant .50€.

Tours

A unique kind of tour is *Wattwandern* (mudflat hiking) at low tide on the floor of the Wattenmeer (see "Walking Across a Sea," p. 535). In addition, boat tours among the Wattenmeer's Ostfriesische Inseln (East Frisian Islands) and day trips to Germany's sole "pelagic" island, Helgoland (p. 565), are available. Staying with water, there are boat tours on the Weser River—upstream around Hameln (p. 515, ❽) and Bad Karlshafen (p. 514, ❹), and downstream at Bremen and Bremerhaven—and boat tours on the Steinhuder Meer (p. 527, ❹) and Maschsee (p. 549, ❹) lakes. On dry land, there are all kinds of tours available in national parks and nature parks (p. 524), for instance hiking and bicycling on the Lüneburger Heide (p. 528, ❻), and hiking and mountain-biking in the Harz Mountains (p. 527, ❸).

Visitor Information

Tourist offices are ubiquitous. They range from multiple branches in big cities all the way down to tiny offices in some villages. In addition to those provided with the individual town listings, other key tourist offices are as follows: SAUERLAND Sauerland Tourism, Postfach 2200; ☎ 01802/403-040; www.sauerland.com; no walk-in service. BREMEN The main office of Bremen-Touristik-Zentrale, Findorffstrasse 105 (at Bürgerpark) has no walk-in service. But two branches are open to the public: one at the Hauptbahnhof (main train station; Mon–Fri 9am–7pm, Sat–Sun 9:30am–6pm), and the other at Obernstrasse/Liebfrauenkirchhof (Mitte; Mon–Fri 10am–6:30pm, Sat–Sun 10am–4pm). The general website is www.bremen-tourism.de, and the tourist information line is ☎ 01805/101-030. GOSLAR Markt 7; ☎ 05321/78060; www.goslar.de; Apr–Oct Mon–Fri 9:15am–6pm, Sat 9:30am–4pm, Sun 9:30am–2pm; Nov–Mar Mon–Fri 9:15am–5pm, Sat 9:30am–2pm. HANNOVER Ernst-August-Platz 8; ☎ 0511/1234-5111; www.hannover.de; Apr–Sept Mon–Fri 9am–6pm, Sat–Sun 9am–2pm; Oct–Mar Mon–Fri 9am–6pm, Sat 9am–2pm). LÜNEBURG Rathaus, Am Markt 7; ☎ 04131/207-6620; www.lueneburg.de; May–Oct & Dec Mon–Fri 9:30am–6pm, Sat 9:30am–4pm, Sun 10am–4pm; Nov & Jan–Apr Mon–Fri 9:30am–6pm, Sat 9:30am–2pm.

12

Hamburg, Schleswig-Holstein & the Baltic Coast

The Best of Northern Germany & the Baltic Coast in 3 Days

Three days isn't a lavish supply of time for a tour in Schleswig-Holstein (Germany's northernmost state) and northern Germany, but it's definitely doable. Hamburg, Lübeck, Wismar, and Schwerin are fairly close to each other and are connected by Germany's excellent Autobahn (highway) net, so traveling between them is a snap. On the first day, you visit Hamburg, world city and major port. The second day takes you to Lübeck, Hamburg's great rival, dating back to the days of the Hanseatic League. On Day 3, you cross into the old East Germany to see how Wismar and Schwerin, two quite different towns, are shaping up.

> *PREVIOUS PAGE The St. Pauli Landungsbrücken in Hamburg Harbor, one of the world's biggest ports.*
> *THIS PAGE The opulent Schweriner Schloss inhabits its own islet on Schweriner See.*

START **Hamburg lies on the Elbe River, 130km (81 miles) southeast of Cuxhaven on the North Sea coast, on B73; 288km (179 miles) northwest of Berlin on A24; 124km (77 miles) northeast of Bremen on A1; and 152km (94 miles) north of Hannover on A7.** TRIP LENGTH **165km (103 miles).**

❶ ★★★ **Hamburg.** Germany's second most populated city (after Berlin) is not that easy to come to grips with, even after you arrive. It sprawls over a large area that encompasses the Elbe River docks of what is among the world's biggest ports. There's a relative lack—yet, fortunately, not an absence—of world-class

1 Hamburg
2 Lübeck
3 Wismar
4 Schwerin

museums and other attractions, and those that exist are scattered around the cityscape, which can make getting to them a problem. Still, Hamburg has plenty going for it. No less than 50% of its surface area is taken up by water, woodlands, farmland, and 1,400 parks and gardens—statistics that add up to it being Germany's greenest city. By the way, much of the water is in the form of canals, but don't take too seriously Hamburg's "Venice of the North" tag. The canals, and their more than 2,000 bridges exist all right; they're just not that spectacular for the most part. Other local waterways, like the Elbe River itself and the Aussenalster and Binnenalster lakes, are noteworthier.

In a day, you could choose to visit the **Hamburger Kunsthalle,** an art gallery that majors in paintings by European artists, from Old Masters down to the 20th century. That should be it for museums, because you'll need a couple of hours at least to get anything out of this one. But should Old Masters, New Masters, and In-Between Masters strike you as equally unappealing, head instead to the **BallinStadt—Das Auswanderermuseum Hamburg** (Emigrants Museum), on the south side of the Elbe River. Subtitled the "Port of Dreams," this outstanding attraction takes as

its theme the waves of European emigrants who sailed to the New World from Hamburg. ⏲ 1 day. For more on Hamburg, including hotel and restaurant recommendations, see p. 594.

On Day 2, try to get going first thing in the morning. If you miss Hamburg's rush hour and stick to the dull, direct route on A24 and A1 northeast to Lübeck (66km/41 miles), you'll do it easily in under an hour. On the other hand, if you can't pass up a chance for some extra driving, stay on A24 east until it hits B207 north to Lübeck (82km/51 miles); that way, you take in the western lakeshore of scenic Ratzeburger See, for the minor cost of adding an hour to the drive.

❷ ★★★ **Lübeck.** This port town and onetime leader of the medieval Hanseatic League (see the "Hanseatic League," p. 578) is Germany's most important town on the Ostsee (East Sea)—the German name for the Baltic Sea. The **Altstadt** (Old Town), centered on Marktplatz, is ringed by the Trave River and connecting canals, giving it the appearance of an oval island, on which stand a thousand medieval red-brick buildings—churches, hospitals, almshouses, guildhalls, and houses—in fact, virtually everything worth seeing in Lübeck.

> *Canals weave elegantly through the 19th- and early 20th-century red-brick buildings of the Speicherstadt district in Hamburg.*

Just across the river from the Altstadt, the massive 15th-century **Holstentor** (Holsten Gate) was once the main town entrance, designed as much to awe visitors as to defend against intruders. The central **Rathaus** (Town Hall, 1230) has been rebuilt several times, but remains of the original structure can be seen in the vaulting and Romanesque pillars in the cellar and the Gothic-arcaded ground floor and foundations. Across Marktplatz, the **Marienkirche** (Church of St. Mary) is the most outstanding church in Lübeck, possibly in northern Germany. It has flying buttresses and towering windows that leave the rest of the city's rooftops at its feet.

On Breitestrasse stands one of Hanseatic Lübeck's last elaborate guild houses, the **Haus der Schiffergesellschaft** (Seafarers Guild House), built in 1535 in Renaissance style, with stepped gables and High Gothic blind windows. It's worth seeing just for the medieval furnishings, beamed ceilings, and hanging sailing-ship models in the main hall, now a restaurant. ⊕1

day. For information on Lübeck, including hotel and restaurant recommendations, see p. 606.

On Day 3, again you have a choice of routes. You can zip directly to Wismar by going south on B207n to A20, and then east on A20, with a final northbound stretch on B208 (67km/42 miles). Or take the coast road, which leads east on B105 to Dassow and then curves north and south on L1 (passing through a village called Klütz—though don't

Taking the Train

For those riding the rails, this itinerary should be straightforward. There are frequent fast trains going between all four towns, and the short distances mean you won't be spending all of your time looking out a train window. Basing yourself in Hamburg or Lübeck and visiting the other places on day trips may make more sense than having to pack up and move every day.

> *Nautical memorabilia contribute to the Hanseatic-era atmosphere at Haus der Schiffergesellschaft restaurant in Lübeck.*

let that put you off) into Wismar (62km/39 miles); this second distance takes an extra half-hour, plus any time you devote to diverting to and stopping at the Baltic Sea.

3 ★ Wismar. Founded in 1229, this Hanseatic-era harbor town can be the briefest stop on your itinerary, if you want it to be. At a minimum, stroll around the central **★★ Markt** (market square) to admire its parade of old buildings, and from there go to the **Alter Hafen** (Old Harbor). Have a bite to eat, and that could easily do it. And yet . . . Wismar's **Altstadt** (Old Town) wasn't awarded UNESCO World Heritage status for nothing. Take time for a stroll here if you can. ☺ At least 1 hr. For more on Wismar, see p. 579, **4**.

From Wismar to Schwerin is just 32km (20 miles) south on B106. You can easily afford to assign a few extra minutes to a diversion through the lakeside villages of Lübstorf, Hundorf, and Seehof, on Schweriner See's western shore, before rolling on into Schwerin.

4 ★★★ Schwerin. Mecklenburg-Vorpommern's elegant state capital stands on the southwest shore of island-speckled Schweriner See, northern Germany's second largest lake—after Müritzsee (p. 590, **5**)—covering an area of 62 sq. km (24 sq. miles).

The town's alpha sight, **Schweriner Schloss** (Schwerin Palace), stands just offshore on its own islet on Schweriner See. This fantastical neo-Renaissance, neo-Gothic, and neo-baroque architectural foppery of turrets, towers, and domes was a highly visible measure of how wealthy the old grand dukes of Mecklenburg-Schwerin were—or at any rate of their ability to squeeze the necessary funding out of their populace. ☺ Half-day. For information on Schwerin, including hotel and restaurant recommendations, see p. 610.

From Schwerin, you can get quickly south on B321 to the east–west Autobahn A24 for a rapid return to Hamburg (109km/68 miles) or the run east toward Berlin (208km/129 miles).

The Best of Northern Germany & the Baltic Coast in 1 Week

With 7 days, covering a grand swath of northern Germany becomes a practical proposition. You start at Hamburg and can either spend 2 days in the city or, on the second day, tour its environs along the Elbe River. A key further decision is whether or not to visit the island of Sylt—doing so is well worthwhile, but it involves a long drive into Schleswig-Holstein's top corner and then back out again. Once you reach Lübeck, you've a fairly easy run east along the Baltic Coast, through Wismar, Rostock, and Stralsund—with a single inland diversion, to Schwerin—before finally crossing over to Rügen.

> *Historic buildings in Rostock's Altstadt were restored to their former beauty after suffering the ravages of World War II.*

START **Hamburg** lies on the Elbe River, 130km (81 miles) southeast of the North Sea port of Cuxhaven, on B73; 288km (179 miles) northwest of Berlin on A24; 124km (77 miles) northeast of Bremen on A1; and 152km (94 miles) north of Hannover on A7. TRIP LENGTH 662km (411 miles).

1 ★★★ **Hamburg.** For recommendations on how to spend your first day in Hamburg, see p. 556, **1**. Having a second day here gives you a chance to take a side trip during the day (see "Hamburg Side Trips," p. 595) and visit the city's St. Pauli entertainment district in the evening. St. Pauli's sin strip, Reeperbahn,

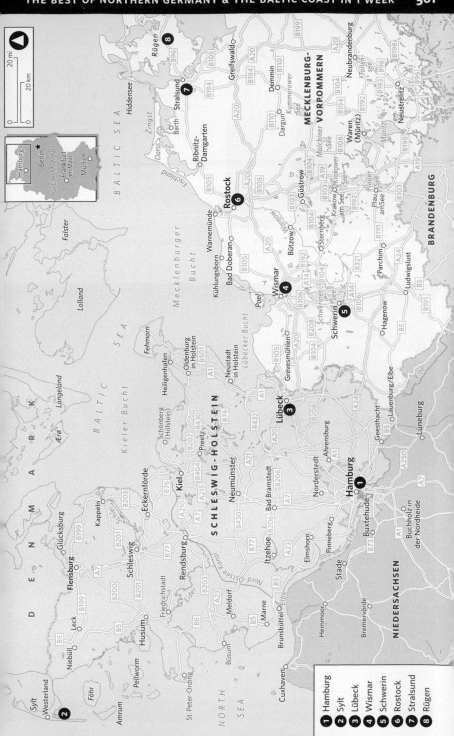

1 Hamburg
2 Sylt
3 Lübeck
4 Wismar
5 Schwerin
6 Rostock
7 Stralsund
8 Rügen

> *Wismar's imposing architecture and twisting streets provided the setting for the atmospheric vampire film classic Nosferatu.*

was named after hempen ropes (for ships) that were made here between the 14th and the 19th centuries. Concern about negatives like AIDS, organized crime, drugs, and human trafficking detract from the Reeperbahn's boost to the city's coffers from legal prostitution. There's a gradual decline evident in the sex trade, as teen hangouts, dance clubs, theaters, and other "normal" kinds of entertainment continue to infiltrate the district. By city ordinance, only men ages 18 and over are permitted to pass the barriers at either end of Herbertstrasse, enabling them to peruse the scantly clad women displaying their wares behind plate-glass windows. ⏲ 2 days. For information on Hamburg, including hotel and restaurant recommendations, see p. 594.

The Beatles in Hamburg

John Lennon famously said, "I may have been born in Liverpool, but I grew up in Hamburg." Between 1960 and 1962, the Beatles learned their trade as musicians by performing in a variety of Hamburg clubs—the Indra, the Kaiserkeller, the Top Ten Club, and the Star-Club—in the Reeperbahn red-light district, while sowing what by all accounts were some pretty wild oats. At that time, the group consisted of John Lennon, Paul McCartney, George Harrison, Stuart Sutcliffe, and Pete Best (Sutcliffe soon left and Best was later fired, being replaced by Ringo Starr). In 2008, Beatles-Platz (Beatles Square) was inaugurated at the entrance to a famous Reeperbahn street, Grosse Freiheit. The circular "square," in the shape of a vinyl record (pictured), has five sculptures representing the six Hamburg Beatles (a single sculpture represents the two drummers, Pete Best and Ringo Starr).

Dining Tip

Any time you are at or near the sea in Germany, be sure to put dining on locally caught seafood high on your list of must-do's.

On Day 3, take A7 north 193km (120 miles) to Niebüll, where you take a train (with your car, if desired) across the causeway to Sylt. Another option is to skip Sylt and spend more time in Lübeck (see "Lingering in Lübeck," p. 564); from Hamburg it's a 66km (41 mile) drive southwest on A1 to Lübeck.

2 ★★★ kids **Sylt.** The island is Germany's most chic seacoast vacation hotspot, and it's just tough cookies that it's tucked away in—offshore from, actually—an awkward-to-reach corner of the country, just below Denmark. Sylt, composed primarily of sand, is fragile, and not much more than 500m (⅓ mile) wide at its narrowest point. Buffeted by North Sea storms, its sand dunes "migrate," and the entire island is in danger of being reclaimed by the sea. One day it may happen, and the party will definitely be over. ⏱ 1 day. For more on Sylt, see p. 571, **5**; for hotel and restaurant recommendations, see p. 575.

Get an early start on Day 4 to maximize your time in Lübeck. Return to Niebüll, and settle down for a long car ride east on B199, south on the fast A7, and finally southeast on B205 and B206 to Lübeck (201km/125 miles).

3 ★★★ **Lübeck.** ⏱ At least 1 day. For information on Lübeck, including hotel and restaurant recommendations, see p. 606.

From Lübeck, go south on B207n, east on A20, and north on B208 to Wismar (67km/42 miles).

4 ★ **Wismar.** So atmospheric are the twisting streets of Wismar's Altstadt (Old Town) that silent filmmaker F. W. Murnau used them as the backdrop for his classic vampire film, *Nosferatu* (1922). Each year, in the middle of June, Wismar celebrates its equally

North Frisian Ferries

Just like the Ostfriesische Inseln (East Frisian Islands; p. 530), the ★★ **Nordfriesische Inseln** (North Frisian Islands) are well worth a visit. But the Wattenmeer (Wadden Sea) is so shallow that it disappears almost entirely at low tide! Ferries to the islands are dependent on the tides, so be sure to check that you have enough time for the trip. The following information should help you to plan. All the ferries listed below ship cars except the one that leaves from Schlüttsiel.

ISLAND	MAINLAND HARBOR	FERRY COMPANY	TRAVEL TIME
Amrum	Dagebüll	WDR ☎ 01805/080-140 www.faehre.de	From Dagebüll 90 min. Via Föhr 120 min.
Föhr	Dagebüll	WDR ☎ 01805/080-140 www.faehre.de	45 min.
Halligen Islets and Amrum	Schlüttsiel	WDR ☎ 01805/080-140 www.faehre.de	Hooge 60 min. Langeness 90 min. Amrum 165 min.
Pellworm	Norden (Strucklahnungshörn)	NPDG ☎ 04844/753 www.faehre-pellworm.de	35 min.
Sylt	Havneby	Rømø-Sylt Linien ☎ 0180/310-3030 www.syltfaehre.de	45 min.

> The vaulted ceilings of Lübeck's Rathaus, Germany's oldest functioning town hall.

Lingering in Lübeck

Anyone who decides against the long run north to Sylt, and in consequence can dedicate part of another day to Lübeck, can head to the nearby Baltic coast at **Timmendorfer Strand.** Lübeck's main beach resort is prized for its long stretch of white sand and its seafood restaurants. Close to the waterfront is **Sea Life Aquarium** at Kurpromenade 5 (☎ 01805/6669-0101; www.sealifeeurope.com; admission 14€ adults, 9.95€ kids 3–14; Mar–June and Sept–Oct daily 10am–6pm, July–Aug daily 10am–7pm, Nov–Feb daily 10am–5pm). A great walk heads east along the coast from nearby Niendorf to Travemünde (see below). It's an easy, signposted hike of 4km (2.5 miles) atop the Brodtener Steilküste (Brodten Seacliffs); take a break halfway, at Café-Restaurant Hermannshöhe (04502/73021).

As its name indicates, **Travemünde** stands at the mouth of the Trave River, and affords good views of big Baltic ferries and other ships heading into and out of Lübeck. It's as popular as Timmendorfer Strand, though less for its beach, which is rather small, than for its shopping, restaurants, and general bustle.

FKK (Nude) Beaches

Many stretches of beach along Germany's North Sea and Baltic Sea coasts—along with lakeside beaches in the interior—have been labeled with the mysterious code FKK. The letters stand for *Freikörperkultur*, or "free body culture"—or, in a word, nudist. Beware of passing an FKK sign while wearing clothes, be they ever so skimpy. The shocking sight of a clothed individual invading this hallowed ground may generate considerable moral outrage from those who have cast aside such artificial trappings. Protected by the powerful fkk juju, the fatherland's naturist sons and daughters strip down to the buff and wave their parts hither and yon with no danger of innocents abroad being injured. So if your apparel of choice on a warm summer's day is your birthday suit, you should fit right in.

ambience-endowed Alter Hafen (Old Harbor) with the Wismarer Hafentage (Wismar Harbor Days), 3 days of open-air music, theater, dance, and general festivities. ⏲ 3 hr. For more on Wismar, see p. 579, ④.

From Wismar, take B106 south to Schwerin (32km/20 miles).

⑤ ★★★ **Schwerin.** Lying inland of the Baltic coast, this town at the southwestern corner of Schweriner See (Lake Schwerin) is set in a fertile, well-irrigated district of small lakes. Schwerin is the proud civic capital and cultural center of this important agricultural district. ⏲ hr. For information on Schwerin, including hotel and restaurant recommendations, see p. 610.

Cross over to the east bank of Schweriner See on B104 and pick up A14 northbound to where it joins A20, then go east to B103 for a final run north into Rostock, a total distance of 95km (59 miles).

High Seas Helgoland

Helgoland proudly proclaims itself Germany's only *Hochseeinsel* (High Seas Island). It lies out in the Deutsche Bucht (German Bight), some 50km (31 miles) from the nearest point on the mainland, and has an area of just 1.7 sq km (⅔ sq. mile) and a permanent population of 1,300. Its red sandstone cliffs tower against the deep-blue pelagic waters and a shoreline fringe of white-sand beaches. A neighboring tiny islet, Düne, consists mainly of sand dunes. Employed as a naval base during both world wars, Helgoland was occupied by Britain from the end of World War II until 1952. Its U-boat (submarine) pens and other military installations were blown up in 1947, in a cataclysmic explosion that collapsed a large part of the island, leaving behind today's *Oberland* (Upper Land) and *Unterland* (Lower Land).

Now a fishing port and car-free vacation center, Helgoland can be reached by excursion boat or fast catamaran from several towns on Germany's North Sea coast and from Hamburg. Once ashore, you can stroll for some hours around the island and its small village of colored timber cottages, while breathing in pollen-free, iodine-rich air. Local sights include the aquarium of a marine biology station, the fishing-boat harbor, and a distinctive, freestanding sandstone rock on the north coast called *Lange Anna* (47m/154 ft. high), reached along a clifftop path. Other pastimes are bird-watching for species that include kittiwakes, guillemots, and gannets, and observing harbor seals and gray seals.

A convenient way to Helgoland is by jet-catamaran from Hamburg (FRS Helgoline; ☎ 0180/320-2025; www.helgoline.de; travel time 3 hr. 45 min.). The jet-cat picks up additional passengers down the Elbe at Wedel (3 hr. 5 min.) and at Cuxhaven at the rivermouth (1 hr. 15 min.), before docking in Helgoland harbor. From May to September, excursion boats depart daily (in most cases) from Cuxhaven (Reederei Cassen Eils; ☎ 04721/350-8284; www.helgolandreisen. de; 2 hr. 30 min.) and Wilhelmshaven (Helgoland Linie; ☎ 01805/228-661; www. helgolandlinie.de; 3 hr.) in Niedersachsen, and from Büsum (Reederei Cassen Eils; ☎ 04834/938-220; www.helgolandreisen. de; 2 hr. 30 min.) in Schleswig-Holstein. The excursion boats don't dock at the island's harbor; instead, passengers are transshipped between the anchored vessels and the harbor aboard small open boats. Out of the summer vacation season, only the boat from Cuxhaven maintains a sea connection with the island, this time to the harbor.

Flights are available in light commercial planes from Hamburg (Air-Hamburg; ☎ 040/7070-8890; www.air-hamburg.de; 40 min.), Bremerhaven (OLT; ☎ 0471/ 77188; www.olt.de; 30 min.), and Büsum (OLT; ☎ 0471/77188; www.olt.de; 20 min.), into a tiny airstrip on Düne. ⏱ 1 day. Tourist information: Helgoland Touristik, Lung Wai 28, Helgoland. ☎ 0180/564-3737. www. helgoland.de.

Northern Germany's National Parks

In addition to the ★★★ **Nationalpark Niedersächsisches Wattenmeer** (Lower Saxony Wadden Sea National Park; p. 529, **7**), two other national parks cover the Wattenmeer's shallow tidal mudflats and low-lying islands bordering the chilly, turbulent North Sea. These are the relatively small ★ **Nationalpark Hamburgisches Wattenmeer** (Hamburg Wadden Sea National Park; ☎ 04721/69271; www.nationalpark-hamburgisches-wattenmeer.de), at the mouth of the Elbe River, and the ★★ **Nationalpark Schleswig-Holsteinisches Wattenmeer** (Schleswig-Holstein Wadden Sea National Park; ☎ 04861/6160; www.wattenmeer-nationalpark.de), Germany's largest national park, stretching up along Schleswig-Holstein's west coast to the border with Denmark.

Moving east, the smooth, gentle Baltic Sea hosts two national parks. The ★★ **Nationalpark Vorpommersche Boddenlandschaft** (West-Pomeranian Lagoon Landscape National Park; ☎ 038234/5020; www.nationalpark-vorpommersche-boddenlandschaft.de) takes in the Zingst peninsula and its white-sand beaches, along with adjoining shallow bays and inlets that are a magnet for migrating birds, and reaches offshore to Hiddensee (p. 585, **8**) and the west coast of Rügen (p. 585, **7**).

On Rügen's north coast, the ★★ **Nationalpark Jasmund** (☎ 038392/661-766. www.nationalpark-jasmund.de), Germany's smallest national park—it covers just 30 sq. km/12 sq. miles—protects a stretch of magnificent white-chalk sea cliffs and an old-growth beech forest that crowns them and reaches some way inland.

Inland, the two separate pieces of ★ **Müritz-Nationalpark** (☎ 039824/2520; www.nationalpark-mueritz.de) cover 322 sq. km (124 sq. miles) of pine forest, lakes (more than a hundred), meadows, and moors in an ecologically diverse part of the Mecklenburg Lake District; one piece reaches west to cover most of Müritzsee's eastern shore. The national park is headquartered at ★ **Schloss Hohenzieritz** (1751), a palace of the dukes of Mecklenburg-Strelitz, in the small town of Hohenzieritz, 13km (8 miles) north of Neustrelitz, off B193. In 1810, Prussia's much-loved Queen Luise died in the palace, her father's summer residence, at age 34. Her remains are interred in a mausoleum in the grounds of Berlin's Schloss Charlottenburg (p. 68, **1**).

These national parks are the jewels in the crown of northern Germany's natural heritage, but they are not its only protected landscapes and seascapes. There are many nature parks and nature reserves. These are likely to be smaller, not quite so spectacular, and maybe not quite so well protected as the national parks. Lovers of nature and the outdoors can easily find out about them by inquiring at local tourist offices; leaflets, brochures, and other information are sure to be available.

> *The beautiful, protected sea island of Rügen is Germany's largest, and its wide variety of popular resorts makes it a popular vacation destination.*

6 ★★ **Rostock.** Following bombing damage in World War II, Rostock has been restored to something approaching its historic splendor. Central Kröpeliner Strasse ends at Kröpeliner Tor, a 14th-century brick gatehouse in the old city walls. On the far side of the walls is a pleasant park with ponds and flower gardens. The Warnow River waterfront makes an attractive sight, and no more so than during the annual Hanse Sail festival (2nd weekend Aug), when around 200 sailing ships line up along Rostock's wharves and those downstream at Warnemünde (p. 584, **4**). ⏱ 4 hr. For more on Rostock, see p. 579, **5**.

From Rostock, go northeast on B105 to Stralsund (74km/46 miles).

7 ★ kids **Stralsund.** The old Hanseatic town is the gateway to the island of Rügen. It's an important Baltic Sea fishing port, with a bustling harbor. The scenic coastline either side of the town along Strelasund, a strait that separates Rügen from the mainland, is worth exploring. ⏱ 2 hr. See p. 580, **6**.

Cross over to Rügen on the road bridge.

8 ★★★ kids **Rügen.** Germany's largest island has known boom times for tourism since the country's reunification, when it was restored to its prewar eminence. Big as the island is, at the height of the tourist season in July and August it can seem downright crowded. That's part reality and part illusion—Rügen is too big to be filled up; at any rate there are always places you can go to escape the crowds. If you have enough time, which can mean as little as a half-day, it's worthwhile renting a bicycle and heading out on country roads into Rügen's wild green yonder. ⏱ At least a half-day. See p. 585, **7**.

Schleswig-Holstein

On this clockwise tour through Germany's most northerly
Land (state), you get to experience Schleswig-Holstein's intriguing mix of
German and Danish elements—much of the territory once belonged to
Denmark. You go up along the North Sea coast, heading offshore to the
Nordfriesische Inseln (North Frisian Islands) along the way, then cut eastward
just below the Danish border to Flensburg, and return south by way of Schleswig
and Kiel on the Baltic Sea. You should be able to visit all the stops on this tour in
a week, but think of this as a general route to follow and either linger longer or
skip stops as your needs and interests dictate.

> *Charming Friedrichstadt offers a glimpse of Holland in northern Germany.*

START Friedrichstadt is 140km (87 miles)
north of Hamburg on A23, B5, and B202.
TRIP LENGTH 274km (170 miles), not including
distances traveled by ferry and train, and
about 7 days.

❶ ★ ★ **kids** **Friedrichstadt.** This little gem of
a town (pop. 2,500) on the Eider River was
founded in 1621 by Protestant Dutch settlers
at the behest of local Duke Friedrich III, who
hoped to create a maritime trading powerhouse
to rival Amsterdam. That didn't pan out, but

the transplanted piece of 17th-century Holland,
complete with *Grachten* (canals), Dutch-style
houses with step gables, and surrounding pol-
derland, is still there to delight. Stroll around
town from Marktplatz, and kick back on a canal-
boat tour with **Friedrichstädter Grachten-
schiffahrt** (☎ 04881/1572; www.grachtenfahrt
de). ⏱ 3 hr. Tourist information: Am Markt 9.
☎ 04881/93930. www.friedrichstadt.de.

**Head north on B202 and B5 to Husum
(17km/11 miles).**

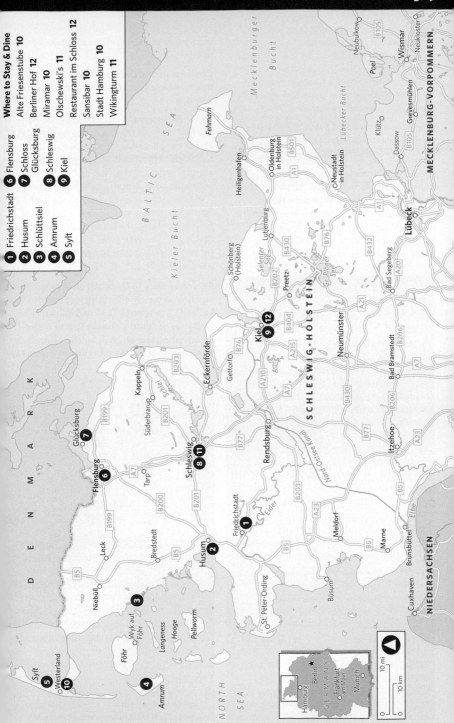

1 Friedrichstadt
2 Husum
3 Schlüttsiel
4 Amrum
5 Sylt
6 Flensburg
7 Schloss Glücksburg
8 Schleswig
9 Kiel

Where to Stay & Dine
Alte Friesenstube 10
Berliner Hof 12
Miramar 10
Olschewski's 11
Restaurant im Schloss 12
Sansibar 10
Stadt Hamburg 10
Wikingturm 11

② Husum. Due to its respectable size (for these parts), a pretty tidal fishing harbor, and a slew of cozy restaurants, bars, and hotels, Husum (pop. 23,000) has become a local tourism center for this part of the seacoast. Take a stroll around the handsome inner harbor. ⏱ 1 hr. www.husum.org.

From Husum, take B5, L278, L11, and L191 north up the coast to Schlüttsiel (36km/22 miles).

③ Schlüttsiel. Ferries (no cars) to the Halligen islets of Langeness and Hooge or to Amrum, depart from here. In addition, tour boats operated by **Halligreederei MS Hauke Haien** (☎ 04841/81481; http://wattenmeerfahrten. inselseiten.de) sail to the islets and may even drop you off for a fascinating stroll on a seal-sanctuary sandbank like Japsand or Norderoogsand that will be underwater when the tide returns. ⏱ Tours last anywhere from 4 to 8 hr.

Continue up the coast to Dagebüll (8km/5 miles), where you can catch a car ferry to Amrum.

④ ★★ kids Amrum. Amrum stands full in the path of whatever the North Sea throws at it. The wind and surf off the long west-coast beach attracts a small army—or navy—of extreme windsurfers. They and other hardy vacationers join a permanent population of 2,400 breeze-buffeted souls on the island's 20 sq. km (8 sq. miles). To get around, rent a bicycle from one of a number of local outlets. ⏱ Half-day. Tourist information: AmrumTouristik, WDR Building, Wittdün. ☎ 04682/94030; www.amrum.de.

Return by ferry to Dagebüll on the mainland and then drive northeast on local roads L9, L6, and L7 to Niebüll (13km/8 miles). Here, load your car onto a railway flatcar at the train station and sit back for the 40-minute ride across the Hindenburgdamm causeway

Ferry Tales

For information on ferry service to the islands off Schleswig-Holstein's Wattenmeer (Wadden Sea) coast, see "North Frisian Ferries," p. 563. The vagaries of ferries, tides, and sailing times mean an island visit will take up a better part of the day, so I've only included Amrum and Sylt on this itinerary. If you have more time, I'd also recommend visits to ★ **Pellworm** and ★ **Föhr.** With a permanent population of just 1,200 on its 37 sq. km (14 sq. miles), Pellworm (www.pellworm.de) sports plenty of peace and quiet, and not much in the way of excitement (if you don't count the threat of devastating storms), which is exactly why people come here. You can bring your car over, but renting a bicycle on the island is a better way to get around its fishing and farming communities. The ferry to Pellworm leaves from Norden.

Sheltered from North Sea winds and storms by neighboring Amrum and Sylt, Föhr (www.foehr.de) has a permanent population of 9,000 souls on its 83 sq. km (32 sq. miles). The island's main village, where the ferry docks, is Wyk auf Föhr. From here a sparse net of country roads—rent a bicycle to get around, if you can—connects more than a dozen hamlets and a patchwork of farms scattered around the landscape. The beaches on the south coast are the best.

Mudflat Hiking

Schleswig-Holstein's shallow Wattenmeer (Wadden Sea) affords opportunities for the fascinating activity of *Wattwandern* (mudflat-hiking) on the seabed when the tide is out, similar to that of Niedersachsen's Wattenmeer coast (see "Walking Across a Sea," p. 535). For information on tours led by a licensed guide, contact local tourist offices or visit the German-language website www.wattenloepers.de. *Warning:* Do not attempt this without an official guide. There is a real danger of being caught by a fast-incoming tide.

> *Windsurfers and sailing enthusiasts flock to the unspoiled, open beaches on the North and Baltic seas in Schleswig-Holstein.*

to Westerland on Sylt; or leave your car in Niebüll and ride a passenger train to Sylt. An alternative is to drive to Havneby in Denmark and take the car ferry across from there (see "North Frisian Ferries," p. 563).

5 ★★★ kids **Sylt.** Some people can't get enough of Sylt (pronounced, more or less, *Zoolt*). They spend every waking hour here—including many hours of bacchanalia—and then come back for more. Germany's most glamorous seacoast resort is sometimes compared to My(as)konos for its hedonism, gay and lesbian scene, and contradictory attitude to clothes—Sylt had Germany's first official nude bathing beach (see p. 564 for more on Germany's *FKK/Freikörperkultur,* or nudist culture), and now most people you'll see here wear either the most expensive designer duds or nothing at all. Just remember, this is the North Sea, not the Aegean. The water is pretty darn cold even on the warmest summer's day. Still, Sylt, which has a permanent population of 22,000 living on its 99 sq. km (38 sq. miles), is much loved for its scenic beauty; healthy, iodine-laden air; and a white-sand beach along the west coast that's 40km (25 miles) long and reaches to Germany's northernmost point at its tip.

Once on the island you have as many colorful choices as a bee in a botanical garden. A string of resorts on the western strip are the main draws, with, from south to north, Hörnum the most threatened by wind and tide, ★★ **Westerland** the largest and most glamorous, Wenningstedt the place for families, ★ **Kampen** the diminutive shopping paradise, and List the harbor for car ferries from Havenby on the island of Rømø, in Denmark (see "North Frisian Ferries," p. 563). Fancy hotels, gourmet restaurants, a casino, bars, nightclubs, sailing, bird-watching, and a general air of being away (*well* away) from it all—that's Sylt. ⊙ 1 day. Tourist information: Sylt Tourismus Zentrale, Keitumer Landstrasse 10B, Tinnum. ☎ 04651/6026. www.sylt-tourismus.de.

Emil Nolde

Expressionist Emil Nolde (1867–1956), a member of the Die Brücke group, is a highly regarded artist in spite of his early support for the Nazi Party. Ironically, the Nazis condemned his art as "degenerate" and removed it from German museums. Nolde lived, worked, and died on a farm at Seebüll, northeast of Neukirchen, close to the Danish border. The Emil Nolde Museum here houses oils, watercolors, and lithographs by the artist, among them his *La Cima della Pala and la Vezzana* (1897). ⊙ 1 hr. Seebüll 31. ☎ 04664/983-930. www.nolde-stiftung.de. Admission 8€ adults, 3€ kids 6–18. June–Sept Fri–Wed 10am–6pm, Thurs 10am–8pm; Oct–May daily 10am–6pm.

> *Flensburg harbor, where you'll find old sailing ships and the Flensburger Schiffahrtsmuseum, which celebrates the area's maritime traditions.*

Return by train to Niebüll, and take B5 north and B199 east to Flensburg (44km/27 miles).

❻ ★ Flensburg. Germany's most Danish-seeming town lies just 7km (4 miles) south of the Danish border. It was actually a part of Denmark until 1864, and it has a Danish minority that accounts for around 25% of its 90,000 inhabitants. Flensburg is centered on its sheltered harbor along Flensburger Förde (Flensburg Fjord); old sailing ships and other floating antiques are tied up here. Visit the **Flensburger Schiffahrtsmuseum** (Flensburg

Maritime Museum), Schiffbrücke 39 (☎ 0461/ 852-970; www.schiffahrtsmuseum.flensburg. de; admission 4€ adults, 1.50€ kids 6–18; Apr–Oct Tues–Sun 10am–5pm; Nov–Mar Tues–Sun 10–4pm), in the harbor, for more local seafaring lore. ⓧ 3 hr. Tourist information: Flensburg Fjord Tourismus, Rathausstrasse 1. ☎ 0461/ 909-0920. www.flensburg-tourismus.de.

Continue east on B199 and K92 to Glücksburg (11km/7 miles).

❼ ★★ kids Schloss Glücksburg. Lovely, white-washed Glücksburg Palace (1587), built as the seat of a local duke and standing in a moat in the heart of the small town of Glücksburg, is one of northern Europe's most outstanding Renaissance palaces. You'll get to see the ornate ducal apartments, banqueting hall, private chapel, and more. ⓧ 2 hr. Schloss Allee. ☎ 04631/442-330; www.schloss-glucksburg. de. Admission 5€ adults, 2.60€ kids 6–16, 10€ families. May–Sept daily 10am–6pm; Oct Tues–Sun 10am–6pm; Nov–Apr Sat–Sun 11am–4pm.

From Glücksburg, backtrack to B199 and take B199, B200, and A7 south, and then B201 east, to Schleswig (51km/32 miles).

Along the Fjord

A drive of just 6km (3¾ miles) northeast from Glücksburg leads onto the Holnis peninsula at the pretty village of Drei. From there it's a short walk to the most northerly point on the German mainland, **Naturschutzgebiet Holnis,** a nature reserve at the cliff-faced peninsula's tip. Your reward—in addition to fresh air—is a scenic outlook across Flensburger Förde (Flensburg Fjord) to Denmark.

> *The popular open-air Wikinger Museum Haithabu is a faithful re-creation of a Viking trading settlement.*

8 ★★ **kids Schleswig.** Though it's a pleasant enough place, with a charming old fishing village forming its Altstadt (Old Town), Schleswig (pop. 24,000) gains much of its appeal from a striking waterfront location at the western end of the Schlei, a long Baltic fjord. ★ **Dom St. Petri** (St. Peter's Cathedral; ☎ 04621/989-595; www.sankt-petri-dom. de), a Romanesque-Gothic church begun in the 12th century, has a spire that's 112m (367 ft.) high and is visible from a long way off. Inside the church, be sure to take in the *Bordesholm Altarpiece* (1521), an intricate oak carving depicting the Passion of Christ. Begun in the 16th century and completed a couple of centuries later, **Schloss Gottorf,** Burgsee (☎ 04621/8130; www.schloss-gottorf.de; admission 8€ adults, 5€ kids 6–16; Apr–Oct Tues–Sun 10am–5pm; Nov–Mar Tues–Fri 10am–4pm, Sat–Sun 10–5pm), was a ducal palace that now houses Schleswig-Holstein's **Landesmuseum** (State Museum) of art and history. Take a small passenger boat across the Schlei, or walk or bicycle around the end of the fjord, to ★★ **Wikinger Museum Haithabu** (☎ 04621/813-222; www.schloss-gottorf. de; admission 6€ adults, 3.50€ kids 6–16; Apr–Oct daily 10am–5pm, Nov–Mar Tues–Sun 10–4pm), an open-air museum and recreation of the important Viking trading settlement of Haithabu, established here in the 9th century. ⏱ 6 hr. Tourist information: Plessenstrasse 7. ☎ 04621/850-050. www.ostseefjordschlei.de.

From Schleswig, continue south on A7 and then east on A210 for a fast highway transfer to Kiel (60km/37 miles). Or take the scenic

Around the Schlei

A great scenic drive from Schleswig is to go along one shore of the Schlei all the way to the Baltic Sea and then return on the opposite shore. It's a long round-trip—a minimum of 120km (75 miles), and more like 200km (124 miles) if you want to visit some of the interesting places along the way—so a full day is needed. You can cross back and forth on little car ferries between Brodersby and Missunde, and Arnis and Sundsacker; and on bridges between Lindau and Stubbe, and Kappeln and Ellenberg. I recommend stopping at Lindau, Arnis, and Kappeln on the north shore and at Missunde, Sieseby, and Opelnitzdorf (at the Baltic Sea) on the south shore.

> *The Baltic port city of Kiel hosts the annual Kieler Woche sailboat regatta, which it claims is the world's largest.*

route to Kiel, southeast on B76 (53km/33 miles)—stop for a stroll around Eckernförde's pretty fishing harbor on the way.

9 ★ **kids Kiel.** The Baltic port city and Schleswig-Holstein state capital (pop. 240,000) stands at the southern end of long Kieler Förde (Kiel Fjord). It is home to one of Germany's two main fleet bases (the other is at Wilhelmshaven on the North Sea; see p. 509, **11**) and in consequence was heavily bombed during World War II, after which it was rebuilt in a modern style. Kiel's maritime assets extend beyond the navy base to an important trade and cruising harbor, a car-ferry port serving destinations around the Baltic, and the eastern terminal of the Nord-Ostsee-Kanal (see "Kiel Canal," below). In addition, it's a center for leisure sailing and hosts the annual Kieler Woche (Kiel Week; last full week in June), which it claims is the world's biggest sailboat regatta. Tour the busy harbor by boat and visit the ★ **Aquarium,** Düsternbrooker Weg 20 (☎ 0431/42700; www.aquarium-kiel.de; admission 3€ adults, 2€ kids 6–18;

Apr–Sept daily 9am–7pm, Oct–Mar daily 9am–5pm). ⊙ 4 hr. Tourist information: Kiel Tourismus, Andreas-Gayk-Strasse 31 (☎ 0431/679-100), or Tourist Service Hauptbahnhof (main train station), www.kurskiel.de.

Kiel Canal

The Nord-Ostsee-Kanal (North-East Sea Canal; better known in English as the Kiel Canal) connects the Baltic Sea at Kiel with the North Sea at Brunsbüttel (see "Hamburg Side Trips," p. 595), a distance of 98km (61 miles) across Schleswig-Holstein's waist. It was dug between 1887 and 1895 (and has since been widened) to aid the movement of warships and merchant vessels between the two seas, avoiding the need to sail around Denmark. Among a constant parade of cargo barges and leisure craft, it's fascinating to watch a large ocean cruise-liner transiting the canal, seeming from a distance to glide past upon the flat land.

Where to Stay & Dine

> Spectacular sea views and recreational facilities are selling points for Sylt's popular Miramar resort.

★★ Alte Friesenstube SYLT FRISIAN

In a thatched-roof house dating from 1648, this old-fashioned eatery turns ultra-chic Sylt upside down. The menu of traditional fish and meat dishes is written in the local Sylter Platt dialect. Gadt 4, Westerland. ☎ 04651/1228. www.altefriesenstube.de. Entrees 16€–22€. No credit cards. Dinner Tues–Sun.

★ Berliner Hof KIEL

Guest rooms are bright and contemporary at this hotel, family-owned since it opened in 1902. It's across the street from Kiel station and close to restaurants, bars, and the tour-boat dock. Ringstrasse 6. ☎ 0431/66340. www.berlinerhof-kiel.de. 103 units. Doubles 95€–125€ w/breakfast. AE, DC, MC, V.

★★ Miramar SYLT

Owned by the same family since 1903, the Miramar lives up to its name with a grand sea view; it has original Art Nouveau elements inside, along with a small modern spa. Friedrichstrasse 43, Westerland. ☎ 04651/8550. www.hotel-miramar.de. 93 units. Doubles 195€–399€ w/breakfast. AE, DC, MC, V.

★ Olschewski's SCHLESWIG

This family-run Altstadt (Old Town) hotel has plain but clean rooms with pine furnishings, one of Schleswig's best restaurants, and views of the Schlei fjord and the harbor. Hafenstrasse 40. ☎ 04621/25577. www.hotelolschewski.de.vu. 7 units. Doubles 77€–95€ w/breakfast. AE, MC, V.

★★ Restaurant im Schloss KIEL CONTINENTAL

Dining in a palace is undeniably romantic—even though 16th-century Kieler Schloss needed to be rebuilt (1965) after wartime destruction. The approach is formal but not excessively so. Wall 74. ☎ 0431/91155. www.restaurant-im-schloss.de. Entrees 12€–21€. AE, DC, MC, V. Lunch & dinner Tues–Sun.

★★★ kids Sansibar SYLT SEAFOOD/CONTINENTAL

This fun beach restaurant has foodie flair, German *"Promis"* (VIPs) to ogle, and a 1,400-label wine cellar in the dunes. Hörnumer Strasse 80, Rantum. ☎ 04651/964-646. www.sansibar.de. Entrees 14€–32€. AE, DC, MC, V. Lunch & dinner daily.

★★★ Stadt Hamburg SYLT

Handy for the next-door casino, this hotel on the main drag to the beach is fitted out like a country mansion in a building dating from 1869 and an annex added in the 1990s. Strandstrasse 2, Westerland. ☎ 04651/8580. www.hotelstadthamburg.com. 72 units. Doubles 145€–300€. AE, DC, MC, V.

★ kids Wikingturm SCHLESWIG CONTINENTAL

The 26th-floor restaurant in the 1960s-"vintage" Wikingturm (Viking Tower) skyscraper, 85m (279 ft.) high, commands fine views over the town and the Schlei fjord, and serves up good food to boot. Wikingeck 5. ☎ 04621/33040. Entrees 14€–32€. No credit cards. Lunch & dinner daily.

The Hanseatic Towns

The North German towns that belonged to the Baltic-
based Hanseatic League trade federation were among the wealthiest in Europe
during the late Middle Ages and into the Renaissance, able to hold their own
with the best of Italy, France, and Spain. This west-to-east itinerary begins
with the museum-piece town of Stade, courses through the league's onetime
competing giants, Hamburg and Lübeck, and moves on to four towns in the old
East Germany—Wismar, Rostock, Stralsund, and Greifswald—that have been
restoring some of their Hansa-era sparkle. All seven towns place the prized
description *Hansestadt* (Hansa Town) before their name.

> *The charming walking paths and river bridges of Stade attract visitors to this North-German town.*

START **Stade,** on the south bank of the Elbe
River, is 96km (60 miles) northeast of
Bremen by way of A27 and B74. TRIP LENGTH
412km (256 miles) and 5 days.

① ★★ Stade. A veritable North-German jewel,
Stade is a well-nigh perfect evocation of a
Hanseatic-era town. ⊙ Half-day. For information on Stade, including hotel and restaurant
recommendations, see p. 612.

From Stade, take B73 southeast to Hamburg
(55km/34 miles). A slightly shorter, slower,
and more interesting route is the one that
hugs the Elbe bank on local roads L140 and
K39, for a distance of 49km (30 miles).
Spend 2 nights in Hamburg.

② ★★★ Hamburg. Even though it eventually
overtook Lübeck and Bremen to become the
Hansa's commercial powerhouse, the Free

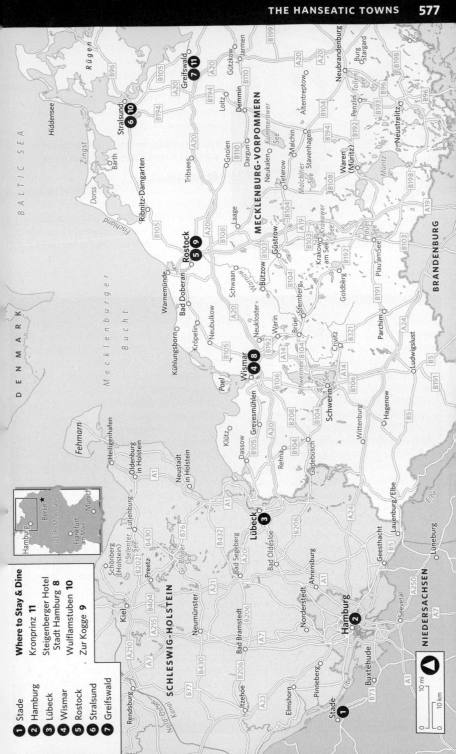

Where to Stay & Dine

Kronprinz **11**
Steigenberger Hotel
Stadt Hamburg **8**
Wulflamstuben **10**
Zur Kogge **9**

1 Stade
2 Hamburg
3 Lübeck
4 Wismar
5 Rostock
6 Stralsund
7 Greifswald

> Rostock's Schiffbau- und Schifffahrtsmuseum commemorates the area's seafaring past.

and Hanseatic City of Hamburg has little in the way of remaining Hanseatic sights. The port city does still have a big mercantile sector and much of every kind of urban attraction imaginable. ⊙ 1½ days. For information on Hamburg, including hotel and restaurant recommendations, see p. 594.

From Hamburg on Day 3, go northeast on A24 and A1 to Lübeck (66km/41 miles).

❸ ★★★ **Lübeck.** For centuries, Lübeck was the principal seat of the Hanseatic League, with trade tentacles that spread through the Baltic and across the North Sea to Norway, London, and Bruges. ⊙ 1 day. For information on Lübeck, including hotel and restaurant recommendations, see p. 606.

The Hanseatic League

Step inside the step-gabled, red-brick Haus der Schiffergesellschaft (Seafarers' Guild House; 1535), on Breite Strasse in Lübeck (p. 606), and you are immediately transported in spirit back to the days of wealthy Hanseatic League merchants. From the 13th to the 17th centuries, this powerful and well-organized association of, at its peak, 170 trading towns and cities in north and northwest Europe controlled trade around the Baltic Sea as far as Russia, and on the North Sea up to Bergen in Norway, west to London, and southwest to Bruges. For much of that time, Lübeck was the league's powerhouse.

Towns in northern Germany and along the Baltic Sea coast—among them Bremen, Hamburg, Lübeck, Rostock, and Wismar—played important roles in the international trade of yesteryear and profited handsomely from their league membership. They proudly bear the title *Hansestadt* (Hanseatic City) to this day. In them you'll find guild houses, civic and religious buildings, warehouses and other mercantile institutions, and the residences of wealthy merchants that date from the Hanseatic period. Many of these survivors of history stand side by side with postwar housing developments and the neon lights of business districts. The *Hanse* (or Hansa in English), as it was known, has

been described, not entirely fancifully, as an early version of the European Union. Around the Baltic Sea today, countries and cities are consciously trying to reestablish Hanseatic trading and cultural links.

The league's most important assets were its *Hansekoggen* (Hansa cogs), square-sailed, broad-beamed wooden merchant ships that could carry 200 tons of cargo. Hundreds of these ships plied the cold northern waters laden with salted herring, Norwegian salted and dried cod and cod-liver oil, Baltic amber, German beer and salt, bales of linen and woolen cloth from the Low Countries and England, coal from England, Russian furs and candle wax, Polish grain and flour, and Swedish timber, pitch, and iron. Lübeck and Rostock have both honored their Hanseatic heritage by building replica Hansa cogs.

As trade increased, the cities and their residents flourished, and the power of the Hanseatic League grew. Such wealth moving slowly on the water naturally attracted pirates, even though the Hansa cogs were well armed and could hold their own in a fight. The most famous privateer was Klaus Störtebeker (c. 1360–1401), a Robin Hood-like figure who was born in Wismar and beheaded in Hamburg.

> *The Deutsches Meersemuseum in Stralsund offers nautical attractions that will captivate the entire family.*

From Lübeck on Day 4, take B207n south to A20, and go east on A20, exiting on B208 to Wismar (67km/42 miles).

4 ★ **Wismar.** Standing on the southern shore of Wismarbucht, a Baltic bay, Wismar (pop. 45,000) consists of two main zones: the moderately attractive **Alter Hafen** (Old Harbor), and the restored Hanseatic ★★ **Altstadt** (Old Town), a UNESCO World Heritage site. Start out at the central ★★ **Markt,** Germany's largest market square, lined with an array of historical buildings. Among these are the **Alter Schwede** (1380), now a restaurant, with a name that recalls a period of Swedish rule, and out on the square, the **Wasserkunst** (Water Art) pavilion (1602). Around the town center are a trio of *Backsteingotik* (brick Gothic)

churches dating from the 13th to the 15th centuries. ⏱ Half-day. Tourist information: Am Markt 11. ☎ 03841/19433. www.wismar.de.

From Wismar, take B105 and A14 southeast to A20, and go northeast on this highway, and then on B103, to Rostock (64km/40 miles).

5 ★★ **Rostock.** Unlike most places in the old East Germany, Rostock (pop. 200,000) was considered a showcase by the Communist regime, since it was the GDR's main port. Money and resources were put in to make good, as far as possible, the heavy damage sustained in World War II bombardments. Rostock's ★ **Altstadt** (Old Town) still bears the signature of its Hanseatic past, even if in a slightly awkward, Stalinist interpretation. The central area around Neuer Markt and Kröpeliner Strasse is especially interesting. Visit the ★ **St.-Marien-Kirche** (Our Lady's Church), Am Ziegenmarkt (☎ 0381/492-3396; www.marienkirche-rostock.de), a masterpiece of the North German

Trading Places

Other North German towns that were members of the Hanseatic League include Braunschweig (p. 507, **8**), Bremen (p. 538), Goslar (p. 544), Hameln (p. 515, **8**), Hannover (p. 546), Hildesheim (p. 507, **7**), and Lüneburg (p. 550). For historical background to the trade federation, see "The Hanseatic League," p. 578.

Taking the Train

You can reach all the towns on this itinerary by train.

> *Baroque and Gothic buildings rim the restored Markt in the beautiful river town of Greifswald.*

style known as *Backsteingotik* (brick Gothic), begun in 1290. It contains a remarkable astronomical clock (1472) decorated with figures of the apostles, an ornate pulpit, and a 13th-century bronze baptismal font. Elements from the Hanseatic past, including model *Hansekoggen* (Hansa cog) sailing ships (see "The Hanseatic League," p. 578), are to be found in the **Schiffbau- und Schifffahrtsmuseum** (Shipbuilding and Shipping Museum), Schmarl-Dorf 40 (☎ 0381/1283-1364; www.schifffahrts-museum-rostock.de; admission 4€ adults,

2.50€ kids 7–14; Apr–June and Sept Tues–Sun 9am–6pm; July–Aug daily 9am–6pm; Oct–Mar Tues–Sun 10–4pm). ⏱ Half-day. Tourist information: Neuer Markt 3. ☎ 0381/381-2222. www.rostock.de.

From Rostock on Day 5, go south on A19, east on A20, and then north on A96 to Stralsund (110km/68 miles). An alternative route that's considerably shorter but takes about as long is to go northeast on B105 (74km/46 miles).

6 ★ kids **Stralsund.** Like Wismar (**4**), Stralsund has a restored Hanseatic **Altstadt** (Old Town) that's a UNESCO World Heritage site, and, also like Wismar, it experienced a long period of rule by Sweden. The town (pop. 58,000) is pretty much surrounded by water and is the gateway to **Rügen island** (p. 585, **7**), which lies just across Strelasund strait. Mementos of its medieval period are to be found in the many Gothic civic, religious, and residential buildings around the town and in the remnants of the city walls. The ★★ **Deutsches Meeresmuseum** (German Oceanographic Museum; ☎ 03831/265-0210; www.meeresmuseum.de; admission 7.50€ adults, 5€ kids 4–16; June–Sept daily 10am–6pm; Oct–May daily 10–5pm) and its trio of nautical attractions—★ **Ozeaneum, Nautineum,** and **Natureum**—are well worth visiting. ⏱ Half-day. Tourist information: Tourismuszentrale, Alter Markt 9. ☎ 03831/24690. www.stralsundtourismus.de.

From Stralsund, go southeast on B96 and B105 to Greifswald (37km/23 miles).

7 ★ **Greifswald.** Set on the Ryck River, 5km (3 miles) from the sea, Greifswald (pop. 54,000) celebrates its civic pride on the ★ **Markt,** a handsome square lined with Gothic and baroque buildings; its Christian virtue in grand medieval churches, like ★ **Dom St. Nikolai** (St. Nicholas's Cathedral, 13th–15th centuries); and its mercantile success at the harbor—though now it's mainly leisure craft that tie up here. ⏱ Half-day. Tourist information: Greifswald Information, Rathaus am Markt. ☎ 03834/521-380. www.greifswald-tourismus.de.

From Greifswald, it's just 13km (8 miles) southwest to the closest point on A20, for a fast return west toward Lübeck and Hamburg or south toward Berlin.

Where to Stay & Dine

> The maritime decor and delicious dishes of Zur Kogge make it one of Rostock's most popular seafood eateries.

★ Kronprinz GREIFSWALD
This hotel in the University (founded 1465) district offers comfortable rooms with contemporary decor and a brasserie that serves seafood and international food. Lange Strasse 22. ☎ 03834/7900. www.hotelkronprinz.de. 31 units. Doubles 99€–112€ w/breakfast. AE, MC, V.

★★ Steigenberger Hotel Stadt Hamburg WISMAR Come here for a desirable location, bright contemporary rooms, a wellness area, and an in-house bistro with Mecklenburg specialties on a broadly Continental menu. Am Markt 24. ☎ 03841/2390. www.steigenberger.com. 104 units. Doubles 105€–165€ w/breakfast. AE, DC, MC, V.

★★ Wulflamstuben STRALSUND *NORTH GERMAN*
It would be hard to get closer to the Hanseatic age than in this brick Gothic building from 1370, on the main square, where you dine on lip-smacking Mecklenburg and Pomeranian fare. Alter Markt 5. ☎ 03831/291-533. www.wulflamstuben.de. Entrees 11€–17€. MC, V. Lunch & dinner daily.

★ Zur Kogge ROSTOCK *SEAFOOD/GERMAN*
The maritime spirit is alive and well in this old-fashioned harbor eatery, decked out with nautical knickknacks and serving local marine specialties like *Mecklenburger Fischsuppe* (fish soup). Wokrenterstrasse 27. ☎ 0381/493-4493. www.zur-kogge.de. Entrees 8€–15€. MC, V. Lunch & dinner Mon–Sat (Sun Apr–Dec).

The Baltic Seacoast & Islands

The old East Germany's Ostsee (Baltic Sea) coast from Wismar east to the Polish border at Usedom has regained its reputation as a vacation playground. Resorts that flourished under the kaisers and declined under the Communists are once again on the European map. National parks and nature reserves protect sensitive stretches of land and sea. By all means, divert from the main route at any points along the coast that take your fancy, and mix and match parts of this itinerary with "The Hanseatic Towns" (p. 576).

> The charming island of Poel, a small, friendly village built on farming, fishing, and tourism.

START **Wismar** is 67km (42 miles) east of Lübeck on B207n and A20. TRIP LENGTH **254km (158 miles)**, not including travel on ferries, and **5 days**.

1 ★ **Wismar.** ☉ 2 hr. See p. 579, **4**.

From Wismar, head up the coast on L12 to Gross Strömkendorf, then west on L121 across the causeway to Fährdorf, on Poel (12km/7½ miles).

2 kids **Poel.** In spite of the causeway from the mainland, Poel is plenty insular. It's a small island; just 3,000 people live permanently on its 36 sq. km (14 sq. miles). Farming, fishing, and tourism are its economic lifelines. A driving tour of around 40km (25 miles) will get you through Poel's handful of villages and into many of its nooks and crannies. Kids will be happy to play for a while on the fine beach at Timmendorfer Strand, on the northwest coast. ☉ 6 hr. Tourist information: Wismarsche Strasse 2. ☎ 038425/20347. www.insel-poel.de.

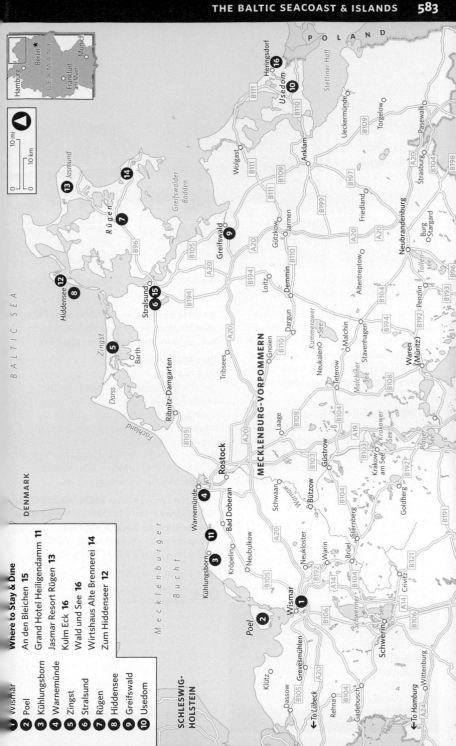

> *The arcades, villas, and hotels in the popular town of Kühlungsborn, a beachfront resort since 1857, were restored after German reunification.*

Return across the causeway, and continue north on L12 to Rakow. Leave L12 and keep heading north on the country road through Roggow to Rerik (gateway to the Wustrow peninsula), and then go east on L122 and north on L12 to Kühlungsborn, a total distance of 36km (22 miles).

❸ ★ **kids Kühlungsborn.** This elegant town (pop. 8,000) traces its origins as a seacoast resort back to 1857. In subsequent decades, grand villas and hotels sprang up. Many of these fell into disrepair under East Germany's postwar regime but have been restored since reunification. Kühlungsborn's popularity today is based on its marvelous beaches and leisure-boating harbor. Just 8km (5 miles) east along the coast, off L12, is Heiligendamm, a restored old aristocratic resort and a good place to spend your first night. ⏱ 2 hr. Tourist information: Touristik Service, Ostseeallee 19, Kühlungsborn. ☎ 038293/8490. www.kuehlungsborn.de.

Travel Tip

Passengers-only ferries operated by **Reederei Hiddensee** (☎ 0180/321-2150; www.reederei-hiddensee.de) cross over to Hiddensee from Schaprode and Wiek on Rügen, from Stralsund (p. 580, ❻) on the mainland, and from Zingst (❺) and Barth, west of Stralsund.

From Heiligendamm, the ubiquitous L12 coast road takes up the itinerary again, leading east to Warnemünde (21km/13 miles).

❹ ★ **Warnemünde.** At the Baltic outlet of the Warnow River, downstream from Rostock (p. 579, ❺), this picturesque small fishing town and beach resort (pop. 7,000) can seem swamped with visitors during the peak travel times in summer. It's especially pretty along the old fishing harbor, Alter Strom, which is lined with restaurants, bars, and boutiques. ⏱ 2 hr. Tourist information: Am Strom 59. ☎ 0381/548-000. www.rostock.de.

Cross the Warnow River on the Warnemünde–Hohe Düne car ferry (☎ 0381/519-860; www.weisse-flotte.de; 5 min.), and follow L22 and L21 up the coast, through Graal-Müritz and Klockenhagen, to Zingst (72km/45 miles).

❺ ★ **Zingst.** The pretty resort town (pop. 3,000) is in the heart of the **Nationalpark Vorpommersche Boddenlandschaft** (West-Pomeranian Lagoon Landscape National Park; see "Northern Germany's National Parks," p. 566). On the way, you pass through Ahrenshoop (p. 28, ❶), a village that's been an artists' colony since 1889. ⏱ 6 hr. Kur und Tourismus, Seestrasse 56, Zingst. ☎ 038232/81580 www.zingst.de.

From Zingst on Day 3, take L21 south and east to just before Neu Lassentin, then hold to the coast road on L213, curving north then south into Stralsund (49km/30 miles).

6 ★ kids **Stralsund.** ⏱ 2 hr. See p. 580, **6**.

Cross over to Rügen on the road bridge or by train to any of multiple island stations, or on a passengers-only ferry to Altefähre (☎ 03831/26810; www.weisse-flotte.de; 15 min.).

7 ★★★ kids **Rügen.** Even a whole day is little enough time for taking in Germany's largest island, which has a great variety of landscapes on its 926 sq. km (358 sq. miles) and a permanent population of 80,000. Roads radiate outward from the main town, Bergen, and rail lines connect the north and east. Along the southeast coast is a constellation of resorts—**Baabe,** ★★ **Binz, Göhren,** and ★ **Sellin**—that trace their glory days back to the 19th century and have restored villas and hotels from that time. Inland, ★ **Putbus,** a small neoclassical town, was conceived and created by a 19th-century prince. A considerable part of Rügen is taken up by protected zones. Parts of the west coast belong to the ★★ **Nationalpark Vorpommersche Boddenlandschaft** (West-Pomeranian Lagoon Landscape National Park; see "Northern Germany's National Parks," p. 566); in the southeast, there's UNESCO's ★ **Biosphärenreservat Südost-Rügen** (Southeast Rügen Biosphere Reserve; www.biosphaerenreservat-suedostruegen.de); and in the north, the ★★★ **Nationalpark Jasmund** (see "Northern Germany's National Parks," p. 566), set around the famous Stubbenkammer chalk cliffs and their most remarkable formation, the Königsstuhl (King's Seat). These were a favorite subject of 19th-century Romantic artist Caspar David Friedrich (see "Caspar David Friedrich," p. 586). From here, the coastline runs around to ★ **Kap Arkona,** a cape at the island's northern tip. ⏱ 1 day. Tourist information: Tourismuszentrale, Bahnhofstrasse 15, Bergen. ☎ 03838/807-780. www.ruegen.de.

From Schaprode or Wiek on Rügen's west coast on Day 4, ride a passengers-only ferry across to Hiddensee island (see the "Travel Tip" for ferry information).

8 ★★ **Hiddensee.** Very nearly car-free, and definitely carefree, Hiddensee is a long, thin island off of Rügen's west coast. At its narrowest points, you can just about stretch out your arms

> *Rügen's towering and historic lighthouse at Kap Arkona is a big draw for seaside visitors.*

and touch the sea on either side. Around 1,000 people are permanent residents on its 19 sq. km (7 sq. miles), living in a few villages and making a living from farming, fishing, and tourism. The few manmade attractions consist of the Leuchtturm (Lighthouse) in the northern Dornbusch district, and the Jugendstil (Art Nouveau) Lietzenburg villa (1905) in Kloster village. But the main attractions are hiking, bicycling, and visiting sights associated with the **Nationalpark Vorpommersche Boddenlandschaft** (West-Pomeranian Lagoon Landscape National Park; see "Northern Germany's National Parks," p. 566). ⏱ 1 day. Tourist information: Insel Information, Norderende 162, Vitte. ☎ 038300/6420. www.seebad-hiddensee.de.

Spend the night on Hiddensee, or return by boat to Rügen and spend the night there. From Rügen on Day 5, either cross back over on the bridge to Stralsund or go to Glewitz on the island's south coast and take the car ferry (☎ 0172/752-6836; www.weisse-flotte.de) across to Stahlbrode on the mainland. Drive southeast to Greifswald on B105 (35km/22 miles from Stralsund; 21km/13 miles from Stahlbrode).

9 ★ **Greifswald.** In addition to spending time in the town of Greifswald itself, you may want to take a brief detour to Wieck and Eldena, pretty villages that face each other on opposite banks of the Ryck River, 5km (3 miles) from Greifswald. Wieck is a working fishing village noted for its fishermen's cottages and photogenic swinging bridge dating from 1887. In Eldena are the ruins of a 12th-century Cistercian abbey painted by Caspar David Friedrich (see "Caspar David Friedrich"). ☺ 2 hr. See p. 580, **7**.

From Greifswald, go southeast on L26 and B111 to Wolgast (29km/18 miles), and cross over on the bridge to Usedom.

Caspar David Friedrich

The great Romantic landscape painter Caspar David Friedrich (1774–1840) was born at Greifswald (p. 580, **7**). He lived and worked in Dresden for most of his career, but many of his most memorable works take the town of his birth, the Baltic Sea coast in general, and the island of Rügen in particular as their subject. These include paintings like his *Ships in Greifswald Harbor* (c. 1810) and *The Sea of Ice* (c. 1818, pictured). Although Friedrich's style was initially popular, he later fell out of favor and was restored in reputation only after his death. Among the museums in Germany where you can view works by the artist are Berlin's Alte Nationalgalerie (p. 80, **17**), Dresden's Galerie Neue Meister (p. 171, **7**), Greifswald's Pommersches Landesmuseum (Rakower Strasse 9, ☎ 03834/83120), Hamburg's Kunsthalle (p. 595, **2**), and Munich's Neue Pinakothek (p. 263, **6**).

> *Ahlbeck pier is a popular point on Usedom, an island divided between Germany and Poland.*

10 ★★ kids **Usedom.** The oddly shaped island is divided between Germany and Poland (its Polish name is Uznam), with Germany owning 373 sq. km (144 sq. miles) out of 445 sq. km (172 sq. miles) and counting 32,000

Wernher von Braun and the V-2

In a way, America's road to a manned landing on the moon in 1969 began at Peenemünde, on the north coast of Usedom, in the years before and during World War II. It was here that the brilliant German rocket engineer, and later U.S. citizen, Wernher von Braun (1912–77), developed the V-2 rocket. Von Braun's interest lay in the conquest of space; the Nazis wanted a ballistic missile to further their war aims by bombarding London and eventually, they hoped, the United States. More than 1,300 V-2 rockets hit London during 1944 and 1945. After the war, von Braun was brought to America, where he developed rockets for the U.S. army and NASA and led the development of the giant Saturn V rocket that took *Apollo 11* to the moon.

inhabitants from a total of 77,000. Like Rügen, Usedom has regained much of its cachet since Germany's reunification. The old *Kaiserbäder* (imperial resorts) of **Bansin,** ★ **Heringsdorf,** and **Ahlbeck**—and their fine beaches—are once again booming in summer. In addition, the island's natural beauty is recognized in its status as a nature park, the **Naturpark Insel Usedom** (☎ 038372/7630; www.naturpark-usedom.de). Germany's World War II V-2 rockets, employed to attack London, Antwerp, and other European towns, were developed and tested at Peenemünde in the north of the island (see "Wernher von Braun and the V-2"). Visit the **Historisch-Technisches Informationszentrum** (Historical-Technical Information Center; ☎ 038371/5050; www.peenemuende.de; admission 6€ adults, 4€ kids 6–18; Apr–Sept daily 10am–6pm; Oct–Mar daily 10am–4pm) to learn the full story. ⏱ 8 hr. Tourist information: Tourismus, Waldstrasse 1, Bansin. ☎ 038378/47710. www.seebad-hiddensee.de.

Where to Stay & Dine

An den Bleichen STRALSUND
On the edge of a wooded area just west of central Stralsund, this tranquil, family-owned hotel from the 1990s has small but well-maintained and comfortable rooms. An den Bleichen 45. ☎ 03831/390-675. www.hotelandenbleichen.de. 23 units. Doubles 60€–75€ w/breakfast. AE, MC, V.

★★★ kids **Grand Hotel Heiligendamm** HEILIGENDAMM Due to its range of amenities, restaurants, and bars, you'll hardly ever need to leave this palatial residence right on the beach. Prof.-Dr.-Vogel-Strasse 6. ☎ 038203/7400. www.grandhotel-heiligendamm.de. 215 units. Doubles 240€–480€ w/breakfast. AE, DC, MC, V.

★★ kids **Jasmar Resort Rügen** RÜGEN Built around a 19th-century mansion, inland from the Jasmund sea cliffs, the hotel has outdoor and indoor pools, a spa, and numerous fine dining options. Am Taubenberg 1, Sagard-Neddesitz. ☎ 038302/95. www.jasmar.de. 243 units. Doubles 105€–160€ w/breakfast. AE, DC, MC, V.

★★ **Kulm Eck** USEDOM CONTINENTAL Brian Seifert, the owner-chef of this gracious restaurant, is as at home with regional Pomernian menus as with ideas for culinary mixing and matching picked up on his travels. Kulmstrasse 17, Seebad Heringsdorf. ☎ 038378/2560. Entrees 18€–24€. V. Dinner Tues–Sun.

★ **Wald und See** USEDOM
This modest, family-run hotel lives up to its name—Wood and Sea—with a leafy location just off the Baltic shore in the island's classiest resort. Rudolf-Breitscheid-Strasse 8, Seebad Heringsdorf. ☎ 038378/47770. www.hotel-waldundsee.de. 43 units. Doubles 69€–119€ w/breakfast. MC, V.

★★ **Wirtshaus Alte Brennerei** RÜGEN NORTH GERMAN Dine on rustic fare in a remarkable setting—the vaulted distillery of Jagdschloss Granitz (1836), a turreted hunting lodge and visitor attraction. Granitzer Strasse (btw. Bintz and Sellin). ☎ 038393/32872. www.alte-brennerei.com. Entrees 12€–22€. No credit cards. Lunch & dinner May–Sept daily, Oct–Apr Tues–Sun. Jagdschloss Granitz is 2.4km (1½ miles) north on a country lane from B196 at Lancken-Granitz (follow the signs).

★ **Zum Hiddenseer** HIDDENSEE NORTH GERMAN The restaurant of the sweet little pension of the same name, in a country house with garden, serves up a nice line in smoked fish and other seafood, along with meat dishes, from a limited menu. Wiesenweg 22, Vitte. ☎ 038300/419. www.hiddenseer.de. Entrees 10€–18€. No credit cards. Lunch & dinner Tues–Sun.

Through the Mecklenburg Lake District

The Mecklenburgische Seenplatte (Mecklenburg Lake District) is a beautiful piece of the natural world, a product of the last Ice Age, which left behind more than a thousand lakes, large and small, on this part of the German state of Mecklenburg-Vorpommern. In addition, this was a heartland of the old Prussian aristocracy, and in their towns and palaces they left behind much of grace and beauty to be admired.

> The impressive, Renaissance-era Schloss Güstrow was once home to the dukes of Mecklenburg.

START Schwerin is 69km (43 miles) southeast of Lübeck on B105 and B104; and 110km (68 miles) east of Hamburg on A24 and B321. TRIP LENGTH 323km (200 miles), or 371km (231 miles) if you include the optional side-trip to Ravensbrück, and 3 days.

1 ★★★ **Schwerin.** ⏱ 6 hr. See p. 610.

From Schwerin, drive northeast on B104 to Güstrow (61km/38 miles). Along the way, you cross over Schweriner See and pass close to several other scenic lakes, among them Grosser Sternbergersee.

1. Schwerin
2. Güstrow
3. Neubrandenburg
4. Neustrelitz
5. Waren
6. Ludwigslust

Where to Stay & Dine
Alte Wache **10**
Klabautermann **7**
Landhotel Broda **8**
Schlossgarten **9**

2 ★ **Güstrow.** Though it doesn't stand right on a shore of a decent-size lake, elegant Güstrow (pop. 31,000) is at the heart of a cluster of such lakes. It was once a residence of the dukes of Mecklenburg, a connection that has given the town a heritage of ducal palaces and other fine buildings. Foremost among these is the magnificent Renaissance palace ★★ **Schloss Güstrow** (1558–89; ☎ 03843/7520; www.schloss-guestrow.de; admission 5€ adults, 3.50€ kids 4–16; mid-Apr to mid-Oct daily 10am–6pm, mid-Oct to mid-Apr Tues–Sun 10am–5pm), set among replicas of period French gardens. It's now a museum, partly of its own history, architecture, and embellishment and partly housing works of art and design from around Mecklenburg. On the central Markt, the 14th-century Gothic **Dom** (cathedral; ☎ 03843/682-433; www.dom-guestrow.de) is noteworthy in itself, and because it houses a replica of the sculpture *Floating Angel* (1927) by Ernst Barlach; the Nazis, who classified Barlach's art as degenerate, destroyed the original. ⏲ 2 hr. Tourist information: Franz-Parr-Platz 10. ☎ 03843/681-023. www.guestrow-tourismus.de.

At the end of Day 1, take B104 southeast to Neubrandenburg (84km/52 miles), where you can spend the night. Along the way, you pass close to scenic Kummerower See.

3 **Neubrandenburg.** By rights, Neubrandenburg (pop. 66,000), on the north shore of Tollensee, should be a jewel, with a medieval Altstadt (Old Town) nestled within a ring of defensive walls. World War II destruction erased much of its historical charm—though the town walls are more or less intact. Going around the walls makes for an interesting stroll of around 2.5km (1½ miles). Check out the four original city gates and several dozen restored small houses, known as *Wiekhäuser,* built into the walls on the inside of the circuit. Boat tours on Tollensee are available in summer, along with other leisure activities on and around the lake, which has a surface area of 17 sq. km (7 sq. miles) and stretches for 10km (6 miles) from the town. ⏲ 3 hr. Tourist information: Touristinfo, Stargarder Strasse 17. ☎ 01805/170-330. www.neubrandenburg-touristinfo.de.

Taking the Train
You can reach all the towns on this itinerary by train.

> The spectacular baroque and neoclassical Schloss Ludwigslust served as a country home for Duke Friedrich von Mecklenburg-Schwerin.

Ravensbrück

It may seem a bit of a stretch to divert south from Neustrelitz toward Berlin to visit **Mahn- und Gedenkstätte Ravensbrück** (Ravensbrück Monument and Memorial; ☎ 033093/6080; www. ravensbrueck.de), just north of Fürstenberg on the Havel River. Since the actual distance is 24km (15 miles), that's more of a psychological issue—a visit to a concentration camp won't be everyone's idea of a vacation jaunt. The women's camp was established in 1938, and between then and 1945 about 90,000 inmates from Germany and countries around Europe perished here. A documentation center occupies the camp commandant's quarters, and the crematorium and other installations can be seen. One of those who died was British agent Violette Szabo (1921–45), captured in occupied France soon after D-day while holding off SS troops to permit her Resistance contacts to escape. She withstood torture by the Gestapo and was brought to Ravensbrück, where she was executed.

From Neubrandenburg on Day 2, go southwest along the east bank of Tollensee on B96, to Neustrelitz (28km/17 miles), where you can spend the night.

④ ★★ **Neustrelitz.** Like Güstrow (②), Neustrelitz (pop. 22,000) owes its beauty to an aristocratic connection. It was purpose-built in the early 18th century as the seat of the duchy of Mecklenburg-Strelitz. Unlike in Güstrow, the grand ducal palace has vanished, a victim of World War II. Only the palace gardens, the Schlosspark, survive, adjoining the town's harbor on Zierker See. By way of compensation, Neustrelitz is an almost perfectly preserved baroque town that repays aimless wandering, and a bustling vacation center come summer. ⏱ 4 hr. Tourist information: Strelitzer Strasse 1. ☎ 03981/253-119. www.neustrelitz.de.

From Neustrelitz on Day 3, go north on B193, then west on B192, skirting the edge of Müritz-Nationalpark, to Waren on the north shore of Müritzsee (44km/27 miles).

⑤ ★ 🄺🄸🄳🅂 **Waren.** For all that it's a neat little place, Waren (pop. 22,000) wouldn't be worth going much out of your way for, except that it's the largest town on the largest lake that lies entirely within Germany, ★★ **Müritz-see** (Lake Müritz). Bodensee (see "Around the Bodensee by Car, Boat & Train," p. 374) is larger, but it is shared with Austria and Switzerland. You get the lowdown on the big lake and its environs at a fascinating aquarium and environmental museum, the **Müritzeum,** Zur Steinmohle 1 (☎ 03991/633-680; www. mueritzeum.de; admission 7.50€ adults, 3€ kids 4–18; Apr–Oct daily 10am–7pm, Nov–Mar daily 10am–6pm). In summer, you can cruise on the lake from Waren harbor (and from other docks around the lakeshore) aboard the tour boats of **Müritz-Linie** (☎ 039931/52797). ⏲ 3 hr. Tourist information: Neuer Markt 21. ☎ 03991/666-183.

From Waren, take B192, B103, and B191 around Müritzsee and Plauer See and then southwest to Ludwigslust (106km/66 miles).

⑥ ★★ **Ludwigslust.** A monument of baroque and neoclassical architecture, this is yet another Mecklenburg town that owes its existence to the desire of some blueblood to put down new roots and a marker for future generations. Ludwigslust (pop. 13,000) developed as a "family town" around the lavish palace, ★★ **Schloss Ludwigslust** (1776; ☎ 03874/57190; www.schloss-ludwigslust. de; admission 5€ adults, 3.50€ kids 6–18; Tues–Sun 10am–5pm), which Duke Friedrich von Mecklenburg-Schwerin constructed as his country *pied-à-terre.* The palace's chambers and salons are filled with art, furnishings, and fittings that show the 18th century at its most lavish, and the building is in a park that covers 135 hectares (334 acres). ⏲ 3 hr. Tourist information: Schlossstrasse 36. ☎ 03874/526-252. www.stadtludwigslust.de.

Where to Stay & Dine

★★ **Alte Wache** LUDWIGSLUST *CONTINENTAL* A restored neoclassical guard post (1853) of the Mecklenburg dragoons houses this grand little cafe-restaurant. Dine inside or under columned arches with courtyard views. Schloss-freiheit 8. ☎ 03874/570-353. Entrees 11€–21€. No credit cards. Lunch & dinner Tues–Sun (daily May–Aug).

★ **Klabautermann** WAREN *FISH* Freshwater fish, caught or farmed in Müritz-see and other nearby lakes and rivers, is the big deal at this great little family restaurant (just 18 seats, and no summer reservations) close to the harbor. Marktstrasse 1. ☎ 03991/662-306. www.klabautermann-waren. de. Entrees 12€–22€. AE, V. Lunch & dinner Tues–Sun.

★ **Landhotel Broda** NEUBRANDENBURG Located between the city walls and Tol-lensee, this country-style hotel overlooking the lake has smart contemporary rooms, a limited-menu restaurant, and a sauna. Oel-mühlenstrasse 29. ☎ 0395/569-170. www. landhotel-broda.de. 13 units. Doubles 65€–84€ w/breakfast. AE, MC, V.

> *Stop in for a bite at the elegant Alte Wache.*

★ **Schlossgarten** NEUSTRELITZ In a tranquil, leafy district, this small family-owned hotel in a neoclassical building with its own garden offers classical comfort in its rooms and a restaurant serving local specialties. Tiergartenstrasse 15. ☎ 03981/24500. www.hotel-schlossgarten.de. 24 units. Doubles 69€–99€ w/breakfast. AE, MC, V.

MEN OF IDEAS
Germany's Most Influential Thinkers

BY KELLY REGAN

GROUNDBREAKING INSIGHT

MARTIN LUTHER (1483-1546)
Priest, theologian, firebrand.

His *95 Theses* questioned the culture of church indulgences (donating money to guarantee salvation). It evolved into a critique of Catholic corruption and a rejection of papal infallibility, sparking the Protestant Reformation. Luther's views spread quickly, thanks to the recent invention of the printing press.

JOHANNES KEPLER (1571-1630)
Astronomer, mathematician, astrologer.

Kepler's laws of planetary motion posited, for the first time, that planets make elliptical orbits around the sun, sweeping out equal areas in equal times. His discoveries were essential to the development of Newton's laws of universal gravitation.

GOTTFRIED LIEBNIZ (1646-1716)
Philosopher, lawyer, diplomat, self-taught mathematician.

First published theory of infinitesimal calculus in 1684; notebooks indicate his first equations employed in 1675, just 3 years after first taking up the study of math. Inspired by the classic Chinese text *I Ching*, invented the binary numerical system, now the basis of all modern computer programming.

JOHANN WOLFGANG VON GOETHE (1749-1832)
Romanticist, poet, playwright, philosopher, scientist.

The towering figure in German literature, his book *The Sorrows of Young Werther* was a seminal inspiration for the Romantic movement. His epic *Faust* inspired such artists as Mozart, Liszt, Beethoven, and Mahler. Nonfiction writing heavily influenced Hegel, Nietzsche, Jung, Darwin, and others.

KARL MARX (1818-1883)
Economist, philosopher, socialist, revolutionary.

In collaboration with Friedrich Engels, built on Hegel's dialectic framework (in which opposing forces clash to form a new paradigm) to advocate the working-class overthrow of capitalist governments and establishment of a classless society, where all people share ownership of property.

FRIEDRICH NIETZSCHE (1844-1900)
Philosopher, philologist, ethicist.

Believed Christianity promoted a "slave morality" in which meekness, submission, and piety are valued. The "death of God" meant it was impossible to know objective, divine truth; against this backdrop of relativism the solitary, exceptional *übermensch* (overman) creates his own inner, superior morality.

ALBERT EINSTEIN (1879-1955)
Nobel Prize–winning theoretical physicist, philosopher, peace activist.

Upended Newton's law of gravity with general & special theories of relativity. Argued that the speed of light remains constant, but space and time aren't absolute; gravity is an expression of how four-dimensional space-time curves around large masses—a simple notion that underpins modern astrophysics & the Big Bang Theory.

THIS GROUP OF GERMANS challenged many of Western Civilization's fundamental life assumptions. Luther questioned man's relationship to God, and Kepler repositioned man's place in the cosmos. Marx raised our collective class consciousness, and Nietzsche attacked organized religion for glorifying weakness. Einstein? Challenged the very building blocks of reality. These rogue philosophers changed our understanding of space, time, and reality. Naming a cookie after one of them is the least we could do.

LITTLE-KNOWN FACT	CONTROVERSY METER (0 TO 5)	QUINTESSENTIAL QUOTE
Met his wife, Katharina von Bora, while abetting her escape from a Cistercian convent; smuggled her out in a wagon filled with herring barrels.	**5** Excommunicated by Pope Leo X and declared heretic/outlaw by Holy Roman Emperor Charles V in 1521; ordained as a monk in 1507, but married in 1525; late in life spouted virulent, violent anti-Semitic views.	"I am more afraid of my own heart than of the pope and all his cardinals. I have within me the great pope, Self."
His novel, *Somnium*, describes a man's voyage to the moon. Displays an uncanny understanding of space travel.	**1** The Catholic Church opposed heliocentrism, but Kepler, a Protestant, avoided the scrutiny that caused his contemporary, Galileo, to be tried for heresy.	"Truth is the daughter of time, and I have no shame in being her midwife."
In 1891, had a butter cookie named in his honor that's still a hot seller today. ▶	**2** Dogged by (still unresolved) controversy over whether he plagiarized calculus theory after seeing Isaac Newton's unpublished writings.	"Even in the games of children there are things to interest the greatest mathematician."
His poem *Der Zauberlehrling* was adapted for "The Sorcerer's Apprentice" in the 1940 animated Disney film *Fantasia*.	**3** Favored a highly sexualized writing style at a time of repressive social mores; some of his poems were suppressed from publication in his lifetime. Werther, one of his first works, was criticized as glorifying suicide.	"Every author in some way portrays himself in his works, even if it be against his will."
Marx, who hailed from Trier, was pictured on Germany's 100 Deutschmark bill from 1964 until 1990.	**3** Died in poverty & obscurity. Political & revolutionary views co-opted unsuccessfully by totalitarians (Lenin, Stalin, Mao). His musings on the failures of capitalism still a rallying cry for pure socialist movements.	"The history of all hitherto existing society is the history of class struggles."
Some historians now believe the sickly Nietzsche went insane not from syphilis, but from a vascular disease.	**4** Intellectual combativeness alienated contemporaries, including Richard Wagner. In life, Nietzsche despised nationalism and anti-Semitism; posthumous reputation suffered when Hitler corrupted the *übermensch* into a Nazi eugenic ideal.	"In individuals, insanity is rare; but in groups, parties, nations and epochs, it is the rule."
In 1952, Einstein was offered the presidency of Israel. He declined, saying, "I lack both the natural aptitude and the experience to deal properly with people."	**2** Fled Nazi Germany in 1933; convinced U.S. to begin developing atomic bomb during World War II; later regretted his role in rise of nuclear technology, becoming a pacifist & fierce civil rights advocate.	"Reality is merely an illusion, albeit a very persistent one."

Hamburg

The metropolis on the Elbe River is Germany's second-
biggest city (pop. 1.8 million), a federal state in its own right, and, despite
being 80km (50 miles) inland, one of Europe's top three ports (up there with
Rotterdam and Antwerp). Crisscrossed by numerous waterways, it has more
canals than Venice and more bridges than Amsterdam. Hamburg was founded
in 825 and grew to be an important member of the medieval Hanseatic League
trade federation. Today, it enjoys the proud title *Freie und Hansestadt Hamburg*
(Free and Hanseatic City of Hamburg)—the *HH* on the city's auto license plates
stands for *Hansestadt Hamburg*. This is a serious world city, with much to take
in and do, even aside from its visitor highlights. You'll want to have 2 days for
Hamburg, and it won't seem like enough.

> *Touring Hamburg's harbor by boat is a great introduction to this important port city.*

START **Hamburg Hauptbahnhof (main train
station)** is the focal point for trains, metro
rail lines (*U-Bahn* and *S-Bahn*), buses, and
taxis. The Museum of Art and Applied Art is
just south of the station on Steintorplatz.

❶ ★ **Museum für Kunst und Gewerbe.** Where
to begin in the Museum of Art and Applied
Art? You could easily believe that most of the

museum's 700,000-object collection, covering 2,000 years of world art and culture, is
out on display, though fortunately that's not
so. Avoid a too-rich experience by focusing
on German medieval religious and classically
influenced sculpture, then move on to Jugendstil (Art Nouveau) design. ◷ 2 hr. Steintorplatz
1. ☎ 040/428-134-2732. www.mkg-hamburg.de

Admission 8€ adults, free for kids 17 and under, 13€ families. Tues and Fri–Sun 11am–6pm, Wed–Thurs 11am–9pm. *U-* or *S-Bahn:* Hauptbahnhof.

❷ ★★★ **Hamburger Kunsthalle.** North Germany's premier art gallery consists of three separate buildings. There's no shortage of paintings by European artists, from Old Masters down to the 20th century. Naturally, works by Rembrandt, Manet, Munch, and others are worth seeking out, but if time is short you might want to focus on German artists. Look for Meister Bertram's *Grabow Altarpiece* (1379) from Hamburg's Petrikirche (❼), depicting 24 biblical scenes. Caspar David Friedrich is represented by spooky Romantic works like *Wanderer Above the Sea of Fog* (1818) and *The Sea of Ice* (1824). ☺ 3 hr.

Glockengiesserwall. ☎ 040/428-131-200. www.hamburger-kunsthalle.de. Admission 8.50€ adults, free for kids 17 and under, 14€ families. Tues–Wed and Fri–Sun 10am–6pm, Thurs 10am–9pm. *U-Bahn:* Hauptbahnhof Nord. *S-Bahn:* Hauptbahnhof.

❸ kids ★★ **Aussenalster.** The outer, larger part of Alstersee (Alster Lake) covers 1.64 sq. km (⅔ sq. mile), stretching north through some of the city's leafiest and toniest residential districts. In good weather, the lake's surface is sure to be studded with sailboats and racing shells. You can stroll or jog around the shore on a waterside path—a round-trip of 7.4km (4½ miles)—and disembark from tour boats at a half dozen jetties. Take the boat (or go by land) to ★ **Alstervorland,** a park on the

Hamburg Side Trips

Between sunrise and sunset, every ship that passes the ★ **Schiffsbegrüssungsanlage Willkomm-Höft** (Welcome Point Ship-Greeting Installation in **Schulauer-Fährhaus** (Schulau Ferry House), Parnasstrasse 29 (☎ 0413/92000; www.schulauer-faehrhaus.de; *S-Bahn:* Wedel), is welcomed or bid farewell in its own language, and Hamburg's flag is dipped in salute. In the case of departing ships of at least 500 gross register tons, their countries' national anthems are played. Schulauer Fährhaus also houses a restaurant, where you can have breakfast, lunch, afternoon tea, or dinner while watching ships glide past on the Elbe. The restaurant has large enclosed and open verandas and a spacious tea garden. In the building's cellar, visit the **Buddelschiff-Museum** (Ship-in-a-Bottle Museum; ☎ 04103/920-0016), where you get to view more than 200 little ships enclosed in bottles. Schulauer-Fährhaus is on the lower Elbe, 22km (14 miles) west of central Hamburg.

A popular day trip destination from Hamburg, handsome ★ **Glückstadt** (pop. 12,000) was founded by the Danes in 1617 as a trading town on the Elbe River's north bank and provides considerable evidence that, even in those days, Danish design sense was to be admired. You can get there on a fast route from Hamburg, northwest on

A23, then west on L112 and L119 (62km/38 miles), or on a slower, scenic route, sticking close to the river, through Blankenese (a centuries-old fishing village that's now a spiffy Hamburg suburb), Rissen, Wedel, and then north on B431, through Elmshorn, to Glückstadt (64km/40 miles). Or go by train to Glückstadt station. If you have time, continue on to **Brunsbüttel,** 34km (21 miles) northwest along the Elbe via B451 and B5. This resort town (pop. 14,000) stands at the mouth of the Elbe and at the southern end of the Nord-Ostsee-Kanal (known as the Kiel Canal in English; see "Kiel Canal," p. 574), connecting the North Sea and the Baltic Sea. The town's position affords you grand views of ships both large and small coming and going on the two waterways.

The small fishing town of ★ **Büsum** (pop. 5,000) is the nearest decent-size seacoast—as opposed to riverside—resort to Hamburg, so come summer it experiences a big tourist influx. In the fishing harbor, the **Museum am Meer** (Museum by the Sea; ☎ 04834/6734; www.museum-am-meer.de) tells of the local relationship to the sea. The ferry (no cars) from Büsum to Helgoland (see "High Seas Helgoland," p. 565) departs from a neighboring quay. From Hamburg, take A23 northwest then B203 west to the coast, a total of 121km (75 miles).

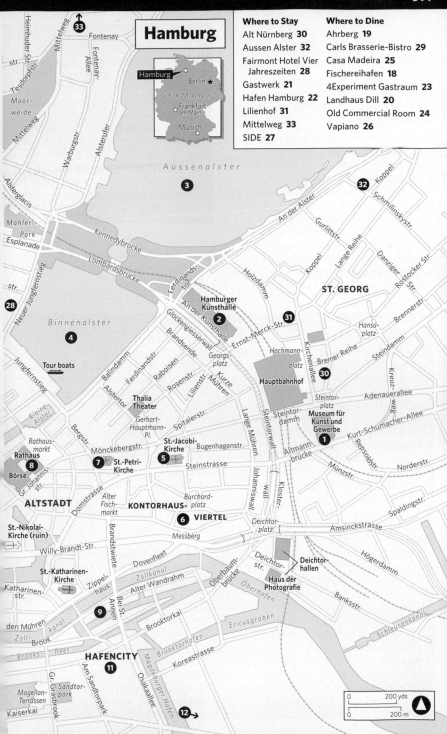

Hamburg

GERMANY

Hamburg

Berlin ★

Frankfurt am Main

Munich

Where to Stay

Alt Nürnberg **30**

Aussen Alster **32**

Fairmont Hotel Vier Jahreszeiten **28**

Gastwerk **21**

Hafen Hamburg **22**

Lilienhof **31**

Mittelweg **33**

SIDE **27**

Where to Dine

Ahrberg **19**

Carls Brasserie-Bistro **29**

Casa Madeira **25**

Fischereihafen **18**

4Experiment Gastraum **23**

Landhaus Dill **20**

Old Commercial Room **24**

Vapiano **26**

northwest shore with manicured lawns, shade trees, cultivated gardens, and cafe-restaurant ★ **Alster-Cliff** (☎ 040/442-719; www.alster-cliff.de) next to the dock. ⏱ 2 hr. Bus: 6 (from Hamburg Hauptbahnhof/main train station) covers most of Aussenalster's eastern shore; 109 from Dammtor *S-Bahn* Station covers most of the western shore.

④ ★ Binnenalster. Far smaller than its neighbor to the north, at just 0.18 sq. km (1/10 sq. mile), inner Alstersee (Alster Lake) is lined on three sides—along Neuer Jungfernstieg, Jungfernstieg, and Ballindamm—by some of Hamburg's most valuable real estate. Standouts among the opulent commercial buildings here are Hotel Vier Jahreszeiten (p. 604), cafe-restaurant Alsterpavillon, and Europa Passage mall. Boat tours on the lake depart from a dock along Jungfernstieg (see "Hamburg by Boat"). On the

Getting Around Hamburg

Don't drive in busy Hamburg. Use its excellent integrated public transportation instead. This consists of *U-Bahn* (subway), *S-Bahn* (city rail), *A-Bahn* (commuter rail), and *R-Bahn* (regional rail) services, along with buses and harbor ferries. Virtually all services in and around Hamburg are run by **HVV** (☎ 040/19449; www.hvv.de); the main exception is the *R-Bahn*, which is run by **Deutsche Bahn** (German Railways; ☎ 11861; www.bahn.de). Consider going by bus—or even by taxi if cost is not an issue—to see as much of the city as possible.

fourth side, the Lombardsbrücke and Kennedybrücke road and rail bridges separate Binnenalster from Aussenalster. ⏱ 30 min. *U-* or *S-Bahn:* Jungfernstieg.

Hamburg by Boat

Since 1189, Hamburg Harbor has been one of the biggest centers for trade on the Continent, making this one of Germany's wealthiest cities. The number of cargo ships sailing into the port rises and falls with the tides of world trade. In recent years, the average has been around 12,000 vessels a year docking at the city's 50km (31 miles) of wharves. An increasing number are container ships rather than bulk dry and liquid carriers. It's not all raw materials and chemicals. Hamburg's warehouses bulge with Oriental carpets, tea, coffee, and spices.

Several tour-boat lines run cruises along the Elbe River and through the harbor from the St. Pauli Landungsbrücken dock. The oldest and most character-rich boats (and skippers) are those of **Glitscher** (☎ 040/737-4343; www.glitscher-hamburg.de), which has 1-hour tours costing 9€ for adults and 5€ for kids 4–16. If you'll need a bigger boat, **HADAG Fährdienst** (☎ 040/311-7070; www.hadag.de) has modern boats that serve snacks and drinks; some even have restaurants. Tours are 11€ for adults, 5.50€ for kids 4–16, 20€–23€ for families, and 12€–16€ for one-parent families. Both lines have a variety of longer tours available.

An alternative to a harbor tour is a boat tour on the Binnenalster and Aussenalster lakes (**③** and **④**). These tours are operated by **ATG Alster-Touristik** (☎ 040/357-4240; www.alstertouristik.de), and depart from a dock on Jungfernstieg (*U-Bahn:* Jungfernstieg), on Binnenalster's south bank. Tours last just under 2 hours and cost 10.50€ for adults and 5.50€ for kids 4–16. A range of different ticket prices allows you to get off the boat and on again at several docks around the lakes, and longer cruises are available.

Getting to Jungfernstieg has the advantage of putting you in central Hamburg, the city's bustling commercial and shopping district and the location of many of its best hotels and restaurants. Many historic buildings that survived World War II are here, among them the **St.-Petri-Kirche** (**⑦**), Hamburg's oldest church, dedicated to St. Peter and founded around 1000. West of the city center, a big attraction is the St. Pauli district, Hamburg's main nightlife area, famed for its neon-lit **Reeperbahn** red-light zone (p. 560, **①**), offering all kinds of nighttime distractions—cafes, bars, dance clubs, music halls, and sex clubs.

> *Hamburg's recently restored Rathaus has 647 rooms, some of which you can see on a guided tour.*

⑤ St.-Jacobi-Kirche (St. James's Church). In this 14th–15th-century Gothic church, a great baroque Arp Schnitger organ (1693) is something of a wonder. In among the Protestant church's ornamentation, look for the outstanding wood carvings on the Trinitätsaltar (Trinity Altar, 1518) in the main choir. ⏱ 30 min. Jakobikirchhof 22. ☎ 040/303-7370.

www.jacobus.de. Free admission. Mon–Sat 10am–5pm (services only on Sun). *U-Bahn:* Mönckebergstrasse.

⑥ ★ Kontorhäuser. These grand 20th-century office buildings around Burchardstrasse include the expressionist Chilehaus (1924), with its brick facade that soars like a ship's prow, and across the street, the Sprinkenhof

> *Miniatur Wunderland features the world's largest scale-model railway, with 830 trains.*

(1927–43). On nearby Deichtorstrasse, the Deichtorhallen (1914; ☎ 040/321-030; www.deichtorhallen.de) is a former indoor market now used for modern-art shows. ⊙ 30 min. *U-Bahn:* Messberg or Steinstrasse.

❼ St.-Petri-Kirche (St. Peter's Church). Hamburg's oldest church was founded around 1000 and has been rebuilt and extended often since then. The now-Protestant church is mostly Gothic, on a Romanesque foundation. It houses works of religious art dating from the Middle Ages up to modern times. In streets around the church, remains of buildings from 9th-century Hammaburg (today's Hamburg) have been excavated. ⊙ 30 min. Speersort. ☎ 040/325-7400. www.sankt-petri.de. Free admission. Mon–Tues and Thurs–Fri 10am–6:30pm, Wed 10am–7pm, Sat 10am–5pm, Sun 9am–9pm. *U-Bahn:* Rathaus.

❽ ★ Hamburger Rathaus (Town Hall). The name may not sound appetizing in English, but Hamburg's recently spruced up Town Hall (1897) is an astonishing confection that back then was intended to showcase the city's wealth and a rising Germany's power. There are 647 rooms—a few too many to take in on the guided tour, though you do get to visit the opulent Kaisersaal (Emperor's Chamber),

Turmsaal (Tower Chamber), and Ratsstube (Senate Chamber), among others. ⊙ 45 min. Rathausmarkt 1. ☎ 040/428-312-064. Admission 3€ adults, 0.50€ kids 13 and under. Guided tours: hourly Mon–Thurs 10:15am–3:15pm, Fri 10:15am–1:15pm, Sat 10:15am–3:15pm, Sun 10:15am–4:15pm. *U-Bahn:* Rathaus.

❾ ★ Speicherstadt (Warehouse City). Canal-threaded Speicherstadt, along the Zollkanal in the old harbor, on and around Dehrwieder and St. Annenufer streets, is a large and surprisingly attractive array of multifloor red-brick warehouses dating from the 19th and early 20th centuries. Museums, attractions, offices, clubs, and restaurants are now housed in what is a protected cultural monument. Among the museums and attractions are kid-oriented **Miniatur Wunderland (❿)** and the district's own **Speicherstadtmuseum,** St. Annenufer 2 (☎ 040/321-191; www.speicherstadtmuseum.de; admission 3.50€ adults, 2€ kids 6–16; Apr–Oct Tues–Fri 10am–5pm, Sat–Sun 10am–6pm; Nov–Mar Tues–Sun 10am–5pm). ⊙ 2 hr. *U-Bahn:* Baumwall. Bus: 3, 4, or 6.

❿ ★★ kids Miniatur Wunderland. The world's largest scale-model railway is awesomely intricate, detailed, and BIG. With 830 trains, 11,000 cars, 200,000 individual figures,

300,000 lights—and counting—this is no Lilliputian attraction. The longest train is 14.5m (48 ft.) long. ⏲ 4 hr. Kehrwieder 2-4, Block D. ☎ 040/3005-1666. www.miniatur-wunderland. de. Admission 10€ adults, 5€ kids 15 and under, free for kids under 1m (3 ft. 4 in.) tall. Mon and Wed-Thurs 9:30am-6pm, Tues 9:30am-9pm, Fri 9:30am-7pm, Sat 8am-9pm, Sun 8:30am-8pm. Bus: 3, 4, or 6.

⑪ ★ **HafenCity.** Apartments, offices, and parks, as well as sports, dining, entertainment, and cultural facilities—like the giant Elbphilharmonie concert hall that's due to open in 2012—are under construction or in planning phases in the vast HarborCity (or City on the Water) redevelopment zone along the Elbe River, south of the city center (www.hafencity. com). The ★ **Internationales Maritimes Museum Hamburg,** Kaispeicher B, Koreastrasse 1 (☎ 040/3009-2300; www.internationales-maritimes-museum.de; admission 10€ adults, 7€ kids 6-18, 12€-22€ families; Apr-Oct Tues-Wed and Fri-Sun 10am-6pm, Thurs 10am-8pm), is a shipping and naval museum. Ocean cruise liners dock at the Hamburg Cruise Center on Chicagokai. Metro (U-Bahn) links are under construction, until they open in 2012 (if all goes well). ⏲ 2 hr. The core HafenCity zone is around Am Kaiserkai, San-Francisco-Strasse, and Uberseeallee. Bus: 3, 4, or 6.

⑫ ★★★ kids **BallinStadt—Das Auswanderermuseum Hamburg.** The stunning Emigrants Museum in "Ballin City," in the Veddel district across the Elbe from downtown Hamburg, is named after Jewish-German shipping magnate Albert Ballin (1857-1918). Ballin built up the Hamburg America Line by transporting European emigrants to America and by creating the concept of specialized cruise liners. Subtitled the "Port of Dreams," the museum is based in three re-creations of the barracks in which emigrants awaited their passage to the New World. It's a hands-on place, re-creating as closely as possible the spirit of the turn of the 20th century and the experience the emigrants underwent. ⏲ At least 2 hr. Veddeler Bogen 2. ☎ 040/3197-9160. www.ballinstadt.de. Admission 12€ adults, 7€ kids 5-12, 25€ families. May-Oct 10am-5:30pm; Oct-Apr daily 10am-4:30pm. S-Bahn: Veddel (BallinStadt).

> St.-Michaelis-Kirche's soaring tower makes it a Hamburg landmark.

⑬ ★ **St.-Michaelis-Kirche (St. Michael's Church).** Dubbed Der Michel (The Michael), the recently refurbished Protestant church (1786), which replaced earlier churches on the same site, is dedicated to the Archangel Michael—a bronze statue above the main entrance depicts the archangel killing the devil. The church tower, 132m (433 ft.) high, has an observation deck at 82m (269 ft.) that affords spectacular views. Composer Carl Philipp Emanuel Bach (1714–88) is interred in the crypt, and there's an exhibit on the church's history. ⏲ 30 min. Englische Planke 1A. ☎ 040/376-780. www.st-michaelis.de. Admission: Church free; Tower 3€ adults, 2€ kids 5-12; Crypt and Exhibit 3€ adults, 2€ kids 5-12; Tower, Crypt, and Exhibit 5€ adults, 3€ kids 5-12. Daily 10am-5:30pm. U-Bahn: St. Pauli.

⑭ ★★ kids **Hamburgmuseum.** Set in a park that occupies open space left behind when the city's fortifications were dismantled in the 19th century, Hamburg's historical and cultural museum has models of the city and depictions of scenes from various periods. These include a model of the Hanseatic-era port in 1497 and recreations of historical rooms and shops. Kids who don't make it to Miniatur Wunderland (⑩) can have fun here with a large model railway. A separate department covers Jewish life in Hamburg, from the first arrivals during the Middle Ages down to the Holocaust. ⊙ 2 hr. Holstenwall 24. ☎ 040/428-132-2380. www.hamburgmuseum.de. Admission 7.50€ (Fri 4€) adults, free for kids 17 and under, 12€ (Fri 6€) families. Tues–Sat 10am–5pm, Sun 10am–6pm. U-Bahn: St. Pauli.

⑮ kids **St. Pauli Landungsbrücken.** Even if you're not interested in doing a boat tour around the harbor (see "Hamburg by Boat," p. 598), this large dock is a great place from which to watch ships and other river traffic on the Elbe, and to kick back at a waterfront cafe. ⊙ 30 min. (longer if you take a boat tour). St. Pauli Hafenstrasse. U- or S-Bahn: Landungsbrücken.

⑯ ★ kids **Planten un Blomen.** The park's name is in Plattdeutsch (Low German), rather than the "Pflanzen und Blumen" it would be if it were in Hochdeutsch (High German). Either way, it means Plants and Flowers—a good description for a park, founded in 1821, that has plenty of both on its 47 hectares (116 acres), along with a botanical garden, a Japanese garden and tea house, and play areas for kids. ⊙ 1 hr. Am Dammtor. ☎ 040/428-232-125. www.plantenunblomen.hamburg.de. Free admission. Apr daily 7am–10pm; May–Sept daily 7am–11pm; Oct–Mar daily 7am–8pm. U-Bahn: Stephansplatz (Oper/CCH). S-Bahn: Dammtor (Messe/CCH).

⑰ ★★ kids **Tierpark Hagenbeck & Tropen-Aquarium.** Hamburg's Hagenbeck Zoo is a superior example of the species. In its landscaped park, unfenced paddocks and moats separate some of its 2,500 animals from visitors. The aquarium puts on dolphin and sealion shows. ⊙ 4 hr. Lokstedter Grenzstrasse. ☎ 040/530-0330. www.hagenbeck-tierpark.de. Admission: Zoo 16€ adults, 11€ kids 4–16, 49€–56€ families; Aquarium 13€ adults, 9€ kids 4–16, 39€–44€ families; combined Zoo and Aquarium 25€ adults, 16€ kids 4–16, 69€–75€ families. U-Bahn: Hagenbecks Tierpark.

Hamburg Nightlife

Hamburg has no shortage of nightlife, and as a big international port city with a long tradition of hosting "entertainment"-starved sailors, it's no surprise that some of it is not entirely wholesome. Still, before you hit the **Reeperbahn's** red-light haunts (p. 560, ①), be advised that you can take in opera and dance at the **Hamburgische Staatsoper** (Hamburg State Opera), Grosse Theaterstrasse 25 (☎ 040/356-868; www.hamburgische-staatsoper.de), and classical-music concerts at the **Laeiszhalle,** Johannes-Brahms-Platz (☎ 040/346-920; www.elbphilharmonie.de/laeiszhalle.en). In 2012, these high-culture institutions are due to be joined by the **Elbphilharmonie,** a stunning waterfront concert hall in HafenCity (p. 601, ⑪). Jazz is served up in copious amounts at the legendary **Cotton Club,** Alter Steinweg 10 (☎ 040/343-878; www.cotton-club.de).

Both high and altitudinally challenged rollers test their luck against the odds at four **Spielbank Hamburg** casinos (www.spielbank-hamburg.de) speckled around town. A cocktail bar, in which you can score a different kind of high, is **20up,** on (what else?) the 20th floor at the trendy **Empire Riverside Hotel,** Bernhard-Nocht-Strasse 97 (☎ 040/311-197-0470; www.empire-riverside.de); ecstatic views are guaranteed. More great cocktails are shaken and stirred at intimate little **Le Lion-Bar de Paris,** Rathausstrasse 3 (☎ 040/334-753-780; www.lelion.net).

Hamburg Shopping

The old Hanseatic League trading town is not often thought of as one of Europe's shopping meccas. Yet the hometown of fashion designers Karl Lagerfeld and Jil Sander has much going for it. Lagerfeld creations are available from (among other places) Alsterhaus (pictured, see below for information) and **Flebbe,** Eppendorfer Baum 7 (☎ 040/476-679); **Jil Sander** is at Neuer Wall 43 (☎ 040/374-1290; www.jilsander.com). A good multilabel fashion store, **Anita Hass,** is at Eppendorfer Landstrasse 60 (☎ 040/4685-6195; www.anitahass.de).

Hamburg's top department store is **Alsterhaus,** Jungfernstieg 16–20 (☎ 040/359-010; www.alsterhaus.de; pictured).

More mainstream shopping in the city center is concentrated around Mönckebergstrasse—dubbed *Die Mö.*

Altona's famously raucous street market, the **Fischmarkt** (Fish Market; www.hamburger-fischmarkt.de; May–Oct Sun 5am–9:30am; Nov–Apr Sun 7am–9:30am), on the waterfront Grosse Elbstrasse, sells far more kinds of food than fish—and far more than food—and is worth getting up early for. Another offbeat option is to be found in the **Krameramtsstuben,** a cluster of cute 17th-century houses around Krayenkamp, in the shadow of St.-Michaelis-Kirche (**13**); many of the houses are now occupied by boutiques, galleries, and craft stores.

Where to Stay

> Despite its large size, baronial Fairmont Hotel Vier Jahreszeiten prides itself on personalized service.

★ Alt Nürnberg ST. GEORG
Housed in a 1930s-vintage building in the heart of town, this hotel brings a taste of modest southern German charm to this northern city—literally so, in its restaurant. Steintorweg 15. ☎ 040/246-023. www.hotelaltnuernberg.de. 12 units. Doubles 95€–125€ w/breakfast. AE, MC, V. *U-* or *S-Bahn:* Hauptbahnhof.

★★ Aussen Alster ST. GEORG
White decor and cool design permeate this exclusive residence on a quiet street close to the Aussenalster lakefront. Schmilinskystrasse 11–15. ☎ 040/241-557. www.aussenalster.eu. 27 units. Doubles 130€–165€ w/breakfast. AE, DC, MC, V. *U-* or *S-Bahn:* Hauptbahnhof.

★★★ Fairmont Hotel Vier Jahreszeiten NEUSTADT
Founded in 1897, the baronial "Four Seasons," along the Binnenalster lakefront, has been a setting for numerous films. Neuer Jungfernstieg 9–14. ☎ 800/257-7544 in North America, or 040/34943151. www.hvj.de. 156 units. Doubles 300€–385€. AE, DC, MC, V. *U-Bahn:* Gänsemarkt.

★★ Gastwerk BAHRENFELD
A "repurposed" gasworks in west Hamburg is the unlikely setting for an ultra-chic designer hotel and its sophisticated fusion restaurant, Mangold. Daimlerstrasse 67. ☎ 040/890-620. www.gastwerk.com. 141 units. Doubles 136€–181€. AE, DC, MC, V. *S-Bahn:* Bahrenfeld.

★★ Hafen Hamburg ST. PAULI
The retired seadogs who lodged here in the 19th century likely wouldn't recognize the old place, updated now to a shipshape contemporary style. Seewartenstrasse 9. ☎ 040/311-130. www.hotel-hamburg.de. 353 units. Doubles 100€–120€. AE, DC, MC, V. *U-* or *S-Bahn:* Landungsbrücken.

Lilienhof ST. GEORG
Close to the city's main train station, this trim little hotel has small rooms that, while not fancy, are at least cozily furnished, bright, and clean. Ernst-Merck-Strasse 4. ☎ 040/241-087. www.hotel-lilienhof.de. 21 units. Doubles 65€–85€. MC, V. *U-* or *S-Bahn:* Hauptbahnhof.

★ Mittelweg HARVESTEHUDE
In the leafy, restaurant-rich Pöseldorf quarter, just west of the Aussenalster lake, this family-owned hotel occupies a 19th-century merchant's villa. Mittelweg 59. ☎ 040/414-1010. www.hotel-mittelweg.de. 39 units. Doubles 125€–168€. AE, MC, V. *U-Bahn:* Klosterstern.

★★ SIDE NEUSTADT
If "cozy" and "comfy" are not critical requirements for you, check out this colorful piece of Milanese modern design, and the panoramic views from its eighth-floor terrace. Drehbahn 49. ☎ 040/309-990. www.side-hamburg.de. 178 units. Doubles 205€–330€. AE, DC, MC, V. *U-Bahn:* Gänsemarkt.

Where to Dine

★★ Ahrberg BLANKENESE *SEAFOOD*
Set among the villas and steep, pedestrians-only streets of a gentrified old fishing village, century-old Ahrberg hauls in fish fanciers from near and far. Strandweg 33. ☎ 040/860-438. www.restaurant-ahrberg.de. Entrees 12€–17€. AE, DC, MC, V. Breakfast, lunch & dinner daily. *U-Bahn:* Gänsemarkt.

★★ Carls Brasserie-Bistro HAFENCITY *CONTINENTAL* Just along the wharf, near the Elbphilharmonie, this chic French-style eatery serves stellar German dishes alongside a wider-ranging menu. Am Kaiserkai 69. ☎ 040/300-322-400. www.carls-brasserie.de. Entrees 13€–33€. AE, MC, V. Lunch & dinner daily. Bus: 3, 4, or 6.

★ Casa Madeira NEUSTADT *PORTUGUESE*
The best among an enclave of authentic Portuguese restaurants relies on native charm and down-home cooking, ahead of fancy decor and place settings. Ditmar-Koel-Strasse 14. ☎ 040/7404-1880. www.casamadeira.de. Entrees 12€–17€. MC, V. Lunch & dinner daily. *U- or S-Bahn:* Landungsbrücken.

★★★ Fischereihafen ALTONA-ALTSTADT *SEAFOOD* A Hamburg institution, this waterfront restaurant has been upholding traditional menus since 1981, to the delight of ordinary folks and VIPs alike. Grosse Elbstrasse 143. ☎ 040/381-816. www.fischereihafenrestaurant.de. Entrees 18€–29€. AE, DC, MC, V. Lunch & dinner daily. *S-Bahn:* Königstrasse.

★★★ 4Experiment Gastraum ST. PAULI *INTERNATIONAL* It's hard to pin down this fashionable eatery. Youthful chefs riff on fresh organic ingredients and rustle up their inspirations in an open kitchen. Karolinenstrasse 32. ☎ 040/4318-8432. www.4experiment.de. Entrees 18€–24€. No credit cards. Dinner Mon–Sat. *U-Bahn:* Messehallen.

★★ Landhaus Dill OTTENSEN *CONTINENTAL*
A few blocks from the Elbe (but with no river views), this handsome restaurant has something of a country villa feel about it, and a garden terrace for summer. Elbchaussee 94.

> *The delicious seafood offerings of Fischereihafen have made it a city institution for nearly 2 decades.*

☎ 040/390-5077. www.landhausdill.com. Entrees 18€–29€. AE, DC, MC, V. Lunch & dinner Tues–Sun. *S-Bahn:* Altona.

★ Old Commercial Room NEUSTADT *NORTH GERMAN* As indelibly Hamburg as an Elbe riverboatman, this seaman's tavern founded in 1643 hits the spot with traditional seafarer meals like *Labskaus* (corned beef) hash. Englische Planke 10. ☎ 040/366-319. www.oldcommercialroom.de. Entrees 12€–32€. AE, DC, MC, V. Lunch & dinner daily. *U-Bahn:* St. Pauli.

★ 🄺🄸🄳🅂 Vapiano NEUSTADT *ITALIAN*
This chain restaurant in the center of town serves fast food with a sense of style. The pasta is freshly made, and the pizzas are a good value. Hohe Bleichen 10. ☎ 040/3501-9975. www.vapiano.com. Entrees 7€–15€. AE, MC, V. Breakfast, lunch & dinner daily. *U-Bahn:* Gänsemarkt.

Lübeck

Lübeck is one of Germany's relatively unknown treasures. The port city (pop. 212,000) was a medieval success story, and from the 13th century on Lübeck was the capital of the Hanseatic League (see the box on p. 578). To recall those glory days, *Hansestadt Lübeck*, as the city proudly names itself, has gabled houses, massive gates, and gilded spires—the "Seven Towers" of its great Gothic churches—and a Burgundian lifestyle reminiscent of the Low Countries' ambience. The Altstadt (Old Town), broadly defined by a ring canal, is a UNESCO World Heritage site.

> *Lübeck's imposing city gate, the Holstentor, houses a museum that features displays of the city's history dating back to the year 800.*

START **Marking the Old Town's western boundary, the massive Holstentor city gate is unmissable. From Lübeck Hauptbahnhof (main train station), it's a walk of just .5km (⅓ mile) east on Konrad-Adenauer-Strasse. Virtually all city buses (nos. 1, 2, 5, 6, 7, 9, 10, 11, 16, 17, 19, 21, 30, 31, 34, and 40) stop at Holstentor.**

① ★★ kids **Museum Holstentor.** The Holstentor (1478) city gate's squat twin towers have become a Lübeck emblem. Note the additional ornamentation of terracotta friezes on the city side. Inside the tower, the city museum covers Lübeck's history, going back to its founding by the Slavs around 800. A fascinating model gives a bird's-eye view of how the city would have looked in the mid-1600s—in the real world, Allied bombs during World War II erased some of what the model depicts, but much has survived. ⏱ 1 hr. Holstentorplatz. ☎ 0451/122-4129. www.die-luebecker-museen. de. Admission 5€ adults, 2€ kids 6–18, 6€–9€ families. Jan–Mar Tues–Sun 11am–5pm; Apr–Dec daily 10am–6pm.

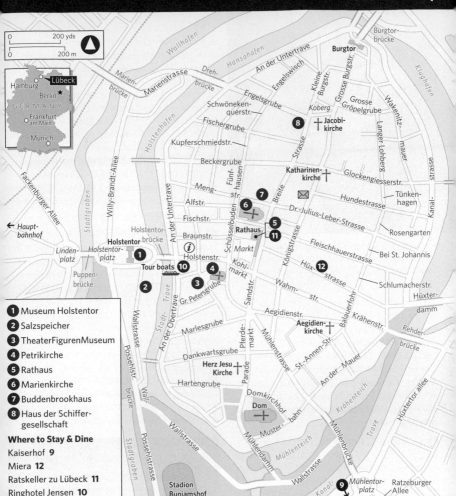

1 Museum Holstentor
2 Salzspeicher
3 TheaterFigurenMuseum
4 Petrikirche
5 Rathaus
6 Marienkirche
7 Buddenbrookhaus
8 Haus der Schiffer-
gesellschaft

Where to Stay & Dine
Kaiserhof **9**
Miera **12**
Ratskeller zu Lübeck **11**
Ringhotel Jensen **10**

2 Salzspeicher. Just behind the Holstentor, along the Trave River, is a group of six venerable warehouses (1579–1745) once used for storing salt from Lüneburg (p. 550). They are still used as warehouses, but now textiles are stored here. Boat tours on the river, with **Stüffh Lübecker Barkassenfahrt** (☎ 0451/707-8222; www.luebecker-barkassenfahrt.de), depart from a dock on the other side of the Trave.

3 ★ kids TheaterFigurenMuseum. Nicely complementing the marvelous Figurentheater-Lübeck (Lübeck Puppet Theater; ☎ 0451/70060; www.figurentheater-luebeck.de) next door, the TheaterFigurenMuseum (Puppet

Theater Museum) claims to own the world's largest collection of marionettes. They come in all styles, shapes, sizes, and colors—very young kids might easily be frightened by some of them. ⏱ 1 hr. Kolk 14. ☎ 0451/78626. www. die-luebecker-museen.de. Admission 4€ adults, 3€ teens 13–18, 2€ kids 4–12, 6€–9€ families. Apr–Oct daily 11am–6pm; Nov–Mar Tues–Sun 11am–5pm.

4 Petrikirche (St. Peter's Church). The cobblestoned alleyways, like Grosse Petersgrube and Kleine Petersgrube, around this 15th-century church are some of the finest restored streets in Lübeck, lined with gabled brick buildings. The red-brick Gothic church is now

> *Lübeck's kid-friendly TheaterFigurenMuseum offers what it claims is the world's largest marionette collection, along with entertaining performances.*

used for occasional exhibits. Its tower is 108m (354 ft.) high, and you can ride an elevator to a viewing platform at 50m (164 ft.) for grand views over Lübeck. ⏱ 45 min. Am Petrikirchhof 1. ☎ 0451/397-7320. www.st-petri-luebeck.de. Church: free admission; Exhibits: admission varies; Mar–Dec Tues–Sun 11am–4pm (and special exhibit times). Tower: 3€ adults, 2€ kids 6–16, 6€ families; Apr–Sept daily 9am–9pm; Oct–Mar daily 10am–7pm.

⑤ ★★ Rathaus (Town Hall). Lübeck's pride and joy got started back in 1230 and is Germany's oldest functioning town hall. If you take the time to peruse its long facade on Markt square and along Breite Strasse, you will see it comprises several different architectural styles, reflecting construction over a 340-year period until completion (and even then some bits weren't finally done until the 1950s). A notable asset here is the Ratskeller (p. 609), a wonderfully atmospheric traditional restaurant in the cellar. ⏱ 1 hr. Breite Strasse (at Markt). ☎ 0451/122-1005. Tours 4€ adults, 2€ kids 6–18. Guided tours (in German) Mon–Fri 11am, noon, and 3pm, Sat–Sun 1:30pm.

⑥ ★ Marienkirche (Church of St. Mary). Just as Lübeck's Hanseatic merchants decorated their homes and civic buildings to show off their wealth, so they supported grand churches—perhaps as a kind of futures contract with the hereafter. The Marienkirche

(1200–1350), adjacent to the Rathaus, is an outstanding example of the North German architectural style known as *Backsteingotik* (brick Gothic). Its two towers soar 125m (410 ft.) above the streets and are visible from a long way off. Look out for a moving World War II memorial—two great bells that smashed to the ground from the south tower as a consequence of Allied bombing. A church tradition of organ recitals that began with composer/organist Dietrich Buxtehude in the 17th century continues to this day. ⏱ 45 min. Marienkirchhof (at Breite Strasse). ☎ 0451/77391. Free admission. Apr–Sept daily 10am–6pm; Oct daily 10am–5pm; Nov–Mar daily 10am–4pm.

⑦ Buddenbrookhaus. Thomas Mann's epic family-saga novel *Buddenbrooks* (1901), set in Mann's hometown, traces the decline and fall of a Lübeck merchant family. This baroque mansion (1758) belonging to Mann's grandparents was the home where Thomas—winner of the 1929 Nobel Prize for Literature—and his elder brother Heinrich, also a successful author, grew up. It now houses the Heinrich-und-Thomas-Mann-Zentrum, a museum dedicated to their lives and work. ⏱ 45 min. Mengstrasse 4. ☎ 0451/122-4129. www.buddenbrookhaus.de. Admission 5€ adults, 2.50€ kids 6–18, 6€–9€ families. Jan–Mar daily 11am–5pm; Apr–Dec daily 10am–6pm.

Marzipan Town

Lübeck is famous for its marzipan, which it has produced, consumed, and exported since the 16th century. Several theories have been advanced to explain how this began. One holds that marzipan was a cheap substitute for bread during a siege; another that it was imported by Lübeck merchants from Persia and the populace developed a taste for it. Whatever the truth, the fact remains that when it comes to marzipan, Lübeck is a byword for quality. The best place to buy marzipan in town is undoubtedly ★ **Niederegger,** Breite Strasse 89 (☎ 0451/530-1126; www.niederegger.de), across the street from the Rathaus (⑤) and in business since 1806. In addition to beautiful marzipan displays and an elegant cafe, Niederegger has a small museum, the Marzipan-Salon (free admission).

8 ★ **Haus der Schiffergesellschaft (Seafarers' Guild House).** You seem to step back in time to Hanseatic Lübeck's heyday in this atmospheric, step-gabled old restaurant from 1535 that once housed a social and welfare society for seafarers. Ship models hang from the ceiling, carved coats of arms of Baltic merchants adorn high-backed wooden booths, and other nautical memorabilia abound. Unsurprisingly, this is one of the most atmospheric restaurants in town, its copious North German food served on scrubbed-oak plank tables. ⏱ 5 min. to look around; longer, of course, if you stay to dine. Breite Strasse 2. ☎ 0451/76776. www.schiffergesellschaft.com. Free admission. Daily 10am–1am.

Where to Stay & Dine

> *The clean, contemporary, and inviting Ringhotel Jensen.*

★★ **Kaiserhof** ST. JÜRGEN
Two former patrician town houses on a tree-lined boulevard have been remodeled into this graceful hotel with individually furnished rooms and a pool. Kronsforder Allee 11–13. ☎ 0451/703-301. www.kaiserhof-luebeck.de. 76 units (some in annexes). Doubles 100€–135€ w/breakfast. AE, DC, MC, V.

★★ **Miera** ALTSTADT *INTERNATIONAL*
The restaurant is part of a complex that includes a bistro, a wine bar, and a delicatessen. An artful fusion of flavors from here, there, and beyond graces your plate in the chic main dining room upstairs. Hüxstrasse 57. ☎ 0451/77212. www.miera-luebeck.de. Fixed-price menus 35€–75€. AE, MC, V. Lunch & dinner Mon–Sat.

★★ **Ratskeller zu Lübeck** ALTSTADT *NORTH GERMAN* Even if the food here was nothing to boast about, this cellar eatery would be worth visiting for its amazing Old Lübeck ambience alone—so it's doubly gratifying to relish the menu's good tastes. Markt 15. ☎ 0451/72044. www.ratskeller-zu-luebeck.de. Entrees 12€–17€. MC, V. Lunch & dinner daily.

★ **Ringhotel Jensen** ALTSTADT
The small- to medium-size rooms are furnished in a homey contemporary style. Breakfast is served in a delightful room with views of the Hanseatic architecture across the Trave River. An der Obertrave 4–5. ☎ 0451/702-490. www.ringhotel-jensen.de. 42 units. Doubles 98€–115€ w/breakfast. AE, DC, MC, V.

Schwerin

Mecklenburg-Vorpommern's state capital (pop. 96,000)

was for centuries the seat of the dukes of Mecklenburg and of Mecklenburg-Schwerin. What with all the various dukes, duchesses, and assorted other bluebloods who came and went in that time, the town is loaded with stately buildings and monuments. The East German Communists just weren't that into keeping up the old haunts of dispossessed aristocrats, but since reunification many have been buffed up, to the delight of Schwerin's many visitors.

> *Romantic Schweriner Schloss stands on its own island and can be reached by two bridges from the mainland.*

START **From Schwerin Hauptbahnhof (main train station), walk east to Alexandrinenstrasse, which runs south along Pfaffenteich, a large rectangular pond lined with elegant buildings. You can't miss the Dom's tall spire, just beyond the south shore.**

① ★ **Dom (Cathedral).** Most of Schwerin's *Backsteingotik* (brick Gothic) cathedral was a work-in-progress for more than 3 centuries, beginning in 1172; the tower, by contrast, was virtually flung up to its full height of 118m (387 ft.) in just 4 years (1889–93). ⏱ 30 min. Am Domhof. ☎ 0385/565-014. www.dom-schwerin. de. Free admission. May–Oct Mon–Sat 10am–5pm, Sun noon–5pm; Nov–Apr Mon–Sat 11am–4pm, Sun noon–4pm.

② **Markt.** Spend a few minutes here to view the English Tudor–style Rathaus (Town Hall).

③ ★★ **Staatliches Museum Schwerin.** The State Museum has a notable collection of paintings by 16th- and 17th-century Dutch, Flemish, and German Old Masters and by later artists. These include Lucas Cranach the Elder's *Portrait of a Young Man with a Beret* (1521), Frans Hals's *Boy Holding a Flute* (1628), and Max Liebermann's *The Granddaughter, Writing* (1923). In addition, there's medieval religious art, fine Dresden china, and much more. ⏱ 2 hr. Alter Garten 3. ☎ 0385/563-090. www.museum-schwerin.de. Admission 5€ adults, free for kids 17 and under, 9€ families. Mid-Apr to mid-Oct Tues–Sun 10am–6pm; mid-Oct to mid-Apr Tues–Sun 10am–5pm.

④ ★ kids **Schweriner See (Lake Schwerin).** Schweriner See is one of the largest of the Mecklenburg lakes, covering 62 sq. km (24 sq. miles). You're likely to be most aware of its waters at Schweriner Schloss (**⑤**) and along the nearby waterfront, yet the lake extends far beyond the town. You can cruise the lake aboard tour boats operated by **Weisse**

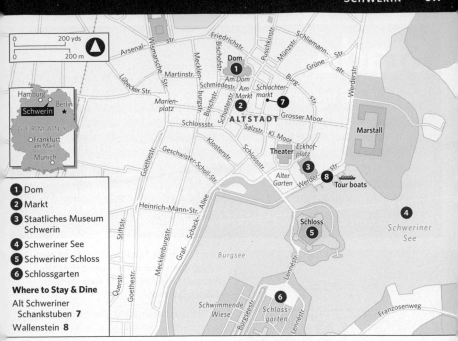

0 200 yds
0 200 m

1 Dom
2 Markt
3 Staatliches Museum Schwerin
4 Schweriner See
5 Schweriner Schloss
6 Schlossgarten

Where to Stay & Dine

Alt Schweriner Schankstuben **7**
Wallenstein **8**

Flotte Schwerin (☎ 0385/55570; www.weisseflotteschwerin.de). ⏱ At least 1 hr.

5 ★★★ **Schweriner Schloss.** Based on the design of a Loire Valley château, this romantic palace (1857) of the grand dukes of Mecklenburg-Schwerin is the jewel in Schwerin's crown and by any measure one of North Germany's most spectacular monuments. It stands on its own little island, reached by a pair of bridges from different points on the mainland. In addition to touring a seemingly endless array of opulent salons and chambers, you can visit the Schlosskirche (Palace Church), which dates from an earlier period (1560), and the English landscape–style Burggarten (Castle Garden). ⏱ 3 hr. Lennéstrasse 1. ☎ 0385/5252-2920. www.schloss-schwerin.de. Admission 6€ adults, free for kids 17 and under, 10€ families. Mid-Apr to mid-Oct daily 10am–6pm; mid-Oct to mid-Apr Tues–Sun 10am–5pm.

6 ★ **Schlossgarten.** The Palace Garden, across the south bridge from Schweriner Schloss, is a baroque garden (1848) in the formal French style, with a cruciform pond, a gallery of heroic sculptures, and trees, flowers, and plants. ⏱ 30 min. Free admission. Open 24/7.

Where to Stay & Dine

★ **Alt Schweriner Schankstuben** CENTRUM
This hotel has colorful guest rooms and Old German–style public areas. The restaurant's menu mirrors the "Meat Market" location. Am Schlachtermarkt 9–13. ☎ 0385/592-530. www.alt-schweriner-schankstuben.de. 16 units. Doubles 78€–94€ w/breakfast. AE, MC, V.

★ **Wallenstein** SCHWERINER SEE CONTINENTAL
A waterside terrace and picture windows looking out on Schweriner See and the Schloss are two draws of this restaurant, with a varied menu and a breezy style. Werderstrasse 140. ☎ 0385/557-7755. www.restaurantwallenstein.de. Entrees 9€–21€. MC, V. Lunch & dinner daily.

Boat Tours

Weisse Flotte Schwerin (☎ 0385/557-770; www.weisseflotteschwerin.de) operates tours of Muritzsee and Ziegelsee, departing from a dock on Werderstrasse.

Stade

One of those towns that can rightly be classified as a dazzling gem, yet possessing few if any outstanding monuments, Stade (pop. 46,000) stands just south of the Elbe between Hamburg and the river's mouth. You should view this picturesque museum-piece—which has maybe been too pristinely burnished—as an ensemble of 17th-century (and earlier) *Fachwerkhäuser* (timber-frame houses) and red-brick buildings, and as perhaps Germany's most perfect surviving example of a late Hanseatic-era town. Visit the "sights" as you go through the town, yet spend some time with your guidebook closed, making your own discoveries.

> Stade's beautiful, ornate Rathaus had its Hanseatic-era design restored after a 1659 fire.

START From the Stade station, cross over Burggraben (the old city moat) into the Altstadt (Old Town), and walk north on Bahnhofstrasse.

❶ **Rathaus (Town Hall).** The Rathaus is a baroque building from 1667, with an elaborate sculpted, arched gateway. An earlier version was lost in the great fire of 1659, which destroyed much of the old center of town and is the reason why not much survives of the original, 13th-century Hanseatic town.

❷ ★★ **Sts. Cosmae et Damiani.** Known locally as the "Cosmae," the Church of Saints Cosmas and Damian dates from the late 13th century, though most of what you see now is 17th-century baroque. The great organ (1675) is the fruit of a collaboration between master organ-builders Berendt Hus and his nephew Arp Schnitger. ⊙ 20 min. Cosmaekirchhof. ☎ 04141/2977. www.cosmae.de. Free admission. Daily, irregular hours.

❸ ★★ **Alter Hafen (Old Harbor).** In the Altstadt's northern reaches, around Fischmarkt and along the Hansehafen (Hanseatic Harbor), is the most photogenic part of town, and this area has inevitably taken on a touristic character. The many restored *Fachwerkhäuser* (timber-frame houses) along waterfront Wasser Ost and Wasser West now host restaurants, cafes, bars, boutiques, and art galleries. Look for the elegantly gabled Burgermeister-Hintze-Haus at Wasser West 23; it now houses Galerie Fündling, an art and antiques gallery. On the

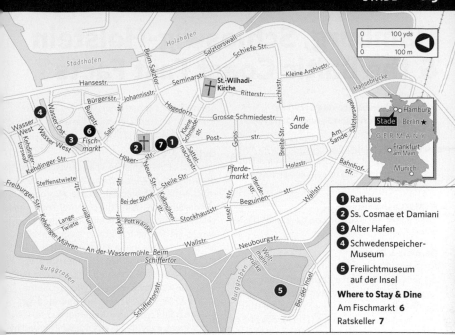

1 Rathaus
2 Ss. Cosmae et Damiani
3 Alter Hafen
4 Schwedenspeicher-Museum
5 Freilichtmuseum auf der Insel
Where to Stay & Dine
Am Fischmarkt 6
Ratskeller 7

dock is a fascinating replica of a centuries-old timber crane, the Holzretkran. ⏱ 1 hr.

4 ★ kids **Schwedenspeicher-Museum.** Housed in a 17th-century warehouse used by Stade's Swedish rulers, this rambling historical museum covers a lot of ground, going back to the earliest known settlers of this low-lying, riverine landscape, around 1000 B.C., before concentrating on the Hanseatic period and the Swedish occupation and then coming more or less up to date. There are hands-on exhibits for children. ⏱ 1 hr. Wasser West 39. ☎ 04141/3222. www.sonderausstellung-schwedenspeicher.de. Admission 3€ adults, 1.50€ kids 6–16, 6€ families. Tues–Fri 10am–5pm, Sat–Sun 10am–6pm.

5 kids **Freilichtmuseum auf der Insel.** An outwork of Stade's 17th-century Swedish fortifications, on an island in the moat, now holds the eminently peaceful Open-Air Museum. Old North German buildings, among them a timber windmill, have been reassembled here. ⏱ 1 hr. Bleicher Ravelin. ☎ 04141/951-821. Admission 1€ adults, free for kids 17 and under. May–Sept Tues–Fri 10am–1pm and 2–5pm, Sat–Sun 10am–1pm and 2–6pm.

Where to Stay & Dine

★ **Am Fischmarkt** ALTSTADT
Enter into the spirit of Hanseatic Stade at this old-fashioned family hotel along Hansehafen. Rooms are small and minimally outfitted but bright and clean, and there's a decent local restaurant. Fischmarkt 2. ☎ 04141/44962. www.hotelamfischmarkt.de. 16 units. Doubles 79€–99€ w/breakfast. MC, V.

★ **Ratskeller** ALTSTADT *NORTH GERMAN*
The restaurant in an arched brick cellar below the Town Hall is about as traditional, in the best sense, as you might expect to find in olde-worlde Stade. Try the Ratskeller's excellent own-brew Gertrude beer. Hökerstrasse 10. ☎ 04141/787-228. www.ratskeller-stade.de. Entrees 9€–16€. MC, V. Lunch & dinner daily.

Hamburg, Schleswig-Holstein & the Baltic Coast Fast Facts

Accommodations Booking Services
Call **Hotel Reservation Service** (☎ 0870/ 243-0003) from anywhere in Germany. Tourist info points at the major train stations and airports can assist with last-minute local hotel bookings. Tourist offices can also arrange accommodation.

ATMs/Cashpoints
The main towns in the region have multiple ATMs from a range of banks.

Dentists & Doctors
Most hotels will be able to refer you to a local doctor (Arzt) or dentist (Zahnarzt) who speaks English. You will be expected to provide proof of either permanent or travel insurance (an EHIC card in the case of most residents of Europe), or to pay for treatment. For a minor injury that requires speedy treatment, go to the Notaufnahme (emergency) department of the nearest Krankenhaus (hospital). For a serious injury, call the doctor/ambulance emergency number (see next item).

Emergencies
To call the police (Polizei), dial ☎ **110.** To report a fire or to summon an emergency doctor (Notarzt) or an ambulance (Krankenwagen), dial ☎ **112.**

Getting There
Hamburg-Fuhlsbüttel (HAM) is the main airport for this region. Berlin's airports, **Berlin-Tegel** (TXL) and **Berlin-Schönefeld** (SXF) are two other good options, in particular for accessing the eastern end of the Baltic and the Mecklenburg Lake District. To a lesser degree, **Hannover** (HAJ) affords access to the region's central belt. Plenty of international and national flights are available to all four airports. All cities and most towns are well served by train. International highways enter the region from Denmark to the north and Poland to the east, and important German highways enter through Hamburg and Berlin. **Eurolines** (www. eurolines.com) international buses stop at Flensburg, Hamburg, Kiel, and Lübeck. There are multiple international car-ferry services to the region from Denmark, Finland, Latvia, Norway, Poland, and Sweden.

Getting Around
In much of the region you can travel fast on the Autobahn (A) roads and Bundesstrasse (B) roads—many of which also have a European (F) designation. Using the comprehensive and efficient train network is undoubtedly the best way to get around by public transportation. Most rail service—and all InterCity trains, including the high-speed ICE (InterCity-Express) trains—are operated by Deutsche Bahn (German Railways; www.bahn.com). Some local and regional services are operated by private train companies. Regional bus service is not great, except in areas not well served by train—parts of Schleswig-Holstein, the Mecklenburg Lake District, and the Baltic islands, for instance. Ferries connect the mainland to the Nordfriesische Inseln (North Frisian Islands) and the Baltic islands of Rügen and Hiddensee. In addition to trains, metro trains (U-Bahn and S-Bahn) and buses, Hamburg has harbor ferries; these depart from the St. Pauli Landungsbrücken dock and connect points in the city center, on the south bank of the Elbe River, and downriver to Teufelsbrück.

Internet Access
Many hotels have one or more terminals for the use of their guests. Wi-Fi and/or broadband is often available, either free or for an hourly or daily charge. Most towns of any size are likely to have at least one Internet cafe.

Pharmacies
In German, a pharmacy is an Apotheke; most operate during normal shopping hours and post details of the nearest 24-hour pharmacy. For cosmetics or toiletries, go to a Drogerie.

Police
To report a lost or stolen article, such as a wallet or passport, visit the local police (Polizei) in your location. To call the police from anywhere in Germany, dial ☎ **110.**

Post Office

You'll recognize branches of **Deutsche Post** (☎ 01802/3333; www.deutschepost.de) by their yellow sign with a black horn. Some centrally located post offices in towns and cities are as follows: **Flensburg:** Schiffbrückstrasse 2 (Harbor); **Hamburg:** Glockengiesserwall 8-10 (Hauptbahnhof/main train station); **Kiel:** Falckstrasse 2 (Altstadt); **Lübeck**: Holstenstrasse 1-3 (Holstentor). Post offices are open Monday to Friday 8am–6pm, Saturday 8am–noon.

Safety

Hamburg, like all big cities—and especially big port cities—has its share of crime, but that's not to say that it is a dangerous city. The major crimes that tourists encounter are pickpocketing and purse- and camera-snatching. Most robberies occur in the big tourist areas, and in particular around the Reeperbahn red-light district and Hauptbahnhof (central station). Around the main train stations in the larger towns it can seem a bit creepy after dark.

Taxis

In Hamburg, call **Taxi Hamburg** (☎ 040/666-666); in Kiel, **Taxi-Kiel** (☎ 0431/680-101); in Lübeck, **Lübecker Funktaxen** (☎ 0451/81122); and in Rostock, **Hanse-Taxi Rostock** (☎ 0381/685-858).

Telephones

Call ☎ 11837 for information and ☎ 11834 for international information. Flensburg's area code is 0461; Hamburg's is 040; Kiel's is 0431; Lübeck's is 0451; and Rostock's is 0381. Dial the area code when calling a town number from outside the town; you don't need to dial it when calling a town number from inside the town. There are public phones in many places—some accept coins and some take phone cards, available at post offices and newsstands.

Toilets

In some places you will find clean public toilets, many of them automatic and wheelchair-accessible; you need a .50€ coin to unlock the door. More convenient and widespread are toilets in cafes, bars, restaurants, hotels, malls, and some stores, and at highway services and rest areas. It is customary to leave the attendant .50€.

Tours

A unique kind of tour is *Wattwandern* (mudflat hiking) at low tide on the floor of the Wattenmeer (Wadden Sea). On the North Sea coast, boat tours are available among the Wattenmeer's Nordfriesische Inseln (North Frisian Islands), as are day trips to Germany's sole "pelagic" island, Helgoland (p. 565). On the Baltic Sea, any number of boat-tour options are available from harbor towns, popular resorts, and the islands. On the Elbe River, many different boat tours are available from Hamburg. The Mecklenburg lakes are a veritable paradise for tour-boat lovers, in particular the larger lakes, such as Müritzsee and Schweriner See. On dry land, all kinds of tours are available in national parks and nature parks (see "Northern Germany's National Parks," p. 566), for instance bird-watching and seal-watching in the seashore national parks, and nature trails and mountain-biking in Müritz-Nationalpark.

Visitor Information

Tourist offices are ubiquitous. They range from multiple branches in Hamburg all the way down to tiny offices in some villages. In addition to those provided with the individual town listings, other key tourist offices are as follows: **HAMBURG** Hamburg has three tourist information offices: Hauptbahnhof (main train station; Kirchenallee; Mon–Sat 8am–9pm, Sun 10am–6pm); Am Hafen (harbor; St. Pauli Landungsbrücken; Apr–Oct daily 8am–6pm; Nov–Mar daily 10am–6pm); and CCH Konzertkasse (Dag-Hammarskjöld-Platz; Mon–Fri 8am–7:45pm, Sat 10am–4pm). The general website is www.hamburg-tourism.de; the tourist information line is ☎ 040/3005-1300. **STADE** Hansestrasse 16; ☎ 04141/409-170; www.stade-tourismus.de; Apr–Sept Mon–Fri 10am–6pm, Sat–Sun 10am–3pm; Oct–Mar Mon–Fri 10am–6pm, Sat 10am–3pm. **LÜBECK** Lübeck und Travemünde Marketing, Holstentorplatz 1 (Holstentor); ☎ 0451/889-9700; www.luebeck-tourismus.de; Jan–May & Oct–Nov Mon–Fri 9:30am–6pm, Sat 10am–3pm; June–Sept Mon–Fri 9:30am–7pm, Sat 10am–3pm, Sun 10am–2pm; Dec Mon–Fri 9:30am–6pm, Sat 10am–3pm, Sun 10am–2pm. **SCHWERIN** Am Markt 14; ☎ 0385/592-5212; www.schwerin.com; Mon–Fri 9am–6pm, Sat–Sun 10am–4pm.

BERLÍN 1990-2009

ASI BLANCH.CAT

13
Germany's History & Culture

Germany: A Brief Overview

> *PREVIOUS PAGE The colorful remains of a dark period—a section of the Berlin Wall near Ostbahnhof.*
> *THIS PAGE Survivors pay tribute to the dead at Buchenwald.*

Germany's long and tumultuous history remains clouded by the horrors of World War II and the Holocaust. How a civilized European nation slipped into the state of barbaric inhumanity that existed during the Nazi era is a question that continues to haunt survivors, occupy historians, and shadow the Germans themselves. Memorials to the victims of the Holocaust are scattered through Germany, perhaps most poignantly at the sites of the Dachau and Buchenwald concentration camps, and November 17 is set aside as a national Day of Prayer and Repentance.

As a result of that harrowing chapter in its modern history, which resulted in the devastation of its cities, the disarmament of its military machine, and the deaths of millions of people, Germany became a strongly pacifist country, and the use of military force in world conflicts always arouses controversy among its citizens.

The other big political issue that has affected Germany's contemporary consciousness is the separation of the country into two opposing regimes—capitalist West, Communist East—from 1961 to 1989. The fall of the Berlin Wall in November 1989 signaled an enormous shift in German life. Although most East Germans embraced the democratic changes that came with reunification, there were many who resented what they saw as a wholesale takeover of their country and who were suddenly exposed to the vagaries, uncertainties, and economic ruthlessness of a free-market economic system and lifestyle vastly different from their own. By the time the wall came down, East Germany was in many respects a broken country, a corrupt police-state with dwindling resources, decaying infrastructure, and a legacy of environmental pollution that will long remain a challenge to clean up. The cost of reunification was far higher than anyone predicted, and it took a toll on people's economic and emotional lives. Outdated, state-controlled industries that could not compete in a free-market economy were scrapped, jobs were lost, crime—most troublingly,

> *Berliners gather at the Berlin Wall shortly after its construction separated neighbors and families in 1961.*

neo-Nazi hate crimes—rose. Yet Germany moved forward, and by the time the celebrations commemorating the 20th anniversary of the fall of the Berlin Wall were held in November 2009, Germany was the most prosperous country in Europe.

Like every other country, Germany was hit by the global recession—but not quite as hard as its neighbors. A nation of savers, it never gave in to the easy-credit credo and had stronger regulations and more oversight in its banking industry than other nations. Germany is a country where labor unions remain strong despite attempts to whittle away at their power.

And when it comes to sponsoring and supporting the arts and culture, Germany is right up there at the top. The generous subsidies that once helped every town and city to operate its own opera house and theater have been reduced and in some cases eliminated, but the arts scene remains strong and vigorous, part of a long tradition that the Germans regard as essential.

A Timeline of German History

EARLY HISTORY

1ST CENTURY A.D. The Roman sphere of influence extends into present-day Germany, with garrisons at Cologne, Koblenz, Mainz, and Trier.

A.D. 400 The Romans withdraw from Germany; in the following centuries, a loose conglomeration of German tribes transforms into what eventually would become the German Empire.

c. 800 Charlemagne (Karl der Grosse, 742–814) is responsible for the earliest large-scale attempt to unite the lands of Germany under one ruler. He also expands the Frankish Empire to include much of western Europe.

c. 900–1500 The power struggles and invasions of the Middle Ages continually disrupt the unity hammered out by Charlemagne. Until the demise of the Holy Roman Empire in 1806, Germany remains a collection of small principalities and free cities.

1400

1471 Albrecht Dürer is born. He and Hans Holbein the Younger (1497–1543) are among the artists who spark an artistic Renaissance in Germany.

1517 Martin Luther (1483–1546) writes the Ninety-Five Theses, triggering the Protestant Reformation (and in response, the Catholic Counter-Reformation). Luther's battle against the excesses of the Roman Catholic Church has far-reaching implications.

1618–48 The culmination of the Counter-Reformation, the Thirty Years War pits the Protestant north against the Catholic south and affects the whole of Europe.

1740 Friedrich der Grosse (Frederick the Great, 1712–86) takes power as king of Prussia. Under his rule, Prussia gains status as a great European power. During this period, the works of German artists, writers, composers, and philosophers usher in the Age of Enlightenment.

1800

1813 Prussian, Austrian, and Russian armies fight French emperor Napoleon I.

1815 Napoleon is defeated in the decisive Battle of Waterloo.

1848 The question of independence and national unity comes to a head in the 1848 revolutions. When that effort fails, the Austrian Hapsburg monarchy reimposes its sovereignty over Prussia and other parts of Germany.

1870–71 After triumphs in the Franco-Prussian War (1870–71), Prussian statesman Otto von Bismarck (1815–98) succeeds in winning over southern German states and, in 1871, becomes first chancellor of the German Empire (Reich).

1900–1948

1914–18 World War I. Military conflict on the eastern front results in the defeat of Russia, while fighting on the western front ultimately leads to German defeat and the abdication of Kaiser Wilhelm II. The war results in severe food shortages throughout the country and intensifies political unrest.

1919–32 In its attempt to establish a democratic and republican government, the so-called Weimar Republic represents a break in dominant traditions of German history. During the "Golden Twenties," Berlin—capital of the republic—blossoms into Germany's economic and cultural center.

1933–1945 Economic crisis in Germany is a major factor in the rise of the Nazi movement, but old authoritarian and nationalistic attitudes also play a part. As the brutal anti-Semitic political agenda of Adolf Hitler (1889–1945) becomes apparent, thousands of German Jews flee the country to escape persecution. In September of 1939, Germany invades Poland, beginning World War II. Millions of Jews and other "undesirables" are systematically exterminated in one of the most horrifying chapters in world history. At the end of the war, with its major cities in smoldering ruins, Germany ceases to exist as an independent state.

1948–2000

1948 West German recovery gets underway with U.S. assistance in the form of the Marshall Plan. The Soviets block railway and road access into West Berlin in an attempt to take control of the entire city, In response, the Western Allies airlift supplies into West Berlin.

1949–61 As the Cold War intensifies, the war's victors divide Germany into two states: The Federal Republic of Germany and the Soviet-ruled German Democratic Republic (GDR). Two Germanys develop with highly different political, economic, and social systems.

1961 In an attempt to slow immigration from East to West Germany, Soviets build the Berlin Wall.

1989 The opening of the Berlin Wall marks for East Germany the culmination of a wave of previously suppressed revolutionary sentiment across central and eastern Europe. Massive demonstrations against the repressive, Stalinist government of the GDR result.

1991 East and West Germany unite under one government. Berlin is made the new capital of a reunified Germany.

2006 Angela Merkel, who grew up in the GDR, becomes Germany's first female chancellor.

2009 Germany celebrates the 20th anniversary of the fall of the Berlin Wall. Angela Merkel is reelected for a second term as chancellor.

Germany's Architecture

> The Porta Nigra, constructed by the Romans in the 3rd century, was the fortified north gate in the city of Trier.

> The Romanesque interior of Dom St. Kilian in Würzburg.

Buildings that you can visit on a trip to Germany span some 1,200 years of architectural history and were created in a number of different styles. (The Porta Nigra, a 1,800-year-old arched gateway in Trier, is Germany's only remaining Roman-era structure of any significance.) Bombing raids in World War II left much of the country's rich architectural heritage in ruins. Some areas, such as the medieval towns along the Romantic Road, escaped damage, but the overall devastation affected nearly the entire country. Many historic buildings are painstaking postwar reconstructions. Here are examples from around Germany of the major architectural trends.

Carolingian & Ottonian (9th–11th c.)

The earliest manifestations of a discernibly Germanic architecture date from the period

of Charlemagne's rule as king of the Franks (768–814) and Emperor of the West (800–14). Constructed around 800, Charlemagne's chapel in Aachen (p. 441, ❹) harks back to earlier Byzantine models of building. During the Ottonian dynasty, architecture developed more complex ground plans and a rational system was devised for dividing churches into a series of separate units, a method that was to be of consequence in Romanesque design.

Romanesque (11th–12th c.)

Simple, clear forms, thick walls, and rounded arches signal Romanesque architecture, a building style adapted from earlier Roman models. The Kaiserdom in Speyer (p. 488, ❶) and Dom St. Kilian in Würzburg (p. 242, ❸) are two of the largest Romanesque churches in Germany.

Gothic (13th–16th c.)

Kölner Dom (Cologne Cathedral, p. 482, ❶) is Germany's greatest example of Gothic architecture, a style developed in France and diffused throughout Europe. Compared to Romanesque, Gothic style is slender and daring, with pointed arches, soaring vaults and spires, and enormous windows. A simpler and more monumental kind of Gothic architecture, built of brick, predominates in northern Germany in cities such as Lübeck (p. 606).

Renaissance (late 15th–17th c.)

Augsburg (p. 218) is one of the best cities in Germany to see Renaissance architecture a style characterized by calm precision, orderly repeating lines, and classical decoration over windows and doors. Renaissance architecture was imported from Italy into southern Germany.

> *Würzburg's Residenz features stunning baroque architecture and ceiling frescoes by Giovanni Battista Tiepolo.*

> *The Greek-inspired architecture of Munich's Propyläen.*

Baroque (17th–18th c.)

The decorative exuberance in curvy baroque architecture sets it apart from the more sober Renaissance style. The baroque flourished in Catholic, Counter-Reformation areas in the south of Germany. The Residenz in Würzburg (p. 240, ❷) and the Neues Palais at Sanssouci in Potsdam (p. 432, ❻) are two of the best examples of baroque architecture in Germany. Munich abounds in the baroque.

Rococo (18th c.)

Notch up the elements of baroque and you have rococo, exemplified by curving walls and staggering amounts of gilded and stucco decoration. One of the most famous examples of flamboyant rococo church architecture in Germany is the Wieskirche in Bavaria (p. 328, ❸). The rococo style was used in two important theaters of the time: the Altes Residenztheater in Munich (p. 275, ❶),

and the Markgräfliches Opernhaus in Bayreuth (p. 223, ❷).

Neoclassical/Neo-Gothic (19th c.)

The neoclassical style was meant to be a rebuke to the excesses of baroque and rococo. As the century wore on, neoclassicism gave way to the more ponderous neo-Gothic style. This fauxmedievalism is what Ludwig's Neuschwanstein castle (p. 338, ❶) is all about.

Jugendstil (late 19th–early 20th c.)

Jugendstil is the German name for Art Nouveau, an early-20th-century European movement that emphasized flowing, asymmetrical, organic shapes. The famous Mädler-Passage arcade in Leipzig shows Jugendstil influence, and the lovely Villa Stuck in Munich (p. 290, ❻) is a perfect example of Jugendstil applied to residential architecture.

Nods to the Neoclassical

Neoclassical architecture has its stylistic roots in the Classical era of Greece. (This style can also be called Greek Revival.) There are several great examples in Berlin, where the Prussian architect Karl Friedrich Schinkel (1781–1841) created a neoclassical avenue called Unter den Linden (p. 54, ❾) and an island of museums, the Museumsinsel (p. 80, ❼). In Munich, the architect Leo von Klenze (1784–1864) designed museums like the Glyptothek (p. 264, ❼) and monuments like the Propyläen (p. 286, ❾), inspired by Greek temples.

> *The resolutely minimalist and functional exterior of Dessau's renowned Bauhaus School of Design.*

Bauhaus (1913–33)
A rigorously modern style, free of frills and unnecessary decoration, Bauhaus was championed by Walter Gropius (1883–1969), who founded the Bauhaus school to create functional buildings and furnishings. Bauhaus museums are found in Weimar (p. 188) and Berlin (p. 45). The school was banned by the Nazis because it didn't promote "German-looking" architecture. The Bauhaus aesthetic was taught and practiced in the United States by European expatriates and their disciples, while the massive and dull German architecture of the 1930s and early 1940s glorified Nazi ideology. For much more on the Bauhaus movement, see "Building Bauhaus," p. 466.

Modernism (1948 onward)
A major housing shortage and rebuilding effort in bombed cities in Germany followed the devastation of World War II. If you walk down the streets or pedestrian zones in just about any major German city, you'll see modernist buildings all around you. It's a simple, functional style with straight lines and square windows, and it learned quite a few lessons from the Bauhaus. One of the most famous German architects of the postwar period is Hans Scharoun, whose daring Philharmonie concert hall in Berlin (p. 128) was completed in 1963.

Postmodernism (1980s onward)
Postmodernism is a style practiced by architects who plunder the past and apply old styles to the buildings of today. British architect James Stirling's Neue Staatsgalerie in Stuttgart (p. 433, ❸) is a reminder of just how uninspired and uninspiring most postmodern buildings are.

A Brief History of German Art

Germany abounds in art museums. You can't escape them, nor should you try. The country's rich artistic heritage is on display in even the smallest cities, while cities like Berlin and Munich boast world-class collections. The chronology below paints the major trends and artists with a brief, broad brushstroke.

Carolingian & Ottonian (9th–10th c.)

During the Carolingian period mosaics based on earlier Roman and Byzantine models were used to decorate Charlemagne's chapel and palace in Aachen (p. 441, ❹), and carved ivory book covers were notable. The first outstanding examples of German painting and sculpture were created during the Ottonian dynasty (c. 960–1060). Splendid illuminated manuscripts were produced in Reichenau (p. 377, ❷); carved in Cologne in the late 10th century, the *Gero Cross* in Kölner Dom (p. 482, ❶) is believed to be the oldest existing large-scale crucifix in the Western world. Fine craftsmanship is apparent in the metalwork of this period as well.

Romanesque (11th–12th c.)

Romanesque art, exemplified more in incised decorative stonework on church buildings than in sculpture or painting, flourished in Germany. Little remains of Romanesque fresco painting, of which Regensburg (p. 200, ❶) was a major

> *The famed sculptures of Adam and Eve by Tilman Riemenschneider, a 16th-century master woodcarver, can be seen at Würzburg's Mainfränkisches Museum.*

center, although there is an example from about 1000 at the Kloster St. Mang in Füssen (p. 204, ❻).

Gothic (13th–14th c.)

With the diffusion of the French Gothic style throughout Europe, notable contributions were made by the Germans, particularly in the field of sculpture, which was used to adorn the portals of the cathedrals at Bamberg (p. 215, ❸) and Cologne (p. 482) and the doors of Augsburg's Dom St. Maria (p. 221, ❻). The *Bamberger Reiter,* an anonymous equestrian sculpture in Bamberg's Kaiserdom (p. 215, ❸), is a masterpiece of 13th-century sculpture. Cologne's Wallraf-Richartz-Museum (p. 485, ❹) has galleries devoted to the Cologne school of painting from this period.

Renaissance (15th–16th c.)

German sculpture, particularly carved wooden altarpieces, reached an artistic highpoint in the late 15th century with the powerfully

> *The ornate painting and gilded, swirling stuccowork of the Wieskirche near Steingaden are definitive characteristics of rococo design.*

and panel painting became more highly developed. Flemish influence is seen in the paintings of Stephan Lochner (1400–51), whose *Adoration of the Magi* altarpiece graces Cologne's cathedral (p. 482, ❶). Hans Holbein the Elder (1465–1524) is another major 15th-century figure.

The artistic genius of the German Renaissance was Albrecht Dürer (1471–1528), who visited Venice and brought elements of Italian Renaissance style to Germany. Dürer's paintings, woodcuts, and engravings influenced all European art of the time; his work is on view in Munich's Alte Pinakothek (p. 262, ❶), Berlin's Gemäldegalerie (p. 78, ❼), and the Germanisches Nationalmuseum (p. 226, ❶) in his native Nuremberg.

Painting was at its height in the 16th century. The great masters of the age—all of whose work can be seen in Munich's Alte Pinakothek (p. 262, ❶)—were Hans Holbein the Younger (1497–1543); Mathias Grünewald (d. 1528); Albrecht Altdorfer (1480–1538), who brought pure landscape painting into vogue; Lucas Cranach the Elder (1472–1553); and Hans Baldung (1484–1545).

Baroque & Rococo (17th–18th c.)

Ceiling paintings and swirling often gilded stuccowork is part and parcel of the decoration in the exuberant baroque and rococo churches and

expressive works of Peter Vischer the Elder (1460–1529), Veit Stoss (1439–1533), Adam Kraft (1460–1508), and Tilman Riemenschneider (1460–1531), a master carver whose genius is on display in Würzburg's Mainfränkisches Museum (p. 243, ❼),

Rothenburg ob der Tauber's St.-Jakobs-Kirche (p. 238, ❹), the Herrgottskirche in Creglingen (p. 208, ❸), and Nuremberg's Germanisches Nationalmuseum (p. 226, ❶). Manuscript illumination and fresco painting declined as stained-glass technique

> *Ernst Ludwig Kirchner's* Self-Portrait with Model.

palaces throughout southern Germany. Two notable examples are the Wieskirche (p. 328, **3**) and the Asamkirche (p. 273 **3**) . The rococo style came to the fore around 1730. At this time, too, small Dresden china figures and groups became popular, with the workshops at Meissen (p. 151, **10**) producing exquisite miniature statuettes of genre subjects.

Romanticism (19th c.)
In the early part of the century, school of German historical painting emerged, and the period brought to the fore genre painters such as Moritz von Schwind (1804–71) and Carl Spitzweg (1808–85). Romantic painters who were influenced by Italian art included Anselm von Feuerbach (1828–80) and Hans von Marées (1837–87). The greatest artist of the romantic period was Caspar David Friedrich (1774–1840), whose famous *Cross in the Mountains* (1808) hangs in Dresden's Gemäldegalerie Alte Meister (p. 166, **1**).

Expressionism (early 20th c.)
In the early years of the 20th century, the sentimental and derivative genre and landscape scenes of the previous century were replaced by a fresh, dynamic, and highly personalized sensibility. The wave of 20th-century artists that emerged created an art known as expressionism for its purposeful distortion of natural forms and attempt to express emotion. The expressionist movement came in three waves. The first, Die Brücke (The Bridge), founded in Dresden in 1905, included Ernst Kirchner (1880–1938), Emil Nolde (1867–1956), and Karl Schmidt-Rottluff (1884–1976). It was followed in 1911 by the Munich-based Blaue Reiter (Blue Rider) group, which included Franz Marc (1880–1916), Gabriele Münter (1877–1962), and several foreign artists, including Swiss-born Paul Klee (1879–1940), American-born Lyonel Feininger (1871–1956), and Russian-born Wassily Kandinsky (1866–1944); their work can be seen in Munich's Lenbachhaus (p. 264, **5**). Die Neue Sachlichkeit (The New Objectivity), a movement founded in the aftermath of World War I by Otto Dix (1891–1969) and George Grosz (1893–1959), was characterized by a more realistic style combined with a cynical, socially critical philosophical stance that was vehemently antiwar. Brilliant, bitter canvases by Dix and Grosz hang in the Neue Nationalgalerie (p. 75, **6**) in Berlin. One artist working in a related style was Käthe Kollwitz (1867–1945), whose haunting sculptures, drawings, and prints can be seen at the Käthe-Kollwitz-Museum in Berlin (p. 75, **4**).

Some of these artists taught at the Bauhaus, which espoused functionalism and encouraged experimentation and abstraction with the ideal of combining artistic beauty with usefulness.

The Nazi regime, which regarded all abstract and expressionist works as degenerate, discouraged and destroyed any art that was not heroic or propagandistic, and the Germany of the 1930s and early 1940s produced nothing of artistic significance.

Post–World War II (1945–present)
Germany hasn't had one predominant school or movement to define its art since World War II, but it has produced internationally recognized artists such as the iconoclastic sculptor and performance artist Joseph Beuys (1921-86), the painter Anselm Kiefer (b. 1945), and the painter-sculptor Georg Baselitz (b. 1938). All three of these artists are represented in Stuttgart's Staatsgalerie (p. 433, **3**) and Bonn's Kunstmuseum (p. 455). Anyone interested in contemporary German art should also visit Cologne's Museum Ludwig (p. 485, **3**).

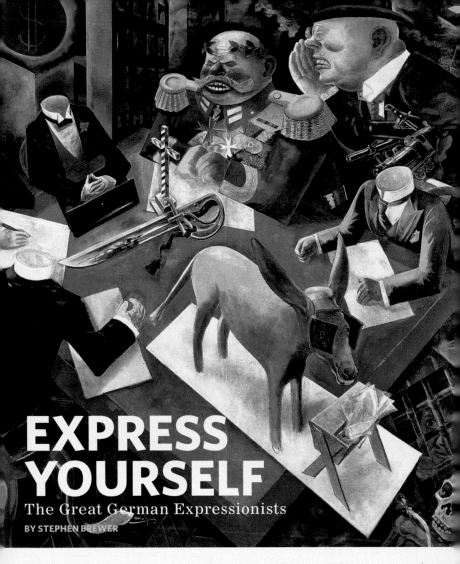

EXPRESS YOURSELF
The Great German Expressionists

BY STEPHEN BREWER

THE EARLY 20TH CENTURY, up until the Nazis took over in 1933, was a time of great artistic ferment and experimentation in Germany. Expressionism, the most compelling art movement to emerge, sought to express emotion and individuality, often by deliberately distorting natural forms and colors. The movement began in Dresden in 1905 with a group known as **Die Brücke** (The Bridge), followed by **Der Blaue Reiter** (Blue Rider), a group that emerged in Munich in 1911. The artists of this period lived in a time of political upheaval and revolutionary politics which grew more intense following Germany's defeat in World War I and the collapse of the German economy. **Die Neue Sachlichkeit** (The New Objectivity), an expressionist movement founded in the aftermath of World War I, was characterized by a more realistic style combined with a socially critical stance that was vehemently antiwar. Several of the expressionist artists taught at the **Bauhaus School of Art and Architecture** (see "The Building of Bauhaus," p. 466), which encouraged experimentation and abstraction with the ideal of combining artistic beauty with usefulness.

Who's Who

GEORGE GROSZ
(1893–1959)

Grosz's experiences in World War I and his observations of life in Weimar-era Berlin had a profound impact and led to his corrosive depictions of piglike business-men, wounded soldiers, prostitutes, sex crimes, and orgies, all done in a deliberately crude form of caricature (*The Eclipse of the Sun*, 1926, shown here). After his emigration to the U.S. in 1933, Grosz rejected the scathing violence of his previous work and painted conventional nudes and landscape watercolors. His greatest works, from the 1920s, hang in the **Neue National-galerie** in Berlin (p. 75, **6**).

KÄTHE KOLLWITZ
(1867–1945)

One of the foremost artists of the 20th century, Kollwitz lived in a working-class neighborhood in Berlin where she saw first-hand the sufferings of ordinary men and women. A socialist and pacifist (both her sons were killed in battle) who believed that art should reflect the times, Kollwitz was the first woman to be elected to the Prussian Academy but was expelled by the Nazis and forbidden to exhibit her work. (Below left, *Group of Children*, 1937–38.) Her haunting sculptures, drawings, and prints, created amidst great hardship and sorrow, can be seen at the **Käthe-Kollwitz-Museum** in Berlin (p. 75, **4**).

OTTO DIX
(1891–1969)

In his early paintings such as *War Cripples*, 1919, he depicted the harsh realities of war, and life in postwar Germany, in a style that was predominantly realist with elements of the grotesque. When the Nazis expelled him from the Dres-den Academy, he began painting landscapes to earn a living. Some of his most powerful works hang in the **Neue Nationalgalerie** in Berlin (p. 75, **6**).

FRANZ MARC
(1880–1916)

Marc spent several years in Paris before returning to his home-town, Munich, where he showed several works in the first Der Blaue Reiter exhibition in 1911. Most of his mature work portrays animals in natural set-tings and is character-ized by bright primary color, stark simplicity, and a profound sense of emotion (below, *Blue Horse I*). In 1936, 20 years after his death at the Battle of Verdun, he was condemned by the Nazis as an *entarteter Künstler* (degenerate artist) and his works were stripped from German museums. In 1999, Marc's painting *Der Wasserfall (The Waterfall)* set a record for 20th-century Ger-man painting when it sold for $5.06 million.

KARL SCHMIDT-ROTTLUFF
(1884–1976)

In 1905 Schmidt-Rottluff founded Die Brücke (The Bridge) in Dresden and gave the movement its name, based on a quote by Nietzsche: "What is great in man is that he is a bridge and not an end." He developed an art of compelling

color and mystical intensity influenced by Fauvism, Cubism, and primitive art (above, *Self-portrait*, 1906). In 1937 hundreds of his paintings were seized from museums by the Nazis and shown in exhibitions of Degenerate Art. In 1947 he was ap-pointed a professor at the University of Arts in Berlin-Char-lottenburg, where he founded Die Brücke Museum in 1967.

The Nazis Take Over

The Nazi regime denounced all abstract and expressionist art as "un-German" or "Jewish-Bolshevik" and purged it from museums. Expressionist artists were dismissed from teaching posts and forbid-den to exhibit their works. As a way to ridicule modern art and enflame the public against all forms of modernism, the Nazis organized an exhibition called *Entartete Kunst* (Degenerate Art) and toured it to several cities. Today the work of German expressionists are prized showpieces in German museums and around the world.

Eating & Drinking in Germany

> *Regensburg's Historische Wurstküche wurst stand has been serving up its famed sausages and sauerkraut for more than 850 years.*

German Cuisine

German cooking tends to be hearty and filling, with many regional variations. Seasonal specialties include *Spargel* (asparagus) in May and June, *Matjes* (herring) in June and July, *Erdbeeren* (strawberries) in spring, *Forelle* (trout) in summer, *Reh* (venison) in fall, and *Gans* (goose) in late fall and early winter. In the country as a whole, you can taste about 150 different types of sausage; Berlin, Munich, and Nuremberg all have their own special kinds, served boiled, broiled, or grilled. By law, German sausage cannot contain "fillers."

Regional specialties in Bavaria include *Leberkäs* (a chilled mold of minced pork, beef, and liver), *Knödel* (dumplings or soaked bread), *Haxen* (pork or veal trotters, usually served with sauerkraut), *Leberknödel*

(liver dumplings served in a clear broth), and *Schweinwurst mit Kraut* (pork sausages with sauerkraut). Fish dishes have long been a staple (but are now more of an expensive specialty) in Hamburg, Lübeck, Bremen, and the towns in the Schleswig-Holstein region of northern Germany: *Aalsuppe* is a sweet-and-sour eel soup flavored with bacon and vegetables; *Labskaus*, a traditional sailor's dish, consists of pork, beef, and salt herring mixed with potatoes and beets and topped by a fried egg; *Rollmops* are pieces of pickled herring rolled in sour cream. Berlin loves *Erbsensuppe* (pea soup) served with rye bread and *Eisbein* (pigs' knuckles). In Baden-Württemburg and south-central Germany look for pasta dishes such as egg-based *Spätzle* tossed with

cheese, and *Maultaschen* (stuffed raviolis). Westphalia and the Black Forest region are famous for their hams. Soups served throughout Germany, but particularly popular in Saxony and Thuringia, include *Kartoffelsuppe* (potato soup with bacon) and *Linsensuppe mit Thüringer Rotwurst* (lentil soup with Thuringian sausage). The Rhineland and the city of Cologne have many regional specialties, such as *Saumagen* (stuffed pork belly with pickled cabbage), *Hämchen* (pork trotters with pickled cabbage and potatoes), and *Sauerbraten* (beef marinated in wine vinegar and spices).

Street vendors in larger cities typically offer hot sausages with *Senf* (mustard) or curry sauce (a spicy red sauce), *Erbsensuppe* (pea soup), and *döner kebab* (meat

> *Local beer from the microbrewery at the Kulturbrauerei Altstadt hotel in Heidelberg.*

Beer with Me: What You Need to Know About German Beer

You don't have to speak German to order a beer. It's spelled *Bier* but it's pronounced *beer*. And it's such a vital part of German culture that the right to drink a beer with lunch is written into some labor contracts. The traditional *Biergarten* (beer garden), with tables set outdoors under trees or trellises, remains popular, especially in southern Germany. A *Bräuhaus* (*broy*-house) serves its own brew along with local food.

When you order a beer in Germany, you have many choices. The range of beer includes *Altbier, Bockbier, Export, Kölsch, Lager, Malzbier, Märzbier, Pils, Vollbier,* and *Weizenbier*. The ratio of ingredients, brewing temperature and technique, alcohol content, aging time, color, and taste all contribute to a German beer's unique qualities. A German law adopted in 1516 dictates that German beer may contain no ingredients other than hops, malt (barley), yeast, and water.

Dark and sweet *Malzbier* (*maltz*-beer; malt beer) contains hardly any alcohol. *Vollbier* (*fole*-beer, or standard beer) has 4% alcohol, *Export* has 5%, and *Bockbier* has 6%. *Pils,* or *Pilsener,* beers are light and contain more hops. *Weizenbier* (*vie*-tsen-beer), made from wheat, is a Bavarian white beer. *Märzbier* (*maertz*-beer), or "March beer," is dark and strong. The most popular beer in Germany is *Pils,* followed by *Export*.

skewers), a traditional Turkish dish that originated with the Turkish "guest workers" who came to Germany in the 1960s. In the pedestrian zones of larger German cities some fast-food restaurants are open to the street; the Nordsee chain sells fresh herring and fish sandwiches.

When it comes to baked goods—bread and pastries—Germany has more variety than any country in the world, with about 300 different types of bread and 1,200 varieties of biscuits and cakes.

And there's been some good news for diners: In 2008, Germany enacted a new nonsmoking policy in public places. You can now enjoy a smoke-free meal in any German restaurant.

Lookin' for Kaffee und Kuchen

The British have their afternoon tea and cakes, and the Germans have their afternoon *Kaffee und Kuchen* (coffee and cake). Until fairly recently, people typically went to a Konditorei, or pastry cafe, for their *Kaffee und Kuchen* fix. Or they bought their delicious afternoon treats at a *Bäckerei* (bakery) and brewed up their own caffeine accompaniment. Now, at least in the larger cities, there's another option: Starbucks. The *Kuchen* part of the K & K tradition may not be kind on the waistline, but with such an extraordinary variety of pastries to choose from—frosted cakes, layer cakes, strudels, fruit-filled tarts—it's hard to resist the temptation. As you travel through Germany, look out for regional specialties to accompany your coffee. Lübeck (p. 606), for example, is where marzipan (almond paste) was invented, and Nuremberg (p. 226) is famous for its *Lebkuchen* (spice cakes).

Make Mine Wine: German Wine

Though perhaps more often associated with beer, Germany is also well-known for its wine production, particularly for its high-quality Rieslings and other whites. The most famous German vineyards are found in the western and southwestern parts of the country, in the Rhine Valley and along the Mosel River, with the Mosel region generally considered the premiere wine-growing region in the country. For more on the country's regions and varietals, see p. 372.

Under German wine law, there are two categories of quality—*Tafelwein* and *Qualitätswein*.

Tafelwein (taf-fel vine; table wine) is made from normally ripe grapes. If you want a simple, inexpensive German table wine, you have two choices: *Deutscher Tafelwein* (a simple table wine) and *Deutscher Landwein* (with more body and character). If the word *Deutscher* is missing on the label of a bottle of *Tafelwein* or *Landwein,* then it is not made solely of German grapes. Instead, it's a foreign wine that may or may not have been blended with German wine. It is likely to have been bottled, but not grown, in Germany.

Made from ripe, very ripe, or overripe grapes, *Qualitätswein* (quality wine) is divided into two types: *Qualitätswein mit Prädikat* (QmP) and *Qualitätswein bestimmter Anbaugebiete* (QbA). If you see QbA on the label, it means the wine comes from one of the 13 specified winegrowing regions and is made from approved grape varieties that have ripened sufficiently to ensure that the wine will have the style and traditional taste of its region. Light, refreshing, and fruity, these wines are meant to be consumed while young, for everyday enjoyment or with meals. QmP wines include all the finest wines of Germany, ranging from light (such as *Kabinett*) to intense (such as *Spätlese*) and from dry to sweet.

The rarest of the QmP wines are *Auslese, Beerenauslese,* and *Trockenbeerenauslese* wines. These are all made of grapes harvested very late in the season, which growing conditions do not always permit. *Auslese* wines are intense and usually (but not always) sweet; *Beerenauslese* and *Trockenbeerenauslese* wines are rich, sweet dessert wines. Also of special note is *Eiswein,* or "ice wine," made from grapes harvested and pressed while frozen to concentrate sugar and acidity. This unique wine has a remarkable concentration of fruity acidity and sweetness.

Ein Bier, Bitte, or How to Order a Beer in Germany

To order a beer, decide whether you want a *dunkles Bier* (*dun*-kles beer; dark beer, brewed with darkly roasted malt and fermented for a long period of time) or a *helles Bier* (*hell*-less beer; light beer, brewed from malt dried and baked by the local brewery). If you want a large glass, you ask for *ein Grosses* (ine *grow*-ses); if you want a small glass, ask for *ein Kleines* (ine *kly*-nis), and tell the waiter or tavernkeeper whether you want *ein Bier vom Fass* (fum *fahss;* from the barrel) or in a *Flasche* (*flah*-shuh; bottle). The beer is always served cold, but not too cold, in an appropriate beer glass or mug, with a long-lasting head of white foam. A proper draft beer, according to the Germans, can't be poured in less than 7 minutes to achieve the proper head.

Germany in Books & Movies

> *Thomas Mann.*

> *Heinrich Böll.*

Books

The fiction and nonfiction books listed below can help you gain a better understanding of German history, culture, personalities, and politics.

Before the Deluge: A Portrait of Berlin in the 1920s, by Otto Friedrich: A fascinating portrait of the political, cultural, and social life of Berlin between the wars.

Berlin Journal 1989–1990, by Robert Darnton: An eyewitness account of the events that led to the opening of the Berlin Wall and the collapse of East Germany's Communist regime.

Berlin Noir, by Philip Kerr: A trilogy of thought-provoking crime novels (*March Violets; The Pale Criminal; A German Requiem*) set in Nazi Germany and postwar Berlin and Vienna and featuring Bernie Gunther as a dyspeptic Berlin detective.

Billiards at Half-Past Nine, by Heinrich Böll: A compelling novel by one of Germany's best-known writers about the compromises made by a rich German family during the Hitler years.

Bismarck, by Edward Crankshaw: An objective and highly readable life of the first chancellor of the German Empire and a seminal figure in Germany's Prussian past.

Buddenbrooks, by Thomas Mann: A classic of German literature, dealing with the transition of a merchant family in Lübeck from 19th-century stability to 20th-century uncertainty.

Europe Central, by William T. Vollman: A bold, brilliant novel that examines the authoritarian cultures of 20th-century Germany and Russia and creates a mesmerizing picture of life during wartime from many different perspectives.

Five Germanys I Have Known, by Fritz Stern: A chronicle of the five distinct eras of Germany's modern history experienced by the family of this well-known Jewish historian.

Frederick the Great, by Nancy Mitford: Frederick—statesman, scholar, musician, and patron of the arts—sketched with wit and humor.

The German Lesson, by Siegfried Lenz: A 1971 bestselling novel that powerfully explores Nazism and its aftermath

> *Willy Brandt in a meeting with U.S. President John F. Kennedy.*

in the northern German provinces.

Germany 1866–1945, by Gordon Craig: One of the best single accounts of the turbulent political, cultural, and economic life in Germany from the foundation of the German Reich through the end of the Third Reich.

Here I Stand: A Life of Martin Luther, by Roland Bainton: A fascinating and meticulously researched account of the Protestant reformer.

Hitler: A Biography, by Ian Kershaw: One of the best of the many biographies of Hitler.

The Last Jews in Berlin, by Leonard Gross: Gripping, true stories of a handful of Jews who managed to remain in Berlin during Word War II by hiding out in the homes of non-Jewish German friends.

My Life in Politics, by Willy Brandt: The political memoirs of Willy Brandt (1913–92), winner of the Nobel Peace Prize in 1971; mayor of West Berlin from 1957 to 1966, during the height of the Cold War; and chancellor of West Germany from 1969 to 1974.

The Tin Drum, by Günter Grass: Perhaps the most famous novel about life in post–World War II Germany, written by a Nobel Prize winner who kept his own Nazi past a secret until 2006.

A Tramp Abroad, by Mark Twain: Twain's account of his travels through Germany, which remains as fresh today as when it first was published in 1899.

The Wall in My Backyard: East German Women in Transition, by Dinah Dodds and Pam Allen-Thompson: A collection of interviews in which East German women describe the excitement, chaos, and frustration of the period between the fall of the Berlin Wall in 1989 and reunification of Germany less than a year later.

When in Germany, Do As the Germans Do, by Hyde Flippo: A short, entertaining crash course in German culture, customs, and heritage.

Witness to Nuremberg, by Richard Sonnenfeldt: The story, told by the chief American interpreter at the war-crimes trials, of his dealings with Hermann Göring, the powerful Nazi official who was subsequently executed for war crimes.

> *A still from Wolfgang Petersen's* Das Boot.

Movies

As with literature, World War II and the Holocaust have dominated the subject matter of recent films about Germany—so much so that German-made films about contemporary German life rarely get a showing outside Germany unless they win a top prize at a festival. Listed below is a selection of German and Germany-themed films available on DVD.

Bent (1997): For this film, Sean Mathias adapted Martin Sherman's powerful play about Max, a gay man sent to Dachau concentration camp under the Nazi regime.

Berlin Alexanderplatz (1980): Rainer Werner Fassbinder's 15-part television adaptation of the novel by Alfred Döblin follows the life of a man released from prison between the two world wars.

The Blue Angel (1930): Josef von Sternberg's film shot Marlene Dietrich to international stardom and remains stark, startling, and provocative.

Cabaret (1972): Bob Fosse's musical is based on Christopher Isherwood's *Berlin Stories* and set in Berlin at the brink of Hitler's rise to power.

The Cabinet of Doctor Caligari (1921): One of the earliest horror films, this classic German silent movie, directed by Robert Weine, used expressionist sets to create a tale of murder and madness.

The Counterfeiters (2007): Based on a true story, Stefan Ruzowitzky's Oscar-winning film (Best Foreign Language Film) tells the story of master forger Salomon "Sally" Sorowitsch and his fellow criminals, who were assigned the job of counterfeiting massive sums of dollars and pounds in an effort by the Nazi regime to weaken the Allies.

Das Boot (1981): This Wolfgang Petersen film tells the story of a German U-Boat crew during World War II. Not for the claustrophobic.

Downfall (2005): Oliver Hirschsbiegel's controversial film stars a frighteningly brilliant Bruno Ganz playing Adolf Hitler during the last days of World War II.

A Foreign Affair (1948): Billy Wilder's cynically hilarious look at postwar occupied Berlin stars Marlene Dietrich as an amoral cabaret singer and Jean Arthur as a self-righteous U.S. congresswoman.

Goodbye, Lenin! (2003): Wolfgang Becker's wry comedy centers on a young man in East Berlin who tries to keep his bedridden mother, a loyal Communist, from learning that the wall has come down and Germany has been reunited.

Heimat (1984–2005): This series created for West German television begins in 1919 with the return of a soldier from Word War I to his village in the northwestern corner of Germany, a rural region known as the Hunsrück, and ends 63 years later; the history of modern Germany is refracted through the experiences of an extended family, the Simons.

The Lives of Others (2006): An Academy Award winner for

> *A scene from* Metropolis, *a Fritz Lang classic.*

> *Actor Ulrich Muhe in* The Lives of Others.

Best Foreign Language Film, this haunting film by Florian Henckel von Donnersmarck, which takes place in East Berlin in 1984, reveals how the East German secret police (the *Stasi*) spied on the country's citizens, destroying lives.

Ludwig (1972): Italian director Luchino Visconti made this turgid epic about the last king of Bavaria, the one who built Neuschwanstein.

The Marriage of Maria Braun (1979): Hanna Schygulla stars as a woman married to a soldier in the waning days of World War II in this film by Rainer Werner Fassbinder.

Metropolis (1927): Fritz Lang directed this classic of German cinema, in which the Workers plan a revolt against the aloof Thinkers who

dominate them in a future dystopia.

Olympiad (1938): Leni Riefenstahl directed this super-Aryan take on the 1936 Olympic games in Berlin.

On the Other Side (2007): This well-acted and well-received contemporary drama by Fatih Akin explores the lives of Turks and Germans living in the multicultural Germany of today.

The Reader (2008): This Hollywood adaptation, directed by Stephen Daldry, of a novel set in postwar Germany deals with the life of an illiterate woman who worked in a concentration camp.

Run, Lola, Run (1999): Writer-director Tom Tykwer's film features fast-paced twists and turns as Lola races

desperately through Berlin seeking 100,000 deutsche marks to save her boyfriend from being rubbed out by a gangster.

Sophie Scholl (2005): Marc Rothemund's film is based on the true story of brother and sister Hans and Sophie Scholl, two students at the University of Munich who resisted the Nazis and paid with their lives.

Triumph of the Will (1934): Leni Riefenstahl filmed the gigantic 1934 Nazi conference and rally in Nuremberg as "image control" propaganda for the Third Reich.

Wings of Desire (1988): In Wim Wenders's film, an angel roaming the streets of Berlin and recording the angst and joy of ordinary life falls in love with a mortal.

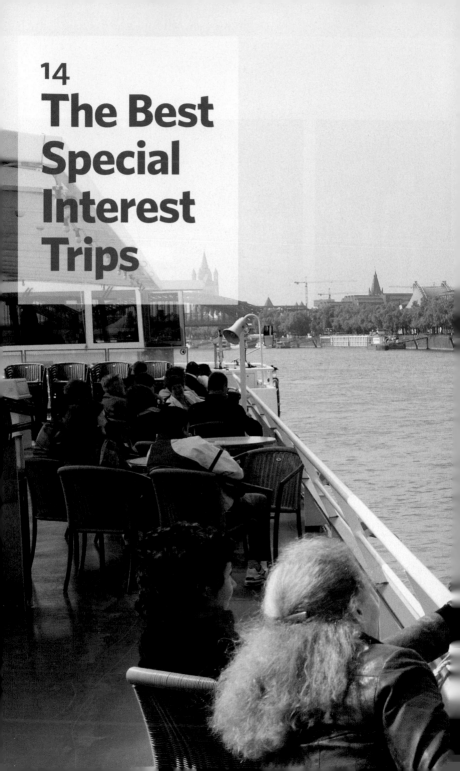

14 The Best Special Interest Trips

> PREVIOUS PAGE *A Rhine River cruise in Cologne.* THIS PAGE *The Nuremberg Christmas Market draws customers from all over Europe.*

Multi-Activity Tours

Luxury travel specialist **Abercrombie & Kent** (☎ 800/554-7016; www.abercrombiekent. com) includes Germany in a series of customized group tours that take in other European cities and countries—Berlin, Prague, and St. Petersburg; Germany and Poland; Central Europe and the Danube (incorporates the Rhine). Comprehensive, unescorted customized package tours to Germany are available from **American Express Vacations** (☎ 800/335-3342; www.americanexpressvacations.com). **Brendan Vacations** (☎ 800/421-8446; www. brendanvacations.com) has a selection of 8- to 15-day tours; the company's Best of Germany tour takes in Frankfurt, Berlin, Nuremberg, Munich, and some Alpine destinations, with accommodations at the better hotels. For a variety of Alpine Countries tours that cover southern Germany, Austria, and Switzerland, contact **Collette Vacations** (☎ 800/340-5158; www.collettevacations.com). **Globus & Cosmos Tours** (☎ 800/338-7092; www. globusandcosmos.com) offers 9- to 16-day escorted tours of various parts of Germany. It also has a budget branch that offers tours at lower rates. **Maupintour** (☎ 800/255-4266; www.maupintour.com) has a selection of upscale tours, such as a Rhine River tour and a tour of Berlin, Dresden, Meissen, Nuremberg,

and Heidelberg. Its most popular tour is a 14-day trip that takes in such cities as Dresden, Berlin, Rothenburg ob der Tauber, Munich, Meissen, Baden-Baden, and Potsdam and includes a Rhine River cruise past the Lorelei Rock. **Virgin Vacations** (☎ 888/937-8474; www.virgin-vacations.com) organizes custom escorted tours of Berlin, Munich, and the Bavarian Alps.

Special Interest Trips A to Z

Archaeology
The British group **Archaeology Safaris** (☎ 44-7815/007128; www.archaeology-safaris.co.uk) occasionally has field trips and "field schools" in Germany, which has a rich heritage of Germanic, Celtic, Roman, Frankish, Carolingian, and medieval sites (and sights).

Architecture
Guided architectural tours in Germany, with the emphasis on modern architecture in cities like Berlin, Hamburg, Dresden, and Leipzig, are offered by Hamburg-based **ArchEX** (☎ 49-40/2281-7363; www.archex.info). For lovers of Bauhaus architecture and design, **Sullivan's Custom Tours** (☎ 713/849-4858; www. sullivanscustomtours.com) has a tour that covers highlights of the style in Berlin, Weimar, Dessau, and other places.

Art Lovers' Tours
American i**Gregory Schaffner** (☎ 49-176/2673-8451; www.privateguidesineurope.com), can guide you through the fine art of museums in Munich, and he also offers other specialized tours of the city and Bavaria.

Auto Industry
Car lovers have plenty to get their hands on in Germany—what with Audi, Mercedes-Benz, VW, and Porsche to choose from. **German Auto Tours** (☎ 800/443-4610; www.germanautotours.com) can get you special access to the automotive plants where cars and engines are produced.

Classical Music
The birthplace of composers like Johann Sebastian Bach, Ludwig van Beethoven, Georg Friedrich Händel, Felix Mendelssohn Bartholdy, Robert Schumann, Richard Strauss, Richard Wagner, and others is never likely to lack for a tune. Both self-guided and guided classical music tours are available from **Allegro Holidays** (☎ 800/838-6860; www.allegroholidays.com). Among a diverse menu of German tours offered by **Conti-Reisen** (☎ 49-221/8019-5250; www.conti-reisen.com) is one that covers opera and classical music in eastern Germany, taking in Berlin, Potsdam, Dresden, and Meissen.

Cruises
The most popular cruises in Germany are along the Rhine, Danube, Mosel, and Elbe rivers. **Jody Lexow Yacht Charters** (☎ 800/662-2628; www.jodylexowyachtcharters.com) rents hotel barges (including crew, food, and beverages) and smaller self-drive craft for touring the canals and rivers of Germany. Canal barge cruises—taking in Berlin, the Mecklenburg lakes, and rivers, as well as canals—are available through **European Barging** (☎ 888/869-7907; www.europeanbarging.com).

Castle Hotels
There are many *Schloss* (castle) hotels in Germany. After reunification, many castles in the old East Germany were restored and opened to the public. Some are rather basic, having more character than comfort, but others are luxurious, with antique furnishings (such as four-poster beds) and a baronial atmosphere often harking back 3 centuries or more. Most of them have installed modern plumbing. Some visitors with a sense of the romantic book castle-hotel packages throughout Germany. The best source for such vacations is Euro-Connection (☎ 800/645-3876; www.euro-connection.com).

Castles
Information on all-inclusive tours of European castles, with a strong focus on the Rhine and Mosel river valleys and Bavaria, is available through **Castles of the World** (no phone; www.castlesoftheworld.com).

Christian Sites
The Reformation may be said to have begun in Germany, with the actions of Martin Luther. You visit sites associated with Luther and other religious reformers on 10-day guided tours from **Reformation Tours** (☎ 800/303-5534; www.reformationtours.com). The Catholics managed to stay in the majority in the southern part of Germany, and you can visit important Catholic sites, like Gothic and baroque cathedrals, with **Globus** (☎ 877/797-8793; www.globusfaith.com).

Christmas Markets
Germany's Christmas markets, like Nuremberg's Christkindlesmarkt (p. 230) and Dresden's Striezelmarkt (p. 173)—and there are plenty more where they come from—are widely recognized to be the state of the art. **ChristmasMarketTours** (☎ 800/942-3301; www.christmasmarkettours.com) can get you to and around some of the best.

Farm Vacations
Growing in its appeal to tourists, a vacation down on the farm—*Urlaub auf dem Bauernhof* in German—cuts costs and is an adventure for children as well. Nearly every local tourist office has a list of farmhouses in its area that take in paying guests. Sometimes only bed and breakfast are offered; at other places a farm-style home-cooked dinner is included if you wish it. For more information, contact DLG (German Agricultural Association; ☎ 49-69/247-880; www.landtourismus.de).

Gay & Lesbian
Gay Travel (☎ 800-GAY-TRAVEL/ (429-8728); www.gaytravel.com) organizes a

Germany tour that culminates at the Oktober-fest Bavarian beer festival. For an insight into Berlin's vibrant gay scene, enlist the aid of **Hank's Berlin Tours** (no phone; www.gayberlintours.com).

Jewish Tours

Berlin-based **Milk & Honey Tours** (☎ 49-30/6162-5761; www.milkandhoneytours.com) has a program of Jewish heritage tours that covers Germany. See also "Jewish Visitors," below.

Napoleonic Battle Reenactments

Germany provided the terrain for two of Napoleon's decisive battles, Jena (1806) and Leipzig (1813), the former a victory for the French emperor and the latter, dubbed the "Battle of the Nations," a defeat. Reenactments of the battles take place some years. Information is available from the tourist offices of both Jena (p. 148) and Leipzig (p. 193).

Railway Tours

General tours that include Germany as part of a wider European itinerary, as well as specific tours, such as traveling by steam train through the Harz Mountains, are organized by **The Society of International Railway Travelers** (☎ 800/478-4881; www.irtsociety.com).

World War II

Ironically, relatively little of Germany suffered heavy ground combat during the war. There were some big exceptions, such as the Battle of Berlin, the Battle of Huertgen Forest (Hürtgenwald), and the Rhine crossing in 1945, and many German towns and cities were destroyed by aerial bombardment. In addition, there are places associated with the Nazi regime, including concentration camps, as well as naval bases and other war-related sites. **Alpenventures World War II Tours** (☎ 888/991-6718; www.worldwar2tours.com) offers tours of such places.

Outdoor Activities A to Z

Biking

Popular bicycling areas in Germany are the Mosel Valley, famed for its vineyards, and the Romantic Road in Bavaria. **Austin-Lehman Adventures** (☎ 800/575-1540; www.austinlehman.com) has guided tours covering both routes. **Breakaway Adventures**

(☎ 800/567-6286; www.breakaway-adventures.com) concentrates on the Mosel. **Classic Adventures** (☎ 800/777-8090; www.classicadventures.com) offers a 10-day Romantic Road tour. **VBT** (☎ 800/245-3868; www.vbt.com) has a 7-day combination bike and barge tour that takes you along the Mosel

Jewish Visitors

Perhaps as many as 200,000 Jews now live in Germany, compared with a prewar high of 500,000. Two Orthodox rabbis were ordained in Munich in 2009—the first such event since World War II. Berlin's Jewish community is the largest, its 20,000 members served by kosher restaurants, a Jewish high school, a child-care center, the Mendelssohn Center at nearby Potsdam University, and weekly and monthly newspapers. Other important Jewish communities are located in Frankfurt, Munich, Düsseldorf, Stuttgart, Cologne, and Hamburg. Another 75 smaller communities are scattered throughout the country.

While anti-Semitism has not disappeared completely—and may even be on the rise, in part due to Middle East issues rather than German ones—in general, postwar Germany has worked hard to confront its past. Some 30 museums deal with Jewish issues, and former concentration camp sites display grisly reminders to visitors. German high schools include Holocaust studies in their curriculum. In politics, there are about 80 extreme-right groups; 20 or so are classified as neo-Nazi, with maybe 65,000 members—a small minority in a country of more than 80 million people.

> *Bicycle tours, like this one in Munich, are commonplace throughout Germany.*

River to Trier and into the Eifel (an additional package includes round-trip airfare to Berlin and pre- and post-tour accommodations). **E.E.I. Travel** (☎ 800/927-3876; www. eeitravel.com) offers a variety of biking tours throughout Germany and can customize your trip. The British **Cyclists Touring Club** (☎ 44-844/736-8450; www.ctc.org.uk) offers guided cycling tours; it charges £36 for an annual membership. The Rhine, the Mosel, the Elbe, and Bavaria are all on the program at **Mercurio Bike Travel** (no phone; www. mercurio-bike-travel.com), in Germany.

Bird-Watching
Spread your wings on a 17-day German Grand Tour that adds sightseeing highlights to basic birding-watching, from **WINGS Birding Tours Worldwide** (☎ 888/293-6443; www. wingsbirds.com).

Canoeing & Kayaking
For guided canoe tours on Bavaria's lakes and rivers, look up Passau-based **Bichlmoser & Oberhofer** (☎ 49-851/966-3603; www. outdoor-outdoor.com). For everything from learning how to hold a paddle to white-water rafting, link up with **Essener Kanuschule** (☎ 49-201/8906-0102; www.kanuschule.de), in the Ruhr region.

Fishing
Germany has complex rules and regulations governing fishing and angling, both on the sea and on inland waters. Some hotels in popular fishing areas—Bavaria, the Harz Mountains, the Mecklenburg lakes, and others—organize packages that take care of these details.

Information is available from the **Verband Deutscher Sportfischer** (German Sportfishing Association; ☎ 49-69/857-0695; www.vdsf. de) and the **Deutscher Anglerverband** (German Anglers Association; ☎ 49-30/9710-4379; www.anglerverband.com).

Golf
Most German golf courses welcome visiting players who are members of golf clubs at home. Weekday green fees are around 50€, rising to as much as 100€ on Saturday and Sunday. For information about golf courses around the country, contact the **Deutscher Golf Verband** (German Golf Association; ☎ 49-611/990-200; www.golf.de/dgv). The Swabian Allgäu region has several good courses. **Golf Oberstaufen Steibis** (☎ 49-8386/8529; www.golf-oberstaufen.de), at Oberstaufen, is an 18-hole course close to a forest and nature park. Ofterschwang, on scenic Tiefenberger Moor, has **Golfresort Sonnenalp** (☎ 49-8321/272-181; www.golfresort-sonnenalp.de). A good 18-hole course is found at **Golfclub Bodensee-Weissensberg** (☎ 49-8389/89190; www.gcbw.de), on the Bodensee (Lake Constance) in southern Germany. Farther north, Augsburg has a fine 18-hole course at **Golfclub Augsburg** (☎ 49-8234/5621; www.golfclub-augsburg.de).

Hiking & Mountain Climbing
These sports are popular in the German uplands. It's estimated that Germany has more than 80,000 marked hiking and mountain-walking tracks. The **Deutscher Wanderverband** (German Hiking Association;

> *Information about Germany's many wellness resorts (such as Nassauer Hof's in Wiesbaden, pictured here) is available from the German Spa Association.*

☎ 49-561/938-730; www.wanderbares-deutschland.de) services the trails and offers details about trails, shelters, huts, and addresses of hiking associations in various regions. Many local tourist offices will supply hiking maps. For sure, the best Alpine hiking is in the Bavarian Alps, especially around the Eckbauer (1,240m/4,068 ft.), on the southern fringe of Garmisch-Partenkirchen (p. 348). Berchtesgaden (p. 344) is the gateway to Berchtesgaden National Park, which offers some of the best-organized hikes; the park's visitor center, Doktorberg 6, Berchtesgaden (☎ 49-8652/968-640; www.nationalpark-berchtesgaden.bayern.de), can hook you up with groups that offer hikes. The **Deutscher Alpenverein** (German Alpine Club; ☎ 49-89/140-030; www.alpenverein.de) owns and operates 50 huts in and around the Alps that are open to all mountaineers, and the club maintains a network of 15,000km (9,300 miles) of Alpine trails. **E.E.I. Travel** (☎ 800/927-3876; www.eeitravel.com) offers a variety of self-guided walking tours. A combined walking and cultural/historic tour in southern Germany (and into neighboring countries) is offered by

Walking Adventures International (☎ 800/779-0353; www.walkingadventures.com). For an easy 1-week walking tour around Füssen (p. 204) in Bavaria, check out the British company **HF Holidays** (☎ 44-20/8732-1250; www.hfholidays.co.uk). The Scottish company **Hooked on Walking** (☎ 44-1501/740-985; www.walking-europe.co.uk) has easy walking tours in the Rhine and Mosel wine country and in the Bavarian Alps.

Motorcycle Tours

British outfit **Bike Bavaria** (☎ 49-9922/502-534 in Germany; www.bikebavaria.com) finds its comfort zone on the winding mountain roads of southern Germany. With German extreme-touring outfit **Wheeltrax** (☎ 49-2688/988-848; www.wheeltrax.com), you get the visor down through the Rhine and Mosel valleys and on the Eifel's famous Nürburgring racing circuit.

Winter Sports

More than 300 winter-sports resorts operate in the German Alps and wooded hill country such as the Harz Mountains, the Black Forest, the Eifel, and the Thuringian Forest. In additior to outstanding ski slopes, trails, lifts, jumps, toboggan slides, and skating rinks, many larger resorts also offer ice hockey, iceboating, and bobsledding. Curling is popular as well, especially in upper Bavaria. The Olympic sports facilities at **Garmisch-Partenkirchen** (p. 348) enjoy international renown. More than 250 ski lifts are found in the German Alps, the Black Forest, and the Harz Mountains. Garmisch-Partenkirchen is Germany's most famous winter-sports center. Set in beautiful Alpine scenery, this picturesque resort is close to the **Zugspitze** (p. 324, ❸), Germany's highest mountain. A mountain railway and a cable car can take you to the peak. In the town is the Olympic Ice Stadium, built in 1936, and the Ski Stadium, which has two jumps and a slalom course. Skiers of every level will be satisfied with the slopes on the mountain above the town. **E.E.I. Travel** (☎ 800/927-3876; www.eeitravel.com) offers a variety of cross-country skiing trips.

Learning Trips & Language Classes

If you want to become proficient in German and have some fun while doing it, take a language course in Germany. There are countless language schools in the country. Explore your options online at **Languages Abroad** (www.languagesabroad.com), **Language-Directory** (www.language-directory.com), and **Language School Abroad** (www.goabroad.com). After your trip, practice your new skills with an online partner at Language Exchange Partner (mylanguageexchange.com).

Wellness Trips

In the 19th century, the heyday of German *Kurort* (spa) construction, a series of resorts was built around dozens of mineral springs bubbling from the soil. Many of these springs had been known since the Middle Ages or even since Roman times—the German word *Kur* (cure) is derived from the Latin *cura,* meaning "care"—and to each was attributed specific power to cure arthritis, gout, infertility, hypertension, gynecological problems, or another condition. For all the various medical claims made at the spas of Germany, the best reason to go is to momentarily escape the stress of everyday life. Baden-Baden (p. 380) in the Black Forest has the waters at its opulent Kurhaus, a casino, sightseeing attractions, deluxe hotels, and good food. Though less grand, Wiesbaden, outside Frankfurt, has a fine open-air thermal pool, and its thermal baths include both indoor and outdoor pools, along with endless massage rooms and solariums. Nearby Bad Homburg in the foothills of the Taunus Mountains, enjoys a reputation for the treatment of heart and circulatory diseases. (For more on Wiesbaden and Bad Homburg, see "Spa Side Trips from Frankfurt," p. 446.) Bad Reichenhall (p. 331) in the Bavarian Alps is known for its saline waters and the treatment of respiratory problems, skin ailments, and rheumatism. More information is available from the Deutscher Heilbäderverband (German Spa Association; ☎ 49-30/2463-6920; www.deutscher-heilbaederverband.de).

Wine & Beer Trips

Wine tours of the Rhine, Mosel, and Saar districts are offered by **Wine Tours of the World** (☎ 888/635-8007; www.winetoursoftheworld.com). Among its large program of international wine tours, **Arblaster & Clarke Wine Tours Worldwide** (☎ 44-1730/263-111; www.winetours.co.uk) has a few that cover the Rhine and the Mosel. Beer is a big deal in Germany—there are 1,300 breweries around the land. Getting to grips with a bottle or a glass of Germany's finest is made easier on an escorted beer tour run by **BeerTrips.com** (☎ 406/531-9109; www.beertrips.com). The outfit offers a Cologne, Bamberg, and Munich tour and includes Germany on tours of European beer countries.

Volunteer & Working Trips

Some of the online resources for finding social, eco, activist, educational, and other volunteer opportunities in Germany (and in other countries) include **www.goabroad.com,** which has extensive listings for jobs throughout Europe and links to study and volunteer options. For resources and tips on volunteering abroad, along with volunteer and paid postings, visit **www.idealist.org.** If you are interested in working on a family farm or on a conservation project, look up **www.transitionsabroad.com.**

> Visitors relaxing in an open-air cafe near Hamburg's beautiful Rathaus.

15
The Savvy
Traveler

Before You Go

Tourist Offices

For more information on Germany, contact a **German National Tourist Board** office. Please note that walk-in offices have been closed worldwide and information is available only by phone or mail, or online at www.germany-tourism.de or www.cometogermany.com. For specific information on a particular city or region, see "Visitor Information" in the Fast Facts sections at the end of every chapter.

IN GERMANY

The German National Tourist Board headquarters is at Beethovenstrasse 69, 60325 Frankfurt am Main (☎ 069/2123-8800).

IN AUSTRALIA

P.O. Box 1461, Sydney NSW 2001 (☎ 02/8296-0487).

IN CANADA

480 University Ave., Suite 1500, Toronto, ON M5G 1V2 (☎ 416/968-1685).

IN SOUTH AFRICA

c/o Lufthansa German Airlines, P.O. Box 10883, Johannesburg 2000 (☎ 011/643-1615).

IN THE UNITED KINGDOM

P.O. Box 2695, London W1A 3TN (☎ 020/7317-0908; fax 020/7317-0917).

IN THE UNITED STATES

122 E. 42nd St., Suite 2000, New York, NY 10168-0072 (☎ 212/661-7200); P.O. Box 59594, Chicago, IL 60659-9594 (☎ 312/644-0723).

Best Times to Go

Germany is a year-round destination and when you travel depends on what you want to see and experience there. The cultural and performing arts scene in the big cities—Berlin, Munich, Hamburg, Cologne, and Dresden—generally kicks off in September and continues into early summer, but there are also major summer festivals and events. If you want to hike in the Alps or bike along the Bodensee, summer is obviously the right time to travel. If you want to schuss down the Zugspitze, plan your trip for between December and February. Every season has it own reasons and rewards.

The high seasons for travel in Germany are from Easter to the end of September with another peak in December (for the Christmas markets). The country is most crowded during May and June; from April to September, the lines for major attractions, such as Neuschwanstein and Linderhof castles in Bavaria, or the Reichstag dome in Berlin, can be more than 2 hours long. July and August may be less expensive because that's when Germans take off on their own holidays, and many hotels consequently offer lower summer rates. October to November and January to March are the low seasons, except in the winter ski and sports resorts, where high season is November to February. In the winter months, museums, castles, and tourist offices have shorter hours and may be closed on certain days.

Festivals and Special Events

Germany hums year-round with festivals and special events of all kinds, some of which are listed here. Verify dates beforehand with the German National Tourist Board (see "Tourist Offices," above) or the tourist board of the city where the event is taking place (see the "Fast Facts" sections of individual chapters).

JANUARY

New Year's Day International Ski Jumping, held on January 1 in Garmisch-Partenkirchen, is one of Europe's major winter sporting events.

FEBRUARY

In Berlin, the well-respected **Berlin International Film Festival** is a weeklong event during the second week in February that showcases the work of international film directors in addition to the latest German films (see "Berlin's Big-Screen Moment," p. 125). **Fasching** (Carnival) festivals take place in Catholic cities throughout Germany, reaching their peak on the Tuesday (Mardi Gras) before Ash Wednesday; celebrations in Cologne and Munich are particularly famous.

Useful Websites

The German National Tourist Board website, www.cometogermany.com, is your best source for general information on German life and culture. Websites for specific cities and regions are listed in every chapter. Many German websites end not with *.com* but with *.de* (for Deutschland).

MAY

Hamburg Summer is the umbrella-name given to a summer-long (May–July) series of cultural events in Hamburg that includes concerts, plays, festivals, and special exhibitions. During the **Historisches Festspiel** (History Festival), Rothenburg ob der Tauber celebrates the story of how a brave mayor saved the town from destruction by drinking a huge tankard of wine, an event called **Der Meistertrunk** (see "The Master Draught," p. 238). The festival takes place over a 4-day period every Whitsuntide (Pentecost, the seventh Sunday after Easter), and also in early September and twice during October. Once every decade from mid-May to early October, the small Bavarian town of Oberammergau becomes the site of a world-famous religious spectacle, the **Passionspiele** (see "Oberammergau's Passion Play," p. 330). It will next be performed in 2020.

JUNE

The renowned **Bachfest/Bach Festival** takes place in mid-June (exact dates vary yearly) in Leipzig; it features performances of Johann Sebastian Bach's work in the famous Thomaskirche, where he was choirmaster, and in other churches and concert halls. In the romantic university city of Heidelberg fireworks enliven the sky for the **Castle Illumination** on a Saturday in early June, mid-July, and early September. Germany's largest **Gay Pride** festivals take place in Berlin (www.berlin.gay-web.de) during the last weekend in June, and Cologne (www.koeln.gay-web.de) during the first weekend in June; they feature parades, performances, and street fairs. On the last weekend in June, enjoy vintages from the Black Forest area during the **Weintagen** (Wine Days) in Freiburg im Breisgau, in the Münsterplatz surrounding the city's magnificent cathedral.

JULY

One of Europe's major opera events, the **Richard-Wagner-Festspiele** (Richard Wagner Festival), takes place from July to late August in the composer's famous Festspielhaus (Festival House) in Bayreuth (see "Music in Bayreuth," p. 223). The **Schleswig-Holstein Music Festival** is one of the best music festivals in Europe; classical concerts take place from mid-July to August or early September in venues in and around the lovely old city of Lübeck.

AUGUST

In July or August, during **Weinkost** (Wine and Food Fair) in Freiburg im Breisgau, local residents and visitors enjoy regional food specialties and the first vintages from grapes grown in the Black Forest district. **Nürnberger Herbstfest** (Fall Festival) is a big Frankish folk festival that takes place in Nuremberg during the last week of August and first week of September, featuring folk music, jazz concerts, and events for the whole family. During the last week of August, arts and pleasure abound at **Alstervergnügen** (Alster Pleasures) in Hamburg; events take place around Binnenalster Lake and include food stalls, fireworks, and shows. At the **Stuttgart Wine Festival** during the last week of August, wine lovers converge on Schillerplatz in Stuttgart to taste a selection of more than 350 Württemberg wines and sample regional food specialties.

SEPTEMBER

Oktoberfest, Germany's most famous festival, happens mostly in September, not October (mid-Sept to first Sunday in Oct), in Munich (see "Oktoberfest," p. 278); most activities occur at Theresienwiese, where local breweries sponsor gigantic tents that can each hold up to 6,000 beer drinkers. Stuttgart's 16-day **Beer Festival,** dating back to 1818, is the second largest in Germany after Munich's Oktoberfest; it begins in late September with a grand procession of horse-drawn beer wagons and people in traditional costumes and features food, rides, and tents for beer drinkers. One of the high points on the cultural calendar of Germany, the **Berliner Festwochen** (Festival Weeks) brings an international roster of performing artists to Berlin from September to mid-October for opera, symphony, and theatrical presentations.

OCTOBER

The **Frankfurt Book Fair** is the largest book fair in Europe and a major event in the world of international book publishing, taking place in mid-October.

NOVEMBER

The annual **Jazz-Fest,** staged at the Philharmonie in Berlin during the first week of November, attracts some of the world's finest jazz artists. **Hamburger Dom** (also called Winter Dom), an annual amusement fair in

GERMANY'S AVERAGE DAYTIME TEMPERATURE & RAINFALL

BERLIN	JAN	FEB	MAR	APR	MAY	JUNE	JULY	AUG	SEPT	OCT	NOV	DEC
Temp. (°F)	30	32	40	48	53	60	64	62	56	49	40	34
Temp. (°C)	1	0	4	9	12	16	18	17	13	9	4	1
Rainfall (in.)	2.2	1.6	1.2	1.6	2.3	2.9	3.2	2.7	2.2	1.6	2.4	1.9
FRANKFURT	JAN	FEB	MAR	APR	MAY	JUNE	JULY	AUG	SEPT	OCT	NOV	DEC
Temp. (°F)	34	36	42	49	57	63	66	66	58	50	41	35
Temp. (°C)	1	2	6	9	14	17	19	19	14	10	5	2
Rainfall (in.)	1.6	1.6	2.0	2.0	2.4	2.8	2.4	2.8	2.0	2.0	2.0	2.0

Hamburg, is the biggest public event in northern Germany, taking place from November 9 to December 9.

DECEMBER

A Christmas Market, generally called a *Weihnachtsmarkt* (*Weihnachten* means Christmas) or a *Christkindlesmarkt* (literally, "Christ Child Market"), takes place in many town squares throughout Germany from the last weekend in November to Christmas. You'll find Christmas Markets in Berlin, Cologne, Dresden, Frankfurt, Heidelberg, Leipzig, Munich, Nuremberg, Rothenburg ob der Tauber, Stuttgart, and Weimar, among other cities. Contact the individual tourist office of each city (see the "Fast Facts" sections of individual chapters) or the German National Tourist Board (see "Tourist Offices," above) for details.

Weather

As in many parts of the world, the weather in Germany has become less predictable. Locals in northern Germany will tell you that they now get less snow and more rain; in southern Germany they'll tell you that the climate is hotter and drier than it used to be. So be prepared for variation. Recent summers brought record-breaking heat waves, and even in autumn many parts of Germany can be warmer than expected.

Overall, Germany has a predominantly mild, temperate climate. Average summer temperatures range from 72°–80°F (22°–27°C). The average winter temperature hovers around 32°F (0°C). That said, bear in mind that the climate is constantly affected by colliding continental and maritime air masses from the Baltic and North seas, resulting in plenty of unpredictable weather, especially in the north.

Cellphones (Mobiles)

In Germany, a cellphone is called a *Handy* (pronounced as it's spelled). If your cellphone is on a GSM (Global System for Mobiles) and you have a world-capable multiband phone, you can make and receive calls across Germany and the rest of Europe. Just call your wireless operator and ask that "international roaming" be activated on your account. Having an unlocked phone will enable you to install a prepaid SIM card (found at local cellphone shops) in Germany; you'll get a local phone number and much lower calling rates. (Not all phones work on all networks, so show your phone to the salesperson.)

You can rent a phone from any number of sites in Germany, including kiosks at airports and car-rental agencies, but it's often more cost-effective to rent one before you leave home. Two good wireless rental companies are **InTouch USA** (☎ 800/872-7626; www.intouchglobal.com) and **Roadpost** (☎ 888/290-1606 or 905/272-5665; www.roadpost.com).

Sustainable Tourism

In the areas of environmental protection and sustainability, Germany is a world leader. Although Germany suffered one of history's most devastating attacks on the environment (World War II), in the postwar years it became a front-runner in preserving the environment and protecting nature. Recycling has been a way of life for decades, and renewable energy sources are regularly being implemented. The country excels in the availability, affordability, and use of its public transportation systems, both national and local. Germans didn't exactly invent walking o hiking across the countryside, but you would think they did when you notice the numbers of citizens who prefer this form of exploration. It's a way to stay in good health, enjoy nature, and avoid harming the environment, all at the same time.

German hotels follow the general environmental waste-reduction plans that are now a part of international travel: Hang up your towel if you want to reuse it (thus saving on detergent use).

Many organizations are devoted to ecotourism. **Biosphere Expeditions,** P.O. Box 917750, Longwood, FL 32791 (☎ 800/407-5671; www.biosphere-expeditions.org), sets up eco-friendly tours to the Bavarian Alps, among other places. **Earthwatch,** 3 Clocktower Place, Ste. 1000, P.O. Box 75, Maynard, MA 01754 (☎ 800/776-0188; www. earthwatch.org), often includes Germany in its 1- to 3-week jaunts to promote conservation of natural resources.

Increasingly popular is spending a holiday on a Germany farm. **Willing Workers on Organic Farms,** Postfach 210259, 01263 Dresden (www.woof.de) charges a membership of 20€; participants get free room and board at a variety of organic farms throughout the country, but they must be willing to work. Another good resource for a Germany farm stay is **www.landtourismus.de.** At some of these farms, guests can help with farm chores; at others, the property has been transformed from a working farm to a charming guesthouse.

For general ecotourism information, **Responsible Travel** (www.responsibletravel. com) is a great source of sustainable travel ideas. **Sustainable Travel International** (www.sustainabletravelinternational.org) promotes responsible tourism practices. **ecotravel.com** is part online magazine and part directory that lets you search for touring companies: water-based, land-based, spiritually oriented, and so on. In the U.K., the **Association of Independent Tour Operators** (AITO; www.aito.co.uk) is a group of interesting specialist operators leading the field in making holidays sustainable.

Getting There

By Plane

The German word for airport is *Flughafen* (*floog*-haf-en). Direct flights from the U.S. and other non-European countries arrive at Frankfurt, Munich, Berlin, Hamburg, and Düsseldorf. You can also fly into Cologne, Stuttgart, Nuremberg, and other cities, but if you're coming from outside Europe, these routes require a change of planes—usually in Frankfurt, Amsterdam, Copenhagen, Paris, or London.

Lufthansa (☎ 800/645-3880 in the U.S., 800/563-5954 in Canada, 01/805-83-84-26 in Germany, 1300/655-727 in Australia, 0800/945-220 in New Zealand; www. lufthansa.com) operates the most frequent service and flies to the greatest number of Germany's airports. From North America, Lufthansa serves 23 gateway cities. The largest of the gateways is the New York City area, where flights depart from both JFK and Newark airports. Lufthansa also offers service from the U.K., Australia, and New Zealand, and is part of the Star Alliance, which also includes Continental, United, US Airways, and Air Canada.

FROM NORTH AMERICA

American Airlines (☎ 800/443-7300; www. aa.com) flies nonstop from Chicago and Dallas to Frankfurt daily, and American's flights connect easily with ongoing flights to many other German cities on Lufthansa or British Airways. **Continental Airlines** (☎ 800/525-0280; www.continental.com) offers daily nonstop service from Newark to Frankfurt. **Delta Airlines** (☎ 800/241-4141; www.delta.com) offers daily connecting service to Hamburg via Paris and nonstop to Frankfurt from Atlanta, Cincinnati, and New York (JFK); to Munich nonstop from Atlanta; and to Berlin nonstop from JFK. **United Airlines** (☎ 800/538-2929; www.ual.com) offers daily nonstops from Los Angeles, New York, and Chicago to Frankfurt and Munich, and because it is a Star Alliance member, all German flights by Lufthansa or Air Canada will also be honored as a part of a United ticket; **US Airways** (☎ 800/428-4322; www.usairways.com) also flies to Frankfurt and Munich daily (with nonstops from Charlotte and Philadelphia). **Air Canada** (☎ 888/247-2262; www.aircanada.com) offers direct flights to Frankfurt from Calgary, Montreal, Ottawa, Toronto, and Vancouver, and to Munich from Toronto.

FROM THE UNITED KINGDOM

From London, **British Airways** (☎ 0870/850-9850; www.britishairways.com) offers direct flights from Heathrow airport to Frankfurt, Munich, Berlin, Düsselfdorf, Hamburg, and Stuttgart. **British Midland** (☎ 0870/607-0555; www.flybmi.com) flies direct from Heathrow to Berlin, Cologne, Düsseldorf, Frankfurt, Hamburg, Hannover, and Munich. Discount airline **Ryanair** (☎ 050/503-770; www.ryanair.com) serves Düsseldorf, Frankfurt, and Bremen from London's Stansted airport. Ryanair also flies direct to Frankfurt from Edinburgh, Dublin, and Kerry. **EasyJet** (www.easyjet.com) flies from Gatwick airport to Berlin, Cologne, Hamburg, and Munich.

FROM AUSTRALIA & NEW ZEALAND

Qantas (☎ 131313; www.qantas.com.au) flies to Frankfurt from Sydney. From New Zealand there are no direct flights; you can go through Sydney with Qantas or take one of Lufthansa's connecting flights.

PACKAGE TOURS

A package tour that includes airfare, hotel, and transportation to and from the airport usually costs less than the hotel alone on a tour you book yourself. **Liberty Travel** (☎ 888/271-1584; www.libertytravel.com) is one of the biggest packagers; several online travel agencies—**Expedia.com, Travelocity. com, Orbitz.com,** and **Lastminute.com**—also offer packages. Other good sources of package deals are the airlines, including: **Continental Airlines Vacations** (☎ 800/301-3800; www.covacations.com); **Delta Vacations** (☎ 800-221-6666; www.deltavacations.com); and **United Vacations** (☎ 800/800-1504; www.unitedvacations.com).

ESCORTED GENERAL-INTEREST TOURS

Several companies offer escorted tours to Berlin, Munich, and destinations elsewhere in Germany (or include Germany in a Europe-wide tour). Many escorted-tour companies cater to special interests, such as castles on the Rhine, while others are more general. A good travel agent can help you find a tour that suits your particular interests. See chapter 14,

"The Best Special Interest Trips," for more on tour operators offering trips in Germany.

By Train

Germany is extremely well connected by train to the rest of Europe. EuroCity (EC) trains connect Germany with neighboring countries, and sleek, high-speed Thalys trains link Cologne and Düsseldorf with Paris and Brussels. When you're traveling between countries, border formalities, such as passport checks, are taken care of on board the train. Major cities, such as Berlin and Hamburg, have more than one station, usually including one main or central inner-city station called a *Hauptbahnhof* (*howpt*-bahn-hof).

Various money-saving rail passes are available through **Rail Europe** (☎ 888/382-7245 in the U.S., 800/361-7245 in Canada; www. raileurope.com). The **German Rail Pass** allows for 4 to 10 consecutive or nonconsecutive days of travel in 1 month within Germany; the **German Rail Twinpass,** for two adults (they do not have to be married and can be of the same sex) traveling together in first or second class represents a 50% savings over single prices. A **German Rail Youth Pass** is valid for those younger than 26 and is available only in second class. Passes for children 6 to 11 are half the adult price; children younger than 6 travel free. A German Rail Pass also entitles the bearer to free or discounted travel on selected bus routes operated by **Deutsche Touring/Europabus,** including destinations not serviced by trains, and free travel on **KD German Line steamers** (day trips only) along the Rhine, Main, and Mosel rivers.

If you'll be traveling in other European countries, the **Eurail Global Pass** is one of Europe's best bargains, offering unlimited first-class rail travel in 20 countries, including Germany. Other options include the **Eurail Global Pass Flexi,** which allows you a certain number of days to travel within a 2-month period; the **Eurail Global Pass Saver** for two to five people traveling together; and the **Eurail Selectpass,** allowing travelers to select three, four, or five adjoining countries linked by rail or ferry. *Note:* Eurail passes can be bought and used only by non-European residents; you cannot buy them in Europe.

By Ship and Ferry

Germany's northern coast lies along the North Sea and the Baltic Sea. International ferry services are available from the United Kingdom, Denmark, Norway, Sweden, Finland, Poland, Russia, Latvia, and Estonia. **DFDS Seaways** (☎ 800/533-3755, ext. 114, in North America; www.seaeurope.com) provides ferry service from Harwich, England, to Hamburg. **Silja Line** (same telephone and website as for DFDS Seaways) sails from Helsinki across the Baltic to Rostock in northern Germany.

There are many cruises that travel down Germany's rivers, sometimes from or to other European cities. **Viking River Cruises** (☎ 800/304-9616 in North America, ☎ 020/8780-7998 in the U.K., ☎ 0800/1887-10033 in Germany; www.vikingrivers.com) sails down the Rhine from Amsterdam to Basel and also on the Elbe in eastern Germany.

Getting Around

By Train

Traveling by train in Germany is fast, efficient, and fun. Service between major German cities is excellent, and you can get to all but the smallest villages by train.

The railway system is operated by **Deutsche Bahn** (German Railways, abbreviated DB). If you need train-related information while you're in Germany, call DB's general information number at ☎ 11861; outside Germany, call ☎ 49-1805/996-633 (regular calling charges apply for both numbers). An English-speaking operator will be available to help you. You also can access train information online, in English, at DB's website, www.bahn.de.

See also the "Getting There" section, above, for information on rail passes.

By Car

The only time you'll really need to rent a car in Germany is if you want to explore more of the countryside or take one of the scenic driving tours, such as the Romantische Strasse (Romantic Road; p. 206) or Deutsche Alpenstrasse (German Alpine Road; p. 332).

RENTALS

Renting a car is fairly easy in Germany. Drivers from the United States, Canada, Australia, and other non-European Union countries must have a valid driver's license, but no other special license is required. It's a good idea to make all the arrangements *before* you leave home, at least 7 days in advance. You can pick up your car at most airports and major train stations, or at an office within German cities. You can often rent a car in one German city and return it in another for no additional charge.

International car-rental firms in Germany include **Alamo** (☎ 800/462-5266 in the U.S., ☎ 0800/272-200 in the U.K.; www.alamo.com); **Auto Europe** (☎ 800/223-5555 in the U.S., ☎ 207/842-2222 in Australia, ☎ 0800/169-6417 in the U.K.; www.autoeurope.com); **Avis** (☎ 800/331-1212 in the U.S., ☎ 136-333 in Australia, ☎ 0870/606-0100 in the U.K.; www.avis.com); **Budget** (☎ 800/527-0700 in the U.S., ☎ 800/472-3325 in Europe; www.budget.com); **Hertz** (☎ 800/654-3001 in the U.S., ☎ 800/263-0600 in Canada, ☎ 01805/333-535 in Germany; www.hertz.com); and **National** (☎ 800/227-7368 in the U.S., ☎ 800/227-3876 in Europe and Australia, ☎ 0990/565-656 in the U.K.; www.nationalcar.com).

You can also rent a car through **Rail Europe** (☎ 877/257-2887 in the U.S., ☎ 800/361-7245 in Canada; www.raileurope.com) at the same time you book your German Rail Pass or Eurail Pass. They offer a **German Rail 'n Drive** option that gives you 2 days of unlimited train travel and 2 days of Hertz car rental within 1 month, and you can purchase extra days for both train travel and car rental.

The A roads that make up the **Autobahn** form Germany's main long-distance highway network. In theory, the Autobahn does not have a speed limit in the left, fast lane, but the government recommends a speed limit of 130kmph (80 mph). A German driver on the Autobahn can be like one possessed, so you may prefer the slower, right lane. The B roads, or **Bundesstrassen** (state roads) vary in quality from region to region. The Bundesstrassen in the major touring areas of the Romantic Road and the Alps in Bavaria, the Rhine Valley, and the Black Forest are smoothly paved and kept in good repair. In eastern Germany, some secondary and local roads are not in such good shape. The best regional **maps** are published by Michelin and Hallweg and are available at major bookstores throughout Germany.

DRIVING RULES

If you're going to drive in Germany, you need to know a few general facts. Signs show distances and speed limits in kilometers (km) and kilometers per hour (kmph). A kilometer is 0.62 of a mile, a mile is 1.62km. Unless posted differently, speed limits are: 50kmph (31 mph) in towns; 100kmph (62 mph) on regular highways; 130kmph (81 mph) on Autobahns. On Autobahns, the left lane is the fast lane. And I mean fast. *Do not drive in this lane unless you are passing another car.* You can pass other vehicles only on the left. German motorists generally flash their lights if they want you to move over so they can pass. The law requires that all passengers wear seat belts. Children younger than 12 must sit on booster seats in the back so that regular seat belts can be used effectively; children younger than 4 must ride in a car seat. You must use low-beam headlights at night and during fog, heavy rain, and snowfalls. You must stop for pedestrians in crosswalks; they have the right of way. Driving while intoxicated and drinking while driving are very serious offenses in Germany. If you've had more than a glass of wine or beer, don't risk driving.

Most of Germany's road signs are standard international signs, but below are a few important words you should know.

Anfang	Start, or beginning
Ausfahrt	Exit
Baustelle	Building site, or roadwork
Einbahnstrasse	One-way street
Einfahrt	Entrance
Ende	End
Gefahr	Danger
Links einbiegen	Turn left
Rechts einbiegen	Turn right
Verengte Fahrbahn	Road narrows
Vorsicht	Attention! Look out!

PARKING

Parking in the center of most big towns is difficult, expensive, or just plain impossible, because most historic town centers are for pedestrians only. Look outside the center for parking lots and parking garages, which are always identified by a large **P**; in some larger cities, signs on the way into town indicate how much space is available in various lots or parking garages. Most parking lots use an automated ticket system. You insert coins (or a credit card) to purchase a certain amount of time.

By Plane

Flying within Germany makes sense if you're traveling from, say, Hamburg or Berlin in the north to Munich in the south. Such a trip normally takes 6 to 7 hours by train or car but only about an hour by plane. Flying doesn't make much sense for short distances, however; when you factor in getting to the airport, going through security, waiting for your departure, and then getting into the city after your plane lands, it's cheaper, more convenient, and just as fast to travel shorter distances via train.

Tips on Accommodations

In general, Germany has high standards for accommodations. Hotel associations, regional tourist associations, and local tourist boards control standards in all categories of accommodations. Even the smallest *pension* must open its doors for inspection to be able to list and rent rooms. These same state agencies and tourist boards rate hotels according to a star system. The system isn't used to recommend hotels but rather simply to categorize them according to their amenities. A 1-star hotel is basic and inexpensive. A 5-star hotel is a luxury property with an on-site spa or pool and a rate at the top end of the price spectrum. *Note:* In this guide, star ratings are based on our personal recommendations, not the system described here.

Breakfast (*Frühstück*) always is included in the price of a room, except at some boutique and high-end luxury hotels. If the word *Garni* is part of the hotel name, breakfast is the only meal it serves.

Smoke-free rooms and smoke-free floors are catching on in Germany, mostly in midrange to high-end hotels. However, Europeans generally are not as committed to smoke-free environments as are Americans. The term for "no smoking" is *nicht rauchen* (nickt *rau-*kin).

Wi-Fi or Internet service is available at almost all hotels in Germany, except in the simplest and cheapest accommodations (although it's usually available at hostels). Charges for this service vary: In higher-end hotels you'll probably have to pay by the hour or day, in others it's a standard amenity.

Booking in Advance

In Germany's large cities, including Berlin, Munich, Frankfurt, and Cologne, booking your hotel room ahead is essential, especially if you're going to be there during the summer or a special event (such as Munich during Oktoberfest). Booking ahead isn't as important in the rest of Germany, but it's still a good idea, especially during high season. Off season, especially in the middle of winter, you won't have a problem booking a room on the spot wherever you are, unless a trade show is going on.

Tourist information centers, located in or near the main train stations in all German cities and towns, can help you find a room. Some charge nothing, some a small fixed fee (usually no more than 4€); others charge 10% of the first night's hotel rate, but you get that back at the hotel, so the service ends up costing nothing. Most tourist information centers also have a free directory of local accommodations.

Types of Accommodations

You find all types of lodging in Germany, from luxury Old World palaces and super-high-tech showoffs to hip boutique hotels, small family-run hotels, cozy inns, chain hotels, rustic guesthouses, and simple rooms in private homes and apartments. A Gasthaus (*gahst*-house) or Gasthof (*gahst*-hofe) is basically an inn with a restaurant that serves breakfast, lunch, and dinner to hotel guests and outside patrons. A pension (pen-see-*own*) is the same as a B&B (bed-and-breakfast): a room in a private home or apartment, with breakfast included in the price. In a small village, finding a room may be as simple as spotting a sign in a house window that reads Zimmer frei (room available); some half-million beds are available in private homes across the country. Keep in mind that many pensions operate on a cash-only basis.

Germany Fast Facts

ATMs/Cashpoints

In German cities, you can easily find 24-hour ATMs in airports and train stations and outside banks. You can get cash 24 hours a day

using your bank card or, if you know your PIN, you can get a cash advance from your credit card. **Cirrus** (☎ 800/424-7787; www. mastercard.com) and **Plus** (☎ 800/843-7587; www.visa.com/atms) are the most popular networks.

Business Hours

Most banks are open Monday through Friday 8:30am to 1pm and 2:30pm to 4pm. Money exchanges at airports and train stations are generally open daily 6am to 10pm. Most businesses are open Monday through Friday 9am to 5pm and Saturday 9am to 1pm. Shops in smaller villages and towns generally are open Monday to Friday 9 or 10am to 6 or 6:30pm and Saturday 9am to 1pm; in larger cities, stores in main shopping areas generally stay open until 8pm or later and also open on Sunday 11am or noon to 5pm.

Credit Cards

American Express, Diners Club, MasterCard, and Visa are accepted at many places throughout Germany, but not universally, and some establishments only accept European cards. Smaller pensions (B&Bs) and restaurants may not accept credit cards at all. If your credit card is lost or stolen, call the following numbers in Germany: **American Express** ☎ 954/503-8850 (collect); **Diners Club** ☎ 702/797-5532 (collect); **MasterCard** ☎ 800/819-1040 (toll-free); **Visa** ☎ 800/811-8440 (toll-free) or 417/581-9994 (collect). You should also call your credit card company before your trip to let them know you'll be using it overseas; some companies will freeze your account if they see unusual charges.

Customs

You can take into Germany most personal effects and the following items duty-free: one video camera or two still cameras with 10 rolls of film each; a laptop PC, provided it shows signs of use; 400 cigarettes, 50 cigars, or 250 grams of tobacco; 2 liters of wine or 1 liter of liquor per person over 17 years old; fishing gear; one bicycle; skis; tennis or squash racquets; and golf clubs.

Rules governing what you can bring back duty-free from Germany vary from country to country and are subject to change. For information on what you're allowed to bring home, contact one of the following agencies:

U.S. CITIZENS

U.S. Customs & Border Protection (CBP), 1300 Pennsylvania Ave. NW, Washington, DC 20229 (☎ 877/287-8667; www.cbp.gov).

CANADIAN CITIZENS

Canada Border Services Agency (☎ 800/461-9999 in Canada, or 204/983-3500; www.cbsa-asfc.gc.ca).

U.K. CITIZENS

HM Customs & Excise at ☎ 0845/010-9000 (from outside the U.K., 020/8929-0152), or consult their website at www.hmce.gov.uk.

AUSTRALIAN CITIZENS

Australian Customs Service at ☎ 1300/363-263, or log on to www.customs.gov.au.

NEW ZEALAND CITIZENS

New Zealand Customs, The Customhouse, 17–21 Whitmore St., Box 2218, Wellington (☎ 04/473-6099 or 0800/428-786; www.customs.govt.nz).

Electricity

Germany uses the 220-volt (50 Hz) system. For U.S. appliances you need a transformer and a converter plug with two round prongs that will fit into German sockets. U.K. 240-volt appliances need a continental adaptor.

Embassies & Consulates

All embassies and consulates are located in Berlin.

The **Australian Embassy** is at Wallstrasse 76–79 (☎ 030/880-0880; www.germany.embassy.gov.au); open Monday, Wednesday, and Friday 9am to 11am.

The **Canadian Embassy** is at Leipziger Platz 17 (☎ 030/203-120; www.berlin.gc.ca); open Monday through Friday 8:30am to 12:30pm and 1:30pm to 5pm.

The **Irish Embassy** is at Friedrichstrasse 200 (☎ 030/220-720; www.embassyofireland.de); open Monday through Friday 9:30am to 12:30pm and 2:30pm to 4:45pm.

The **New Zealand Embassy** is at Friedrichstrasse 60 (☎ 030/206-210; www.nzembassy.com/germany); Monday through Friday 9am to 1pm and 2pm to 5:30pm.

The **South African Embassy** is at Tiergartenstrasse 18 (☎ 030/220-730; www.suedafrika.org/de); open Monday through Friday 8am to 12:45pm and 1:30pm to 4:30pm.

The **United Kingdom Embassy** is at Wilhelmstrasse 70–71 (☎ 030/204-570; www.ukingermany.fco.gov.uk/de); open Monday through Friday 8am to noon and 1pm to 4:30pm.

The **United States Embassy** is at Pariser Platz 2 (☎ 030/238-5174; http://berlin.usembassy.gov/germany). The office for passport, visa, and U.S. citizen services is at Clayallee 170 (☎ 030/832-9223); open Monday through Friday 8:30am to noon.

Emergencies

Throughout Germany, dial ☎ 110 for police, ☎ 112 for fire or to call an ambulance.

Family Travel

The website of the **German National Tourist Office** (www.cometogermany.com) has a section on family travel and is a good place to begin researching your trip. You can find good family-oriented vacation advice on the Internet from sites like the **Family Travel Forum** (www.familytravelforum.com), **Family Travel Network** (www.familytravelnetwork.com), **Travel with Your Kids** (www.travelwithyourkids.com), and **Family Travel Files** (www.thefamilytravelfiles.com). For a list of other family-friendly travel resources, visit www.frommers.com/planning.

Look for the kids icon as you flip through this book, which highlights hotels, restaurants, and attractions that are particularly family friendly.

Admission prices for attractions throughout Germany are reduced for children 6 to 14; kids younger than 6 almost always get in for free. If you're traveling with children, always check to see whether the attraction offers a money-saving **family ticket,** which considerably reduces the admission price for a group of two adults and two or more children. The same is true for public transportation: Low-priced family or group tickets usually are available. On trains, children 6 to 11 pay half the adult fare, and children younger than 6 travel free.

Gay & Lesbian Travelers

Germany is one of the most "developed" countries in the world when it comes to gay pride, gay culture, and gay tourism. In 2008, Berlin's openly gay mayor and the German Minister of Culture unveiled a memorial to the homosexual victims of Nazi persecution.

Located between Potsdamer Platz and the Brandenburg Gate, in Tiergarten park, the simple concrete structure has a window with a continuous film loop showing two men kissing.

Berlin, Munich, Hamburg, Frankfurt, and Cologne all have large gay communities, but gay life flourishes outside the big cities, too. A network of gay or gay-friendly restaurants, cafes, stores, bars, dance clubs, and community centers exists throughout the country, in small towns and large.

Gay (*schwul*) and lesbian (*lesbisch*) couples (or friends) qualify for family tickets on public transportation in many German cities. With most family, or *Gruppen* (group), tickets, all that matters is that two (or more) individuals travel together.

Every summer, parades and special events celebrate gay pride. Berlin holds its annual Gay & Lesbian Street Festival in mid-June, celebrates its Christopher Street Day and Parade around the third weekend in June, and stages its famous Loveparade in mid-July. Munich celebrates Christopher Street Day in mid-July. Hamburg celebrates with a Gay Pride Parade and Festival around June 8 to 10. Cologne's Christopher Street Weekend usually is the first weekend in June. Frankfurt's Christopher Street Weekend takes place around the third weekend in July.

The **German National Tourist Office** website (www.cometogermany.com) has a section on gay and lesbian travel and is a good place to begin researching your trip. Other websites you may want to check out include: www.pinkpassport.com and www.stadt.gay-web.de. For information on specific cities go to: www.berlin.gay-web.de; www.munich.gay-web.de; www.hamburg.gay-web.de; www.frankfurt.gay-web.de; and www.koeln.gay-web.de or www.gaykoeln.com.

Holidays

Many museums and attractions close on the following public holidays: January 1, Easter (including Good Friday and Easter Monday), Labor Day (May 1), Ascension Day (10 days before Pentecost/Whitsunday, the seventh Sunday after Easter), Whitmonday (the day after Pentecost/Whitsunday), Day of German Unity (October 3), Day of Prayer and Repentance (November 17), and December 25–26. In addition, some German states observe the following holidays: Epiphany (January 6), Corpus Christi (10 days after Pentecost), Assumption (August 15), and All Saints' Day (November 1).

Internet Access

Almost all hotels in Germany now offer Internet or Wi-Fi. There are also cybercafes in the larger cities; for locations, ask at the local tourist office or your hotel.

Liquor Laws

Officially, you must be 18 to consume any kind of alcoholic beverage in Germany. Bars and cafes may request proof of age. Local authorities treat drinking while driving as a very serious offense.

Medical Assistance

Most major hotels have a physician on staff or on call. If you can't get hold of a doctor and your situation is life threatening, dial the emergency service, ☎ **112.** Medical and hospital services aren't free, so be sure that you have appropriate insurance coverage before you travel.

Money

Since 2002, Germany has used the euro (€) as its currency; 1€ is divided into 100 cents. Coins come in denominations of 1¢, 2¢, 5¢, 10¢, 20¢, 50¢, 1€, and 2€. Notes are available in 5€, 10€, 20€, 50€, 100€, 200€, and 500€. As with any unfamiliar currency, euros take a bit of getting used to. The coins have varying sizes, shapes, and weights; each banknote denomination has its own color. Before departing, consult a currency exchange website such as www.oanda.com/convert/classic to check up-to-the-minute rates.

Currency exchanges, called *bureaux de change* or *Geldwechsel*, are found in airports, railway stations, post offices, and many banks.

Passports

A valid passport is the only legal form of identification accepted around the world. If you're a citizen of the United States, Australia, New Zealand, or Canada, you must have a valid passport to enter Germany. U.K. residents need an EU identity card. Getting a passport is easy, but the process takes some time.

FOR RESIDENTS OF AUSTRALIA Contact the Australian Passport Information

Service at ☎ 131-232, or visit the government website at www.passports.gov.au.

FOR RESIDENTS OF CANADA
Contact the central Passport Office, Department of Foreign Affairs and International Trade, Ottawa, ON K1A 0G3 (☎ 800/567-6868; www.ppt.gc.ca).

FOR RESIDENTS OF IRELAND
Contact the Passport Office, Setanta Centre, Molesworth Street, Dublin 2 (☎ 01/671-1633; www.irlgov.ie/iveagh).

FOR RESIDENTS OF NEW ZEALAND
 Contact the Passports Office at ☎ 0800/225-050 in New Zealand or ☎ 04/474-8100, or log on to www.passports.govt.nz.

FOR RESIDENTS OF THE UNITED KINGDOM
Visit your nearest passport office, major post office, or travel agency or contact the United Kingdom Passport Service at ☎ 0870/521-0410 or search its website at www.ukpa.gov.uk.

FOR RESIDENTS OF THE UNITED STATES
To find your regional passport office, either check the U.S. State Department website or call the National Passport Information Center toll-free number (☎ 877/487-2778) for automated information.

Pharmacies
A pharmacy is called an *Apotheke* (ah-po-*tay*-kuh); the trained staff can recommend over-the-counter medications for many common ailments. German pharmacies take turns staying open nights, on Sunday, and on holidays, and each Apotheke posts a list of those that are open during their off-hours.

Police
The German word for police is *Polizei* (po-lit-*sigh*). Throughout the country, dial ☎ **110** for emergencies.

Post Offices
The words *Deutsche Post* identify a post office. Post offices are open Monday through Friday 8am to 6pm and Saturday 8am to noon. In larger cities, the post office in the main train station may be open longer hours and on Sunday. Street mailboxes are yellow. To find international postage rates and services from Germany, check out the website for Deutsche Post, **www.deutschepost.de.**

Safety
Germany is generally a safe country to travel in, with the usual caveats to use common sense and be aware of your surroundings. At night, avoid areas around the large railway stations in Frankfurt, Munich, Berlin, and Hamburg, and take the same types of precautions against pickpockets and thieves you would in any large city.

For more information and updates on travel safety in Germany and around the world, consult the U.S. State Department's website at www.travel.state.gov; in the U.K., consult the Foreign Office's website, www.fco.gov.uk; and in Australia, consult the government travel advisory service at www.smartraveller.gov.au.

Senior Travelers
Germany won't present any problems for you if you're a senior who gets around easily. If not, be aware that not all hotels—particularly smaller, less-expensive pensions and guesthouses—have elevators. When you reserve a hotel, ask whether you'll have access to an elevator (in German *Fahrstuhl,* pronounced *far*-shtool).

Seniors (usually 60 and over) are entitled to travel bargains, including lower prices for German Rail Passes and reduced admission at museums and other attractions. Always ask about a senior discount, even if one isn't posted, and carry an ID with proof of age. *Note:* In Germany, you may find that some discounts are available only for German or EU (European Union) residents.

AARP, 601 E St. NW, Washington, DC 20049 (☎ 866/687-2277; www.aarp.org), charges an annual membership of $12.50 (anyone 50 or older can join) and offers members a wide range of benefits, including discounts on US Airways flights to Frankfurt and Munich from several U.S. cities; discounts on escorted tours from Globus and Cosmos, major tour operators offering trips to Germany; and discounts on car rentals and hotels. **Elderhostel,** 75 Federal St., Boston, MA 02110-1941 (☎ 877/426-8056), offers seniors 55 and older a variety of university-based education programs in Berlin and throughout Germany. These courses are value-packed, hassle-free ways to learn while traveling. The price includes airfare, accommodations, meals, tuition, tips, and insurance.

Taxes

Germany imposes a *Mehrwertsteuer* (MWST), or value-added tax (VAT), of 16% on most goods and services. Prices in restaurants and hotels include the VAT.

If you're not a resident of the European Union, you can get a VAT refund on purchases you make in Germany (excluding hotel and restaurant bills). There is usually a minimum amount you must spend to qualify for the refund. To receive a refund, shop at stores displaying a **TAX-FREE SHOPPING** sign. When you make a qualifying purchase, you receive a **tax-free voucher,** completed by the store, with a copy of your sales receipt attached. Before checking your luggage upon your departure from Germany, have the voucher stamped by German Customs to confirm that the goods have been exported. Then, redeem the voucher for cash (euros or dollars) at a **Europe Tax-Free Shopping** window, located at all major airports, border crossings, ferry ports, and railroad stations.

Telephones

The country code for Germany is 49. Every city or town also has its own city code. To call Germany from outside the country, dial the international access code 011, then 49, then the city code (without the initial zero), then the phone number, which may have from four to nine digits. The phone numbers as given in this book are for calling within Germany, when it is necessary to dial 0 before the city code.

Place local and long-distance calls from post offices or telephone booths (you can also call through a hotel switchboard, although the cost is significantly more). The unit charge is .20€. Most phones in Germany now require a *Telefonkarte* (telephone card), available at post offices and newsstands in increments of 5€, 10€, and 20€; coin-operated phones are increasingly rare. To make an international call from a public phone, look for a phone marked *Inlands und Auslandsgespräche;* most have instructions in English.

To call the U.S. or Canada from Germany, dial 01, followed by the country code (1), then the area code, and then the number.

Alternatively, you can dial the various telecommunication companies in the States for cheaper rates: Access numbers are ☎ 0800/225-5288 for **AT&T** and ☎ 0800/888-8000 for **MCI.**

Time Zone

Germany operates on Central European Time (CET), which means that the country is 6 hours ahead of Eastern Standard Time in the United States and 1 hour ahead of Greenwich Mean Time (GMT). Daylight saving time begins in April and ends in October—there's a slight difference in the dates from year to year.

Tipping

If a restaurant bill says *Bedienung,* a service charge has already been added, so just round your bill up to the nearest euro. If not, add 5% to 10%, depending on your satisfaction. Round up to the nearest euro for taxis. Bellhops get 1€ per bag, as does the doorperson at a hotel, restaurant, or nightclub. It is customary to give a small tip to the room-cleaning staff and to concierges who perform special favors such as obtaining theater or opera tickets. Tip hairdressers or barbers 5% to 10%.

Toilets

A women's *Toilette* (twah-*leh*-teh) is usually marked with an F for *Frauen* and a men's with an H for *Herren.* Restrooms in train stations sometimes require a .50€ or 1€ coin to enter. Many restrooms have an attendant who expects a small tip (never more than .20€); the attendant in a men's *Toilette* may be female.

Water

Tap water is safe to drink in all German towns and cities; still, drinking bottled water is a way of life. Restaurants do not freely offer water with your meal. You order and pay for *Sprudelwasser* (shprew-dil-vos-er; water with gas) or *Still* (shtill; noncarbonated water).

Weights and Measures

Germany uses the metric system. Heights are given in centimeters (cm) and meters (m), distances in kilometers (km), and weights in grams (g) or kilograms (kg). Temperature is measured in degrees Celsius (0°C = 32°F).

Useful Phrases & Menu Terms

Phrases

ENGLISH	GERMAN	PRONUNCIATION
please	bitte	*bit*-eh
thank you	danke	*dunk*-eh
you're welcome	gern geschehen	gairn geh-*shee*-en
yes	ja	*yahh*
no	nein	*nine*
hello	hallo	hah-*loh*
goodbye	auf wiedersehen	ouf *vee*-dehr-she-hen
good morning	guten morgen	*goo*-ten *mor*-ghenn
good evening	guten abend	*goo*-ten *ahh*-bend
How are you?	Wie geht es Ihnen?	vee *ghehht* as eehnen
Fine, thanks.	Gut, danke.	*goot, dunk*-eh
excuse me	entschuldigung	ennt-*shooll*-dee-ghoong
sorry	tut mir leid	toot mere *lyde*
My name is ____.	Ich heisse ____.	ee(ch) *hye*-sseh
What's your name?	Wie heissen Sie?	vee hye-ssenn *zee*
Do you speak English?	Sprechen Sie Englisch?	Shpre-(ch)en zee *eng*-lish
I don't speak German.	Ich spreche kein Deutsch	ee(ch) *shpre*-(ch)eh kyne doytsh
Where	wo	*voh*
how many/how much	wie viele	vee *fee*-leh
hotel	hotel	ho-*tell*
restaurant	restaurant	ress-toh-*rohng*
left	links	*links*
right	rechts	*re(ch)ts*
next to	neben	*neh*-ben
today	heute	*hoy*-the
tomorrow	morgen	*morr*-ghenn
yesterday	gestern	*ghess*-tehrn

Emergencies

Please call an ambulance!	Rufen Sie bitte einen Krankenwagen!	Roofen see bit-eh eye-nen *krahnk*-en-vah-ghenn!
Police	polizei	poli-*tsaih*
I've been robbed!	Ich wurde ausgeraubt!	Ee(ch) voorr-deh *ous*-gheh-raubt
My child disappeared.	Mein Kind ist verschwunden.	Mine *kin*-d isst fair-shwoonn-den

Numbers

ENGLISH	GERMAN	PRONUNCIATION
1	eins	*aihnts*
2	zwei	*tsvaih*
3	drei	*drrye*
4	vier	*feer*
5	fünf	*f(ue)nff*
6	sechs	*zechs*
7	sieben	*zee-ben*
8	acht	*a(ch)t*
9	neun	*noyn*
10	zehn	*tsehn*
11	elf	*ellf*
12	zwölf	*tsv(oe)llf*
13	dreizehn	*drrye-tshen*
14	vierzehn	*feer-tsehn*
15	fünfzehn	*f(ue)nff-tsehn*
16	sechzehn	*ze(ch)-tsehn*
17	siebzehn	*zeeb-tsehn*
18	achtzehn	*a(ch)-tsehn*
19	neunzehn	*noyn-tsehn*
20	zwanzig	*tsvann-tsigg*
21	einundzwanzig	*aihnn-oonnd-tsvann-tsigg*
30	dreissig	*drrye-sigg*
40	vierzig	*feer-tsigg*
50	fünfzig	*f(ue)nff-tsigg*
60	sechzig	*ze(ch)-tsigg*
70	siebzig	*zeeb-tsigg*
80	achtzig	*a(ch)-tsigg*
90	neunzig	*noyn-tsigg*
100	einhundert	*aihn-hoonn-dehrt*
200	zweihundert	*tsvaih-hoonn-dehrt*
1,000	eintausend	*aihn-towsend*

Days of the Week

ENGLISH	GERMAN	PRONUNCIATION
Sunday	Sonntag	*zonn*-tahgg
Monday	Montag	*mohn*-tahgg
Tuesday	Dienstag	*deens*-tahgg
Wednesday	Mittwoch	*mitt*-voh(ch)
Thursday	Donnerstag	*donn*-airs-tahgg
Friday	Freitag	*frye*-tahgg
Saturday	Samstag	*zamms*-tahgg

Restaurant Phrases

A table for ____, please.	Einen Tisch für ____ Personen, bitte.	Eye-nen *tish* f(ue)hr ____ pehr-soh-nen, bit-eh
The menu, please.	Die Karte, bitte.	dee *kahrr*-the, bit-eh
main courses	hauptgerichte	*howpt*-guh-rick-tuh
desserts	nachspeisen	*nock*-shpeye-zen
Check, please.	Zahlen, bitte.	*tsah*-len, bit-eh
Is the tip included?	Ist das inclusive Trinkgeld?	Isst dahs in-kloo-see-veh *trink*-gelld
fork	gabel	*gah*-bull
glass	glas	*glahss*
spoon	löffel	*leu*-ful
knife	messer	*mes*-sir
napkin	serviette	sare-vee-*et*-uh
plate	teller	*tel*-ler
breakfast	frühstück	*froo*-shtook
lunch	mittagessen	*mit*-tog-essen
dinner	abendessen	*ah*-bent-essen

Menu Items

apple	apfel	*ahp*-fell
cherries	kirschen	*keer*-shen
vegetables	gemüse	guh-*muse*-uh
salad	Salat	sa-*lot*
potato	kartoffel	car-*toff*-el
potato salad	kartoffelsalat	car-*toff*-el-saw-lot
soup	Suppe	*zoo*-pa
egg	ei	*eye*

Menu Items *continued*

ENGLISH	GERMAN	PRONUNCIATION
meat	fleisch	*flysch*
beef	rindfleisch	*rint*-flysch
sausage	wurst	*voorst*
duck	ente	*en*-tuh
fish	fisch	*fish*
beefsteak	fleischsteak	*flysch*-shtake
goose	gans	*gahnz*
chicken	geflügel or hühnchen	guh-*flew*-gull or *hen*-shen
veal	kalbfleisch	*callb*-flysch
seasoned pork cutlet	schnitzel	*shnit*-sul
marinated beef, oven- or pot-roasted	sauerbraten	*sour*-bra-ten
potato-based pasta	spätzle	*shpay*-tzell
flaky fruit pastry	strudel	*shtrew*-del
chewy white breakfast rolls	brötchen	*bro*-chen
dumplings	knödel	kuh-*no*-del
cake	kuchen	*koo*-kin
pancake	pfannkuchen	*fon*-koo-kin

Drinks

beer	bier	*beer*
Coca-Cola	Coke	*co*-ca
coffee	kaffee	caff-*ay*
milk	milch	*miltsch*
juice	saft	*zoft*
sparkling wine, champagne	sekt	*sect*
sparkling water	sprudelwasser	*shproodel*-vahs-sir
tea	tee	*tay*
water	wasser	*vahs*-sir
wine	wein	*vine*

Index

A

Aachen, 441–42, 495
  staying/dining in, 443
Aachener Dom, 442, 622, 625
Abtei Blaubeuren, 408
Accommodations, 654–55. *See also*
  specific hotels/areas; Fast Facts for
    specific areas
  apartment rentals (Berlin), 138
  best, by type, 14–15
Adlon Kempinski (Berlin), 14, 114, 115
  Gourmet Restaurant Lorenz
    Adlon, 106, 111
Ägyptisches Museum (Berlin),
  58–59, 81
Ahrenshoop, 28, 30, 584
Albers, Anni, 467
Albertinum (Dresden), 171
Albrecht-Dürer-Haus (Nuremberg),
  199, 229
Albrechtsburg (Meissen), 151, 155
Alexandrowka (Potsdam), 132, 134
Allerheiligen, 362, 364
All Quiet on the Western Front
  (Remarque), 510–11
Alois Dallmayr (Munich), 292, 296,
  298, 299
Alpine Road. *See* German Alpine
  Road
Alpirsbach, 364
Alps, Bavarian. *See* Southern Bavaria
  and the Bavarian Alps
Alpspitz, 8, 350–51
Alster-Cliff restaurant (Hamburg),
  598
Alsterhaus (Hamburg), 603
Alstersee (Hamburg), 595, 598
Alstervorland (Hamburg), 595, 598
Alte Brücke (Heidelberg), 400, 427
Alte Hofhaltung (Bamberg), 216
Alte Kapelle (Regensburg), 202, 234
Alte Mainbrücke (Würzburg), 198,
  243
Alte Nationalgalerie (Berlin), 65, 78,
  81, 130, 586
Altenburg, 149
Alte Oper (Frankfurt), 479
Alte Pinakothek (Munich), 23, 36,
  249, 255, 262, 277, 322, 324, 626
  site guide to, 265
Alter Hafen (Stade), 612–13
Alter Hafen (Wismar), 559
Alter Markt (Potsdam), 132
Alter Schwede (Wismar), 579
Altes Museum (Berlin), 58, 73, 81

Altes Rathaus
  in Bamberg, 216
  in Braunschweig, 507
  in Göttingen, 506
  in Leipzig, 182, 184
  in Lindau, 392
  in Lüneburg, 550
  in Munich, 286
  in Nuremberg, 199, 228
  in Passau, 217
  in Regensburg, 202, 235
Altes Residenztheater (Munich),
  261, 275, 314, 623
Altes Schloss and Neues Schloss
  (Meersburg), 379
Alte Synagoge (Erfurt), 148
Alte Thorschenke (Cochem), 15, 461
Alte Werrabrücke (Hann. Münden),
  502
Alt Luxemburg (Berlin), 16, 106, 107
Altstadt (Old Town) districts. *See*
  specific cities
Altstadtmarkt (Braunschweig), 507
Amalienburg (Schloss
  Nymphenburg), 277
Am Markt (Tübingen), 402–3
Amphitheater (Trier), 493
Amrum (island), 563, 570
Ana e Bruno (Berlin), 106, 107
Andreaskirche (Hildesheim), 507
Anette Petermann (Berlin), 100, 104
Anne Frank Zentrum (Berlin), 90
Annweiler am Trifels, 458
Antikensammlungen (Berlin), 81
Antikensammlungen (Munich), 258,
  264, 287
AquaDom/Sea Life Berlin, 90
Aquariums/Sea life attractions. *See*
  also Marine attractions/museums
  AquaDom/Sea Life Berlin, 90
  Deutsches Meeresmuseum
    (Stralsund), 580
  in Helgoland, 565
  in Kiel, 574
  Müritzeum (Waren), 591
  Nordsee-Aquarium (Langeoog),
    534–35
  Sea Life Aquarium (Lübeck), 564
  seal-watching, 532, 533, 570, 615
  Seehundstation (Norddeich), 533
  Tropen-Aquarium (Hamburg),
    602
  Zoo am Meer (Bremerhaven), 42,
    522, 523, 543
  at Zoo Berlin, 47, 64, 90
Archaeological attractions
  Archäologisches Landesmuseum
    (Konstanz), 377

Bärenhöhle, 31, 418
Dinopark, 522
Historisches Museum der Pfalz
  (Speyer), 407, 488–89
Kurpfälzisches Museum
  (Heidelberg), 424
Landesmuseum Württemberg
  (Stuttgart), 402, 433–34
Museum für Pre- und
  Vorgeschichte (Berlin), 81
Neanderthal Museum, 470
Pfahlbaumuseum
  Unteruhldingen, 378
Rheinisches Landesmuseum
  (Trier), 492
Römisch-Germanisches Museum
  (Cologne), 22, 484
Rosgartenmuseum (Konstanz),
  376
Urwelt-Museum Hauff, 31, 416
Varusschlacht Museum und
  Park, 511
Wikinger Museum
  Haithabu, 573
Archaeology tours, 495, 640
Architecture, 622–24. *See also*
  specific architects; see also
    Bauhaus
  baroque, 212–17, 412–15, 623
  Gothic, 622
  modern/postmodern, 82–87, 624
  of Nazi regime, 87
  neoclassical/neo-Gothic, 623
  tours of, 640
Art, 625–29. *See also specific artists*
  and art movements
  expressionism, 466, 571, 627,
    628–29
  under Nazi regime, 500, 627, 629
  Renaissance, 625–26
  Romantic, 627
Arte Luise Kunsthotel (Berlin), 114,
  115
Art tours, 641
Asam, Cosmas and Egid, 258, 273
Asamkirche (Munich), 248–49, 258,
  273, 286, 627
Assmannshausen, 449, 452, 453
ATMs/Cashpoints, 655. *See also* Fast
  Facts *for specific areas*
A-Trane (Berlin), 124, 129
Augsburg, 204, 209, 218–21, 245,
  622, 643
  staying/dining in, 221
August II of Saxony (Augustus the
  Strong), 151, 155, 168, 172
  equestrian statue of (Dresden),
    172, 174